The Letters of Robert Browning and Elizabeth Barrett Barrett 1845–1846

Volume I
January 1845–March 1846

This portrait was executed at Rome, in 1859,
as a companion to that of E. B. B. now in the
National Portrait Gallery, by Field Talfourd; & there
properly it remained. I rejoice that it now belongs
to my friend Gosse.   Robert Browning
Apr. 10ᵗ 85

Robert Browning, 1859
From a drawing by Field Talfourd

The
Letters
of
Robert Browning
and
Elizabeth Barrett Barrett
1845-1846

Edited by Elvan Kintner

The Belknap Press of
Harvard University Press
Cambridge, Massachusetts
1969

To the Memory of Howard Foster Lowry
Mentor and Friend

Acknowledgments

This edition of the Barrett–Browning letters began in connection with the preparation of a doctoral dissertation. A preliminary version of the undertaking was accepted in 1953 by the faculty of the Graduate School of Yale University in partial fulfillment of the requirements for a Ph.D. degree. Since then I have tried to augment that study so as to produce an edition of the letters that would make them genuinely available both to scholars and to interested readers in general.

The debts contracted in so lengthy a process are beyond remembering, let alone chronicling, but these are the chief: I am deeply grateful to Sir John Murray, of 50, Albemarle Street, London W.1, for permission to print a corrected text of these letters. Sir John claims copyright on all unpublished material written by either of the Brownings and I am therefore his debtor for all such material.

There is a very particular debt to Wellesley College for permission to transcribe the manuscript letters of this correspondence and to study the manuscript of *Aurora Leigh,* unpublished letters of Browning, Mrs. Browning, and John Kenyon, as well as for the facilities and assistance afforded me on numerous visits. Yale University has given me access to and permission to print all or parts of unpublished letters of Harriet Martineau, Mary Russell Mitford, and Walter Savage Landor, and to quote from unpublished letters of the Brownings.

Lady Martineau of Melville Hall, Birmingham, Mr. Gaston Martineau of Chipping Camden, and Lieutenant-Colonel J. W. Landor of Bournemouth were kind enough to approve my use of letters by their kinsmen. Professor R. H. Super, of the University of Michigan, Mr. D. Wyn Evans, Rare Book Librarian of the University of Birmingham, and Professor R. K. Webb, of Columbia University, have helped me trace the heirs of Landor, Miss Martineau, and Miss Mitford.

Acknowledgments

The Baylor Browning Library, through the kindness of the late Dr. A. J. Armstrong, made available in photostat an important fragment of a letter by Landor. I wish to thank the British Museum for making available and permitting quotation from materials amassed by the late W. Hall Griffin in the preparation of his life of Browning and for access to Sir Frederic Kenyon's typescript of E.B.B.'s letters.

Individual members of the staffs at the institutions I have named have been notably helpful. What this book owes to the intelligence, information, patience, and good will of Miss Hannah D. French, Research Librarian of the Wellesley College Library, is beyond calculation. Her assistant, Mrs. Hazel Godfrey, has augmented that kindness frequently. Among others at the Yale Library the Misses Marjorie Karlson and Marjorie Wynne and Professor Carl F. Schreiber and Mrs. Hedwig Dijon were most kind. The British Museum staff in Great Russell Street and at Colindale made my work much easier and more pleasant.

The late Professor G. Lincoln Hendrickson of Yale gave most generously of his time and his great knowledge of the classics and mythology, and Professor Thomas G. Bergin helped with Italian references and quotations. Professor Richard L. Purdy, who was my dissertation adviser, gave unstintingly of his time and placed at my disposal valuable materials in his possession. To my colleagues Professors Scott Elledge, now of Cornell, and Owen Jenkins and Charles Messner of Carleton, I am indebted for help of various kinds.

I wish to acknowledge gratefully financial aid from the Lilly Foundation, made available through Carleton College, and from the Carleton Faculty Research and Assistance Fund, which helped with necessary travel and secretarial help. I wish to thank President Emeritus Laurence M. Gould and the trustees of Carleton College for the year's leave during which this work was drawn together, and President Gould, his successor President John W. Nason, and former Deans Richard Gilman, now President of Occidental College, and Philip Phenix, now of Teachers College, Columbia, for their interest and help at many points.

At the Harvard University Press my debts are especially to Mrs. T. J. Wilson, who managed my copy and a sense of humor simultaneously, and to Mrs. L. J. Kewer, who suggested ways of avoiding some awkwardnesses in my original format.

My daughter Sherry and my wife Sibyl have helped with patience,

viii

secretarial help, and proofreading, but the latter's indispensable contribution was planning so careful and frugal it managed largely to offset my spectacular unsuccess at getting grants. There is "I can't live without you" in the best modern scholarly idiom: "You're my grant from the foundation."

Finally, I wish to thank my typists—Mrs. Marguerite Brodersen, Mrs. Margaret Carlson, Mrs. Marion Christopherson, Mrs. Victoria Hanson, Mrs. Betty McGuire, and Miss Robin Miller.

E. K.

Northfield, Minnesota
June 1968

Contents

Volume I

Contents

Volume II

Illustrations
Volume I

(1844): "a detestable engraving—as like Robert as Flush"—*Letters of EBB*, I,
335–336. Nevertheless, a copy of this engraving was hanging on the wall of
E.B.B.'s room before her first meeting with R.B. Reproduced through the
courtesy of Wellesley College.

Sketched by Sir George Scharf from a portrait bust by Thomas Crawford made
in Rome in 1841. Scharf had been secretary of the National Portrait Gallery from
its beginning in 1857; he became its Director in 1882, and served with devotion
and distinction until shortly before his death in 1895. His sketch is reproduced
by permission of the National Portrait Gallery.

Volume II

From a drawing made by Field Talfourd, in Rome, in 1859. Reproduced by
permission of the National Portrait Gallery, London.

Another example of emotion reflected in handwriting. From the original manuscript, courtesy of the Wellesley College Library.

From a portrait by William Fisher, painted at Rome in 1854 and now at Wellesley
College: "an admirable likeness"—E.B.B. to Miss Mitford, *Letters of EBB*, II, 160.
Courtesy of the Wellesley College Library.

E.B.B.'s outings frequently took her to Regent's Park; John Kenyon lived for
years in York Terrace. Reproduced from a portion of a plate in the Crace Collection by permission of the Trustees of the British Museum.

The church in which E.B.B. and R.B. were married, seen from Regent's Park.
Wash drawing by T. Shepherd, 1828; reproduced by permission of the City of
Westminster, Archives Department, Public Library, Marylebone Road, through
the courtesy of Miss V. R. Readman, Assistant Archivist.

Entry in the marriage register of St. Marylebone Parish, showing that the wit-
nesses were R.B.'s cousin, James Silverthorne, and E.B.B.'s maid, Wilson.
Reproduced by permission of the Rector of St. Marylebone, the Rev. Dr. Frank
Coventry.

The last letter of this correspondence, written the night before their departure
for Europe. From the original manuscript, courtesy of the Wellesley College
Library.

Short-Title Bibliography

Browning Collections: The Browning Collections. Catalogue of Oil Paintings, Drawings and Prints: Autograph Letters and Manuscripts: Books . . . the Property of R. W. Barrett Browning, Esq. Sotheby Catalogue, 1913.

D & K: William C. DeVane and Kenneth L. Knickerbocker, eds., *New Letters of Robert Browning.* New Haven: Yale University Press, 1950.

DeVane: William C. DeVane, *A Browning Handbook.* 2nd ed., New York: Appleton-Century-Crofts, 1955.

Dowden: Edward Dowden, *The Life of Robert Browning.* Everyman edition. London and New York: E. P. Dutton, n.d.

EBB: Letters to Her Sister: Elizabeth Barrett Browning: Letters to Her Sister, 1846–1859, ed. Leonard Huxley. London: John Murray, 1929.

EBB to MRM: Elizabeth Barrett to Miss Mitford, ed. Betty Miller. London: John Murray, 1954.

G & M: W. Hall Griffin and H. C. Minchin, *The Life of Robert Browning.* 3rd ed., London: Methuen, 1938.

Hood: Thurman L. Hood, ed., *Letters of Robert Browning Collected by Thomas J. Wise.* New Haven: Yale University Press, 1933.

Kenyon TpS: Typescripts of Letters of Elizabeth Barrett Browning made for F. G. Kenyon's two-volume edition of her correspondence. British Museum Add. MSS. 42228–31.

Letters of EBB: The Letters of Elizabeth Barrett Browning, ed. Frederic G. Kenyon. 2 vols., New York: Macmillan, 1897.

Letters of EBB to RHH: Letters of Elizabeth Barrett Browning Addressed to Richard Hengist Horne, ed. R. S. Townshend Mayer. 2 vols., London, 1877.

Letters to Geo. Barrett: Letters of the Brownings to George Barrett, ed. Paul Landis and Ronald E. Freeman. Urbana: University of Illinois Press, 1958.

McAleer: Edward C. McAleer, ed., *Dearest Isa: Browning's Letters to Isa Blagden.* Austin: University of Texas Press, 1951.

Macmillan ed.: *The Complete Poetical Works of Robert Browning.* New Edition with Additional Poems First Published in 1914. New York: The Macmillan Company, 1915.

Miss Marks: Jeannette Marks, *The Family of the Barrett.* New York: Macmillan, 1938.

Short-Title Bibliography

Mrs. Orr: Mrs. Sutherland Orr, *Life and Letters of Robert Browning,* revised by
   Frederic G. Kenyon. Boston: Houghton Mifflin, 1908.
New Poems: New Poems by Robert Browning and Elizabeth Barrett Browning, ed. Sir
   Frederic G. Kenyon. London: Smith, Elder, 1914.
New Spirit of the Age: A New Spirit of the Age, ed. R. H. Horne, 2 vols., London,
   1844.
Orr Handbook: Mrs. Sutherland Orr. *A Handbook to the Works of Robert Browning.*
   Revised edition. London: George Bell & Sons, 1937.
Robert Browning and Alfred Domett: Robert Browning and Alfred Domett, ed. Frederic
   G. Kenyon. London: Smith, Elder, 1906.
Tennyson: A Memoir: Hallam Tennyson, *Alfred Lord Tennyson: A Memoir.* 2 vols.,
   London, 1897.
W. Hall Griffin Papers: Various materials compiled by W. Hall Griffin in preparing
   his biography of Browning. British Museum Add. MSS. 45558–45564.

Line-number references to Mrs. Browning's poems and translations are based
on the one-volume *Poetical Works,* ed. Kenyon (London: Smith, Elder, 1897); those
to Browning's on the ten-volume Centenary Edition, ed. Kenyon (London: Smith,
Elder, 1912); and those to Shakespeare on the three-volume Oxford edition of
1911–1912.

A Note on the Text

The line across the page is not a symbol, but Browning's own device for signaling a change in subject, and usually in mood.

Where dates are supplied for letters, they have been arrived at by comparing the writer's indication of the day of the week with the postmark and a calendar for 1845 or 1846. Since the sequence of the letters is too tight to permit mistakes as to the week, this is a trustworthy technique except where one or the other correspondent errs as to the day. These slips are corrected in subsequent letters or betrayed by the necessary sequence of letters or by inconsistency with their postmarks. Many conjectures are corroborated by references to a Browning visit, for which the dates are known. Where a postmark is the only hard evidence, that alone is supplied, even though fairly dependable inferences might be drawn from it. As a general rule, Browning's letters are written and postmarked on the same day and there is a one-day lag in Miss Barrett's. In addition, she is given to journal letters written over a period of several days. A few special problems are dealt with in the notes.

Most of these letters, despite their often considerable length, were sent in very tiny envelopes—E.B.B.'s about $1\frac{1}{2} \times 4$ and Browning's about $2\frac{1}{2} \times 3\frac{1}{2}$. Browning's first two letters and one or two thereafter are exceptions, written on stationery about two or three times as large. Most of the correspondence went by Penny Post, but several letters were enclosed in parcels of books or proof. Presumably these too went by mail, though Browning made up a parcel as a blind for Letter 237, which he delivered in person. The enclosure letters are usually not addressed; for the rest, E.B.B.'s bear the address "Robert Browning Esqre / New Cross / Hatcham / Surrey" and his "Miss Barrett, / 50 Wimpole St." Since the correspondents maintained the same residences throughout, postmarks have been noted only where they throw light on the text or where they are the only means of dating a letter. If a letter lacks postmark or address, the fact is noted and explained. Except where otherwise indicated, the letters are written in ink.

In several instances it has been necessary to reverse the order of two letters as they appeared in 1899. Where that edition, however, interpreted as two letters the contents of a single envelope, this one follows suit, both because the grounds for doing so are defensible and because continuing the practice will simplify finding a particular letter for anyone familiar with the earlier text. In such instances the Wellesley number is followed by [a] and [b] and the details are supplied in a note.

A Note on the Text

Brief biographies of those people whose names occur constantly throughout the text are not given in the footnotes, but may be found in the Biographical Appendix.

Although Browning and E.B.B. usually wrote their Greek without accents, it is here printed in standard form.

The following symbols are used in presenting the text of the letters:

⟨ ⟩   Cancellation.

↑ ↓   Insertion.

‖···‖   Unrecovered matter. Three dots, one to five words; four dots, six to fifteen words; five dots, sixteen to thirty words. Conjectural readings are supplied between parallels.

⟨‖···‖⟩   Unrecovered cancelled matter.

[ ]   Editorial insertion.

⌈ ⌉   Passages oddly or significantly placed in the manuscript letter. Details are given in a note.

/ ⟩ /   Original and altered readings. Used where one word has been superimposed upon another or the original retraced so as to alter it.

/‖···‖⟩ /   Alteration or superimposition has made the original illegible.

W1, W1°   The W stands for Wellesley, and the number is that assigned the manuscript letter by the Wellesley Library, which uses the superscript ° to distinguish Miss Barrett's letters.

Introduction

Introduction

This collection of letters offers a reader some bonuses that most correspondences do not, but it is only proper to warn him that unless he is careful he may find that the dividends have cheated him of the principal. Here we have not only both sides of the correspondence but contained within it, in the words of the two lovers themselves, both of them poets, one of the few love stories from real life that can compete in plot interest with the art of the fictioner. Indeed, the story itself has been retold many times, in ways as varied as Virginia Woolf's *Flush* and Rudolph Besier's *The Barretts of Wimpole Street*. Its inherent interest is only partly that it is so unlike routine human experience; it lies rather in the fact that Browning and Miss Barrett reënact an archetypal myth. Miss Dormer Creston called her 1929 retelling of the story *Andromeda in Wimpole Street*. Dean DeVane has shown how the legend of Andromeda became Browning's "private myth" and can be traced in his work from *Pauline* all the way to the *Parleying with Francis Furini*, and how readily the myth assimilated Elizabeth Barrett in his mind.[1] DeVane at least suggests that Browning is at his best as a poet when, as in *Men and Women*, the myth retires a bit and the insights become subtler. That is a cognate of the point relevant to the reader of these letters.

It is true to some degree of all fiction and in the extreme of myth that they call for a reductive simplification of character, whereas a man's letters are most rewarding when, like Keats's, they take us inside his mind. In ways and for reasons to be discussed later, Browning takes a rather self-conscious stand much of the time in these letters, though less so than in anything that he ever wrote to any other correspondent

---

1. William C. DeVane, "The Virgin and the Dragon," *Yale Review*, N.S. XXXVII (September 1947), 33–46. Reprinted in Boyd Litzinger and K. L. Knickerbocker, eds., *The Browning Critics* (Lexington: University of Kentucky Press, 1965), pp. 181–196.

we know of. Even so, our sense of the man himself comes at times as obliquely as it does for some of his most notable imaginative creations. If the roll of events keeps suggesting Perseus or St. George, Browning will escape us altogether. The myth has probably coöperated with her husband's portrait of her as Pompilia and the least felicitous parts of her own poetry to give the impression so widely encountered that E.B.B. was a kind of hothouse flower. Those who know her letters well—these or others—know that the best of her is in them: warm, humorous, lively. There are rich elements of high comedy in the development of her relationship with Browning and in the situation the two of them are in, and her awareness of these elements is enjoyable, as are the deftness and sympathy she exhibits in dealing with a sometimes difficult lover. She is an interesting human being worth our attention in her own right and not as Andromeda or Pompilia-to-be. In short, these letters have much to give of the charm one has learned to expect of all good letters, but the reader has some problems.

I. *Letters from the Cherokee*

When Robert Wiedemann Barrett Browning published his parents' love letters in 1899, the event attracted wide and often scandalized attention. More than half a century had passed since England's most famous woman poet had run off to Italy with a young man who just missed being an obscure poet in one sense by being so in another. At the time almost no one knew that Elizabeth Barrett and Robert Browning had ever set eyes on one another, much less fallen in love and married. It was common, if somewhat inexact, knowledge that she was an incurable invalid, incapable even of leaving her room. In the years that followed, when she had borne a son and become one of the lights of the Anglo-American artistic circle in Florence, the story began to acquire its mythic quality. By 1899 it was generally known that the romance had surprised her father and her family even more than it had the rest of the world and that there had been bad blood about the matter. Thus the two volumes of letters announced for the 1899 Easter trade by Smith, Elder in Britain and Harper & Brothers in America appealed to the romantic in some, to the gossip in others, and to both in many more.

Yet the event was not answerable. There was nothing that was sensational and much that was confusing. The fears or hopes of those who felt that R. W. Barrett Browning had been indiscreet were short-lived. Many were inclined to agree with G. K. Chesterton that these would be private letters even if published a hundred times over and that "as far as any third person is concerned, Browning might as well have been expressing the most noble and universal sentiment in the dialect of the Cherokees."[2] It is very true that in these letters, as elsewhere, Browning is given to what E.B.B. laughingly calls "Sordelloisms," but the real problems lay partly in looking for what the letters do not have to offer and principally in serious inadequacies in the 1899 edition. That edition has sometimes misled and misinformed scholars as well as confused and disappointed the common reader. There was no editor in 1899 and apparently only the most casual supervision. Barrett Browning supplied a signed note to Letter 451 to say that the gardener's son had not after all been killed at Aliwal, and someone got Sir Frederic Kenyon to identify some Greek passages from Aeschylus and supply E.B.B.'s translations of them. One or two other Greek phrases were translated, but not all of them, and some bits of flora which turned up as enclosures were duly noted. Printed or written enclosures were passed along, though the transmitter did not always fasten on their real point. Beyond that, the reader was left comfortless. The text had its errors, too, rather more notable for their naïveté than their numbers. The very little evidence still with the manuscript letters now that they have been properly filed and catalogued at Wellesley seems to show that they were copied out by a staff of workers, each assigned singly and at random the bundles of twenty letters from one correspondent or the other in which Browning and E.B.B. kept them. Because of the sealing wax the envelopes still tend to cohere in bundles of twenty, and there are penciled notes that a particular group of twenty, indicated by numbers, are "in the safe." It appears, then, that each copyist worked with no awareness of the whole correspondence or even of both sides of it at any given point. Browning's word "boots," for example, in Letter 31 would hardly have been misread as "paste" by an editor who knew of E.B.B.'s response to it. If one has nothing else to go on, the word does look like "paste," but read so it not only makes a hash of the allusion to *Luria* of which it is a part, but leaves Miss Barrett's ensuing play on "boots" and "Bootes" utterly confusing. That at least one copyist was amusingly unsophisticated in literary matters is implied by

2. *Robert Browning*, English Men of Letters (New York: Macmillan, 1903), p. 64.

the opening of Letter 22 in the 1899 text, where Browning's head is put under the bag instead of the bay.

The present edition attempts to translate these letters from the Cherokee. One aspect of the process is an annotation that undertakes not only to identify people, places, and literary allusions, but to furnish bits of biography, quotations from newspapers and periodicals, cross-references between letters, and even exegesis at a point or two where Browning's prose gets confusing. It is unlikely that any reader will need or want all these helps. Some are for the Browning specialist, others for the interested layman; some for the serial reader, others for the reference-seeker. Whatever the success, there has been an earnest attempt to make so many notes available but not officious. The need for relatively heavy annotation stems in part from the fact that these letters are in effect part of a running conversation. One telling bit of evidence is the way both correspondents ignore, with increasing frequency, conventional ceremony. Headings and often signatures drop away as the momentum rises. In fact, beginning in May 1845 the record we have is actually incomplete because what was said in the increasingly frequent visits was of course not committed to paper. This interchange, furthermore, stretches through some twenty months of the lives of two well-read people living in a literary and historical context markedly unlike our own. The extensive annotation tries to provide the necessary continuity and context. As for the text, it attempts something more than correctness. The holograph letters are full of variant readings, alterations, and cancellations, some of them dramatically decisive, others still legible. Some of these are directly alluded to in the text itself; others provide a reading in depth that clarifies the meaning or the tone or both of a sentence or a letter. Cumulatively they provide some of the overtones of a personality. Symbols developed at Harvard University Press for transcribing manuscript have made it possible to report all significant alterations without clogging the natural flow of this extended conversation on paper.

II. *The Past as Prologue*

Tracing briefly the lives of our two principals up to the day in January 1845 when E.B.B. opened Browning's first letter will help us to understand both the letters and the writers. When that first letter arrived Browning was thirty-two and E.B.B. thirty-eight. Both had been highly romantic children, capable of imagining a story like the one they were to live, but childhood was long past. Browning had decided upon a celibate career, and the combination of her age and her invalid condition had long since made E.B.B. wryly humorous about the occasional gallantries by mail to which she was subjected.

Elizabeth Barrett Moulton-Barrett was born March 6, 1806, at Coxhoe Hall, County Durham. When she was three her family moved to Hope End, near Malvern in Herefordshire. Besides leading the active life usual for a child in the country, she wrote precocious verses and learned to love Homer in Pope's translation. When her brother Edward began to study Greek her fondness for him and for Homer led her to share the lessons. At eleven or twelve she produced her own epic poem in four books, *The Battle of Marathon*, much influenced by both Homer and Pope. Her proud father had fifty copies printed in early 1820.

In 1821 a serious illness interrupted her physical activity. Her contemporaries and even some of her collateral descendants for a century or more attributed it to a spinal injury incurred in an accident with her pony Moses. Browning had corresponded with her for some time before he learned better. It is clear now that she was suffering from tuberculosis in 1821 and that her illness seventeen years later was a recurrence of it.[3] After recovering from the first attack, she resumed an active, even tomboyish life, but the enforced idleness while she was ill seems to have fortified her natural love of reading and writing.

In 1826 she published a second volume, this time anonymously, *An Essay on Mind, with Other Poems*. The title poem confesses its debt to Pope, but the fourteen others, some written as long as seven years before publication, are very different. There are experiments with various verse forms and styles of diction, and poems on Byron's death and on Greek and Spanish patriots. The title poem elicited three published comments, one kindly, another derogatory, the third a summary dismissal in two sentences as a "bluestocking affair."[4] It also attracted the attention of the blind classical scholar Hugh Stuart Boyd and led to an acquaintance with him that greatly increased E.B.B.'s facility in Greek. That, in sum, was probably the volume's greatest importance.

Two years later, in 1828, Mrs. Moulton-Barrett died, and shortly

3. See *Letters to Geo. Barrett*, pp. 341–348.
4. Letter 193, note 4.

thereafter her husband told his children that the family fortunes had been declining. By 1832 the family relinquished Hope End and moved to Sidmouth, in Devon. There E.B.B. was attracted by the eloquence of George Barrett Hunter, a widowed Independent minister who fell in love with her and eventually followed her to London.[5] It is doubtful that she ever shared his passionate feelings, but if so she had ceased to by the time Browning entered her life. When she read Browning's *A Soul's Tragedy* in 1846 she discovered in it the portrait of just such a man, and her later letters to the poet refer to Hunter as "my Chiappino."

Her intensified interest in the classics led to a rather too-hasty translation of the *Prometheus* of Aeschylus, published in 1833. The anonymous volume identified its author only as having written *An Essay on Mind*. It contained nineteen original poems, in some of which one first hears the strongly religious note common in her later poetry and hints of a somewhat morbid preoccupation with death. The *Athenæum* of June 8, 1833, cited the translation as a horrible example to prospective translators of Aeschylus. Nine weeks before, the same periodical had carried a brief but generally encouraging notice of another anonymous volume, *Pauline,* the first appearance in print of Robert Browning.

The new poet was six years Miss Barrett's junior, having been born at Camberwell on May 7, 1812, of middle-class parents. His father was a Bank of England clerk, though originally slated for relatively greater wealth and prestige. The elder Browning's mother had some holdings in a sugar plantation at St. Kitt's, and after her death his father had sent him there as an overseer; but his moral revulsion at slavery was so strong that he had broken with his father and altogether abandoned his financial advantages. He was fond of out-of-the-way books, and his library of over a thousand volumes was the source of much of his son's varied and esoteric information. The poet's mother, though born in Scotland, was of German ancestry—a forceful, matriarchal woman, deeply pious. Browning inherited from her both his love of music and an enthusiasm for animals that embraced spiders and newts as well as more familiar pets. These affectionate parents indulged their precocious son in his love for art, music, and poetry. After a brief experience of the

5. See Betty Miller, *Robert Browning: A Portrait* (London: John Murray, 1952), pp. 99–100, Gardner B. Taplin, *The Life of Elizabeth Barrett Browning* (New Haven: Yale University Press, 1957), *passim*, and Mrs. Miller's article in the *Cornhill Magazine* (Spring 1951), pp. 83–96.

Reverend Mr. Ready's school at Peckham, he was tutored privately, partly by his father. A sister, Sarianna, two years young Robert's junior, completed the small circle of his domestic admirers. In 1829 he entered the new University of London, but left after one unhappy term. He had decided to be a poet.

With an Ossian imitation at five to his credit, Browning was, if anything, a more precocious versifier than E.B.B., but his closest approach to publication had come when Eliza Flower, his mother's friend and the ward of his father's old friend W. J. Fox, copied out his verses from a manuscript volume entitled *Incondita*. He was then about fourteen. In 1833 his Aunt Silverthorne underwrote the publication of *Pauline*. In addition to the *Athenæum* notice by Alan Cunningham, already mentioned, the poem got a very kind, if not altogether spontaneous, welcome from Fox in his *Monthly Repository*.[6] The *Literary Gazette* and *Tait's Edinburgh Magazine* dismissed it contemptuously. There were no sales. No doubt this was all somewhat disappointing to the poet, but for a maiden effort, *Pauline* made a fair critical showing.

But the most important criticism was never published. Fox distributed a dozen review copies for Browning, one of which he gave to John Stuart Mill. Though he never wrote the review, Mill marked his copy in some detail and it found its way back to Browning.[7] In three paragraphs Mill developed this thesis: "With considerable poetic powers, the writer seems to me possessed with a more intense and morbid self-consciousness than I ever knew in a sane human being." The critique was a stinging blow, and Browning thereafter adopted a mask rarely laid aside for the rest of his career, though he sometimes professed a desire to do so. Furthermore, he carefully directed attention to his mask by labeling his works "dramatic" and explaining the term, as in the advertisement to *Dramatic Lyrics:* "so many utterances of so many imaginary persons, not mine." This line of defense was so instinctive that when Browning, after his first visit, wrote a too-hasty profession of love and E.B.B. insisted on its withdrawal, he incorporated in his tense and overwrought retraction in Letter 31 this parenthesis: "(all my writings are purely dramatic as I am always anxious to say)."

6. Browning in effect asked for the review. See Mrs. Orr, pp. 51–52.

7. Mill returned the copy through Fox. It is now in the Forster and Dyce Collection in the Victoria and Albert Museum. (DeVane, pp. 45–46.)

Pauline was an acute embarrassment for the rest of his life, hidden whenever possible and "explained" when not. When the fear of piracy led him to reprint it in 1868, he carefully prefaced it with "an exculpatory word." The effects of Mill's remarks are observable in two famous and completely contradictory remarks about Browning— Macready's in 1835 that he was "more like a youthful poet than any man I ever saw" and Lockhart's in 1854 that he liked Browning for being so unlike "a damned literary man."[8] The mask, not yet very discernible two years after *Pauline*, had in another nineteen become a settled habit. Henry James's fascination with the disparity between the Browning he saw and the Browning he read was the origin of his story *The Private Life*. By 1845–46 Browning was wearing the mask with some assurance, but in his new role as lover he often tried, not always successfully, to put it aside.

In 1835 he published *Paracelsus,* the first work to bear his name. In a review for the *Examiner* John Forster hailed it as "a work of unequivocal power." Though Browning was somewhat perversely given to attributing the poem's modest success entirely to Forster, there were several other friendly and encouraging notices of it. It made no money but gained the attention of some important people, among them Landor, Macready, and Harriet Martineau. It led Thomas Noon Talfourd to invite Browning to a supper celebrating the stage success of his own tragedy *Ion*. There Wordsworth drank to his health, and John Kenyon introduced himself as both an admirer of *Paracelsus* and a sometime schoolmate of Browning senior. That taste of success was so pleasant and unusual that Browning's title pages a decade later still identified him as the "Author of 'Paracelsus.'" His bride even thought the phrase might appear in the newspaper advertisement of their wedding.

In the year *Paracelsus* was published the Barretts moved to London, where John Kenyon introduced himself to E.B.B. and arranged for her to meet some of his famous friends, including Landor, Wordsworth, and Mary Russell Mitford. Shortly thereafter some of E.B.B.'s poems attracted favorable attention in the *New Monthly Magazine,* which at about the same time was praising the author of *Paracelsus*.[9] She also

8. G & M, p. 75; D & K, pp. 73–74.

9. In the March issue John Forster praised the poem in "Evidences of a New Genius for Dramatic Poetry—No. 1," and the September issue contained Euphrasia Haworth's "Sonnets to the Author of 'Paracelsus.'" E.B.B.'s *Romaunt of Margret* appeared in July and her *Poet's Vow* in October.

contributed to the *Athenæum* and to the annual *Finden's Tableaux,* edited by Miss Mitford. These pieces were collected in an 1838 volume, *The Seraphim and Other Poems.* It was her fourth appearance in print but the first since 1820 to bear her name. The book's preface described the title poem as an attempt to deal as Aeschylus might have with the story of the Crucifixion. Except for a very few occasional verses, the thirty-eight other poems share a like moral and religious cast, and the preface draws attention to the fact. The collection was rather widely reviewed. Critics praised the title poem for learning, promise, and some spots of beauty but found it as a whole rather diffuse and uncontrolled. The few who mentioned the shorter poems preferred them. Browning, who loves to allude to E.B.B.'s poems in his letters to her, almost entirely overlooks this collection.

Though this 1838 volume was not an unqualified success it served to enroll Miss Barrett by name in the ranks of England's feminine poets and initiate her reputation for erudition. In the normal course of things it would certainly have done for her socially what *Paracelsus* had for Browning, but the London climate had weakened her lungs so alarmingly that shortly after the book appeared her doctor ordered her removed to Torquay.

Along with all its happy results, *Paracelsus* had one unfortunate effect on Browning's career. It led Macready in May of 1836 to ask for a play. Browning responded with *Strafford,* produced in 1837. It was just successful enough to be a false start. Browning's first two dramatic monologues, *Porphyria's Lover* and *Johannes Agricola,* had appeared anonymously in the *Monthly Repository* for January 1836, but he let them go unacknowledged for six years. From our vantage point either poem is more noteworthy, but of course the play drew far more contemporary attention.

Though he had begun planning it while still at work on *Paracelsus,* Browning's next major poem did not appear until 1840. In the course of preparing it, he made his first trip to Italy in 1838. *Sordello* was such a crushing popular failure that the jokes it engendered are all most people know about it.[10] Browning's most sustained effort proved the greatest possible disaster to a promising career. His frustration was not untouched by bitterness. Macready noted that Browning betrayed

10. For a discussion of its composition and the complications at least partly responsible for its failure, see DeVane, pp. 72–87.

irritation on the subject even toward his old friend Fox.[11] Their special circumstances do not exempt these letters from a touch of it: E.B.B., who clearly appreciates the poem's good points, does have the temerity to jest mildly about its obscurities, but as late as Letter 223 Browning reacts a bit warmly to Miss Mitford's reported strictures on it. In 1845-46 he was still in the shadow of *Sordello's* failure, and it still galled.

By October of 1839 E.B.B. was so ill that she was not permitted even to stand, and only with difficulty persuaded her doctor to let her be lifted from the bed to the sofa for one hour a day. Nevertheless, she continued to write. Her greatest consolation at Torquay was the company of her brother Edward, who, at her plea, was not sent off to Jamaica on business as her father had intended. A younger brother, Samuel, who did go, died there in 1840 of yellow fever. If his death occasioned any shock on his sister's part, it was soon overwhelmed by a much greater. E.B.B.'s strongest human tie before Browning was to Edward. One day about five months after Samuel's death he went sailing on the bay at Torquay and never returned. She reacted so strongly that Miss Mitford, for one, despaired of her life. Torquay became a nightmare she could escape only in work. She wrote a great deal, advised R. H. Horne by correspondence on a volume of Chaucer modernizations he was editing, to which she contributed, and planned with him the never-completed play mentioned in Letter 21.

In the spring of 1841, still too weak to move, she was returned to London in a specially built carriage and carried up three flights of steps to the room in Wimpole Street that she rarely left until the summer of 1846. In this restricted life her pleasures were confined largely to her spaniel Flush, the attentions of a large family that had always in some degree centered upon her, and her work. Visitors were limited to family and old friends, so that she saw few literary people, but the list of her famous correspondents grew. Horne was joined by the painter Benjamin Robert Haydon, the American editor Cornelius Mathews, and Harriet Martineau. Mathews kept her in touch with the world of contemporary American literature and purchased some of her poems for American periodicals. Miss Mitford, since her friendship antedated the invalidism, was both caller and correspondent, and John Kenyon came regularly with news of his many literary friends and brought

11. *The Diaries of William Charles Macready, 1833–1851,* ed. William Toynbee (2 vols., London: Chapman & Hall, 1912), II, 76 (August 27, 1840).

away E.B.B.'s manuscript pieces to show them. Shortly after her return from Torquay he asked to bring his friend Browning, but the moment had not yet come. She refused because of "a blind dislike to seeing strangers."[12] During 1842 she published both poetry and prose in the *Athenæum,* and the next year her *Cry of the Children* appeared in *Blackwood's*. From the first it was one of her most popular pieces and attracted wide attention. At the same time she was helping Horne with his *New Spirit of the Age,* two volumes of essays on noteworthy contemporaries published in 1844. Unknown to her Horne had another, less active, collaborator—Robert Browning. By the end of 1843 she had begun another long poem, eventually to be called *A Drama of Exile,* designed to be the nucleus of a new collection.

The failure of *Sordello* led Browning to reconsider his plans and concentrate his efforts. He had had a play staged with partial success, most of the compliments he had gathered from critics and friends had stressed his dramatic gifts, and ever since *Pauline* he had himself been insisting on the dramatic character of his work. Thus it was altogether logical, however unfortunate, that he decided to concentrate on plays. His publisher, Edward Moxon, suggested a comparatively inexpensive format for them—a double-column pamphlet in fine print on inexpensive paper and with paper covers—and the series Browning called *Bells and Pomegranates* was launched in 1841 with *Pippa Passes* as the first number. That play impressed even Miss Mitford[13] and, had it come before instead of after *Sordello,* would probably have enhanced Browning's reputation; but in 1841 it could at most effect only a mild rehabilitation. The odd series title disquieted a reading public already skittish because of *Sordello;* the wary critic for *Tait's Edinburgh Magazine* pronounced only an interim judgment, in the belief that he was dealing with a serial story in dramatic form.[14]

With his plays really designed for staging Browning fared badly. Macready had rejected *King Victor and King Charles,* the play that appeared in 1842 as the second number of *Bells and Pomegranates,* even before *Sordello,* perhaps realizing that Browning's undeniable dramatic gifts were not the same thing as a sense of theater. Furthermore, Macready was in no financial condition to take chances with a play-

12. *Letters of EBB,* I, 288.
13. See Letter 6.
14. N.S. VIII (June 1841), 405.

wright whose "obscurity" threatened to become a legend, and was therefore all the more deeply shaken by the *Sordello* disaster. He rejected *The Return of the Druses* in 1840 and it appeared in 1843 as the fourth number of the pamphlet series. Browning thereupon undertook to tailor a play that would specifically avoid Macready's objections to these two. The result was *A Blot in the 'Scutcheon*. After two years of desperate evasive action Macready scheduled production, but he then engaged in still wilder maneuvers during rehearsal to induce Browning to withdraw the play. It was finally staged, but at the expense of what little civility still existed between its author and its producer. Browning and Moxon rushed it into print the day the play opened as the fifth number of *Bells and Pomegranates* in an attempt to forestall Macready's extensive alterations.[15]

The unpleasantness with Macready left Browning with one slim theatrical tie, which was soon severed. On the strength of an offer from Charles Kean he wrote *Colombe's Birthday* and delivered it in March 1844. But Kean wanted to delay production for a year, and that was much too long for Browning's purposes. When he bundled the play off to Moxon to become the sixth number of *Bells and Pomegranates* Browning symbolically washed his hands of the theater. The play was produced in 1853 and again in 1885 with some success, but Browning never again wrote for the theater. In less than four years he had reached the dead end of the road he took when *Sordello* failed. Fortunately, however, Moxon had suggested varying the original intention of making the pamphlet series exclusively plays. The third number in 1842 was called *Dramatic Lyrics* and consisted of fourteen short poems. Eight of them are now standard favorites of thousands of people who have scarcely heard of any of the works mentioned so far. *Porphyria's Lover* and *Johannes Agricola* were at last collected and published beside *Cavalier Tunes, My Last Duchess, Incident of the French Camp, Soliloquy of the Spanish Cloister, Cristina,* and *The Pied Piper of Hamelin*. Critics were still oversensitive about obscurity, but the pamphlet was kindly— though not widely—reviewed.

Soon after sending *Colombe's Birthday* to Moxon, Browning set off on his second trip to Italy. Before leaving he submitted four short poems to *Hood's Magazine*.[16] These, unlike his contributions to the

15. For a full account, see DeVane, pp. 137–145.
16. For Browning's contributions to *Hood's,* see Letter 63, note 2.

Monthly Repository eight years earlier, were signed.

Just about the time Browning's play was submitted to Kean, E.B.B.'s *A Drama of Exile* and enough accompanying poems to fill two volumes were in the press for Moxon, and their author had acquired enough transatlantic reputation that a New York bookseller planned to publish simultaneously and pay her 10 per cent of profits. *Poems* (1844) appeared in England in August and was greeted by a flood of critical praise, one that was still running high at the time of her marriage. Even critics who found technical fault were impressed by her profundity and moral earnestness. When the American edition (*A Drama of Exile and Other Poems*) appeared, the enthusiastic Poe hailed her in the dedication of *The Raven and Other Poems* (1845) as the "Noblest of her Sex."

There was more than one reason for this success. The new poems were in general better than those of 1838, but matters wholly independent of poetic value conspired in their favor with the public. One of the chief was the essay about E.B.B. in Horne's *New Spirit of the Age,* widely grumbled about by disgruntled authors and their friends but widely read nevertheless. A modern press agent could hardly have aroused more interest than Horne's picture of her as a fabulous invalid of great learning who corresponded with many important people but lived in an "almost hermetically sealed" apartment and saw no one.[17] Another was the fact that she had published in the very influential *Blackwood's,* which regularly took care of its own critically. It praised the new collection at length. In addition, several of the poems had rather special appeals. *The Cry of the Children,* which had already attracted favorable attention in *Blackwood's* in 1843, and *The Cry of the Human,* published in America in November 1842, were both addressed to contemporary political and social problems and enlisted the partisan interest of reformers like Cobden and Fox and their followers. *Lady Geraldine's Courtship,* a last-minute addition,[18] proved to be most popular of all. In the trochaic rhythm of *Locksley Hall,* later adopted by Poe in *The Raven,* it told a sentimental short story of the kind popular with Tennyson's early readers. But a third appeal was probably more important than either of these. An age that itched to see its own reflection in art liked the poem's references to current history and con-

17. See Letter 6, note 1.
18. *Letters of EBB,* I, 176–177.

temporary figures: Tennyson, the journalist Howitt, the sculptor Lough—and Browning. Save that the sexes were reversed, it was the simplest of Cinderella stories, but the stage properties succeeded in making a surprising number of readers and critics think it realistic.

The triumph was complete: letters arrived from the great and the humble; many asked to call but few were admitted. By January 1845 Elizabeth Barrett Barrett had been accepted in many quarters as England's leading poetess. Still in seclusion in that single Wimpole Street room with the carefully controlled temperature, she was laying plans. In view of the particular and surprising success of *Lady Geraldine's Courtship,* she began plotting a modern novel in verse, announced to Miss Mitford on December 30, 1844.[19] Eleven days later Browning's first letter arrived and began the train of events that were to make *Aurora Leigh* so completely unlike *Lady Geraldine.*

Though she had refused to see him in 1841, Browning and Miss Barrett had thereafter maintained fairly regular indirect contact through John Kenyon. Browning relayed his approval of the papers she published in the *Athenæum* in 1842,[20] and his note to Kenyon praising a poem he had seen in manuscript so pleased E.B.B. that she asked to keep it.[21] Privately she commended his work to her friends; publicly she expressed, in an *Athenæum* review of Wordsworth, her hope for poetry in an unpoetic age: "The Tennysons and the Brownings ... will work, wait on."[22] The best, however, was yet to be. About the time Browning returned from Italy in late 1844, John Kenyon gave Sarianna Browning the two green volumes of *Poems* (1844). There, in stanza xli of *Lady Geraldine,* Browning found a still warmer compliment. E.B.B.'s poet-hero reads to his high-born lady from Spenser, the Italian poets, and some moderns—from Wordsworth, Howitt, Tennyson, "Or from Browning some 'Pomegranate,' which, if cut deep down the middle, / Shows a heart within blood-tinctured, of a veined humanity." Browning's gratitude softened his diffidence about corresponding directly, and Kenyon first assured and then by note

19. *EBB to MRM,* pp. 231–232. The reference is pretty certainly to *Aurora Leigh,* and there are numerous bits of evidence in these letters that much of that work was written in 1845–46. These are cited in the notes.

20. Her four papers on *The Greek Christian Poets* appeared on February 26 and March 5, 12, and 19, 1842. They are reprinted in her *Works,* ed. F. G. Kenyon (London, 1897), pp. 590 ff.

21. *Letters of EBB,* I, 143.

22. *Athenæum,* August 27, 1842. Reprinted in *Works,* ed. Kenyon, p. 650.

"re-assured" him that E.B.B. would be pleased by a letter. Only then, "on *account of my purely personal obligation*" and "on the whole, UNWILLINGLY," as he puts it in Letter 151, Browning took up his pen and began the headlong letter that opens this correspondence.

III. *" The Noblest of Her Sex"*

That letter's bold and prophetic profession of love for a woman Browning had yet to see is indeed remarkable even by later standards of decorum. One wonders how it was received. Apparently with less surprise than one would expect, even though E.B.B. seems never to have interpreted it as another of the irresponsible gallantries that sometimes turned up in her mail. One of the most regularly recurrent formulas in E.B.B.'s letters is her claim to be the supreme favorite of one person or another. There is evidence that this is not the egotistical delusion it may seem; Miss Mitford, Kenyon, the members of her family, and dozens of people who met her afterward in Italy—many and various persons testify to a marked partiality for her, and many of them do so too early to be explained away as influenced by any pity for an invalid. Something about the tiny dark-haired woman often generated real and spontaneous affection. For instance, although she was the oldest of the Barrett children and regarded by the outside world as an erudite bluestocking, she was treated by her brothers and sisters, and often by her father, with something like the affection reserved for a particularly winning child. She was the center of a large family's affections.

As we have already seen, her mother and two brothers had already died; in addition a sister, Mary, had died in early childhood. Even so there were ten immediate family members in Wimpole Street. The two nearest in age to Elizabeth were her sisters, Henrietta (1809-60) and Arabella (1813-68). Henrietta was pretty, lively, and restive under her father's restrictions on social life. In 1850 she married Captain Surtees Cook, the second cousin glimpsed in these letters as her furtive but persevering suitor, and was disowned by her father. Arabella was especially close to E.B.B. and then to Browning after her death. She was a deeply religious woman. There were six surviving brothers. The eldest was Charles John (1814-1905), known as "Stormie" in the family and afflicted with a speech impediment that prevented his taking the degree for which he studied at Glasgow. George Goodin (1817-95) did take an A.B. at Glasgow and became a barrister-at-law in 1839. His work led to a fairly broad social acquaintance. Henry (1819-96) enters his sister's letters mainly as a negotiator on two occasions when Flush was being held for ransom. Alfred Price (1820-1904) was an amateur artist who hoped to become secretary to an official of the Great Western Railway and was studying accounting for the purpose. He was disappointed in this hope, and his sister's later letters indicate that he was dogged by ill luck. In 1855 he married his cousin Lizzie, who was a regular member of the Wimpole Street household in 1845-46. Like his two sisters, he was disowned for it. The two remaining brothers were Septimus James (1822-70), "Sette" or "Set," and Octavius Butler (1824-1910), "Occy" or "Occyta," who studied architecture with Barry, the designer of the then-building Houses of Parliament.

The glimpses we are afforded show them a lively, amusing, and affectionate family; they must have lightened the invalid's lot notably. Yet it is instructive to listen to her own account of that life after her delivery from it. From Italy she wrote to her old friend Mrs. Martin: "My family had been so accustomed to the idea of my living on and on in that room, that while my heart was eating itself, their love for me was consoled, and at last the evil grew scarcely perceptible. It was no want of love in them, and quite natural in itself: we all get used to the thought of a tomb; and I was buried . . . Nobody quite understood this of me, because I am not morally a coward, and have a hatred of all the forms of audible groaning . . . Even my poetry . . . was a thing on the outside of me . . . A thoroughly morbid and desolate state it was, which I look back to now with the sort of horror with which one would look to one's graveclothes, if one had been clothed in them by mistake during a trance.[23]

Probably that paradoxical feeling of being at once loved and entombed in the Wimpole Street room owed less to the rest of her family than to her enigmatic father, whose felt presence throughout these letters makes him the third character in the myth. Edward Barrett Moulton-Barrett (1785-1857) was born in Jamaica on the extensive Barrett family estates which he managed as absentee landlord and from which, despite a few serious reverses, he drew wealth enough to be mildly affluent. The Barretts were his mother's family; she had

23. *Letters of EBB*, I, 288.

separated from her husband, Charles Moulton, a restless, philandering man, when her children were still very young. Her sons Edward and Samuel, in accordance with their grandfather's will, added Barrett to their names in 1798 and, except for some likely psychological residue, dropped their father almost entirely from their lives. They were then in England, where their mother had taken them in 1795 for their education. Edward was enrolled at Harrow but withdrawn after being flogged by an older boy.[24] Later he spent a very short time at Trinity College, Cambridge, but never matriculated. In 1805 he married Mary Graham-Clarke, and their daughter Elizabeth was born in April of the next year.

In the twenty-nine years from his wife's death to his own, Mr. Barrett held the bulk of his family together by strictly forbidding them to marry. Elizabeth and the other two defectors were summarily disowned and seemingly forgotten. The man is a very complicated riddle we must not expect fully to unravel. "Not one of his children will ever marry without a breach," E.B.B. wrote after her own marriage but before Henrietta's and Alfred's, "which we all know, *though he probably does not.*"[25] His strangeness showed itself in other ways than the marriage taboo. Even though John Kenyon was a relative, a college acquaintance, and E.B.B.'s great benefactor, Mr. Barrett never invited him to dinner. It was probably not personal coolness or ingratitude: Mr. Barrett once called personally upon R. H. Horne in gratitude for a kindness to his daughter but, to her chagrin, did not ask him to dinner either.[26] This might suggest a recluse or a social grotesque, but he was a member of the Reform Club, and Mary Russell Mitford, who somehow was asked to dinner, found him charming. "Mr. Barrett," she wrote her friend Miss Anderdon, "looks younger than Mr. Dawson, much younger, and has the same animation and flow of conversation."[27] At her suggestion, in fact, Miss Anderdon called on the Barretts but was rebuffed, which led Miss Mitford to remark, "I doubt if any of the family except the young lawyer . . . visit much—and yet Mr. Barrett is an exceedingly clever agreeable man with easy highbred manners."[28] Four months later the topic was still alive: "It seems to me that Mr.

24. Browning's "Prefatory Note," in E.B.B.'s *Works,* ed. Kenyon, p. viii.
25. *Letters of EBB,* I, 292; italics added.
26. *EBB to MRM,* p. 183.
27. Manuscript letter, November 1841, at Yale.
28. Manuscript letter, December 5, 1841, at Yale.

Barrett, delightful person as he is, shirks [?] from any extension of his acquaintance" and desires no visitors "beyond his family connexion."[29] There seems to have been a moral paradox as well as a social one. This man who held his own sons and daughters in a sort of slavery—"using one's children as one's chattels" is E.B.B.'s description of it in Letter 256 —"willingly assisted in his own undoing [as a West Indian proprietor] by petitioning for emancipation."[30]

These complexities in Mr. Barrett's personality sometimes make those who deal with him on paper seem disingenuous. It is hard, for instance, to square E.B.B.'s praise of her father in the dedication to *Poems* (1844) with the implications of some of these letters, written less than two years later. She saw the problem herself; in Letter 214, after telling Browning her father would rather see her dead than married, she asks, "Do you ever wonder at me . . that I should write such things, and have written others so different? *I have thought* THAT *in myself very often."* When this correspondence was first published in 1899 "Stormie" Moulton-Barrett protested in a letter to the *Standard:* "The careless indifference of Mr. Robert [Wiedemann Barrett] Browning . . . was no excuse for the sacrilege. His mother would have been horrified. She loved her father. The notices of the book have been . . . cruelly unjust to [my father]."[31] Indeed E.B.B. did love her father, so much that her failure to effect a reconciliation was bitterly painful, as a letter to Miss Mitford, apparently written after a miscarriage, testified: "perhaps, after all, if I had to choose between additional comforts, I should choose the smile of my own father to that of my own child . . if I could have either."[32] Perhaps his undying bitterness is explained by what "Stormie" went on to say: "He had loved her from childhood. He never recovered it."

These letters are indeed unjust to Mr. Barrett, not from malice or falsehood, but from the reductive operation of the myth. When Mr. Besier actually translated the letters into fiction in *The Barretts of Wimpole Street* he did exactly what his form demanded—he provided a crude but easy and coherent account of Edward Moulton-Barrett. Biographically it was libelous nonsense but it made the play possible,

29. Manuscript letter, April 10, 1842, at Yale.
30. Manuscript letter, E.B.B. to Cornelius Mathews, April 30, 1845, at Yale.
31. *Literary Digest,* XVIII (May 20, 1899), 578.
32. Kenyon TpS, April 15 [1848].

whereas a character as complex as the original would have overwhelmed the plot. Sea monsters and dragons are notably uncomplicated. People nearer the situation than Besier and not faced with writing problems have been tempted into similar simplifications. Browning in Letter 531 interprets Mr. Barrett as a mixture of Jehovah complex and slave-owner's instincts, and Browning's friend Arnould called him a Calvinistic hypocrite.[33] Besier is more sensational but not more inaccurate.

No simple account of the man will wash, including the one that undertakes to make him look better by suggesting that he was just a Victorian father with a willful daughter.[34] The view advanced by Miss Jeannette Marks in *The Family of the Barrett,* from which many of the biographical data in this section are drawn, is the most nearly adequate. It cannot be altogether satisfactorily extracted from the mass of background material she supports it with, but some of her points can be summarized. She concludes that a number of eccentricities eventually intensified to the point where Mr. Barrett was in fact insane, but that they were recognizable products of his life and background. Jamaican families tended to be socially self-contained (the Barrett family's social contacts were largely confined to other Jamaican families in London) and to intermarry, probably as a means of holding family fortunes together. Miss Marks feels that Mr. Barrett's financial reverses and the emotional effects of having spent all his adult life away from his native country, where all his family roots were, had darkened these tendencies into xenophobia. Furthermore, his very early separation from his father and his reaction to an awareness of the infidelities that brought it about may account both for his own excessive paternalism and for a morbid sense of sin about sexual matters so strong that he reacted irrationally to the idea of marriage for any of his children. However hypocritical this may sound in a man who married at twenty and sired twelve children, it squares with such things as his approving characterization of Elizabeth as "the purest woman he ever knew," which she reports in Letter 562. She must have seemed the safest from marriage of all his children.

Assuredly, Mr. Barrett was no monster, and there is abundant

---

33. *Robert Browning and Alfred Domett,* p. 133.
34. See Phyllis Browne, "De-Bunking Mr. Barrett," *Courier,* XXIX (October, 1957), pp. 67–69.

evidence that he was, or had been, an affectionate and usually good-natured father. He seems never to have committed his side of this story to paper, so that we are very unlikely ever to resolve the enigma he presents. Several years ago Mr. Lachlan Philip Kelley had reason to believe that E.B.B.'s unavailing letters seeking her father's forgiveness were still in existence. Even if they are found, of course, we shall not have the answering voice, and it can never be proved that Mr. Barrett read them. But that he did not summarily destroy them would in some degree strengthen the impression in his son's letter of a grieving rather than malignant father: "He never recovered it." Since E.B.B. herself never resolved the enigma of her father, it is, happily, no bar to enjoying her letters and Browning's. It is necessary only to realize that she could love the tyrant and even for a time feel a sort of security in his tyranny, yet recognize it, to use her own metaphor, as something like premature graveclothes.

E.B.B.'s surprise and delight at her delivery from this quasi–death are clearly enough reflected in her image of Browning as the delivering angel, which moves from Letter 143 into Sonnet XLII of *Sonnets from the Portuguese*. But it returns us to the distorting mirror of myth, which simplifies her father into villainy and transmutes into pure hero a human being who, as we shall see, was too much marked by his time and his circumstances to assume the role easily. And it gives us the very bad exchange of another suffering Victorian heroine for a woman with genuine gaiety, humor, and intelligence in the process of discovering that life stretches ahead of her, not behind her. It is thus well to remember that this is Perseus and Andromeda with a difference.

IV. The "New Cross Knight"

Our concern is not to deny that we are dealing with a very remarkable story, but to make sure that we do not dehumanize the principals. Such a process, quite apart from these letters, influenced the popular picture of Browning for a long time. The interpretation that confused him with the assured and incorrigible optimist who inhabits some of his poetry has been seriously questioned, particularly in the last two decades. Carefully read, his love letters alone would discredit it. As has already been suggested in tracing his early career, he was not a man patiently waiting for posterity to vindicate his rather daring choice of career. His very real courage was not uncloudedly optimistic and self-assured, but human enough to include hours, days, and weeks of frustration, and moments of petulance, despair, and awkwardness. *Rabbi Ben Ezra* may "prize" doubt in a tone that makes it sound like another thing, but Browning knew the agonizing reality of it, and all the more intensely for the gamble he had taken with life. If one misses that fact there are some unnecessary puzzles about him—for instance, his early and continuing feeling almost of abhorrence for *Pauline* and his adoption of a set formula to "explain" the poem.[35] Not to sense his occasional frustration and his self-consciousness is to ignore or put a less charitable construction on bits of affectation and flashes of ill temper.[36] It is also to miss enjoying the remarkable tact and understanding with which E.B.B. responds.

Until his marriage Browning depended upon his father for support and for the expense of publishing his poetry. There can be no doubt of his father's willingness, but it is hard to suppose that the situation did not trouble Browning. Two bits of evidence in these letters show that it did not pass without comment. Browning tells in Letter 102 how Basil Montagu repeatedly urged him to study law, and in Letter 311 E.B.B. reports Mrs. Procter's regret that he "had not seven or eight hours a day of occupation." Nineteenth-century England found the idea of a young man's setting up in business as a full-time poet a bit preposterous. When E.B.B. reviewed Wordsworth's 1842 volume she praised the old man's dedication of a whole life to poetry and contrasted the practice of his successors: "'Art,' it was said long ago, 'requires the whole man,' and 'Nobody,' it was said later, 'can be a poet who is anything else;' but the present idea of Art requires the segment of a man, and everybody who is anything at all is a poet in a parenthesis."[37] In the refusal of "the

---

35. See Letter 207, note 5.

36. Though affectation is rather rare in these letters, it is common in surviving Browning letters before 1846, except perhaps those to Domett. It is noteworthy in the unpublished correspondence with Comte Amédée de Ripert-Monclar, which I have read through the kindness of its owner, Professor Richard L. Purdy of Yale. It is very clear in the preface and notes ɔ *Pauline* and *Paracelsus*. Harriet Martineau noted "some little affectations" (G & M, p. 137); as late as 1852 Mrs. Carlyle thought Browning "a fluff of feathers" (*New Letters and Memorials of Jane Welsh Carlyle* [2 vols., London and New York: John Lane, 1903], II, 39, 108); Miss Mitford's unrestrained remarks are quoted in the Biographical Appendix entry for her. The temper is apparent enough even in these letters, where Browning must have wanted very much to control it.

37. See above, note 18.

Tennysons and the Brownings" to be mere parenthetical poets she found hope for poetry's survival. But she was a rare dissenting voice in the choir of Montagus and Mrs. Procters.

Browning's irregular choice of career was the more egregious because he was not a university man and because his family was not nobility, gentry, or even clergy. In fact his social position was much like that of Keats, one of whose critics, it will be recalled, reminded him of his "place" and counseled him to return to gainful employment. Lockhart was anachronistic as well as unjust, for the line between upper middle class and gentry was blurring; but it had yet to disappear, and one senses Browning's lurking awareness of it. It was, however, in no sense a hat-in-hand awareness. The Browning of 1845–46 danced the newly fashionable polka, moved with apparent ease among titles and celebrities, and generally led an active, even strenuous, social life, as he had since publishing *Paracelsus*. The third and fourth *Sonnets from the Portuguese* and some of her first letters to Browning show that in E.B.B.'s mind his social bent seemed to open a gulf between them: "but what a strange world you seem to have," she remarks in Letter 17, "to me at a distance—what a strange husk of a world!" Browning replied that he too thought it a husk; he cultivated it at the expense of an aching head when what he most wanted was the simplest life possible. In Letter 305 a defense of dueling leads him to discuss the uses of society as he sees them: "There are uses in it, great uses, for purposes quite beyond its limits—you pass thro' it, mix with it, to get something by it: you do *not* go into the world to live on the breath of every fool there, but you reach something *out* of the world by being let go quietly, if not with a favourable welcome, among them." Surely one meaning of this is that Browning thought part of his battle for acceptance was social and had to be fought in drawing rooms and salons. And it attests to the mask mentioned earlier and to his discomfort with it.

The legendary figure with unflagging courage, optimism, and moral energy sometimes mistaken for Browning is credited as well with robust and extraordinary health, and the reader familiar with him may be somewhat surprised to find in these letters so many references to disabling headaches. His first impulse will be to attribute them to the special tensions of an unusual love affair. But Browning's ill health neither began in 1845 nor ended in 1846. In 1842 E.B.B. wrote Miss Mitford that Browning was "weak in health," and on another occasion that he feared that his horse would be taken away from him, presumably for reasons of health.[38] Mrs. Orr says explicitly that Browning was much less healthy than his father: "he was conscious of . . . a nervousness of nature . . . He imputed to an undue physical sensitiveness to mental causes of irritation, his proneness to deranged liver, and . . . asthmatic conditions."[39] The very different impression given by Griffin and Minchin's *Life* is probably owing to Pen Browning's complaint to Griffin that Mrs. Orr had misrepresented his father's health and that "he was the healthiest man I ever knew!"[40] However true that may have been for the part of his father's life that Pen remembered, there is strong support for Mrs. Orr in the evidence from an earlier period. For example, E.B.B. feared that the strain of seeing *Bells and Pomegranates* VIII through the press would trigger the disabling headaches; in Letter 293 she writes: "You are sure not to be well. That is to be accepted as a necessary consequence—it cannot be otherwise." Later, in Italy, worry over his wife's health brought on more such headaches. Several times in the letters E.B.B. speaks, as if she were clairvoyant, of headache or annoyance not reflected in Browning's words themselves. The clue she is reading is the size of Browning's hand, normally miniscule in his letters to her (after the first) but larger than average in some written when he is known to be ill. When the larger hand appears unheralded, she understands. Sometimes, when Browning touches on a matter that agitates him, the change is strikingly evident in the course of a single letter.

It is clear that Browning's headaches—and his flashes of temper as well—came of tension and frustration, but both cause and effect preceded the love affair and did not conveniently disappear with marriage. The fact is that the course of Browning's early career would have exasperated many men, and the physiological testimony is that it did in fact exasperate Browning.[41] Letter 529 quotes the epithet used by Mr. Hunter, E.B.B.'s unsuccessful suitor, for Browning: the "New Cross Knight." Even Hunter saw the outline of the myth in this story, but with the malice of an interested and unhappy party. The resultant irony has the not unwelcome ring of truth. This mid-nineteenth-

38. *EBB to MRM,* pp. 136, 140.
39. Mrs. Orr, pp. 19–20.
40. Manuscript letter of October 30, 1903, W. Hall Griffin Papers.
41. John Kenyon believed Browning was discouraged by his lack of success. See *Letters to Geo. Barrett,* pp. 81–82.

century love story has its real reflections of St. George, of Perseus and Andromeda, but in that age as in ours such things cannot pass untouched by irony.

The Letters

R.B. to E.B.B.

[*Postmarked January 10, 1845, a Friday*]

New Cross, Hatcham, Surrey.

I love your verses with all my heart, dear Miss Barrett,—and this is no off-hand complimentary letter that I shall write,—whatever else, no prompt matter-of-course recognition of your genius, and there a graceful and natural end of the thing: since the day last week when I first read your poems,[1] I quite laugh to remember how I have been turning and turning again in my mind what I should be able to tell you of their effect upon me—for in the first flush of delight I thought I would this once get out of my habit of purely passive enjoyment, when I do really enjoy, and thoroughly justify my admiration—perhaps even, as a loyal fellow-craftsman should, try and find fault and do you some little good to be proud of hereafter!—but nothing comes of it all—so into me has it gone, and part of me has it become, this great living poetry of yours, not a flower of which but took root and grew—oh how different that is from lying to be dried and pressed flat, and prized highly and put in a book with a proper account at top and bottom, and shut up and put away . . and the book called a 'Flora,' besides! After all I ⟨shall be⟩ need not give up the thought of doing that, too, in time; because even now, talking with whoever is worthy, I can give a reason for my faith in one and another excellence, the fresh strange music, the affluent language, the exquisite pathos and true new brave thought—but in this addressing myself to you—your own self, and for the first time, my feeling rises altogether. I do, as I say, love these books with all my heart—and I love you too: do you know I was once not very far from seeing—really seeing you? Mr. Kenyon said to me one morning "Would you like to see Miss Barrett?"—then he went to announce me,—then he returned . . you were too unwell—and now it is years ago[2]—and I feel as at some untoward passage in my travels—as if I had been close, so close, to some

3

world's-wonder in chapel or crypt, ⟨‖ · · · ‖⟩↑only↓ a screen to push and I might have entered, but there was some slight . . so it now seems . . slight and just-sufficient bar to admission; and the half-opened door shut, and I went home my thousands of miles, and the sight was never to be!

Well, these Poems were to be—and this true thankful joy and pride with which I feel myself

Yours ever faithfully,

Robert Browning

1. *Poems* (1844). 2 vols. John Kenyon had given the set to Browning's sister.
2. "Mr. Kenyon proposed also to introduce to my sofa-side—Mr. Browning the poet—who was so honor-giving as to wish something of the sort. I was pleased at the thought of his wishing it—for the rest, *no!*" E.B.B., March 30, 1842, *Letters to Geo. Barrett*, p. 81.

2 (W1°)   **E.B.B. to R.B.**

[*Saturday*]

50 Wimpole Street:
Jan. 11, 1845.

I thank you, dear Mr. Browning, from the bottom of my heart. You meant to give me pleasure by your letter—and even if the object had not been answered, I ought still to thank you. But it is thoroughly answered. Such a letter from such a hand! Sympathy is dear—very dear to me: but the sympathy of a poet, & of such a poet, is the quintessence of sympathy to me! Will you take back my gratitude for it?—agreeing, too, that of all the commerce done in the world, from Tyre to Carthage, the exchange of sympathy for gratitude is the most princely thing?

For the rest you draw me on with your kindness. It is difficult to get rid of people when you once have given them too much pleasure—*that* is a fact, & we will not stop for the moral of it. What I was going to say . . after a little natural hesitation . . is, that if ever you emerge without inconvenient effort from your "passive state," & will *tell* me of such faults as rise to the surface and strike you as important in my poems, (for of course, I do not think of troubling you with criticism in detail) you will confer a lasting obligation on me, and one which I shall value so much, that I covet it at a distance. I do not pretend to any extra-ordinary meekness under criticism, & it is possible enough that I might not be altogether obedient to yours. But with my high respect for your power in your Art & for your experience as an artist, it w^d be quite impossible for me to hear a general observation of yours on what appear to you my master-faults, without being the better for it hereafter in some way. I ask for only a sentence or two of general observation—and I do not ask even for *that*, so as to teaze you—but in the humble, low voice, which is so excellent a thing in women[1]—particularly when they go a-begging! The most frequent general criticism I receive, is, I think, upon the style, "if I *would* but change my style"! But *that* is an objection (isn't it?) to the writer bodily? Buffon says, and every sincere writer must feel, that '*Le style c'est l'homme;*' a fact, however, scarcely calculated to lessen the objection with certain critics.

It is indeed true that I was so near to the pleasure and honour of making your acquaintance?—& can it be true that you look back upon the lost opportunity with any regret? BUT . . . you know . . if you had entered the 'crypt,' you might have caught cold, or been tired to death, & *wished* yourself 'a thousand miles off'—which w^d have been worse than travelling them. It is not my interest however to put such thoughts in your head about its' being "all for the best"—and I would rather hope (as I do) that what I lost by one chance I may recover by some future one. Winters shut me up as they do dormouse's eyes: in the spring, *we shall see*: & I am so much better that I seem turning round to the outward world again. And in the meantime I have learnt to know your voice, not merely from the poetry but from the kindness in it. Mr. Kenyon often speaks of you—dear Mr. Kenyon!—who most un-speakably, or only speakably with tears in my eyes, . . has been my friend & helper, & my book's friend & helper! critic & sympathiser, true friend of all hours! You know him well enough, I think, to understand that I must be grateful to him.

I am writing too much—& ₊notwithstanding₊ that I am writing too much, I will write of one thing more. I will say that I ₊am₊ your debtor, not only for this cordial letter & for all the pleasure which came with it, but in other ways, & those the highest: & I will say that while I live to follow this divine art of poetry . . in proportion to my love for it and my devotion to it, I must be a devout admirer & student of your works. This is in my heart to say to you—& I say it.

And, for the rest, I am proud to remain
                 Your obliged and faithful
                                              Elizabeth B. Barrett

   1. *Lear* V. iii. 273–274.

3 (W2)   R.B. *to* E.B.B.

_____

[*Monday*]

                                   New Cross, Hatcham, Surrey.
                                              Jany 13, 1845.

Dear Miss Barrett,
      I just shall say, in as few words as I can, that you make me very
happy, and that, now the beginning is over, I dare say I shall do better . .
because my poor praise, number one, was nearly as felicitously brought
out, as a certain tribute to no less a personage than Tasso, which I was
amused with at Rome some weeks ago, in a neat pencilling on the
plaister-wall by his tomb at Sant' Onofrio—"Alla cara memoria—di—
(please fancy solemn interspaces and grave capital letters at the new
lines)—di—Torquato Tasso—il Dottore Bernardini—offriva—il
seguente Carme—*O tu*"[1] . . and no more, the good man, it should
seem, breaking down with the overload of love here! But my "O tu"—
was breathed out most sincerely, and now you have taken it in gracious
part, the rest will come after. Only,—and which is why I write now—it
looks as if I have introduced some phrase or other about "your faults"
so cleverly as to give exactly the opposite meaning to what I meant,
which was, that in my first ardour I had thought to tell you of *everything*
which impressed me in your verses, down, even, to whatever "faults"
I could find—a good earnest, when I had got to *them,* that I had left out
not much between: as if some Mr. Fellows[2] were to say, in the overflow
of his first enthusiasm of rewarded adventure, "I will describe you all
the outer life and ways of these Lycians, down to their very sandal-
thongs," whereto the be-corresponded one rejoins—"Shall I get next
week, then, your dissertation on sandal-thongs"? Yes, and a little about
the 'Olympian Horses,' and god-charioteers as well!
      What "struck me as faults," were not matters on the removal of

which, one was to have—poetry, or high poetry,—but the very highest poetry, so I thought, and that, to universal recognition: for myself, or any artist, in many of the cases there would be a positive loss of true, peculiar artist's pleasure . . for an instructed eye loves to see where the brush has dipped twice in a lustrous colour, has lain insistingly along a favorite outline, dwelt lovingly in a grand shadow—for these "too muches" for the everybody's picture are so many helps to the making out the real painter's-picture as he had it in his brain; and all of the Titian's Naples Magdalen must have ‹once› been golden in its degree to justify that heap of hair in her hands—the *only* gold effected now!

But about this soon—for night is drawing on and I go out, yet cannot, quiet at conscience, till I repeat (to *myself* . . for I never said it to you, I think) that your poetry must be, cannot but be, infinitely more to me than mine to you—for you *do* what I always wanted, hoped to do, and only seem now likely to do for the first time. You speak out, *you*,—I only make men & women speak—give you truth broken into prismatic hues, and fear the pure white light, even if it is in me:[3] but I am going to try . . so it will be no ⟨‖ · · · ‖⟩ small comfort to have your company just now,—seeing that when you have your men & women aforesaid, you are busied with them, whereas it seems bleak melancholy work, this talking to the wind[4] (for I have begun)—yet I don't think I shall let *you* hear, after all, the savage things about Popes and imaginative religions that I must say.[5]

See how I go on and on to you,—I who, whenever now and then pulled, by the head and hair, into letter-writing, get sorrowfully on for a line or two, as the cognate creature urged on by stick and string, and then come down "flop" upon the sweet haven of page one, line last, as serene as the sleep of the virtuous! You will never more, I hope, talk of 'the honor of my acquaintance,' but I will joyfully wait for the delight of your friendship, and the spring, and my Chapel-sight after all! Ever yours most faithfully,

R. Browning

For Mr. Kenyon—I have a convenient theory about *him,* and his otherwise quite unaccountable kindness to me—but 'tis quite night now, and they call me.

1. "To the dear memory of Torquato Tasso—Dr. Bernardini—offered—the following poem—*O thou*—"

2. Charles Fellows (1799–1860), archaeologist, had lately discovered the Xanthian Marbles in Lycia and brought them to the British Museum. He was knighted in May of 1845.

3. W. O. Raymond says *Numpholeptos* (1876) is very like a commentary in allegory on this passage *(The Infinite Moment* [Toronto: University of Toronto Press, 1950], p. 205).

4. In other words, writing non-dramatic poetry.

5. Dowden (p. 123) suggests that this refers to *Christmas Eve* and *Easter Day.* Nothing in *Dramatic Romances and Lyrics,* then in progress, fits this description, but *St. Praxed's,* critical but not savagely so of a Bishop, was sent to *Hood's Magazine* on February 18 (D & K, pp. 35–36). Of all Browning's work *The Pope and the Net* best fits this account. Perhaps like the *Cardinal and the Dog,* which was set just before it in *Asolando* (1889) and is similar to it in a number of ways, it had been written long before it was published.

4 *(W2°)* **E.B.B. to R.B.**

[*Wednesday*]

50 Wimpole Street:
Jan. 15, 1845.

Dear Mr. Browning,

The fault was clearly with me & not with you.

When I had an Italian master, years ago, he told me that there was an unpronounceable English word which absolutely expressed me, & which he would say in his own tongue, as he could not in mine, . . "*testa lunga.*" Of course, the signor meant *headlong*—and now I have had enough to tame me, & might be expected to stand still in my stall. But you see I do not. Headlong I was at first, and headlong I continue—precipitously rushing forward through all manner of nettles & briars instead of keeping the path,—guessing at the meaning of unknown words instead of looking into the dictionary . . tearing open letters, and never untying a string,—and expecting everything to be done in a minute, & the thunder to be as quick as the lightning. And so, at your half word I flew at the whole one, with all its possible consequences, & wrote what you read. Our common friend, as I think he is, Mr. Horne, is often forced to entreat me into patience & coolness of purpose,—though his only intercourse with me has been by letter. And, by the way, you will be sorry to hear that during his stay in Germany *he* has been 'headlong' (out of a metaphor) twice,—once, in falling from the Drachenfels, when he only just saved himself by catching at a vine,—and once quite lately, at Christmas, in a fall on the ice of the Elbe in skating, when he dislocated his left shoulder in a very painful manner. He is doing quite well, I believe—but it was sad to have such a shadow from the German Christmas tree, & he a stranger.

In art, however, I understand that it does not do to be headlong, but patient & laborious—& there is a love strong enough, even in me, to overcome nature. I apprehend what you mean in the criticism you just intimate, & shall turn it over & over in my mind until I get practical good from it. What no mere critic sees, but what you, an artist, know, is the difference between the thing desired & the thing attained, between the idea in the writer's mind & the ἐΐδωλον¹ cast off in his work. All the effort—the quickening of the breath & beating of the heart in pursuit, which is ruffling & injurious to the general effect of ₊a₊ composition; all which you call 'insistency,' & which many wᵈ call superfluity, and which *is* superfluous in a sense . . *you* can pardon, because you understand. The great chasm between the thing I say, & the thing I would say, wᵈ be quite dispiriting to me, in spite even of such kindnesses as yours, if the desire did not master the despondency. "Oh for a horse with wings!" It is wrong of me to write so of myself—only you put your finger on the root of a fault, which has, to my fancy, been a little misapprehended. I do not *say everything I think* (as has been said of me by master-critics) but I *take every means to say what I think,* which is different!—or I fancy so!

In one thing, however, you are wrong. Why shᵈ you deny the full measure of my delight & benefit from your writings? I could tell you why you should not. You have in your vision two worlds—or to use the language of the schools of the day, you are both subjective & objective in the habits of your mind. You can deal both with abstract thought & with human passion in the most passionate sense. Thus, you have an immense grasp in Art; and no one at all accustomed to consider the usual forms of it, could help regarding with reverence & gladness the gradual expansion of your powers. Then you are 'masculine' to the height—and I, as a woman, have studied some of your gestures of language & intonation wistfully, as a thing beyond me far! & the more admirable for being beyond.

Of your new work I hear with delight. How good of you to tell me. And it is not dramatic ⊦in the strict sense⊦ I am to understand . . (am I right in understanding so?) and you speak in your own ⟨‖ ··· ‖⟩ ⊦person⊦ 'to the winds'? no—but to the thousand living sympathies which will awake to hear you. A great dramatic power may develop itself otherwise than in the formal drama; & I have been guilty of wishing, before this hour, (for reasons which I will not thrust upon you after all my tedious writing), that you w^d give the public a poem unassociated ⊦directly or indirectly⊦ with the stage, for a trial on the popular heart. I reverence the drama, but—

But I break in on myself out of consideration for you. I might have done it you will think, before. I vex your 'serene sleep of the virtuous' like a nightmare. Do not say . . "No." I am *sure* I do! As to the vain parlance of the world, I did not talk of the 'honor of your acquaintance' without a true sense of honor, indeed; but I shall willingly exchange it all (& *now*, if you please, at this moment, for fear of worldly muta[bilities) for the 'delight of your friendship.'

Believe me, therefore, dear Mr. Browning.

Faithfully yours & gratefully,

Elizabeth B. Barrett

For Mr. Kenyon's kindness, as *I* see it . . no 'theory' will account. I class it with mesmerism for that reason.]²

1. "Image."
2. Written in the throat of the envelope.

5 (W3)   *R.B. to E.B.B.*

[*January 27, 1845.*]

New Cross, Hatcham
Monday Night

Dear Miss Barrett,

Your books lie on my table here, at arm's length from me, in this old room where I sit all day: and when my head aches or wanders or strikes work, as it now or then will, I take my chance for either green covered volume, as if ⟨there⟩ it were so much fresh trefoil to feel in one's hands this winter-time,—and round I turn, and, putting a decisive elbow on three or four half-done-with 'Bells'[1] of mine, read, read, read, and just as I have shut up the book and walked to the window, I recollect that you wanted me to find faults there, and that, in an unwise hour, I engaged to do so. Meantime, the days go by (the whitethroat is come and sings now) and as I would not have you "look down on me from your white heights" as promise breaker, evader, or forgetter, if I could help . . and as, if I am very candid & contrite, you may find it in your heart to write to me again . . who knows? . . I shall say at once that the said faults cannot be lost, must be *somewhere*, and shall be faithfully brought you back whenever they turn up,—as people tell one of missing matters. I am rather exacting, myself, with my own gentle audience, and get to say spiteful things about them when they are backward in their duties of appreciation—but really, *really*—could I be quite sure that anybody as good as . . I must go on, I suppose, and say—as myself, even, were honestly to feel ↕towards me↕ as I do, towards the writer of Bertha, and the Drama, and the Duchess, and the Page[2] and—the whole two volumes, I should be paid after a fashion, I know.

One thing I can do . . pencil, if you like, and annotate, and dissertate upon that I love most and least—I think I can do it, that is.

Here an odd memory comes—of a friend who,—volunteering such a service to a sonnet-writing somebody, gave him a taste of his quality in a side-column of short criticisms on sonnet the First, and starting off the beginning three lines with, of course, 'bad, worse, worst'—made by a generous mintage of words to meet the sudden run on his epithets, 'worser, worserer, worserest' pay off the second terzet in full . . no 'badder, badderer, badderest' fell to the *Second's* allowance, and 'worser' &c. answered the demands of the Third—'worster, worsterer, worsterest' supplied the emergency of the Fourth; and, bestowing his last 'worserestest and worstestest' on lines 13 and 14, my friend (slapping his forehead like an emptied strong-box) frankly declared himself bankrupt, and honourably incompetent, to satisfy the reasonable expectations of the rest of the series.

What an illustration of the law by which opposite ideas suggest opposite, and contrary images come together!

See now, how, of that "Friendship" you offer me (and here Juliet's word[3] rises to my lips)—I feel sure once and for ever—I have got already, I see, into this little pet-handwriting of mine (not anyone else's) which scratches on as if theatrical copyists (ah me!) and BRADBURY AND EVANS' READER[4] were not! But you shall get something better than this nonsense one day, if you will have patience with me . . hardly better, tho', because this does me real good, gives real relief, to write. After all, you know nothing, next to nothing of me, and that stops me. Spring is to come, however!

If you hate writing to me as I hate writing to nearly everybody, I pray you never write—if you do, as you say, care for anything I have done,—I will simply assure you, that meaning to begin work in deep earnest, BEGIN without affectation, God knows—I do not know what will help me more than hearing from you,—and therefore, if you do not so very much hate it, I know I *shall* hear from you—and very little more about your "tiring me."

Ever yours faithfully,

Robert Browning

1. Poems for *Bells and Pomegranates* VII, *Dramatic Romances and Lyrics,* published November 1845.

2. All from E.B.B.'s 1844 *Poems: Bertha in the Lane, A Drama of Exile, Rhyme of the Duchess May, The Romaunt of the Page.*

3. Perhaps "It is an honour that I dream not of." *Romeo and Juliet* I. iii. 66.

4. The copyists who made up play-books from Browning's manuscript and the reader for the firm which printed *Bells and Pomegranates* for Moxon, Browning's publisher. Browning traced the words here capitalized in a large and exaggeratedly clear hand.

6 *(W3°)* **E.B.B. to R.B.**

[*Monday*]

50 Wimpole Street

Feb. 3, 1845

Why how could I hate to write to you, dear Mr. Browning? Could you believe in such a thing? If nobody likes writing to everybody (except such professional letter writers as you & I are *not*) yet everybody likes writing to somebody, & it w^d be strange and contradictory if I were not always delighted both to hear from *you* and to write to *you* . . this talking upon paper being as good a social pleasure as another, when our means are somewhat straightened. As for me, I have done most of my talking by post of late years—as people shut up in dungeons, take up with scrawling mottos on the walls. Not that I write to many in the way of regular correspondence, as our friend Mr. Horne predicates of me in his romances[1] (which is mere romancing!—) but that there are a few who will write & be written to by me without a sense of injury. Dear Miss Mitford, for instance—you do not know her, I think, personally, although she was the first to tell me (when I was very ill & insensible to all the glories of the world except poetry) of the grand scene in Pippa Passes,[2]—she has filled a large drawer in this room with delightful letters, heart-warm & soul-warm, . . driftings of nature (if sunshine c^d drift like snow)—& which, if they sh^d ever fall the way of all writing, into print, w^d assume the folio shape as a matter of course, & take rank on the lowest shelf of libraries, with Benedictine editions of the Fathers, $\kappa.\tau.\lambda.$[3] I write this to you to show how I can have pleasure in letters, and never think them too long, nor too frequent, nor too illegible from being written in little "pet hands." I can read any ⟨thing⟩ ↑MS.↓ except the writing on the pyramids. And if you will only promise to treat me 'en bon camarade,' without reference to the conventionalities of 'ladies & gentlemen,' taking no thought for your sentences, (nor for mine) nor for your blots, (nor for mine), nor for your blunt speaking (nor for mine), ↑nor for your badd speling (nor for mine),↓ & if you agree to send me a blotted thought whenever you are in the mind for it, & with as little ceremony & less legibility than you would think it necessary to employ towards your printer . . why, *then*, I am ready to sign & seal the contract, and to rejoice in being 'articled' as your correspondent. Only *don't* let us have any constraint, any ceremony! *Don't* be civil to me when you feel rude,—nor loquacious when you incline to silence,— nor yielding in the manners when you are perverse in the mind. See how out of the world I am! Suffer me to profit by it in almost the only profitable circumstance . . & let us rest from the bowing and the courtesying, you & I, on each side. You will find me an honest man on the whole, if rather hasty & prejudging, . . which is a different thing from prejudice at the worst. And we have great sympathies in common, & I am inclined to look up to you in many things, & to learn as much of everything as you will teach me. On the other hand you must prepare yourself to forbear & to forgive—will you? While I throw off the ceremony, I hold the faster to the kindness.

Is it true, as you say, that I 'know so "little"' of you? And is it true, as others say, that the productions of an artist do not partake of his real nature, . . that in the minor sense, man is not made in the image of God? It is *not* true, to my mind—& therefore it is not true that I know little of you, except in as far as it is true (which I believe) that your greatest works are to come. Need I assure you that I shall always hear with the deepest interest every word you will say to me of what you are doing or about to do? I hear of the 'old room' & the '"bells" lying about,' with an interest . . which you may guess at, perhaps. And when you tell me besides, . . of *my poems being there;* & of your caring for them so much beyond the tide-mark of my hopes, . . the pleasure rounds itself into a charm, & prevents its own expression. Overjoyed I am with this cordial sympathy—but it is better, I feel, to try to justify it by future work, than to thank you for it now. I think,—if I may dare to name myself with you in the poetic relation,—that we ⟨have⟩ both have high views of the art we follow, and stedfast purpose in the pursuit of it, & that we should not, either of *us,* be likely to be thrown from the course, by the casting of any Atalanta-ball of speedy popularity. But I do not know, I cannot guess, . . whether you are liable to be pained deeply by hard criticism & cold neglect . . such as original writers like yourself, are too often exposed to—or whether the love of Art is enough for you, & the exercise of Art the filling joy of your life. Not that praise must not always, of necessity, be delightful to the artist, but that it may be redundant to his content. Do you think so? or not? It appears to me that poets who, like Keats, are highly susceptible to criticism, must be jealous, in their own persons, of the ↑future↑ honour of their works. Because, if a work is worthy, honour must follow it—though the worker should not live to see that following or overtaking. Now, is it not enough that the work be honoured—enough I mean, for the worker? And is it not enough to keep down a poets ordinary wearing anxieties, to think, that if his work be worthy it will have honour, &, if not, that 'Sparta must have nobler sons than he'?[4] I am writing nothing applicable, I see, to anything in question—but when one falls into a favorite train of thought, one indulges oneself in thinking on. I began in thinking & wondering what sort of artistic constitution you had—being determined, as you may observe (with a sarcastic smile at the impertinence!), to set about knowing as much as possible of you immediately. Then you spoke of your 'gentle audience'—(you began!)

& I who know that you have not one but many enthusiastic admirers, the 'fit & few' in the intense meaning, yet not the *diffused* fame which will come to you presently,—wrote on, down the margin of the subject, till I parted from it altogether. But, after all, we are on the ˇproperˇ matter of sympathy. And after all, & after all that has been said and mused upon the 'natural ills,' the anxiety, & wearing out experienced by the true artist, . . is not the *good* immeasurably greater than the *evil?* Is it not great good, & great joy? For my part, I wonder sometimes . . I ⟨find⟩ ˇsurpriseˇ myself wondering . . how without such an object & purpose of life, people find it worth while to live at all. And, for happiness . . why my only idea of happiness, as far as my personal enjoyment is concerned, (but ⟨not⟩ I have been straightened in some respects and in comparison with the majority of livers!) lies deep in poetry & its associations. And then, the escape from pangs of heart & bodily weakness . . when you throw off *yourself* . . what you feel to be *yourself*, . . into another atmosphere & into other relations, where your life may spread its wings ˇoutˇ new, & gather on every ⟨feather⟩ separate plume a brightness from the sun of the sun! Is it possible that imaginative writers sh^d be so fond of depreciating & lamenting over their own destiny? Possible, certainly—but reasonable, not at all—& grateful, less than anything!

My faults, my faults—Shall I help you? Ah—you see them too well, I fear. And do you know that *I* also have something of your feeling about 'being about to *begin*'—or I should dare to praise you for having it. But in you, it is different—it is, in you, a virtue. When Prometheus had recounted a long list of sorrows to be endured by Io, & declared at last that he was μηδέπω ἐν προοιμίοις,[5] poor Io ⟨began to cry⟩ burst ˇoutˇ crying. And when the author of 'Paracelsus' and the 'Bells and Pomegranates' says that he is only 'going to begin' we may well (to take 'the opposite idea' as you write) rejoice & clap our hands. Yet I believe that, whatever you may have done, you *will* do what is greater. It is my faith for you.

And how I sh^d like to know what poets have been your sponsors, 'to promise & vow' for you,—and whether you have held true to early tastes, or leapt violently from them—& what books you read, & what hours you write in. How curious I could prove myself!—(if it isn't proved already).[6]

But this is too much indeed—past all bearing, I suspect. Well—but if I ever write to you again, . . I mean, if you wish it,—it may be in the other extreme of shortness. So do not take me for a born heroine of Richardson, or think that I sin always to this length! else,—you might indeed repent your quotation from Juliet . . which I guessed at once—& of course.

> "I have no joy in this contract to-day!
> It is too unadvised, too rash and sudden."[7]

Ever faithfully yours,
Elizabeth B. Barrett

1. "The latter lady [E.B.B.] or 'fair shade'—whichever she may be—is not known personally to anybody; but her poetry is known to a highly intellectual class, and she 'lives' in constant correspondence with many of the most eminent persons of the time . . . Confined entirely to her own apartment, and almost hermetically sealed, in consequence of some extremely delicate state of health, the poetess . . . is scarcely ever seen by any but her own family." *A New Spirit of the Age,* II, 132–134.
2. She had apparently called the Ottima-Sebald scene "exquisite." *EBB to MRM,* pp. 80–81.
3. "Etc."
4. "And be the Spartan's epitaph on me—Sparta hath many a worthier son than he." Byron, *Childe Harold* IV. x.
5. "'Not yet reached the prelude.' Aeschylus, *Prometheus Bound,* 741." Footnote, 1899 edition. Cf. E.B.B.'s translation, ll. 865–866.
6. The words in parentheses are circled in the manuscript.
7. *Romeo and Juliet* II. ii. 117–118.

7 *(W4)*   **R.B. to E.B.B.**

[February 11, 1845.]

Hatcham, Tuesday.

Dear Miss Barrett,
    People would hardly ever tell falsehoods about a matter, if they had been let tell truth in the beginning—for it is hard to prophane one's very self, and nobody who has, for instance, used certain words and ways to a mother or a father *could* . . even if by the devil's help he *would* . . reproduce or mimic them with any effect to anybody else that was to be won over; and so, if "I love you" were always outspoken when it might be, there would, I suppose, be no fear of its desecration at any after time:

but lo! only last night, I had to write, on the part of Mr. Carlyle, to a
certain ungainly foolish gentleman who keeps back from him, with all
the fussy impotence of stupidity (not bad feeling, alas; for *that* we could
deal with) a certain MS. letter of Cromwell's which completes the
collection now going to press[1]—and this long-ears had to be "dear
Sir'd" and "obedient servanted" till I *said* (to use a mild word)
"commend me to the sincerities of this kind of thing"! When I spoke
of you knowing little of me, one of the senses in which I meant so was
this .. that I would not well vowel-point my common-place letters and
syllables with a masoretic[2] *other* sound and sense, make my "dear"
something intenser than "dears" in ordinary, and "yours ever" a
thought more significant than the run of its like; and all this came of your
talking of "tiring me," "being too curious," &c. &c. which I should
never have heard of had the plain truth looked out of my letter with its
unmistakeable eyes: *now*, what you say of the "bowing," and convention that is to be, and *tant de façons* that are not to be, helps me once and
for ever—for have I not a right to say simply that, for reasons I know,
for other reasons I don't exactly know, but might if I chose to think a
little, and for still other reasons, which, most likely, all the choosing and
thinking in the world would not make me know, I had rather hear from
you than see anybody else Or [Oh?] never you care, dear noble Carlyle,
nor you, my own friend Alfred[3] over the sea, nor a troop of true lovers!
—Are not these fates written? There! Don't you answer this, please, but,
mind it is on record, and now then, with a lighter conscience I shall
begin replying to your questions. First then,—what I have printed gives
no knowledge of me—it evidences abilities of various kinds, if you will
—and a dramatic sympathy with certain modifications of passion .. *that*
I think: but I never have begun, even, what I hope I was born to begin
and end,—'R.B. a poem.' And next, if I speak (and, God knows, feel)
as if what you have read were sadly imperfect demonstrations of even
mere ability, it is from no absurd vanity, though it might seem so—
these scenes and song-scraps *are* such mere and very escapes of my inner
power, which lives in me like the light in those crazy Mediterranean
phares I have watched /from⟩at/ sea, wherein the light is ever revolving
in a dark gallery, bright and alive, and only after a weary interval leaps
out, for a moment, from the one narrow chink, and then goes on with
the blind wall between it and you; and, no doubt, *then,* precisely, does
the poor drudge that carries the cresset set himself most busily to trim

the wick—for don't think I want to say I have not worked hard—(this head of mine knows better)—but the work has been *inside,* and not when at stated times I held up my light to you—and, that there is no self-delusion here, I would prove to you, (and nobody else) even by opening this desk I write on, and showing what stuff, in the way of wood, I *could* make a great bonfire with, if I might only knock the whole clumsy top off my tower!—Of course, every writing body says the same, so I gain nothing by the avowal; but when I remember how I have done what was published, and half done what may never be, I say with some right, you can know but little of me. Still, I *hope* sometimes, though phrenologists will have it that I *cannot,* and am doing better with this darling "Luria"—so safe in my head, & a tiny slip of paper I cover with my thumb!

Then you inquire about my "sensitiveness to criticism," and I shall be glad to tell you exactly, because I have, more than once, taken [a] course you might else not understand. I shall live always,—that is for me—I am living here this 1845, that is for London. I write from a thorough conviction that it is the duty of me, and with the belief that, after every drawback & shortcoming, I do my best, all things con-sidered—that is for *me,* and, so being, the not being listened to by one human creature would, I hope, in nowise affect me. But of course I must, if for merely scientific purposes, know all about this 1845, its ways and doings, and something I do know, as that for a dozen cabbages, if I pleased to grow them in the garden here, I might demand, say, a dozen pence at Covent Garden Market,—and that for a dozen scenes, of the average goodness, I may challenge as many plaudits at the theatre close by; and a dozen pages of verse, brought to the Rialto where verse-merchants most do congregate, ought to bring me a fair proportion of the Reviewers' gold-currency, seeing the other traders pouch their winnings, as I do ⟨see⟩: well, when they won't pay me for my cabbages, nor praise me for my poems, I may, if I please, say "more's the shame," and bid both parties 'decamp to the crows,' in Greek phrase, and YET go very lighthearted back to a garden-full of rose-trees, and a soul-full of comforts; if they had bought my greens I should have been able to buy the last number of "Punch," and go thro' the toll-gate of Waterloo Bridge, and give the blind clarionet-player a trifle, and all without changing my gold—if they had taken to my books, my father and mother would have been proud of this and the other 'favourable

critique,' and . . at least so folks hold . . I should have to pay Mr. Moxon
less by a few pounds—whereas . . but you see! Indeed, I force myself to
say ever and anon, in the interest of the market-gardeners regular, and
Keats's proper,—"It's nothing to *you*,—critics & hucksters, all of you,
if I *have* this garden and this conscience,—I might go die at Rome, or
take to gin and the newspaper, for what *you* would care"! So I don't
quite lay open my resources to everybody. But it does so happen, that I
have met with much more than I could have expected in this matter of
kindly and prompt recognition. I never wanted a real set of good hearty
praisers—and no bad reviewers—I am quite content with my share.
No—what I laughed at in my "gentle audience" is a sad trick the real
admirers have of admiring at the wrong place—enough to make an
apostle swear. *That* does make me savage,—*never* the other kind of
people; why, think now: take your own "Drama of Exile" and let *me*
send it to the first twenty men & women that shall knock at your door
to-day and after—of whom the first five are—the Postman, the seller of
cheap sealing-wax, Mr. Hawkins Junr, the Butcher for orders, and the
Tax gatherer—will you let me, by Cornelius Agrippa's assistance,[4]
force these five and their fellows to read, and report on, this drama—
and, when I have put these faithful reports into fair English, do you
believe they would be better ⁺than⁺, if as good, as, the general run of
Periodical criticisms? Not they, I will venture to affirm. But then,—
once again, I get these people together and give them your book, and
persuade them, moreover, that by praising it, the Postman will be
helping its author to divide Long Acre into two beats, one of which she
will take with half the salary and all the red collar,—that a sealing wax-
vendor will see red wafers brought into vogue, and so on with the rest—
and won't you just wish for your Spectators and Observers and
Newcastle-upon-Tyne—Hebdomadal Mercuries back again! You see
the inference—I do sincerely esteem it a perfectly providential and
miraculous thing that they are so well-behaved in ordinary, these
critics; and for Keats and Tennyson to "go softly all their days"[5] for a
gruff word or two is quite inexplicable to me, and always has been.
Tennyson reads the "Quarterly" and does as they bid him, with the
most solemn face in the world—out goes this, in goes that, all is changed
and ranged . . Oh me!—

Out comes the sun, in comes the "Times" and eleven strikes
(it *does*) already, and I have to go to Town, and I have no alternative but

that this story of the Critic and Poet, "the Bear and the Fiddle," should 'begin but break off in the middle'⁶—yet I donot—nor will you henceforth, I know, say, "I vex you, I am sure, by this lengthy writing" —mind that spring is coming, for all this snow; and know me for yours ever faithfully,

R. Browning

I don't dare—yet I will—ask *can* you read this? Because I *could* write a little better, but not so fast. Do you keep writing just as you do now!

1. *Oliver Cromwell's Letters and Speeches, with Elucidations* was published in November 1845. Carlyle wrote Browning in May 1844: "This Mr. X——, Oliver's descendant, seems to be a kind of fool; and I find I shall have to attack him thro' you . . . he is known to some friends of yours." *New Letters of Thomas Carlyle,* ed. Alexander Carlyle (2 vols., London and New York: John Lane, 1904.), I, 311–312. "Mr. X——" was named Field; see *Browning Collections,* p. 46.

2. The Masoretes added vowel points and accents to the purely consonantal traditional text of Hebrew Scriptures. "In [some] cases the vowel points attached to the written word . . . belong to the word which is to be substituted for it, the latter being placed in the margin . . . in some instances the suggested reading really affects the sense of the passage." "Bible," *Encyclopaedia Britannica,* 11th ed., III, 855.

3. Domett.

4. [Heinrich] Cornelius Agrippa [von Nettesheim] (1486?–1535), noted German mystic and occultist, whose most famous work, *Occult Philosophy,* was in Browning's father's library (G & M, p. 22) and furnished the preface to *Pauline.*

5. Isaiah 38:5: "I shall go softly all my years in the bitterness of my soul." Cf. *Fears and Scruples* (1876), st. ix.

6. "Argument of the First Canto," Samuel Butler's *Hudibras.*

---

8 (W4°)   **E.B.B. to R.B.**

[Monday]

50 Wimpole Street,
February 17, 1845.

Dear Mr. Browning,

To begin with the end (which is only characteristic of the perverse like myself), I assure you I read your handwriting as currently as I could read the clearest type from font. If I had practised the art of reading your letters all my life, I couldn't do it better. And then I approve of small

MS. upon principle. Think of what an immense quantity of physical energy must go to the making of those immense sweeping handwritings achieved by some persons. . . Mr. Landor, for instance, who writes as if he had the sky for a copybook & dotted his *i*'s in proportion. People who do such things sh^d wear gauntlets,— yes, and have none to wear,— or they wouldn't waste their strength so. People who write . . by profession . . shall I say? . . never should do it . . or what will become of them when most of their strength retires into their head & heart, (as is the case with some of us & may be the case with all) & when they have to write a poem twelve times over, as Mr. Kenyon says I should do if I were virtuous? Not that I do it. Does anybody do it, I wonder? Do *you*, ever? From what you tell me of the trimming of the light, I imagine not. And besides, one may be laborious as a writer, without copying twelve times over. I believe there are people who will tell you in a moment what three times six is, without 'doing it' on their fingers; and in the same way one may work one's verses in one's head quite as laboriously as on paper—I maintain it. I consider myself a very patient, laborious writer—though dear Mr. Kenyon laughs me to scorn when I say so. And just see how it could be otherwise. If I were netting a purse I might be thinking of something else & drop my stitches,—or even if I were writing verses to please a popular taste, I might be careless in it. But the pursuit of an Ideal acknowledged by the mind, *will* draw and concentrate the powers of the mind—and Art, you know, is a jealous god & demands the whole man . . or woman. I cannot conceive of a sincere artist who is also a careless one—though one may have a quicker hand than another, in general,—& though all are liable to vicissitudes in the degree of facility . . & to entanglements in the machinery, notwithstanding every degree of facility. You may write twenty lines one day— or even three like Euripides in three days—and a hundred lines in one more day—& yet on the hundred, may have been expended as much good work, as on the twenty & the three. And also, as you say, the lamp is trimmed behind the wall—and the act of utterance is the evidence of foregone study still more than it is the occasion to study. The deep interest with which I read all that you had the kindness to write to me of yourself, you must trust me for, as I find it hard to express it. It is sympathy in one way, and interest every way! And now, see! Although you proved to me with admirable logic that, for reasons which you know & reasons which you don't know, I couldn't possibly know anything about you, . . though that is all true . . & proven (which is better than true) I really did understand of you before I was told, exactly what you told me. Yes—I did indeed. I felt sure that as a poet you fronted the future—& that your chief works, in your own apprehension, were to come. Oh—I take no credit of sagacity for it,—as I did not long ago to my sisters & brothers, when I professed to have knowledge of all their friends whom I never saw in my life, by the image coming with the name; and threw them into shouts of laughter by giving out all the blue eyes & black eyes & hazel eyes & noses Roman & Gothic ticketed aright for the Mr. Smiths & Miss Hawkinses—& hit the bull's eye & the true features of the case, ten times out of twelve. But *you* are different. *You* are to be made out by the comparative anatomy system. You have thrown out fragments of ⟨bone⟩ *os* . . *sublime* . . indicative of soul-mammothism—and you live to develop your nature, . . *if* you live. That is easy & plain. You have taken a great range—from those high faint notes of the mystics which are beyond personality . . to dramatic impersonations, gruff with nature, 'gr-r-r- you swine'; & when these are thrown into harmony, as in a manner they are in 'Pippa Passes' (which I could find in my heart to covet the authorship of, more than any of your works—), the combinations of effect must always be striking & noble—and you must feel yourself drawn on to such com-binations more and more. But I do not, you say, know yourself . . you. I only know abilities and faculties. Well, then! teach me yourself . . you. I will not insist on the knowledge—and, in fact, you have not written the R. B. poem yet—your rays fall obliquely rather than directly straight. I see you only in your moon. Do tell me all of yourself that you can & will . . before the R. B. poem comes out. And what is *Luria*? A poem and not a drama? I mean, a poem not in the dramatic form? Well! I have wondered at you sometimes, not for daring, but for bearing to trust your noble works into the great mill of the "rank, popular" play-house, to be ground to pieces between the teeth of vulgar actors and actresses. I, for one, would as soon have "my soul among lions."[1] 'There is a fascination in it,' says Miss Mitford, & I am sure there must be, to account for it. Publics in the mass are bad enough; but to distil the dregs of the public & baptise oneself in that acrid moisture, where can be the temptation[?] I could swear by Shakespeare, as was once sworn "by those dead at Marathon," that I do not see where. I love the drama too. I look to our old dramatists as to our Kings & princes in poetry. I love them through all the deeps of their abominations. But the theatre in those days was a better medium between the people and the poet; and the press in those days was a less sufficient medium than now. Still, the poet suffered by the theatre even then; & the reasons are very obvious.

　　How true—how true .. is all you say about critics. My convictions follow you in every word. And I delighted to read your views of the poet's right aspect towards criticism—I read them with the most complete appreciation & sympathy. I have sometimes thought that it would be a curious & instructive process, as illustrative of the wisdom & apprehensiveness of critics, if anyone would collect the critical soliloquies of every age touching its own literature, (as far as such may be extant) and *confer* them with the literary product of the said ages. Professor Wilson[2] has begun something of the kind apparently, in his ⁺initiatory⁺ paper of the last Blackwood number on critics, beginning with Dryden—but he seems to have no design in his notice—it is a mere critique on the critic. And then, he sh^d have begun earlier than Dryden —earlier even than Sir Philip Sydney, who in the noble 'Discourse on Poetry,' gives such singular evidence of being stone-critic-blind to the gods who moved around him. As far as I can remember, he saw even Shakespeare but indifferently.[3] Oh, it was in his eyes quite an unillumed age, that period of Elizabeth which *we* see full of suns! and few can see what is close to the eyes though they run their heads against it: the denial of contemporary genius is the rule rather than the exception. No one counts the eagles in the nest, till there is a rush of wings—and lo! they are flown. And here we speak of understanding men, such as the Sydneys and the Drydens. Of the great body of critics you observe rightly, that they are better than might be expected of their badness— only the fact of their *influence* is no less undeniable than the reason why they should not be influential. The brazen kettles will be taken for oracles all the world over. But the influence is for to-day, for this hour— not for to-morrow & the day after—unless indeed as you say, the poet do himself perpetuate the influence by submitting to it. Do you know Tennyson?—that is, with a face to face knowledge? I have great admiration for him. In execution, he is exquisite,—and, in music, a most subtle weigher out to the ear of fine airs. That such a poet sh^d submit blindly to the suggestions of his critics, (I do not say that suggestions from without may not be accepted with discrimination sometimes, to

the benefit of the acceptor) blindly & implicitly to the suggestions of his
critics, . . is much as if Babbage were to take my opinion & undo his
calculating machine by it.[4] Napoleon called poetry '*science creuse*'—
which, although he was not scientific in poetry himself, is true enough.
But anybody is qualified, according to everybody, for giving opinions
upon poetry. It is not so in chymistry and mathematics. Nor is it so, I
believe, in whist and the polka. But then these are more serious things.

Yes—and it does delight me to hear of your 'garden full of roses
and soul full of comforts.' You have the right to both—you have the
key to both. You have written enough to live by, though only beginning
to write, as you say of yourself. And this reminds me to remind you that
when I talked of coveting most of the authorship of your 'Pippa,' I did
not mean to call it your finest work (you might reproach me for *that*)
but just to express a personal feeling. Do you know what it is to covet
your neighbour's poetry?—not his fame, but his poetry?—I dare say
not. You are too generous. And, in fact, beauty is beauty, and, whether
it comes by our own hand or another's, blessed be the coming of it! *I*,
besides, feel *that*. And yet—and yet, I have been aware of a feeling within
me which has spoken two or three times to the effect ⟨that⟩ of a wish,
that I had been visited with the vision of 'Pippa', before you—and
confiteor tibi[5]—I confess the baseness of it. The conception is, to my mind,
most exquisite & altogether original—and the contrast in the working
out of the plan, singularly expressive of various faculty.

Is the poem under your thumb, emerging from it? and in what
metre? May I ask such questions?

And does Mr. Carlyle tell you that he has forbidden all 'singing' to
this perverse & froward generation, which should work & not sing?
And have you told Mr. Carlyle that song is work, and also the condition
of work? I am a devout sitter at his feet—and it is an effort to me to think
him wrong in anything—and once when he told me to write prose and
not verse,[6] I fancied that his opinion was I had mistaken my calling, . . a
fancy which in infinite kindness & gentleness he stooped immediately
to correct. I never shall forget the grace of that kindness—but then! For
him to have thought ill of *me*, would not have been strange—I often
think ill of myself, as God knows. But for Carlyle to think of putting
away, even for a season, the poetry of the world, was wonderful, and
has left me ruffled in my thoughts ever since. I do not know him
personally at all. But as his disciple I ventured (by an exceptional motive)

to send him my poems, and I heard from him as a consequence. 'Dear and noble' he is indeed—and a poet unaware of himself; all but the sense of music. You feel it so—do you not? And the 'dear sir' has let him have the 'letter of Cromwell,' I hope; and satisfied 'the obedient servant.' The curious thing in this world is not the stupidity, but the upper-handism of the stupidity. The geese are in the Capitol, and the Romans in the farmyard[7]—and it seems all quite natural that it should be so, both to geese & Romans!

But there are things you say, which seem to me supernatural . . for reasons which I know and for reasons which I don't know. You will let me be grateful to you, . . will you not? You must, if you will or not. And also . . I would not wait for more leave . . if I could but see your desk . . as I do your death's heads and the spider-webs appertaining; but the soul of Cornelius Agrippa fades from me.

Ever faithfully yours,
Elizabeth B. Barrett

1. Psalms 57:4.

2. John Wilson (1785–1854), better known as "Christopher North." E.B.B. refers to the first of eight articles (February–September 1845).

3. When Sidney wrote the *Defense of Poesy* Shakespeare was only sixteen.

4. Charles Babbage (1792–1871), mathematician and scientist, built the first calculating machine on modern principles in 1820–21.

5. "I confess to you."

6. Carlyle's standard advice to poets. See Letter 99 and note 5 and *Mary Russell Mitford: Correspondence with Charles Boner and John Ruskin,* ed. Elizabeth Lee (London: T. Fisher Unwin, 1914), p. 154.

7. The sacred geese kept at the Capitol saved it from invasion by the Gauls, 390 B.C.

9 (W5)   ### R.B. to E.B.B.

[*February 26, 1845.*]

Wednesday morning—Spring!

Real warm Spring, dear Miss Barrett, and the birds know it; and in Spring I shall see you, surely see you . . for when did I once fail to get whatever I had set my heart upon?—as I ask myself sometimes, with a strange fear.

I took up this paper to write a great deal—now, I don't think I shall write much—"I shall see you," I say!

That 'Luria' you enquire about, shall be my last play .. for it is but a play, woe's me! I have one done here, "A Soul's Tragedy," as it is properly enough called, but *that* would not do to end with—(end I will) —and Luria is a Moor, of Othello's country, and devotes himself to something he thinks Florence, and the old fortune follows—all in my brain, yet, but the bright weather helps and I will soon loosen my Braccio and Puccio (a pale discontented man), and Tiburzio (the Pisan, good true fellow, this one), and Domizia the Lady .. loosen all these on dear foolish (ravishing must his folly be) golden-hearted Luria, all these with their worldly-wisdom and Tuscan shrewd ways,—and, for me, the misfortune is, I sympathise just as much with these as with him,—so there can no good come of keeping this wild company any longer, and 'Luria' and the other sadder ruin of one Chiappino,—these got rid of, I will do as you bid me, and .. but first I have some Romances and Lyrics, all dramatic, to dispatch, and *then*, I shall stoop of a sudden under and out of this dancing ring of men & women hand in hand; and stand still awhile, should my eyes dazzle,—and when that's over, they will be gone and you will be there, *pas vrai?*—For, as I think I told you, I always shiver involuntarily when I look .. no, glance .. at this First Poem of mine to be. '*Now*,' I call it, what, upon my soul,—for a solemn matter it is,—what is to be done *now*, believed *now*,—so far as it has been revealed to me—solemn words, truly,—and to find myself writing them to any one else! Enough now.

I know Tennyson "face to face,"—no more than that. I know Carlyle and love him—know him so well, that I would have told you he had shaken that grand head of his at 'singing,' so thoroughly does he love and live by it. When I last saw him, a fortnight ago, he turned, from I don't know what other talk, quite abruptly on me with, 'Did you never try to write a *Song*? Of all things in the world, *that* I should be proudest to do.' Then came his definition of a song—then, with an appealing look to Mrs. C., 'I always say that some day in *spite of nature and my stars,* I shall burst into a song' (he is not mechanically 'musical,'— he meant, and the music is the poetry, he holds, and should enwrap the thought as Donne says "an amber-drop enwraps a bee"),[1] and then he began to recite an old Scotch song, stopping at the first rude couplet, "The beginning words are merely to set the tune, they tell me"—and then again at the couplet about—or, to the effect that—'give me' (but in broad Scotch) "give me but my lass, I care not for my cogie." "*He says*," quoth Carlyle magisterially, "that if you allow him the love of his lass, you may take away all else,—even his cogie, his cup or can, and he cares not"—just as a professor expounds Lycophron. And just before I left England, six months ago, did not I hear him croon, if not certainly sing, 'Charlie is my darling' ('my *darling*' with an adoring emphasis) and then he stood back, as it were, from the song, to look at it better, and said 'How must that notion of ideal wondrous perfection have impressed itself in this old Jacobite's "young Cavalier"—("They go to save their land, and the *young Cavalier!*")—when I who care nothing about such a rag of a man, cannot but feel as he felt, in speaking his words after him!' After saying which, he would be sure to counsel everybody to get their heads clear of all singing!—Don't let me forget to clap hands—we got the letter, dearly bought as it was by the 'Dear Sirs,' &c., and insignificant scrap as it proved—but still it is got, to my encouragement in diplomacy.

Who told you of my sculls and spider webs—Horne?[2] Last year I petted extraordinarily a fine fellow, (a *garden* spider—there was the singularity,—the thin clever-even-for a spider-sort, and they are *so* "spirited and sly," all of them—this kind makes a long cone of web, with a square chamber of vantage at the end, and there he sits loosely and looks about)—a great fellow that housed himself, with real gusto, in the jaws of a great scull, whence he watched me as I wrote, and I remember speaking to Horne about his good points. Phrenologists look gravely at that great scull, by the way, and hope, in their grim manner, that its owner made a good end. It looks quietly, now, out at the green little hill behind. I have no little insight to the feelings of furniture, and treat books and prints with a reasonable consideration—how some people use their pictures, for instance, is a mystery to me—very revolting all the same: portraits obliged to face each other for ever,—prints put together in portfolios . . my Polidoro's perfect Andromeda[3] along with "Boors Carousing," by Ostade,—where I found her,—my own father's doing, or I would say more.

And when I have said I like "Pippa" better than anything else I have done yet, I shall have answered all you bade me. And now may *I* begin questioning? No,—for it is all a pure delight to me, so that you do but write. I never was without good, kind, generous friends and lovers, so they say—so they were and are—perhaps they came at the wrong time—I never wanted them,—though that makes no difference in my gratitude, I trust—but I know myself—surely—and always have done so—for is there not somewhere the little book I first printed when a boy, with John Mill, the metaphysical head, *his* marginal note that 'the writer possesses a deeper self-consciousness than I ever knew in a sane human being'[4]—So I never deceived myself much, nor called my feelings for people other than they were; and who has a right to say, if I have not, that I had, but I said that, supernatural or no. /But⟩Pray/ tell me, too, of your present doings and projects, and never write yourself "grateful" to me who *am* grateful, very grateful to you,—for none of your words but I take in earnest—and tell me if Spring *be not* coming, come—and I will take to writing the gravest of letters—because this beginning is for gladness' sake, like Carlyle's song couplet. My head aches a little to-day too, and, ↑as↓ poor dear Kirke White[5] said to the moon, from his heap of mathematical papers, "I throw aside the learned sheet,—I cannot choose but gaze she looks so—mildly sweet." Out on the foolish phrase, but there's hard rhyming without it.

> Ever yours faithfully,
>
> Robert Browning

1. "To the Countess of Bedford," *Verse Letters to Severall Personages*. ("Honour is so sublime perfection . . . .")

2. See note 8 to Letter 10.

3. This painting by Polidoro di Caravaggio is alluded to in *Pauline* (ll.656–667) and *Sordello* (II, 211). An engraving of it hung over Browning's desk (Orr Handbook, p. 21n.).

4. For the influence on Browning's development of this famous copy of *Pauline*, now in the Forster and Dyce Collection in the Victoria and Albert Museum, see Introduction, p. xxvii.

5. Henry Kirke White (1775–1806). The quotation is from the fifth of twelve "Fragments" in his *Remains* (2nd ed.; London, 1808, p. 100). A note there says that the poems were "written upon the back of his mathematical papers, during the last year of his life."

10 (W5°)   *E.B.B. to R.B.*

_____

[*Thursday*]

50 Wimpole Street
Feb. 27, 1845.

Yes, but, dear Mr. Browning, I want the spring according to the
new 'style' (mine), & not the old one of you & the rest of the poets. To
me unhappily, the snowdrop is much the same as the snow—it feels as
cold underfoot—and I have grown sceptical about "the voice of the
turtle," the east winds blow so loud. April is a Parthian with a dart, &
May (at least the early part of it) a spy in the camp. *That* is my idea of
what you call spring; mine, in the *new style!* A little later comes my
spring,—and indeed after such severe weather, from which I have just
escaped with my life, I may thank it for coming at all. How happy you
are, to be able to listen to the "birds" without the commentary of the
east wind,—which, like other commentaries, spoils the music. And how
happy I am to listen to you, when you write such kind open-hearted
letters to me!—I am delighted to hear all you say to me of yourself, &
'Luria,' & the spider, & to do him no dishonour in the association, of the
great teacher of the age, Carlyle, who is also yours & mine. He fills the
office of a poet—does he not?—by analyzing humanity back into its
elements, to the destruction of the conventions of the hour. That is—
strictly speaking . . the office of the poet, is it not?—and he discharges it
fully,—and with a wider intelligibility perhaps as far as the contemporary period is concerned, than if he did forthwith 'burst into a song.'

But how I do wander!—I meant to say, and I will call myself back
to say, that spring will really come some day I hope & believe, & the
warm settled weather with it, and that then I shall be probably fitter for
certain pleasures than I can appear even to myself, now.

And, in the meantime, I seem to see 'Luria' instead of you,—I have
visions & dream dreams. And the 'Soul's Tragedy,' which sounds to me
like the step of a ghost of an old Drama! & you are not to think that I
blaspheme the Drama, dear Mr. Browning; or that I ever thought of
exhorting you to give up the 'solemn robes' & tread of the buskin. It is
the theatre which vulgarizes these things; the modern theatre in which
we see no altar!—where the thymele[1] is replaced by the caprice of a

popular actor. And also, I have a fancy that your great dramatic power would work more clearly & audibly in the less definite mould—but you ride your own faculty as Oceanus did his sea-horse, 'directing it by your will';[2] and woe to the impertinence, which would dare to say "turn this way" or "turn from that way"—it should not be MY impertinence. Do not think I blaspheme the /theatre⟩Drama/. I have gone through "all such reading as should never be read" (that is, by women!)—through my love of it on the contrary. And the dramatic faculty is strong in you—& therefore, as 'I speak unto a wise man, judge what I say.'

For myself & my own doings, you shall hear directly what I have been doing, & what I am about to do. Some years ago, as perhaps you may have heard, (but I hope not . . for the fewer who hear of it the better . .)—some years ago, I translated or rather *undid* into English, the Prometheus of Æschylus. To speak of ↑this production↓ moderately (not modestly), it is the most miserable of all miserable versions of the class. It was completed (in the first place) in thirteen days—the iambics ↑thrown↓ into blank verse, the lyrics into rhymed octosyllabics & the like—and the whole ⟨‖ · · ‖⟩ together as cold as Caucasus, & as flat as the nearest plain. To account for this, the haste may be something; but if my mind had been properly awakened at the time, I might have made still more haste & done it better. Well,—the comfort is, that the little book was unadvertised & unknown, & that most of the copies (through my entreaty of my father) are shut up in the wardrobe of his bedroom.[3] If ever I get well I shall show my joy by making a bondfire of them. In the meantime, the recollection of this sin of mine, has been my nightmare & daymare too, and the sin has been the 'Blot on my escutcheon.' I could look in nobody's face, with a "Thou canst not say I did it"[4]—I know, I did it. And so I resolved to wash away the transgression, and translate the tragedy over again. It was an honest straightforward proof of repentance—was it not? and I have completed it, except the transcription & last polishing. If Æschylus stands at the foot of my bed now, I shall have a little breath to front him. I have done my duty by him, not indeed according to his claims, but in proportion to my faculty. Whether I shall ever publish ⟨‖ · · ‖⟩ or not (remember) remains to be considered—that is a different side of the subject. If I do, it *may* be in a magazine[5] . . or . . this is another ground. And then, I have in my head to associate with the version . . a monodram of my own—not a long poem, . . but a monologue of Æschylus as he sate a blind exile on the flats of Sicily and recounted the past to his own soul, just before the eagle cracked his great massy skull with a stone.[6]

But my chief *intention* just now is the writing of a sort of novel-poem[7]—a poem as completely modern as "Geraldine's Courtship," running into the midst of our conventions, & rushing into drawing-rooms & the like "where angels fear to tread"; & so, meeting face to face & without mask ↑the↓ Humanity of the age, & speaking the truth as I conceive of it, out plainly. That is my intention. It is not mature enough yet to be called a plan. I am waiting for a story, & I won't take one, because I want to make one, & I like to make my own stories, because then I can take liberties with them in the treatment.

Who told me of your skulls and spiders? Why, couldn't I know it without being told? Did Cornelius Agrippa know nothing without being told? Mr. Horne—never spoke it to my ears—(I never saw him face to face in my life, although we have corresponded for long and long), & he never wrote it to my eyes. Perhaps he does not know that I know it. Well, then! if I were to say that *I heard it from you yourself*, . . how would you answer? AND IT WAS SO.[8] Why, are you not aware that these are the days of Mesmerism & clairvoyance? Are you an infidel? I have believed in your skulls for the last year, for my part.

And I have some sympathy in your habit of feeling for chairs & tables. I remember, when I was a child & wrote poems in little clasped books, I used to kiss the books & put them away tenderly because I had been happy near them, & take them out by turns when I was going from home, to ⟨‖· · ·‖⟩ ↑cheer↓ them by the change of air & the pleasure of the new place. This, not for the sake of the verses written in them, & not for the sake of writing more verses in them, but from pure gratitude. Other books I used to treat in a like manner—and to talk to the trees & the flowers, was a natural inclination—but between me & that time, the cypresses grow thick & dark.

Is it true that your wishes fulfil themselves?—And when they *do*, are they not bitter to your taste—do you not wish them *un*fulfilled? Oh—this life, this life! There is comfort in it, they say, & I almost believe—but the brightest place in the house, is the leaning out of the window!—at least, for me.

⌈Of course you are *self-conscious*—How c[d] you be a poet otherwise? Tell me. Ever faithfully yours, E. B. B.

And was the little book written with Mr. Mill pure metaphysics, or what?⌉[9]

1. An altar to Dionysus in the orchestra of the Greek theater.
2. *Prometheus Unbound*, ll. 336–338 of E.B.B.'s 1850 translation.
3. This version was published with some original poems in 1833.
4. *Macbeth* III. iv. 50.
5. She approached *Blackwood's* (Letter 516), but the second translation first appeared in the 1850 *Poems*.
6. Apparently never completed; but Browning either undertook the same subject (Macmillan ed., p. 1339) or copied E.B.B.'s fragment. The authorship of "Aeschylus' Soliloquy" is discussed by Martha H. Shackford in the *Times Literary Supplement*, March 21, 1942, and G. D. Hobson, *ibid.*, April 11, 1942.
7. *Aurora Leigh*, published in 1856.
8. This bit of mystification is explained by Horne's having sent E.B.B. a letter from Browning (printed in Hood, p. 8). Browning made a rough sketch of the jaw of a skull, the spider, and its web, with the note: "N.B. (A picturesque bit of ghastliness: in this little writing-room of mine are two sculls, each on its bracket by the window . . .)" See *Letters to Geo. Barrett*, p. 104.
9. Written in the throat of the envelope.

11 *(W6)*   **R.B. to E.B.B.**

[*1845*]

Sat[y] Night, March 1.

Dear Miss Barrett—I seem to find of a sudden— . . surely I knew before . . anyhow, I *do* find now,—that with the octaves on octaves of quite new golden strings you enlarged the compass of my life's harp with, there is added, too, such a tragic chord—that which you touched, so gently, in the beginning of your letter I got this morning—"just escaping" &c. But if my truest heart's wishes avail, as they have hitherto done, you shall laugh at East winds yet, as I do! See now: this sad feeling is so strange to me, that I must write it out, *must*—and you might give me great, the greatest pleasure for years and yet find me as passive as a stone used to wine-libations, and as ready in expressing my sense of them—but when I am pained, I find the old theory of the uselessness of communicating the circumstances of it, singularly untenable. I have been "spoiled" in this world—to such an extent, indeed, that I often *reason* out . . make clear to myself . . that I might very properly . . so far as myself am concerned . . take any step that would peril the whole of my future happiness—because the past is gained, secure, and on record; and, tho' not another of the old days should dawn on me, I shall not have lost my life, no—Out of all which you are—please—to make a sort of sense, if you can, ⸢so as to express⸥ that I have been deeply struck to find a new real unmistakable sorrow along with these as real but not so new joys you have given me—How strangely this connects itself in my mind with another subject in your note! I looked at that translation for a minute, not longer, years ago, knowing nothing about it or you— and I *only* looked to see what rendering a passage had received that was often in my thoughts.[1] I forget your version (it was not YOURS, my " YOURS" *then;* ⸢I mean I had no extraordinary interest about it)⸥ but the original makes Prometheus (telling over his bestowments towards human happiness) say, as something περαιτέρω τῶνδε, that he stopped mortals μὴ προδέρκεσθαι μόρον — τὸ ποῖον εὑρών, asks the Chorus, τῆσδε φάρμακον νόσου? Whereto he replies, τυφλὰς ἐν αὐτοῖς ἐλπίδας κατῴκισα (what you hear men dissertate upon by the hour, as proving the immortality of the soul apart from revelation, undying yearnings, restless longings, instinctive desires which, unless to be eventually in- dulged, it were cruel to plant in us, &c. &c.). But, μέγ' ὠφέλημα τοῦτ' ἐδωρήσω βροτοῖς! concludes the chorus, like a sigh from the admitted Eleusinian Æschylus was! You cannot think how this foolish circum- stance struck me this evening; so I thought I would e'en tell you at once and be done with it—are you not my dear friend already, and shall I not use you? And pray you not to "lean out of the window" when my own foot is only on the stair—do wait a little for

Yours EVER,

R. B.

1. "The following is the version of the passage in Mrs. Browning's later translation of the 'Prometheus' (ll. 250-253 of the original).

Prom.	I did restrain besides
	My mortals from premeditating death.
Cho.	How didst thou medicine the plague-fear of death?
Prom.	I set blind hopes to inhabit their house.
Cho.	By that gift thou didst help thy mortals well."

Footnote, 1899 edition.

In adopting Sir Frederic Kenyon's 1899 notes I have silently changed line- number references to Greek texts to conform to the Loeb Library numbering. Line numbers in E.B.B.'s translation are 293–297.

12 *(W6°)*   *E.B.B. to R.B.*

[*Wednesday*]

March 5th, 1845.

But I did not mean to strike a 'tragic chord'; indeed I did not! Sometimes one's melancholy will be uppermost & sometimes one's mirth,—the world goes round, you know—& I suppose that in that letter of mine the melancholy took the turn. As to 'escaping with my life,' it was just a phrase—at least it did not signify more than that the sense of mortality, & [the] discomfort of it, is peculiarly strong with me when east winds are blowing & waters freezing. For the rest, I am *essentially better,* & have been for several winters,—and I feel as if it were intended for me to live & not die, & I am reconciled to the feeling. Yes! I am satisfied to 'take up' with the blind hopes again, & have them in the house with me, for all that I sit by the window. By the way . . did the chorus utter scorn in the μέγ' ὠφέλημα. I think not. It is well to fly towards the light, even where there may be some fluttering & bruising of wings against the windowpanes!—is it not?

There is an obscurer passage, on which I covet your thoughts— where Prometheus, after the sublime declaration that, with a full knowledge of the penalty reserved for him, he had sinned of free will & choice, goes on to say . . or to seem to say—that he had *not,* however, foreseen the extent & detail of the torment . . the skiey rocks . . & the friendless desolation. See v. 275[1]. The intention of the poet might have been to magnify to his audience the torment of the martyrdom—but the heroism of the martyr diminishes in proportion—& there appears to be a contradiction—and oversight. Or is my view wrong? Tell me. And tell me too, if Æschylus is not the divinest of all the divine Greek souls? People say after Quintilian[2], that he is savage & rude; a sort of poetic Orson[3], with his locks all wild. But I will not hear it of my master!—He is strong as Zeus is—& not as a boxer—and tender as Power itself; which always is tenderest.

But to go back to the view of Life with the blind Hopes—you are not to think,—whatever I may have written or implied,—that I lean either to the philosophy or affectation which beholds the world through darkness instead of light, & speaks of it wailingly. Now, may

God forbid that it sh^d be so with me. I am not desponding by nature—
and after a course of bitter mental discipline & long bodily seclusion, I
come out with two ✝learnt✝ lessons (as I sometimes say & oftener feel) . .
the wisdom of cheerfulness—& the duty of social intercourse. Anguish
has instructed me in joy—and solitude in society—it has been a wholesome & not unnatural reaction. And altogether, I may say that the earth
looks the brighter to me in proportion to my own deprivations: the
laburnum trees & rose trees are plucked up by the roots—but the sunshine is in their places—and the root of the sunshine is above the
storms. What we call Life is a condition of the soul—and the soul must
improve in happiness & wisdom, except by its own fault. These tears
in our eyes—these faintings of the flesh, . . will not hinder such improvement.

    And I do like to hear ⟨such⟩ testimonies like yours, to *happiness*—
& I feel it to be a testimony of a higher sort than the obvious one. Still,
it is obvious ✝too✝ that you have been spared, up to this time, the great
natural afflictions, against which we are nearly all called, sooner or
later, to struggle and wrestle—or your step would not be "on the
stair" quite so lightly. And so, we turn to you, dear Mr. Browning, for
comfort & gentle spiriting! Remember ⟨you⟩ that as you owe your
unscathed joy to God, you should pay it back to his world. And I
thank you for some of it already.

    Also . . writing as from friend to friend—as you say rightly that we
are,—I ought to confess that of one class of griefs, (which has been
called too the bitterest) I know as little as you. The cruelty of the world,
& the treason of it—the unworthiness of the dearest,—of these griefs I
have scanty knowledge. It seems to me from my personal experience
that there is kindness everywhere in different proportions, & more
goodness & tenderheartedness than we read of in the moralists. People
have been kind to ME, even without understanding me, & pitiful to me,
without approving of me—nay, have not the very critics tamed their
beardom for me, & roared delicately as sucking doves[4], on behalf of
me? I have no harm to say of your world, though I am not of it, as you
see!—And I have the cream of it in your friendship, . . and a little more
—and I do not envy much the milkers of the cows.

    How kind you are!—how kindly & gently you speak to me!—
Some things you say are very touching, & some, surprising—& although I am aware that you unconsciously exaggerate what I can be to

you, yet it is delightful to be broad awake & think of you as my friend.
May God bless you.

Faithfully yours,

Elizabeth Barrett Barrett

1. E.B.B.'s line numbers for the Greek correspond to those in the edition of Bishop Charles James Blomfield (Cambridge, 1810), a copy of which was in the Browning's library; the passage is ll. 267–271 in the Loeb Library text. She ultimately translated the passage thus:

> By my choice, my choice,
> I freely sinned—I will confess my sin—
> And helping mortals, found my own despair.
> I did not think indeed that I should pine
> Beneath such pangs against such skyey rocks.
> Doomed to this drear hill and no neighbouring
> Of any life . . .

(ll. 313–319)

2. *Institutio Oratoria* X. i. 66.
3. Who was suckled and reared by a bear in the French romance *Valentine and Orson*.
4. *Midsummer-Night's Dream* I. ii. 81.

13 *(W7)*   *R.B. to E.B.B.*

[March 11, 1845.]

Tuesday Morning.

Your letter made me so happy, dear Miss Barrett, that I have kept quiet this while; is it too great a shame if I begin to want more good news of you, and to say so? Because there has been a bitter wind ever since. Will you grant me a great favour? Always when you write, tho' about your own works, not Greek plays merely, put me in, *always,* a little official bulletin-line that shall say "I am better" or "still better," will you? That is done, then—and now, what do I wish to tell you first? The poem you propose to make, for the times,—the fearless fresh living work you describe,—is the *only* Poem to be undertaken now by you or anyone that *is* a Poet at all,—the only reality, only effective piece of service to be rendered God and man—it is what I have been all my life intending to do, and now shall be much, much nearer doing, since you will be along with me. And you *can* do it, I know and am sure—so sure, that I could find in my heart to be jealous of your stopping in the way even to translate the Prometheus; tho' the accompanying monologue will make amends too—Or shall I set you a task I meant for myself once upon a time?—which, oh, how you would fulfil! Restore the Prometheus πυρφόρος as Shelley did the Λυόμενος—when I say "restore," I know, or very much fear, that the πυρφόρος was the same with the πυρκαεύς[1] which, by a fragment, we sorrowfully ascertain to have been a Satyric Drama—but surely the capabilities of the subject are much greater than in this, we now wonder at; nay, they include all those of this last—for just see how magnificently the story unrolls itself. The beginning of Jupiter's Dynasty, the calm in Heaven after the storm, the ascending . . (stop, I will get the book and give the words), ὅπως τάχιστα τὸν πατρῷον εἰς θρόνον καθέζετ', εὐθὺς δαίμοσιν νέμει γέρα ἄλλοισιν ἄλλα . . κ.τ.λ.,[2] all the while Prometheus being the first among the first in honour, as καίτοι θεοῖσι τοῖς νέοις τούτοις γέρα τίς ἄλλος, ἢ 'γώ, παντελῶς διώρισε?[3]—then the one black hand-cloudlet storming the joyous blue and gold everywhere, βροτῶν δὲ τῶν ταλαιπώρων λόγον οὐκ ἔσχεν οὐδένα,[4] and the design of Zeus to blot out the whole race, and plant a new one. And Prometheus with his grand solitary ἐγὼ δ'ἐτόλμησα,[5] and his saving them . . as the *first* good . . from annihilation. Then comes the darkening brow of Zeus, and estrangement from the benign circle of grateful gods, and the dissuasion of old confederates, and all the Right that one may fancy in Might, the strongest reasons παύεσθαι τρόπου φιλανθρώπου,[6] coming from the own mind of the Titan, if you will,—and all the while he shall be proceeding steadily in the alleviation of the sufferings of mortals whom, νηπίους ὄντας τὸ πρίν, ἔννους καὶ φρενῶν ἐπηβόλους ἔθηκε,[7] while still, in proportion, shall the doom he is about to draw on himself, manifest itself more and more distinctly, till at the last, he shall achieve the salvation of man, body (by the gift of fire) and soul (by even those τυφλαὶ ἐλπίδες,[8] hopes of immortality) and so having rendered him utterly . . according to the mythos here . . *independent* of Jove—for observe, Prometheus in the play never talks of helping mortals more, of fearing for them more, of even benefitting them more by his sufferings—the rest is between Jove and himself . . he will reveal the master-secret to Jove when he shall have released him, &c—there is no stipulation that the gifts to mortals shall be continued . . indeed . . by the fact that it is Prometheus who hangs on

Caucasus while "the ephemerals possess fire," one sees that somehow mysteriously *they* are past Jove's harming now. Well, this wholly achieved, the price is as wholly accepted, and off into the darkness passes in calm triumphant grandeur the Titan—with Strength and Violence, and Vulcan's silent and downcast eyes—and then the gold clouds and renewed flushings of felicity shut up the scene again, with Might in his old throne again, yet with a new element of mistrust, and conscious shame, and fear, that writes significantly enough above all the glory & rejoicing that all is not as it was, nor will ever be. Such might be the framework of your Drama—just what cannot help striking one at first glance, and would not such a Drama go well before your translation? Do think of this and tell me—it nearly writes itself. (You see, I meant the μέγ' ὠφέλημα [9] to be a deep great truth; if there were no life beyond this, I think the hope in one ⟨and belief⟩ would be an incalculable blessing *for* this life, which is melancholy for one like Æschylus to feel, if he could *only* hope, because the argument as to the ulterior good of those hopes is, cut clean away, and what had he left?)

   I do not find it take away from my feeling of the magnanimity of Prometheus that he should . . in ⟨plain⟩ truth . . complain (as he does from beginning to end) of what he finds himself suffering. He could have prevented all, and can stop it now—of that he never thinks for a moment. That was the old Greek way—they never let an antagonistic passion neutralise the other which was to influence the man to his praise or blame. A Greek hero fears exceedingly and battles it out—cries out when he is wounded and fights on, does not say his love or hate makes him see no danger or feel no pain—Æschylus from first word to last (ἴδεσθέ με, οἷα πάσχω[10] to ἐσορᾷς με, ὡς ἔκδικα πάσχω[11]) insists on the unmitigated reality of the punishment which only the sun, and divine ether, and the godhead of his mother can comprehend—still, still—that is only what I suppose Æschylus to have done,—in your poem you shall make Prometheus our way.

   And now enough of Greek, which I am fast forgetting (for I never look at books I loved once—it was your mention of the translation that brought out the old fast fading outlines of the Poem in my brain—the Greek poem, that is)—You think . . for I must get to *you* . . that I "unconsciously exaggerate what you are to me"—now you don't know what *that* is, nor can I very well tell you, because the language with which I talk to myself of these matters is spiritual Attic, and "loves contractions," as grammarians say; but I read it myself, and well know what it means . . that's why I told you I was self-conscious,—I meant that I never yet mistook my own feelings, one for another—there! Of what use is talking? Only, do you stay here with me in the 'House' these few short years. Do you think I shall see you in two months, three months? I may travel, perhaps. So you have got to like society, and would enjoy it, you think? For me, I always hated it,—have put up with it these six or seven years past, lest by foregoing it I should let some unknown good escape me, in the true time of it, and only discover my fault when too late,—and now, that I have done most of what is to be done, *any* lodge in a garden of cucumbers for me! I don't even care about reading now—the world,—and pictures of it, rather than writings about the world! but you must read books in order to get words and forms for "the public" if you *write,* and *that* you needs must do, if you fear God. I have no pleasure in writing myself—none, in the mere act— tho' all pleasure in the sense of fulfilling a duty—whence, if I have done my real best, judge how heartbreaking a matter ↑must it be↓ to be pro- nounced a poor creature by Critic This and acquaintance the other. But I think you like the operation of writing as I should like that of painting or making music, do you not? After all, there is a great delight in the heart of the thing; and use and forethought have made me ready at all times to set to work—but—I don't know why—my heart sinks when- ever I open this desk, and rises when I shut it. Yet but for what I have written you would never have heard of me—and *thro'* what you have written, not properly *for* it, I love and wish you well! Now, will you remember what I began my letter by saying—how you have promised to let me know if my well wishing takes effect, and if you still continue better? And not even . . (since we are learned in magnanimity . .) don't even tell me that or anything else, if it teases you,—but wait your own good time, and know me for . . if these words were but my own, and fresh-minted for this moment's use! . .

> Yours ever faithfully,
>
> R. Browning

1. "Fire-Bearer," "Unbound," "Fire-Bearer," and "Fire-Kindler."
2. "Aeschylus, *Prometheus,* 230ff.:
> 'When at first
> He filled his father's throne, he instantly
> Made various gifts of glory to the gods.'"

Footnote, 1899 edition. Line numbers in E.B.B., 271–273.

3. "*Ib.* 439–440: 'For see—their honours to these new-made gods, / What other gave but I?'" 1899 ed. Line numbers in E.B.B., 508–509.

4. "*Ib.* 233–234: 'Alone of men, / Of miserable men, he took no count.'" 1899 ed. Line numbers in E.B.B., 274–275.

5. "*I* dared it." Line 279 in E.B.B. Line 237 in the Greek text cited in other notes.

6. "Aeschylus, *Prometheus* 11: 'Leave off his old trick of loving man.'" 1899 ed. Line 12 in E.B.B.

7. "*Ib.* 443–444: 'Being fools before, / I made them wise and true in aim of soul.'" 1899 ed. Line numbers in E.B.B., 513–514.

8. "*Ib.* 252 'Blind hopes.'" 1899 ed. Line 296 in E.B.B.

9. "*Ib.* 253: 'A great benefit.'" 1899 ed. E.B.B.'s translation—line 297—is rather free: "By that gift thou didst help thy mortals well."

10. "Behold me, . . . what I endure . . . !" Line 103 of E.B.B.'s translation, 92 of Greek text.

11. "Aeschylus, *Prometheus*, 1093: 'Dost see how I suffer this wrong?'" 1899 ed. Line 1287, the closing line, of E.B.B.'s translation.

14 (W7°)   **E.B.B. to R.B.**

[*Thursday*]

50 Wimpole Street
March 20, 1845.

Whenever I delay to write to you, dear Mr. Browning, it is not, be sure, that I take my "own good time" but submit to my own bad time. It was kind of you to wish to know how I was, & not unkind of me to suspend my answer to your question—for indeed I have not been very well, nor have had much heart for saying so. This implacable weather! —this east wind that seems to blow through the sun & moon! who can be well in such a wind? Yet for me, I should not grumble. There has been nothing very bad the matter with me, as there used to be—I only grow weaker than usual, & learn my lesson of being mortal, in a corner— & then all this must end!—April is coming. There will be both a May & a June if we live to see such things, & perhaps, after all, we may. And as to seeing *you* besides, I observe that you distrust me, & that perhaps you penetrate my morbidity & guess how when the moment comes to see a living human face to which I am not accustomed, I shrink & grow pale in the spirit—Do you?—You are learned in human nature, & you know the consequences of leading such a secluded life as mine . . notwithstanding all my fine philosophy about social duties & the like—well—if you have such knowledge or if you have it not, I cannot say—but I do say that I will indeed see you when the warm weather has revived me a little, & put the earth "to rights" again so as to make pleasures of the sort possible. For if you think that I shall not *like* to see you——you are wrong, for all your learning. But I shall be afraid of you at first—though I am not, in writing thus. You are Paracelsus, and I am a recluse, with nerves that have been all broken on the rack, & now hang loosely, . . quivering at a step and breath.

And what you say of society draws me on to many comparative thoughts of your life & mine. You seem to have drunken of the cup of life full, with the sun shining on it. I have lived only inwardly,—or with *sorrow*, for a strong emotion. Before this seclusion of my illness, I was secluded still—& there are few of the youngest women in the world who have not seen more, heard more, known more, of society, than I, who am scarcely to be called young now. I grew up in the country . . had no social opportunities, . . had my heart in books & poetry, . . & my experience, in reveries. My sympathies drooped towards the ground like an untrained honeysuckle—& but for *one* . . in my own house . . but of this I cannot speak. It was a lonely life—growing green like the grass around it. Books and dreams were what I lived in—& domestic life only seemed to buzz gently around, like the bees about the grass. And so time passed, and passed—and afterwards, when my illness came & I seemed to stand at the edge of the world with all done, & no prospect (as appeared at one time) of ever passing the threshold of one room again,—why then, I turned to thinking with some bitterness (after the greatest sorrow of my life[1] had given me room & time to breathe) that I had stood blind in this temple I was about to leave . . that I had seen no Human nature, that my brothers & sisters of the earth were *names* to me, . . that I had beheld no great mountain or river—nothing in fact. I was as a man dying who had not read Shakespeare . . & it was too late!—do you understand? And do you also know what a disadvantage this ignorance is to my art— Why, if I live on & yet do not escape from this seclusion, do you not perceive that I labour under signal disadvantages . . that I am, in a manner, as a *blind poet*? Certainly, there is a compensation to a degree. I have had much of the inner life—& from the habit of selfconsciousness of selfanalysis, I make great guesses at Human Nature in the main. But how willingly I would as a poet exchange some of this lumbering, ponderous, helpless knowledge of books, for some experience of life & man, for some . . .

But /this⟩all/ grumbling is a vile thing. We should all thank God for our measures of life, & think them enough for each of us. I write so, that you may not mistake what I wrote before in relation to society, although you do not see from my point of view; and that you may understand what I mean fully when I say, that I have lived all my chief *joys*, & indeed nearly all emotions that go warmly by that name & relate to /me⟩myself/ personally, in poetry & in poetry alone. Like to write? Of course, of course I do. I seem to live while I write—it is life, for me. Why what is to live? Not to eat & drink & breathe, . . but to feel the life in you down all the fibres of being, passionately & joyfully. And thus, one lives in composition surely . . not always . . but when the wheel goes round & the procession is uninterrupted. Is it not so with you? oh—it must be so. For the rest, there will be necessarily a reaction; & in my own particular case, whenever I see a poem of mine in print, or even smoothly transcribed, the reaction is most painful. The pleasure, . . the sense of power, . . without which I could not write a line, is gone in a moment; & nothing remains but disappointment and humiliation. I never wrote a poem which you could not persuade me to tear to pieces if you took me at the right moment! I have a *seasonable* humility, I do assure you.

How delightful to talk about oneself—but as you 'tempted me and I did eat,'[2] I entreat your longsuffering of my sin—& Ah—if you would but sin back so in turn!—You and I seem to meet in a mild contrarious harmony . . as in the 'si . . no . . si . . no' of an Italian duet. I want to see more of men—& you have seen too much, you say. I am in ignorance, & you, in satiety. "You don't even care about reading now." Is it possible? And I am as 'fresh' about reading, as ever I was—as long as I keep out of the shadow of the dictionaries & of theological controversies, and the like. Shall I whisper it to you under the memory of the last rose of last summer . . . *I am very fond of romances* . . yes! and I read them not only as some wise people are known to do, for the sake of the eloquence here & the sentiment there, & the graphic intermixtures here & there, . . but for the story!—just as little children would, sitting on their papa's knee. My childish love of a story never wore out with my love of plumbcake—& now there is not a hole in it. I make it a rule, for the most part, to read all the romances that other people are kind enough to write—& woe to the miserable wight who tells me how the third volume endeth. Have you in you any surviving innocence of this sort? or do you call it idiocy?—If you do, I will forgive you, only smiling to myself—I give you notice—

with a smile of superior . . pleasure! Mr. Chorley made me quite laugh the other day by recommending Mary Howitt's 'Improvisatore,'[3] with a sort of deprecating reference to the *descriptions* in the book—just as if I never read a novel—*I!*—I wrote a confession back to him which made him shake his head perhaps—& now I confess to *you*, unprovoked. I am one who could have forgotten the plague, listening to Boccaccio's stories,—& I am not ashamed of it. I do not even 'see the better part,' I am so silly.

Ah—you tempt me with a grand vision of Prometheus! *I*, who have just escaped with my life, after treading Milton's ground,[4] you would send me to Æschylus's. No—*I do not dare*. And besides . . . I am inclined to think that we want new *forms* . . as well as thoughts. The old gods are dethroned. Why should we go back to the antique moulds . . classical moulds, as they are so improperly called? If it is a necessity of Art to do so, why then those critics are right who hold that Art is exhausted and the world too ⟨old⟩ ↑worn out↓ for poetry. I do not, for my part, believe this: & I believe the so-called necessity of Art ⟨but⟩ ↑to be the↓ mere feebleness of the artist. Let us all aspire rather to *Life*—& let the dead bury their dead. If we have but courage to face these conventions, to touch this low ground, we shall take strength from it instead of losing it; & of that, I am intimately persuaded. For there is poetry *everywhere* . . the "treasure" (see the old fable) lies all over the field.[5] And then Christianity is a worthy *myth*, & poetically acceptable.

I had much to say to you . . or at least something . . of the 'blind hopes' &c . . but am ashamed to take a step into a new sheet. If you mean "to travel," why, I shall have to miss you—do you really mean it? How is the play going on? & the poem?

May God bless you!

Ever & truly yours,

E. B. B.

[P.S. Are you aware that in a l[at]e American publication comprising the poets of England, you are included, with a critical essay?—or biography, or personal notice of some sort—?][6]

1. The death of her oldest brother, see Letter 87.
2. Cf. Genesis 3:13 and *Paradise Lost* X. 162.
3. An English translation of the popular novel (1835) by Hans Christian Andersen (1805–75) had just appeared. For E.B.B.'s reply to Chorley's letter, see

Letters of E.B.B., I, 234–235.

4. *A Drama of Exile* (1844) dealt with the expulsion from Eden.

5. In the fable of *The Husbandman and His Sons,* attributed to Aesop, the mysterious treasure the father bequeaths his boys proves to be the soil itself.

6. Written in the throat of the envelope. The publication was probably Rufus W. Griswold's *Poets and Poetry of England in the Nineteenth Century* (Philadelphia, 1844), which printed *Incident of the French Camp* as "An Incident at Ratisbon," along with excerpts from *Paracelsus* and *Sordello,* and included a brief critical note.

15 *(W8)*   R.B. to E.B.B.
                   ───────────────────────

[*March 31, 1845.*]

                                              Monday Morning
When you read Don Quixote, my dear romance-reader, do you ever notice that flower of an incident of good fellowship where the friendly Squire of Him of the Moon, or the Looking glasses, (I forget which) passes to Sancho's dry lips,[1] (all under a cork-tree one morning) —a plump wine-skin,—and do you admire dear brave Miguel's knowledge of thirsty nature when he tells you that the Drinker, having seriously considered for a space the pleiads, or place where they should be, fell, as he slowly returned the shrivelled bottle to its donor, into a deep musing of an hour's length, or thereabouts, and then . . mark . . only *then,* fetching a profound sigh, broke silence with . . such a piece of praise as turns pale the labours in that way of Rabelais and the Teian (if he wasn't a Byzantine monk, alas!)[2] and our Mr. Kenyon's stately self—(since my own especial poet *à moi,* that can do all with anybody, only "sips like a fly,"[3] she says, and so cares not to compete with these behemoths that drink up Jordan)[4]—Well, then . . (oh, I must get quick to the sentence's end, and be brief as an oracle-explainer!)—the giver is you and the taker is I, and the letter is the wine, and the stargazing is the reading the same, and the brown study is—how shall I deserve and be grateful enough to this new strange friend of my own, that has taken away my reproach among men, that have' each and all their friend, so they say (. . not that I believe all they say—they boast too soon sometimes, no doubt,—I once was shown a letter wherein the truth stumbled out after this

fashion "Dere Smith,—I calls you *"dere"* . . because you are so in your shop!")—and the great sigh is,—there is no deserving nor being grateful at all,—and the breaking silence is, and the praise is . . ah, there, enough of it!

    This sunny morning is as if I wished it for you—10 strikes by the clock now—tell me if at 10 this morning you feel any good from my heart's wishes for you—I would give you all you want out of my own life and gladness and yet keep twice the stock that should by right have sufficed the thin white face that is laughing at me in the glass yonder at the fancy of its making anyone afraid . . and now, with another kind of laugh, at the thought that when its owner "travels" next, he will leave off Miss Barrett along with port-wine—Dii meliora piis,[5] and, among them to

        Yours every where, and at all times yours

R. Browning

    I have all to say yet—next letter.

    1. Browning's embellishment of *Don Quixote* II. xii–xiii.
    2. Anacreon. Browning alludes to the dwindling of his canon as scholars discovered an increasing number of late imitations.
    3. Cf. E.B.B.'s *Wine of Cyprus* (1844):

> If old Bacchus were the speaker,
>   He would tell you with a sigh
> Of the Cyprus in this beaker
>   I am sipping like a fly . . .

    4. Job 40:23.
    5. "May the Gods grant better things to the upright."

16 (W9)   ### R.B. to E.B.B.

[*April 15, 1845.*]

Tuesday Night.

    I heard of you, dear Miss Barrett, between a Polka and a Cellarius[1] the other evening, of Mr. Kenyon—how this wind must hurt you! And yesterday I had occasion to go your way—pass, that is, Wimpole Street, the end of it,—and, do you know, I did not seem to have leave from you to go down in yet, much less count number after number till I came to yours,—much least than less, look up when I did come there. So I went on to a viperine she-friend of mine who, I think, rather loves me she does so hate me, and we talked over the chances of certain ⸤other⸥ friends who were to be balloted for at the "Athenæum" last night,— one of whom, it seems, was in a fright about it—"to such little purpose" said my friend—"for he is so inoffensive—now, if one were to style *you* that!"—"Or you"—I said—and so we hugged ourselves in our grimness like tiger-cats. Then there is a deal in the papers to-day about Maynooth,[2] and a meeting presided over by Lord Mayor Gibbs, and the Reverend Mr. Somebody's speech—And Mrs. Norton has gone and book-made at a great rate about the Prince of Wales,[3] pleasantly putting off till his time all that used of old to be put off till his mother's time—altogether, I should dearly like to hear from you, but not till the wind goes, and sun comes—because I shall see Mr. Kenyon next week and get him to tell me some more. By the way, do you suppose anybody else looks like him? If you do, the first room full of real London people you go among you will fancy to be lighted up by a saucer of /lightning⟩ burning/ salt & spirits of wine in the background.

Monday—Last night when I could do nothing else I began to write to you, such writing as you have seen—strange! The proper time & season for good sound sensible & profitable forms of speech—when ought it to have occurred, and how did I evade it in these letters of mine? For people begin with a graceful skittish levity, lest you should be struck all of a heap with what is to come, and *that* is sure to be the stuff and staple of the man, full of wisdom and sorrow,—and then again comes the fringe of reeds and pink little stones on the other side, that you may put foot on land, and draw breath, and think what a deep pond you have swum across. But *you* are the real deep wonder of a creature,—and I sail these paper-boats on you rather impudently. But I always mean to be very grave one day,—when I am in better spirits and can go *fuori di me*.[4]

And one thing I want to persuade you of, which is, that all you gain by travel is the discovery that you have gained nothing, and have done rightly in trusting to your innate ideas—or not rightly in distrusting them, as the case may be; you get, too, a little . . perhaps a considerable, good, in finding the world's accepted *moulds* every where, into which you may run & fix your own fused metal,—but not a grain Troy-weight do you get of new gold, silver or brass. After this, you go boldly on your own resources, and are justified to yourself, that's all. Three scratches with a pen,[5] even with this pen,—and you have the green little Syrenusa

Letter 16, pages 1 and 4

R.B. illustrates a point

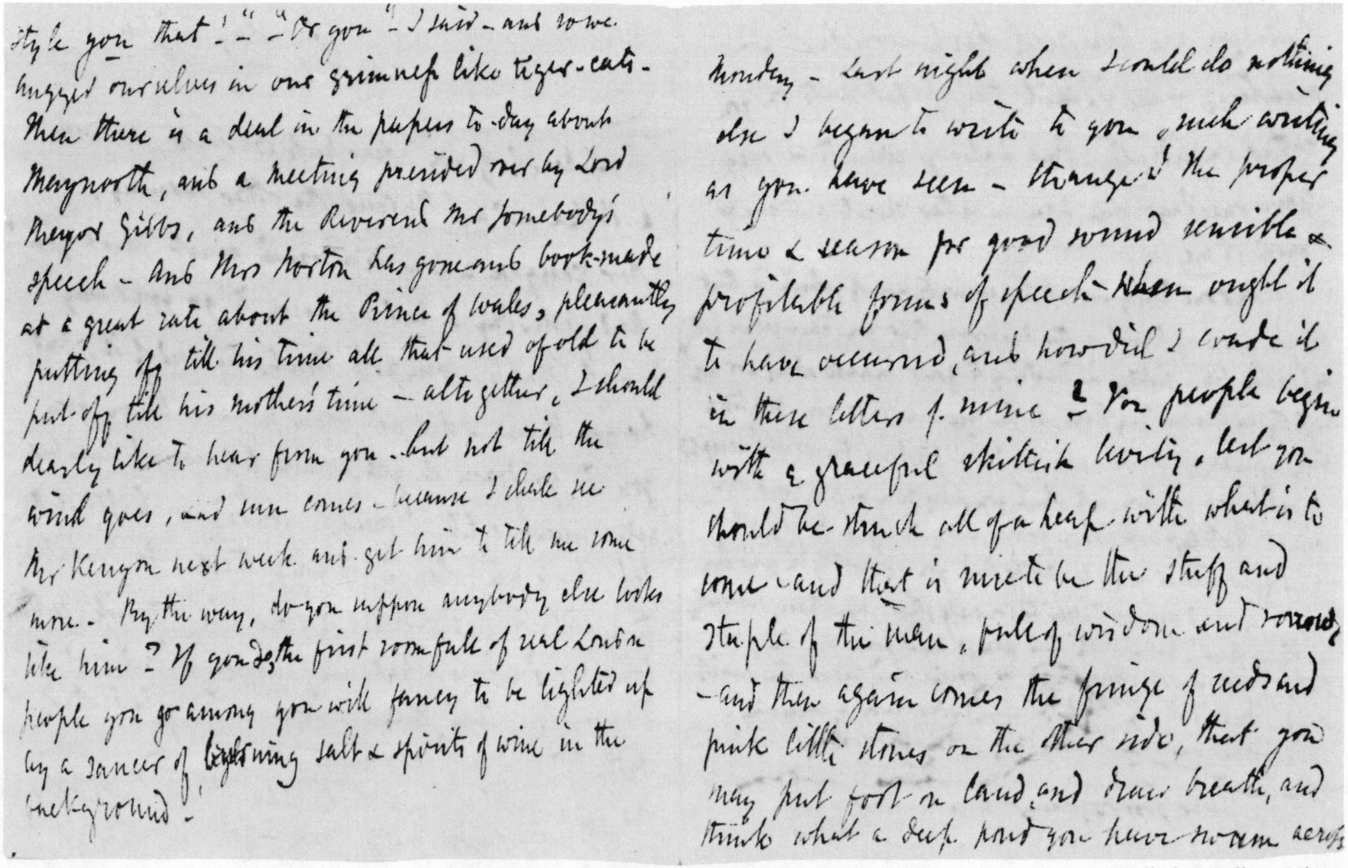

Letter 16, pages 2 and 3

where I have sate and heard the quails sing. One of these days I shall describe a country I have seen in my soul only, fruits, flowers, birds and all.

Ever yours, dear Miss Barrett,

R: Browning

1. A form of waltz named for, and presumably devised by, the Austrian dancing master who brought the polka to Paris in 1840. It had reached London by mid-November 1844 and was a sensation, but faded too rapidly to be noted in the *OED*. Cf. *Aurora Leigh,* I, 424.

2. The Royal Catholic College at Maynooth, County Kildare, a seminary for Irish Catholic priests, had fallen into decay, and a bill to grant it funds had just come up for a second reading in Parliament. There was a great national boiling-up of bigotry on the issue, in *Times* editorials, debates, and mass protest meetings. Eventually, however, the bill passed.

3. Caroline Elizabeth Sarah Norton (1808–77) was a granddaughter of R. B. Sheridan. Browning refers to her *Child of the Islands* in three-hundred and seventy-one Spenserian stanzas which had been planned for publication on the Prince's first birthday, November 9, 1842, but had just appeared. For more on Mrs. Norton, see Letter 444, note 4.

4. "Outside myself."

5. The rest of the text covers a sketch which clearly represents the largest of the "Syranusae," the small, uninhabited islands just off Sorrento once thought to be the home of the Sirens (see *Aeneid* V. 864), which under their modern name, Li Galli, figure in Browning's *The Englishman in Italy* (first published in November 1845 as *England in Italy*): "Those isles of the siren, your Galli . . ." (l. 199). Browning's sketch depicts ". . . the strange square black turret / With never a door . . ." (219–220). It seems clear that Browning was then at work upon the poem.

17 *(W8°)*   *E.B.B. to R.B.*

[April 17, 1845.]

Thursday Morning.

If you did but know dear Mr. Browning how often I have written . . not this letter I am about to write, but another better letter to you, . . in the midst of my silence, . . you w^d not think for a moment that the east wind, with all the harm it does to me, is able to do the great harm of putting out the light of the thought of you to my mind,—for this, indeed, it has no power to do. I had the pen in my hand once to write,—

& why it fell out, I cannot tell you. And you see, . . all your writing will not change the wind! You wished all manner of good to me one day as the clock struck ten,—yes, & I assure you I was better that day—& I must not forget to tell you so though it is so long since. /But⟩And/ *therefore,* I was logically bound to believe that you had never thought of me since . . unless you thought east winds of me! *That* was quite clear; was it not?— or would have been,—if it had not been for the supernatural conviction, I had above all, of your kindness, which was too large to be taken in the hinge of a syllogism. In fact I have long left off thinking that logic proves anything—it *doesn't,* you know.

But your Lamia[1] has taught you some subtle 'viperine' reasoning & *motiving,* for the turning down one street instead of another. It was conclusive.

Ah—but you will never persuade me that I am the better, or as well, for the thing that I have not. We look from different points of view, & yours is the point of attainment. Not that you do not truly say that, when all is done, we must come home to place our engines, & act by our own strength. I do not want material as material,—no one does. But every life requires a full experience, a various experience—& I have a profound conviction that where a poet has been shut from most of the ₊outward₊ aspects of life, he is at a lamentable disadvantage. Can you, speaking for yourself, separate the results in you from the external in- fluences at work around you, that you say so boldly that you get nothing from the world? You do not *directly,* I know—but you do indirectly & by a rebound. Whatever acts upon you, becomes *you*—& whatever you love or hate, whatever charms you or is scorned by you, acts on you & becomes *you*. Have you read the 'Improvisatore'? or will you?—The writer seems to feel, just as I do, the good of the outward life,—and he is a poet in his soul. It is a book full of beauty & had a great charm to me.

As to the Polkas and Cellariuses, . . I do not covet them of course . . but what a strange world you ₊seem to₊ have, to me at a distance—what a strange husk of a world! How it looks to me like mandarin-life or something as remote; nay, not mandarin-life but mandarin *manners,* . . life, even the outer life, meaning something deeper, in my account of it. As to dear Mr. Kenyon I do not make the mistake of fancying that many can look like him or talk like him or *be* like him. I know enough to know otherwise. When he spoke of me he sh[d] have said that I was better not- withstanding the east wind. It is really true—I am getting slowly up from the prostration of the severe cold, & feel stronger in myself.

But Mrs. Norton discourses excellent music—& for the rest, there are fruits in the world so over-ripe, that they will fall, . . without being gathered. Let Maynooth witness to it!—*if you think it worth while!*

Ever yours,

Elizabeth B. Barrett

⌐And *is it* nothing to be 'justified to one's self in one's resources?' '*That's all*,' indeed! For the 'soul's country' we will have /it⟩that/ also— and I know how well the birds sing in it. How glad I was by the way to see your letter!⌐[2]

1. The "viperine she-friend" of Letter 16. The epithet is used for Lady Waldemar, the "villainess" of *Aurora Leigh* (see, e.g., VII, 147).
2. Written above the heading on the first page of the letter.

18 (W10)   **R.B. to E.B.B.**

_____

[*April 30, 1845.*]

Wednesday Morning.

If you did but know, dear Miss Barrett, how the "full stop" after "Morning" just above, has turned out the fullest of stops,—and how for about a quarter of an hour since the ink dried I have been reasoning out the why & wherefore of the stopping, the wisdom of it, and the folly of it . . .

—By this time you see what you have got in me—You ask me questions, "if I like novels," "if the Improvisatore is not good," "if travel and sightseeing do not effect this and that for one," and "what I am devising—play or poem,"—and I shall not say I could not answer at all manner of lengths—but, let me only begin some good piece of writing of the kind, and . . no, you shall have it, have what I was going to tell you stops such judicious beginnings,—in a parallel case, out of which your ingenuity shall, please, pick the meaning— There is a story of D'Israeli's, an old one, with an episode of strange interest,[1] or so I found it years ago,—well, you go breathlessly on with the people of it, page after page, till at last the end *must* come, you feel—and the tangled threads draw to one, and an out-of-door feast in the woods helps you . . that is, helps them, the people, wonderfully on,—and, lo, dinner is done, and Vivian Grey is here, and Violet Fane there,—and a detachment of the party is drafted off to go catch butterflies, and only two or three stop behind. At this moment, Mr. Somebody, a good man and rather the lady's uncle, "in answer to a question from Violet, drew from his pocket a small neatly written manuscript, and, seating himself on an inverted wine-cooler, proceeded to read the following brief remarks upon the characteristics of the Mæso-gothic literature"—this ends the page,—which you don't turn at once! But when you *do,* in bitterness of soul, turn it, you read—"On consideration, I" (Ben, himself) "shall keep them for Mr. Colburn's New Magazine[2]—and deeply you draw thankful breath! (Note this "parallel case" of mine is pretty sure to meet the usual fortune of my writings—you will ask what it means,—and this it means, or should mean, all of it, instance and reasoning and all,—that I am naturally earnest, in earnest about whatever thing I do, and little able to write about one thing while I think of another)—

I think I will really write verse to you some day ⟨‖ ⁻· · · · ‖⟩ *this* day, it is quite clear I had better give up trying.

No, spite of all the lines in the world, I will make an end of it, as Ophelia with her swan's-song,—for it grows too absurd. But remember that I write letters to nobody but you, and that I want method and much more. That book you like so, the Danish novel, must be full of truth & beauty, to judge from the few extracts I have seen in Reviews. That a Dane should write so, confirms me in an old belief—that Italy is stuff for the use of the North,[3] and no more: pure Poetry there is none, nearly as possible none, in Dante even—materials for Poetry in the pitifullest romancist of their thousands, on the contrary—strange that those great wide black eyes should stare nothing out of the earth that lies before them! Alfieri,[4] with even grey eyes, and a life of travel, writes you some fifteen tragedies as colourless as salad grown under a garden glass with matting over it—as free, that is, from local colouring, touches of the soil they are said to spring from,—think of 'Saulle,' and his Greek attempts!

I expected to see Mr. Kenyon, at a place where I was last week, but he kept away. Here is the bad wind back again, and the black sky. I am sure I never knew till now whether the East or West or South were the quarter to pray for—But surely the weather was a little better last week, and you, were you not better? And do you know—but it's all self-flattery I believe,—still I cannot help fancying the East wind does *my* head harm too!

Ever yours faithfully

R. Browning

1. *Vivian Grey,* Bk. V, chap. xv. Characteristically the minute details here are Browning's own—e.g., the prefix "Mæso-" to "gothic"—and the remarks were to have been on architecture, not literature. See Letter 20.

2. The *New Monthly Magazine,* was published by Henry Colburn (d. 1855), the man who first published Pepys's and Evelyn's diaries.

3. Though Browning softens this when E.B.B. demurs, he wrote in the same vein to Isa Blagden in 1866 (McAleer, p. 238), and E.B.B. herself came to a similar view: "The roots of thought, here in Italy, seem dead in the ground. It is well they have great memories—nothing else lives." *Letters of E.B.B.,* I, 309.

4. Count Vittorio Alfieri (1749-1803) was the author of nineteen tragedies in classical forms, of which *Saul* is the best known.

19 (W9°)   **E.B.B. to R.B.**

[May 1, 1845.]

Thursday.

People say of you & of me, dear Mr. Browning, that we love the darkness & use a sphinxine idiom in our talk,—and really you do talk a little like a sphinx in your argument drawn from Vivian Grey. Once I sate up all night to read 'Grey,'—but I never drew such an argument from him. Not that I give it up (nor *you* up) for a mere mystery. Nor that I can '*see what you have got in you,*' from a mere guess. But just observe! If I ask questions about novels, is it not because I want to know how much elbow-room there may be for our sympathies . . & whether there is room for my loose sleeves, & the lace lappets, as well as for my elbows,—& because I want to see *you* by the refracted lights as well as by the direct ones,—& because I am willing for you to know *me* from the beginning, with all my weaknesses & foolishnesses, . . as they are accounted by people who say to me 'no one would ever think, without

knowing you, that you were so & so.' Now if I send all my idle questions to Colburn's Magazine, with other Gothic literature, & take to
standing up in a perpendicular personality like the angel on the school-
man's needle, in my letters to come, without further leaning to the left
or the right—why the end would be that *you* w^d take to 'running after
the butterflies,' for change of air & exercise. And then . . oh . . then, my
'small neatly written manuscripts' might fall back into my desk . . . !
(*Not* a 'full stop'!.)

Indeed . . I do assure you . . I never for a moment thought of
'making conversation' about the 'Improvisatore' or novels in general,
when I wrote what I did to you. I might, to other persons . . perhaps.
Certainly not to *you*. I was not dealing round from one pack of cards to
you & to others. That's what you meant to reproach me for, you know
—& of that, I am not guilty at all. I never could think of 'making conversation' in a letter to *you*—never. Women are said to partake of the
nature of children—& my brothers call me 'absurdly childish' sometimes: and I am capable of being childishly 'in earnest' about novels, &
straws, & such 'puppydogs tails' as my Flush's![1] Also I write more
letters than you do, . . I write in fact almost as you pay visits, . . & one
has to 'make conversation' in turn, of course. *But*—give me something
to vow by—whatever you meant in the Vivian Grey argument, you
were wrong in it! & you never can be much more wrong—which is a
comfortable reflection.

Yet you leap very high at Dante's crown—or ⟨perhaps⟩ you do
not leap, . . you simply ⌈extend your hand to it, & make a rustling among
the laurel leaves, which is somewhat prophane. Dante's poetry only
materials for the northern rhymers!—I must think of that . . if you please
. . before I agree with you. Dante's poetry seems to come down in hail,
rather than in rain—but count me the drops congealed in one hailstone!
Oh! the 'Flight of the Duchess'[2]—do let us hear more of her! Are you
(I wonder) . . . not a 'self-flatterer,' . . but . . a flatterer.
                              Ever yours

                                                        E. B. B.⌉[3]

1. A spaniel given to E.B.B. in January 1841 by Mary Russell Mitford, who
owned the sire.

2. E.B.B. had apparently just come upon the first nine sections of the poem in
the April 1845 *Hood's Magazine*.

3. The bracketed text is written inside the envelope flap.

R.B. to E.B.B.

[*May 3, 1845.*]

Saturday Morning.

Now shall you see what you shall see—here shall be "sound speech not to be reproved,"—for this morning you are to know that the soul of me has it all her own way, dear Miss Barrett, this green cool nine-in-the-morning time for my chestnut-tree over there, and for me who only coaxed my good-natured—(really)—body up, after its three-hours night-rest on condition it should lounge, or creep about, incognito and without consequences—and so it shall, all but my right-hand which is half-spirit and "cuts" its poor relation, and passes itself off for somebody (that is, some soul) and is doubly active & ready on such occasions—Now I shall tell you all about it, first what last letter meant, and then more. You are to know, then, that for some reason, that looked like an instinct, I thought I ought not to send shaft on shaft, letter-plague on letter, with such an uninterrupted clanging . . that I ought to wait, say a week at least, having killed all your mules for you, before I shot down your dogs: but not being exactly Phoibos Apollon,[1] you are to know further that when I *did* think I might go modestly on, . . ὤμοι,[2] let me get out of this slough of a simile, never mind with what dislocation of ancles! Plainly, from waiting and turning my eyes away (not from *you,* but from you in your special capacity of being *written*-to, not spoken-to) when I turned again you had grown formidable somehow—tho' that's not the word,—nor are you the person, either,—it was my fortune, my privilege of being your friend this one way, that it seemed a shame for me to make no better use of than taking it up with talk about books and I don't know what: write what I will, you would read for once, I think —well, then,—what I shall write shall be—something on this book, and the other book, and my own books, and Mary Howitt's books,[3] and at the end of it—good bye, and I hope here is a quarter of an hour rationally spent. So the thought of what I should find in my heart to say, and the contrast with what I suppose I ought to say . . all these things are against me. But this is very foolish, all the same, I need not be told—and is part & parcel of an older—indeed primitive folly of mine, which I shall never

wholly get rid of, of desiring to do nothing when I cannot do all; seeing
nothing, getting, enjoying ⁺nothing,↓ where there is no seeing & getting
& enjoying *wholly*—and in this case, moreover, you are *you*, and know
something about me, if not much, and have read Bos on the art of supplying Ellipses,[4] and (after, particularly, I have confessed all this, why &
how it has been) you will *subaudire*[5] when I pull out my Mediæval-
Gothic-Architectural-Manuscript (so it was, I remember now,) and
instruct you about corbeils and ogives . . tho', after all, it was none of
Vivian's doing, that,—all the uncle kind of man's, which I never professed to be. Now you see how I came to say some nonsense (I very
vaguely think *what*) about Dante—some desperate splash I know I made
for the beginning of my picture, as when a painter at his wits' end and
hunger's beginning says 'Here shall the ⁺figures↓ hand be'—and spots
that down, meaning to reach it naturally from the other end of his canvass,—and leaving off tired, there you see the spectral disjoined thing,
and nothing between it and rationality: I intended to shade down and
soften off and put in and leave out, and, before I had done, bring Italian
Poets round to their old place again in my heart, giving new praise if I
took old,—anyhow Dante is out of it all, as who knows but I, with all of
him in my head and heart? But they do fret one, those tantalizing creatures, of fine passionate class, with such capabilities, and such a facility of
being made pure mind of. And the special instance that vexed me, was
that a man of sands and dog-roses and white rock and green sea-water
just under, should come to Italy where my heart lives, and discover the
sights and sounds . . certainly discover them. And so do all Northern
writers; for take up handfuls of sonetti, rime, poemetti, doings of those
who never did anything else,—and try and make out, for yourself,
what . . say, what flowers they tread on, or trees they walk under,—as
you might bid *them*, those tree & flower loving creatures, pick out of
our North poetry a notion of what *our* daisies and harebells and furze
bushes and brambles are—"Odorosi fioretti, rose porporine, bianchis-
simi gigli."[6] And which of you eternal triflers was it called yourself
'Shelley' and so told me years ago that in the mountains it was a feast
"When one should find those globes of deep red gold—Which in the
woods the strawberry-tree doth bear, Suspended in their emerald atmosphere."[7] So that when my Mule walked into a sorb-tree, not to tumble
sheer over Monte Calvano,[8] and I felt the fruit against my face, the little
ragged bare-legged guide fairly laughed at my knowing them so well—

"Niursi—sorbi!"[9] No, no,—does not all Naples-bay and half Sicily, shore and inland, come flocking once a year to the Piedigrotta fête[10] only to see the blessed King's Volanti, or livery servants all in their best, as tho' heaven opened? and would not I engage to bring the whole of the Piano (of Sorrento) in likeness to a red velvet dressing gown properly spangled over, before the priest that held it out on a pole had even begun his story of how Noah's son Shem, the founder of Sorrento, threw it off to swim thither, as the world knows he did? Oh, it makes one's soul angry, so enough of it. But never enough of telling you—bring all your sympathies, come with loosest sleeves and longest lace-lappets, and you and yours shall find "elbow room," oh, shall you not! For never did man woman or child, Greek, Hebrew, or as Danish as our friend, like a thing, not to say love it, but I liked and loved it, one liking neutralizing the rebellious stir of its fellow, so that I do'n't go about now wanting the fixed stars before my time; this world has not escaped me, thank God; and—what other people say is the best of it, may not escape me after all, tho' until so very lately I made up my mind to do without it;—perhaps, on that account, and to make fair amends to other people,—who, I have no right to say, complain without cause. I have been surprised, rather, with something not unlike illness of late—I have had a constant pain in the head for these two months, which only very rough exercise gets rid of, and which stops my "Luria" and much besides. I thought I never could be unwell. Just now all of it is gone, thanks to polking all night and walking home by broad daylight to the surprise of the thrushes in the bush here. And do you know I said "this must *go*, cannot mean to stay, so I will not tell Miss Barrett why this & this is not done,"—but I mean to tell you all, or more of the truth, because you call me "flatterer," so that my eyes widened again! I, and in what? And of whom, pray? not of *you*, at all events,—of whom then? *Do* tell me, because I want to stand with you—and am quite in earnest there. And "The Flight of the Duchess," to leave nothing out, is only the beginning of a story written some time ago, and given to poor Hood in his emergency[11] at a day's notice,—the true stuff and story is all to come, the '*Flight*' and what you allude to is the mere introduction—but the Magazine has passed into other hands and I must put the rest in some "Bell" or other—it is one of my Dramatic Romances. So is a certain '*Saul*' I should like to show you one day—an ominous liking,—for nobody ever sees what I do till it is printed. But as you *do* know the printed little part of me, I should not be sorry if, in justice, you knew all I have *really* done,—written in the portfolio there,—tho' that would be far enough from *this* me, that writes to you now. I should like to write something in concert with you—how I would try!

I have read your letter thro' again. Does this clear up all the difficulty, and do you see that I never dreamed of "reproaching you for dealing out one sort of cards to me and everybody else"—but that . . why, "*that*" which I have, I hope, said, so need not resay. I will tell you— Sydney Smith laughs somewhere at some Methodist or other whose wont was, on meeting an acquaintance in the street, to open at once on him with some enquiry after the state of his soul[12]—Sydney knows better now, and sees that one might quite as wisely ask such questions as the price of Illinois stock or the condition of glebe-land,—and I *could* say such

———

——— "could" . . the plague of it! So no more at present from your loving . . Or, let me tell you that I am going to see Mr. Kenyon on the 12 inst.—that you do not tell me how you are, and that yet if you do not continue to improve in health . . I shall not see you—not—not—not —what "knots" to untie! Surely the wind that sets my chestnut-tree dancing, all its baby-cone-blossoms, green now, rocking like fairy castles on a hill in an earthquake,—that is South West, surely! God bless you, and me in that—and do write to me soon, and tell me who was the "flatterer," and how he never was

Yours

R. B.

1. *Iliad* I.
2. "Alas!"
3. The wife of William Howitt and translator of European writers.
4. Lambertus Bos, an eighteenth-century Dutch classical scholar, was author of the standard work on interpreting elliptical constructions in Greek.
5. ". . . *understand, supply* an omitted word." Lewis and Short's *Latin Dictionary* (Oxford, 1879).
6. "Sweet blossoms, red roses, whitest lilies."
7. Shelley, *Marenghi*, st. xiii, slightly misquoted.
8. At Sorrento. See *The Englishman in Italy*, ll. 229–232.
9. "Yes, sir—sorb apples!"
10. The feast of the Madonna di Piedigrotta, celebrated on September 8 at the

church of that name near the Grotto of Posilipo, originated in Charles III's victory over the Austrians in 1744. In Browning's time it was a military feast in which 40,000 soldiers lined the streets from the palace to the church while the Royal Family drove there in silver-gilt coaches *(volanti)* to thank the Virgin for Charles's victory. (B. Pellerano, *Handbook of Naples* [Naples, 1885], pp. 9–10; Alexander Polovtsoff, *The Call of the Siren* [London: Selwyn & Blount, 1939], pp. 189–193.)

11. Thomas Hood (1799–1845), remembered now for *The Song of the Shirt* and *The Bridge of Sighs* but better known as a humorist in his own day, was editor of *Hood's Magazine* from its inception until shortly before his death, which occurred on the day this letter was written. During his last illness his friends kept the magazine going.

12. Sydney Smith (1771–1845), English clergyman and humorist. In an article in the *Edinburgh Review* (1808), Smith printed the following as an extract from "Meth. Mag. p. 247," "Whenever he met me in the street, his salutation used to be 'Have you free and lively intercourse with God to-day?'" *The Works of the Rev. Sydney Smith* (4th ed.; 3 vols., London, 1848), I, 189. Browning's ensuing remark refers to Smith's death three months earlier.

21 (W10°) *E.B.B. to R.B.*

[May 5–6, 1845.]

Monday—& Tuesday.

So when wise people happen to be ill, they sit up till six o'clock in the morning & get up again at nine? Do tell me how Lurias can ever be made out of such ungodly imprudences. If the wind blows east or west, where can any remedy be, while such evil / things>deeds / are being committed? And what is to be the end of it? And what is the reasonableness of it in the meantime, when we all know that thinking, dreaming, creating people like yourself, have two lives to bear instead of one, & therefore ought to sleep more than others, . . throwing over ↑& buckling in↓ that fold of death, to stroke the life-purple smoother. You have to live your own personal life, & also Luria's life—& therefore you sh^d^ sleep for both. It is logical indeed—& rational, . . which logic is not always,—and if I had 'the tongue of men & of angels,' I would use it to persuade you. Polka, for the rest, may be good,—but sleep is better. I think better of sleep than I ever did, now that she will not easily come near me except in a red hood of poppies. And besides . . praise your 'goodnatured body' as you like, . . it is only a seeming

goodnature! Bodies bear malice in a terrible way, be very sure!—
appear mild & smiling for a few short years, and then .. out with a cold
steel,—and the soul *has it,* 'with a vengeance,' .. according to the
phrase! You will not persist, (—will you?—) in this experimental
homicide. Or tell me if you will, that I may do some more teazing. It
really, really is wrong. Exercise is one sort of rest & you feel relieved by
it—and sleep is another: one being as necessary as the other.

　　This is the first thing I have to say. The next is a question. *What do
you mean about your manuscripts .. about 'Saul' & the portfolio?* for I am
afraid of hazardously supplying ellipses—& your 'Bos' comes to βοῦς
ἐπὶ γλώσσῃ.[1] I get half bribed to silence by the very pleasure of fancying. But if it could be possible that you should mean to say you would
show me ... Can it be? or am I reading this 'Attic contraction' quite
the wrong way? You see I am afraid of the difference between flattering
myself & being flattered,—the fatal difference. And now will you
understand that I sh^d be too overjoyed to have revelations from the
"Portfolio," .. however incarnated with blots & pen-scratches, .. to be
able to ask impudently of them now? Is that plain?

　　It must be, .. at any rate, .. that if *you* would like to 'write something together' with me, *I* should like it still better. I should like it for
some ineffable reasons. And I should not like it a bit the less for the
grand supply of jests it w^d ⟨‖ · · · ‖⟩ ↑administer↓ to the critical Board of
Trade, about visible darkness, multiplied by two, mounting into palpable obscure.[2] We should not mind .. should we? *you* would not mind,
if you had got over certain other considerations deconsiderating to
your coadjutor. Yes—but I dare not do it, .. I mean, think of it, .. just
now, if ever: and I will tell you why in a Mediæval-Gothic-architec-
tural manuscript.

　　The only poet by profession (if I may say so) except yourself, with
whom I ever had much intercourse even on paper, ↑(if this is near to
'much')↓ has been Mr. Horne. We approached ↑each other↓ on the
point of one of Miss Mitford's annual editorships,—& ever since, he
has had the habit of writing to me occasionally,—& when I was too ill
to write at all, in my dreary Devonshire days, I was his debtor for
various little kindnesses, .. for which I continue his debtor. In my
opinion he is a truehearted & generous man. Do you not think so?
Well—long & long ago, he asked me to write a drama with him on the
Greek model,[3]—that is, for me to write the choruses, and for him to

do the dialogue. Just then it was quite doubtful in my own mind, ⟨‖ · · · ‖⟩ & worse than doubtful, whether I ever sh^d write again,—& the very doubtfulness made me speak my 'yes' more readily. Then I was desired to make a subject, . . to conceive a plan; & my plan was of a man, haunted by his own soul, . . (making her a separate personal Psyche, a dreadful, beautiful Psyche)—the man ↑being↓ haunted & terrified through all the turns of life by her. Did you ever feel afraid of your own soul, as I have done? I think it is a true wonder of our humanity—& fit subject enough for a wild lyrical drama. I should like to ⟨‖ · · · ‖⟩ ↑write↓ it by myself at least, well enough. But with him I will not now. It was delayed . . delayed. He cut the plan up into scenes . . I mean into a list of scenes . . a sort of ↑ground↓ map to work on— ↑& there it lies. Nothing more was done.↓ It all lies in one sheet—& I have offered to give up my copyright of idea in it—if he likes to use it alone—or I sh^d not object to work it out alone on my own side, since it comes from me: only I will not consent now to a *double work* in it. There are objections—none . . be it well understood . . in Mr. Horne's disfavour—for I think of him as well at this moment, & the same in all essential points, as I ever did. He is a man of / high⟩fine / imagination, & is besides good & generous. In the course of our acquaintance (on paper—for I never saw him!) I never was angry with him except once, —& then, *I* was quite wrong & had to confess it. But this is being too "mediæval." Only you will see from it that I am a little entangled on the subject of compound works, & must look where I tread . . & you will understand (if you ever hear from Mr. Kenyon or elsewhere that I am going to write a compound-poem with Mr. Horne) how it *was* true, & isn't true any more.

Yes—you are going to Mr. Kenyon's on the 12th—& yes—my brother & sister are going to meet you & your sister there one day to dinner. Shall I have courage to see you soon, I wonder! If you ask me, I must ask myself. But oh, this make-believe May—it cant be May after all! If a south-west wind sate in your chestnut tree, it was but for a few hours—the east wind 'came up this way' by the earliest opportunity of succession. As the old 'mysteries' showed 'Beelzebub with a bearde,'[4] even so has the east wind had a 'bearde' of late, in a full growth of bristling exaggerations—the English spring-winds have excelled themselves in evil this year; & I have not been down stairs yet.—*But* I am certainly stronger & better than I was—that is undeni-

able—& I *shall* be better still. You are not going away soon—are you?
In the meantime you do not know what it is to be . . a little afraid of
Paracelsus. So right about the Italians! & the 'rose porporine' which
made me smile. How is the head? Ever yours

E. B. B.

⌈Is the 'Flight of the Duchess' in the portfolio? Of course you
must ring the Bell. That poem has a strong heart in it, to begin so
strongly. Poor Hood!⁵ And all those thoughts fall mixed together.
May God bless you.⌉⁶

    1. "Aeschylus, *Agamemnon* 36: 'An ox hath trodden on my tongue'—a Greek
proverb implying silence." 1899 ed.
    2. See *Paradise Lost* I. 63 and II. 406.
    3. To have been called *Psyche Apocalypte*; see *Letters of EBB to RHH*, II, 61–110,
and *Elizabeth Barrett Browning: Hitherto Unpublished Poems and Stories*, ed. H. Buxton
Forman (2 vols., Bibliophile Society, Boston, 1914), II, 203–220.
    4. Apparently mystery plays. Some were first printed in the 1830's and 1840's,
but none with this phrase.
    5. See note 10 to the preceding letter.
    6. The postscript is squeezed in at the top of the first page of manuscript.

22 (W11°)   *E.B.B. to R.B.*

[May 11, 1845.]

Sunday—in the last hour of it.

May I ask how the head is? just under the bay? Mr. Kenyon was
here to-day & told me such bad news that I cannot sleep to-night
(although I did think once of doing it) without asking such a question
as this, dear Mr. Browning.

Let me hear how you are—will you? and let me hear (if I can) that
it was prudence or some unchristian virtue of the sort, & not a dreary
necessity, which made you put aside the engagement for Tuesday—
for Monday. I had been thinking so of seeing you on Tuesday . . with
my sister's eyes—for the first sight.

And now if you have done killing the mules & the dogs, let me have a straight quick arrow for myself, if you please. Just a word, to say how you are. I ask for no more than a word, lest the writing should be hurtful to you.

May God bless you always.

Your friend
E. B. B.

23 (W12)   *R.B. to E.B.B.*

[May 12, 1845.]

Monday.

My dear, own friend, I am quite well now, or next to it—but this is how it was,—I have gone out a great deal of late, and my head took to ringing such a literal alarum that I wondered what was to come of it; and at last, a few evenings ago, as I was dressing for a dinner some-where, I got really bad of a sudden, and kept at home to my friend's heartrending disappointment—Next morning I was no better—and it struck me that I should be really disappointing dear kind Mr. Kenyon, and wasting his time, if that engagement, too, were broken with as little warning,—so I thought it best to forego all hopes of seeing him, at such a risk. And that done, I got rid of every other promise to pay visits for next week and next, and told everybody, with considerable dignity, that my London season was over for this year, as it assuredly is—and I shall be worried no more, and let walk in the garden, and go to bed at ten o'clock, and get done with what is most expedient to do, and my "flesh shall come again like a little child's,"[1] and one day, oh the day, I shall see you with my own, own eyes . . for, how little ↑you↓ understand me; or rather, your self,—if you think I would dare see you, without your leave, that way! Do you suppose that your power of giving & refusing ends when you have shut your room-door? Did I not tell you I turned down another street, even, the other day, and why not down your's? And often as I see Mr. Kenyon, have I ever dreamed of asking any but the merest conventional questions about you; your health, and no more?

61

I will answer your letter, the last one, to-morrow—I have said nothing of what I want to say.

Ever yours

R. B.

1. II Kings 5:14, the story of Naaman the Leper.

24 (*W13*)   *R.B. to E.B.B.*

[*May 13, 1845.*]

Tuesday Morning.

Did I thank you with any effect in the lines I sent yesterday, dear Miss Barrett? I know I felt most thankful, and, of course, began reasoning myself into the impropriety of allowing a "more" or a "most" in feelings of that sort towards you. I am thankful for you, all about you—as, do you not know?

Thank you, from my soul.

Now, let me never pass occasion of speaking well of Horne, who deserves your opinion of him,—it is my own, too. He has unmistakeable genius, and is a fine, honest, enthusiastic chivalrous fellow—it is the fashion to affect to sneer at him, of late, I think—the people he has praised fancying that they "pose" themselves sculpturesquely in playing the Greatly Indifferent, and the other kind shaking each other's hands in hysterical congratulations at having escaped such a dishonour:[1] *I* feel grateful to him, I know, for his generous criticism, and glad & proud of in any way approaching such a man's standard of poetical height. And he might be a disappointed man, too—for the players trifled with and teazed out his very earnest nature, which has a strange aspiration for the horrible tin-&-lacquer 'crown' they give one from their clouds (of smooth shaven deal done over blue)—and he don't give up the bad business yet, but thinks a "small" theatre would somehow not be a theatre, and an actor not quite an actor . . I forget in what way, but the upshot is, he bates not a jot in that rouged, wigged, padded, empty headed, heartless tribe of grimacers that came and canted me; not I, them,—a thing he cannot understand—*so,* I am not the one he would

have picked out to praise, had he not been *loyal*. I know he admires your
poetry properly—God help him, and send some great artist from the
country, (who can read & write beside comprehending Shakspeare,
and who "exasperates his H's" when the feat is to be done)—to undertake the part of Cosmo, or Gregory,[2] or what shall most soothe his spirit!
The subject of your play is tempting indeed—& reminds one of that wild
Drama of Calderon's which frightened Shelley just before his death[3]—
also, of Fuseli's theory with reference to his own Picture of Macbeth in
the witches' cave[4] . . wherein the apparition of the armed head from the
cauldron is Macbeth's own.

"If you ask me, I must ask myself"—that is, when I am to see you—
I will *never* ask you! You do *not* know what I shall estimate that permission at,—nor do I, quite—but you do—do not you? know so much of
me as to make my "asking" worse than a form—I do not "ask" you to
write to me—not *directly* ask, at least.

I will tell you—I ask you *not* to see me so long as you are unwell,
⟨or mistrustful of⟩

No, no, that is being too grand! Do see me when you can, and let
me not be only writing myself

Yours

R. B.

["Next letter" to say how you must help me with all my new
Romances and Lyrics, and Lays & Plays, and read them and heed them
and end them and mend them!"][5]

A kind, so kind, note from Mr. Kenyon came. We, I & my sister, are
to go in June instead . . I shall go nowhere till then; I am nearly well—all

save one little wheel in my head that keeps on its

That you are better I am most thankful.

1. As being written about in *A New Spirit of the Age*. The book was assaiied by
most critics as having too much of the clique or coterie about it. The *New Monthly
Magazine* (May 1844) said that "Even those whom it praises are uneasy under its
approbation."
2. *Cosmo de' Medici* (1837), a tragedy, and *Gregory VII* (1840), an historical
drama. None of Horne's plays was ever acted.
3. Shortly before his death Shelley awakened the household at San Lorenzo

one night by screaming in his sleep. "On waking him, he related that he had had a vision. He thought that a figure wrapped in a mantle came to his bedside, and beckoned to him. He got up and followed it, and when in the hall, the phantom lifted up the hood of his cloak, and showed the phantasm of himself—and saying 'Siete satisfatto'—vanished." Shelley had been reading Calderón's *El embozado, O el encapotado,* in which the protagonist encounters his own phantasm, and Medwin attributes the dream to that fact. [Thomas Medwin], "Memoir of Shelley," *Athenæum*, August 18, 1832, p. 536.

    4. Henry Fuseli (born Johann Heinrich Füssli, 1741–1825) was fond of painting grotesque and supernatural subjects, especially from Milton and Shakespeare. Of this picture of Macbeth he told his biographer: "I have endeavoured to shew a colossal head rising out of the abyss, and that head Macbeth's likeness. What, I would ask, would be a greater object of terror to you, if, some night on going home, you were to find yourself sitting at your own table . . .? Would not this make a powerful impression on your mind?" John Knowles, *The Life and Writings of Henry Fuseli, Esq., M.A.R.A.* (3 vols., London, 1830), I, 189–190.

    5. This sentence was apparently squeezed in after the rest had been finished.

25 *(W12°)*   *E.B.B. to R.B.*

[*May 15, 1845.*]

Thursday.

    But how 'mistrustfulness'? And how "that way"? What have I said or done, *I,* who am not apt to be mistrustful of anybody & sh^d be a miraculous monster if I began with *you!* What can I have said, I say to myself again & again.

    One thing, at any rate, I have done, "that way" or this way! I have made what is vulgarly called a 'piece of work' about little; or seemed to make it. Forgive me. I am shy by nature:—& by position and experience, . . by having had my nerves shaken to excess, & by leading a life of such seclusion, . . by these things together & by others besides, I have appeared shy & ungrateful to you. Only not mistrustful. You could not mean to judge me so. Mistrustful people do not write as I write . . surely! for wasn't it a Richelieu or Mazarin (or who?) who said that with five lines from anyone's hand, he c^d take off his head for a corollary?[1] I think so.

    Well!—but this is to prove that I am not mistrustful, & to say, that if you ⟨do⟩ care to come to see me you can come; & that it is my gain (as I feel it to be) & not yours, whenever you do come. You will not talk of having come afterwards I know, because although I am 'fast bound' to see one or two persons this summer² (besides yourself, whom I receive of choice & willingly) I *cannot* admit visitors in a general way—& putting the question of health quite aside, it w^d be unbecoming to lie here on the sofa & make a company-show of an infirmity, & hold a beggar's hat for sympathy. I sh^d blame it in another woman—& the sense of it has had its weight with me sometimes.

For the rest, . . when you write that "*I* do not know how you w^d value, &c. *nor yourself quite,*" you touch very accurately on the truth, . . & *so* accurately in the last clause, that to read it, made me smile 'tant bien que mal.' Certainly you cannot "quite know," or know at all, whether the least straw of pleasure can ⟨come⟩ go to you from knowing me otherwise than on this paper—& I, for my part, 'quite know' my own honest impression, dear Mr. Browning, that none is likely to /do⟩go/ to you. There is nothing to see in me; nor to hear in me—I never learnt to talk as you do in London,—although I can admire that brightness of carved speech in Mr. Kenyon & others. If my poetry is worth anything to any eye,—it is the flower of me. I have lived most & been most happy in it, & so it has all my colours; the rest of me is nothing but a root, fit for the ground & the dark. And if I write all this egotism, . . it is for shame; & because I feel /afraid⟩ashamed/ of having made a fuss about what is not worth it,—and because you are extravagant in caring so for a permission, which will be nothing to you afterwards. Not that I am not touched by your caring so at all!—I am deeply touched now,—& presently, . . I shall understand. Come then. There will be truth & simplicity for you in any case,—& a friend. And do not answer this—I do not write it as a flytrap for compliments. Your spider would scorn me for it too much.

Also . . as to the how and when. You are not well now, & it cannot be good for you to do anything but be quiet & keep away that dreadful musical note in the head. I entreat you not to think of coming until *that* is all put to silence satisfactorily. When it is done, . . you must choose whether you w^d like best to come with Mr. Kenyon or to come alone—& if you would come alone, you must just tell me on what day, & I will see you on any day unless there sh^d be an unforeseen obstacle, . . any day after two, or before six. And my sister will bring you up stairs to me,—& we will talk; or *you* will talk; & you will try to be indulgent, & like me as well as you can. If, on the other hand, you w^d rather come with Mr. Kenyon, you must wait, I imagine, till June,—because he goes away on Monday & is not likely immediately to return—no, on Saturday, tomorrow.

In the meantime, why I sh^d be '*thanked*,' is an absolute mystery to me—but I leave it!

You are generous & impetuous,—*that,* I can see & feel,—and so far from being of an inclination to mistrust you or distrust you, I do profess to have as much faith in your full, pure loyalty, as if I had known you personally as many years as I have appreciated your genius. Believe this of me—for it is spoken truly.

In the matter of Shakespeare's "poor players" you are severe—& yet I was glad to hear you severe—it is a happy excess, I think. When men of intense reality, as all great poets must be, give their hearts to be trodden on and tied up with ribbons ⟨by⟩ in turn, by men of masks, there will be torture if there is not desecration. Not that I know much of such things—but I have HEARD. Heard from Mr. Kenyon; heard from Miss Mitford; who however is passionately fond of the theatre as a writer's medium—*not at all,* from Mr. Horne himself, . . except what he has printed on the subject.

Yes—he has been infamously used on the point of the 'New Spirit'³ —only he sh^d have been prepared for the infamy—it was leaping into a gulph, . . not to 'save the republic,' but '*pour rire*': it was not merely putting one's foot into a hornet's nest, but taking off a shoe and stocking to do it. And to think of Dickens being dissatisfied! To think of Tennyson's friends grumbling!—he himself did not, I hope & trust. For you, you certainly were not adequately treated—& above all, you were not placed with your *peers* in that chapter⁴—but that there was an intention to do you justice, and that there *is* a righteous appreciation of you in the writer, I know & am sure,—& that *you* sh^d be sensible to this, is only what I should know & be sure of *you.* Mr. Horne is quite above the narrow, vicious, hateful jealousy of contemporaries, which we hear reproached, too justly sometimes, on men of letters.

I go on writing as if I were not going to see you—soon perhaps.— Remember that the how & the when rest with you—except that it cannot be before next week at the soonest. You are to decide.

Always your friend,

E. B. B.

1. The remark, probably apocryphal, is ascribed to Richelieu.
2. One was apparently Chorley, whom E.B.B. had agreed to see at the behest of Mary Russell Mitford (*EBB to MRM,* pp. 239, 247–249).
3. See Letter 24, note 1. Certain very oblique references in letters of the time indicate that Horne suffered socially because of the book, but Dickens' only recorded complaint is about his portrait and none of Tennyson's friends is on record. The chapter on Tennyson was largely E.B.B.'s work (see Letter 373).
4. Browning shared a chapter with his acquaintance John Westland Marston (1819–90), whose play *The Patrician's Daughter* had been produced by Macready. The material on Browning had already appeared in an article in the *Church of England Quarterly Review* for October 1842.

26 (W14)   **R.B. to E.B.B.**

_____

[*May 16, 1845.*]

Friday Night.

My friend is not 'mistrustful' of me, no, because she don't fear I shall make mainprize of the stray cloaks & umbrellas down-stairs, or turn an article for "Colburn's" on her sayings & doings up-stairs,—but, spite of that, she does mistrust . . *so* mistrust my common sense,—nay, uncommon and dramatic-poet's sense, if I am put on asserting it!—all which pieces of mistrust I could detect, and catch struggling, and pin to death in a moment, and put a label on, with name, genus and species, just like a horrible entomologist; only I won't, because the first visit of the Northwind will carry the whole tribe into the Red Sea—and those horns and tails and scalewings are best forgotten altogether. And now will I say a cutting thing and have done: have I trusted *my* friend so,—or said even to myself, much less to her, she is even as—"Mr. Simpson" who desireth the honour of the acquaintance of Mr. B. whose admirable works have long been his, Simpson's, especial solace in private—and who accordingly is led to that personage by a mutual friend—Simpson blushing as only adorable ingenuousness can, and twisting the brim of his hat like a sailor giving evidence. Whereupon Mr. B. beginneth by remarking that the rooms are growing hot—or that he supposes Mr. S. has not heard if there will be another adjournment of the House to-night—whereupon Mr. S. looketh up all at once, brusheth the brim smooth again with his sleeve, and takes to his assurance once

more, in something of a huff, and after staying his five minutes out
for decency's sake, noddeth familiarly an adieu, and spinning round
on his heel ejaculateth mentally—'Well, I *did* expect to see something
different from that little yellow commonplace man . . and, now I
come to think, there *was* some precious trash in that book of his'—
Have *I* said 'so will Miss Barrett ejaculate?'

⟨And, remember, before you call any wish of mine extravagant,
that I⟩ ⟨You will⟩

Dear Miss Barrett, I thank you for the leave you give me, and for
the infinite kindness of the way of giving it. I will call at 2 on Tuesday—
not sooner, that you may have time to write should any ⊦adverse⊦ circumstances happen . . not that they need inconvenience you, because . .
what I want particularly to tell you for now and hereafter,—do not
mind my coming in the least, but,—should you be unwell, for instance,
—just send or leave word, and I will come again, and again, and again—
my time is of *no* importance, and I have acquaintances thick in the
vicinity.

Now if I do not seem grateful enough to you, *am* I so much to
blame? ⟨Don't forget to let me say that⟩ You see it is high time you
saw me, for I have clearly written myself *out!*

Ever yours,

R. B.

27 *(W 13°)*   **E.B.B. to R.B.**

[*May 17, 1845.*]

Saturday.

I shall be ready on Tuesday I hope, but I hate & protest against your
horrible "entomology." Beginning to explain, w^d thrust me lower and
lower down the circles of some sort of an "Inferno"; only with my
dying breath I w^d maintain that I never could, consciously or unconsciously, mean to distrust you; or, the least in the world, to Simpsonize
you. What I said, . . . it was *you* that put it into my head to say it—for
certainly, in my usual disinclination to receive visitors, such a feeling
does not enter. There, now!—There, I am a whole 'giro'[1] lower! Now,

you will say perhaps that I distrust *you*, & nobody else! . . So it is best to be silent, & bear all the "cutting things" with resignation!—*that* is certain.

Still I must really say, under this dreadful incubus-charge of Simpsonism, . . that you, who know everything, or at least make awful guesses at everything in one's feelings & motives, & profess to be able to pin them down in a book of classified inscriptions, . . should have been able to understand better, or misunderstand less, in a matter like this— Yes! I think so. I think you sh^d have made out the case in some such way as it was in nature—viz. that you had lashed yourself up to an exorbitant wishing to see me, . . (you who could see, /any day⟩every day/, people who are a hundredfold & to all social purposes, my superiors!—) because I was unfortunate enough to be shut up in a room & silly enough to make a fuss about opening the door,—& that I grew suddenly abashed by the consciousness of this. How different from a distrust of *you*!—how different!—

Ah—if, after this day, you ever see any interpretable sign of distrustfulness in me, you may be "cutting" again, & I will not cry out. In the meantime here is a fact for your 'entomology.' I have not so much *distrust,* as will make a *doubt,* as will make a *curiosity* for next Tuesday. Not the simplest modification of *curiosity* enters into the state of feeling with which I wait for tuesday—: and if you are angry to hear me say so, . . why, you are more unjust than ever.

ₜLet it be three instead of two—if the hour be as convenient for yourself.ᵥ[2]

Before you come, try to forgive me for my "infinite kindness" in the manner of consenting to see you. Is it 'the cruellest cut of all' when you talk of infinite kindness, yet attribute such villainy to me? Well!— but we are friends till Tuesday—& after perhaps.

Ever yours,

E. B. B.

[If on Tuesday you should be not well, *pray do not come*—Now, that is my request to your kindness.][3]

1. Dante's "circle."
2. Inserted after the letter was completed.
3. Written inside the envelope flap.

Browning did call on Tuesday, and, in the fashion that became standard

procedure, entered a two-line summary of the meeting on the face of the envelope of E.B.B.'s most recent letter—in this instance the preceding one. The note reads:
+Thursday, May 20, 1845
3–4$\frac{1}{2}$ p.m.

28 (W15)   R.B. to E.B.B.

[*May 20, 1845.*]

Tuesday ⟨Night⟩ Ev^g

I trust to you for a true account of how you are—if tired, if not tired, if I did wrong in any thing,—or, if you please, *right* in any thing—(only, not one more word about my "kindness," which, to get done with, I will grant is excessive)—but, let us so arrange matters if possible, —and why should it not be?—that my great happiness, such as it will be if I see you, as this morning, from time to time,— may be obtained at the cost of as little inconvenience to you as we can contrive. For an instance—just what strikes me—they all say here I speak very loud—(a trick caught from having often to talk with a deaf relative of mine).[1] And did I stay too long?

I will tell *you* unhesitatingly of such "corrigenda"—nay, I will again say, do not humiliate me—*do not* again,—by calling me "kind," in that way.

I am proud & happy in your friendship—now and ever. May God bless you!

R. B.

1. His uncle, Reuben Browning, whose hearing had been damaged by a cricket ball. (Mrs. Orr, p. 370, n.)

29 (W14°)   E.B.B. to R.B.

[*May 21, 1845.*]

Wednesday Morning.

Indeed there was nothing wrong—how sh^d there be? And there

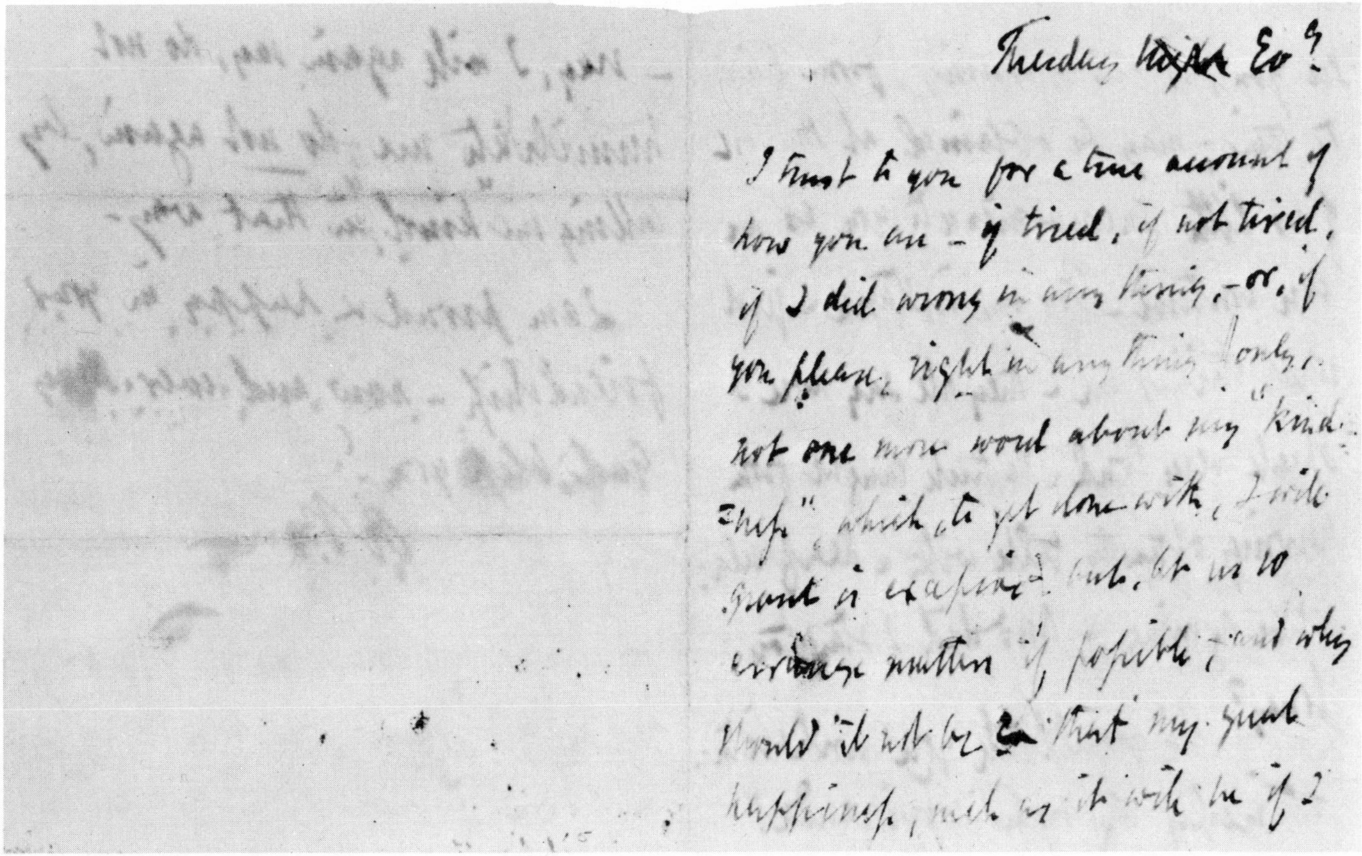

Letter 28, pages 1 and 4

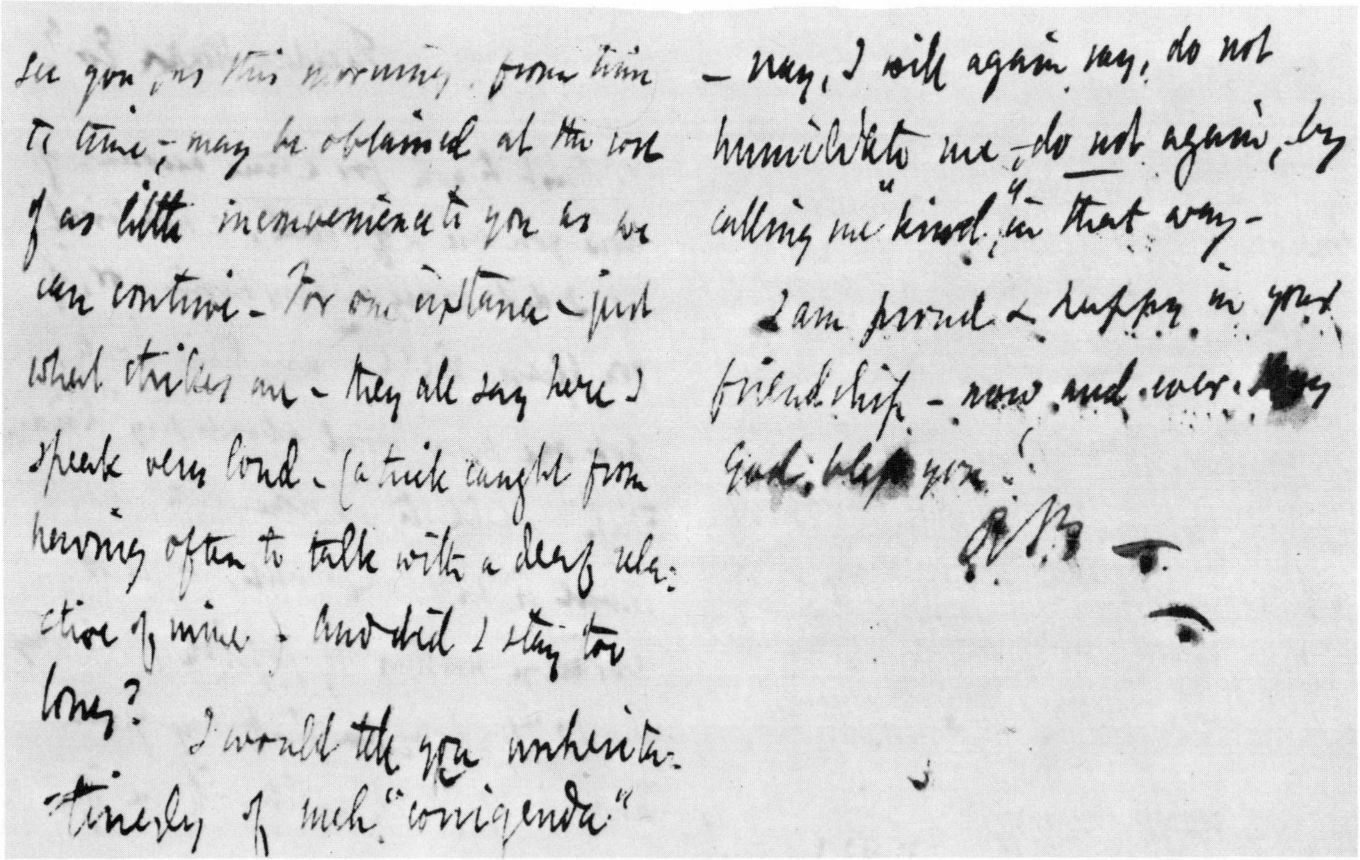

Letter 28, pages 2 and 3

R. R. shows increasing emotion

was everything right—as how should there not be? And as for the 'loud speaking,' I did not hear any!—and, instead of being worse, I ought to be better for what was certainly (to speak it, or be silent of it,) happiness & honour to me yesterday.

Which reminds me to observe that you are so restricting our vocabulary, as to be ominous of silence in a full sense, presently. First, one word is not to be spoken—and then, another is not. And why? Why deny me the use of such words as have natural feelings belonging to them—and how can the use of such be "humiliating" to *you?* If my heart were open to you, you c^d see nothing offensive to you in any thought there or trace of thought that has been there—but it is hard for you to understand, with all your psychology (and to be reminded of it I have just been looking at the preface of some poems by some Mr. Gurney[1] where he speaks of "the reflective wisdom of ↑a↓ Wordsworth and the ↑profound↓ psychological utterances of a Browning") it is hard for you to understand what my mental position is after the peculiar experience I have suffered, & what τί ἐμοὶ καὶ σοί[2] a sort of feeling is irrepressible from me to you, when, from the height of your brilliant happy sphere, you ask, as you did ask, for personal intercourse with me. What words but 'kindness' . . but "gratitude"—but I will not in any case be *un*kind ⟨‖ · · · ‖⟩ & *un*grateful, and do what is displeasing to you. And let us both leave the subject with the words—because we perceive ↑in it↓ from different points of view; we stand on the black & white sides of the shield,—& there is no coming to a conclusion.

But you will come really on Tuesday—& again, when you like & can together—& it will not be more "inconvenient" to me to be pleased, I suppose, than it is to people in general—will it, do you think? Ah—how you misjudge!—Why it must obviously & naturally be delightful to me to receive you here when you like to come, & it cannot be necessary for me to say so in set words—believe it of

Your friend,

E. B. B.

1. Archer Thompson Gurney (1820–87), a clergyman and writer, had been Browning's friend for some time. (Mrs. Orr, p. 78.) E.B.B. probably refers to *Love's Legends* (1845), of which there is no recorded copy in America nor any at the British Museum.

2. "What have I to do with thee?" Mark 5:7, Luke 8:28.

As E.B.B.'s response in the following letter shows, Browning's sixteenth letter offended—presumably by proposing marriage—and Browning asked (Letter 31) to have it returned, whereupon he destroyed it (see Letter 146). Wellesley follows E.B.B.'s numbering as far as possible, and thus there is no extant Browning letter numbered W 16.

30 (W15°)   **E.B.B. to R.B.**

[*May 23, 1845.*]

Friday Evening.

I intended to write to you last night & this morning, & could not,— you do not know what pain you give me in speaking so wildly—And if I disobey you my dear friend, in speaking, (I for my part) of your wild speaking, I do it, not to displease you, but to be in my own eyes, & before God, a little more worthy, or less unworthy, of a generosity from which I recoil by instinct & at the first glance, yet conclusively,—& because my silence w^d be the most disloyal of all means of expression, in reference to it. Listen to me then in this. You have said some intemperate things . . . fancies,—which you will not say over again, nor unsay, but *forget at once, & for ever, having said at all,*—& which (so) will die out between *you & me alone,* like a misprint between you and the printer. And this you will do *for my sake* who am your friend,—(& you have none truer)—& this I ask, because it is a condition necessary to our future liberty of intercourse. You remember—surely you do—that I am in the most exceptional of positions; & that, just *because of it,* I am able to receive you as I did on Tuesday; and that, for me to listen to "unconscious exaggerations," is as unbecoming to the humilities ↑of my position,↓ as unpropitious (which is of more consequence) to the prosperities of yours—Now, if there sh^d be one word of answer attempted to this,—or of reference; *I must not . . I* WILL *not see you again*—& you will justify me later in your heart . . So for my sake you will not say it—I think you will not—& spare me the sadness of having to break through an intercourse just as it is promising pleasure to me,—to me who have so many sadnesses & so few pleasures. You will—! & I need not be uneasy—& I shall owe you that tranquillity, as one gift of many—For, that I have much to receive from you in all the free gifts of thinking, teaching, master-spirits, . . *that,* I know!—it is my own ⟨/peace⟩praise/⟩↑praise↓ that I appreciate you, as none can more. Your influence & help in poetry will be full of good & gladness to me—for with many to love me in this house, there is no one to judge me . . *now*. Your friendship & sympathy will be dear and precious to me all my life, if you indeed leave them with me so long or so little. Your mistakes in me . . which *I* cannot mistake (—& which have humbled me by too much honouring—) I put away gently, & with grateful tears in my eyes,—because *all that hail* will beat down & spoil crowns ⟨‖ · · · ‖⟩, as well as "blossoms."

If I put off next Tuesday to the week after—I mean your visit, . . shall you care much?—For the relations I named to you, are to be in London next week; and I am to see one of my aunts whom I love,[1] & have not met since my great affliction—& it will all seem to come over again, & I shall be out of spirits & nerves. On tuesday week you can bring a tomahawk & do the criticism, & I shall try to have my courage ready for it—Oh, you will do me so much good—and Mr. Kenyon calls me "docile" sometimes I assure you; when he wants to flatter me out of being obstinate—and in good earnest, I believe I shall do everything you tell me. The Prometheus is done—but the monodram is where it was—& the novel, not at all.[2] But I think of some half promises half given, about something I read for 'Saul'—& the Flight of the Duchess—where is she?

You are not displeased with me? *no—that* w^{d} be hail & lightning together—I do not write as I might, of some words of yours—but you know that I am not a stone, even if silent like one. And if in the *un*silence, I have said one word to vex you, pity me for having ↑had↓ to say it—and for the rest, may God bless you far beyond the reach of vexation from my words or my deeds! ⟨‖ · · · ‖⟩

Your friend in grateful regard,

E. B. B.

1. Mrs. Jane Hedley; see Letter 34.
2. See Letter 10, and notes 5 and 6.

31 (W17)   *R.B. to E.B.B.*

———————————

[*May 24, 1845.*]

Saturday M^g

Don't you remember I told you, once on a time, that you "knew
nothing of me"? whereat you demurred—but I meant what I said, &
knew it was so. To be grand in a simile, for every poor speck of a
Vesuvius or a Stromboli in my microcosm there are huge layers of
ice and pits of black cold water—and I make the most of my two
or three fire-eyes, because I know by experience, alas, how these
tend to extinction—and the ice grows & grows—still this last is true
part of me, most characteristic part, *best* part perhaps, and I disown
nothing—only,—when you talked of '*knowing* me'!—Still, I am
utterly unused, of these late years particularly, to dream of communicating anything about *that* to another person (all my writings are
purely dramatic as I am always anxious to say) that when I make
never so little an attempt, no wonder if I *bungle* notably—"language,"
too, is an organ that never studded this heavy heavy head of mine.
Will you not think me very brutal if I tell you I could almost smile
at your misapprehension of what I meant to write?—Yet I *will* tell
you, because it will undo the bad effect of my thoughtlessness, and at
the same time exemplify the point I have all along been honestly
earnest to set you right upon . . my real inferiority to you; just that
and no more. I ⟨spoke⟩ wrote to you, in an unwise moment, on the
spur of being again "thanked," and, unwisely writing just as if thinking to myself, said what must have looked absurd enough ↑as seen↓
apart from the horrible counterbalancing never-to-be-written *rest of
me*—by the side of which, could it be written & put before you,
my note would sink to its proper & relative place, and become a
mere "thank you["] for your good opinion—which I assure you is
far too generous,—for I really believe you to be my superior in many
respects, and feel uncomfortable till *you* see that, too—since I hope
for your sympathy & assistance, and frankness is everything in such
a case. I do assure you, that had you read my note, *only* having
"*known*" so much of me as is implied in having inspected, for
instance, the contents, merely, of that fatal and often-referred-to
"portfolio" there (Dii meliora piis!),[1] you would see in it, (the note

74

not the portfolio) the blandest utterance ever mild gentleman gave
birth to: but I forgot that one may make too much noise in a silent
place by playing the few notes on the 'ear piercing fife' which in
Othello's regimental band ✦might✦ have been thumped into decent
subordination by his "spirit stirring drum"[2]—to say nothing of
gong and ophicleide. Will you forgive me, on promise to remember
for the future, and be more considerate? Not that you must too
much despise me, neither; nor, of all things, apprehend I am attitudini-
zing à la Byron, and giving ✦you✦ to understand unutterable some-
things, longings for Lethe and all that—far from it! I never committed
murders, and sleep the soundest of sleeps—but "the heart is desperately wicked,"[3] that is true, and tho' I dare not say "I know"
mine, yet I have had signal opportunities, I who began life from
the beginning, and can forget nothing (but names, and the date of
the battle of Waterloo,) and have known good & wicked men and
women, gentle & simple, shaking hands with Edmund Kean and
Father Mathew, you and—Ottima![4] Then, I had a certain faculty
of self-consciousness, years, years ago, at which John Mill wondered,[5] and which ought to be improved by this time, if constant use
helps at all—and, meaning, on the whole, to be a Poet, if not *the* Poet . .
for I am vain and ambitious some nights,—I do myself justice, and dare
call things by their names to myself, and say boldly, this I love, this I
hate, this I would do, this I would not do, under all kinds of circumstances,—and talking (thinking) in this style *to myself,* and beginning,
however tremblingly, in spite of conviction, to write in this style *for
myself*—on the top of the desk which contains my "Songs of the Poets—
No. 1 M.P.,"[6] I wrote,—what you now forgive, I know! Because I am,
from my heart, sorry that by a foolish fit of inconsideration I should
have given pain for a minute to you, towards whom, on every account,
I would rather soften and "sleeken every word as to a bird"[7] . . (and,
not such a bird as my black self that go ⟨schreek⟩ ✦screeching✦ about the
world for "dead horse"—corvus (picus)—mirandola!)[8] I, too, who
have been at such pains to acquire the reputation I /have in⟩enjoy/ in the
world,—(ask Mr. Kenyon,) & who dine, and wine, and dance and en-
hance the company's pleasure till they make me ill and I keep house, as
of late: Mr. Kenyon, (for I only quote where you may verify if you
please) *he* says my common sense strikes him, and its contrast with my
muddy metaphysical poetry! And so it shall strike you—for tho' I am

glad that, since you *did* misunderstand me, you said so, and have given me an opportunity of doing by another way what I wished to do in *that*, —yet, if you had *not* alluded to my writing, as I meant you should not, you would have certainly understood *something* of its drift when you found me next Tuesday precisely the same quiet (no, for I feel I speak too loudly, in spite of your kind disclaimer, but—) the same mild man-about-town you were gracious to, the other morning—for, indeed, my own way of worldly life is marked out long ago, as precisely as yours can be, and I am set going with a hand, winker-wise, on each side of my head, and a directing finger before my eyes, to say nothing of an instinctive dread I have that a certain whip-lash is vibrating somewhere in the neighbourhood in playful readiness! So "I hope here be proofs,"[9] to Dogberry's satisfaction that, first, I am but a very poor creature compared to you and entitled by my wants to look up to you,—all I meant to say from the first of the first—and that, next, I shall be too much punished if, for this piece of mere inconsideration, you deprive me, ₊more or less, or↓ sooner or later, of the pleasure of seeing you—, a little over boisterous gratitude for which, perhaps, caused all the mischief! The reasons you give for deferring my visits next week are too cogent for me to dispute—that is too true—and, being now & henceforward "on my good behaviour," I will at once cheerfully submit to them, if needs must—but should your mere kindness and forethought, as I half suspect, have induced you to take such a step, you will now smile, with me, at this new and very unnecessary addition to the "fears of me" I had got so triumphantly over in your case! Wise man, was I not, to clench my first favorable impression so adroitly . . like a recent Cambridge worthy, my sister heard of; who, being on his theological (or rather, scripture-historical) examination, was asked by the Tutor, who wished to let him off easily, "who was the first King of Israel?"—"Saul," answered the trembling youth. "Good!" nodded approvingly the Tutor. "Otherwise called *Paul*," subjoined the youth in his elation! Now I have begged pardon, and blushingly assured you *that* was only a slip of the tongue, and that I did really *mean* all the while, (Paul or no Paul), the veritable son of Kish, he that owned the asses, and found listening to the harp the best of all things for an evil spirit! Pray write me a line to say, 'Oh . . if *that's* all!' and remember me for good (which is very compatible with a moment's stupidity) and let me not for one fault, (and that the only one that shall be), lose *any pleasure* . . for your friendship I am sure I have not lost—God bless you, my dear friend!   R. Browning

⌈And by the way, will it not be better, as co-operating with you more effectually in your kind promise to forget the "printer's error" in my blotted proof, to send me back that same "proof," if you have not inflicted proper and summary justice on it? When Mephistopheles last came to see us in this world outside here, he counselled sundry of us "never to write a letter,—and never to burn one"—do you know that? But I never mind what I am told! Seriously, I am ashamed . . I shall next ask a servant for my boots in the "high fantastical" style of my own "Luria."⌉[10]

1. "May the gods grant better things to the upright!"
2. *Othello* III. iii. 352–355.
3. Jeremiah 17:9.
4. Edmund Kean (1787–1833), the famous tragedian, had a profound influence on Browning (G & M, pp. 45–46). Father Theobald Mathew (1790–1856) was a saintly Franciscan whose temperance movement had extraordinary results in Ireland. His open-air meetings in London in 1843 were highly successful. Browning "stood on the scaffold with him, and heard him preach." *Robert Browning and Alfred Domett*, pp. 92–93. Ottima, of course, is the adultress in *Pippa Passes*.
5. See Introduction, p. 00.
6. This mystifying phrase may refer to *Pauline*. Browning said on several occasions that it was to have been the first in a series of poems, novels, operas, and the like, in which he would "assume and realize I know not how many different characters." It might thus be considered the first of a series of songs by various hands, this one being—as Mill guessed—confessional in its self-revelation: "The present abortion was the first work of the *Poet* of the batch, who would have been more legitimately *myself* than most of the others." (See note 5 to Letter 207.) Perhaps, therefore, "M.P." stands for something like *me poeta*.
7. An echo of E.B.B.'s *A Portrait* (1844), ll. 52–54.
8. *Corvus,* the Latin for "crow," is also the generic term for a class of birds. "Picus" turns this to a play on Linnaeus's term for the magpie, *corvus pica;* and *mirandola*—Italian for "looking at her"—turns the whole thing to a pun on the name of the Italian philosopher Pico della Mirandola. The wild train of association is an interesting glimpse at the working of Browning's mind and the extent of his nervous excitement.
9. A confused recall of Pompey, *Measure for Measure* II. i. 129: "I hope here be truths." Browning may have been confused by Hazlitt, who quotes this correctly as the motto for his *Character of the Country People* but also attributes it to Dogberry.
10. Written inside the envelope flap.

The envelope of the following letter is not addressed or stamped, probably because it was sent in a wrapper with the rejected Browning letter it refers to.

32 (W16°)   E.B.B. to R.B.

[May 25, 1845.]

Sunday

I owe you the most humble of apologies dear Mr. Browning, for having spent so much solemnity on so simple a matter, & I hasten to pay it,—confessing at the same time (as why sh^d I not?) that I am quite as much ashamed of myself as I ought to be, which is not a little. You will find it difficult to believe me perhaps when I assure you that I never made such a mistake (I mean of over-seriousness to indefinite compliments), no, never in my life before—indeed my sisters have often jested with me (in matters of which they were cognizant) on my supernatural indifference to the superlative degree in general, as if it meant nothing in grammar. I usually know well that " boots " may be called for in this world of ours, just as you called for yours,—& that to bring ' *Bootes*,'[1] were the vilest of mal-à-pro-pos-ities. Also, I sh^d have understood " boots " where you wrote it, in the letter in question; if it had not been for *the relation of two things* in it—& now I perfectly seem to see HOW I mistook that relation; ("*seem to see*,"—because I have not looked into the letter again since your last night's commentary, & will not—) inasmuch as I have observed before in my own mind, that a good deal of what is called obscurity in you, arises from a habit of very subtle association,—so subtle, that you are probably unconscious of it, . . and the effect of which is to throw together on the same level & in the same light, things of likeness & unlikeness—till the reader grows confused as I did, & takes one for another. I may say however, in a poor justice to myself, that I wrote what I wrote so unfortunately, *through reverence for you*, & not at all from vanity on my own account . . although I do feel palpably while I write these words here & now, that I might as well leave them unwritten,—for that no man of the world who ever lived in the world (not even *you*) could be expected to believe them, though said, sung, & sworn.

For the rest, it is scarcely an apposite moment for you to talk, even " dramatically," of my 'superiority' to you, . . unless you mean, which perhaps you do mean, my superiority in *simplicity*—&, verily, to some of the " adorable ingenuousness," sacred to the shade of Simpson, I may put in a modest claim, . . "& have my claim allowed." "Pray do not mock me"[2] I quote again from your Shakespeare to you who are a dramatic poet, . . & I will admit anything that you like, (being humble just now)—even that I DID NOT KNOW YOU. I was certainly innocent of the knowledge of the "ice & cold water" you introduce me to, and am only just shaking my head, as Flush w[d], after a first wholesome plunge—Well—if I do not know you, I shall learn, I suppose, in time. I am ready to try humbly to learn—& I may perhaps—if you are not done in Sanscrit, which is too hard for me, . . . notwithstanding that I had the pleasure yesterday to hear, from America, of my profound skill in "various languages less known than Hebrew"!—a liberal paraphrase on Mr. Horne's large fancies[3] on the like subject, & a satisfactory reputation in itself—as long as it is not necessary to deserve it. So I here enclose to you your letter back again, as you wisely desire,—although you never c[d] doubt, I hope, for a moment, of its safety with me in the completest of senses: and then, from the heights of my superior . . stultity, & other qualities of the like order, . . I venture to advise you . . however (to speak of the letter critically, & as the dramatic composition it is) it is to be admitted to be very beautiful, and well worthy of the rest of its kin in the portfolio, . . 'Lays of the poets,' or otherwise, . . . I venture to advise you to burn it at once. And then, my dear friend, I ask you (having some claim) to burn at the same time the letter I was fortunate enough to write to you on friday, & this present one—don't send them back to me; I hate ↑to have↓ letters ⟨‖ · · · ‖⟩ sent back—but burn them for me & never mind Mephistopheles. After which friendly turn, you will do me the one last kindness of forgetting all this exquisite nonsense, & of refraining from mentioning it, by breath or pen, TO ME OR ANOTHER. Now I trust you so far—: you will put it with the date of the battle of Waterloo—& I, with every date in chronology; seeing that I can remember none of them. And we will shuffle the cards, & take patience, & begin the game again, if you please—& I shall bear in mind that you are a dramatic poet, which is not the same thing, by any means, with *us* of the primitive simplicities, who dont tread on cothurns[4] nor shift the mask in the scene. And I will reverence you both as "a poet" & as "*the* poet,"—because it is no false "ambition," but a right you have—& one which those who live longest, will see justified to the uttermost. . In the meantime I need not ask Mr. Kenyon if you have any sense, because I have no doubt that you have quite sense enough—& even if I had a doubt, I shall prefer judging for myself ⟨lest⟩ without interposition; which I can do, you know, as long as you like to come and see me. And you can come this week if you do like it—because our relations dont come till the end of it, it appears—not that I made a pretence "out of kindness"—pray dont judge me so outrageously—but if you like to come .. not on tuesday .. but on wednesday at three oclock, I shall be very glad to see you,—& I, for one, shall have forgotten everything by that time,—being quick at forgetting my own faults usually—If Wednesday does not suit you, I am not sure that I *can* see you this week—but it depends on circumstances. Only don't think yourself *obliged* to come on Wednesday. You know I *began* by entreating you to be open & sincere with me—& no more—I *require* no 'sleekening of every word' or of any word. I love the truth & can bear it—whether in word or deed—& those who have known me longest would tell you so fullest. Well!—May God bless you. We shall know each other some day perhaps—and I am

Always & faithfully your friend,

E. B. B.

1. The constellation which includes Arcturus.
2. *Lear* IV. vii. 59.
3. "[Miss Barrett] has read Plato, in the original, from beginning to end, and the Hebrew Bible from Genesis to Malachi (nor suffered her course to be stopped by the Chaldean)." *New Spirit of the Age,* II, 35. American articles at this time frequently merely paraphrased or pirated English books or articles.
4. Buskins.

33 *(W18)*   *R.B. to E.B.B.*

[*May 26, 1845.*]

Nay—I *must* have last word—as all people in the wrong desire to have—and then, no more of the subject. You said I had given you *great pain*—so long as I stop *that,* think anything of me you choose or can! But *before* your former letter came, I saw the pre-ordained uselessness of mine: speaking is to some *end,* (apart from foolish self-relief,—which, after all, I can do without)—and where there is *no* end—you see! or, to finish characteristically—since the offering to cut off one's right-hand to save anybody a headache, is in vile taste, even for our melodrames, see-ing that it was never yet believed in on the stage or off it,—how much worse to really make the ugly chop, and afterwards come sheepishly in, one's arm in a black sling, and find that the delectable gift had changed aching to nausea! There! And now, "exit, prompt-side, nearest door, Luria"—and enter RB—next Wednesday,—as boldly as he suspects most people do just after they have been soundly frightened!

I shall be most happy to see you on the day and at the hour you mention. ⟨I w⟩

God bless you, my dear friend,

R. B.

34 (W17°)   *E.B.B. to R.B.*

[*May 26, 1845.*]

Monday Morning.

You will think me the most changeable of all the changeable,—but indeed it is *not* my fault that I cannot, as I wished, receive you on wednes-day. There was a letter this morning,—and our friends not only come to London but come to this house on tuesday (to-morrow) to pass two or three days, until they settle in an hotel for the rest of the season. There-fore, you see, it is doubtful whether the two days may not be three, & the three days four; but if they go away in time, & if Saturday sh^d suit you, I will let you know by a word; & you can answer by a yea or nay. While they are in the house, I must give them what time I can—& in-deed, it is something to dread altogether.

Tuesday [May 27].

I send you the note I had begun before receiving yours of last night, & also a fragment from Mrs. Hedley's herein enclosed,[1] a full & com-plete certificate, .. that you may know .. quite *know*, .. what the real & only reason of the obstacle to wednesday is. On Saturday perhaps, or on Monday more certainly, there is likely to be no opposition, .. at least not on the 'côté *gauche*' (*my* side!) to our meeting—but I will let you know more.

For the rest, we have both been a little unlucky, there's no denying, in overcoming the embarrassments of a first acquaintance—but suffer me to say as one other last word, (& *quite, quite the last this time!*) in case there sh^d have been anything approaching, however remotely, to a distrustful or unkind tone in what I wrote on sunday, (& I have a sort of consciousness that in the process of my selfscorning I was not in the most sabbatical of moods perhaps—) that I do recall & abjure it, & from my heart entreat your pardon for it, & profess, notwithstanding it, neither to 'choose' nor 'to be able' to think otherwise of you than I have done, . . as of one MOST generous and MOST loyal; for that if I chose, I could not; & that if I could, I should not choose.

Ever and gratefully your friend, E. B. B.

—And now we shall hear of 'Luria,' shall we not? & much besides. And Miss Mitford has sent me the most high comical of letters to read, addressed to her by "R. B. Haydon[2] historical painter" which has made me quite laugh,—and w^d make *you;* expressing his ⟨‖ · · ‖⟩ ↑righteous↓ indignation at the "great fact" and gross impropriety of any man who has "thoughts too deep for tears" agreeing to wear a 'bag wig' . . the case of poor Wordsworth's going to court,[3] you know.—Mr. Haydon being infinitely serious all the time, & yet holding the doctrine of the divine right of princes in his left hand!—

How is your head? may I be hoping the best for it? May God bless you.

1. An enclosure in the letter reads: "me on Tuesday, or Wednesday? if on Tuesday, I shall come by the three o'clock train; if on Wednesday, *early* in the Morn^g, as I shall be anxious to secure rooms . . so that y^r Uncle and Arabel may come up on Thursday."

2. A slip of the pen for B. R. Haydon.

3. After missing his first Court ball as Poet Laureate, Wordsworth traveled three-hundred miles to go to another on April 25, 1845. Haydon wrote in his journal for May 16: "[Talfourd] said Wordsworth went to court in [Samuel] Rogers's clothes, buckles, and stockings, and wore [David Wilkie's] sword. Moxon had hard work to make the dress fit." On May 22 he wrote Wordsworth: "I wish you had not gone to court . . . I can't bear to associate a bag-wig and sword, ruffles and buckles with Helvellyn and the Mountain solitudes." *Life of Benjamin Robert Haydon . . . from His Autobiography and Journals,* ed. Tom Taylor (2nd ed.; 3 vols., London, 1853), III, 305–306.

35 (*W19*)   *R.B. to E.B.B.*

                    _____

[*Wednesday, May 28, 1845.*]

Saturday, Monday, as you shall appoint: no need to say that, or my thanks—but this note troubles you, out of my bounden duty to help you, or Miss Mitford, to make the Painter run violently down a steep place into the sea, if that will amuse you, by further informing him, what I know on the best authority, that Wordsworth's "bag-wig," or at least, the more important of his court-habiliments, were considerately furnished for the nonce by *Mr. Rogers* from his own wardrobe, to the manifest advantage of the Laureate's pocket, but more problematic improvement of his person, when one thinks on the astounding difference of 'build' in the two Poets:—the fact should be put on record, if only as serving to render less chimerical a promise sometimes figuring in the columns of provincial newspapers—that the two apprentices, some grocer or other advertises for, will be "boarded and *clothed* like *one* of the family." May not your unfinished (really good) head of the great man[1] have been happily kept waiting for the body which can now be added on, with all this picturesqueness of circumstances? Precept on precept . . but then, *line upon line,* is allowed by as good authority, and may I not draw *my* confirming black line after yours, yet not break pledge? I am most grateful to you for doing me justice—doing yourself your own judgment, justice, since even the play-wright of Theseus & the Amazon found it one of his hardest devices to "write me a speech, lest the lady be frightened, wherein it shall be said that I, Pyramus, am not Pyramus, but &c. &c."[2] God bless you—one thing more, but one— you *could never have* misunderstood the *asking for the letter again,* I feared you might refer to it "pour constater le fait"—

                    And now I am yours—

                              R. B.

My head is all but well now; thank you.

1. In 1842 Haydon sent his "Wordsworth on Helvellyn" to E.B.B. and in 1843 substituted a "less finished" portrait for it. *Letters from Elizabeth Barrett to B. R. Haydon,* ed. Martha H. Shackford (New York: Oxford University Press, 1939), pp. 23–24.
   2. *Midsummer-Night's Dream* III. i. 15ff.

36 (W18°)   E.B.B. to R.B.

[*May 30, 1845.*]

Friday Morning.

Just one word to say that if Saturday, to-morrow, sh^d be fine—because in the case of its raining I *shall not expect you,*—you will find me at three oclock.

Yes—the circumstances of the costume were mentioned in the letter,—Mr. Rogers' bagwig & the rest, and David Wilkie's sword[1]—& also that the Laureate, so equipped, fell down upon both knees in the superfluity of etiquette, & had to be picked up by two lords in waiting.[2] It is a large exaggeration I do not doubt—and then I never sympathized with the sighing kept up by people about that acceptance of the Laureateship which drew the bagwig as a corollary after it. Not that the Laureateship honoured *him,* but that he honored it; & that, so honoring it, he preserves a symbol instructive to the masses, who are children & to be taught by symbols now as formerly. Isn't it true? or at least may it not be true? And won't the court laurel (such as it is) be all the worthier of *you* for Wordsworth's having worn it first?

And in the meantime I shall see you to-morrow perhaps? or if it sh^d rain, on Monday at the same hour.

Ever yours, my dear friend,

E. B. B.—

1. See Letter 34, n. 3. Samuel Rogers (1763–1855) was the poet, banker, and connoisseur of art; Sir David Wilkie (1785–1841), the painter, had been a friend of both Haydon and Wordsworth.

2. "Hallam told me, with great gusto, that when Wordsworth went to the Levee (1845) he was passing before the Queen, when Lord Delawarr said, 'Kneel, kneel.' Wordsworth, ignorant of Court etiquette, plumped down on both knees, and when he was too feeble to get up again himself, Lord Delawarr and Lord Lansdowne helped him up. The Queen was much touched." *Benjamin Robert Haydon: Correspondence and Table-Talk* (2 vols., London, 1876), II, 476–477.

On the envelope of Letter 36 Browning noted two visits:

+Saturday May 31

and   3–5 p.m.

+Thursday June 5

3–4½ p.m.

[June 6, 1845.]

Friday Morning.

When I see all you have done for me in this Prometheus,[1] I feel more than half ashamed both of it & of me for using your time so, & forced to say in my own defence (not to you but myself) that I never thought of meaning to inflict such work on you who might be doing so much better things in the meantime both for me & for others—because, you see, it is not the mere reading of the MS., but the / "conferring"⟩"comparing" / of the text, & the melancholy comparisons between the English and the Greek, . . . quite enough to turn you from your φιλανθρώπου τρόπου,[2] that I brought upon you,—& indeed I did not mean so much, nor so soon!—Yet as you have done it for me—for me who expected a few jottings down with a pencil & a general opinion,—it is of course of the greatest value, besides the pleasure & pride which come of it; & I must say of the translation, (before putting it aside for the nonce), that the circumstance of your paying it so much attention & seeing any good in it, is quite enough reward for the writer & quite enough motive for self-gratulation, if it were all torn to fragments at this moment—which is a foolish thing to say because it is so obvious, & ⟨that⟩ ₊because₊ you would know it if I said it or not.

And while you were doing this for me, you thought it unkind of me not to write to you,—yes, and you think me at this moment the very princess of apologies & excuses & depreciations & all the rest of the small family of distrust . . or of hypocrisy . . who knows? Well!—but you are wrong . . wrong . . to think so; & you will let me say one word to show where you are wrong—not for you to controvert, . . because it must relate to myself especially, & lies beyond your cognizance, & is something which *I must know best* after all. And it is, . . that you persist in putting me into a false position, with respect to *fixing days* & the like, & in making me feel somewhat as I did when I was a child, & Papa used to put me up on the chimney-piece & exhort me to stand up straight like a hero, which I did, straighter and straighter, and then suddenly "was 'ware" (as we say in the ballads) of the walls' growing alive behind me & extending two stony hands to push me

down that / frighten⟩frightful / precipice to the rug, where the dog
lay . . . dear old Havannah, . . & where he & I were likely to be dashed
to pieces together & mix our uncanonised bones,—Now my present
false position . . which is not the chimney-piece's, . . is the necessity
you provide for me in the shape of my having to name this day, or
that day, . . & of your coming because I ⟨pick it⟩ name it, & of my having to think & remember that you come because I name it. Through a
weakness, perhaps, or morbidness, or ⟨apathy⟩ one knows not how to
define it, I *cannot help* being uncomfortable in having to do this,—it is
impossible. Not that I distrust *you*—you are the last in the world I
could distrust: and then (although you may be sceptical) I am naturally
given to trust . . to a fault . . as some say—or to a sin, as some reproach
me:—& then again, if I were ever such a distruster, it could not be of
you. But if you knew me—! I will tell you! if one of my brothers omits
coming to this room for two days, . . I never ask why it happened! if
my own father omits coming up stairs to say 'good night,' I never say
a word,—& not from indifference. Do try to make out these readings
of me as a "dixit Casaubonus";[3] & don't throw me down as a corrupt
text!—nor convict me for an infidel which I am not. On the contrary
I am grateful & happy to believe that you like to come here; & even if
you came here as a pure act of charity & pity to me, as long as you
CHOSE TO COME I should not be too proud to be grateful & happy still.
I could not be proud to *you*, & I hope you will not fancy such a possibility, which is the remotest of all. Yes, & I am anxious to ask you to be
wholly generous & leave off such an interpreting philosophy as you
made use of yesterday, & forgive me when I beg you to fix your own
days for coming for the future. Will you? It is the same thing in one
way. If you like to come really every week, there is no hinderance to it
—you can do it—& the privilege & obligation remain equally mine:—
& if you name a day for coming on any week, where there is an obstacle on my side, you will learn it from me in a moment. Why I
might as well charge *you* with distrusting *me,* because you persist in
making me choose the days. And it is not for me to do it, but for you—
I must feel that—and I cannot help chafing myself against the thought
that for me to begin to fix days in this way, just because you have quick
impulses (like all imaginative persons), & wish me to do it now, . . may
bring me to the catastrophe of asking you to come when you would
rather not, . . which, as you say truly, w^d not be an important vexation

to you; but to me would be worse than vexation; to *me*—& therefore I shrink from the very imagination of the possibility of such a thing, & ask you to bear with me & let it be as I prefer . . left to your own choice of the moment. And bear with me above all—because this shows no want of faith in you . . none . . but comes from a simple fact (with its ramifications) . . that you know little of me personally yet, and that you *guess*, even, but very little of the influence of a peculiar experience over me & out of me—and if I wanted a proof of this, we need not seek further than the very point of discussion, & the hard worldly thoughts you thought I was thinking of you yesterday,—I, who thought not one of them! But I am so used to discern the correcting & ministering angels by the same footsteps on the ground, that it is not wonderful I sh^d look down there at any approach of a φιλία τάξις,[4] whatever, to this personal *me*. Have I not been ground down to browns & blacks? & is it my fault if I am not green?—Not that it is ↑my↓ *complaint*—I sh^d not ↑be↓ justified ↑in complaining↓; ⟨∥ · · · ∥⟩ I believe, as I told you, that there is more gladness than sadness in the world—that is, generally: & if some natures have to be refined by the sun, & some by the furnace (the less genial ones) both means are to be recognised as *good*, . . however different in pleasurableness & painfulness, & ⟨∥ · · · ∥⟩ tho' furnace-fire leaves scorched streaks upon the fruit—. I assured you there was nothing I had any power of teaching you: & there *is* nothing, except grief!—which I would not teach you, you know, if I had the occasion granted.

It is a multitude of words about nothing at all, . . this!—but I am like Mariana in the moated grange and sit listening ↑too often↓ to the mouse in the wainscot.[5] Be as forbearing as you can—& believe how profoundly it touches me that you should care to come here at all, much more, so often! & try to understand that if I did not write as you half asked, it was just because I failed at the moment to get up enough pomp & circumstance to write on purpose to certify the important fact of my being a little stronger or a little weaker on one particular morning. That I am always ready & rejoiced to write to you, you know perfectly well, & I have proved, by 'superfluity of naughtiness' and prolixity through some twenty posts:—& this, and therefore, ⟨∥ · · · ∥⟩ you will agree altogether to attribute no more to me on these counts, & determine to read me no more backwards with your Hebrew, putting in your own vowel points without my leave?[6] Shall it be so?

Here is a letter grown from a note which it meant to be—& I have been interrupted in the midst of it, or it sh^d have gone to you earlier. Let what I have said in it of myself pass unquestioned & unnoticed; because it is of *me* & not of *you*, . . &, if in any wise lunatical, all the talking & writing in the world will not put the implied moon into another quarter. Only be patient with me a little, . . & let us have a smooth ground for the poems which I am foreseeing the sight of with such pride & delight—Such pride & delight!

And one thing . . which is chief, though it seems to come last! . . you *will* have advice (—will you not?—) if that pain does not grow much better directly?—It cannot be prudent or even *safe* to let a pain in the head go on so long, & no remedy be attempted for it, . . & you cannot be sure that it is a merely nervous pain & that it may not have consequences; & this, quite apart from the consideration of suffering. So you will see some one with an opinion to give, & take it? *Do, I* beseech you—you will not say 'no'? Also . . if on wednesday you sh^d be less well than usual, you will come on thursday instead, I hope, . . seeing that it must be right for you to be quiet & silent when you suffer so, & a journey into London can let you be neither. Otherwise, I hold to my day . . Wednesday. And may God bless you my dear friend—

Ever yours
E. B. B.

You are right I see, nearly everywhere, if not quite everywhere in the criticisms—but of course I have not looked very closely—that is, I have read your papers but not in connection with a *my* side of the argument—but I shall lose the post after all.

1. These notes of Browning's were sold as part of Lot #142 in 1913 (*Browning Collections,* p. 32). As in these letters—e.g., the next—he seems to have avoided suggestions about expression and confined himself to matters of text and meanings.
2. "Aeschylus, *Prometheus* 11.: "trick of loving men . . ." Footnote, 1899 edition. Line 12 of E.B.B.'s translation.
3. A trustworthy reading, so called after Isaac Casaubon (1559–1614).
4. "Friendly force."
5. E.B.B. is recalling not *Measure for Measure* but Tennyson's *Mariana* (1830): "the mouse / Behind the mouldering wainscot shriek'd" (ll. 63–64). She also alludes to this passage in Letter 77.
6. See Letter 7 and its note 2.

38 (W20)   *R.B. to E.B.B.*

[*June 7, 1845.*]

Saturday M^g

Saturday M^{g}

I ventured to hope this morning might bring me news of you—First East-winds on you, then myself, then those criticisms!—I do assure you I am properly apprehensive. How are you? May I go on Wednesday without too much αὐθαδία.[1]

Pray remember what I said & wrote, to the effect that my exceptions were, in almost every case, to the "reading"—not to your version of ⟨that⟩ ↑it↓: but I have not specified the particular ones—, not written down the Greek, of my suggested translations—have I? And if you do not find them in the margin of your copy, how you must wonder! Thus, in the last speech but one, of Hermes, I prefer Porson and Blomfield's εἰ μηδ' ἀτυχῶν τι χαλᾷ μανιῶν,[2]—to the old combinations that include εὐτυχῇ—though there is no MS. authority for emendation, it seems. But in what respect does Prom. "fare *well*," or "better" even, since the beginning? And is it not the old argument over again, that when a man *fails* he should repent of his ways?—And while thinking of Hermes, let me say that "μηδέ μοι διπλᾶς ὁδοὺς προσβάλῃς" is surely—"Don't subject me to the trouble of a second journey . . by paying no attention to the first."[3] So says Scholiast A, and so backs him Scholiast B, especially created, it should appear, to show there could be in rerum naturâ such another as his predecessor. A few other remarks occur to me, which I will tell you if you please—*now*, I really want to know how you are, and write for that.

Ever yours

R. B.

1. "Self-will," "arrogance."
2. Richard Porson (1759–1808), the great Cambridge classicist, published an Aeschylus in 1794 and his pupil, Bishop Charles James Blomfield (1786–1857), a *Prometheus Vinctus* in 1810. There was a copy of the latter in the Brownings' library (*Browning Collections,* p. 68, Lot #312). Εὐτυχῇ means "good fortune," whereas ἀτυχῶν is an adjective ("unfortunate") modifying μανιῶν ("madness"). E.B.B. (ll. 1251–52) seems to adopt a third reading: "If the Fate who hath bound him should loose not the links / He were utterly mad." Her version seems closer to an 1805 Leipzig edition by F. H. Bothe, which was also in the Browning library.

3. Browning's translation is close to those in general acceptance, but the portion after the two points is explanatory, not inherent. E.B.B. translated: "Never cast / Ambiguous paths, Prometheus, for my feet" (ll. 1129–30).

39 (W21)   *R.B. to E.B.B.*

_____

[*Postmarked June 9, 1845.*]

Just after my note left, yours came . . I will try so to answer it as to please you; and I begin by promising cheerfully to do all you bid me about naming days &c. I do believe we are friends now & for ever,— there can be no reason, therefore, that I should cling tenaciously to any one or other time of meeting, as if, losing that, I lost everything—and, for the future, I will provide against sudden engagements, outrageous weather &c., to your heart's content. Nor am I going to except against here & there a little wrong I could get up . . as when you *imply* from my "quick impulses" & the like . . no, my dear friend—for I seem sure I shall have quite, quite time enough to do myself justice in your eyes— let time show!

Perhaps I feel none the less sorely, when you "thank" me for such company as mine, that I cannot avoid confessing to myself that it would not be so absolutely out of my power, perhaps, to contrive really & deserve thanks in a certain acceptation: I *might* really *try,* at all events, and amuse you a little better, when I do have the opportunity, —and I *do not*—but there is the thing! It is all of a piece—I *do not* seek your friendship in order to do you good—any good—only to do myself good. Tho' I *would,* God knows, do that too—

Enough of this!—

I am much better, indeed,—but will certainly follow your advice should the pain return: and you—you have tried a new journey from your room, have you not?

Do recollect, at any turn, any chance so far in my favour,—that I am here & yours should you want any fetching & carrying in this out- side London world—your brothers may have their own business to mind, Mr. Kenyon is at New York, we will suppose, . . here am I— what else, *what else* makes me count my cleverness to you, as I know I have done more than once, by word & letter, but the real wish to be set at work? ⟨Don't you⟩ ↟I should have,↡ I hope, better taste than to tell any everyday acquaintance, who could not go out, one single morning even, on account of a headache, that the weather was delightful, much less that I had been walking five miles and meant to run ten: yet to you I boasted once of polking & waltzing and more—but then would it not be a very superfluous piece of respect in the four-footed bird[1] to keep his wings to himself because his Master Oceanos could fly forsooth? Whereas he begins to wave & flap and show how ready they are to be off—for what else were the good of him? Think of this—and

Know me for yours

R. B.

For good you are, to those notes—you shall have more,—that is, the rest—on Wednesday then, at 3, except as you except. God bless you.

Oh, let me tell you—I suppose Mr. Horne must be in town—as I rec^d a letter two days ago, from the contriver of some literary society or other who had before written to get me to belong to it, protesting *against* my reasons for refusing, and begging that "at all events I would suspend my determination till I had been visited by Mr. H. on the subject"—and, as they can hardly ⟨‖ · · · ‖⟩ ↟mean to bring↡ him express from the Drachenfels for just that, he is returned no doubt:[2] & as he is your friend, I take the opportunity of mentioning the course I shall pursue with him or any other friend of yours I may meet,—(and everybody else, ⟨‖ · · · ‖⟩ ↟I may add↡—) the course I understand you to desire, with respect to our own intimacy: while I may acknowledge, I believe, that I correspond with you, I shall not, in any case, suffer it to be known that I see, or have seen you. This I just remind you of, lest any occasion of embarrassment should arise, for a moment, from your not being quite sure how *I* had acted in any case.—Con che, le bacio le mani—a rivederla![3]

---

1. "Lo, my four-footed bird sweeps smooth and wide." *Prometheus Bound,* l. 459 of E.B.B.'s translation.
2. Horne had just returned from a stay in Germany. See the following letter and Letter 58.
3. "With which, I kiss your hand—until we meet!"

40 (W20°)   *E.B.B. to R.B.*

[*June 10, 1845.*]

Tuesday Morning.

I must thank you by one word for all your kindness & consideration—which c^d not be greater,—nor more felt by me,—In the first
place, afterwards (if that should not be Irish dialect) do understand that
my letter passed from my hands to go to yours on *friday,* but was
thrown aside carelessly down stairs & "covered up" they say, so as not
to be seen until late on saturday; & I can only humbly hope to have
been cross enough about it (having conscientiously tried) to secure a
little more accuracy another time.—And then, . . if ever I sh^d want anything done or found . . (a roc's egg or the like) you may believe me that
I shall not scruple to ask you to be the doer⟨?⟩—but at this moment I
want nothing, indeed, except your poems;—and that is quite the truth.
Now do consider & think what I could possibly want in your "outside
London world,"—you, who are the 'genius of the lamp'!—Why if
you light it & let me read your romances, &c by it, is not that the best
use for it, & am I likely to look for another? Only I shall remember
what you say, gratefully & seriously,—& if ever I should have a good
fair opportunity of giving you trouble (as if I had not done it already!)
you may rely upon my evil intention, . . even though dear Mr. Kenyon
sh^d not actually be at New York, . . which he is not, I am glad to say, as
I saw him on Saturday.

Which reminds me that *he* knows of your having been here . . of
course!—& will not mention it; as he understood from me that *you*
would not.—Thank you! Also there was an especial reason which constrained me, on pain of appearing a great hypocrite, to tell Miss Mitford
the bare fact of my having seen you—& reluctantly I did it, though
placing ⟨little⟩ some hope in her promise of discretion. And how
necessary the discretion is, will appear in the awful statistical fact of our
having at this moment . . as my sisters were calculating yesterday . .
some forty relations in London—to say nothing of the right wing of
the enemy. For Mr. Horne, I c^d have told you, & really I thought I *had*
told you of his being in England.

Last paragraph of all is, that I *don't want to be amused* . . or rather

92

that I *am* amused by everything & anything. Why surely, surely, you have some singular ideas about me!! So, till to-morrow,

E. B. B.

⌈Instead of writing this note to you yesterday, as sh^d have been, I went down stairs—or rather was carried—and am not the worse.⌉[1]

1. Written above and at right angles to the first line of the letter.

Browning marked the envelope of Letter 40:
+ Wed. June
11, 3—5
He took with him a copy of Prolusiones Academicae *(Cambridge, 1829), the pamphlet in which were reprinted all the Cambridge prize poems for the year, including Tennyson's* Timbuctoo *which had won the Chancellor's Medal.*

41 (W21°)   *E.B.B. to R.B.*

[*June 13, 1845.*]

Friday.
Yes, the poem *is* too good in certain respects for the prizes given in colleges . . (when all the pure parsley goes naturally to the rabbits) . . and has a great deal of beauty here and there in image & expression. Still I do not quite agree with you that it reaches the Tennyson standard any wise; & for the blank verse, I cannot for a moment think it comparable to one of the grand passages in Œnone, & Arthur and the like. In fact I seem to hear more in that latter blank verse than you do, . . to hear not only a "mighty line" as in Marlowe, but a noble full orbicular wholeness in complete passages—which always struck me as the mystery of music & great peculiarity in Tennyson's versification, inasmuch as he attains to these complete effects without that shifting of the pause practised by the masters, . . Shelley & others. A 'linked music' . . in which there are no links! . . *that*, you w^d take to be a contradiction—& yet something like that, my ear has always

93

seemed to perceive; & I have wondered curiously again & again how there could be so much union & no fastening. Only of course it is not model versification—& for dramatic purposes, it must be admitted to be bad.

Which reminds me to be astonished for the second time how you c^d think such a thing of me as that I wanted to read only your lyrics . . or that I "preferred the lyrics" . . or something barbarous in that way? You dont think me 'ambidexter,' or 'either-handed' . . & both hands open for what poems you will vouchsafe to me,—& yet if you w^d let me see anything you may have in a readable state by you, . . The Flight of the Duchess . . or act or scene of The Soul's Tragedy, . . I shall be so glad & grateful to you! Oh—if you change your mind & choose to be "bien prié," I will grant it is your right, & begin my liturgy directly. But this is not teazing (in the intention of it!—)—and I understand all about the transcription, & the inscrutableness of rough copies,—that is, if you write as I do, so that my guardian angel or M. Champollion[1] cannot read what is written. Only whatever *they* can, (remember!) *I* can! and you are not ⌈to mind trusting me with the cacistography possible to mortal readers.

The sun shines so that nobody dares complain of the East wind—& indeed I am better altogether . . May God bless you, my dear friend.

E. B. B.⌉[2]

1. Jean François Champollion (1790–1832) solved Egyptian hieroglyphics by deciphering the Rosetta Stone.
2. Completed above the opening text of the letter.

42 (W 22)   *R.B. to E.B.B.*

———————

[*Saturday*]

June 14, 1845.[1]

When I ask my wise self what I really do remember of the Prize poem, the answer is—both of Chapman's lines a-top, quite worth any prize for their quoter—then, the good epithet of 'green Europe' contrasting with Africa—then, deep in the piece, a picture of a Vestal in a vault, where I see a dipping & winking lamp plainest, and last of all the ominous "all was dark" that dismisses you: I read the poem many years ago, and never since—tho' I have an impression that the versification is good, yet from your commentary I see I must have said a good deal more in its praise than that. But have you not discovered by this time that I go on talking with my thoughts away?

I know, I have always been jealous of my own musical faculty (I can write music).—Now that I see the uselessness of such jealousy, and am for loosing & letting it go, it may be cramped possibly. Your music is more various & exquisite than any modern writer's to my ear. One should study the mechanical part of the art, or nearly all that there is to be studied—for the more one sits and thinks over the creative process, the more it confirms itself as "inspiration," nothing more nor less. Or, at worst, you write down old inspirations, what you remember of them —but with *that* it begins: "Reflection" is exactly what it names itself—a *re*-presentation, in scattered rays from every angle of incidence, of what first of all became present in a great light, a whole one. So tell me how these lights are born, if you can! But I can tell anybody how to make melodious verses—let him do it therefore—it should be exacted of all writers.

You do not understand what a new feeling it is for me to have someone who is to like my verses or I shall not ever like them after! So far differently was I circumstanced of old, that I used rather to go about for a subject of offence to people; writing ugly things in order to warn the ungenial & timorous off my grounds at once. I shall never do so again at least! As it is, I will bring all I dare, in as great quantities as I can —if not next time, after then—certainly. I must make an end, print this Autumn my last four "Bells," Lyrics, Romances, The Tragedy, & Luria,[2] and then go on with a whole heart to my own Poem—indeed, I have just resolved not to begin any new song, even, till this grand clearance is made—I will get the Tragedy transcribed to bring—

"To bring!" Next Wednesday—if you knew how happy you make me! may I not say *that*, my dear friend, when I feel it from my soul?

I thank God that you are better: do pray make fresh endeavours to profit by this partial respite of the weather! All about you must urge that: but even from my distance some effect might come of such wishes. But you *are* better—look so & speak so! God bless you.

R. B.

You let "flowers be sent you in a letter,"[3] every one knows, and this hot day draws out our very first yellow rose—eccola[4]—

1. Dated by Browning on the reverse of the last leaf. The placement of dates has been regularized, even though short notes were usually dated beneath the text and to the left. Any other departure from the norm is, as here, indicated in a note.

2. What Browning here calls his "last four 'Bells'" became the last two numbers of *Bells and Pomegranates—Dramatic Romances and Lyrics* (No. VII), published in November 1845, and *Luria* and *A Soul's Tragedy* (No. VIII), published in April 1846. His enumeration seems to indicate that Browning made his last two numbers of materials originally intended for four.

3. *A Flower in a Letter* was one of E.B.B.'s 1844 *Poems*.

4. "Look at it."

43 *(W22°)*　　　　　　　　　**E.B.B. to R.B.**

[*June 16, 1845.*]

Monday.

　　Yes, I quite believe as you do that what is called the 'creative process' in works of Art, is just inspiration & no less—which made somebody say to me not long since,—" And so, you think that Shakespeare's Othello was of the effluence of the Holy Ghost"—? rather a startling deduction, . . only not quite as final as might appear to somebodies perhaps. At least it does not prevent my going on to agree with the saying of *Spiridion*[1] . . do you remember? . . "Tout ce que l'homme appelle inspiration, je l'appelle aussi revelation," . . if there is not something too selfevident in it after all—my sole objection! And is it not true that your inability to analyze the mental process in question, is one of the proofs of the fact of inspiration?—as the gods were known of old by not being seen to move their feet . . coming & going in an equal sweep of radiance.—And still more wonderful than the first transient great light you speak of . . & far beyond any work of *reflection*, except in the pure analytical sense in which you use the word, . . appears that gathering of light on light upon particular points, as you go (in composition) step by step, till you get intimately near to things, & see them in a fulness & clearness, & an intense trust in the truth of them which you have not in any sunshine of noon ↑(called real!)↓ but which you have *then* . . & struggle to communicate—: an ineffectual struggle with most writers (oh, how ineffectual!) & when effectual, issuing in the "Pippa Passes," & other master pieces of the world.

You will tell me what you mean exactly by being jealous of your own music? You said once that you had had a false notion of music, or had practised it according to the false notions of other people: but did you mean besides that you ever had meant to despise music altogether—because *that*, it is hard to set about trying to believe of you indeed. And then, you *can* praise my verses for music?—Why, are you aware that people blame me constantly for wanting harmony—from Mr. Boyd who moans aloud over the indisposition of my 'trochees' . . and no less a person than Mr. Tennyson, who said to somebody who repeated it, that in the want of harmony lay the chief defect of the poems . . "although it might verily be retrieved, as he c^d fancy that I had a[n] ear by nature." Well—but I am pleased that you sh^d praise me—right or wrong —I mean, whether I am right or wrong in being pleased!—and I say so to you openly, although my belief is that you are under a vow to our Lady of Loretto to make giddy with all manner of high vanities, some head, . . not too strong for such things, but too low for them, . . before you see again the embroidery on her divine petticoat. Only there's a flattery so far beyond praise . . even YOUR praise—as where you talk of your verses being liked &c &c, & of your being happy to bring them here, . . that is scarcely a lawful weapon; and see if the Madonna may not signify so much to you!—Seriously . . you will not hurry too uncomfortably, or uncomfortably at all, about the transcribing? Another day, you know, will do as well—& patience is possible to me, if not "native to the soil."

Also I am behaving very well in going out into the noise,—not quite out of doors yet, on account of the heat—& I am better as you say, without any doubt at all, & stronger—only my looks are a little deceitful,—& people are apt to be heated & flushed in this weather, one hour, to look a little more ghastly an hour or two after. Not that it is not true of me that I am better, mind!—Because I am.

The "flower in the letter" was from one of my sisters—from Arabel (though many of these poems are ⟨‖ · · · ‖⟩ *ideal* . . will you understand?) & your rose came quite alive & fresh, though in act of dropping its beautiful leaves, because of having to come to me instead of living on in your garden, as it intended. But I thank you—for this, & all, ⟨‖ · · · ‖⟩ my dear friend.   E. B. B.

1. By George Sand (1838).

On the envelope of the foregoing letter Browning recorded his next visit:
+Wedn. Ju. 18.
3–4½

44 *(W23)*   **R.B. to E.B.B.**

_____

[*June 19, 1845.*]

Thursday Morning.
When I next see you, do not let me go on & on to my confusion
about matters I am more or less ignorant of, but always ignorant: I tell
you plainly I only trench on them, and intrench in them, from
gaûcherie, pure and respectable—I should certainly grow instructive
on the prospects of hay-crops and pasture-land, if deprived of this
resource. And now here is a week to wait before I shall have any
occasion to relapse into Greek literature when I am thinking all the
while, "now I will just ask simply, what flattery there was," &c &c
which, as I had not courage to say then, I keep to myself for shame
now. This I will say, then—wait and know me better, as you will
one long day at the end.
Why I write now, is because you did not promise, as before, to let
me know how you are—this morning is miserably cold again—Will
you tell me, at your own time?
God bless you, my dear friend.

R. B.

45 *(W23°)*   **E.B.B. to R.B.**

_____

[*June 19, 1845.*]

Thursday evening.
If on Greek literature or anything else it is your pleasure to cultivate
a reputation for ignorance, I will respect your desire—& indeed the
point of the deficiency in question being far above my sight I am not

qualified either to deny or assert the existence of it,—so you are free to
have it all your own way.

About the "flattery" however, there is a difference,—& I must deny
a little having ever used such a word . . as far as I can recollect, & I have
been trying to recollect, . . as that word of flattery. /Though⟩Perhaps/ I
said something about your having vowed to make me vain by writing
this or that of my liking your verses & so on—& perhaps I said it too
lightly . . which happened because when one doesn't know whether to
laugh or to cry, it is far best, as a general rule, to laugh. ⟨‖ · · · · ‖⟩ But
the serious truth is that it was all nonsense together what I wrote, &
that, instead of talking of your making me vain, I sh^d have talked (if
it had been done sincerely) of your humbling me—inasmuch as nothing does humble anybody so much as being lifted up too high. You
know what vaulting Ambition did once for himself?[1] and when it is
done for him by another, his fall is still heavier. And one moral of all
this general philosophy is, that if when your poems come, you persist
in giving too much importance to what I may have courage to say of
this or of that in them, you will make me a dumb critic & I shall have
no help for my dumbness. So I tell you beforehand—nothing extenuating nor exaggerating nor putting down in malice.[2] I know so much
of myself as to be sure of it. Even as it is, the "insolence" which
people blame me for & praise me for, . . the 'recklessness' which my
friends talk of with mitigating countenances . . seems gradually
going & going—& really it would not be very strange (without that)
if *I* who was born a hero worshipper & have so continued, & who
always recognised your genius, should find it impossible to bring out
critical doxies on the workings of it. Well—I shall do what I can—as
far as *impressions* go, you understand—& *you* must promise not to
attach too much importance to anything said—So that is a covenant,
my dear friend!—

And I am really gaining strength—& I will not complain of the
weather. As long as the thermometer keeps above sixty I am content
for one; & the roses are not quite dead yet, ↑which they w^d have
been in the heat↓. And last & not least . . may I ask if you were told
that the pain in the head was not important (or was) in the causes, . .
& was likely to be well soon? or was not? I am at the end.[3]

E. B. B.

[Upon *second* or *third* thoughts, isn't it true that you are a little suspicious of me ? . . suspicious at least of ⟨my suspicions⟩ suspiciousness ?⟧[4]

1. *Macbeth* I. vii. 27–28.
2. *Othello* V. ii. 341–342.
3. Of the paper; the last sentence is crammed into a half-inch.
4. Added at the top of the first page.

46 (W24)   R.B. to E.B.B.
                    _____

                    [*June 22, 1845.*]

Sunday Afternoon.
And if I am "suspicious of your suspiciousness," who gives cause, pray? The matter was long ago settled, I thought, when you first took exception to what I said about higher & lower, and I consented to this much—that you should help seeing, if you could, our true intellectual & moral relation each to the other, so long as you would allow *me* to see what *is* there, fronting me. "Is my eye evil because yours is not good?" My own friend, if I wished to "make you vain," if having 'found the Bower'[1] I did really address myself to the wise business of spoiling its rose-roof,—I think that at least where there was such a will, there would be also something not unlike a way,—that I should find a proper hooked stick to tear down flowers with, and write you other letters than these—quite, quite others, I feel—tho' I am far from going to imagine, even for a moment, what might be the precise prodigy—like the notable Son of Zeus, that *was* to have been, and done the wonders, only he did not, because &c &c.[2]

But I have a restless head to-day and so let you off easily. Well, you ask me about it, that head, and I am not justified in being positive when my Doctor is dubious—as for the causes, they are neither superfluity of study, nor fancy, nor care, nor any special naughtiness that I know how to amend. So if I bring you "nothing to signify" on Wednesday . . tho' I hope to do more than that . . you will know exactly why it happens. I will finish & transcribe the "Flight of the Duchess" since you spoke of that first.

I am truly happy to hear that your health improves still.

For me, going out does me good—reading, writing, &,—what is

odd,—infinitely most of all, *sleeping* do me the harm,—never any very
great harm. And all the while I am yours ever.

R. B.

1. See E.B.B.'s *The Lost Bower* (1844).
2. Possibly a reference to Prometheus's secret—that Zeus would be overthrown
by his son, should one be born of Thetis.

47 (W 24°)   **E.B.B. to R.B.**

———————————

[June 23, 1845.]

Monday.

I had begun to be afraid that I did not deserve to have my questions
answered, . . & I was afraid of asking them over again. But it is worse to
be afraid that you are not better at all in any essential manner (after all
your assurances) & that the medical means have failed so far. Did you go
to somebody who knows anything?—because there is no excuse, you
see, in common sense, for not having the best & most experienced
opinion when there is a choice of advice—& I am confident that that
pain sh^d not be suffered to go on without something being done.
What I said about *nerves*, related to what you had told me of your
mother's suffering & what you had fancied of the relation of it to
your own,[1] & not that I could be thinking about imaginary complaints—I wish I could. Not (either) that I believe in the relation . .
because such things are not hereditary . . are they? & the bare coincidence is improbable.—Well, but, I wanted particularly to say this—
Don't bring the Duchess with you on Wednesday. I shall not expect anything, I write distinctly to tell you—& I would far far rather that you
did not bring it. You see it is just as I thought—for that whether too
much thought or study did or did not bring on the illness, . . yet you
admit that reading and writing increase it . . as they w^d naturally do
any sort of pain in the head—therefore if you will but be in earnest
& try to get well *first*, we will do the "Bells" afterwards, & there
will be time for a whole peal of them, I hope & trust, before the
winter. Now do admit that this is reasonable, & agree reasonably to
it. And if it does you good to go out & take exercise, why not go out
& take it? nay, why not go *away* & take it? Why not try the effect of

101

a little change of air—or even of a great change of air—if it sh^d be necessary . . or even expedient?—Anything is better, you know . . or if you
don't know, *I* know—than to be ill, really, seriously—I mean for *you* to
be ill, who have so much to do & to enjoy in the world yet . . & all those
bells waiting to be hung! So that if you will agree to be well first, I will
promise to be ready afterwards to help you in any thing I can do . .
transcribing or anything . . to get the books through the press in the
shortest of times—and I am capable of a great deal of that sort of work
without being tired, having the habit of writing in any sort of position,
& the long habit, . . since, before I was ill even, I never used to write at a
table (or scarcely ever) but on the arm of a chair, or on the seat of one,
sitting, myself on the floor, calling myself a Lollard for dignity. So you
will put by your 'Duchess' . . will you not? or let me see just that one
sheet—if one sh^d be written—which is finished? . . up to this moment,
you understand? finished *now*.

   And if I have tired & teazed you with all these words it is a bad
opportunity to take—and yet I will persist in saying through good &
bad opportunities that I never did "give cause" as you say, to your being
"suspicious of my suspiciousness" as I believe I said before. I deny my
'suspiciousness' altogether—it is not one of my faults. Nor is it quite my
fault ↑that↓ you and I sh^d always be quarrelling about over-appreciations
& under-appreciations—& after all I have no interest nor wish, I do
assure you, to depreciate myself—& you are not to think that I have the
remotest claim to the Monthyon prize[2] for good deeds in the way of
modesty of selfestimation. Only when I know you better, as you talk of
. . & when *you* know *me* too well, . . the right & the wrong of these conclusions will appear in a fuller light than ever so much arguing can produce now. Is it unkindly written of me? *no*—I *feel* it is not!—and that
"now & ever we are friends," (just as you think) *I* think besides, & am
happy in thinking so, & could not be distrustful of you if I tried. So may
God bless you, my ever dear friend—& mind to forget the 'Duchess' &
to remember every good counsel!—Not that I do particularly confide
in the medical oracles. They never did much more for *me* than . . when
my pulse was above a hundred and forty with fever . . to give me digitalis
to make me weak,—&, when I could not move without fainting (with
weakness) . . to give me quinine to make me feverish again. Yes—& they
could tell from the stethoscope, how very little was really wrong in me . .
if it were not on a vital organ—& how I sh^d certainly live . . if I didn't die

sooner. But then, nothing *has* power over affections of the chest, except God & his winds—& I do hope that an obvious quick remedy may be found for your head. But *do* give up the writing & all that does harm!— Ever yours, my dear friend,

E. B. B.

Miss Mitford talked of spending Wednesday with me—& I have put it off to Thursday:—and if you sh^d hear from Mr. Chorley that he is coming to see *her and me together*[3] *on any day* .. do understand that it was entirely her proposition & not mine, & that certainly it won't be acceded to, as far as *I* am concerned,—as I have explained to her finally. I have been vexed about it—but she can see him down stairs as she has done before—& if she calls me perverse and capricious ⊦(which she will do)↓ I shall stop the reflection by thanking her again & again (as I can do sincerely) for her kindness & goodness in coming to see me herself, so far!—

1. Mrs. Orr (p. 19) says that Browning's mother suffered from anemia and neuralgia. For the relation between this and her son's illness see Letter 514.

2. Antoine Jean Baptiste Robert Auget, Baron de Montyon (1733–1820) bequeathed money for several perpetual prizes, including *the prix de vertu,* for the most courageous act performed by a Frenchman in modest circumstances.

3. See Letter 25, note 2.

48 (W25)   **R.B. to E.B.B.**

[*June 24, 1845.*]

Tuesday Morning,
(in the spirit)

(So my friend did not in the spirit see me write that *first* letter, on Friday, which was too good & true to send, & met, five minutes after, its natural fate accordingly: then on Saturday I thought to take health by storm, and walked myself half dead all the morning—about town too: last post-hour from this Thulé[1] of a suburb—4 p.m. on Saturdays, next expedition of letters, 8 a.m. on Mondays;—and then my real letter set out with the others—and, it should seem, set at rest a "wonder whether my friend's questions deserved answering"—de-served—answer-ing—!)

Parenthetically so much—I want most, though, to tell you—(leaving out any slightest attempt at thanking you) that I am much better, quite well to-day—that my doctor has piloted me safely thro' two or three illnesses, and knows all about me, I do think—and that he talks, confidently of getting rid of all the symptoms complained of—and *has* made a good beginning if I may judge by to-day: as for going abroad, that is just the thing I most want to avoid, (for a reason not so hard to guess, perhaps, as why my letter was slow in arriving)

So, till To-morrow,—my light through the dark week.

God ever bless you, dear friend,

R. B.

1. The ancients used this name for the northernmost end of the world.

49 (*W25°*)   **E.B.B. to R.B.**

[*June 24, 1845.*]

Tuesday evening.

What will you think when I write to ask you *not* to come to-morrow, wednesday; but . . on friday perhaps . . instead? But do see how it is; & judge if it is to be helped.

I have waited hour after hour, hoping to hear from Miss Mitford that she w^d agree to take thursday in change for wednesday,—& just as I begin to wonder whether she can have received my letter at all, or whether she may not have been vexed by it into taking a vengeance & adhering to her own devices; (for ⟨‖ · · · ‖⟩ it appealed to her esprit de sexe on the undeniable axiom of women having their way . . & she might choose to act it out!) . . just as I wonder over all this, & consider what a confusion of the elements it w^d be if you came & found her here, & Mr. Chorley at the door perhaps, waiting for some of the light of her countenance;—comes a note from Mr. Kenyon, to the effect that *he* will be here at four oclock p.m. & comes a final note from my aunt Mrs. Hedley (supposed to be at Brighton for several months) to the effect that *she* will be here at twelve oclock m.!! So do observe the constellation of adverse stars . . or the covey of 'bad birds,' as the Romans called them—and that there is no choice, but to write as I am writing. It can't be helped—can it? For take away the doubt about Miss Mitford, & Mr. Kenyon remains—& take away Mr. Kenyon, and there is Mrs. Hedley—and thus it *must be for friday* . . which will learn to be a fortunate day for the nonce —unless saturday sh^d suit you better. I do not speak of thursday, because of the doubt about Miss Mitford—& if any harm sh^d happen to friday, I will write again; but if you do not hear again, & are able to come then, you *will* come perhaps then.

In the meantime I thank you for the better news in your note—if it is really, really to be trusted in—but you know, you have said so often that you were better & better, without being really better, that it makes people . . "suspicious." Yet it is full amends for the disappointment to hope . . here I must break off or be too late. May God bless you my dear friend.

E. B. B.

50 *(W 26)*   **R.B. to E.B.B.**

[*June 25, 1845.*]

12. Wednesday

Pomegranates you may cut deep down the middle[1] & see into, but not hearts,—so why should I try & speak?

Friday is best day because nearest, but Saturday is next best—it is next near, you know: if I get no note, therefore, Friday is my day.

Now is Post-time,—which happens properly.

God bless you, & so your own R. B.

1. "Or from Browning some 'Pomegranate,' which, if cut deep down the middle / Shows a heart within blood-tinctured, of a veined humanity." E.B.B.'s *Lady Geraldine's Courtship* (1844), st. xli.

June, 1845

51 (W26°)   *E.B.B. to R.B.*

[June 26, 1845.]

Thursday evening.

After all it must be for Saturday, as Mrs. Hedley comes again on friday, to-morrow, from *New Cross,*—or just beyond it, Eltham Park, —to London for a few days, on account of the illness of one of her children. I write in the greatest haste after Miss Mitford has left me . . and / go⟩so / tired!! . . to say this—that if you can & will come on saturday, . . or if not on Monday or tuesday, there is no reason against it.   Your friend always

E. B. B.—

52 (W27)   *R.B. to E.B.B.*

[June 27, 1845.]

Friday Morning.

Let me make haste & write down *To-morrow,* Saturday, & not later, lest my selfishness be thoroughly got under in its struggle with a better feeling that tells me you must be far too tired for another visitor this week.

What shall I decide on?

Well—Saturday is said—but I will stay not quite so long, nor talk nearly so loud as of old-times—nor will you—if you understand anything of me—fail to send down word should you be at all indisposed: I should not have the heart to knock at the door unless I really believed you would do that. Still saying this & providing against the other does not amount, I well know, to the generosity, or justice rather, of staying away for a day or two altogether—But—what "a day or two" may not bring forth! Change to you, change to me—

Not all of me, however, can change, thank God—

Yours ever

R. B.

June, 1845

Or, write, as last night,—if needs be: Monday, Tuesday is not so long to wait. Will you write?

53 (*W 27°*)   *E.B.B. to R.B.*

_____

[*June 27, 1845.*]

Friday ev^g

You are very kind & [as?] always—but really *that* does not seem a good reason against your coming to-morrow—so come, if it should not rain. If it rains, it CONCLUDES for Monday . . or tuesday,—whichever may be clear of rain. I was tired on Wednesday by the confounding confusion of more voices than usual in this room; but the effect passed off, & though Miss Mitford was with me for hours yesterday I am not unwell today. And pray speak *bona verba* about the awful things which are possible between this now & Wednesday. You continue to be better, I do hope? I am forced to the brevity you see, by the post on one side, & my friends on the other, who have so long overstayed the coming of your note—but it is enough to assure you that you will do no harm by coming—only give pleasure—

Ever yours, my dear friend,

E. B. B.

On the envelope of Letter 53, Browning noted his sixth visit:
+ Sat^y 28 June
3^{1}–$4\frac{1}{4}$ p.m.

Letter 54 was an enclosure in the package with Prolusiones Academicae, *which Browning had lent E.B.B. (see the editorial note preceding Letter 41).*

54 (W28°)   *E.B.B. to R.B.*

[*June 30, 1845.*]

Monday.

I send back the prize poems which have been kept far too long even if I do not make excuses for the keeping—but our sins are not always to be measured by our repentance for them. Then I am well enough this morning to have thought of going out till they told me it was ⊹not⊹ at all a right day for it . . too windy . . soft & delightful as the air seems to be—particularly after yesterday, when we had some winter back again in an episode. And the roses do not die,—which is quite magnanimous of them considering their 'reverses'; & their buds are coming out in most exemplary resignation—like birds singing in a cage. Now that the windows may be open, the flowers take heart to live a little in this room.

And think of my forgetting to tell you on saturday that I had known of a letter being received by somebody from Miss Martineau, who is at Ambleside at this time & so entranced with the lakes and mountains as to be dreaming of taking or making a house among them, to live in for the rest of her life. Mrs. Trollope,[1] you may have heard, had something of the same nympholepsy—no, her daughter was 'settled' in the neighbourhood—*that* is the more likely reason for Mrs. Trollope!—& the spirits of the hills conspired against her the first winter & almost slew her with a fog & drove her away to your Italy where the Oreadocracy has gentler manners. And Miss Martineau is practising mesmerism & miracles on all sides she says, & counts on Archbishop Whately[2] as a new adherent. I even fancy that he has been to see her in the character of a convert. All this from Mr. Kenyon.

There's a strange wild book called the Autobiography of Heinrich Stilling[3] . . one of those true devout deep-hearted Germans who believe everything, and so are nearer the truth, I am sure, than the wise who believe nothing,—but rather over-German sometimes, and redolent of saurkraut—and *he* gives a ⟨⊹personal⊹⟩ tradition . . somewhere between mesmerism & mysticism, . . of a little spirit with gold shoebuckles, who was his familiar spirit and appeared only in the sunshine I think . . mottling it over with its feet, perhaps, as a child

might snow. Take away the shoebuckles and I believe in the little spirit
—dont *you?* But these ↑English↓ mesmerists make the shoebuckles
quite conspicuous & insist on them broadly,—& the Archbishops
Whately may be drawn by *them* (who can tell?) more than by the little
spirit itself. How is your head to-day? now really, & nothing extenuating? I will not ask of poems, till the 'quite well' is *authentic.* May
God bless you always! my dear friend!

E. B. B.

[After all the book must go another day . . I live in chaos do you
know? & I am too hurried at this moment . . yes it is here.]⁴

 1. Frances Trollope (1780–1863), the mother of Anthony and his near equal in
sheer literary fecundity.
 2. Richard Whately (1787–1863), Archbishop of Dublin, known as a very
matter-of-fact clergyman. On February 8, 1846, Miss Martineau wrote E.B.B.: "I
have been intrusted by the Archbᵖ of Dublin with some papers of his on the nature
and *morale* of Mesᵐ, & the objections of those who fear supernaturalism in it. These
papers may be shown to anyone I please, on a clear promise that no copy shall be
taken" (manuscript in Yale Library).
 3. Pen name of Johann Heinrich Jung (1740–1817), oculist, surgeon, physician,
teacher, and friend of Goethe. The *Autobiography* was published in English translation
in 1835–36.
 4. Added at the top of the first page.

55 (W28)   *R.B. to E.B.B.*

[*July 1, 1845.*]

Tuesday Morning.

How are you—may I hope to hear soon?
 I don't know exactly what possessed me to set my next day so far
off as Saturday—as it was said, however, so let it be. And I will bring
the rest of the 'Duchess'—four or five hundred lines,—"heu, herba
mala crescit"¹—(as I once saw mournfully pencilled on a white wall at
Asolo)—but will you tell me if you quite remember the main of the
first part—(*parts* there are none except in the necessary process of chop-
ping up to suit the limits of a magazine—& I gave them as much as I

could transcribe at a sudden warning)—because, if you please, I can bring the whole,—of course.

After seeing *you,* that Saturday, I was caught up by a friend and carried to see Vidocq[2]—who did the honours of his museum of knives & nails and hooks that have helped great murderers to their purposes— he scarcely admits, I observe, an implement with only one attestation to its efficacy; but the one or two exceptions rather justify his latitude in their favour—thus one little sort of desert-knife *did* only take *one* life. . . "but then," says Vidocq, "it was the man's own mother's life, with fifty-two blows, and all for" (I think) "fifteen francs she had got?" So prattles good-naturedly Vidocq—one of his best stories is of that Lacénaire—'jeune homme d'un caractère fort avenant—mais c'était un poète,' quoth he, turning sharp on *me* out of two or three other people round him.

Here your letter breaks in, & sunshine too.

Why do you send me that book—not let me take it? What trouble for nothing!

An old French friend of mine,[3] a dear foolish, very French heart & soul, is coming presently—his poor brains are whirling with mes-merism in which he believes, as in all other unbelief. He & I are to dine alone (—I have not seen him these two years)—and I shall never be able to keep from driving the great wedge right thro' his breast and, descending lower, from riveting his two foolish legs to the wintry chasm,—for I that stammer and answer at hap-hazard with you, get proportionately valiant & voluble with a mere cupful of Diderot's rinsings—, and a man into the bargain.

If you were prevented from leaving the house yesterday, as-suredly to-day you will never attempt such a thing—the wind, rain— all is against it: I trust you will not make the first experiment except under really favourable auspices . . for by its success you will naturally be induced to go on or leave off—Still you are *better!* I fully believe, dare to believe, *that* will continue. As for me, since you ask—find me but something *to do,* and see if I shall not be well!—Tho' I *am* well now almost.

How good you are to my roses—they are not of my making, to be sure: never by the way, did Miss Martineau work such a miracle as I now witness in the garden—I gathered at Rome, close to the fountain of Egeria,[4] a handful of *fennel*-seeds from the most indisputable plant of fennel I ever chanced upon—and, lo, they are come up . . hemlock, or something akin! In two places, moreover. Wherein does hemlock resemble fennel? How could I mistake? No wonder that a stone's cast off from that Egerias fountain is the Temple of the God Ridiculus.

Well, on Saturday then—at 3: & I will certainly bring the verses you mention—and trust to find you still better.

Vivi felice—my dear friend, God bless you!

R. B.

1. "Alas, the evil weed flourishes!"
2. François Eugene Vidocq (1775–1857), the famous French detective who learned his trade partly by having been a criminal, was holding a public exhibition and sale in Regent Street. "[There] are to be seen the costumes of all the various grades of society in Paris among which swindlers, rogues, thieves, and plunderers . . . associate, which . . . M. Vidocq [wears] in his professional capacity, [for] discovering and arresting criminals . . . . There is also a variety of daggers, sanguinary weapons, knives, and other horrible implements of murder or mutilation taken from the [criminals]; and in addition . . . manacles or fetters with which M. Vidocq himself was secured . . . . But the principal curiosity in the collection will be found to be M. Vidocq himself." *The Times*, June 9, 1845.
3. This must have been "C. Caillard" to whom Browning wrote on June 27, 1845. See Broughton, Northup, and Pearsall, *Robert Browning: A Bibliography* (Ithaca, N.Y.: Cornell University Press, 1953), p. 344.
4. An ancient fountain sacred to the nymph Egeria, said by tradition to have advised Numa Pompilius, had recently been located within the Roman wall; but Browning refers to an earlier supposed site, near a ruin mistakenly thought to be the Temple of the Divus Ridiculus, built in gratitude for Hannibal's retreat. See Murray's *Handbook of Rome and Its Environs* (11th ed.; London, 1872), pp. 38, 90.

56 (W29°)   *E.B.B. to R.B.*

[*July 2–3, 1845.*]

Wednesday-Thursday Evening.

Yes—I know the first part of the 'Duchess' & have it here—& for the rest of the poem, dont mind about being very legible, or even legible in the usual sense; & remember how it is my boast to be able to read all such manuscript writing as never is read by people who dont like caviare. Now you wont mind? really I rather like blots than other-wise—being a sort of patron-saint of all manner of untidyness . . if Mr.

Kenyon's reproaches (of which there's a stereotyped edition) are justified by the fact—and he has a great organ of order, & knows 'disorderly persons' at a glance, I suppose. But you wont be particular with *me* in the matter of transcription? *that* is what I want to make sure of. And even if you are not ↑particular↓, I am afraid you are not well enough to be troubled by writing & writing & the thinking that comes with it—it w^d be wiser to wait till you are quite well—now wouldn't it?—& my fear is that the 'almost well' means 'very little better.' And why . . when there is no motive for hurrying . . run any risk? Dont think that I will help you to make yourself ill. That I refuse to do even so much work as the "little desert-knife" in the way of murder, . . *do* think! So upon the whole, I expect nothing on saturday from this distance—and if it comes unexpectedly (I mean the Duchess and not saturday) *let* it be at no cost, or at the least cost possible—will you? I am delighted in the meanwhile to hear of the quantity of 'mala herba'; & hemlock does not come up from every seed you sow, though you call it by ever such bad names.

Talking of poetry, I had a newspaper 'in help of social & political progress' sent to me yesterday from America—addressed to—just my name . . *poetess, London!* Think of the simplicity of those wild Americans in "calculating" that 'people in general' here in England knew what a poetess ⟨was⟩ is!—Well—the post office authorities, after deep meditation, I do not doubt, on all probable varieties of the chimpanzee, & a glance to the Surrey Gardens on one side, & the Zoological department of Regent's Park on the other, thought of 'Poet's Corner,' perhaps, & wrote at the top of the parcel, 'Enquire at Paternoster Row'!—whereupon the Paternoster Row people wrote again . . 'Go to Mr. Moxon'—& I received my newspaper.

And talking of poetesses, I had a note yesterday (again) which quite touched me . . from Mr. Hemans—Charles . . the son of Felicia[1] —written with so much feeling, that it was with difficulty I could say my perpetual 'no' to his wish about coming to see me. His mother's memory is surrounded to him, he says, "with almost a divine lustre" —& "as it cannot be to those who knew the writer alone & not the woman." Do you not like to hear such things said? and is it not better than your tradition about Shelley's son? & is it not pleasant to know that that poor noble pure-hearted woman, the Vittoria Colonna[2] of our country, sh^d be so loved & comprehended by some . . by one at least . .

of her own house? Not that, in naming Shelley, I meant for a moment to make a comparision—there is not equal ground for it. Vittoria Colonna does not walk near Dante—no. And if you promised never to tell Mrs. Jameson . . nor Miss Martineau . . I would confide to you perhaps my secret profession of faith—which is . . which is . . that let us say & do what we please & can . . there *is* a natural inferiority of mind in women—of the intellect . . not by any means, of the moral nature—& that the history of Art ⟨‖···‖⟩ & of genius testifies to this fact openly. Oh—I would not say so to Mrs. Jameson for the world! I believe I was a coward to her altogether—for when she denounced ⟨‖···‖⟩ ↑carpet↓ work as "injurious to the mind," because it led the workers into "fatal habits of reverie," I defended the carpet work as if I were striving *pro aris et focis,*[3] (*I,* who am so innocent of all that knowledge!) & said not a word for the poor reveries which have frayed away so much of silken time for me . . & let her go away repeating again & again . . 'Oh, but *you* may do carpet work with impunity—yes! *because* you can be writing poems all the /time⟩ while/.'!

Think of people making poems & rugs at once. There's complex machinery for you!

I told you that I had a sensation of cold blue steel from her eyes!—And yet I really liked & like & shall like her. She is very kind I believe—↑& it was my mistake—↓ & I correct my impressions of her more & more to perfection, as *you* tell me who know more of her than I.

Only I sh^d not dare, . . *ever* . . I think . . to tell her that I believe women . . all of us in a mass . . to have minds of quicker movement, but less power & depth . . & that we are under your feet, because we can't stand upon our own—Not that we sH^d either be quite under your feet!—so you are not to be too proud, if you please—& there is certainly some amount of wrong—: but it never will be righted in the manner & to the extent contemplated by certain of our own prophetesses . . nor ought to be, I hold in intimate persuasion. One woman indeed now alive . . & only *that* one down all the ages of the world . . seems to me to justify for a moment an opposite opinion—that wonderful woman George Sand; who has something monstrous in combination with her genius, there is no denying at moments (for she has written one book, Leila, which I could not read,[4] though I am not ⟨‖···‖⟩ easily turned back,) but whom, ⟨‖····‖⟩ ↑in her↓ good & evil together,

I regard with infinitely more admiration than all other women of genius who are or have been. Such a colossal nature in every way—with all that breadth & scope of faculty which women want—magnanimous, & loving the truth & loving the people—and with that "hate of hate"[5] too, which you extol—so eloquent, & yet earnest as if she were dumb—so full of a living sense of beauty, & of noble blind instincts towards an ideal purity—& so proving a right even in her wrong. By the way, what you say of the Vidocq museum reminds me of one of the chamber of masonic trial scenes in Consuelo.[6] Could you like to see those knives?

I began with the best intentions of writing six lines—& see what is written!—And all because I kept my letter back . . from a *doubt about saturday*—but it has worn away, & the appointment stands good . . for me: I have nothing to say against it.

But ↑belief in↓ mesmerism is not the same thing as ↑general↓ unbelief—to do it justice—now is it? It may be super-belief as well. Not that there is not something ghastly & repelling to me in the thought of Dr. Elliotson's[7] great boney fingers seeming to 'touch the stops' of a whole soul's harmonies—as in phreno-magnetism. And I sh^d have liked far better than hearing & seeing *that,* to have heard *you* pour the "cupful of Diderot's rinsings," out,—& indeed, I can fancy a little that you & how you could do it—& break the cup too afterwards!

Another sheet—& for what?

What is written already, if you read, you do so meritoriously—and it's an example of bad writing, if you want one in the poems. I am ashamed, you may see, of having written ⟨‖ · · · ‖⟩ too much, (besides) —which is *much* worse—but one writes & writes: *I* do at least—for *you* are irreproachable. Ever yours my dear friend, as if I had not written . . or *had!*   E. B. B.

1. Felicia Hemans (1793–1835), a minor poetess popular in her day, now best remembered for *The Pilgrim Fathers* and the much-parodied *Casabianca* ("The boy stood on the burning deck"). There was a poem to her memory in E.B.B.'s 1844 collection. Her youngest son, Charles (1817–76), was an antiquary and the founder (1846) of Rome's first English-language newspaper.

2. Vittoria Colonna (1490–1547) was an Italian poetess and friend of Michelangelo. Widowed at twenty-five, after six years of married life, she devoted the twenty-two years of her life that remained largely to sonnets in memory of her husband or on sacred and moral subjects. In 1818 Mrs. Hemans and her husband

parted for the rest of their lives, apparently for reasons of poverty rather than estrangement. This "widowhood" is the likeliest parallel.

3. "For altar and hearth."

4. Published 1833. ". . . a serpent book both for language-color and soul-slime and one which I could not read through for its vileness myself." *EBB to MRM*, p. 156.

5. Tennyson, *The Poet*, l. 3.

6. Another George Sand novel (1842–43).

7. John Elliotson (1791–1868) was professor of physic in London University and physician to University College Hospital until his interest in phrenology and mesmerism aroused the ire of his colleagues and led to his resignation in 1838. Thackeray dedicated *Pendennis* (1848) to him.

Browning's seventh visit is noted on the envelope of Letter 56:

+ Sat^y July 5

3–4½ p.m.

57 *(W 29)*   **R.B. to E.B.B.**

—————————————

[*July 7, 1845.*]

Monday Afternoon.

While I write this,—3 o'clock,—you may be going out, I will hope —for the day is very fine, perhaps all the better for the wind: yet I got up /today⟩this/ morning sure of bad weather. I shall not try to tell you how anxious I am for the result, and to know it. You will of course feel fatigued at first—but persevering, as you mean to do, do you not?— persevering, the event must be happy.

I thought, and still think, to write to you about George Sand, and the vexed question, a very Bermoothes[1] of the 'Mental Claims of the Sexes relatively considered' (so was called the . . I do believe . . worst poem I ever read in my life—) and Mrs. Hemans, and all and some of the points referred to in your letter—but 'by my fay, I cannot reason,'[2] to-day: and, by a consequence, I feel the more—so I say how I want news of you . . which, when they arrive, I shall read "meritoriously"—do you think? My friend, what ought I to tell you on that head (or the re-verse rather)—of your discourse? I should like to match you at a fancy-flight; if I could, give you nearly as pleasant an assurance that "there's no merit in the case," but the hot weather and lack of wit get the better of my good will—besides, I remember once to have admired a certain enticing simplicity in the avowal of the Treasurer of a Charitable Institution at a Dinner got up in its behalf—the Funds being at lowest, Debt at highest . . in fact, this dinner was the last chance of the Charity, and this Treasurer's speech the main feature in the chance—and our friend, inspired by the emergency, went so far as to say, with a bland smile— "Do not let it be supposed that we—*despise* annual contributors,—we *rather*—solicit their assistance." All which means, do not think that I take any "merit" for making myself supremely happy, I rather—&c &c

Always rather mean to deserve it a little better—but never shall: so it should be, for you and me—and as it was in the beginning so it is still . . you are the ⟨∥ · · · ∥⟩—But you know and why should I teaze myself with words?

Let me send this off now—and to-morrow some more, because I trust to hear you have made the first effort and with success.

Ever yours, my dear friend—

R. B.

1. *Tempest* I. ii. 229.
2. *Hamlet* II. ii. 267

58 (W30°)   *E.B.B. to R.B.*

[*July 7, 1845.*]

Monday.

Well—I have really been out,—and am really alive after it—which is more surprising still—alive enough I mean, to write even *so,* to-night. But perhaps I say so ↑with more emphasis,↓ to console myself for failing in my great ambition of getting into the Park & of reaching Mr. Kenyon's door[1] just to leave a card there vaingloriously, . . all which I did fail in, & was forced to turn back from the gates of Devonshire Place. The next time it will be better perhaps—& this time there was no fainting nor anything very wrong . . not even cowardice on the part of the victim (be it recorded!) for one of my sisters was as usual in authority & ordered the turning back just according to her own prudence & not my selfwill. Only you will not, any of you, ask me to admit that it was all delightful—pleasanter work than what you wanted to spare me in taking care of your roses on Saturday!—don't ask *that*, & I will try it again presently.

I ought to be ashamed of writing this I- and me-ism—but since your kindness made it worth while asking about, I must not be over-wise & silent on my side.

Tuesday.—Was it fair to tell me to write though, & be silent of the Duchess—& when I was sure to be so delighted,—& *you knew it? I* think not indeed. And, to make the obedience possible, I go on fast to say that I heard from Mr. Horne a few days since & that *he* said—" your envelope reminds me of"—*you*, he said . . & so, asked if you were in England still, & meant to write to you. To which I have answered that I believe you to be in England—thinking it strange about the envelope,—which, as far as I remember, was one of those long ones, used, the more conveniently to enclose to him back again a MS. of his own I had offered with another of his, by his desire, to Colburn's Magazine, as the productions of a friend of mine, when he was in Germany & afraid of his proper fatal onymousness,[2] yet in difficulty how to approach the magazines as a nameless writer—(you will not mention this of course—). And when he was in Germany, I remember, . . writing just as your first letter came, . . that I mentioned it to him, & was a little frankly proud of it!—but since, your name has not occurred once—not once, certainly!—& it is strange. . . Only he *cant* have heard of your having been here, & it *must* have been a chance-remark—altogether!—taking an imaginary emphasis from my evil conscience perhaps. Talking of evils, how wrong of you to make that book for me!—& how ill I [thanked you after all! Also, I couldn't help feeling more grateful still for the Duchess . . who is under ban: and for how long I wonder?

My dear friend, I am ever yours, E. B. B.]³

1. At 40 York Terrace, Regent's Park, just under a half mile from 50 Wimpole Street.
2. The *OED* defines onymous as "having or bearing a name." The sense is pretty clearly that Horne's name is poison because of the reception of *A New Spirit of the Age.*
3. Written at the top of the first page.

[*July 9, 1845.*]

Wednesday M^g

You are all that is good & kind: I am happy and thankful the beginning (and worst of it) is over and so well. The Park, & Mr. Kenyon's all
in good time—and your sister was most prudent—and you mean to try
again—God bless you!—all to be said or done—but, as I say it, no vain
word. No doubt it was a mere chance-thought, and *à-propos de bottes* of
Horne—neither he or any other *can* know or even fancy how it is: indeed, tho' on other grounds I should be all so proud of being known for
your friend by everybody, yet there's no denying the deep delight of
playing the Eastern Jew's part here in this London—they go about, you
know by travel-books, with the tokens of extreme destitution & misery,
and steal by blind ways & by-paths to some blank dreary house, one
obscure door in it—which being well shut behind them, they grope on
thro' a dark corridor or so, and then, a blaze follows the lifting a curtain
or the like, for they are in a palace-hall with fountains and light, and
marble and gold, of which the envious are never to dream!¹ And I, too,
love to have few friends, and to live alone, and to see you from week to
week—Do you not suppose I am grateful?

And you do like the "Duchess," as much as you have got of it? that
delights me, too—for every reason. But I fear I shall not be able to bring
you the rest to-morrow—Thursday, my day—because I have been
broken in upon more than one morning; nor, tho' much better in my
head, can I do /much⟩anything/ at night just now. All will come right
eventually, I hope,—and I shall transcribe the other things you are to
judge.

To-morrow then: only—(and that is why I would write)—do, do
know me for what I am and treat me as I deserve in that *one* respect, and
GO OUT, without a moment's thought or care, if to-morrow should suit
you—leave word to that effect and I shall be as glad as if I saw you or
more—*reasoned* gladness, you know. Or you can write—tho' that is not
necessary at all,—do think of all this! I am yours ever, dear friend,

R. B.

1. No such account has come to light, but whatever it was, ll. 73–77 of Browning's *How It Strikes a Contemporary* (1855) must owe something to it.

Between the foregoing letter and the following, Browning made the call noted on the envelope of Letter 58 :

+Thursday July 10

3–4½ p.m.

60 (W31°)   *E.B.B. to R.B.*

[*Friday, July 11, 1845.*]

You understand that it was not a resolution passed in favour of formality, when I said what I did yesterday about not going out at the time you were coming—surely you do,—whatever you might signify to a different effect,—If it were necessary for me to go out every day, or most days even, it w^d be otherwise—but as it is, I may certainly keep the day you come, free from the fear of carriages, let the sun shine its best or worst,—without doing despite to you or injury to me—and that's all I meant to insist upon indeed & indeed. You see, Jupiter Tonans was good enough to come to-day on purpose to deliver me—one evil for another! —for I confess with shame & contrition, that I never wait to enquire whether it thunders to the left or the right, to be frightened most ingloriously. Isn't it a disgrace to anyone with a pretension to poetry? Dr. Chambers,[1] a part of whose office it is, Papa says, "to reconcile foolish women to their follies," used to take the side of my vanity—& discourse at length on the passive obedience of some nervous systems to electrical influences—but perhaps my faint-heartedness is besides traceable to a ↑half–↓ reasonable terror of a great storm in Herefordshire . . where great storms most do congregate . . (such storms!) round the Malvern hills, those mountains of England. We lived four miles from their roots, thro' all my childhood & early youth, in a Turkish house my father built himself, crowded with minarets & domes, & crowned with metal spires & crescents, to the provocation (as people used to observe) of every lightning of heaven. Once a storm of storms happened, & we all thought the house was struck—& a tree was so really, within two hundred yards of the windows while I looked out—the bark, rent from the top to the bottom . . torn into long ribbons by the dreadful fiery hands, & dashed out into the air, over the heads of other trees, or left twisted in their branches—torn into shreds in a moment, as a flower might be, by a child!—Did you ever see a tree after it has been struck by lightning? The whole trunk of that tree was bare & peeled—& up that new whiteness of it, ran the finger-mark of the lightning in a bright beautiful rose-colour (none of your roses brighter or more beautiful!) the fever-sign of the certain death—Though the branches themselves were for the most part untouched, & spread from the peeled trunk in their full sum-mer foliage,—and birds singing in them three hours afterwards! And, in that same storm, two young women belonging to a festive party were killed on the Malvern hills—each sealed to death in a moment with a sign on the chest which a common seal w^d cover—only the sign on them was not rose-coloured as on our tree . . but black as charred wood. So I get 'possessed' sometimes with the effects of these impressions—& so does one, at least, of my sisters, in a lower degree—and oh!—how amus-ing & instructive all this is to you! When my father came into the room to-day & found me hiding my eyes from the lightning, he was quite angry & called "it disgraceful to anybody who had ever learnt the alpha-bet"—to which I answered humbly that "I knew it was"—but if I had been impertinent, I MIGHT have added that wisdom does not come by the alphabet but in spite of it? Don't you think so in a measure? non obstantibus Bradbury and Evans?[2] There's a profane question—& un-grateful too . . after the Duchess—I except the Duchess & her peers—& be sure she will be the world's Duchess & received as one of your most striking poems. Full of various power the poem is . . I cannot say how deeply it [has impressed me—but though I want the conclusion, I don't *wish* for it; and in this, am reasonable for once!! You will not write & make yourself ill—will you? or read Sybil[3] at unlawful hours even? Are you better at all?—What a letter! & how very foolishly to-day I am

Yours, E. B. B.][4]

1. William Frederick Chambers (1786–1855), an F.R.S. and physician in ordinary to Queen Victoria, described by the *DNB* as "the leading physician in London" at this time, had been E.B.B.'s doctor for almost a decade.

2. "Bradbury and Evans notwithstanding." See Letter 5 and its note 4.

3. Disraeli's novel, published in May 1845.

4. The letter was completed at the top of the first page.

Edward Barrett Moulton-Barrett

Painting by H. W. Pickersgill, R.A.

The Barrett house at 50 Wimpole Street

61 (W31)   *R.B. to E.B.B.*

[*July 13, 1845.*]

Sunday Morning.

Very well—I shall say no more on the subject—tho' it was not any
piece of formality on your part that I deprecated; nor even your over-
kindness exactly—I rather wanted you to be really, wisely kind, & do
me a greater favor than the next great one in degree—but you must
understand this much in me—how you can lay me under deepest obligation. I daresay you think you have some—perhaps many,—to whom
your well-being is of deeper interest than to me—Well, if that be so, do
for their sakes make every effort with the remotest chance of proving
serviceable to you,—nor *set yourself against* any little irksomeness these
carriage-drives may bring with them just at the beginning; and you
may say, if you like, "how I shall delight those friends, if I can make this
newest one grateful"—and, as from the known quantity one reasons
out the unknown, this newest friend will be one glow of gratitude, he
knows that, if you can warm your finger-tips and so do yourself that
much real good, by setting light to a dozen "Duchesses": why ought I
not to say this when it is so true? Besides, people profess as much to their
merest friends—for I have been looking thro' a poem-book just now,
and was told, under the head of Album-verses alone, that for A. the
writer would die, & for B. die too but a crueller death, and for C. too, &
D. and so on. I wonder whether they have since wanted to borrow
money of him on the strength of his professions. But you must remember we are in July; the 13th it is, and summer will go and cold weather
stay ("*come*" forsooth!)—and now is the time of times: still I feared the
rain would hinder you on Friday—but the thunder did not frighten me
—for you: your father must pardon me for holding most firmly with
Dr. Chambers—his theory is quite borne out by my own experience,
for I have seen a man it were foolish to call a coward, a great fellow too,
all but die away in a thunderstorm, though he had quite science enough
to explain why there was no immediate danger at all—whereupon his
↑younger↓ brother suggested that he should just go out and treat us to a
repetition of Franklin's experiment with the cloud and the kite—a well-
timed proposition which sent the Explainer down with a white face into

121

the cellar. What a grand sight your tree was—*is*, for I see it—My father
has a print of a tree so struck—torn to ribbons, as you describe—but the
rose-mark is striking and new to me: we had a good storm on our last
voyage, but I went to bed at the end, as I thought—and only found there
had been lightning next day by the bare poles under which we were
riding: but the finest mountain fit of the kind I ever saw has an unfortunately ludicrous association. It was at Possagno, among the Euganean-
Hills, and I was at a poor house in the town—an old woman was before
a little picture of the Virgin, and at every fresh clap she lighted, with the
oddest sputtering muttering mouthful of prayer imaginable, an inch of
guttery candle, which, the instant the last echo had rolled away, she as
constantly blew out again for saving's sake—having, of course, to *light
the smoke* of it, about an instant after that: the expenditure in wax at
which the elements might be propitiated, you see, was a matter for
curious calculation: I suppose I ought to have bought the whole taper
for some four or five centesimi (100 of which make *8d*. English) and so
kept the countryside safe for about a century of bad weather. Leigh Hunt
tells you a story he had from Byron, of kindred philosophy in a Jew who
was surprised by a thunderstorm while he was dining on bacon—he
tried to eat between-whiles, but the flashes were as pertinacious as he, so
at last he pushed his plate away, just remarking with a compassionate
shrug, "All this fuss about a piece of pork!" By the way, what a characteristic of an Italian *late* evening is Summer-lightning—it hangs in broad
slow sheets, dropping from cloud to cloud, so long in dropping and dying off. The "bora," which you only get at Trieste,[1] brings wonderful
lightning—you are in glorious June-weather, fancy, of an evening,
under green shock-headed acacias, so thick and green, with the cicalas
stunning you above, and all about you men, women, rich & poor, sitting,
standing & coming & going—and thro' all the laughter & screaming &
singing, the loud clink of the spoons against the glasses, the way of calling for fresh 'sorbetti'[2]—for all the world is at open-coffee-house at
such an hour—when suddenly there is a stop in the sunshine, a /dark-
ness>blackness/ drops down, then a great white column of dust drives
strait on like a wedge, and you see the acacia heads snap off, now one,
then another—and all the people scream "la bora, la bora!"—and you
are caught up in their whirl and landed in some interior, the man with
the guitar on one side of you, and the boy with a cageful of little brown
owls for sale, on the other—meanwhile, the thunder claps, claps, with

such a persistence, and the rain, for a finale, falls in a mass, as if you had knocked out the whole bottom of a huge tank at once—then there is a second stop—out comes the sun—somebody clinks at his glass, all the world bursts out laughing, and prepares to pour out again,—but *you*, the stranger, *do* make the best of your way out, with no preparation at all; whereupon you infallibly put your foot (and half your leg) into a river, really that, of rainwater—that's a *Bora* (and that comment of yours, a justifiable pun!) Such things you get in Italy, but better, better, the best of all things you do not (*I* do not) get those. And I shall see you on Wednesday, please remember, and bring you the rest of the poem— that you should like it, gratifies me more than I will try to say, but then, do not you be tempted by that pleasure of pleasing which I think is your besetting sin—may it not be?—and so cut me off from the other pleasure of being profited: as I told you, I like so much to fancy that you see, and will see, what I do as *I* see it, while it is doing, as nobody else in the world should, certainly,—even if they thought it worth while to want—but when I try and build a great building I shall want you to come with me and judge it and counsel me before the scaffolding is taken down, and while you have to make your way over hods of mortar & heaps of lime, and trembling tubs of size, and those thin broad whitewashing brushes I always had a desire to take up and bespatter with. And now goodbye— I am to see you on Wednesday I trust—and to hear you say you are better, still better, much better? God grant that, and all else good for you, dear friend, and so for R.B. ever yours.

    1. A violent, cold, north to northeast wind.
    2. Ices or iced drinks.

The visit noted by Browning on the envelope of Letter 60
+ Wednesday July 16
$3-4\frac{1}{4}$ *p.m.*
occurred while the following letter was in progress.

E.B.B. to R.B.

[*July 16–17, 1845.*]

I suppose nobody is ever expected to acknowledge his or her "be-setting sin "—it w^d be unnatural—& therefore you will not be surprised to hear me deny the one imputed to me for mine. I deny it quite & directly. And if my denial goes for nothing,—which is but reasonable, . . I might call in a great cloud of witnesses,[1] . . a thundercloud, . . (talking of storms!) & even seek no further than this table for a first witness,— this letter,[2] I had yesterday, which calls me . . let me see how many hard names . . "unbending," . . "disdainful," . . "cold hearted," . . "arro-gant," . . yes, "arrogant, as women always are when men grow humble " . . there's a charge against all possible & probable petticoats beyond mine & through it! Not that either they or mine deserve the charge—we do not,—to the lowest hem of us!—for I don't pass to the other extreme, mind, & adopt besetting sins 'over the way' & in antithesis. It's an un-deserved charge, & unprovoked!—& in fact, the very flower of selflove selftormented into ill temper; & shall remain unanswered, for *me*, . . & *should*, . . even if I could write mortal epigrams, as your Lamia[3] speaks them. Only it serves to help my assertion that people in general who know something of me, my dear friend, are not inclined to agree with you in particular, about my having an "over-pleasure in pleasing," for a besetting sin. If you had spoken of my sister Henrietta indeed, you w^d have been right—*so* right!—but for *me,* alas, my sins are not half as ami-able, nor given to lean to virtue's side with half such a grace. And then I have a pretension to speak the truth like a Roman, even in matters of literature, where Mr. Kenyon says falseness is a fashion—& really & honestly I should not be afraid . . I sh^d have no reason to be afraid, . . if all the notes & letters written by my hand for years & years about pre-sentation copies of poems & other sorts of books were brought together & 'conferred,' as they say of manuscripts, before my face—I sh^d not shrink & be ashamed. Not that I always tell the truth as I see it—*but* I *never do* speak falsely with intention & consciousness,—never—& I do not find that people of letters are sooner offended than others are, by the truth told in gentleness;—I do not remember to have offended anyone in this relation, & by these means. Well!—but *from me to you,*—it is all different, you know—you must know how different it is. I can tell you truly what I think of this thing & of that thing in your 'Duchess'—but I must of a necessity hesitate & fall into misgiving of the adequacy of my truth, so called. To judge at all of a work of yours, I must *look up to it,*—& *far up*—because whatever /power⟩faculty/ *I* have is included in your faculty, & with a great rim all round it besides! And thus, it is not at all from an over-pleasure in pleasing *you,* not at all from an inclination to depreciate myself, that I speak & feel as I do & must on some occasions— it is simply the consequence of a true comprehension of you & of me—& apart from it, I sh^d not be abler, I think, but less able, to assist you in any- thing. I do wish you w^d consider all this reasonably, & understand it as a third person would in a moment, & consent not to spoil the real pleasure I have & am about to have in your poetry, by nailing me up into a false position with your gold-headed nails of chivalry, which wont hold to the wall through this summer. Now you will not answer this?—you will only understand it & me—& that I am not servile but sincere—but earn- est—but meaning what I say—& when I say I am afraid, you will believe that I am afraid, . . and when I say I have misgivings, . . you will believe that I have misgivings—you will *trust* me so far, & give me liberty to breathe & feel naturally . . according to my own nature. Probably or certainly rather, I have one advantage over you . . one, of which women are not fond of boasting—that of *being older by years*—for the Essay on Mind, which was the first poem published by me,—(and rather more printed than published after all) the work of my earliest youth, half childhood half womanhood, was published in 1826 I see—and if I told Mr. Kenyon not to let you see that book, it was not for the date, but because Coleridge's daughter[4] was right in calling it a mere "girl's exercise,"—because it is just *that* and no more, . . no expression whatever of my nature as it ever was, . . ⟨‖ · · · ‖⟩ pedantic, & in some things, pert, . . & such as altogether, & to do myself justice (which I w^d fain do of course) I was not in my whole life. Bad books are never like their writers, you know—& those under-age books are generally bad. Also I have found it hard work to *get into expression,* though I began rhyming from my very infancy, much as you did (& this, with no sympathy near to me—I have had to do without sympathy in the full sense—) & even in my 'Seraphim' days,[5] my tongue clove to the roof of my mouth . . from leading so conventual recluse a life, perhaps—& all my /bitterness[?]⟩ better/ poems were written last year, the very best being to come

⟨‖ · · · ‖⟩ if there sh^d be any life or courage to come—: I scarcely know.
Sometimes—it is the real truth, . . I have haste to be done with it all. It is
the real truth; however ↑to say so may be an↓ ungrateful return for your
kind & generous words, . . which I DO feel gratefully, let me otherwise
feel as I will, . . or must. But then you know you are liable to such prodigious mistakes about besetting sins & even besetting virtues—to such
a set of small delusions, that are sure to break one by one, like other
bubbles, as you draw in your breath, . . as I see by the law of my own
star, my own particular star, the star I was born under, the star *Worm-
wood*[6] . . on the opposite side of the heavens from the constellations of
'the Lyre & the Crown.'[7] In the meantime, it is difficult to thank you, or
not to thank you, for all your kindnesses— ἄλγος δὲ σιγᾶν.[8] Only Mrs.
Jameson told me of Lady Byron's saying "that she knows she is burnt
every day in effigy by half the world, but that the effigy is so unlike herself as to be inoffensive to her"[9]—and just so, or rather just in the converse of *so,* is it with me & your kindnesses. They are meant for quite
another than I, or are too far to be so near. The comfort is . . in seeing you
throw all those ducats out of the window, . . (& how many ducats go in
a figure to a "dozen Duchesses," it is profane to calculate) the comfort is
that you will not be the poorer for it in the end; since the people beneath,
are honest enough to push them back under the door. Rather a bleak
comfort & occupation though!—& you may find ⟨‖ · · · ‖⟩ better work
for your friends, who are (some of them) weary even unto death of the
uses of this life. And now, you who are generous, BE generous, . . & take
no notice of all this. I speak of myself, not of you—so there is nothing
for you to contradict or discuss—& if there were, you w^d be really kind
& give me my way in it. Also you may take courage; for I promise not
to vex you by thanking you against *your* will,—more than may be helped.

    Some of this letter was written before yesterday & in reply of course
to yours—so it is to pass for two letters, being long enough for just six.
Yesterday you must have wondered at me for being in such a maze altogether about the poems—& so now I rise to explain that it was assuredly the wine song & no other which I read of yours in Hood's.[10] And
then, what did I say of the Dante & Beatrice? Because what I referred to
was the exquisite page or two or three on that subject in the "Pentameron."[11] I do not remember anything else of Landor's with the same
bearing—do you? As to Montaigne, with the threads of my thoughts
smoothly disentangled, I can see nothing coloured by him . . nothing. Do

bring all the Hood poems of your own—inclusive of the 'Tokay,' because I read it in such haste as to whirl up all the dust you saw, from the wheels of my chariot. The Duchess is past speaking of here—but you will see how I am delighted. And we must make speed—only taking care of your head . . for I heard to-day that Papa & my aunt are discussing the question of sending me off either to Alexandria or Malta for the winter. Oh—it is quite a passing talk & thought, I dare say! and it w^d not *be* in any case, until September or October; tho' in every case, I suppose, *I* /shall⟩should/ not be much consulted . . & all cases and places ↑w^d↓ seem better to me ↑(if I were)↓ than Madeira which the physicians used to threaten me with long ago. So take care of your headache & let us have the 'Bells' rung out clear before the summer ends—& pray don't say again anything about clear consciences or unclear ones, in granting me the privilege of reading your manuscripts—which is all clear privilege to me, with pride & gladness waiting on it. May God bless you always my dear friend!

E. B. B.

You left behind your sister's little basket—but I hope you did not forget to thank her for my carnations.

1. Hebrews 12:1.
2. Undoubtedly from the Rev. George Barrett Hunter.
3. See Letter 17.
4. Sara Coleridge (1802–52) married a cousin whom she succeeded as editor of her father's works. She also published some original works and translations of her own. The remark, perhaps relayed verbally by John Kenyon, seems lost. An unpublished portion of a letter from E.B.B. to Miss Mitford (MS. in Wellesley Library) in April 1845 refers, however, to some recent correspondence with Mrs. Coleridge. Her largely unfavorable remarks on the 1844 *Poems,* expressed in a letter to Kenyon, are reprinted in *Sara Coleridge: A Memoir and Letters,* ed. by her daughter (New York, 1874), p. 213.
5. *The Seraphim and Other Poems* was published in 1838, when E.B.B. was thirty-two.
6. Revelations 8:11. The star is twice mentioned in *The Ring and the Book,* Bk. XII (ll. 12 and 828) as a symbol of Pompilia's story, and there is an allusion to it in *Aurora Leigh,* V, 917–918. E.B.B. had also used the figure in an uncollected poem, *A Night-Watch by the Sea,* in the *Monthly Chronicle* for April 1840.
7. "It is certain . . . that a work like mine depends . . . on the intelligence and sympathy of the reader for its success;—indeed, were my scenes stars, it must be his coöperating fancy which, supplying all chasms, shall connect the scattered lights into one constellation—a Lyre or a Crown." Preface to *Paracelsus* (first edition only).
8. "To suffer pain in silence."

9. Mrs. Jameson, who was a close friend of the poet's wife from 1834 until they quarreled in 1852, undoubtedly heard much of the distaff point of view on the sensationally unsuccessful marriage whose other side Byron had pointedly underscored in some of his works. After an initial alignment that favored Lady Byron, public sympathy in the 1840's began gravitating to the dead poet.

10. *Claret and Tokay* (now the first two sections of *Nationality in Drinks*) was first published in *Hood's Magazine* for June 1844.

11. W. S. Landor's *Pentameron and Pentalogia* (London, 1837), pp. 237–240 (Fourth Day).

Since it was enclosed in the parcel of poems from Hood's Magazine, *referred to in its close, the following letter is not postmarked.*

63 (W32)   R.B. to E.B.B.

─────────────────

[*Not postmarked*]

I shall just say, at the beginning of a note as at the end, I am yours *ever*, and not till summer ends & my nails fall out, and my breath breaks bubbles,—ought you to write thus having restricted me as you once did, and do still? You tie me like a Shrove-Tuesday fowl to a stake and then pick the thickest cudgel out of your lot, and at my head it goes—I wonder whether you remembered having predicted exactly the same horror once before. "I was to see you—and you were to understand"—*Do* you? do you understand—my own friend—with that superiority in years, too! For I confess to that—you need not throw that in my teeth . . as soon as I read your "Essay on Mind"—⸗(which of course I managed to do about 12 hours after Mr. K's positive refusal to keep his promise, and give me the book)↓ from preface to the "Vision of Fame" at the end, and reflected on my own doings about that time, 1826—I did indeed see, and wonder at, your advance over me in years—what then? I have got nearer you considerably—(if only nearer—) since then,—and prove it by the remarks I make at favorable times—such as this, for instance, which occurs in a poem you are to see—written some time ago—which advises nobody who thinks nobly of the Soul, to give, if he or she can help, such a good argument to the materialist as the owning that any great choice of that Soul, which it is born to make and which—(in its determining, as it must, the whole future course and impulses of that soul)—which must endure for ever, even tho' the object that induced the choice should disappear)—owning, I say, that such a choice may be scientifically determined and produced, at any operator's pleasure, by a definite number of ingredients, so much youth, so much beauty, so much talent &c &c, with the same certainty and precision that another kind of operator will construct you an artificial volcano with so much steel filings and flower of sulphur and what not: there is more in the soul than rises to the surface and meets the eye; whatever does *that,* is for this world's immediate uses; and were this world *all, all* in us would be pro-ducible and available for use, as it *is* with the body now—but with the soul, what is to be developed *afterward* is the main thing, and instinctively asserts its rights—so that when you hate (or love) you shall not be so able to explain "why" ("You" is the ordinary creature enough of my poem—*he* might not be so able.)[1]

There, I will write no more. You will never drop *me* off the golden hooks, I dare believe—and the rest is with God—whose finger I see every minute of my life. Alexandria! Well, and may I not as easily ask leave to come "to-morrow at the Muezzin" as next Wednesday at 3?

God bless you—do not be otherwise than kind to this letter which it costs me pains, great pains to avoid writing better, as truthfuller—this you get is not the first begun. Come, you shall not have the heart to blame me; for, see, I will send all my sins of commission with Hood[2]—blame *them,* tell me about them, and meantime let me be, dear friend, yours

R. B.

---

1. Though this passage sketches a recurrent Browning theme, it is hard to identify with any particular poem. Yet Browning's implied satisfaction must mean that it was published. At this time Browning was working on *Dramatic Romances and Lyrics,* and *Pictor Ignotus,* which gained the second place in that collection has certain notable ties to this account. Its narrator and the "youth, men praise so" are equals in talent (and perhaps, by implication, in beauty), yet their careers diverge utterly because the former's insight rejects the latter's worldly success; in the words Browning uses here, his soul "instinctively asserts its rights." The difficulties—apart from a reading of the poem not universally acceptable—are that the passage suggests a poem that directly "advises" the reader and one that employs the metaphor of the operator and his artificial volcano. There are, however, other notable, though less striking, occasions when Browning modified his original in detailed and concrete ways in the retelling. See, e.g., Letter 18.

2. *The Laboratory* and *Claret and Tokay* (June 1844), the two *Garden Fancies* (July 1844), *The Boy and the Angel* (August 1844), *The Tomb at St. Praxed's* (March 1845), and the first nine sections of *The Flight of the Duchess* (April 1845).

64 (W33°) **E.B.B. to R.B.**

_____

[*July 21, 1845.*]

Monday.

But I never *did* strike you or touch you—& you are not in earnest in the complaint you make—& this is really all I am going to say to-day. What I said before was wrung from me by words on your part, which you know far too well how to speak so as to make them go deepest, & which sometimes it becomes impossible, or overhard to bear without deprecation :—as when, for instance, you talk of being "grateful" to *me!!*—Well! I will try that there shall be no more of it—no more pro-vocation of generosities—& so, (this once) as you express it, I 'will not have the heart to blame' you[1]

except for reading my books against my will, which was very wrong indeed. Mr. Kenyon asked me, I remember, (he had a mania of sending my copybook literature round the world to this person & that person—& I was roused at last into binding him by a vow to do so no more) I remember he asked me . . "Is Mr. Browning to be excepted "—to which I answered that nobody was to be excepted—& thus he was quite right in resisting to the death . . or to dinner-time . . just as you were quite wrong ⸝after dinner⸝. Now, could a woman have been more curious?—Could the very author of the book have done worse? But I leave my sins & yours gladly, to get into the Hood poems which have delighted me so—& first to the St. Praxed's which is of course the finest & most powerful . . & indeed full of the power of life . . and of death. It has impressed me very much. Then the 'Angel & Child,' with all its beauty & significance!—and the 'Garden Fancies' . . some of the stanzas about the name of the flower, with such exquisite music in them, & grace of every kind—& with that beautiful & musical use of the word 'meandering,' which I never remember having seen ⸝used⸝ in relation to *sound* before. It does to mate with your '*simmering* quiet' in Sordello,[2] which brings the summer air into the room as sure as you read it. Then I like your burial of the pedant so much!—you have quite the damp smell of funguses and the sense of creeping things through and through it. And the Laboratory is hideous as you meant to make it:—only I object a little to your tendency . . which is almost a habit . . & is very observable in this poem I think, . . of making lines difficult for the reader to read . . see the opening lines of this poem. Not that ⟨you want⟩ music ↑is required↓ everywhere, nor in *them* certainly, but that ↑the uncertainty of rhythm↓ throws the reader's mind off the *rail* . . & interrupts ↑his progress with you and↓ your influence with him. Where we have not direct pleasure from rhythm, ⟨we⟩ & where no peculiar impression is to be produced by the changes in it, we sh^d be encouraged by the poet to *forget it altogether;* should we not? I am quite wrong perhaps—but you see how I do not conceal my wrongnesses where they mix themselves ↑up↓ with my sincere impressions. And how c^d it be that no one within my hearing ever spoke of these poems? Because it is true that I never saw one of them—never!—except the 'Tokay,' which is inferior to all; ↑& that↓ I was quite unaware of your having ⟨written⟩ printed so much with Hood—or at all, except this 'Tokay,' & this 'Duchess'! The world is very deaf & dumb, I think—but in the end, we need not be afraid of its not learning its lesson.

Could you come—for I am going out in the carriage, & will not stay to write of your poems even, any more to-day—could you come on thursday or friday (the day left to your choice) instead of on wednesday? If I could help it I w^d not say so—it is not a caprice. And I leave it to you, whether thursday or friday. And Alexandria seems discredited just now for Malta—and 'anything but Madeira,' I go on saying to myself. These *Hood* poems are all to be in the next 'Bells' of course—of necessity?

May God bless you my dear friend, my ever dear friend!—

E. B. B.

1. This unconventional break in the text occurs in the manuscript letter.
2. "Flittered in the cool some azure damsel-fly / Born of the simmering quiet, there to die." *Sordello*, I, 909–910.

65 *(W33)*   **R.B. to E.B.B.**

[*July 22, 1845.*]

Tuesday M^g

I will say, with your leave, Thursday—(nor attempt to say anything else without your leave)—

The temptation of reading the 'Essay' was more than I could bear: and a wonderful work it is every way—the other poems and their music —wonderful!

And you go out still—so continue better!

I cannot write this morning—I should say too much and have to be sorry and afraid—let me be safely yours ever, my own dear friend—

R. B.

I am but too proud of your praise—when will the blame come— at Malta?

The following letter was written the day after the visit noted on the envelope of Letter 64:

+ Thursday 24 July
3–4¼ p.m.

66 *(W34°)*   **E.B.B. to R.B.**

[*July 25, 1845.*]

Are you any better to-day? and will you say just the truth of it? & not attempt to do any of the writing which does harm—nor of the reading even, which may do harm—and something does harm to you, you see—& you told me not long ago that you knew how to avoid the harm .. now did you not? & what could it have been last week which you did not avoid, & which made you so unwell? Beseech you not to think that I am going to aid & abet in this wronging of yourself, for I will not indeed—& I am only sorry to have given you my querulous queries[1] yesterday . . & to have omitted to say in relation to them, too, how they were to be accepted in any case as just passing thoughts of mine for *your* passing thoughts, . . some right, it may be . . some wrong, it must be . . & none, insisted on even by the thinker!—just impressions, & by no means pretending to be judgments—now WILL you understand? Also, I intended (as a proof of my fallacy) to strike out one or two of my doubts before I gave the paper to you—so *whichever strikes you as the most foolish of them, of course must be what I meant to strike out*—(there's ingenuity for you!—) ⟨It⟩ The poem did, for the rest, as will be suggested to you, give me the very greatest pleasure, & astonish me in two ways . . by the versification, mechanically considered,—& by the successful evolution of pure beauty from all that roughness & rudeness of the son of the boar-pinner . . successfully evolved, without softening one hoarse accent of his voice. But there is to be a pause now—you will not write any more—no, nor come here on wednesday . . if coming into the roar of this London should make the pain worse, as I cannot help thinking it must—& you were not well yesterday morning, you admitted. You *will* take care? And if there sh^d be a wisdom in going away . . !

　　Was it very wrong of me, doing what I told you of yesterday?[2] Very imprudent, I am afraid—but I never knew how to be prudent—& then, there is not a sharing of responsibility in any sort of imaginable measure,—but a mere going away of so many thoughts, apart from the thinker, or of words, apart from the thinker, . . just as I might give away a pocket-handkerchief to be newly marked & mine no longer. I did not do—& w^d not have done, . . one of those papers singly. It w^d have been unbecoming of me in every way. It was simply a writing of notes . . of slips of paper . . now on one subject, & now on another . . which were thrown into the great cauldron & boiled up with other matter,—& re-translated from my idiom where there seemed a need for it. And I am not much afraid of being ever guessed at . . except by those Œdipuses who astounded me once for a moment & were after all, I hope, baffled by the Sphinx—or ever betrayed; because besides the black Stygian oaths & indubitable honour of the editor, he has some interest, even as I have the greatest, in being silent & secret. And nothing IS MINE . . if something is *of me* . . or *from* me, rather. Yet it was wrong & foolish, I see plainly—wrong in all but the motives. How dreadful to write against time, & with a side ways running conscience!—And then the literature of the day was wider than his knowledge, all round! And the booksellers were barking distraction on every side!—I had some of the mottos to find too! But the paper relating to you I never was consulted about—or in *one particular way* it w^d have been better,—as easily it might have been. May God bless you, my dear friend, E. B. B.

1. This is E.B.B.'s first reference to her influential role as critic before the fact of *Dramatic Romances and Lyrics*. Besides the remarks in these letters, she wrote fifty-six manuscript pages covering that collection and *Luria* and *A Soul's Tragedy (Browning Collections*, p. 32, Lot #143). A somewhat inaccurate transcription in *New Poems by Robert Browning and Elizabeth Barrett Browning*, ed. F. G. Kenyon (London: Smith, Elder & Co., 1914) is reprinted in the Macmillan edition of Browning's works. The major item in the fifty-six pages, however—eleven and one-half devoted to *The Flight of the Duchess*—were somehow omitted and have never been printed. The original papers are now in the possession of Dr. Frederic Palmer, who kindly allowed the editor to inspect but not to publish them. See Frederic Palmer and Edward Snyder, "New Light on the Brownings," *Quarterly Review*, CCLXIX (July 1937), 48–63.

2. E.B.B. is speaking here of her participation in Horne's *New Spirit of the Age*. Particularly in the papers on Carlyle, Landor, and Tennyson, Horne drew heavily on her contributions. *Letters of EBB to RHH*, I, 131–272; II, 1–57; Letter 373 and its note 3.

67 (W34)   R.B. to E.B.B.

[*July 25, 1845.*]

Friday Morning.

You would let me *now*, I dare say, call myself grateful to you—yet such is my jealousy in these matters,—so do I hate the material when it puts down, (or tries,) the immaterial in the offices of friendship; that I could almost tell you I was *not* grateful, and try if that way I could make you see the substantiality of those other favours you refuse to recognise, and reality of the other gratitude you will not admit. But truth is truth, and you are all generosity, and will draw none but the fair inference, so I thank you as well as I can for this *also*—this last kindness. And you know its value, too—how if there were another *you* in the world, who had done all you have done and whom I merely admired for that; if such an one had sent me such a criticism, so exactly what I want and can use and turn to good; you know how I would have told you, my *you* I saw yesterday, all about it; and been sure of your sympathy and gladness:— but the two in one!

For the criticism itself, it is all true, except the overrating—all the suggestions are to be adopted, the improvements accepted: I so thoroughly understand your spirit in this, that, just in this beginning, I should really like to have found some point in which I could coöperate with your intention, and help my work by disputing the effect of any alteration proposed, if it ought to be disputed—*that* would answer your purpose exactly as well as agreeing with you,—so that the benefit to me were apparent; but this time I cannot dispute one point—All is for best.

So much for this "Duchess"—which I shall ever rejoice in—wherever was a bud, even, in that strip of May-bloom, a live musical bee hangs now. I shall let it lie, (my poem) till just before I print it; and then go over it, alter at the places, and do something for the places where I (really) wrote anyhow, almost, to get done. It is an odd fact, yet characteristic of my accomplishings one and all in this kind, that of *the poem,* the real conception of an evening (two years ago; fully)—of *that,* not a line is written,[1]—tho' perhaps after all, what I am going to call the accessories in the story are real though indirect reflexes of the original idea, and so supersede properly enough the necessity of its personal appearance,—so to speak: but, as I conceived the poem, it consisted entirely of the gipsy's description of the life the Lady was to lead with her future gipsy lover—a *real* life, not an unreal one like that with the Duke—and as I meant to write it, all their wild adventures would have come out and the insignificance of the former vegetation have been deducible only—as the main subject has become now—of course it comes to the same thing, for one would never show half by half like a cut orange.—

Will you write to me?—caring, though, so much for my best interests as not to write if you can work for yourself, or save yourself fatigue: I *think* before writing . . or just after writing,—such a sentence,—but reflection only justifies my first feeling; I WOULD rather go without your letters, without seeing you at all, if that advantaged you—my dear, first and last friend; my friend! And now—surely I might dare say you may if you please get well thro' God's goodness—with persevering patience, surely—and this next winter abroad—which you must get ready for now, every sunny day, will you not? If I venture to weary you again with all this, is there not the cause of causes, and did not the prophet write that "there was a tide in the affairs of men, which taken at the E. B. B." led on to the fortune[2] of Your R. B.

Oh, let me tell you in the bitterness of my heart, that it was only

4 o'clock—that clock I enquired about—and that, . . no, I shall never say with any grace what I want to say . . and now dare not . . that you all but owe me an extra quarter of an hour next time: so in the East you give a beggar something for a few days running—then you miss him; and next day he looks indignant when the regular dole falls and murmurs— "And, for yesterday?"—Do I stay too long, I WANT to know,—too long for the voice and head and all but the spirit that may not so soon tire,—knowing the good it does. If you would but tell me. God bless you—R. B.

1. Browning began *The Flight of the Duchess* in 1842, was interrupted at his work, and finally followed a suggestion by his friend Kinglake for concluding it—or so he told Dr. Furnivall (Hood, p. 217). Palmer and Snyder (note 1 to the preceding letter) suggest that the poem was really a calculated move in the complicated courtship.
2. An allusion to *Julius Caesar* IV. iii. 216–217.

68 (W35°)   E.B.B. to R.B.

───────────────

[*July 26, 1845.*]

Saturday.

    You say too much indeed in this letter which has crossed mine—& particularly as there is not a word in it of what I most wanted to know & want to know . . *how you are*—for you must observe, if you please, that the very paper you pour such kindness on, was written after your own example & pattern, when, in the matter of my Prometheus, (such different wearying matter!), you took trouble for me & did me good. Judge from this, if even in inferior things, there can be gratitude from you to me!—or rather, do not judge—but listen when I say that I am delighted to have met your wishes in writing as I wrote; only that you are surely wrong in refusing to see a single wrongness in all that heap of weedy thoughts, & that when you look again, you must come to the admission of it. One of the thistles is the suggestion about the line
            'Was it singing, was it saying,'[1]
which you wrote so, & which I proposed to amend by an intermediate

'or.' Thinking of it at a distance, it grows clear to me that you were right, & that there should be and must be no 'or' to disturb the listening pause. Now *sh^d* there? And there was something else, which I forget at this moment—& something more than the something else. Your account of the production of the poem interests me very much—& proves just what I wanted to make out from your statements the other day, & they refused, I thought, to let me, . . that you are more faithful to your first *Idea* than to your first *plan*. Is it so? or not? 'Orange' is orange—but *which half* of the orange is not predestinated from all eternity—: is it *so?*

    Sunday.—I wrote so much yesterday & then went out, not knowing very well how to speak or how to be silent (is it better today?) of some expressions of yours . . & of your interest in me—which are deeply affecting to my feelings—whatever else remains to be said of them. And you know that you make great mistakes, . . of fennel for hemlock,[2] of four oclocks for five oclocks, & of other things of more consequence, one for another; & may not be quite right besides as to my getting well '*if I please!*' . . which reminds me a little of what Papa says sometimes when he comes into this room unexpectedly & convicts me of having dry toast for dinner, & declares angrily that obstinacy & dry toast have brought me to my present condition, & that if I *pleased* to have porter & beefsteaks instead, I sh^d be as well as ever I was, in a month! . . But where is the need of talking of it? What I wished to say was this—that if I get better or worse . . as long as I live & to the last moment of life, I shall remember with an emotion which cannot change its character, all the generous interest & feeling you have spent on me—*wasted* on me I was going to write—but I would not provoke any answering—& in one obvious sense, it need not be so. I never shall forget these things, my dearest friend; nor remember them more coldly. God's goodness!—I believe in it, as in His sunshine here—which makes my head ache a little, while it comes in at the window, & makes most other people gayer—it does *me* good too in a different way. And so, may God bless you! & me in this . . just this, . . that I may never have the sense, . . intolerable in the remotest apprehension of it . . of being, in any way, directly or indirectly, the means of ruffling your smooth path by so much as one of my flint-stones!—In the meantime you do not tire me indeed even when you go later for sooner . . & I do not tire myself even when I write longer & duller letters to you (if the last is possible) than the one I am ending now . . as the most grateful (leave me that word) of your friends. E. B. B.

[How c^d you think that I sh^d speak to Mr. Kenyon of the book? All I ever said to him has been that you had looked through my Prometheus for me—& that I was *not 'disappointed in you,'* these two things on two occasions. I do trust that your head is better.]^3

    1. *The Flight of the Duchess,* l. 512. Despite this recantation, Browning made the proposed emendation.
    2. See Letter 55.
    3. Added at the top of the first page.

69 (W35)   R.B. to E.B.B.

[*Monday, July 28, 1845.*]

    How must I feel, & what can, or could I say even if you let me say all? I am most grateful, most happy—most happy, come what will!
    Will you let me try and answer your note to-morrow . . before Wednesday when I am to see you? I will not hide from you that my head aches now; and I have let the hours go by one after one—I am better all the same, and will write as I say—"Am I better" you ask!
    Yours I am, ever yours my dear friend R. B.

    The quarter hour lost on July 24, of which Browning complained at the close of Letter 67, was recovered at this point; he marked the time of his call on the envelope of Letter 68:
        + Wednesday July 30
        3-4$\frac{3}{4}$ p.m.

70 (W36)   R.B. to E.B.B.

[*July 31, 1845.*]

                                  Thursday.
In all I say to you, write to you, I know very well that I trust to

your understanding me almost beyond the warrant of any human capacity—but as I began, so I shall end. I shall believe you remember what I
am forced to remember—you who do me the superabundant justice on
every possible occasion,—you will never do me injustice when I sit by
you and talk about Italy and the rest.

     —To-day I cannot write—tho' I am very well otherwise—but I
shall soon get into my old self-command and write with as much
"ineffectual fire" as before: but meantime, *you* will write to me, I hope
—telling me how you are? I have but one greater delight in the world
than in hearing from you.

     God bless you, my best, dearest friend—think what I would speak—

Ever yours
R. B.

71 (W 36°)   *E.B.B. to R.B.*

———————————

[*July 31, 1845.*]

Thursday.

     Let me write one word .. not to have it off my mind .. because it is
by no means heavily *on* it; but lest I sh^d forget to write it at all by not
writing it at once. What could you mean, .. I have been thinking since
you went away, .. by applying such a grave expression as having a thing
'off your mind' to that foolish subject of the stupid book, (mine)[1] & by
making it worth your while to account logically for your wish about
my not mentioning it to Mr. Kenyon? You could not fancy for one
moment that I was vexed in the matter of the book?—or in the other
matter of your wish?—Now just hear me. I explained to you that I had
been silent to Mr. Kenyon, first because the fact was so,—& next & a
little, because I wanted to show how I anticipated your wish by a wish
of my own .. though from a different motive ⟨perhaps⟩. *Your* motive I
really did take to be (never suspecting my dear kind cousin of treason) to
be a natural reluctancy of being convicted (forgive me!) of such an
arch-womanly curiosity. For my own motive .. motives .. they are
more than one .. you must trust me,—& refrain as far as you can from
accusing me of an over-love of Eleusinian mysteries when I ask you to

say just as little about your visits here & of me as you find possible, . .
even to Mr. Kenyon . . as *to every other person whatever.* As you know . . &
yet more than you know . . I am in a peculiar position—& it does not
follow that you should be ashamed of my friendship or that I should not
be proud of yours, if we avoid making it a subject of conversation in
high places, or low places . . There! *that* is my request to you—or commentary on what you put 'off your mind' yesterday—probably quite
unnecessary as either request or commentary; yet said on the chance of
its not being so,—because you seemed to mistake my remark about
Mr. Kenyon.

And your head? how is it? And do consider if it would not be wise
& right on that account of your health, to go with Mr. Chorley? You
can neither work nor enjoy while you are subject to attacks of the kind—
& besides, & without reference to your present suffering & inconvenience, you *ought not* to let them master you & gather strength from time
& habit; I am sure you ought not. Worse last week than ever, you see!—
And no prospect, perhaps, of bringing out your bells this autumn, without paying a cost too heavy!—Therefore . . the *therefore* is quite plain
and obvious!—

Friday [August 1, 1845].—Just as it is how anxious Flush & I
⟨‖ · · · ‖⟩ ↑are↓, to be delivered from you, . . by these sixteen heads of the
discourse of one of us, written before your letter came. Ah, but I am
serious—& you will consider—will you not?—what is best to be done?
& do it—you could write to me, you know, from the end of the world,
—if you could take the thought of me so far,—

And *for* me—no—& yet yes,—I *will* say /so⟩this/ much—for I am
not inclined to do you injustice, but justice, when you come here—the
justice of wondering to myself how you can possibly, possibly, care to
come—Which is true enough to be *unanswerable*, if you please—or I
should not say it. '*As I began, so I shall end*—' ⟨‖ · · · · · ‖⟩ Did you, as I
hope you did, thank your sister for Flush & for me? When you were
gone, he graciously signified his intention of eating the cakes—brought
the bag to me & emptied it without a drawback, from my hand, cake
after cake. And I forgot the basket once again—

And talking of Italy & the cardinals, and thinking of some cardinal
points you are ignorant of, did you ever hear that I was one of
'those schismatiques
of Amsterdam'[2]

whom your Dr. Donne w^d have put into the dykes?—unless he meant the Baptists, instead of the Independents, the holders of the Independent church principle. No—not "*schismatical*," I hope—hating as I do from the roots of my heart all that rending of the garment of Christ, which Christians are so apt to make the daily week-day of this Christianity so called—& caring very little for most dogmas & doxies in themselves—too little, as people say to me sometimes, (when they send me 'New Testaments' to learn from, with very kind intentions—) & believing that there is only one church in heaven & earth, with /the⟩one/ divine High Priest to it,—let exclusive religionists build what walls they please & bring out what chrisms—But I used to go with my father always, when I was able, to the nearest dissenting chapel of the Congregational-ists—from liking the simplicity of that praying and speaking without books—& a little too from disliking the theory of state churches. There is a narrowness among the dissenters which is wonderful,—an arid, grey Puritanism in the clefts of their souls: but it seems to me clear that they know what the "liberty of Christ" *means,* far better than those do who call themselves 'churchmen'; & ⟨so⟩ stand altogether, as a body, on higher ground. And so, you see, when I talked of the sixteen points of my discourse, it was the /preshadowing⟩forshadowing/ of a coming event, & you have had it at last in the /full⟩whole/ length & breadth of it. But it is not my fault if the wind began to blow so that I could not go out—as I intended—as I shall do to-morrow; and that you have received my dulness ⟨mixed⟩ in a full libation of it, in consequence. My sisters said of /your⟩the/ roses you blasphemed ⟨‖···‖⟩ yesterday, that they "never saw such flowers anywhere—anywhere here in London—" & therefore if I had thought so myself before, it was not so wrong of me— I put your roses, you see, against my letter, to make it seem less dull—& yet I do not forget what you say about caring to hear from me—I mean, I do not *affect* to forget it.

May God bless you, far longer than I can say so—E. B. B.

1. Probably Browning's reading the *Essay on Mind.* See Letter 63.
2. Donne's *The Will,* st. iii.

[*August 3, 1845.*]

Sunday Evening.

I said what you comment on, about Mr. Kenyon, because I feel I *must* always tell you the simple truth—and not being quite at liberty to communicate the whole story—(tho' it would at once clear me from the charge of over-curiosity . . if I much cared for *that!*)—I made my first request in order to prevent your getting at any part of it from *him* which should make my witholding seem disingenuous for the moment —that is, till my explanation came, if it had an opportunity of coming: and then, when I fancied you were misunderstanding the reason of that request—and supposing I was ambitious of making a higher figure in *his* eyes than your own,—I then felt it "on my mind" and so spoke . . a natural mode of relief surely! For, dear friend, I have *once* been *untrue* to you—when, and how, and why, you know—but I thought it pedantry and worse to hold by my words and increase their faults: you have for-given me that one mistake, and I only refer to it now because if you should ever make *that* a precedent, and put any least, most trivial word of mine under the same category, you would wrong me as you never wronged human being:—and that is done with. For the other matter,— the talk of my visits,—it is impossible that any hint of them can ooze out of the only three persons in the world to whom I ever speak of them— my father, mother and sister—to whom ⟨the⟩ my appreciation of your works is no novelty since some years, and whom I made comprehend exactly your position and the necessity for the absolute silence I enjoined respecting the permission to see you: you may depend on them,—and Miss Mitford is in your keeping, mind,—and dear Mr. Kenyon, if there should be never so gentle a touch of "garrulous God-innocence"[1] about those kind lips of his. Come, let me snatch at *that* clue out of the maze, and say how perfect, absolutely perfect, are those three or four pages in the "Vision" which present the Poets—a line, a few words, and the man there,—one twang of the bow and the arrowhead in the white— Shelley's "white ideal all statue-blind" is—perfect,—how can I coin words? And dear deaf old Hesiod—and—all, all are perfect, perfect! But "the Moon's regality will hear no praise"—well then, will she hear

142

blame? Can it be you, my own you past putting away, *you* are a schismatic and frequenter of Independent Dissenting Chapels? And you confess this to *me*—whose father and mother went this morning to the very Independent Chapel where they took me, all those years back, to be baptized—and where they heard, this morning, a sermon preached by the very minister who officiated on that other occasion! Now will you be particularly encouraged by this successful instance to bring forward any other point of disunion between us that may occur to you? Please do not—for so sure as you begin proving that there is a gulf fixed between us, so sure shall I end proving that . . . Anne Radcliffe[2] avert it! . . that you are just my sister: not that I am much frightened, but there are such surprizes in novels!—Blame the next,—& yes, now this *is* to be real blame!—and I meant to call your attention to it before: why, why, do you blot out, in that unutterably provoking manner, whole lines, not to say words, in your letters—(and in the criticism on the "Duchess")—if it is a fact that you have a second thought, does it cease to be as genuine a fact, that first thought you please to efface? Why give a thing and take a thing? Is there no significance in putting on record that your first impression was to a certain effect and your next to a certain other, perhaps completely opposite one? If any proceeding of yours could go near to deserve that harsh word "impertinent" which you have twice, in speech and writing, been pleased to apply to your observations on me,—certainly *this* does go as near as can be—as there is but one step to take from Southampton pier to New York quay, for travellers Westward. Now will you lay this to heart and perpend—lest in my righteous indignation I ⟨‖ · · · ‖⟩! For my own health—it improves, thank you! And I shall go abroad all in good time, never fear: for my Bells, Mr. Chorley tells me there is no use in the world of printing them before November at earliest —and by that time I shall get done with these Romances and certainly one Tragedy[3] (*that* could go to press next week)—in proof of which I ⟨‖ · · · ‖⟩ ↑will↓ bring you, if you let me, a few more hundreds of lines next Wednesday: but, 'my poet,' if I would, as is true, sacrifice all my works to do your fingers, even, good—what would I not offer up to prevent you staying . . . perhaps to correct my very verses . . perhaps read and answer my very letters . . staying the production of more Berthas and Caterinas and Geraldines, more great and beautiful poems of which I shall be—how proud! Do not be punctual in paying tithes of thyme, mint, anise and cummin, and leaving unpaid the real weighty dues of the Law;[4] nor affect a scrupulous acknowledgment of "what you owe me" in petty manners, while you leave me to settle such a charge, as accessory to the hiding the Talent, as best I can! I have thought of this again and again, and would have spoken of it to you, had I ever felt myself fit to speak of any subject nearer home and me and you than Rome and Cardinal Acton[5]—for, observe, you have not done . . yes, the Prometheus, no doubt . . but with that exception *have* you written much lately, as much as last year when "you wrote all your best things" you said, I think? Yet you are better now than then. Dearest friend, *I* intend to write more, and very likely be praised more, now I care less than ever for it, but still more to [do] I look to have you ever before me, in your place, and with more poetry and more praise still, and my own heartfelt praise ever on the top, like a flower on the water. I have said nothing of yesterday's storm . . *thunder* . . may you not have been out in it! The evening draws in, and I will walk out. May God bless you, and let you hold me by the hand till the end—Yes, dearest friend!

R. B.

1. E.B.B.'s *A Vision of Poets* (1844), l. 297; by "three or four pages" to which Browning later refers, he means from that line to 497. Hesiod is at line 310, Shelley at 406.
2. Mrs. Radcliffe (1764–1823), the Gothic novelist.
3. *A Soul's Tragedy;* see Letter 9.
4. Matthew 23:23.
5. Charles Januarius Edward Acton (1803–47), the son of a baronet, had become a cardinal in 1842.

A note on the envelope of Letter 71 records a visit at this point:
+ Wednesday Aug. 6
$3-4\frac{1}{2}$

73 (W37°)   E.B.B. to R.B.

[*Postmarked August 8, 1845.*]

Just to show what may be lost by my crossings out, I will tell you the story of the one in the 'Duchess'—& in fact it is almost worth telling

to a metaphysician like you, on other grounds, that you may draw perhaps some psychological good from the absurdity of it. Hear, then.
When I had done writing the sheet of annotations & reflections on your
poem I took up my pencil to correct the passages reflected on with the
reflections, by the crosses you may observe, just glancing over the writing as I did so. Well! and, where that erasure is, I found a line purporting
to be extracted from your 'Duchess,' with sundry acute criticisms &
objections quite undeniably strong, following after it,— only, to my
amazement, as I looked & looked, the line so acutely objected to & purporting, as I say, to be taken from the 'Duchess,' was by no means to be
found in the Duchess, . . nor anything like it, . . & I am certain indeed
that, in the Duchess or out of it, you never wrote such a bad line in your
life. And so it became a proved thing to me that I had been enacting, in a
mystery, both poet & critic together—& one so neutralizing the other,
that I took all that pains you remark upon to cross myself out in my
double capacity, . . & am now telling the story of it notwithstanding.
And there's an obvious moral to the myth, isn't there?—for critics who
bark the loudest, commonly bark at their own shadow in the glass, as
my Flush used to do long & loud, before he gained experience & learnt
the $\gamma\nu\hat{\omega}\theta\iota$ $\sigma\epsilon\alpha\upsilon\tau\acute{o}\nu$[1] in the apparition of the brown dog with the glittering dilating eyes, . . & as *I* did, under the erasure. And another moral
springs up of itself in this productive ground; for, you see, . . 'quand je
m'efface il n'y a pas grand mal'[2]

And I am to be made to work very hard,—am I?—But you should
remember that if I did as much writing as last summer, I should not be
able to do much else, . . I mean, to go out & walk about . . for really I
think I *could* manage to read your poems & write as I am writing now,
with ever so much head-work of my own going on at the same time.
But the bodily exercise is different—& I do confess that the novelty of
living more in the outer life for the last few months than I have done for
years before, make me idle & inclined to be idle—& everybody is idle
sometimes—even *you* perhaps—are you not?—For me, you know, I do
carpet-work . . ask Mrs. Jameson[3]—& I never pretend to be in a perpetual motion of mental industry. Still it may not be quite as bad as you
think: I have done some work since Prometheus—only it is nothing
worth speaking of & not a part of the romance-poem which is to be
some day if I live for it—lyrics for the most part, which lie written illeg-
ibly in pure Ægyptian—oh, there is time enough, & too much perhaps!

& so let me be idle a little now, & enjoy your poems while I can. It is pure enjoyment & must be—but you do not know how much, or you would not talk as you do sometimes . . so wide of any possible application.

And do *not* talk again of what you would 'sacrifice' for ME. If you affect me by it, which is true, you cast me from you farther than ever in the next thought—*That* is true.

The poems . . yours . . which you left with me . . are full of various power & beauty & character, & you must let me have my own gladness from them in my own way.

Now I must end this letter. Did you go to Chelsea & hear the divine philosophy?

Tell me the truth always . . will you? I mean such truths as may be painful to me *though* truths . .

May God bless you, ever dear friend.

E. B. B.

1. "Know thyself."
2. A pun; the literal meaning is "It is no great harm when I blot myself," the idiomatic "It is no great harm when I stay in the background."
3. See Letter 56.

74 (W38)   R.B. to E.B.B.

[*August 8, 1845.*]

Friday Afternoon.

Then there is one more thing "off my mind": I thought it might be with you as with *me*—not remembering how different are the causes that operate against us; different in kind as in degree:—(*so* much reading hurts me, for instance,—whether the reading be light or heavy, fiction or fact, and *so* much writing, whether my own, such as you have seen, or the merest compliment-returning to the weary tribe that exact it of one). But your health—that before all! . . as assuring all eventually . . and ⁺on⁺ the other accounts you must know! Never, pray, *pray,* never lose one sunny day or propitious hour to 'go out or walk about'—But do not surprise *me*, one of these mornings, by "walking" up to me when I am introduced . . or I shall infallibly, in spite of all the after repentance and begging pardon,—I shall ⟨‖ · · · ‖⟩ . . so here you learn the first 'painful truth' I have it in my power to tell you!

I sent you the last of our poor roses this morning—considering that I fairly owed that kindness to them.

Yes, I went to Chelsea and found dear Carlyle alone—his wife is in the country where he will join her as soon as his ↑book's↓ last sheet returns corrected and fit for press—which will be at the month's end about —He was all kindness and talked like his own self while he made me tea—and, afterward, brought chairs into the little yard, rather than garden, and smoked his pipe with apparent relish; at night he would walk as far as Vauxhall Bridge on my way home.

If I used the word "sacrifice," you do well to object—I can imagine nothing ever to be done by me worthy such a name.

God bless you, dearest friend—shall I hear from you before Tuesday?

Ever your own R.B.

75 (W 38°)   *E.B.B. to R.B.*

———————————

[*August 8, 1845.*]

Friday.

It is very kind to send these flowers—too kind—why are they sent? and without one single word . . which is not too kind certainly. I looked down into the heart of the roses & turned the carnations over & over to the peril of their leaves, & in vain! Not a word do I deserve to-day, I suppose!—And yet if I dont, I dont deserve the flowers either. There should have been an equal justice done to my demerits, O Zeus with the scales!

After all I do thank you for these flowers—& they are beautiful—& they came just in a right current of time, just when I wanted them, or something like them—so I confess *that* humbly, & do thank you, at last, rather as I ought to do. Only you ought not to give away all the flowers of your garden to *me;* & your sister thinks so, be sure . . if as silently as you sent them. Now I shall not write any more, not having been written to. What with the wednesday's flowers & these, you may think how I in this room, look down on the gardens of Damascus, let *your Jew*[1] say what he pleases of *them*—& the wednesday's flowers are as fresh & beautiful, I must explain, as the new ones. They were quite supererogatory . . the new ones . . in the sense of being flowers. Now, the sense of what I am writing seems questionable, does it not?—at least, more so, than the nonsense of it.

  Not a word—even under the little blue flowers!!!—

                                                           E. B. B.—

1. A manuscript notation by Browning identifies "R[abbi] Benjamin of Tudela," whose twelfth-century *Massa'oth (Itinerary)* is an account of his travels from Spain to the frontiers of China. The Rabbi says of Damascus: "[It] is very large and handsome, enclosed by a wall and surrounded by beautiful country, which in a circuit of fifteen miles presents the richest gardens and orchards, in such quantity and beauty as to be without equal upon earth." (*The Itinerary of Benjamin of Tudela,* tr. and ed. by A. Asher, 2 vols.; London and Berlin, 1840–41.)

76 (*W39*)   R.B. to E.B.B.

                        ─────────────────

                      [*August 10, 1845.*]

                                                   Sunday Afternoon.

  How good you are to the smallest thing I try and do—(to show I *would* please you for an instant if I could, rather than from any hope such poor efforts as I am restricted to, ↑can please↓ you or ought.) And that you should care for the note that was not there!—But I was surprised by the summons to seal & deliver, since time & the carrier were peremptory—and so, I dared divine, almost, I should hear from you by our mid-day post—which happened—and the answer to *that*, you received on Friday Night, did you not? I had to go to Holborn, of all places,—not to pluck strawberries in the Bishop's Garden like Richard Crouchback,[1] but to get a book—and there I carried my note, thinking to expedite its delivery: this notelet of yours, quite as little in its kind as my blue flowers, —this came last evening—and here are my thanks, dear E. B. B.— dear friend.

  In the former note there is a phrase I must not forget to call on you to account for—that where it confesses to having done "some work— only nothing worth speaking of." Just see,—will you be first and only

compact-breaker? Nor misunderstand me here, please . . as I said, I am
quite rejoiced that you go out now, "walk about" now, and put off the
writing that will follow thrice as abundantly, all because of the stopping
to gather strength . . so I want no new word, not to say poem, not to say
the romance-poem—let the "finches in the shrubberies grow restless in
the dark "[2]—*I* am inside with the lights and music: but what is done, is
done, *pas vrai?* And "worth" is, dear my friend, pardon me, not in your
arbitration quite.

Let me tell you an odd thing that happened at Chorley's the other
night: I must have ⟨‖ · · · ‖⟩ ₊mentioned to you that₊ I forget my own
verses so surely after they are once on paper, that I ought, without affectation, to mend them infinitely better, able as I am to bring fresh eyes to
bear on them—(when I say "once on paper" that is just what I mean
and no more, for after the sad revising begins they do leave their mark,
distinctly or less so according to circumstances)—well, Miss Cushman,[3]
the new American actress (clever and truthful-looking) was talking of a
new novel by the Dane Andersen, he of the "Improvvisatore," which
will reach us, it should seem, in translation, *viâ* America—she had
looked over two or three proofs of the work in the press, and Chorley
was anxious to know something about its character. The Title, she said,
was capital—"Only a Fiddler!"[4]—and she enlarged on that word,
"Only," and its significance, so put: and I quite agreed with her for
several minutes, till first one reminiscence flitted to me, then another
and at last I was obliged to stop my praises and say "but, now I think of
it, *I* seem to have written something with a similar title—nay, a play, I
believe—yes, and in five acts—"Only an Actress"—and from that time,
some two years or more ago to this, I have been every way relieved of
it"!—And when I got home, next morning, I made a dark pocket in
my russett horror of a portfolio give up its dead—and there fronted me
"Only a Player-girl" (the real title) and the sayings and doings of her,
and the others—such others! So I made haste and just tore out one sample-
page, being Scene the First, and sent it to our friend as earnest & proof I
had not been purely dreaming, as might seem to ⟨‖ · · · ‖⟩ ₊be₊ the case.
And what makes me recall it now is, that it was Russian, and about a fair
on the Neva, and booths and droshkies and fish-pies and so forth, with
the Palaces in the background: and in Chorley's "Athenæum" of yesterday you may read a paper of *very* simple moony stuff about the death
of Alexander, and that Sir James Wylie[5] I have seen at St. Petersburgh

(where he chose to mistake me for an Italian—"M. l'Italien" he said ⟨‖···‖⟩ ↟another time↡, looking up from his cards) . . So I think to tell you.

Now I may leave off—I shall see you start, on Tuesday—hear perhaps something definite about your travelling.

Do you know, "Consuelo"[6] wearies me—oh, wearies—and the fourth volume I have all but stopped at—there lie the three following: but who cares about Consuelo after that horrible evening with the Venetian scamp, ↟(where he bullies her, and it does answer, after all she says)↡ as we say? And Albert wearies too—it seems all false, all writing—(not the first part, though). And what easy work these novelists have of it! a Dramatic poet has to *make* you love or admire his men and women, —they must *do* and *say* all that you are to see and hear—really do it in your face, say it in your ears, and it is wholly for *you*, in *your* power, to *name*, characterize and so praise or blame, *what* is so said and done . . ↟if you don't perceive of yourself,↡ there is no standing by, for the Author, and telling you: but with these novelists, a scrape of the pen—out blurting of a phrase, and the miracle is achieved—"Consuelo possessed to perfection this and the other gift"—what would you more? Or, to leave dear George Sand, pray think of Bulwer's beginning a "character" by informing you that Ione, or somebody in "Pompeii,"[7] "was endowed with *perfect* genius"—"genius"! What tho' the obliging informer might write his fingers off before he gave the pitifullest proof that the poorest spark of that same, that genius, had ever visited *him?* *Ione* has it "*perfectly*"—perfectly—and that is enough! Zeus with the scales? with the false weights!

And now—till Tuesday good bye, and be willing to get well as★ soon as may be! and may God bless you, ever dear friend.

R. B.

★—letting me send *porter* instead of flowers—and beefsteaks too—

1. *Richard III* III. iv. 31–33.
2. *Lady Geraldine's Courtship*, st. xxi.
3. Charlotte Cushman (1816–76) had toured America with Macready in 1843–44, scoring notable triumphs in tragedy. She was making her first English tour in 1845.
4. Published in Danish in 1837, in Mary Howitt's English translation in 1845.
5. Wylie (1768–1854), an Englishman, was physician to the Russian court from 1798 until his death. The *Athenæum* (August 2 and 9) printed "The Last Days of the

Emperor Alexander," by Robert Lee, M.D., F.R.S., in which Wylie figures prominently. Mrs. Orr (p. 7) tells a variant of this story.

    6. The George Sand novel mentioned by E.B.B. in Letter 56.

    7. Bulwer-Lytton's *Last Days of Pompeii* (1834).

77 (W39°)   **E.B.B. to R.B.**

[*Postmarked August 11, 1845.*]

    But if it 'hurts' you to read & write ever so little, why should I be asked to write . . for instance . . 'before tuesday?' And I did mean to say before to-day, that I wish you never w^d write to me when you are not *quite well,* as once or twice you have done if not much oftener,—because there is not a necessity, . . & I do not choose that there should ever be, or *seem,* a necessity, . . do you understand? And as a matter of personal pre-ference, it is natural for me to like the ⸿silence⸿ that does not hurt you, better than the speech that does. And so, remember.

    And talking of what may 'hurt' you & me, you would smile, as I have often done in the midst of my vexation, if you knew the persecu-tion I have been subjected to by the people who call themselves (lucus a non lucendo)[1] "the faculty," & set themselves against the exercise of other people's faculties, as a sure way to death & destruction. The mod-esty ⸿and simplicity⸿ with which one's physicians tell one not to think or feel, just as they would tell one not to walk out in the dew, would be quite amusing, if it were not too tryingly stupid sometimes. I had a doctor once who thought he had done everything because he had carried the inkstand out of the room—"Now," he said, "you will not have such a pulse to-morrow." He gravely thought poetry a sort of disease . . a sort of fungus of the brain—& held as a serious opinion, that nobody could be properly well who exercised it as an art—which was true (he maintained) even of men—he had studied the physiology of poets, 'quotha'—but that for women, it was a mortal malady & incompatible with any common show of health under any circumstances. And then came the damnatory clause in his experience . . that he had never known "a system" approaching mine in "excitability" . . except Miss Garrow's[2] . . a young lady who wrote verses for Lady Blessington's annuals[3] . . & who was ⟨‖ · · · ‖⟩ the only other female rhymer he had

had the misfortune of attending. And she was to die in two years, though she was dancing quadrilles then (& has lived to do the same by the Polka), & *I*, of course, much sooner, if I did not ponder these things, & amend my ways, & take to reading "a course of history"—!! Indeed I do not exaggerate. And just so, for a long while I was persecuted & pestered . . vexed thoroughly sometimes . . my own family, instructed to sing the burden out all day long—until the time when the subject was suddenly changed by my heart being broken by that great stone that fell out of Heaven.[4] Afterwards I was let do anything I could best . . which was very little, until last year—& the working, last year, did much for me in giving me stronger roots down into life, . . much. But think of that absurd reasoning that went before!—the *niaiserie* of it! For, granting all the premises all round, it is not the *utterance* of a thought that ↑can↓ hurt⟨s⟩ anybody, —while only the utterance is dependent on the will,—& so, what can the taking away of an inkstand do? Those physicians are such metaphysicians! It's curious to listen to them. And it's wise to leave off listening: though I have met with excessive kindness among them, . . & do not refer to Dr. Chambers in any of this, of course.

I am very glad you went to Chelsea—& it seemed finer afterwards, ↑on purpose↓ to make room for the divine philosophy. Which reminds me (the going to Chelsea) that my brother Henry confessed to me yesterday, with shame & confusion of face, to having mistaken & taken your umbrella for another belonging to a cousin of ours then in the house. He saw you . . without conjecturing, just at the moment, who you were. Do *you* conjecture sometimes that I live all alone here like Mariana in the moated Grange?[5] It is not quite so—: but where there are many, as with us, every one is apt to follow his own devices—& my father is out all day & my brothers & sisters are in & out, & with too large a public of noisy friends for me to bear, . . & I see them only at certain hours, . . except, of course, my sisters. And then as you have "a reputation" & are opined to talk generally in blank verse, it is not likely that there sh^d be much irreverent rushing into this room when you are known to be in it.

The flowers are . . . so beautiful! Indeed it was wrong, though, to send me the last. It was not just to the lawful possessors & enjoyers of them. That it was kind to *me* I do not forget.

You are too teachable a pupil in the art of obliterating—and omne ignotum pro terrifico[6] . . & therefore I wont frighten you by walking to meet you for fear of being frightened myself.

So goodbye until tuesday. I ought not to make you read all this, I know, whether you like to read it or not: and I ought not to have written it, having no better reason than because I like to write on & on. *You* have better reasons for thinking me . . very weak—& I, too good ones for not being able to reproach you for that natural & necessary opinion. May God bless you my dearest friend.

E. B. B.

1. "A grove because unlighted"—a standard comment on faulty reasoning.
2. Theodosia Garrow (1825–65), later (1848) Mrs. Thomas Adolphus Trollope was a linguist, musician, journalist, and minor poetess.
3. Marguerite, Countess of Blessington (1789–1849), author of *Conversations with Lord Byron* (1834), edited two annuals, *The Book of Beauty* and *The Keepsake*.
4. The death of "Bro"; for E.B.B.'s account, see Letter 87.
5. For the source of E.B.B.'s allusion, see Letter 37, note 5.
6. "Everything unknown is thought to be fearful." Cf. Tacitus, *Agricola* 30: "Omne ignotum pro magnifico est."

The following letter was written after the visit noted on the envelope of Letter 77:

Tuesday
+Aug 12, 1845
3–½ past 4 p.m.

78 (W40)   **R.B. to E.B.B.**

[*August 12, 1845.*]

Tuesday Evening.

What can I say, or hope to say to you when I see what you do for me?

This—for myself, (nothing for *you!*)—*this,* that I think the great, great good I get by your kindness strikes me less than that kindness.

—All is right, too—

Come, I WILL have my fault-finding at last! So you can decypher my *utterest* hieroglyphic? Now droop the eyes while I triumph: the plains *Cower, Cower*[1] beneath the mountains their masters—and the

Priests stomp[2] over the clay ridges, (a palpable plagiarism from two lines of a legend that delighted my infancy, and now instruct my maturer years in pretty nearly all they boast of /that⟩the/ semi-mythologic era referred to—"In London town, when reigned King Lud, His lords went stomping thro' the mud"—would all historic records were half as picturesque!)

But you know, (yes, *you*)—know you are too indulgent by far—and treat these roughnesses as if they were advanced so many a stage! Meantime the pure gain is mine, and better, the kind generous spirit is mine, (mine to profit by)—and best—best—best, the dearest friend is mine,

So be happy R. B.

1. This letter replies to E.B.B.'s critical notes on *England in Italy,* apparently given to Browning at his visit on Thursday. On lines 189–191, she wrote:
> "How the soft plains they look on and love so
> As they would pretend
> Tower beneath them—(lower).
"I do not see the contruction. Is 'lower' put he.e as a verb? and, if correctly, is it clearly, so put." (Macmillan ed., p. 1343.)
2. Of line 272, E.B.B. wrote:
> "And now come out, come out, &c.
> The priests mean to stamp.
"But is this word 'stamp,' and is it to rhyme to 'pomp.' I object to that rhyme—*I!!*" Next the offending word Browning wrote "(stomp). R.B." (*Ibid.*, p. 1344.)

79 *(W40°)*   **E.B.B. to R.B.**

[August 13, 1845.]

Yes, I admit that it was stupid to read that word so wrong. I thought there was a mistake somewhere, but that it was *your's,* who had written one word, meaning to write another. 'Cower' puts it all right of course. But is there an English word of a significance different from 'stamp,' in 'stomp'? Does not the old word King Lud's men stomped withal, claim identity with our "stamping." The *a* & *o* used to 'change about,' you know, in the old English writers—see Chaucer for it. Still the "stomp" with the peculiar significance, is better of

course⹁ than the 'stamp' even with a rhyme ready for it, & I dare say
you are justified in daring to put this old wine into the new bottle; &
we will drink to the health of the poem in it. It *is* 'Italy in England'—
isn't it?[1] But I understand & understood perfectly, through it all, that
it is *unfinished,* & in a rough state round the edges. I could not help
seeing *that,* even if I were still blinder than when I read 'Lower' for
'Cower'—

But do not, I ask of you, speak of my "kindness" . . my kindness!
—mine! It is "wasteful & ridiculous excess" ⟨‖ · · · ‖⟩ ↑and mis-
application↓ to use such words of me. And therefore, talking of
'compacts' & the 'fas' and 'nefas'[2] of them, I entreat you to know for
the future that whatever I write of your poetry, if it isn't to be called
"impertinence," isn't to be called "kindness," any more, . . *a fortiori,*
as people say when they are sure of an argument. Now, will you try
to understand?

And talking still of compacts, how & where did I break any
compact? I do not see.

It was very curious, the phenomenon about your 'Only a player-
girl.' What an un-godlike indifference to your creatures though—your
worlds, breathed away from you like soap bubbles, & dropping &
breaking into russet portfolios unobserved! ⟨‖ · · · ‖⟩ Only a god for
the Epicureans, at best,—can you be? That Miss Cushman went to
Three Mile Cross the other day, & visited Miss Mitford, & pleased her
a good deal, I fancied from what she said, . . and with reason, from
what *you* say. And "Only a fiddler," as I forgot to tell you yesterday,
is announced, you may see in any newspaper, as about to issue from
the English press by Mary Howitt's editorship. So we need not go to
America for it. /And⟩But/ if you complain of George Sand for want
of art, how could you bear Andersen, who can see a thing under his
eyes & place it under yours, & take a thought separately into his soul
& express it insularly, but has ↑no sort of↓ instinct towards wholeness
& unity,—and writes a book by putting so many pages together, . .
just so!—For the rest, there can be no disagreeing with you about the
comparative difficulty of novel-writing & drama-writing. I disagree
a little, lower down in your letter—because I could ↑not↓ deny (in my
own convictions) a certain ⟨gift⟩ ↑proportion↓ of genius to the author
of 'Ernest Maltravers,' and 'Alice'[3] (did you ever read those books?),
even if he had more impotently tried (supposing it to be possible) for

the dramatic laurel. In fact his poetry, dramatic or otherwise, is "nought"; but for the prose romances, and for 'Ernest Maltravers' above all, I must lift up my voice & cry. And I read the Athenæum about your Sir James Wylie who took you for an Italian . .

> "Poi vi dirò Signor, che ne fu causa
> Ch' avrò fatto al ⟨cantar⟩ scriver debita pausa."[4]

Ever your E. B. B.

1. It was *England in Italy.*
2. Right and wrong from the standpoint of divine law.
3. *Alice, or the Mysteries* (1838) was Bulwer-Lytton's sequel to *Ernest Maltravers* (1837).
4. "Hereafter, sir when I have made a suitable pause in my ⟨singing⟩ writing, I shall tell you the cause of it." Altered from Ariosto, *Orlando Furioso* III. lxxvii.

80 (W41)   **R.B. to E.B.B.**
                     ────────────────

[*August 15, 1845.*]

Friday Morning.

Do you know, dear friend, it is no good policy to stop up all the vents of my feeling, nor leave one for safety's sake, as you will do, let me caution you never so repeatedly; I know, quite well enough, that your "kindness" is not *so* apparent, even, in this instance of correcting my verses, as in many other points—but on such points, you lift a finger to me and I am dumb. . . Am I not to ⸱be⸱ allowed a word then neither?

—I remember—in the first season of German Opera here,[1] when "Fidelio's" effects were going—going up to the gallery in order to get the best of the last chorus,—get its oneness which you do—and, while perched there an inch under the ceiling, I was amused with the enormous enthusiasm of an elderly German (we thought,—I and a cousin of mine)—whose whole body broke out in billow, heaved and swayed in the perfection of his delight, hands, head, feet, all tossing and striving to utter what possessed him: well—next week, we went again to the Opera, and again mounted at the proper time, but the crowd was greater, and our mild greatfaced white haired red cheeked

German was not to be seen—not at first—for as the glory was at its full,—my cousin twisted me round and made me see an arm, only an arm, all the body of its owner being amalgamated with a dense crowd on each side, before, and—not behind because they, the crowd, occupied the last benches, over which we looked—and this arm waved and exulted ↟as if↟ "for the dignity of the whole body,"—relieved it of its dangerous accumulation of repressed excitability: when the crowd broke up all the rest of the man disengaged itself by slow endeavours, and there stood our friend confessed—as we were sure!

—Now, you would have bade him keep his arm quiet? "Lady Geraldine, you *would!*"[2]

I have read those novels—but I must keep that word of words, "genius"—for something different—"talent" will do here surely.

There lies Consuelo—done with!

I shall tell you frankly that it strikes me as precisely what in conventional language with the customary silliness is styled a *woman's-*book, in its merits & defects,—and supremely timid in all the points where one wants, and has a right to expect, some *fruit* of all the pretence and George Sand*ism:* there are occasions when one does say, in the phrase of her school, "que la Femme parle"! or what is better, let her act! and how does Consuelo comfort herself on such an emergency? Why, she bravely lets the uninspired people throw down one by one their dearest prejudices at her feet, and then, like a very actress, picks them up, like so many flowers, returning them to the breast of the owners with a smile & a courtesy and trips off the stage with a glance at the Pit. Count Christian, Baron Frederic, Baroness—what is her name—all open their arms, and Consuelo will not consent to entail disgrace &c &c No, you say,—she leaves them in order to solve the problem of her true feeling, whether she can really love Albert; but remember that this is done, (that is, so much of it as ever *is* done, and as determines her to accept his hand at the very last)—this is solved sometime about the next morning—or earlier—I forget—and in the meantime, Albert gets that "benefit of the doubt" of which chapter the last informs you: as for the hesitation and selfexamination on the matter of that Anzoleto—the writer is turning over the leaves of a wrong dictionary, seeking help from Psychology, and pretending to forget there is such a thing as Physiology. Then, that horrible Porpora! —if George Sand gives *him* to a Consuelo for an absolute master, in consideration of his services specified, and ⟨‖ · · · ‖⟩ ↑is of opinion↓ that *they* warrant his conduct, or at least, oblige submission to it,—then, I find her objections to the fatherly rule of Frederic perfectly imperti-nent—he having a few claims upon the gratitude of Prussia also, in his way, I believe! If the strong ones *will make* the weak ones lead them— then, for Heaven's sake, let this dear old all-abused world keep on its course without these outcries and tearings of hair, and don't be for ever goading the Karls and other trodden-down creatures till they get their carbines in order (very rationally,) to abate the nuisance—when you make the man a long speech against some enormity he is about to commit, and adjure and beseech and so forth, till he throws down the aforesaid carbine, falls on his knees, and lets the Frederic go quietly on his way to keep on killing his thousands after the fashion that moved your previous indignation.—Now is that right, consequential—that is *inferential;* logically deduced, going straight to the end—, *manly?*

The accessories are not the Principal, the adjuncts—the essence, nor the ornamental incidents the book's self, so what matters it if the portraits are admirable, the descriptions eloquent, (eloquent, there it is —that is her characteristic—what she *has* to speak, she *speaks out,* speaks volubly *forth,* too well, inasmuch as you say, advancing a step or two, "And now speak as completely *here*"—and she says nothing) —but all *that,* another could do, as others have done—but 'la femme qui parle'—Ah, that, is this all? So I am not George Sand's—she teaches me nothing—I look to her for nothing—

I am ever yours, dearest friend. How I write to you—page on page! But Tuesday—who could wait till then! Shall I not hear from you? God bless you ever

R. B.

1. In the spring of 1832, at the King's Theatre; *Fidelo* was performed on May 18. Eric Walter White, *The Rise of English Opera* (New York: Philosophical Library, 1951), pp. 80, 279.
2. *Lady Geraldine's Courtship,* st. lix.

[August 16, 1845.]

Saturday.

But what likeness is there between opposites; & what has "M. l'Italien" to do with the said "elderly German"?—See how little!— For to bring your case into point, somebody should have been playing on a Jew's harp for the whole of the orchestra; & the elderly German should have quoted something about "Harp of Judah" to the Venetian behind him!—And there, you w^d have proved your analogy!— Because you see my dear friend, it was not the expression, but the thing expressed, I cried out against—the exaggeration in your mind. I am sorry when I write that what you do not like—but I have instincts & impulses too strong for me when you say things which put me into such a miserably false position in respect to you—as for instance, when in this very last letter (oh, I *must* tell you!) you talk of my "correcting your verses"!—My correcting your verses! ! !—Now is *that* a thing for you to say?—And do you really imagine that if I kept that happily imagined phrase in my thoughts, I should be able to tell you one word of my impressions from your poetry, ever, ever again? Do you not see at once what a disqualifying and paralysing phrase it must be, of simple necessity? So it is *I* who have reason to complain, . . it appears to *me*, . . & by no means *you*—& in your 'second consideration' you become aware of it, I do not at all doubt—

As to 'Consuelo' I agree with nearly all that you say of it,—though George Sand, we are to remember, is greater than Consuelo, & not to be depreciated according to the defects of that book, nor classified as 'femme qui parle,' . . she who is man & woman together, . . judging her by the standard of even that book in the nobler portions of it. For the inconsequency of much in the book, I admit it of course—& *you* will admit that it is the rarest of phenomena when men . . men of logic . . follow their own opinions into their obvious results—nobody, you know, ever thinks of doing such a thing: to pursue one's own inferences is to rush in where angels . . perhaps . . do *not* fear to tread, . . but where there will not be much other company. So the want of practical logic shall be a human fault rather than a womanly one . . if you please . . & you must please also to remember that Consuelo is only "half the orange";[1] and that when you complain of its not being a whole one, you overlook that hand which is holding to you the 'Comtesse de Rudolstadt' in three volumes![2] Not that I, who have read the whole, profess a full satisfaction about Albert & the rest—& Consuelo is made to be happy by a mere clap-trap at last: and M[dme] Dudevant[3] has her specialities,—in which, other women, I fancy, have neither part nor lot, . . even *here!*—Altogether, the book is a sort of rambling Odyssey, a female Odyssey, if you like, but full of beauty & nobleness, let the faults be where they may. And then, I like those long, long books, one can live away into . . leaving the world & above all oneself, quite at the end of the avenue of palms—quite out of sight & out of hearing!—Oh, I have felt something like *that* so often—so often!—and *you* never felt it, & never will, I hope.

But if Bulwer had written nothing but the Ernest Maltravers books, you w[d] think perhaps more highly of him. Do you *not* think it possible now? It is his most impotent struggling into poetry, which sets about proving a negative of genius on him—*that,* which the Athenæum *praises* as "respectable attainment in various walks of literature"—! *like* the Athenæum, isn't it? & worthy praise, to be administered by professed judges of art? What is to be expected of the public, when the teachers of the public teach *so?*—

When you come on Tuesday, do not forget the MS. if any is done—only dont let it be done so as to tire and hurt you—mind! And goodbye until tuesday, from E. B. B.

1. Browning's phrase in Letter 67.
2. Published in 1843.
3. George Sand, who was actually baronne Dudevant.

82 *(W42°)*   *E.B.B. to R.B.*

[*August 17, 1845.*]

Sunday.

I am going to propose to you to give up tuesday, & to take your choice of two or three other days, say friday, or saturday, or to-morrow

. . Monday. Mr. Kenyon was here to-day & talked of leaving London on friday, and of visiting me again on 'tuesday' . . he said, . . but that is an uncertainty, & it may be tuesday or wednesday or thursday. So I thought (wrong or right) that out of the three remaining days you would not mind choosing one. And if you do choose the Monday, there will be no need to write—nor time indeed—; but if the friday or saturday, I shall hear from you perhaps. Above all things remember, my dear friend, that I shall not expect you tomorrow, except as by a *bare possibility*. In great haste, signed & sealed this sunday evening by

E. B. B.

83 (W42)   *R.B. to E.B.B.*

[*August 18, 1845.*]

Monday, 7 p.m.

I this moment get your note—having been out since the early morning—and I must write fast to catch the post. You are pure kindness & considerateness, *no* thanks to you!—(since you will have it so—). I choose Friday, then,—but I shall hear from you before / that⟩ thursday /, I dare hope? I have all but passed your house to-day—with an Italian friend,[1] from Rome, whom I must go about with a little on weariful sight seeing, so I shall earn Friday.—Bless you

R. B.

1. Letter 85 speaks of a husband and wife who had been kind to Browning in Rome, and Letter 86 calls the wife "Countess." She was probably the Countess Carducci, with whom Browning and his traveling companion "spent most of their evenings" in Rome in 1844. Mrs. Orr, p. 127.

84 (W43°)   *E.B.B. to R.B.*

[*August 19, 1845.*]

Tuesday.

I fancied it was just *so*—as I did not hear & did not see you on Monday. Not that you were expected particularly—but that you would have written your own negative, it appeared to me, by some post in the day, if you had received my note in time. It happened well too, altogether, as you have a friend with you, though Mr. Kenyon does not come, & will not come, I dare say; for he spoke like a doubter at the moment,—and as this Tuesday wears on, I am not likely to have any visitors on it after all, & may as well, if the rain quite ceases, go and spend my solitude on the park a little. Flush wags his tail at that proposition when I speak it loud out. And I am to write to you before Friday, & so, am writing, you see . . which I should not, should not have done if I had not been told,—because it is not my turn to write, . . did you think it was?

Not a word of Malta!—except from Mr. Kenyon who talked homilies of it last Sunday & wanted to / speak⟩talk / them to Papa—but it would not do in any way—now especially—& in a little time there will be a decision for or against,—I am afraid of *both* . . which is a happy state of preparation. Did I not tell you that early in the summer I did some translations / from⟩for / Miss Thomson's[1] 'Classical Album' . . from Bion & Theocritus, & Nonnus the author of that large (not great) poem in some forty books of the 'Dionysiaca' . . & the paraphrases from Apuleius? Well—I had a letter from her the other day, full of compunction & ejaculation, & declaring the fact that Mr. Burges[2] had been correcting all the proofs of the poems,—leaving out & emending generally, according to his own particular idea of the pattern in the mount—is it not amusing? I have been wicked enough to write in reply that it is happy for her and all readers . . 'sua si bona norint'[3] . . if during some half hour which otherwise might have been dedicated by Mr. Burges to putting out the lights of Sophocles & his peers, he was satisfied with the humbler devastation of E. B. B. upon Nonnus. You know it is impossible to help being amused. This correcting is a mania with that man! And then I, who wrote what I did from the Dionysiaca, with no respect for 'my author,' & an arbitrary will to 'put the case' of Bacchus & Ariadne as well as I could, for the sake of the art-illustrations, . . those subjects Miss Thomson sent me, . . & did it all with full liberty and persuasion of soul that nobody would think it worth while to compare English with Greek & refer me back to Nonnus & detect my wanderings from the text! ! But the critic was not to be cheated so!—And I do not doubt that he has set me all 'to rights' from beginning to end; & combed Ariadne's hair close to her cheeks for me. Have *you* known Nonnus, . . *you* who forget nothing? and have known everything, I think? For it is quite startling, I must tell you, quite startling & humiliating, to observe how you combine such large tracts of experience of outer & inner life, of books & men, of the world & the arts of it; curious knowledge as well as general knowledge . . & deep thinking as well as wide acquisition, . . & you, looking none the older for it all!—yes, & being besides a man of genius & working your faculty & not wasting yourself over a surface ↑or away from an end↓. Dugald Stewart[4] said that genius made naturally a lopsided mind —did he not? He ought to have known *you*.—And *I* who do . . a little . . (for I grow more loth than I was to assume the knowledge of you, my dear friend)—*I* do not mean to use that word 'humiliation' in the sense of having felt the thing myself in any *painful* way, . . because I never for a moment did, or *could,* you know,—never could . . never did . . except indeed when you have over praised me, which forced ⟨‖ · · · ‖⟩ another personal feeling in. Otherwise it has always been quite pleasant to me to be "startled & humiliated"—& more so perhaps than to be startled & exalted, if I might choose.

Only I did not mean to write all this, though you told me to write to you. But the rain which keeps one in, gives one an example of pouring on . . & you must endure as you can or will. Also . . as you have a friend with you 'from Italy' . . 'from Rome,' & commended me for my "kindness & considerateness" in changing / monday⟩tuesday / to friday . . (wasn't it? . .) ⟨kind you do not⟩ shall I still be more considerate & put off the visit-day to next week?—mind, you let it be as you like it best to be—I mean, as is most convenient 'for the nonce' to you & your friend—because all days are equal, as to that matter of convenience, to your other friend of this ilk, ...

E. B. B.—

1. Miss Thomson, later Mrs. Emil Braun, was the niece of John Kenyon's good friend, Miss Bayley. Except for Bion's *Lament for Adonis* and Sappho's *Song of the Rose,* everything planned for her "Album" was first to be published in 1862, in *Last Poems.* The Bion and Sappho translations were to be in *Poems* (1850).

2. George Burges (1786–1864) edited several classics and translated Plato and the Greek Anthology for the Bohn Library. He was fond of emending texts and, sometimes, forging them (see Letter 86, note 5). When Browning published *Aurora and Tithonus* in 1862 he appended a pointedly ambiguous note: "Rendered after Mr. Burges' reading, in some respects—not quite all."

3. "If only they knew their good." Virgil, *Georgics* II. 458.

4. Stewart (1753–1828), was a professor of moral philosophy at the University of Edinburgh. E.B.B. may be thinking of Stewart's discussion of "The Poet" in his *Elements of the Philosophy of the Human Mind*, Part III, where he speaks of poetical genius or imagination to this effect but not in these words. See the *Collected Works of Dugald Stewart*, ed. Sir William Hamilton (11 vols., Edinburgh, 1854), IV, 222–238.

85 (W43)   R.B. to E.B.B.
                        ─────────────────

[*August 20, 1845.*]

Wednesday M^g

Mauvaise, mauvaise, mauvaise, you know as I know, just as much, that your "kindness & considerateness" consisted, not in putting off Tuesday for another day, but in caring for my coming at all,—for my coming and being told at the door that you were engaged, and I might call another time—And you are NOT, NOT my "other friend," any more than this head of mine is my *other* head, seeing that I have got a violin which has a head too! All which, beware lest you get fully told in the letter I will write this evening, when I have done with my Romans—who are, it so happens, here at this minute; that is, have left the house for a few minutes with my sister—but are not "with me," as you seem to understand it,—in the house to stay. They were kind to me in Rome, (husband & wife), and I am bound to be of what use I may during their short stay. Let me lose no time in begging & praying you to cry "hands off" to that dreadful Burgess; have not I got a . . but I will tell you to-night—or on Friday which is my day, please— Friday,—Till when, pray believe me, with respect and esteem,

Your most obliged and disobliged at these blank endings—what have I done? God bless you ever dearest friend.

86 (W44)   R.B. to E.B.B.
                        ─────────────────

[*August 21, 1845.*]

Thursday, 7 o'clock.

I feel at home, this blue early morning, now that I sit down to

write (or, *speak,* as I try & fancy) to you, after a whole day with those
"other friends"—dear good souls, whom I should be so glad to serve,
& to whom service must go by way of last will & testament, if a few
more hours of "social joy," "kindly intercourse," &c, fall to my portion: my friend the Countess began proceedings ↑when I first saw her,
not yesterday↓ by asking "if I had got as much money as I expected by
any works published of late?"—to which I answered, of course,
'exactly as much'—é grazioso![1] (All the same, if you were to ask her,
or the like of her, "how much the stone-work of the Coliseum would
fetch, properly burned down to lime?"—she would shudder from
head to foot and call you "barbaro" with good Trojan heart.) Now
you suppose—(watch my rhetorical figure here)—you suppose I am
going to congratulate myself on being so much for the better, *en pays
de connaissance,* with my "other friend," E. B. B., number 2—or 200,
why not?—whereas I mean to "fulmine over Greece,"[2] since thunder
frightens you, for all the laurels,[3]—and to have reason for your taking
my own part and lot to yourself—I do, will, must, and WILL, again,
wonder at *you* and admire *you,* and so on to the climax. It is a fixed,
immoveable thing: so fixed that I can well forego talking about it. But
if ↑to↓ talk you once begin, "the King shall enjoy (or receive quietly,)
his own again"—⟨I know nothing about all the heap of marvels in⟩
↑I wear no bright weapon out of that Panoply . . or↓ Panoplite, as I
think you call Nonnus, nor ever, like Leigh Hunt's "Johnny, ever
blythe and bonny, went singing Nonny, nonny"[4] and see to-morrow,
what a vegeance I will take for your "mere suspicion in that kind"!
But to the serious matter . . nay, I said yesterday, I believe—keep off
that Burgess—he is stark staring mad—mad, do you know? The last
time I met him he told me he had recovered I forget how many of the
lost books of Thucydides—found them imbedded in Suidas (I think),
and had disengaged them from *his* Greek, without loss of a letter, "by
an instinct he, Burgess, had"—(I spell his name wrongly to help the
proper *hiss* at the end). Then, once on a time, he found in the "Christus
Patiens,"[5] an odd dozen of lines, clearly dropped out of the "Prometheus," and proving that Æschylus was aware of the invention of
gunpowder: he wanted to help Dr. Leonhard Schmitz in his
"Museum"[5]—and scared him, as Schmitz told me. What business has
he, Burges, with English verse—and what on earth, or under it, has
Miss Thomson to do with *him*. If she must displease one of two, why is

Mr. B., not to be thanked and "sent to feed," as the French say prettily? At all events, do pray see what he has presumed to alter . . you can alter at sufficient warrant, profit by suggestion, I should think! But it is all Miss Thomson's shame & fault; because she is quite in her propriety, saying to such intermeddlers, gently for the sake of their poor weak heads, "very good, I dare say, very desirable emendations, only the work is not mine, you know, but my friend's, and you must no more alter it without her leave, than alter this sketch, this illustration, because you think you could mend Ariadnes face or figure,—Fecit Tizianus, scripsit E. B. B."[7] Dear friend, you will tell Miss Thomson to stop further proceedings, will you not? ⟨I could talk on it⟩ There! only, do mind what I say!

And now—till to-morrow! It seems an age since I saw you. I want to catch our first post . . (this phrase I ought to get stereotyped—I need it so constantly). The day is fine . . you will profit by it, I trust. "Flush, wag your tail and grow restless & scratch at the door!"

God bless you,—my one friend, without an "other"—bless you ever—   R. B.

1. "You are most gracious."
2. *Paradise Regained* IV. 270.
3. Pliny, *Natural History* XV. 30, says lightning will not strike the laurel. Tiberius wore a wreath of it during thunderstorms. Cf. *Sonnets from the Portuguese*, V:
>   . . . those laurels on thine head
>   O my Belovèd, will not shield thee so,
>   That none of all the fires shall scorch and shred
>   The hair beneath.
4. Slightly misquoted from *To J. H., Four Years Old, A Nursery Song.*
5. A Greek tragedy whose authorship E.B.B. had discussed in *The Greek Christian Poets.* "[Burges] had in 1832 contributed to the *Gentleman's Magazine* (under a pseudonym) some lines purporting to be a newly discovered portion of the *Bacchae,* but really composed by himself on the basis of a parallel passage in the *Christus Patiens.*" Kenyon's note, *Letters of EBB,* I, 102.
6. Schmitz (1807–1890), a German-born historical writer, founded the *Classical Museum,* a journal of philology and of ancient history and literature (London, 1844–50).
7. The sense is that E.B.B.'s signature, like Titian's, puts a work beyond the reach of "improvers."

August, 1845

The visit Browning chronicled on the envelope of Letter 84
                    + Friday Aug 22.
                    3–4½ p.m.
*occurred after E.B.B. had written the first two paragraphs of the following
letter.*

87 (W44°)   *E.B.B. to R.B.*

[*August 20, 1845.*]

Wednesday.

But what have *I* done that you should ask what have *you* done? I
have not brought any accusation, have I . . no, nor *thought* any, I am
sure—& it was only the 'kindness and considerateness'—argument
/which⟩that/ was irresistable as a thing to be retorted, when your thanks
came so naturally & just at the corner of an application. And then, you
know, it is gravely true, seriously true, sadly true, that I am always
⟨prepared⟩ expecting to hear or to see how tired you are at last of me!—
sooner or later, you know!—But I did not mean any seriousness in that
letter. No, nor did I mean . . (to pass to another question . .) to provoke
you to the
                    "Mister Hayley . . so are *you* . ."
reply complimentary.[1] All I observed concerning yourself, was the
combination—which not an idiom in chivalry could treat grammatically
as a thing common to *me* & you, inasmuch as everyone who has known
me for half a day, may know that, if there is anything peculiar in me, it
lies for the most part in an extraordinary deficiency in this & this & this,
. . there is no need to describe what. Only nuns of the strictest sect of the
nunneries are rather wiser /in⟩on/ some points, & have led less restricted
lives than /mine⟩I have/ in others. And if it had not been for my
'carpet-work'——

Well—& do you know that I have, for the last few years, taken
quite to despise book-knowledge & its effect on the mind—I mean
/what⟩when/ people *live by it* as most readers by profession do, . .
cloistering their souls under these roofs made with hands, when they
might be under the sky. Such people grow dark & narrow & low,
with all their pains. . . .

Friday [August 22]—I was writing you see before you came—& now I go on in haste to speak "off my mind" some things which are on it. First . . of yourself,—how can it be that you are ⟨ill⟩ unwell again, . . & that you should talk (now did you not?—did I not hear you say so?) of being "weary in your soul" . . *you?* What should make *you*, dearest friend, weary in your soul; or out of spirits in any way?—Do . . tell me . . I was going to write without a pause—and almost I might, perhaps, . . even as one of the two hundred of your friends, . . almost I might say out that 'Do tell me.' Or is it (which I am inclined to think most probable,) that you are tired of a same life and want change?—it may happen to anyone sometimes, & is independent of your will & choice, you know— & I know, & the whole world knows: & would it not therefore be wise of you, in that case, to fold your life new again & go abroad at once? What can make you weary in your soul, is a problem to me. You are the last from whom I should have expected such a word. And you did say so, I *think*. I *think* that it was not a mistake of mine. And *you*, . . with a full liberty, & the world in your hand for every purpose & pleasure of it!—Or is it that, being unwell, your spirits are affected by *that?* But then you must be more unwell than you like to admit—. And I am teasing you with talking of it . . am I not?—and being disagreeable is only one third of the way towards being useful, it is good to remember in time.

And then the next thing to write off my mind is . . that you must not, you must not, make an unjust opinion out of what I said to-day. I have been uncomfortable since, lest you should—& perhaps it would have been better if I had not said it apart from all context in that way,— only that you could not long be a friend of mine without knowing & seeing what so lies on the surface. But then, . . as far as I am concerned, . . no one cares less for a "will" than I do (& this though I never had one, . . in clear opposition to your theory which holds generally nevertheless) for a will in the common things of life. Every now & then there must of course be a crossing & vexation—but in one's mere pleasures & fantasies, one w^d rather be crossed & vexed a little than vex a person one loves . . & it is possible to get used to the harness & run easily in it at last—& there is a side-world to hide one's thoughts in, & 'carpet-work' to be immoral on in spite of Mrs. Jameson, . . & the word 'literature' has, with me, covered a good deal of liberty as you must see . . real liberty which is never enquired into—& it has happened throughout my life by an accident (as far as anything is accident) that my own sense of right & happi-

ness on any important point of overt action, has never run contrariwise
to the way of obedience required of me . . while in things not exactly
overt ⟨we are all⟩ ↑I and all of us are↓ apt to act sometimes up to the limit
of our means of acting, with shut doors & windows, & no waiting for
cognizance or permission. Ah—& that last is the worst of it all perhaps—!
to be forced into concealments from the heart naturally nearest to us . . &
forced away from the natural source of counsel and strength!—and then,
the disingenuousness—the cowardice—the 'vices of slaves'!—And
everyone you see . . all my brothers, . . constrained *bodily* into submission
. . apparent submission at least . . by that worst & most dishonoring of
necessities, the necessity of *living:* everyone of them all, except myself,
being dependent in money-matters on the inflexible will . . do you see?
But what you do NOT see, what you *cannot* see, is the deep tender affection behind & below all those patriarchal ideas of governing grownup
children 'in the way they *must* go!'—and there never was (under the
strata) a truer affection in a father's heart . . no, nor a worthier heart in
itself . . a heart loyaller & purer, & more compelling to gratitude &
reverence, than his, as I see it!—The evil is in the system—& he simply
takes it to be his duty to rule, & to make happy according to his own
views of the propriety of happiness—he takes it to be his duty to rule
like the Kings of Christendom, by divine right. But he loves us through
& through it—& *I*, for one, love *him!* & when, five years ago, I lost what
I loved best in the world beyond comparison & rivalship . . far better
than himself as he knew . . for everyone who knew *me* could not choose
but know what was my first & chiefest affection . . when I lost *that,* . . I
felt that he stood the nearest to me on the closed grave . . or by the un-
closing sea . . I do not know which nor could ask. And I will tell you that
not only he has been kind & patient & forbearing to me through the
tedious trial of this illness (far more trying to standers by than you have
an idea of perhaps) but that he was generous & forbearing in that hour of
bitter trial, & never reproached me as he might have done & as my own
soul has not spared—never once said to me then or since, that if it had
not been for *me,* the crown of his house w^d not have fallen. He *never did* . .
& he might have said it, & more—& I could have answered nothing.
Nothing, except that I had paid my own price . . & that the price I paid
was greater than his loss . . his!! For see how it was—& how, "not with
my hand but heart," I was the cause or occasion of that misery—&
/not⟩though/ not with the intention of my heart but with its weakness,

yet the *occasion*, any way!

 They sent me down you know to Torquay—Dr. Chambers saying that I could not live a winter in London—The worst . . —what people call the worst—was apprehended for me at that time. So I was sent down with my sister to my aunt[2] there—and he, my brother whom I loved so,[3] was sent too, to take us there & return. And when the time came for him to leave me, *I*, to whom he was the dearest of friends & brothers in one . . the only one of my family who . . well, but I cannot write of these things; & it is enough to tell you that he was above us all, ⬐better than us all⬎ & kindest & noblest & dearest to *me*, beyond comparison, any comparison, as I said—& when the time came for him to leave me *I*, weakened by illness, could not master my spirits or drive back my tears—& my aunt kissed them away instead of reproving me as she should have done; & said that *she* would take care that I should not be grieved . . *she!* . . and so she sate down & wrote a letter to Papa to tell him that he would "break my heart" if he persisted in calling away my brother—As if hearts were broken *so!* I have thought bitterly since that my heart did not break for a good deal more than *that!* And Papa's answer was—burnt into me, as with fire, it is—that "under such circumstances he did not refuse to suspend his purpose, but that he considered it to be *very wrong in me to /ask⟩exact/ such a thing.*" So there was no separation *then*: & month after month passed—& sometimes I was better & sometimes worse—& the medical men continued to say that they w^d not answer for my life . . they! if I were agitated—& so there was no more talk of a separation. And once *he* held my hand, . . how I remember! & said that he "loved me better than them all & that he *would not* leave me . . till I was well," he said! how I remember *that!* And ten days from that day the boat had left the shore which never returned; never—& he *had* left me! gone! For three days we waited—& I hoped while I could—oh—that awful agony of three days! And the sun shone as it shines to-day, & there was no more wind than now; and the sea under the windows was like this paper for smoothness—& my sisters drew the curtains back that I might see for myself how smooth the sea was, & how it could hurt nobody—& other boats came back one by one.

 Remember how you wrote in your Gismond

   'What says the body when they spring
   Some monstrous torture-engine's whole
   Strength on it? No more says the soul—'[4]

Two pages of letter 87

The letter betrays great agitation as E.B. writes of her brother's death

Elizabeth Barrett Browning
Drawing by Rudolf Lehmann

and you never wrote anything which *lived* with me more than *that*. It is such a dreadful truth. But you knew it for truth, I hope, by your genius, & not by such proof as mine—I, who could not speak or shed a tear, but lay for weeks & months half conscious, half unconscious, with a wandering mind, & too near to God under the crushing of His hand, to pray at all. I expiated all my weak tears before, by not being able to shed then one tear—and yet they were forbearing—& no voice said 'You have done this.'

Do not notice what I have written to you, my dearest friend. I have never said so much to a living being—I never *could* speak or write of it. I asked no question from the moment when my last hope went: & since then, it has been impossible for me to speak what was in me. I have borne to do it today & to you, but perhaps if you were to write—so do not let this be noticed between us again—*do not!*—And besides there is no need—! I do not reproach myself with such acrid thoughts as I had once —I *know* that I would have died ten times over for *him,* & that therefore though it was wrong of me to be weak, & I have suffered for it ↑and shall learn by it I hope—↓ *remorse* is not precisely the word for me—not at least in its full sense. Still you will comprehend from what I have told you how the spring of life must have seemed to break within me *then;* —& how natural it has been for me to loath the living on—& to lose faith (even without the loathing) to lose faith in myself . . which I have done on some points utterly. It is not from the cause of illness—no. And you will comprehend too that I have strong reasons for being grateful to the forbearance. . . It would have been *cruel,* you think, to reproach me. Perhaps so!—yet the kindness & patience of the desisting from reproach, are positive things all the same.

Shall I be too late for the post, I wonder? Wilson[5] tells me that you were followed upstairs yesterday (I write on saturday this latter part) by somebody whom you probably took for my father. Which is Wilson's idea—& I hope not yours. No—it was neither father nor other relative of mine, but an old friend in rather an ill temper.[6]

And so goodbye until tuesday. Perhaps I shall . . not . . hear from you tonight. Dont let the tragedy or aught else do you harm—will you? & try not to be 'weary in your soul' any more—& forgive me this gloomy letter I half shrink from sending you, yet will send——May God bless you.

E. B. B.

1. Perhaps a reference to William Blake's attacks on his whilom friend William Hayley; see *On Friends and Foes*.

2. Arabella Graham-Clarke; see *EBB to MRM*, p. 34. For biographical information, see note 1 to Letter 407.

3. Edward ("Bro").

4. Lines 64–66 of the poem Browning later retitled *Count Gismond*. At its first appearance, in *Bells and Pomegranates* II (1842), it was paired with the poem now known as *My Last Duchess* under the covering title *Italy and France* and bore the subtitle *France*. The handwriting of the whole letter, but especially for a page or so at this point betrays very intense nervous agitation.

5. Elizabeth Wilson had been in E.B.B.'s service just over a year, her predecessor, Crow, having left in March or April of 1844, when it was discovered that she and the butler were secretly married (*EBB to MRM*, pp. 214–216). Despite some misgivings on her mistress's part, Wilson proved an invaluable confidante and help during the courtship and flight to Italy, as succeeding letters will show. She remained in service with the Brownings until 1857, marrying their man-servant, Ferdinando Romagnoli in 1855. In 1887 Pen Browning took the then indigent Romagnolis into the Palazzo Rezzonico. She died in 1902. These and other details of Wilson's later life are available in McAleer, pp. 9–10.

6. The Rev. George Barrett Hunter, whose angry letter is quoted in Letter 62. On July 12 he had omitted his "regular" Saturday visit, probably from annoyance at Browning's calling so often (*Letters of EBB*, I, 265).

A visit intervenes here, as noted on the envelope of Letter 87:
+ Tues. Aug 26.
3–4-10 min. p.m.
Browning brought with him the manuscript of the incomplete Saul, *of which he was to publish the first nine sections in November 1845.*

88 (W45)   R.B. to E.B.B.
_____

[*August 27, 1845.*]

Wednesday M^g

On the subject of your letter,—quite irrespective of the injunction in it—I would not have dared speak; now, at least: But I may permit myself, perhaps, to say I am *most* grateful, *most grateful,* dearest friend, for this admission to participate, in my degree, in /your⟩these/ feelings. There is a better thing than being happy in your happiness; I feel, now that you teach me, it is so. I will write no more now; tho' that sentence of "what you are *expecting*,—that I shall be tired of you &c,"—tho' I *could* blot that out of your mind for ever by a very few words *now*,—for you *would believe* me at this moment, close on the other subject:—but I will take no such advantage—I will wait.

I have many things (indifferent things, after those) to say; will you write, if but a few lines, to change the association for that purpose? Then I will write too.—

May God bless you,—in what is past and to come! I pray that from my heart, being yours

R. B.

89 (W45°)   *E.B.B. to R.B.*

[*August 27, 1845.*]

Wednesday Morning.

But your 'Saul' is unobjectionable as far as I can see, my dear friend. He was tormented by an evil spirit—but how, we are not told . . & the consolation is not obliged to be definite . . is it? A singer was sent for as a singer—& all that you are called upon to be true to, are the general characteristics of David the chosen, standing between his sheep & his dawning hereafter, between innocence & holiness, & with what you speak of as the 'gracious gold locks' besides the chrism of the prophet, on his own head—and surely you have been happy in the tone & spirit of these lyrics . . broken as you have left them. Where is the wrong in all this? For the right & beauty, they are more obvious—& I cannot tell you how the poem holds me & will not let me go until it blesses me . . & so, where are the 'sixty lines' thrown away?[1] I do beseech you . . you who forget nothing, . . to remember them directly, & to go on with the rest . . *as* directly (be it understood) as is not injurious to your health. The whole conception of the poem, I like . . & the execution is exquisite up to this point—& the sight of Saul in the tent, just struck out of the dark by that sunbeam, "a thing to see," . . not to say that afterwards when he is visibly 'caught in his pangs' like the king serpent, . . the sight is grander still. How could you doubt about this poem. . .

At the moment of writing which, I receive your note. Do *you* receive my assurances from the deepest of my heart that I never did otherwise than " BELIEVE " *you* . . never did nor shall do . . & that you completely
misinterpreted my words if you drew another meaning from them.
Believe *me* in this—will you? I could not believe *you* any more for anything you could say, now or hereafter—and so do not avenge yourself
on my unwary sentences by remembering them against me for evil. I
did not mean to vex you . . still less to suspect you—indeed I did not!—
and moreover it was quite your fault that I did not blot it out after it was
written, whatever the meaning was.[2] So you forgive me (altogether)
for your ↑own↓ sins: you must!—

For my part, though I have been sorry since to have written you
such a gloomy letter, the sorrow unmakes itself in hearing you speak so
kindly—Your sympathy is precious to me, I may say. May God bless
you. Write and tell me among the 'indifferent things' something not
indifferent, how you are yourself, I mean . . for I fear you are not well
and thought you were not looking so yesterday.

Dearest friend, I remain yours

E. B. B.

1. This may mean that Browning had already worked out section x of the poem.
The section now contains thirty-one lines, but those in the 1845 text were only half
the present length.
2. As E.B.B. notes in the succeeding letter, Browning (Letter 72) objected to
her cancellations.

90 *(W46°)*   *E.B.B. to R.B.*

[*August 29, 1845.*]

Friday Evng—
I do not hear,—& come to you to ask the alms of just one line, having taken it into my head that something is the matter. It is not so much
exactingness on my part, as that you spoke of meaning to write as soon
as you ⟨hear⟩ received a note of mine . . which went to you five minutes
afterwards . . which is three days ago, or will be when you read this. Are
you not well—or what? Though I have tried & *wished* to remember

having written in the last note something very or even a little offensive to you, I failed in it and go back to the worse fear. For you could not be vexed with me for talking of what was "your fault" . . "your own fault," viz: in having to read sentences which, but for your commands, w^d have been blotted out. You c^d not very well take *that* for serious blame! from *me* too, who have so much reason & provocation for blaming the archangel Gabriel.—No—you could not misinterpret so,—and if you could not, & if you are not displeased with me, you must be unwell, I think. I took for granted yesterday that you had gone out as before—but to-night it is different—& so I come to ask you to be kind enough to write one word for me by some post to-morrow. Now remember . . I am not asking for a letter—but for a *word* . . ⸤or line⸥ strictly speaking—

Ever yours, dear friend,

E. B. B.

91 (W46)   *R.B. to E.B.B.*

[August 29, 1845.]

This sweet Autumn Evening, Friday, comes all golden into the room and makes me write to you—not think of you—yet what shall I write?

It must be for another time, . . after Monday, when I am to see you, you know, and hear if the headache be gone, since your note would not round to the perfection of kindness and comfort, and tell me so.

God bless my dearest friend.

R. B.

I am much better—well, indeed—thank you.

92 (W47)   *R.B. to E.B.B.*

[August 30, 1845.]

Can you understand me *so,* dearest friend, after all? Do you see

175

me,—when I am away, or with you,—"taking offence" at words, "being vexed" at words, or deeds of yours, even if I could not immediately trace them to their source of entire, pure kindness—, as I have hitherto done in every smallest instance?

I believe in *you* absolutely, utterly—I believe that when you bade me, that time, be silent,—that such was your bidding, and I was silent—dare I say I think you did not know at that time the power I have over myself, that I could sit and speak and listen as I have done since—Let me say now—*this only once*—that I loved you from my soul, and gave you my life, so much of it as you would take,—and all that is *done,* not to be altered now: it was, in the nature of the proceding, wholly independent of any return on your part: I will not think on extremes you might have resorted to; as it is, the assurance of your friendship, the intimacy to which you admit me, now,—make the truest, deepest joy of my life—a joy I can never think fugitive while we are in life, because I KNOW, as to me, I *could* not willingly displease you,—while, as to you, your goodness and understanding will always see to the bottom of involuntary or ignorant faults—always help me to correct them. I have done now: if I thought you were like other women I have known, I should say so much —but—(my first and last word—I *believe* in you!)—what you could and would give me, of your affection, you would give nobly and simply and as a giver—you would not need that I tell you—(*tell* you!)—what would be supreme happiness to me in the event—however distant—

I repeat . . I call on your justice to remember, on your intelligence to believe . . that this is merely a more precise stating the *first* subject; to put an end to any possible misunderstanding—to prevent your henceforth believing that because I *do not write,* from thinking too deeply of you, I am offended, vexed &c &c I will never recur to this ⟨again⟩, nor shall you see the least difference in my manner next Monday: it is indeed, always before me . . how I know nothing of you and yours: but I think I ought to have spoken when I did—and to speak clearly . . or more clearly what I do—as it is my pride and duty to fall back, now, on the feeling with which I have been in the meantime—Yours

God bless you—R. B.

Let me write a few words to lead into Monday—and say, you have probably received my note. I am much better—with a little headache, which is all, and fast going this morning: of yours you say nothing—I trust you see your . . dare I say . . your *duty* in the Pisa affair, as all else *must* see it—shall I hear on Monday? And my Saul that you are so lenient to.

Bless you ever—

The following letter was enclosed in a packet of the books mentioned in its postscript. Browning's visit occurred after the letter proper had been written, but before the postscript:

+Monday Sepr 1, 1845

3–4½ p.m.

(note on the envelope of Letter 90).

93 (W47°)   *E.B.B. to R.B.*

[*August 31, 1845.*]

Sunday.

I did not think you were angry—I never said so. But you might reasonably have been wounded a little, if you had suspected me of blaming you for any bearing of yours towards myself—& this was the amount of my fear, . . or rather hope . . since I conjectured most that you were not well. And after all you did think . . do think . . that in some way or for some moment I blamed you, disbelieved you, distrusted you—or why this letter? How have I provoked this letter? Can I forgive myself for having even seemed to have provoked it?— & will you believe me that if for the past's sake you sent it, it was unnecessary, & if for the future's, irrelevant? Which I say from no want of sensibility to the words of it—your words always make themselves felt—but in fulness of purpose not to suffer you to hold to words because they have been said, nor to say them as if to be holden by them. Why, if a thousand more such words were said by you to me, how could they operate upon the future or present, supposing me to choose to keep the possible modification of your feelings, as a probability, in my sight & yours? Can you help my sitting with the doors all open if I think it right? I do attest to you . . while I trust you, as you must see, in word & act, & while I am confident that no human being ever stood higher or purer in the eyes of another, than you do in mine . . that you would still stand high & remain unalterably my friend, if the probability in question became a fact, as now at this moment. And this I must say, since you have said other things: & this alone, which *I* have said, concerns the future, I remind you earnestly.

My dearest friend—you have followed the most *generous* of impulses in your whole bearing to me—& I have recognized & called by its name, in my heart, each one of them. Yet I cannot help adding that, of us two, yours has not been quite the hardest part, . . I mean, to a generous nature like your own, to which every sort of nobleness comes easily. Mine has been more difficult—& I have sunk under it again & again: & the sinking & the effort to recover the duty of a lost position, may have given me an appearance of vacillation and lightness, unworthy at least of *you,* & perhaps of both of us. Notwithstanding which appearance, it was right & just (only just) of you, to believe in me—in my truth—because I have never failed to you in it, nor been capable of *such* failure:—the thing I have said, I have meant . . always: & in things I have not said, the silence has had a reason somewhere different perhaps from where you looked for it. And this brings me to complaining that you, who profess to believe in me, do yet obviously believe that it was only merely silence, which I required of you on one occasion—& that if I had 'known your power over yourself,' I should not have minded . . no!—In other words you believe of me that I was thinking just of my own—(what shall I call it for a motive base & small enough?) my own scrupulousness . . freedom from embarrassment . . ! of myself in the least of me; in the tying of my shoestrings, say! . . so much & no more!—Now this is so wrong, as to make me impatient sometimes in feeling it to be your impression—I asked for silence—but ALSO & chiefly for the putting away of . . you know very well what I asked for. And / it⟩this / was sincerely done, I attest to you. You wrote once to me . . oh, long before May & the day we met— that you "had been so happy, you should be now justified to yourself in taking ⟨a⟩ ↑any↓ step most hazardous to the happiness of your life" —but if you were justified, c^d *I* be therefore justified in abetting such a step,—the step of wasting, in a sense, your best feelings . . of emptying your water gourds into the sand?—What I thought then I think now —just what any third person, knowing you, w^d think, I think & feel.

I thought too, at first, that the feeling on your part was a mere generous impulse, likely to expend itself in a week perhaps—It affects me & has affected me, very deeply—more than I dare attempt to say . . that you should persist so—& if sometimes I have felt, by a sort of instinct, that after all you w^{d} not go on to persist, & that (being a man, you know) you might mistake, a little, unconsciously, the strength of your own feeling,—you ought not to be surprised; when I felt it was more advantageous & happier ⟨‖ · · · ‖⟩ for you ⟨if⟩ ↑that it should↓ be so—*In any case,* I shall ⟨‖ · · · ‖⟩ ↑never↓ regret my own share in the events of this summer, & your friendship will be dear to me to the last. You know I told you so—not long since. And as to what you say otherwise, you are right in thinking that I would not hold by unworthy motives in avoiding to speak what you had any claim to hear. But what could I speak that w^{d} not be unjust to you? Your life! . . if you gave it to me & I put my whole heart into it; what should I put but anxiety, & more sadness than you were born to? What could I give you, which it would not be ungenerous to give? Therefore we must leave this subject—& I must trust you to leave it without one word more;[1] too many have been said already—but I could not let your letter pass quite silently . . as if I had nothing to do but to receive all as matter of course *so!*) while you may well trust *me* to remember to my life's end, as the grateful remember,—& to feel, as those do who have felt sorrow, (for where these pits are dug, the water will stand), the full price of your regard. May God bless you my dearest friend—I shall send this letter after I have seen you, & hope you may not have expected to hear sooner.

Ever yours, E. B. B.

Monday [September 1]. 6 *p.m.*—I send in *dis*obedience to your commands, Mrs. Shelley's book[2]—but when books accumulate and when besides, I want to / lend⟩let / you have the American edition of my poems[3] . . famous for all manner of blunders you know; what is to be done but have recourse to the parcel-medium? You were in jest about being at Pisa *before or as soon as we / were⟩are /* ?—oh no—that must not be indeed—we must wait a little!—even if you determine to go at all which is a question of doubtful expediency. Do take more exercise, this week, & make war against those dreadful sensations in the head—now, will you? ⟨After all the first volume of Mrs. Shelley is not to be found—& must go afterwards—⟩

1. It is tempting to suppose Browning was recalling this phrase in this context when he used it as title of the tribute to E.B.B. which closes *Men and Women* (1855).

2. Probably *Rambles in Germany and Italy* . . .; see Letter 100.

3. Published October 1844, but dated 1845, by Henry G. Langley, New York, under the title originally planned for the English edition: *A Drama of Exile: and Other Poems.*

94 *(W48)*   *R.B. to E.B.B.*

_____

[*September 2, 1845.*]

Tuesday E^g

I rather hoped . . with no right at all . . to hear from you this morning or afternoon—to know how you are—that, "how are you," there is no use disguising, is,—vary it how one may,—my own life's question—

I had better write no more, now. Will you not tell me something about you—the head,—and that too, *too* warm hand . . or was it my fancy? Surely the report of Dr. Chambers is most satisfactory,—all seems to rest with yourself: you know, in justice to me, you *do* know that *I* know the all but mockery, the absurdity of anyone's counsel "to be composed," &c &c—But try, dearest friend!

God bless you—

I am yours

R. B.

95 *(W49)*   *R.B. to E.B.B.*

_____

[*September 2, 1845.*]

Tuesday night

Before you leave London, I will answer your letter—all my attempts end in nothing now—

Dearest friend—I am yours ever

R. B.

But meantime, you will tell me about yourself, will you not?

The parcel came a few minutes after my note left—Well, I can thank you for *that*—, for the Poems,—tho' I cannot wear them round my neck—and for the too great trouble. ⟨What cool⟩ My heart's friend! Bless you—

96 (W48°)   **E.B.B. to R.B.**

[*Postmarked September 4, 1845.*]

Indeed my headaches are not worth enquiring about—I mean, they are not of the slightest consequence & seldom survive the remedy of a cup of coffee. I only wish it were the same with everybody—I mean, with every *head!* Also there is nothing the matter otherwise—and I am going to prove my right to a "clean bill of health" by going into the park in ten minutes. Twice round the inner enclosure is what I can compass now—which is equal to once round the world—is it not?

I had just time to be afraid that the parcel had not reached you. The reason why I sent you the poems was that I had a few copies to give to my personal friends, & so, wished you to have one; & it was quite to please myself & not to please *you* that I made you have it,—& if you put it into the 'plum-tree'[1] to hide the errata, I shall be pleased still, if not rather more. Only let me remember to tell you this time in relation to those books & the question asked of yourself by your noble Romans[2] . . that just as I was enclosing my sixty-pounds debt to Mr. Moxon, I did actually and miraculously receive a remittance of fourteen pounds from the selfsame bookseller of New York[3] who agreed last year to print my poems at his own risk & give me 'ten per cent on the profit.' Not that I ever asked for such a thing! They were the terms offered. And I always considered the 'per centage' as quite visionary . . put in for the sake of effect, to make the agreement look better!—But no—you see! One's poetry has a real 'commercial value,' ⟨elsewhere⟩ if you dɔ but take it far away enough from the 'civilization of Europe.' When you get near the backwoods & the red Indians, it turns out to be nearly as good for something as 'cabbages,' after all! Do you remember what you said to me of cabbages *versus* poems, in one of the first letters you ever wrote to me?—of selling cabbages and buying 'Punches'?[4]

People complain of Dr. Chambers & call him rough and unfeeling
—neither of which *I* ever found him for a moment—& I like him for
his truthfulness, which is the nature of the man, though it is essential to
medical morality never to let a patient think himself mortal while it is
possible to prevent it, & even Dr. Chambers may incline to this on
occasion. Still he need not have said all the good he said to me on
saturday—he *used* not to say any of it; & he must have thought some
of it: &, any way, the Pisa-case is strengthened all round by his opinion
& injunction, so that all my horror & terror at the thoughts of his visit,
(& it's really true that I would rather *suffer* to a certain extent than be
cured by Many of those doctors!) had some compensation. How are
you? do not forget to say!—I found among some papers to-day, a note
of yours which I asked Mr. Kenyon to give me for an autograph, two
years ago.[5]

May God bless you, dearest friend. [And I have a dispensation
from 'beef and porter' εἰς τοὺς αἰῶνας.[6] 'On no account' was the
answer!—][7]

1. See Browning's *Sibrandus Schafnaburgensis* (*Garden Fancies* II, 1845), st. iii.
2. Letter 83 and note 1, and the opening of Letter 86.
3. Henry G. Langley.
4. Letter 7.
5. See *Letters of EBB*, I, 143.
6. "For all time."
7. Added at the top of the first page.

97 (W50)   **R.B. to E.B.B.**

[*September 5, 1845.*]

Friday Afternoon.
What you tell me of Dr. Chambers', "all the good of you" he
said, and all I venture to infer,—this makes me most happy and thankful: do you use to attach our old τυφλὰς ἐλπίδας[1] (and the practice of
instilling them) to that medical science in which Prometheus boasted
himself proficient? I had thought the "faculty" dealt in fears, on the
contrary, and scared you into obedience: but I know most about the

doctors in Molière. However the joyous truth is . . must be, that you are better . . and if one could transport you quietly to Pisa,—save you all worry,—what might one not expect!

When I know your own intentions,—measures, I should say, respecting your journey—mine will of course be submitted to you—it will just be "which day next—month"?—Not week, alas.

I can thank you now for this edition of your poems—I have not yet taken to read it, though—for it does not, each volume of it, open obediently to a thought, here, and here, and here, like my green books . . no, my Sister's they are[2]—, so these you give me are really mine. And America, with its ten per cent., shall have my better word henceforth and for ever . . for when you calculate, there must have been a really extraordinary circulation,—and in a few months: it is what newspapers call "a great fact." Have they reprinted the "Seraphim"? Quietly, perhaps!

I shall see you on Monday, then—

And my all-important headaches are tolerably kept under—headaches proper they are not—but the noise and slight turning are less troublesome—will soon go altogether.

         Bless you ever—ever dearest friend

                               R. B.

Oh, oh, oh! As many thanks for that precious card-box and jewel of a flower-holder as are consistent with my dismay at finding you *only* return *them* . . and not the costly brown paper wrappages also . . to say nothing of the inestimable pins ✝with✝ which my sister uses to fasten the same!

1. "Blind hopes." The phrase is recalled from Letter 13 (note 8).
2. See Letter 1, note 1.

98 (W49°)   *E.B.B. to R.B.*

[*September 6, 1845.*]

                                Saturday—
I am in the greatest difficulty about the steamers. Will you think a

little for me & tell me what is best to do? It appears that the direct Leg-horn steamer will not sail on the third, & may not until the middle of October, & if forced to still further delay, which is possible, will not at all. One of my brothers has been to Mr. Andrews of St. Mary Axe & heard as much as this. What shall I do? The middle of October, say my sisters . . & I half fear that it may prove so . . is too late for me—to say nothing for the uncertainty which completes the difficulty.

On the 20th of September (on the other hand) sails the Malta vessel; & I hear that I ⟨can⟩ ↑may↓ go in it to Gibraltar & find a French steamer there to proceed by. Is there an objection to this—except the change of steamers . . repeated . . for I must get down to Southampton—& the leaving England so soon? Is any better to be done? Do think for me a little. And now that the doing comes so near . . & in this dead silence of Papa's . . it all seems impossible, . . & I seem to see the stars *constellating* against me, & give it as my serious opinion to you that I shall not go. Now, mark.

But I have had the kindest of letters from dear Mr. Kenyon, urging it—

Well—I have no time for writing any more—& this is only a note of business to bespeak your thoughts about the steamers. My wisdom looks back regretfully . . only rather too late . . on the Leghorn vessel of the third of September. It w^d have been wise if I had gone *then*. May God bless you, dearest friend.

E. B. B.

But if your head turns still, . . *do* you walk enough?—Is there not fault in your not walking, by your own confession?—Think of this first—& then, if you please, of the steamers.

So, till Monday!—

Browning's visit at this point is noted on the envelope of Letter 98:
+Monday Sept 8, 1845
3–4½ p.m.

99 (W50°)   E.B.B. to R.B.

[September 9, 1845.]

Tuesday.

One reason against printing the tragedies now, is your not being well enough for the necessary work connected with them, . . a sure reason & strong . . nay, chiefest of all. Plainly you are unfit for work now—& even to complete the preparation of the lyrics & take them through the press, may be too much for you I am afraid,—& if so, why you will not do it—will you? . . you will wait for another year, . . or at least be satisfied for this, with bringing out a number of the old size,[1] consisting of such poems as are fairly finished & require no retouching. 'Saul' for instance, you might leave— —! You will not let me hear when I am gone, of your being ill—you will take care . . will you not? Because you see . . or rather *I* see . . you are *not* looking well at all—no, you are not!—and even if you do not care for that, you should & must care to consider how unavailing it will be for you to hold those golden keys of the future with a more resolute hand than your contemporaries, should you suffer yourself to be struck down before the gate . . should you lose the physical power while keeping the heart & will. Heart & will are great things, & sufficient things in your case—but after all we carry a barrow-full of clay about with us, & we must carry it a little carefully if we mean to keep to the path & not run zigzag into the border of the garden. A figure which reminds me . . & I wanted no figure to remind me . . to ask you to thank your sister for me & from me for all her kindness about the flowers. Now you will not forget? you must not . . When I think of the repeated trouble she has taken week after week, & all for a stranger, I must think again that it has been very kind—& I take the liberty of saying so moreover . . *as I am not thanking you.* Also these flowers of yesterday, which yesterday you disdained so, look full of summer & are full of fragrance, & when they seem to say that it is not September, I am willing to be lied to just *so.* For I wish it were not September. I wish it were July . . or November . . two months before or after: & that this journey /was⟩were/ thrown behind or in front . . any-where to be out of sight. You do not know the courage it requires to hold the intention of it fast through what I feel sometimes—if it ↑(the courage)↓ had been prophesied to me only a year ago, the prophet w^d have been laughed to scorn. Well!—but I want you to see George's letter, & how he & Mrs. Hedley, when she saw Papa's note of consent to me, gave unhesitating counsel. Burn it when you have read it. It is addressed to me . . which you will doubt from the address of it perhaps . . seeing that it goes βα . . ρβαρίζων. We are famous in this house for what are called nic-names . . though a few of us have escaped rather by a caprice than a reason: and I am never called anything else (never at all) except by the nom de *paix* which you find written in the letter,—proving as Mr. Kenyon says, that I am just "half a Ba-by" . . no more nor less:—and in fact the name has that precise definition.[2] Burn the note when you have read it.

And then I take it into my head, as you do not distinguish my sisters, you say, one from the other, to send you my own account of them in these enclosed 'sonnets'[3] which were written a few weeks ago, & though only pretending to be 'sketches,' pretend to be like, as far as they go, & *are* like—my brothers thought—when I "showed them against" a profile drawn in pencil by Alfred, on the same subjects. I was laughing & maintaining that mine should be as like as his—& he yielded the point to me. So it is mere portrait-painting—& you who are in 'high art,' must not be too scornful. Henrietta is the elder, ⟨‖ · · · ‖⟩ & the one who brought you into this room first—& Arabel, who means to go with me to Pisa, has been the most with me through my illness & is the least wanted in the house here, . . & perhaps . . perhaps—is my favorite— though my heart smites me while I write that unlawful word. They are both affectionate & kind to me in all things, & good & loveable in their own beings—very unlike, for the rest,—one, most caring for the Polka, . . & the other for the sermon preached at Paddington Chapel, . . *that* is Arabel . . so if ever you happen to know her you must try not to say before her how 'much you hate &c' Henrietta always "managed" everything in the house even before I was ill, . . because she liked it & I didn't, & I waived my right to the sceptre of dinner-ordering.

I have been thinking much of your 'Sordello' since you spoke of it—& even, I *had* thought much of it before you spoke of it yesterday,— feeling that it might be thrown out into the light by your hand, and greatly justify the additional effort. It is like a noble picture with its face to the wall just now—or at least, in the shadow. And so worthy as it is of you in all ways!—individual all through: you have *made* even the darkness of it! And such a work as it might become if you chose . . if you put your will to it—!—What I meant to say yesterday was not that it wanted more additional verses than the 'ten per cent' you spoke of[4] . . though it does perhaps . . so much as that (to my mind) it wants drawing together & fortifying in the connections & associations . . which hang as loosely every here & there, as those in a dream, & confound the reader who persists in thinking himself awake.

How do you mean that I am 'lenient'? Do you not believe that I tell you what I think, & as I think it? I may *think wrong*, to be sure—but *that* is not my fault:—& so there is no use reproaching me generally, unless you can convict me definitely at the same time:—is there, now?—

And I have been reading & admiring these letters of Mr. Carlyle, & receiving the greatest pleasure from them in every way. He is greatly *himself always*—which is the hardest thing for a man to be, perhaps. And what his appreciation of you is, it is easy to see—& what he expects from you:—notwithstanding that prodigious advice of his, to write your next work in prose[5]—! Also Mrs. Carlyle's letter[6]—thank you for letting me see it—I admire *that* too! It is as ingenious 'a case' against poor Keats, as could well be drawn—but nobody who knew very deeply what poetry *is, could,* you know, draw any case against him. A poet of the senses, he may be & is, just as she says—but then it is of the senses idealized; & no dream in a 'store-room' w^d ever be like the 'Eve of St. Agnes,' unless dreamed by some 'animosus infans,' like Keats himself. Still it is all true . . isn't it? . . what she observes of the want of thought as thought. He was ↑a↓ *seer*—strictly speaking.—And what noble oppositions—(to go back to Carlyle's letters) . . he writes to the things you were speaking of yesterday! These letters are as good as Milton's picture for convicting & putting to shame. Is not the difference between the men of our day & 'the giants which were on the earth,' less . . far less . . in the faculty . . in the gift, . . or in the general intellect, . . than in the stature of the soul itself? Our inferiority is not in what we can do, but in what we are. We should write poems like Milton if [we] lived them like Milton.

I write all this just to show, I suppose, that I am not industrious as you did me the honour of /supposing⟩apprehending/ that I was going to be . . packing trunks perhaps . . or what else in the way of 'active usefulness.'

Say how you are—will you? And do take care, & walk & do what is good for you. I shall be able to see you twice before I go. And oh, this going! Pray for me, dearest friend. May God bless you. E. B. B.

1. ". . . it was agreed that each poem [i.e., number of *Bells and Pomegranates*] should form a separate brochure of just one sheet—sixteen pages in double columns." Edmund Gosse, *Personalia* (Boston and New York, 1890), p. 53. In practice, however, only I, III, and V were so small.

2. These words have misled many to think the nickname was pronounced "Bay," but the contrary evidence is overwhelming: George's Greek transliteration here, E.B.B.'s remark that people say the name "quite naturally and pastorally" *(Letters of EBB,* I, 50), Browning's indication that it rhymes with the French *oies* (Letter 323), and Dorothy Hewlett's report of the family tradition *(Elizabeth Barrett Browning* [London: Cassell, 1953], p. xiii). But the finishing touch comes from a woman who heard the name but never saw it in print: ". . . I felt inclined to address her by the name of 'Bar,' the pet name of her own sweet poem." *Mary Boyle: Her Book,* ed. Sir Courtenay Boyle (New York: E. P. Dutton, 1902), p. 219.

3. The sonnets entitled *Two Sketches,* first published in *Blackwood's* for June 1847 and collected in 1850.

4. Browning undertook to recast *Sordello* in 1855–56, without success (G & M, p. 208). After being omitted from the 1849 collection it was included in the 1863 *Works.* There had been some attempts at clarification, including a very few added lines, but the dedication to Milsand indicates that Browning had given up any attempt to make the poem popular: "I lately gave time and pains to turn my work into what the many might,—instead of what the few must,—like: but after all, I imagined another thing at first, and therefore leave as I find it." (Macmillan ed., p. 103.)

5. "If ever your choice happened to point that way, I for one should hail it as a good omen that your next work were written in prose." Carlyle to Browning, June 21, 1841 *(Browning Collections,* p. 45, Lot #202.)

6. Her letter has not been traced.

---

100 (W51)　　　　　　**R.B. to E.B.B.**

[*September 11, 1845.*]

Thursday M^g

Here are your beautiful, and I am sure *true* sonnets; they look true— I remembered the light hair, I find. And who paints, and dares exhibit, E. B. B's self? And surely "Alfred's" pencil has not foregone its best privilege, not left *the* face unsketched? Italians call such an "effect defective"[1]—'l'andar a Roma senza vedere il Papa.'[2] He must have begun by seeing his Holiness, I know, and . . *he* will not trust me with the result, that my sister may copy it for me, because we are strangers, he and I, and I could give him nothing, nothing like the proper price for it—but *you* would lend it to me, I think, nor need I do more than thank you in my usual effective and very eloquent way—for I have already been allowed to visit you seventeen times, do you know; and this last letter of yours, Fiftieth is the same! So all my pride is gone, pride ↑in↓ *that* sense—and I mean to take of you for ever, and reconcile myself with my lot in this life. Could, and would you give me such a sketch?—It has been on my mind to ask you ever since I knew you if nothing in the way of *good* portrait existed—and this occasion bids me speak out, I dare believe: the more, that you have also quieted—have you not?—another old obstinate and very likely impertinent questioning of mine—as to the little name which was neither Orinda, nor Sacharissa³ (for which thank providence) and is never to appear in books, though you write them. Now I know it and write it—'Ba'—and thank you, and your brother George, and only burned his kind letter because you bade me who know best. So, wish by wish, one gets one's wishes!—at least I do—for one instance, you will go to Italy

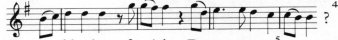

Why, 'lean and harken after it' as Donne says—⁵

Don't expect Neapolitan Scenery at Pisa, quite in the North, remember. Mrs. Shelley found Italy for the first time, real Italy, at Sorrento, she says. Oh that book⁶—does one wake or sleep?⁷ The "Mary dear" with the brown eyes, and Godwin's daughter and Shelley's wife, and who surely was something better once upon a time—and to go thro' Rome & Florence & the rest, after what I suppose to be Lady Londonderry's fashion:⁸ the intrepidity of the commonplace quite astounds me. And then that way, when she and the like of her are put in a new place, with new flowers, new stones, faces, walls, all new—of looking wisely up at the sun, clouds, evening star, or mountain top and wisely saying "who shall describe *that* sight!"—Not *you,* we very well see—but why dont you tell us that at Rome they eat roasted chestnuts, and put the shells into their aprons, the women do, and calmly empty the whole on the heads of the passengers in the street below; and that at Padua when a man drives his waggon up to a house and stops, all the mouse-coloured oxen that pull it from a beam against their foreheads sit down in a heap and rest. But once she travelled the country with Shelley on arm; now she plods it, Rogers in hand[9]—to such things & uses may we come at last! Her remarks on art, once she lets go of Rio's skirts,[10] are amazing— Fra Angelico, for instance, only painted Martyrs, Virgins &c.—she had no eyes for the divine *bon-bourgeoisie* of his pictures; the dear common folk of his crowds, those who sit and listen (spectacle at nose and bent into a comfortable heap to hear better) at the sermon of the Saint—and the children, and women,—divinely pure they all are, but fresh from the streets and market place—but she is wrong every where, that is, not right, not seeing what is to see, speaking what one expects to hear—I quarrel with her, for ever, I think.

I am much better, and mean to be well as you desire—I shall correct the verses you have seen, and make them do for the present—

Saturday, then! And one other time only, do you say?

God bless you, my own, best friend.

Yours ever R. B.

1. *Hamlet* II. ii. 103.
2. "Going to Rome without seeing the Pope."
3. E.B.B.'s *The Pet Name* (1838), st. ii:

> It never did to pages wove
> For gay romance belong;
> It never dedicate did move .
> As 'Sacharissa' unto love,
> 'Orinda' unto song.

Sacharissa was Waller's poetic name for Lady Dorothy Sidney, Orinda the pen name of Mrs. Katherine Philips.

4. This is the opening phrase of *Che faro senza Eurydice* from Gluck's *Orfeo*, apparently set down from memory, since it is slightly altered. The literal sense of the Italian—"What shall I do without Eurydice [EBB]?"—can be read into the sentence.

5. *A Valediction: forbidding mourning,* l. 31.

6. The context indicates pretty clearly that Browning refers to Mary Wollstonecraft Shelley's *Rambles in Germany and Italy in 1840, 1842, and 1843* (2 vols., London, 1844).

7. Browning for the moment confuses the close of Keats's *Ode to a Nightingale* and Shelley's *Skylark*.

8. Browning alludes to C. W. Vane, Marquis of Londonderry, *A Steam Voyage to Constantinople, by the Rhine and the Danube, in 1840–41, and to Portugal, Spain, &c. in 1839* (2 vols., London, 1841). Lady Londonderry looms large in a dull account of a very commonplace tour enlivened, if that is the word, only by the snobbery and ill temper of its principals.

9. Samuel Rogers' long travel poem *Italy* (1822) often served as a guide book.

10. Alexis François Rio, *De la poésie chrétienne dans son principe, dans sa matière, et dans ses formes* (Paris, 1836).

101 (W51°)   E.B.B. to R.B.

[September 11, 1845.]

Thursday.

Will you come on friday ↑ . . to-morrow . .↓ instead of saturday—
will it be the same thing? Because I have heard from Mr. Kenyon, who
is to be in London on friday evening he says, & therefore may mean to
visit me on saturday I imagine. So let it be friday—if you should not, for
any reason, prove Monday to be better still.
May God bless you—Ever yours,

E. B. B.

*A note on the envelope of the preceding letter indicates another visit before
Letter 102:*

+Friday, Septr. 12, 1845
3–5 p.m.

102 (W52)   R.B. to E.B.B.

[September 13, 1845.]

Saturday M^g

Now, dearest, I will try and write the little I shall be able, in reply
to your letter of last week[1]—and first of all I have to intreat you, now
more than ever, to help me and understand from the few words the
feelings behind them—(I should *speak* rather more easily, I think—but
I dare not run the risk: and I know, after all, you will be just & kind
where you can.) I have read your letter again & again: I will tell you—
no, not *you*, but any imaginary other person, who should hear what I
am going to avow; I would tell that person most sincerely there is not
a particle of fatuity, shall I call it, in that avowal; cannot be, seeing that
from the beginning and at this moment I never dreamed of winning
your *love* . . I can hardly write this word, so incongruous & impossible

does it seem; such a change of our places does it imply—nor, next to that, tho' long after, *would* I, if I *could,* supplant one of any of the affections that I know to have taken root in you—*that* great & solemn one, for instance . . I feel that if I could get myself *remade,* as if turned to gold, I WOULD not even then desire to become more than the mere setting to *that* diamond you must always wear: the regard and esteem you now give me, in this letter, and which I press to my heart & bow my head upon, is all I can take & all too embarrassing, ⟨‖ · · ‖⟩ ↑using↓ *all* my gratitude: and yet, with that contented pride in being infinitely your debtor as it is, bound to you for ever as it is,—when I read your letter with all the determination to be just to us both; I dare not so far withstand the light I am master of, as to refuse seeing that whatever is recorded as an objection to your disposing of that life of mine I would give you—has reference to some supposed good in that life which your accepting it would destroy (—of which fancy I shall speak presently)— I say, wonder as I may at this, I cannot but find it there, surely there: I could no more " bind *you* by words," than you have bound me, as you say—but if I misunderstand you, one assurance to that effect will be but too intelligible to me—but, as it *is,* I have difficulty in imagining that while one of so many reasons, which I am not obliged to repeat to myself, but which any one easily conceives; while *any one* of those reasons would impose silence on me *for ever*—(for, as I observed, I love you as you now are, and *would* not remove one affection that is already part of you,)—*would* you, being able to speak *so,* only say *that you* desire not to put " more sadness than I was born to," into my life?— that you " could give me only what it were ungenerous to give " ?

Have I your meaning here? In so many words, is it on my account that you bid me " leave this subject " ? I think if it were so, I would for once call my advantages round me. I am not what your generous self-forgetting appreciation would sometimes make me out—but it is not since yesterday, nor ten nor twenty years before, that I began to look into my own life, and study its end, and requirements, what would turn to its good or its loss—and I *know,* if one may know anything, that ↑to↓ make that life yours and increase it by the union with yours, would render me *supremely happy,* as I said, and say, and feel. My whole suit to you is, in that sense, *selfish*—not that I am ignorant that *your* nature would most surely attain happiness in / finding⟩being / conscious that it made another / happy⟩happier / —but *that best, best end of all,* would, like the rest, come from yourself, be a reflection of your own gift.

Dearest, I will end here—words, persuasion & arguments,—if they were at my service I would not use them—I believe in you, altogether have faith in you—in you. I will not think of insulting by trying to reassure you on one point which certain phrases in your letter might at first glance seem to imply—you do not understand me to be living and labouring and writing (and *not* writing) in order to be successful in the world's sense? I even convinced the people *here* what was my true 'honorable position in society,' &c. &c. +therefore+ I shall not have to inform *you* that I desire to be very rich, very great; but not in reading Law gratis with dear foolish old Basil Montagu,[2] as he ever & anon bothers me to do;—⟨much less⟩—enough of this nonsense.

"Tell me what I have a claim to hear": I can hear it, and be as grateful as I was before and am now—your friendship is my pride and happiness. If you told me your love was already bestowed elsewhere, and that it was in my power to serve you *there,* to serve you there would still be my pride and happiness. I look on and on over the prospect of my love, it is all *on*wards,—and all possible forms of unkindness . . I quite laugh to think how they are *behind* . . cannot be encountered in the route we are traveling!—I submit to you and will obey you implicitly . . obey what I am able to conceive of your least desire, much more of your expressed wish—But it was necessary to make this avowal, among other reasons, for one which the world would recognize too—My whole scheme of life, (with its wants, material wants at least, closely cut down,) was long ago calculated—and it supposed *you,* the finding such an one as you, utterly impossible —because in calculating one goes upon *chances,* not on providence—how could I expect you? So for my own future way in the world I have always refused to care—any one who can live a couple of years & more on bread and potatoes as I did once on a time,[3] and who prefers a blouse and a blue shirt (such as I now write in) to all manner of dress and gentlemanly appointment, and who can, if necessary, groom a horse not so badly, or at all events would rather do it all day long than succeed Mr. Fitzroy Kelly in the Solicitor-Generalship,[4] . . such an one need not very much concern himself beyond considering the lilies how they grow: but now I see you near this life, all changes—and at a word, I will do all that ought to be done,—that every one used to say could be done, and let "all my powers find sweet employ" as Dr. Watts sings,[5] in getting whatever is to be got—not very much, surely. I would print these things, get them away, and do this now, and go to you at Pisa with the news—at Pisa where one may live for some £100 a year—while, lo, I seem to remember, I *do* remember, that Charles Kean offered to give me 500 of those pounds for any play that might suit him[6]—to say nothing of Mr. Colburn saying confidentially that he wanted more than his dinner "a novel on the subject of *Napoleon" !!!* So may one make money, if one does not live in a house in a row, and feel impelled to take the Princesses' Theatre for a laudable development and exhibition of one's faculty.

Take the sense of all this, I beseech you, dearest—all you shall say will be best—I am yours—

Yes—Yours ever—God bless you for all you have been, and are, and will certainly be to me, come what He shall please—!

R. B.

1. Actually Letter 93, almost two weeks earlier.
2. Montagu (1770–1851) was a highly successful bankruptcy and chancery lawyer, intimate of Wordsworth and Coleridge, and an editor of Bacon.
3. This may have been a period of Shelley-inspired vegetarianism. G & M, pp. 51–52 (the connection to this letter is much clearer in the editions of 1910 and 1911 than in the revised and enlarged edition of 1938).
4. Sir Fitzroy Kelly (1796–1880) became Solicitor-General on June 29, 1845, was then knighted, and held the office until the following July. He held the same post twice again, in 1852 and in 1858–59.
5. A version of the 92nd Psalm by Isaac Watts (1674–1748), the great dissenting hymn-writer. When Browning was a small boy, weekly hair-brushing at Mr. Ready's school was accompanied by Watts's hymns. G & M, p. 31.
6. Charles (1811–68), for whom Browning wrote *Colombe's Birthday,* was the son of the more famous Edmund. He never staged the play.

103 (W52°)   **E.B.B. to R.B.**

[*Postmarked September 16, 1845.*]

I scarcely know how to write what is to be written nor indeed why it is to be written & to what end. I have tried in vain—& you are wait-

ing to hear from me. I am unhappy enough even where I am happy—
but ungrateful nowhere—& I thank you from my heart—profoundly
from the depths of my heart . . which is nearly all I can do.

One letter I began to write & asked in it how it could become me
to speak at all if '*from the beginning & at this moment you never dreamed of*'
. . & there, I stopped & tore the paper, . . because I felt that you were
too loyal & generous, for me to bear to take a moment's advantage of
the same, & bend down the very flowering branch of your generosity
(as it might be) to thicken a little the fence of a woman's caution &
reserve. You will not say that you have not acted as if you "dreamed"
—& I will answer therefore to the general sense of your letter & former
letters, & admit at once that I *did* state to you the difficulties most difficult to myself . . though not all . . & that if I had been worthier of you
I should have been proportionably less in haste to 'bid you leave that
subject,' I do not understand how you can seem at the same moment
to have faith in my integrity & to have doubt whether all this time I
may not have felt a preference for another . . which you are ready "to
serve," you say. Which is generous in you—but in *me*, where were
the integrity? Could you really hold me to be blameless? & do you
think that true-hearted women act usually so? Can it be necessary for
me to tell you that I could not have acted so, & did not? And shall I
shrink from telling you besides . . ⟨to⟩ YOU who have been generous
to me & have a right to hear it . . & have spoken to me in the name of
an affection & memory most precious & holy to me, in this same letter
. . that neither now nor formerly has any man been to my feelings
what you are . . & that if I were different in some respects and free in
others by the providence of God, I would accept ⟨‖ · · ‖⟩ the great
trust of your happiness, gladly, proudly, & gratefully; & give away
my own life & soul to that end. I *would* do it . . *not, I do* . . observe! it is a
truth without a consequence; only meaning that I am not all stone—
only proving that I am not likely to consent to help you in wrong
against yourself. You see in me what is not:—*that*, I know: & you
overlook in me what is unsuitable to you . . *that* I know, & have sometimes told you. Still, because a strong feeling from some sources is
self-vindicating & ennobling to the object of it, I will not say that, if it
were proved to me that you felt this for me, I would persist in putting
the sense of my own unworthiness between you & me—not being
heroic you know, nor pretending to be so. But something worse than

even a sense of unworthiness, GOD has put between us! & judge yourself if to beat your thoughts against the immovable marble of it, can be
anything but pain & vexation of spirit, waste & wear of spirit to you . .
judge!—The present is here to ↑be↓ / fact⟩seen / . . speaking for itself! &
the best future you can imagine for me, what a precarious thing it
must be . . a thing for making burdens out of . . only not for your
carrying; as I have vowed to my own soul. As dear Mr. Kenyon said
to me to-day in his smiling kindness . . "In ten years you may be strong
perhaps"—or 'almost strong'! that being the encouragement of my
best friends! What would he say, do you think, if he could know or
guess . . ! what *could* he say but that you were . . a poet!—& I . . still
worse!—*Never* let him know or guess!—

    And so if you are wise & would be happy (and you have excellent
practical sense after all & should exercise it) you must leave me—these
thoughts of me, I mean . . for if we might not be true friends for ever,
I sh^d have less courage to say the other truth. But we may be friends
always . . & cannot be so separated, that your happiness, in the knowledge of it, will not increase mine. And if you will be persuaded by me,
as you say, you will be persuaded *thus* . . & consent to take a resolution
& force your mind at once into another channel. Perhaps I might bring
you reasons of the class which you tell me "would silence you for
ever." I might certainly tell you that my own father, if he knew that
you had written to me so, & that I had answered you—*so,* even . .
would not forgive me at the end of ten years—& this, from none of the
causes mentioned by me here & in no disrespect to your name & your
position . . though he does not over-value poetry even in his daughter,
& is apt to take the world's measures of the means of life . . but for the
singular reason that he never *does* tolerate in his family (sons or
daughters) the development of one class of feelings. Such an objection
I could not bring to you of my own will—it rang hollow in my ears—
perhaps I thought even too little of it:—& I brought to you what I
thought much of, & cannot cease to think much of equally. Worldly
thoughts, these are not at all, nor have been: there need be no soiling
of the heart with any such:—& I will say, in reply to some words of
yours, that you cannot despise the gold & gauds of the world ↑more↓
than I do, & should do even if I found a use for them. And if I *wished* to
be very poor, in the world's sense of poverty, I *could not,* with three or
four hundred a year of which no living will can dispossess me. And is it

not the chief good of money, the being free from the need of thinking of it? It seems so to me.

The obstacles then are of another character, & the stronger for being so. Believe that I am grateful to you—*how* grateful, cannot be shown in words nor even in tears . . grateful enough to be truthful in all ways. You know I might have hidden myself from you—but I would not: & by the truth +told+ of myself, you may believe in the earnestness with which I tell the other truths—of you . . & of this subject. The subject will not bear consideration—it breaks in our hands. But that God is stronger than we, cannot be a bitter thought to you but a holy thought . . while He lets me, as much as I can be any-one's, be only yours.

E. B. B.

104 (W53)   **R.B. to E.B.B.**

————————

[*Tuesday, September 16, 1845.*]

I do not know whether you imagine the precise effect of your letter on me—very likely you do, and write it just for that—for I con-ceive *all* from your goodness: but before I tell you what is that effect, let me say in as few words as possible what shall stop any fear—tho' only for a moment and on the outset,—that you have been misunder-stood,—that the goodness *outside,* and round and over all, hides all or any thing: I understand you to signify to me that you see, at this present, insurmountable obstacles to that . . can I speak it . . entire gift, which I shall own, was, while I dared ask it, above my hopes—and wishes, even, so it seems to me . . and yet could not but be asked, so plainly was it dictated to me, by something quite out of those hopes & wishes—Will it help me to say that once in this Aladdin-cavern I knew I ought to stop for no heaps of jewel-fruit on the trees from the very beginning, but go on to the lamp, *the* prize, the last and best of all? Well, I understand you to pronounce that at present you believe this gift impossible—and I acquiesce entirely—I submit wholly to you; repose on you in all the faith of which I am capable: those obstacles are solely for *you* to see and to declare . . had *I* seen them, be sure I should never have mocked you or myself by affecting to pass them over . .

what *were* obstacles, I mean: but you *do* see them, I must think,—and perhaps they strike me the more from my true, honest unfeigned inability to imagine what they are,—not that I shall endeavour: after what you *also* apprise me of, I know and am joyfully confident that if ever they cease to be what you now consider them, you who see now *for me,* whom I implicitly trust in to see for me; you will *then,* too, see and remember me, and how I trust, and shall then be still trusting: and until you see, and so inform me, I shall never utter a word—for that would / be⟩involve / the vilest of implications. I thank God—I *do* thank him, that in this whole matter I have been, to the utmost of my power, not unworthy of his introducing you to me, in this respect that, being no longer in the first freshness of life, and having for many years now made up my mind to the impossibility of loving any woman . . having wondered at this in the beginning, and fought not a little against it, having acquiesced in it at last, and accounted for it all to myself, and become, if anything, rather proud of it than sorry . . I say, when real love, making itself at once recognized as such, *did* reveal itself to me at last, I *did* open my heart to it with a cry—nor care for its overturning all my theory—nor mistrust its effect upon a mind set in ultimate order, so I fancied, for the few years ⟨of⟩ more—nor apprehend in the least that the new element would harm what was already organized without its help: nor have I, either, been guilty of the more pardonable folly, of treating the new feeling after the pedantic fashions and instances of the world . . I have not spoken when *it* did not speak, because "one" might speak, or has spoken, or *should* speak, and "plead" and all that miserable work which after all, I may well continue proud that I am not called to attempt: here ↑for instance↓ *now* . . "one" should despair; but "try again" first, and work blindly at removing those obstacles (—if I saw them, I should be silent, and only speak when a month hence, ten years hence, I could bid you look where they *were*)—and "one" would do all this, not for the *play–acting's* sake, or to "look the character" . . (*that* would be something quite different from folly . .) but from a not unreasonable anxiety lest by too sudden a silence, too complete an acceptance of your will; the earnestness and endurance and unabatedness . . the *truth,* in fact, of what had already been professed, should get to be questioned—But I believe that you believe me—and now that all is clear between us I will say, what you will hear, without fearing for me or yourself, that I am

utterly contented . . ("grateful" I have done with . . it must go—) I
accept what you give me, what those words deliver to me, as—not all
I asked for . . as I said . . but as more than I ever hoped for,—*all,* in the
best sense, that I desire. That phrase in my letter which you objected to,
and the other—may stand, too—I never attempted to declare, describe
my feeling for you—one word of course stood for it all . . but having
to put down some one *point,* so to speak, of it—you could not wonder
if I took any extreme one *first* . . never minding all the untold portion
that *led* up to it, made it possible and natural—it is true, 'I could not
dream of *that'*—that I was eager to get the horrible notion away from
never so flitting a visit to you, that you were thus and thus to me *on
condition* of my proving just the same to you—just as if we had waited
to acknowledge that the moon lighted us till we ascertained within
these two or three hundred years that the earth happens to light the
moon as well! But I felt that, and so said it:—now you have declared
what I should never have presumed to hope—and I repeat to you that
I, with all to be thankful for to God, am most of all thankful for this
the last of his providences . . which is no doubt, the natural and inevitable feeling, could one always see clearly. Your regard for me is *all*
success—let the rest come, or not come. In my heart's thankfulness I
would . . I am sure I would promise anything that would gratify you
. . but it would *not* do that, to agree, in words, to change my affections,
put them elsewhere &c &c That would be pure foolish talking, and
quite ⟨impracticable⟩ ↑foreign to the↓ practical results which you will
attain in a better way from a higher motive: I will cheerfully promise
you, however, to be "bound by no words," blind to no miracle,—in
sober earnest, it is not because I renounced once for all oxen and the
owning and having to do with them, that I will obstinately turn away
from any unicorn[1] when such an apparition blesses me . . but meantime I shall walk at peace on our hills here nor go looking in all corners
for the bright curved horn! And as for you . . if I did not dare "to dream
of that"—, now it is mine, my pride & joy prevent in no manner my
taking the whole consolation of it at once, *now*—I will be confident
that, if I obey you, I shall get no wrong for it—if, endeavouring to
spare you fruitless pain, I do not eternally revert to the subject,—do
indeed "quit" it just now, when no good can come of dwelling on it
to you; you will never say to yourself—"so I said—" the "generous
impulse"[2] *has* worn itself out . . time is doing his usual work—this was

to be expected" &c &c You will be the first to say to me "such an obstacle has ceased to exist . . or is now become one palpable to *you,* one *you* may try and overcome"—and I shall be there, and ready— ten years hence as now—if alive.

One final word on the other matters—the "worldly matters"—I shall own I alluded to them rather ostentatiously, because—because *that would be* the *one* poor sacrifice I could make you—one I would cheerfully make,—but a sacrifice, and the only one; this careless "sweet habitude of living"—this absolute independence of mine, which, if I had it not, my heart would starve and die for, I feel, and which I have fought so many good battles to preserve—for that has happened, too—this light rational life I lead, and know so well that I lead; this I could give up for nothing less than ⟨our⟩—what you know —but I *would* give it up, not for you merely, but for those whose dis- appointment might re-act on you—and I should break no promise to myself—the money getting would not be for the sake of *it;* "the labour not for that which is nought"—indeed the necessity of doing this, if at all, *now,* was one of the reasons which make me go on to that *last request of all* . . at once; one must not be too old, they say, to begin their ways: but, in spite of all the babble, I feel sure that whenever I make up my mind to that, I can be rich enough and to spare—because along with what you have thought *genius* in me, is certainly talent, what the world recognizes as such; and I have tried it in various ways, just to be sure that I *was* a little magnanimous in never intending to use it: thus, in more than one of the reviews & newspapers that laughed my "Paracelsus" to scorn ten years ago—in the same column, often, of these reviews, would follow a most laudatory notice of an Elemen- tary French book, on a new plan, which I '*did*' for my old French Master,[3] and he published—"*that* was really an useful work"!—So that when the only obstacle is only that there is so much *per annum* to be producible, you will tell me: ⟨‖ · · · · · ‖⟩ ↑after all it would be unfair in me not to confess . . that this was always intended to be *my* own single stipulation—"an objection" which I could see, certainly,—but meant to treat myself to the little luxury of removing.↓

So, now, dearest—let me once think of that, and of you as my own, my dearest—this once—dearest, I have done with words for the present: I will wait: God bless you and reward you—I kiss your hands *now.* This is my comfort, that if you accept my feeling as all but *un-*

expressed now,—more and more will become spoken—or understood, that is—we both live on—you will know better *what* it was, how much and manifold, what one little word had to give out.

God bless you—
Your R. B.

On Thursday,—you remember?

This is Tuesday Night—

I called on Saturday at the Office in St. Mary Axe—all uncertainty about the vessel's sailing again for Leghorn—"it could not sail before the middle of the month—and only then *if* &c But if I would leave my card &c &c"

   1. This begins a recurrent motif in the correspondence; for Browning "unicorn" means E.B.B., for her, something exotic or attractive. Browning's allusion, pretty surely, is to Donne's *Elegy* IV, "The Perfume," ll. 47–50:

> But as wee in our Ile emprisoned,
> Where cattell onely, and diverse dogs are bred,
> The pretious Unicornes, Strange monsters call,
> So thought he good, strange, that had none at all.

The poem is a vituperative outburst against a jealous father, so that a Donne enthusiast like Browning might logically recall it in connection with the letter he is answering. One wonders whether E.B.B. caught the special overtone, but she knew the poem well enough to have recommended just these lines to Horne as a motto for the essay on Sir Henry Taylor in *A New Spirit of the Age*. *Letters of EBB to RHH*, I, 136–137.

   2. See Letter 93.

   3. Professor Lionel Stevenson (*Modern Language Notes*, XLII [May 1927], 299–305) identified the volume as *Le Gil Blas de la Jeunesse* (London, 1835), one of whose joint editors was "A. Loradoux, Professeur de Langues, Walworth," presumably the same Loradoux with whom Browning studied for two years. (G & M, p. 47). Stevenson found only one periodical that reviewed the French text and *Paracelsus* in the same issue. Additional reviews of both have been turned up but no other simultaneous ones.

105 (W53°)   **E.B.B. to R.B.**

[*September 17, 1845.*]

Wednesday Morning.

I write one word just to say that it is all over with Pisa; which was a

probable evil when I wrote last, & which I foresaw from the beginning
—being a prophetess, you know. I cannot tell you now how it has all
happened—*only do not blame me,* for I have kept my ground to the last, &
only yield when Mr. Kenyon & all the world see that there is no standing. I am ashamed almost of having put so much earnestness into a
personal matter—& I spoke face to face & quite firmly—so as to pass
with my sisters for the "bravest person in the house" without con-
testation.

Sometimes it seems to me as if it *could not* end so—I mean, that the
responsibility of such a negative must be reconsidered . . & you see how
Mr. Kenyon writes to me. Still, as the matter lies, . . no Pisa!—And, as I
said before, my prophetic instincts are not likely to fail, such as they
have been from the beginning.

If you wish to come, it must not be until saturday at soonest. I have
a headache & am weary at heart with all this vexation—& besides there
is no haste now: & when you do come, IF *you do,* I will trust to you not
to recur to one subject, which must lie where it fell . . must! I had begun
to write to you on saturday, to say how I had forgotten to give you your
MSS. which were lying ready for you . . the Hood poems.[1] Would it
not be desirable that you made haste to see them through the press, &
went abroad with your Roman friends[2] at once, to try to get rid of that
uneasiness in the head? Do think of it—& more than think.

For me, you are not to fancy me unwell. Only, not to be worn a
little with the last week's turmoil, were impossible—and Mr. Kenyon
said to me yesterday that he quite wondered how I could bear it at all,—
do anything reasonable at all, & confine my misdoings to sending letters
addressed to him at Brighton, when he was at Dover! If anything
changes, you shall hear from—

E. B. B.

[Mr. Kenyon returns to Dover immediately. His kindness is impotent in the case.][3]

1. In other words, those printed in *Hood's Magazine*.
2. See Letter 83, note 1.
3. Added at the top of the first page.

_____

[*September 17, 1845.*]

Wednesday evening.—
But one word before we leave the subject, and then to leave it
finally,—but I cannot let you go on to fancy a mystery anywhere, in
obstacles or the rest. You deserve at least a full frankness; & in my letter
I meant to be fully frank. I even told you what was an absurdity, so absurd that I should far rather not have told you at all, only that I felt the
need of telling you all: and no mystery is involved in that, except as an
'idiosyncrasy' is a mystery. But the "insurmountable" difficulty is for
you & everybody to see,— —& for me to feel, who have been a very
byword among the talkers, for a confirmed invalid through months &
years, & who, even if I were going to Pisa & had the best prospects possible to me, should yet remain liable to relapses & stand on precarious
ground to the end of my life. Now that is no mystery for the trying of
"faith"; but a plain fact, which neither thinking nor speaking can make
less a fact. But DON'T let us speak of it.
I must speak, however (before the silence) of what you said and
repeat in words for which I gratefully thank you—& which are *not*
'ostentatious' though unnecessary words—for, if I were in a position to
accept sacrifices from you, I would not accept *such* a sacrifice .. amount-
ing to a sacrifice of duty & dignity as well as of ease & satisfaction .. to
an exchange of higher work for lower work .. & of the special work you
are called to, for that which is work for anybody. I am not so ignorant of
⁺the⁺ right uses & destinies of what you have & are. You will leave the
Solicitorgeneralships to the Fitzroy Kellys, & justify your own nature;
& besides, do me the little right, (*over* the *over*-right you are always
doing me) of believing that I would not bear or dare to do *you* so much
wrong, if I were in the position to do it.
And for all the rest I thank you—believe that I thank you .. & that
the feeling is not so weak as the word. That *you* should care at all for *me*
has been a matter of unaffected wonder to me from the first hour until
now—& I cannot help the pain I feel sometimes, in thinking that it
would have been better for you if you never had known me .. May God
turn back the evil of me!—Certainly I admit that I cannot expect you ..

just at this moment, . . to say more than you say, . . & I shall try to be at ease in the consideration that you are as accessible to the "unicorn" now as you ever could be at any former period of your life. And here I have done. I had done *living,* I thought, when you came & sought me out! and why? & to what end? *That,* I cannot help thinking now. Perhaps just that I may pray for you—which were a sufficient end. If you come on saturday I trust you to leave this subject untouched,—as it must be indeed henceforth.

I am yours,
E. B. B.

No word more of Pisa—I shall not go, I think.

107 (W54)   **R.B. to E.B.B.**

[*September 17, 1845.*]

Words!—it was written I should hate and never use them to any purpose. I will not say one word here—very well knowing neither word nor deed avails—from me.

My letter will have reassured you on the point you seem un-decided about—whether I would speak &c

I will come whenever you shall signify that I may . . whenever, acting in my best interests, you feel that it will not hurt ↑you↓ (weary ↑you↓ in any way) to see me—but I fear that on Saturday I must be otherwhere . . I enclose the letter from my old foe,[1]—which could not but melt me for all my moroseness[?] and I can hardly go and return for my sister in time. Will you tell me?

It is dark—but I want to save the post—

Ever yours
R. B.—

1. John Forster had become a "foe" after taking a very magisterial tone in his *Examiner* (June 22, 1844) review of *Colombe's Birthday.* Forster was one of an amateur group headed by Dickens who performed *Every Man in His Humour* at Miss Kelly's Theater. (John Forster, *The Life of Charles Dickens,* Memorial Edition [2 vols., London, 1911], I, 396ff.) Presumably his letter contained tickets for the performance, which was given on September 20, 1845; Forster errs on the date.

108 (W55°)   E.B.B. to R.B.

_____

[*September 18, 1845.*]

Wednesday [for Thursday].
Of course you cannot do otherwise than go with your sister—or it
will be 'Every man *out* of his humour' perhaps—& you are not so very
'savage' after all.

On Monday then, if you do not hear—to the contrary.

Papa has been walking to & fro in this room, looking thoughtfully
& talking leisurely—& every moment I have expected I confess, some
word (that did not come) about Pisa. Mr. Kenyon thinks it cannot end
so—& I do sometimes—& in the meantime I do confess to a little
'savageness' also—at heart!—All I asked him to say the other day, was
that he was not displeased with me—*& he wouldn't;* & for me to walk
across his displeasure spread on the threshold of the door, & moreover
take a sister & brother with me, & ⟨make⟩ do such a thing for the sake
of going to Italy & securing a personal advantage, were altogether impossible, obviously impossible! So poor Papa is quite in disgrace with
me just now—if he would but care for *that!*——

May God bless you. Amuse yourself well on saturday. I could not
see you on thursday any way, for Mr. Kenyon is here every day . . staying in town just on account of this Pisa business, in his abundant kindness—On Monday then.

Ever yours,
E. B. B.

109 (W55)   R.B. to E.B.B.

_____

[*September 18, 1845.*]

Thursday M^g
But you, too, will surely want, if you think me a rational creature,
my explanation—without which all that I have said and done would be
pure madness, I think: it *is* just "what I see" that I *do* see,—or rather it

has proved, since I first visited you, that the reality was infinitely worse than I know it to be . . for at and after the writing of *that first letter,* on my first visit,[1] I believed—thro' some silly or misapprehend[ed] talk, collected at second hand too—that your complaint was of quite another nature—a spinal injury irremediable in the nature of it: had it been *so*— now speak for *me,* for what you hope I am, and say how *that* should affect or neutralize what you *were,* what I wished to associate with myself in you? But *as you now are*—: then if I had married you seven years ago, and this visitation came now first, I should be "fulfilling a pious duty," I suppose, in enduring what could not be amended—a pattern to good people in not running away . . for where were *now* the use and the good & the profit and— —

I desire in this life (with very little fluctuation for a man & too weak a one) to live and just write out certain things which are in me, and so save my soul. I would endeavour to do this if I were forced to "live among lions" as you once said[2]—but I should best do this if I lived quietly with myself and with you. That you cannot dance like Cerito[3] does not materially disarrange this plan—nor that I might (beside the perpetual incentive and sustainment and consolation) get, over and above the main reward, the incidental, particular and unexpected happiness of being allowed when not working to rather occupy myself with watching you, that ˄with˅ certain other pursuits I might be ˄otherwise˅ addicted to—*this*, also, does not constitute an obstacle, as I see obstacles—

But *you* see them—and I see *you*, and know my first duty and do it resolutely if not cheerfully.

As for referring again, till leave by word or letter—you will see—

And very likely, the tone of this letter even will be misunderstood —because I studiously cut out all vain words, protesting &c:—No— will it?

I said, unadvisedly, that Saturday was taken from me . . but it was dark and I had not looked at the tickets—the hour of the performance is later than I thought: if to-morrow ˄does not˅ suit you, as I infer, let it be Saturday—at 3—and I will leave earlier, a little, and all will be quite right here: one hint will apprise me.

God bless you, dearest friend.

R. B.

⌈Something else just heard, makes me reluctantly strike out *Saturday—*

    Monday then?⌉[4]

1. The letter E.B.B. returned to be destroyed. See Letter 30 and the note which precedes it.
2. Letter 8.
3. Fanny Cerito was the current sensation of the opera ballet and one of four great dancers of her generation, the others being Marie Taglioni, Carlotta Grisi, and Lucille Grahn.
4. This is an enclosure, written in pencil.

110 (W56°)   **E.B.B. to R.B.**

[*September 19, 1845.*]

                          Friday Morning.

It is not 'misunderstanding' you to know you to be the most generous & loyal of all in the world—you overwhelm me with your generosity—only while you see from above & I from below, we cannot see the same thing in the same light. Moreover, if we DID, I should be more beneath you in one sense, than I am. Do me the justice of remembering this whenever you recur in thought to the subject which ends here in the words of it.

I began to write last Saturday to thank you for all the delight I had had in Shelley,[1] though you beguiled me about the pencil-marks which are few—Besides the translations, some of the original poems /were⟩are/ not in my copy & /are⟩were/, so, quite new to me. 'Marianne's Dream' I had been anxious about to no end—I only know it now.—

On Monday at the usual hour. As to coming twice into town on saturday, that would have been quite foolish if it had been possible. Dearest friend

                         I am yours, E. B. B.

1. Browning seems to have lent E.B.B. his copy of Shelley's *Posthumous Poems* (1824; *Browning Collections*, p. 129, Lot #1079).

A visit noted on the envelope of Letter 110 occurred at this point:
+Monday Sepr 22,
3–4$\frac{1}{2}$ p.m.

111 (W57°)   **E.B.B. to R.B.**

_____

[*September 23, 1845.*]

I have nothing to say about Pisa, . . but a great deal (if I could say it) about *you*, who do what is wrong by your own confession & are ill because of it & make people uneasy . . . now *is* it right altogether? is it right to do wrong? . . for it comes to *that*:—& is it kind to do so much wrong? . . for it comes almost to *that* besides. Ah—you should not indeed!—I seem to see quite plainly that you will be ill in a serious way, if you do not take care & take exercise; & so you must consent to be teazed a little into taking both. And if you will not take them here . . or not so effectually as in other places,—*why not go with your Italian friends?*[1] Have you thought of it at all? *I* have been thinking since yesterday that it might be best for you to go at once, now that the probability has turned quite against me. If I were going, I sh^d ask you not to do so immediately . . but you see how unlikely it is!—although I mean still to speak my whole thoughts—I *will do that* . . even though for the mere purpose of self-satisfaction. George came last night—but there is an adverse star this morning, & neither of us has the opportunity necessary. Only both he and I WILL *speak*—that is certain. And Arabel had the kindness to say yesterday that if I liked to go, she would go with me at whatever hazard —which is very kind—but you know I could not—it w^d not be right of me. And perhaps after all we may gain the point lawfully,—& if not . . at the worst . . the winter may be warm (it is better to fall into the hands of God, as the Jew said)[2] & I may lose less strength than usual, . . having more than usual to lose . . and altogether it may not be so bad ⟨as⟩ an alternative. As to being the cause of any anger against my sister, you would not advise me into such a position, I am sure—it would be untenable for one moment.

But *you* . . in that case, . . would it not be good for your head if you went at once? I praise myself for saying so to you—yet if it really is good

for you, I don't deserve the praising at all. And how was it on saturday?
—that question I did not ask yesterday—with Ben Jonson & the amateurs?—I thought of you at the time—I mean, on that saturday evening,
nevertheless.

You shall hear when there is any more to say. May God bless you,
dearest friend!—I am ever yours

E. B. B.

1. See Letter 83, note 1.
2. Not identified.

112 (W56)   **R.B. to E.B.B.**

[*September 24, 1845.*]

Wednesday E^g

I walked to town, this morning, and back again—so that when I
found your note on my return, and knew what you had been enjoining
me in the way of exercise, I seemed as if I knew, too, why that energetic
fit had possessed me and why I succumbed to it so readily. You shall
never have to intimate twice to me that such an insignificant thing,
even, as the taking exercise should be done. Besides, I have many
motives now for wishing to continue well—But Italy *just now*—Oh,
no! My friends would go thro' Pisa, too.

On that subject I must not speak—And you have "more strength
to lose," and are so well, evidently so well; that is, so much better, so
sure to be still better—can it be that you will not go!

Here are your new notes on my verses.[1] Where are my words for
the thanks? But you know what I feel, and shall feel—ever feel—for
these and for all. The notes would be beyond price to me if they came
from some dear Phemius[2] of a teacher—but from you!

The Theatricals "went off" with great éclat, and the performance
was really good, really clever or better. Forster's 'Kitely' was very em-
phatic and earnest, and grew into great interest, quite up to the poet's
allotted tether, which is none of the longest. He pitched the character's
key note too gravely, I thought; *beginning* with certainty, rather than
mere suspicion, of evil. Dickens' "Bobadil" *was* capital—with perhaps

a little too much of the consciousness of entire cowardice . . which I
don't so willingly attribute to the noble would-be pacificator of Europe,
besieger of Strigonium &c—but the end of it all was really pathetic, as it
should be, for Bobadil is only too clever for the company of fools he
makes ⟨∥ · · · ∥⟩ ⊦wonderment⊦ for—having once the misfortune to
relish their society, and to need but too pressingly their "tobacco-
money," what can he do but suit himself to their capacities?—And D.
Jerrold[3] was very amusing and clever in his 'Country Gull'—And Mr.
Leech[4] superb in the Town Master Mathew. All were good, indeed,
and were voted good, and called on, and cheered off, and praised heartily
behind their backs & before the curtain. Stanfield's[5] function had exercise solely in the touching up (very effectively) sundry "Scenes"—
painted scenes—and the dresses, which were perfect, had the advantage
of Mr. Maclise's[6] experience. And—all is told!

    And now; I shall hear, you promise me, if anything occurs—with
what feeling, I wait and hope, you know. If there is *no* best of reasons
against it, Saturday, you remember, is my day—This fine weather, too!

    May God bless my dearest friend—

Ever yours R. B.

    1. See Letter 66, note 1.

    2. The minstrel (*Odyssey* I) who sings of the Greek return from Troy.

    3. Douglas William Jerrold (1803–57) was a comic playwright, magazine
writer, and editor (at this time of *Douglas Jerrold's Shilling Magazine*). His best-
remembered work is *Mrs. Caudle's Curtain Lectures* (collected 1846).

    4. John Leech (1817–64), caricaturist and illustrator of Dickens's *Christmas
Carol,* was a famous contributor to *Punch*.

    5. William Clarkson Stanfield (1794–1867), famous as a painter of seascapes,
began as a scene painter at Old Royalty, a sailors' theater in London.

    6. David Maclise (1806–70), an Irish painter known for his portraits and scenes
drawn from literature and history. One of his pictures suggested the lines that
Browning later expanded into *In a Gondola* (G & M, p. 128; Mrs. Orr, p. 193).

113 (W59°)   **E.B.B. to R.B.**

[*Postmarked September 25, 1845.*]

I have spoken again, & the result is that we are in precisely the same position,—only with bitterer feelings on one side. If I go or stay they *must* be bitter⟨er⟩: words have been said that I cannot easily forget, nor remember without pain—& yet I really do almost smile in the midst of it all, to think how I was treated this morning as an undutiful daughter because I tried to put on my gloves . . for there was no worse provocation. At least he complained of the undutifulness & rebellion (! ! !) of everyone in the house—& when I asked if he meant that reproach for ME, the answer was that he meant it for all of us, one with another. And I could not get an answer. He would not even grant me the consolation of thinking that I sacrificed what I supposed to be good, to HIM. I told him that my prospects of health seemed to me to depend on taking this step, but that ↑through my affection for him,↓ I was ready to sacrifice those to his pleasure if he exacted it—only it was necessary to my self-satisfaction in future years, to understand definitely that the sacrifice *was* exacted by him & *was* made to him, . . & not thrown away blindly & by a misapprehension. And he would not answer *that*. I might do my own way, he said—*he* would not speak—*he* would not say that he was not displeased with me, nor the contrary:—I had better do what I liked:—for his part, he washed his hands of me altogether—

And so I have been very wise—witness how my eyes are swelled with annotations & reflections on all this! The best of it is that now George himself admits I can do no more in the way of speaking, . . I have no spell for charming the dragons, . . & allows me to be passive & enjoins me to be tranquil, and not "make up my mind" to any dreadful exertion for the future. Moreover he advises me to go on with the preparations for the voyage, & promises to state the case himself at the last hour to the "highest authority"; & judge finally whether it be possible for me to go with the necessary companionship. And it seems best to go to Malta on the 3rd of October—if at all . . from steam-packet reasons . . without excluding Pisa . . remember . . by any means.

Well!—& what do you think? Might it be desirable for me to give up the whole? Tell me. I feel aggrieved of course & wounded—& whether I go or stay that feeling must last—I cannot help it. But my spirits sink altogether at the thought of leaving England *so*—& then I doubt about Arabel & Stormie . . & it seems to me that I *ought not* to mix them up in a business of this kind where the advantage is merely personal to myself. On the other side, George holds that if I give up & stay even, there will be displeasure just the same, . . & that, when once gone, the irritation will exhaust & smooth itself away—which however does not touch my chief objection. Would it be better . . more *right* . . to give it up? Think for me. Even if I hold on to the last, at the last I shall be thrown off—*that* is my conviction. But . . shall I give up *at once?* Do think for me—

And I have thought that if you like to come on friday instead of saturday . . as there is the uncertainty about next week, . . it w^d divide the time more equally: but let it be as you like & according to circumstances as you see them. Perhaps you have decided to go at once with your friends—who knows? I wish I could know that you were better to-day—May God bless you Ever yours, E. B. B.

114 *(W57)*   *R.B. to E.B.B.*

[*Postmarked September 25, 1845.*]

You have said to me more than once that you wished I might never know certain feelings *you* had been forced to endure. I suppose all of us have the proper place where a blow should fall to be felt most—and I truly wish *you* may never feel what I have to bear in looking on, quite powerless, and silent, while you are subjected to this treatment, which I refuse to characterize—so blind is it *for* blindness. I think I ought to understand what a father may exact, and a child should comply with— and I respect the most ambiguous of love's caprices if they give never so slight a clue to their all-justifying source: did I, when you signified to me the probable objections . . you remember what . . to myself, my own happiness,—did I once allude to . . much less argue against, or refuse to acknowledge those objections? For I wholly sympathize, however it go against me, with the highest, wariest, pride & love for you, and the proper jealousy and vigilance they entail—but now, and here, the jewel is not being over guarded, but ruined, cast /off⟩away/. And whoever is privileged to interfere should do so in the possessor's own interest—all common sense interferes—all rationality against absolute no-reason at all . . and you ask whether you ought to obey this no-reason?—I will tell you: all passive obedience and implicit submission of will and in-

tellect is by far too easy, if well considered, to be the course prescribed
by God to Man in this life of probation—for they *evade* probation altogether, tho' foolish people think otherwise: chop off your legs, you will
never go astray,—stifle your reason altogether and you will find it is
difficult to reason ill: "it is hard to make these sacrifices!"—Not so hard
as to lose the reward or incur the penalty of an Eternity to come; "hard
to effect them, then, and go through with them"—*not* hard, when the
leg is to be *cut off*⟨or⟩—that it is rather harder to keep it quiet on a stool,
I know very well. The partial indulgence, the proper exercise of one's
faculties, there is the difficulty and problem for solution, set by that
Providence which might have made the laws of Religion as indubitable
as those of vitality, and ↑revealed↓ the articles of belief as certainly as that
condition, for instance, by which we breathe so many times in a minute
to support life: but there is no reward proposed for the feat of breathing,
and a great one for that of believing—consequently there must go a
great deal more ↑of voluntary↓ effort to this latter than is implied in the
getting absolutely rid of it at once, by adopting the direction of an infallible church, or private judgment of another—for all our life is some
form of religion, and all our action some belief, and there is but one
law, however modified, for the greater and the less—In your case I do
think you are called upon to do your duty to yourself; that is, to God in
the end: your own reason should examine the whole matter in dispute
by every light which can be put in requisition; and every interest that
appears to be affected by your conduct should have its utmost claims
considered—your father's in the first place; and that interest, not in the
miserable limits of a few days' pique or whim in which it would seem
to express itself,—but in its whole extent . . the *hereafter* which all
momentary passion prevents him seeing . . indeed, the *present* on either
side which everyone else must see—And this examination made, with
whatever earnestness you will, I do think and am sure that on its conclusion you should act, in confidence that a duty has been performed . .
difficult, or how were it a duty? Will it *not* be infinitely harder to act so
than to blindly adopt his pleasure, and die under it? Who can *not* do
that? ⟨∥ · · · ∥⟩

    I fling these hasty rough words over the paper, fast as they will fall—
knowing to whom I cast them, and that any sense they may contain or
point to, will be caught and understood, and presented in a better light:
the hard thing . . this is all I want to say . . is to act on one's own best

conviction—not to abjure it and accept another will, and say "*there* is my plain duty"—easy it is, whether plain or no!

How "all changes!" When I first knew you,—you know what followed. I supposed you to labour under an incurable complaint—and, of course, to be completely dependent on your father for its commonest alleviations; the moment after that inconsiderate letter,[1] I reproached myself bitterly with the selfishness apparently involved in any proposition I might then have made—for tho' I have never been at all frightened of the world, nor mistrustful of my power to deal with it, and get my purpose out of it if once I thought it worth while, yet I could not but feel the consideration, of WHAT failure would *now* be, paralyse all effort even in fancy: when you told me lately that "you could never be poor" —all my solicitude was at an end—I had but myself to care about, and I told you, what I believed and believe, that I can at any time amply provide for that, and that I could cheerfully & confidently undertake the removing *that* obstacle. Now again the circumstances shift—and you are in what I should wonder at as the veriest slavery—and I who *could* free you from it, I am here—scarcely daring to write . . tho' I know you must feel for me and forgive what forces itself from me . . what retires so mutely into my heart at your least word . . what *shall not* be again written or spoken, if you so will . . that I should be made happy beyond all hope of expression by—Now while I *dream,* let me once dream! I would marry you now and thus—I would come when you let me, and go when you bade me—I would be no more than one of your brothers— "*no more*"—that is, instead of getting to-morrow for Saturday, I should get Saturday as well—two hours for one—when your head ached I should be *here.* I deliberately choose the realization of that dream (—of sitting simply by you for an hour every day) rather than any other, excluding you, I am able to form for this world, or any world I know— And it will continue but a dream. God bless my dearest E.B.B. ⟨‖ · · · ‖⟩
                                                            R. B.

⌈You understand that I see you to-morrow, Friday, as you propose. I am better—thank you—and will go out to-day.
You know what I am, what I would speak, and all I would do.⌉[2]

---

1. See Letter 30 and the note which precedes it.
2. The postscript is actually a separate enclosed note. The final sentence has so light a line drawn through it that it cannot be considered a genuine cancellation.

The following letter was written shortly after Browning's visit noted on the envelope of Letter 113:

+ Friday, Sepr 26

3–4$\frac{1}{2}$ p.m.

It marks the important turning point in the relationship between E.B.B. and Browning. The letters of the preceding month have been carefully reviewing that whole relationship, just as had been done earlier, on the occasion of Browning's indiscreetly romantic letter after their first meeting. Letter 103, for instance, repeats less adamantly E.B.B.'s earlier request to avoid romantic complications. Edward Barrett's lack of concern for his daughter, however, led Browning to declare himself openly once more in Letter 114, apparently written and mailed in haste after he had read E.B.B.'s account of the scene in which her father " washed his hands of me." This potentially offensive letter was not discussed on Friday afternoon, but E.B.B., writing that evening, relents somewhat in her refusal to consider Browning more than a friend.

It is noteworthy that after this emotional turning point we begin to encounter in these letters phrases and ideas which parallel Sonnets from the Portuguese. *For example, the third paragraph of the following letter may remind the reader of the second sonnet.*

115 (W59°)　　　　　　　*E.B.B. to R.B.*

[*September 26, 1845.*]

Friday evening.

I had your letter late last night, everyone almost, being out of the house by an accident, so that it was left in the letter-box, and if I had wished to answer it before I saw you, it had scarcely been possible.

But it will be the same thing—for you know as well as if you saw my answer, what it must be, what it cannot choose but be, on pain of sinking me so infinitely below not merely your level but my own, that the depth cannot bear a glance down. Yet, though I am not made of such clay as to admit of my taking a base advantage of certain noble extravagances, (& that I am not I thank God for your sake) I will say, I must say, that your words in this letter have done me good & made me happy, . . that I thank & bless you for them, . . & that to receive such a proof of attachment from YOU, not only overpowers every present evil, but seems to me a full and abundant amends for the merely personal sufferings of my whole life. When I had read that letter last night I *did* think so. I looked round & round for the small bitternesses which for several days had been bitter to me—& I could not find one of them. The tear-marks went away in the moisture of new, happy tears. Why, how else could I have felt? how else do you think I could?—How would any woman have felt . . who could feel at all . . hearing such words said (though "in a dream" indeed) by such a speaker?—

And now listen to me in turn. You have touched me more profoundly than I thought even *you* could have touched me—my heart was full when you came here to-day. Henceforward I am yours for everything but to do you harm—and I am yours too much, in my heart, ever to consent to do you harm in that way— —If I could consent to do it, not only should I be less loyal . . but in one sense, less yours. I say this to you without drawback and reserve, because it is all I am able to say, & perhaps all I *shall* be able to say. However this may be, a promise goes to you in it that none, except God & your will, shall interpose between you & me, . . I mean, that if He should free me within a moderate time from the trailing chain of this weakness, I will then be to you whatever at that hour you shall choose . . whether friend or more than friend . . a friend to the last in any case. So it rests with God & with you—Only in the meanwhile you are most absolutely free . . "unentangled" (as they call it) by the breadth of a thread—& if I did not know that you considered yourself so, I would not see you any more, let the effort cost me what it might. You may force me to *feel:* . . but you cannot force me to *think* contrary to my first thought . . that it were better for you to forget me at once in one relation. And if better for *you,* can it be bad for *me?*— which flings me down on the stone-pavement of the logicians.

And now if I ask a boon of you,[1] will you forget afterwards that it ever was asked?—I have hesitated a great deal; but my face is down on the stone-pavement ⟨‖ · · · ·‖⟩—no I will not ask today—It shall be for another day—& may God bless you on this & on those that come after, my dearest friend.[2]

---

1. The return of the destroyed letter, not fully stated until November (Letter 145).

2. The last three words are nervously retraced.

Letter 115, E.B.B. to R.B., pages 2 and 3

A turning point in their relations

Wimpole Street at the turn of the century

116 (W58)   R.B. to E.B.B.
                    _____

[September 27, 1845.]

Think for me, speak for me, my dearest, *my own!* You that are all
great-heartedness and generosity, do that one more generous thing!
God bless you for

                                                    R. B.

What can it be you ask of me!—'a boon'—once my answer to *that*
had been the plain one—but now . . when I have better experience of—
No, now I have BEST experience of how you understand my interests; that at last we *both* know what is my true good—so ask, ask! *My
own, now!* For there it is!—oh, do not fear I am *"entangled"*—my crown
is loose on my head, not nailed there—my pearl lies in my hand—I may
return it to the sea, if I will!

What is it you ask of me, this first asking?

117 (W60°)   E.B.B. to R.B.
                    _____

[September 29, 1845.]

Then *first*, . . first, I ask you not to misunderstand. Because we do
not . . no, we do not . . agree (but disagree) as to "what is your true
good" . . but disagree, & as widely as ever indeed.

The other asking shall come in its season . . some day before I go if
I go. It only relates to a restitution—and you cannot guess it if you try . .
so don't try!—and perhaps you cant grant it if you try—and I cannot
guess.

Cabins and berths all taken in the Malta steamer for both third &
twentieth of October!—see what dark lanterns the stars hold out, &
how I shall stay in England after all as I think!—And thus we are thrown
back on the old Gibraltar scheme with its shifting of steamers . . unless
we take the dreary alternative of Madeira!—or Cadiz!—Even suppose
Madeira, . . why it were for a few months alone—& there w^d be no
temptation to loiter as in Italy.

DON'T think too hardly of poor Papa—You have his wrong side . . his side of peculiar wrongness . . to you just now. When you have walked round him you will have other thoughts of him.

Are you better, I wonder? & taking exercise & trying to be better? May God bless you! Tuesday need not be the last day if you like to take one more besides—for there is no going until the fourth or seventh, . . and the seventh is the more probable of those two. But now you have done with me until tuesday. Ever yours, E. B. B.

Browning came to call the day before the following letter was written; on the envelope of Letter 117 he noted:

+Tuesday Sepr 30
3–4½ p.m.

118 (W61°)   **E.B.B. to R.B.**
_____

[*October 1, 1845.*]

Wednesday.

I have read to the last line of your Rosicrucian;[1] & my scepticism grew & grew through Hume's process of doubtful doubts, and at last rose to the full stature of incredulity . . for I never could believe Shelley capable of such a book (call it a book!), not even with a flood of boarding-school idiocy dashed in by way of dilution. Altogether it roused me to deny myself so far as to look at the date of the book, & to get up and travel to the other end of the room to confront it with other dates in the "Letters from Abroad" . . . (I, who never think of a date except the 'AD,' and am inclined every now & then to write *that* down as 1548 . .) well! & on comparing these ⟨two⟩ dates in these two volumes before my eyes, I find that your Rosicrucian was "printed for Stockdale" in *1822*, & that Shelley *died in the July of the same year!!*—There, is a vindicating fact for you! And unless the 'Rosicrucian' went into more editions than one, & dates ↑here↓ from a latter one, . . which is not ascertainable from this fragment of a titlepage, . . the innocence of the great poet stands proved—now doesn't it? For nobody will say that he published

such a book in the last year of his life, in the maturity of his genius, &
that Godwin's daughter helped him in it!—That 'dripping dew' from
the skeleton is the only living word in the book!—which really amused
me notwithstanding, from the intense absurdity of the whole composition . . descriptions . . sentiments . . & morals.

Judge yourself if I had not better say 'No' about the cloak! I would
take it if you wished such a kindness to me—& although you might find
it very useful to yourself . . or to your mother or sister . . still if you
wished me to take it I should like to have it, & the mantle of the prophet
might bring me down something of his spirit!—but do you remember
. . do you consider . . how many talkers there are in this house, & what
would be talked—or that it is not worth while to provoke it all? And
Papa, knowing it, would not like it—& altogether it is far better, believe
me, that you should keep your own cloak, & I, the thought of the kindness you meditated in respect to it. I have heard nothing more—nothing.

I was asked the other day by a very young friend of mine . . the
daughter of an older friend who once followed you up stairs in this
house . . Mr. Hunter, an Independent minister . . for "Mr. Browning's
autograph." She wants it for a collection . . for her album—& so, will
you write out a verse or two on one side of note paper . . not as you write
for the printers . . & let me keep my promise & send it to her? I forgot to
ask you before. Oh one verse will do . . anything will do . . and dont let
me be bringing you into vexation. It need not be of MS. rarity.

You are not better . . really . . I fear. And your mother's being ill
affects you more than you like to admit, I fear besides. Will you, when
you write, say how *both* are . . nothing extenuating, you know. May
God bless you, my dearest friend—ever yours, E. B. B.

1. *St. Irvyne: or the Rosicrucian* was published in 1811, as written by "a Gentleman
of the University of Oxford," by J. J. Stockdale, who, as Browning conjectures in
the following letter, issued his remainders in 1822 with a new title page. H. Buxton
Forman, *The Prose Works of Percy Bysshe Shelley* (4 vols., London, 1880), I, [162].

[*October 2, 1845.*]

Thursday.

Well, let us hope against hope in the sad matter of the novel—yet, yet,—it *is* by Shelley, if you will have the truth—as I happen to *know*—proof *last* being that Leigh Hunt told me he unearthed it in Shelley's own library at Marlow once, to the writer's horror & shame—"He snatched it out of my hands"—said H—yet I thrust it into yours . . so much for the subtle fence of friends who reach your heart by a side-thrust, as I told you on Tuesday, after the enemy has fallen back breath-less and baffled. As for the date, that Stockdale was a notorious pirate and raker-up of rash publications . . and, do you know, I suspect the *title-page* is all that boasts such novelty,—see if the *book,* the inside leaves, be not older evidently!—a common trick of the "trade" to this day: the history of this and 'Justrozzi,' as it is spelt,—the other novel,—may be read in Medwin's conversations[1]—and, as I have been told, in Lady Ch. Bury's "Reminiscences" or whatever she calls them[2] . . the "Giustrozzi" was *certainly* "written in concert with"—somebody or other . . for I confess the whole story grows monstrous, and even the froth of wine strings itself in bright bubbles,—ah, but this was the scum of the fermenting vat, do you see? I am happy to say I forget the novel entirely, or almost—and only keep the exact impression which you have gained . . thro' me! "The fair cross of gold *he dashed on the floor*"—(*that* is my pet-line . . because the "chill dew" of a place not commonly sup-posed to favour humidity is a plagiarism from Lewis's 'Monk,' it now flashes on me![3] Yes, Lewis, too, puts the phrase into intense italics.) And now, please read a chorus in the "Prometheus Unbound" or a scene from the "Cenci"—and join company with Shelley again!

—From "chill dew" I come to the *cloak*—you are quite right—and I give up that fancy. Will you, then, take one more precaution when *all* proper safeguards have been adopted; and, when *everything* is sure, con-trive some one /surety⟩sureness/ besides, against cold or wind or sea-air; and say "*this*—for the cloak which is not here, and to help the heart's wish which *is*"—so I shall be there *palpably*. Will you do this? Tell me you will to-morrow—and tell me all good news.

My Mother suffers still . . I hope she is no worse—but a little better
—certainly better. I am better too, in my unimportant way.

Now I will write you the verses . . some easy ones out of a paper-full
meant to go between poem & poem ↑in my next number↓ and break
the shock of collision.

Let me kiss your hand—dearest! My heart and life—all is yours,
and forever—God make you happy as I am thro' you—Bless you

R. B.

1. "It was from an early acquaintance with German writers that [Shelley]
probably imbibed a romantic turn of mind; at least, we find him before fifteen
publishing two Rosa-Matilda-like novels called 'Justrozzi' [*Zastrozzi*] and 'The
Rosicrucian' [*St. Irvyne*]." Thomas Medwin, *Journal of the Conversations of Lord
Byron* (London, 1824), p. 248 n.

2. Lady Charlotte Bury's *Diary Illustrative of the Times of George the Fourth*
(2 vols., London, 1838) mentions *St. Irvyne* but not *Zastrozzi*. Browning corrects
Medwin's un-Italian spelling but perpetuates his error about the title.

3. *The Monk* (1796) by Matthew Gregory Lewis (1775–1818) was one of the
wildest and most satanic of Gothic novels.

*A note on the envelope of Letter 118 indicated that Browning visited
E.B.B. the day before she wrote the following letter:*
+ Friday, Oct. 3. 1845
3–4¼ p.m.

120 (W62°)   **E.B.B. to R.B.**

[*October 4, 1845.*]

Saturday.

Tuesday is given up in full council. The thing is beyond doubting
of, as George says & as you thought yesterday. And then George has it
in his head to beguile the Duke of Palmella out of a smaller cabin, so that
I might sail from the Thames on the twentieth—and whether he succeeds or not, I humbly confess that one of the chief advantages of the
new plan if not the very chief (as *I* see it) is just in the *delay*.

Your spring-song[1] is full of beauty as you know very well—&

"that's the wise thrush," so characteristic of you (& of the thrush too) that I was sorely tempted to ask you to write it "twice over," . . & not send the first copy to Mary Hunter notwithstanding my promise to her. And now when you come to print these fragments, would it not be well if you were to stoop to the vulgarism of prefixing some word of introduction, as other people do, you know, . . a title . . a name? You perplex your readers often by casting yourself on their intelligence in these things—and although it is true that readers in general are stupid & cant understand, it is still more true that they are lazy & wont understand . . & they dont catch your point of sight at first unless you think it worth while to push them by the shoulders & force them into the right place. Now these fragments . . you mean to print them with a line between . . & not one word at the top of it . . now don't you!—And then people will read

"Oh, to be in England"

and say to themselves . . "Why who is this? . . who's out of England?" Which is an extreme case of course; but you will see what I mean . . & often I have observed how some of the very most beautiful of your lyrics have suffered just from your disdain of the usual tactics of writers in this one respect.

And you are not better, still—you are worse instead of better . . are you not? Tell me—And what can you mean about 'unimportance,' when you were worse last week . . this expiring week . . than ever before, by your own confession? And now?—And your mother?

Yes—I promise! And so, . . /I⟩*Elijah*/ will be missed instead of /the cloak⟩his mantle/[2] . . which will be a losing contract after all. But it shall be as you say. May you be able to say that you are better! God bless you.

Ever yours.

[Never think of the "White Slave."[3] I had just taken it up. The trash of it is prodigious—far beyond Mr. Smythe. Not that I can settle upon a book just now, in all this wind, to judge of it fairly.][4]

---

1. The autograph verses for Mary Hunter were *Home-Thoughts from Abroad*.
   2. A reference to the offer by Browning to lend E.B.B. a cloak for her projected Italian trip (see Letters 118 and 119). A variation of this same playful allusion to II Kings 2:13 appears in *Aurora Leigh*, III, 53–54.
   3. *The White Slave; or, The Russian Peasant Girl,* " by the author of ' Revelations

of Russia'" (Charles Frederick Hennigren, 1815–77) had been published a week or so earlier.

4. This last paragraph is written on a separate sheet of paper.

121 (W60)   **R.B. to E.B.B.**

──────────────

[*October 6, 1845.*]

Monday M^g

I should certainly think that the Duke of Palmella may be induced, and with no great difficulty, to give up a cabin under the circumstances —and *then* the plan becomes really objection-proof, so far as mortal plans go: but now you must think all the boldlier about whatever difficulties remain, just because they are so much the fewer: it *is* cold already in the mornings and evenings—cold and (this morn^g) foggy—I did not ask if you continue to go out from time to time . . I am sure you *should,*— you would so prepare yourself properly for the fatigue and change— yesterday it was very warm & fine in the afternoon, nor is this noontime so bad, if the requisite precautions are taken: and do make "journeys across the room," and out of it, meanwhile, and *stand* when possible— get all the strength ready, now that so much is to be spent. Oh, if I were by you!

Thank you, thank you—I will devise titles—I quite see what you say, now you do say it. I am (this Monday morning, the prescribed day for efforts & beginnings) looking over & correcting what you read—to press they shall go, and then the plays can follow gently, and then . . "Oh to be in Pisa. Now that E. B. B. is there!"—And I *shall* be there—! I am much better to-day;—and my mother better—and to-morrow I shall see you—So come good things together!

Dearest—till to-morrow and ever I am yours, wholly yours— May God bless you!

R. B.

You do not ask me that "boon"[1]—why is that?—Besides, I have my own *real* boons to ask too, as you will inevitably find, and I shall perhaps get heart by your example.

1. See Letter 115, note 1.

122 (W63°)   E.B.B. to R.B.

[October 6, 1845.]

Ah but the good things do *not* come together—for just as your letter comes I am driven to asking you to leave tuesday for wednesday. On tuesday Mr. Kenyon is to be here or not to be here, he says—there's a doubt . . & you would rather go to a clear day. So if you do not hear from me again I shall expect you on *Wednesday* unless I hear to the contrary from you:—and if anything happens to wednesday you shall hear. Mr. Kenyon is in town for only two days, or three. I never could grumble against him, so good & kind as he is:—but he may not come after all to-morrow—so it is not grudging the obolus to Belisarius,[1] but the squandering of the last golden days at the bottom of the purse.

Do I 'stand'—Do I walk? Yes—'most uprightly.' I 'walk uprightly every day.' Do I go out?—no, never. And I am not to be scolded for *that,* because when you were looking at the sun to-day, I was marking the east wind—and perhaps if I had breathed a breath of it . . farewell Pisa. People who can walk don't always walk into the lion's den as a consequence—do they? should they? Are you "sure that they should"? I write in great haste. So Wednesday then . . perhaps!——

And yours every day.

You understand. Wednesday—if nothing to the contrary.

1. The Roman general Belisarius was dismissed by Justinian for supposed complicity in a plot. There is a legend that says that he was blinded and became a beggar, asking passersby, "Obolum da mihi." (Sir Thomas Browne, *Pseudodoxia Epidemica* VII. xvii, and Nathaniel Wanley, *Wonders of the Little World* VI. xv. 22.) The phrase is a favorite with E.B.B. and turns up often in her letters and poems.

123 (W64°)   E.B.B. to R.B.

[October 7, 1845.]

Wednesday [Tuesday] Evening.
Mr. Kenyon never came. My sisters met him in the street, &

he had been 'detained all day in the city & would certainly be here to-morrow' . . wednesday! And so you see what has happened to wednesday.! Moreover he may come besides on thursday, . . I can answer for nothing. Only if I do not write & if you find thursday admissible, will you come then? In the case of an obstacle, you shall hear. And it is not (in the meantime) my fault—now is it?—I have been quite enough vexed about it, indeed.

Did the Monday work work harm to the head, I wonder? I do fear so that you wont get through those papers with impunity . . especially if the plays are to come after . . though ever so "gently." And if you are to suffer, it would be right to tongue-tie that silver Bell, & leave the congregations to their selling of cabbages.[1] Which is unphilanthropic of me perhaps, . .ὦ φίλτατε;[2]

Be sure that I shall be 'bold' when the time for going comes—& both bold & capable of the effort. I am desired to keep to the respirator & the cabin for a day or two, while the cold can reach us, . . & midway in the bay of Biscay some change of climate may be felt, they say. There is no sort of danger for me; except that I shall *stay in England*. And why is it that I feel tonight more than ever almost, as if I should stay in England? Who can tell? *I* can tell ⟨‖ · · · ‖⟩ one thing. IF I stay, it will not be from a failure in my resolution—*that will* not be—*shall* not be. Yes—& Mr. Kenyon & I agreed the other day that there was something of the tigress-nature very distinctly cognizable under what he is pleased to call my "Ba-lambishness."

Then, on thursday! . . unless something happens to *thursday* . . and I shall write in that case. And I trust to you (as always) to attend to your own convenience—just as you may trust to me to remember my own 'boon.' Ah—you are curious, I think! Which is scarcely wise of you—because it MAY, you know, be the roc's egg[3] after all. But no, it *isn't*—I will say just so much. And besides I *did* say that it was a 'restitution',—which limits the guesses if it does not put an end to them. Unguessable, I choose it to be.

And now I feel as if I should *not* stay in England. Which is the difference between one five minutes and another. May God bless you ——Ever yours, E. B. B.

1. An allusion to Letter 7.
2. "O Beloved."
3. An allusion to Letter 40.

October, 1845

124 *(W61)* R.B. to E.B.B.

[*October 8, 1845.*]

12—Wednesday.

Well, dearest, at all events I get up with the assurance I shall see you, and go on till the fatal 11¼ p.m. believing in the same, and *then*, if after all there *does* come such a note as this with its instructions, why, first, it is such a note and such a gain, and next it makes a great day out of to-morrow that was to have been so little of a day, that is all. Only, only, I am suspicious, now, of a real loss to me in the end; for, *putting* off yesterday, I dared put off (on your part) Friday to Saturday . . while *now* . . what shall be said to that?

Dear Mr. Kenyon to be the smiling inconscious obstacle to any pleasure of mine, if [it] were merely pleasure!

But I want to catch our next post—to-morrow, then, excepting what is to be excepted!

Bless you, my dearest—
Your own
R. B.

The "exceptions" did not materialize; Browning noted his visit on the envelope of Letter 123:

+ Thursday Octr 9
3–4½

125 *(W65°)* E.B.B. to R.B.

[*October 10–11, 1845.*]

Dear Mr. Kenyon has been here again & talking so (in his kindness too) about the probabilities as to Pisa being against me . . about all depending 'on one throw' & the 'dice being loaded' &c. . . . that I looked at him aghast as if he looked at the future through the folded curtain & was licensed to speak oracles:—& ever since I have been out of spirits . .

oh, out of spirits, . . & must write myself back again, or try. After all he may be wrong like another—& I should tell you that he reasons altogether from the delay . . and that " the cabins will therefore be taken " & the "circular bills" out of reach! He *said* that one of his purposes in staying in town, was to '*knout*' me every day—didn't he?

Well—George will probably speak before *he* leaves town, which will be on monday!—and now that the hour approaches, I do feel as if the house stood upon gunpowder, & as if I held Guy Fawkes's lantern in my right hand.—And no! I shall not go. The obstacles will not be those of Mr. Kenyon's finding—and what their precise character will be I do not see distinctly. Only that they will be sufficient, & thrown by one hand just where the wheel sh^d turn, . . *that,* I see—& you will, in a few days.—

Did you go to Moxon's & settle the printing matter?[1] Tell me. And what was the use of telling Mr. Kenyon that you were 'quite well' when you know you are not? Will you say to me how you are, saying the truth?—& also how your mother is—?

To show the significance of the omission of those evening or rather night visits of Papa's . . for they came sometimes at eleven, and sometimes at twelve, . . I will tell you that he used to sit & talk in them, & then *always* kneel & pray with me and for me—which I used of course to feel as a proof of very kind & affectionate sympathy on his part, & which has proportionably pained me in the withdrawing. They were no ordinary visits, you observe, . . & he could not well throw me further ⟨off⟩ from him than by ceasing to pay them—the thing is quite expressively significant. Not that I pretend to complain, nor to have reason to complain. One should not be grateful for kindness, only while it lasts: *that* would be a short-breathed gratitude. I just tell you the fact, . . proving that it cannot be accidental.

Did you ever, ever tire me?—Indeed no—you never did. And do understand that I am not to be tired "in that way," though as Mr. Boyd said once of his daughter, one may be so "far too effeminate." No—if I were put into a crowd I should be tired soon—or, apart from the crowd, if you made me discourse orations De Coronâ[2] . . concerning your bay even . . I should be tired soon—though peradventure not very much sooner than you who heard.—But on the smooth ground of quiet conversation (particularly when three people dont talk at once as my brothers do . . to say the least!) I last for a long while:—not to say that I have the pretention of being as good & inexhaustible a listener to your own speaking as you could find in the world. So please not to accuse me of being tired again. I cant be tired, & wont be tired you see.

And now, since I began to write this, there is a new evil & anxiety—a worse anxiety than any—for one of my brothers is ill; had been unwell for some days & we thought nothing of it, till today Saturday: & the doctors call it a fever of the typhoid character . . not typhus yet . . but we are very uneasy. You must not come on wednesday if an infectious fever be in the house—*that* must be out of the question. May God bless you—I am quite heavy-hearted to-day, but never less yours, E. B. B.

1. Arrangements for the forthcoming publication of *Dramatic Romances and Lyrics,* the seventh number of *Bells and Pomegranates.*
2. *De Corona* was Demosthenes' successful defense of Ctesiphon, who had been indicted for awarding him a golden crown for public service.

126 (W62)   **R.B. to E.B.B.**

[*October 12, 1845.*]

Sunday.

These are bad news, dearest—all bad, except the enduring comfort of your regard; the illness of your brother is worst . . that *would* stay you, and is the first proper obstacle: I shall not attempt to speak and prove my feelings,—you know what even Flush is to me thro' you: I wait in anxiety for the next account.

If after all you do *not* go to Pisa,—why, we must be cheerful and wise, and take courage and hope: I cannot but see with your eyes and from your place, you know,—and will let this all be one surprizing and deplorable mistake of mere love and care . . but no such another mistake ought to be suffered, if you escape the effects of this—I will not cease to believe in ↑a↓ better event, till the very last, however, and it is a deep satisfaction that all has been made plain and straight up to this strange and sad interposition like a bar. You have done *your* part, at least—with all that forethought and counsel from friends and adequate judges of the case—so, if the bar *will* not move, you will consider,—will you not, dearest?—where one may best encamp in the unforbidden country and wait the spring and fine weather—would it be advisable to go where Mr. Kenyon suggested? or elsewhere? Oh, these vain wishes . . the will here, and no means!

My life is bound up with yours—my own, first and last love. What wonder if I feared to tire you—I who,—knowing you as I do, admiring what is so admirable (let me speak), loving what must needs be loved, fain to learn what you only can teach; proud of so much, happy in so much of you,—I, who, for all this, neither come to admire, nor feel proud, nor be taught,—but only, only to live with you and be by you— *that* is love—for I *know* the rest, as I say. I know those qualities are in you . . but at them I could get in so many ways . . I have your books, here are my letters you give me,—you would answer my questions were *I* in Pisa—well, and it all would amount to nothing, infinitely much as I know it is; to nothing if I could not sit by you and see you . . I can stop at that, but not before and it seems strange to me how little . . less than little I have laid open of my feelings, the nature of them to you —I smile to think how if all this while I had been acting with the profoundest policy in intention, so as to pledge myself to nothing I could not afterwards perform with the most perfect ease & security, I should have done not much unlike what I *have* done—to be sure, one word includes many or all . . but I have not said . . what I will not even even now say . . you will *know*—in God's time to which I trust.

I will answer your note now—the questions. I did go—(it may amuse you to write on)—to Moxon's: first let me tell you that when I called there the Saturday before, his brother (in his absence) informed me, replying to the question when it came naturally in turn with a round of like inquiries, that your poems continued to sell "singularly well"— they would "end in bringing a clear profit," he said: I thought to catch him, and ask if they *had* done so . . "Oh,—not at the beginning . . it takes more time"—he answered. On Thursday I saw Moxon—he spoke rather encouragingly of my own prospects. I send him a sheetful tomorrow, I believe, and we are 'out' on the 1st. of next month. Tennyson, by the way, has got his pension, £200 per annum[1]—by the other way, Moxon has bought the MSS. of Keats in the possession of Taylor the publisher, and is going to bring out a complete edition;[2] which is pleasant to hear.

After settling with Moxon I went to Mrs. Carlyle's—who told me characteristic quaintnesses of Carlyle's father and mother over the tea she gave me. And all yesterday, you are to know, I was in a permanent mortal fright—for my uncle came in the morning to intreat me to go to Paris in *the evening* about some urgent business of his,—a five-minutes' matter with his brother there,[3]—and the affair being really urgent and material to his and the brother's interest, and no substitute being to be thought of, I was forced to promise to go—in case a letter, which would arrive ∗in Town∗ at noon, should not prove satisfactory: so I calculated times, and found I could be at Paris to-morrow, and back again, *certainly* by Wednesday—and so not lose you on that day—Oh, the fear I had!—but I was sure then & now, that the 17th would not /be your⟩*see* you/ depart. But night came, and the last Dover train left, and I drew breath freely—this morning I find the letter was all right—so may it be with all worse apprehensions!—What you fear, precisely that, never happens, as Napoleon observed and thereon grew bold. I had stipulated for an hour's notice, if go I must—and that was to be wholly spent in writing to you—for in quiet consternation my mother cared for my carpet bag.

And so, I shall hear from you to-morrow . . that is, you will write *then,* telling me ALL about your brother. As for what you say, with the kindest intentions, "of fever-contagion" & keeping away on Wednesday on *that* account, it is indeed "out of the question,"—for a first reason,—which dispenses with any second,—because I disbelieve altogether in contagion from fevers, and especially from typhus fevers—as do much better-informed men than myself—I speak quite advisedly: if there should be only *that* reason, therefore, you will not deprive me of the happiness of seeing you next Wednesday.

I am not well—have a cold, influenza or some unpleasant thing, but am better than yesterday—My mother is much better, I think (she and my sister are resolute non-contagionists, mind you that!)

God bless you and all you love! dearest, I am your R. B.

1. Tennyson had learned of it on September 24. *Tennyson: A Memoir,* I, 224.

2. John Taylor of Taylor and Hesse threatened to prosecute for infringement of copyright when Moxon announced an edition of Keats for early 1845, but then sold both the copyright and manuscripts he had collected for a complete edition. Hyder E. Rollins, ed., *The Keats Circle: Letters and Papers, 1816–1878* (2 vols., Cambridge, Mass.: Harvard University Press, 1948), II, 115–116, 128–129. Moxon published his new edition in 1846 and the *Life, Letters, and Literary Remains* (ed. Lord Houghton) in 1848.

3. The two half-brothers of Robert Browning, Sr., were employed by the House of Rothschild. Reuben, the younger, was in the London office and William

October, 1845

Shergold Browning in Paris. The urgent matter perhaps related to the latter's return to England (G & M, pp. 6–7). See the close of Letter 130.

127 (W66°) **E.B.B. to R.B.**

[*October 11, 1845.*]

Saturday.

It was the merest foolishness in me to write about fevers and the rest as I did ⟨yest⟩ to-day, just as if it could do any good, all the wringing of hands in the world. And there is no typhus *yet* . . & no danger of any sort I hope & trust!—and how weak it is that habit of spreading the cloud which is in you all around you, how weak & selfish . . & unlike what *you* would do . . just as you are unlike Mr. Kenyon. And you *are* unlike him—& you were right on thursday when you said so, & I was wrong in setting up a phrase on the other side . . only what I said came by an instinct because you seemed to be giving him all the sunshine to use & carry, which should not be after all. But you are unlike him & must be . . seeing that the producers must differ from the 'nati consumere fruges'[1] in the intellectual as in the material. You create & he enjoys, & the work makes you pale & the pleasure makes him ruddy, & it is so of a necessity. So differs the man of genius from the man of letters—& then dear Mr. Kenyon is not even a man of letters in a full sense . . he is rather a Sybarite of letters. Do you think he ever knew what mental labour is? I fancy not. Not more than he has known what mental inspiration is!— And not more than he has known what the strife of the heart is . . with all his tenderness & sensibility. He seems to me to *evade* pain, & where he suffers at all to do so rather negatively than positively . . if you understand what I mean by that . . rather by a want than by a blow: the secret of all being that he has a certain latitudinarianism (not indifferentism) in his life & affections, & has no capacity for concentration & intensity. Partly by temperament & partly by philosophy he contrives to keep the sunny side of the street—though never inclined to forget the blind man at the corner. Ah, dear Mr. Kenyon: he is magnanimous in toleration, & excellent in sympathy—& he has the love of beauty & the reverence of genius—but the faculty of *worship* he has not: he will not worship aright either your heroes or your gods . . & while you do it he only 'tolerates' the act in you. Once he said . . not to me . . but I heard of it: "What, if genius should be nothing but scrofula?"—and he doubts (I very much fear) whether the world is not governed by a throw of those very same 'loaded dice,' & no otherwise. Yet he /reverences⟩reveres/ genius in the acting of it, & recognizes a God in creation—only it is but 'so far,' & not farther. At least I think not—& I have a right to think what I please of him, holding him as I do, in such true affection.—One of the kindest & most indulgent of human beings has he been to me, & I am happy to be grateful to him.

Sunday [October 12].—The Duke of Palmella takes the whole vessel for the 20th, & therefore if I go it must be on the 17th. Therefore (besides) as George must be on sessions tomorrow, he will settle the question with Papa to-night. In the meantime our poor Occy is not much better . . though a little . . & is ordered leeches on his head, & is confined to his bed & attended by physician & surgeon. It is not decided typhus . . but they will not answer for it not being infectious . . & although he is quite at the top of the house . . two stories above me . . I shall not like you to come indeed. And then there will be only room for a farewell, & I who am a coward shrink from the saying of it.—No— Not being able to see you to-morrow, (Mr. Kenyon is to be here to-morrow, he says) let us agree to throw away wednesday. I will write, . . you will write perhaps—& above all things you will promise to write by the 'Star' on Monday, that the captain may give me your letter at Gibraltar. You promise?—But I shall hear from you before then, & oftener than once, & you will acquiesce about wednesday & grant at once that there can be no gain, no good, in that miserable good-bye-ing. I do not want the pain of it to remember you by—I shall remember very well without it, be sure. Still it shall be as you like . . as you shall choose . . & if you are *disappointed* about wednesday (if it is not vain in me to talk of disappointments) why do with Wednesday as you think best . . . . always understanding that there's ⟨‖ · · · ‖⟩ no risk of infection.

Monday [October 13].—All this I had written yesterday—& today it all is worse than vain. Do not be angry with me—do not think it my fault—but I *do not go to Italy* . . it has ended as I feared. What passed between George & Papa there is no need of telling: only the latter said that I "might go if I pleased, but that going it would be under his heaviest displeasure." George, in great indignation, pressed the question fully . . .

but all was vain . . & I am left in this position . . to go, if I please, with his displeasure over me, (which after what you have said & after what Mr. Kenyon has said, and after what my own conscience & deepest moral convictions say aloud, I would unhesitatingly do at this hour!) and ⟨so⟩ necessarily run the risk of exposing my sister and brother to that same displeasure . . from which risk I shrink & fall back & feel that to incur it, is impossible. Dear Mr. Kenyon has been here & we have been talking—& he sees what I see . . that I am justified in going myself, but not in ⟨to⟩ bringing others into difficulty. The very kindness & goodness with which they desire me (both my sisters) "not to think of them," naturally makes me think more of them.—And so, tell me that I am not wrong in taking up my chain again & acquiescing in this hard necessity. The bitterest 'fact' of all is, that I had believed Papa to have loved me more than he obviously does—: but I never regret knowledge . . I mean I never would *un*know anything . . even were it the taste of the apples by the Dead sea—& this must be accepted like the rest. In the meantime your letter comes—and if I could seem to be very unhappy after reading it . . why it would be 'all pretence' on my part, believe me: Can you care for me so much . . YOU? Then *that* is light enough to account for all the shadows, & to make them almost unregarded,—the shadows of the life behind. Moreover dear Occy is somewhat better—with a pulse only at ninety: & the doctors declare that visitors may come to the house without any manner of danger. Or I should not trust to your theories—no, indeed!—it was not that I expected you to be afraid, but that *I* was afraid—and if I am not ashamed for THAT, why at least I am, for being 'lache' about wednesday, when you thought of hurrying back from Paris only for it!—You *could* think *that!*—You *can* care for me so much!—(I come to it again!)—When I hold some words to my eyes . . such as these in this letter . . I can see nothing beyond them . . no evil, no want. There IS no evil & no want. Am I wrong in the decision about Italy? Could I do otherwise? I had courage & to spare—but the question, you see, did not regard myself wholly. For the rest, the "unforbidden country" lies within these four walls. Madeira was proposed in vain—& any part of England would be as objectionable as Italy, & not more advantageous to *me* than Wimpole Street. To take courage & be cheerful, as you say, is left as an alternative—& (the winter may be mild!) to fall into the hands of God rather than of man: & *I shall be here for your November number.*[2]

And now that you are not well, will you take care?—& not come on Wednesday unless you are better?—and never again bring me *wet flowers,* which probably did all the harm on thursday?—I was afraid for you then, though I said nothing. May God bless you. Ever yours I am— your own.

Ninety is not a high pulse .. for a fever of this kind—is it?—and the heat diminishes: & his spirits are better—& we are all much easier .. have been both today & yesterday indeed—

1. "Ones born to consume the fruits." See Horace, *Epistles* I. ii. 27. The phrase is Homeric in origin (*Iliad* VI. 142).
2. Number VII of *Bells and Pomegranates—Dramatic Romances and Lyrics.*

128 (W63)   *R.B. to E.B.B.*

[*October 14, 1845.*]

Tuesday M^g

Be sure, my own, dearest love, that this is for the best,—will be seen for the best in the end. It is hard to bear now—but *you* have to bear it; any ⟨us⟩ other person ⟨who⟩ could not,—and you will, I know, knowing you—*will* be well this one winter if you can, and then—& since I am *not* selfish in this love to you, my own conscience tells /you⟩me/—I desire, more earnestly than I ever knew what desiring was, to be yours and with you and, ⸝as far⸜ as may be in this life & world, YOU—and no hindrance to that, but one, gives me a moment's care or fear,—but that one is just your little hand, as I could fancy it raised in any least interest of yours—and before that, I am, and would ever be, still silent. But now—what is to make you raise that hand? I will not speak *now ;* not seem to take advantage of your present feelings,—we will be rational, and all-considering and weighing consequences, and foreseeing them—but first I will prove .. if *that* has to be done, ⟨why⟩ but I begin speaking, and I should not, I know.

Bless you, love!

R. B.

To-morrow I see you, without fail. I am rejoiced as you can imagine, at your brother's improved state.

129 (W67°)   *E.B.B. to R.B.*

[*October 14, 1845.*]

Tuesday.

Will this note reach you at the 'fatal hour' .. or sooner? At any rate it is forced to ask you to take thursday for wednesday, inasmuch as Mr. Kenyon in his exceeding kindness has put off his journey just for *me,* he says, because he saw me depressed about the decision, & wished to come & see me again to-morrow & talk the spirits up, I suppose. It is all so kind and good, that I cannot find a voice to grumble about the obligation it brings of writing thus—And then, if you suffer from cold & influenza, it will be better for you not to come for another day, .. I think THAT, for comfort. Shall I hear how you are tonight, I wonder?—Dear Occy "turned the corner," the physician said, yesterday evening, & although a little fluctuating today, remains on the whole considerably better. They were just in time to keep the fever from turning to typhus—

How fast you print your book, for it is to be out on the first of November! Why it comes out suddenly like the sun. Mr. Kenyon asked me if I had seen anything you were going to print,—& when I mentioned the second part of the 'Duchess' & described how your perfect rhymes, perfectly new, & all clashing together as by natural attraction, had put me at once to shame & admiration, he began to praise the first part of the same poem (which I had heard him do before, by the way) & extolled it as one of your most striking productions.

And so until Thursday! May God bless you—
& as the heart goes, ever yours.

I am glad for Tennyson, & glad for Keats.[1] It is well to be able to be glad about something—is is it not?—about something out of ourselves. And (*in* myself) I shall be most glad, if I have a letter to-night. Shall I?

1. See Letter 126.

130 (W64)   *R.B. to E.B.B.*

[*October 15, 1845.*]

Thanks, my dearest, for the good news—of the fever's abatement —it is good, too, that you write cheerfully, on the whole: what is it to *me* that you write of *me* . . I shall never say *that!* Mr. Kenyon is all kindness, and one gets to take it as not so purely natural a thing, the showing kindness to those it concerns, and belongs to,—well! On Thursday, then,—to-morrow! Did you not get a note of mine, a hurried note, which was meant for yesterday-afternoon's delivery?

Mr. Forster came yesterday & was very profuse of graciosities: ↑he↓ may have, or must have meant well, so we will go on again with the friendship,[1] as the snail repairs his battered shell—

My poems went duly to press on Monday night—there is not much *correctable* in them,—you make, or you spoil, one of these things,—that is, *I* do. I have adopted all your emendations, and thrown in lines and words, just a morning's business; but one does not write plays so. You may like some of my smaller things, which stop interstices, better than what you have seen . . I shall wonder to know: I am to receive a *proof* at the end of the week—will you help me & over-look it. ("Yes"—she says . . my thanks I do not say!)

While writing this, the "Times" catches my eye (it just came in)— and something from the "Lancet" is extracted,[2] a long article against quackery—and, as I say, this is the first and only sentence I read— "⟨We⟩ There is scarcely a peer of the realm who is not the patron of some quack pill or potion: and the literati, too, are deeply tainted. We have heard of barbarians who threw quacks & their medicines into the sea: but here in England we have Browning, a prince of poets, touching the pitch which defiles and making Paracelsus the hero of a poem: Sir E. L. Bulwer writes puffs for the water doctors[3] in a style worthy of imitation by the scribe that does the poetical for Moses & Son:[4] Miss Martineau makes a finessing servant girl her physician-general: & Richard Howitt & the Lady aforesaid stand Godfather & mother to the contemptible mesmeric vagaries of Spencer Hall."[5]—Even the sweet incense to me fails of its effect if Paracelsus is to figure on a level with Priessnitz, and "Jane"!

What weather, now at last! Think for yourself and for me—could you not go out on such days?

I am quite well now—cold, over & gone. Did I tell you my Uncle arrived from Paris on Monday, as they hoped he would—so my travel would have been to great purpose!

Bless my dearest—my own!

R. B.

1. See Letter 107, note.

2. The extract was a review reprinted from the *Lancet* (October 11, 1845) of *Hints on Consumption and Its Relief: Gout and Its Cure: Indigestion and the Means of Avoiding It, Rheumatism and Its Cure: with Hints on Diet and Digestion,* by the late Sir Henry Halford, Bart.

3. Bulwer-Lytton, after a nervous and physical crisis, underwent treatment by the Austrian hydropath Preissnitz and published a laudatory article in the *New Monthly Magazine* for September 1845.

4. Moses and Son, 86, Aldgate, and 154, Minories, were "drapers, tailors, and general outfitters," whose ads in the London papers were in execrable verse. For a sample, see the *New Yorker,* May 24, 1952, p. 89.

5. For Miss Martineau's relation to Spencer Timothy Hall and to her "finessing servant girl," Jane, see the entry on her in the Biographical Appendix. Richard Howitt was a minor writer, the brother of William Howitt; his connection with Hall is unclear.

131 (W68°)   *E.B.B. to R.B.*

[*October 15, 1845.*]

Wednesday.

Your letter which should have reached me in the morning of yesterday, I did not receive until nearly midnight—partly through the eccentricity of our new postman whose good pleasure it is to make use of the letter-box without knocking,—& partly from the confusion in the house, of illness in different ways . . the very servants being ill, . . one of them breaking a bloodvessel—for there is no new case of fever; . . & for dear Occy, he grows better slowly day by day. And, just so late last night, five letters were found in the letter-box, & mine . . yours . . among them—which accounts for my beginning to answer it only now.

What am I to say but this . . that I know what you are . . & that I know also what you are to *me*,—& that I should accept that knowledge as more than sufficient recompense for worse vexations than these late ones. Therefore let no more be said of them: & no more *need* be said,— even if they were not likely to prove their own end good, as I believe with you. You may be quite sure that I shall be well this winter, if in any way it should be possible, & that I *will not* be beaten down, if the will can do anything. I admire how . . if all had happened ↑so↓ but a year ago . . (yet it could not have happened quite *so!*), I should certainly have been beaten down—& how it is different now, . . & how it is only gratitude to you, to *say* that it is different now—My cage is not worse but better since you brought the green groundsel to it—& to dash oneself against the wires of it will not open the door—We shall see . . & God will oversee. And in the meantime you will not ⟨‖ · · · ‖⟩ ↑talk of↓ extravagances; & then nobody need hold up the hand— because, as I said & say, I am yours—your own—only not to *hurt you*. So now let us talk of the first of November & of the poems which are to come out then, & of the poems which are to come after them—and of the new avatar of 'Sordello'[1] for instance, which you taught me to look for. And let us both be busy & cheerful—& you will come & see me throughout the winter, . . if you do not decide rather on going abroad, which may be better . . better for your health's sake?—in which case I shall have your letters—

And here is another . . just arrived. How I thank you. Think of the Times!—Still it was very well of them to recognise your principality. Oh yes—do let me see the proof—I understand too about the 'making & spoiling.'

Almost you forced me to smile by thinking it worth while to say that you are *"not selfish."* Did Sir Percival say so to Sir Gawaine across the Round Table, in those times of chivalry to which you belong by the soul?—Certainly you are not selfish!—May God bless you.

Ever your
E. B. B.

The fever may last, they say, for a week longer, or even a fortnight —but it *decreases*. Yet he is hot still, and very weak.

To to-morrow!—

1. See Letter 99 and note 4.

Browning recorded on the envelope of the preceding letter the visit which came between it and Letter 132:

+Thursday, Oct. 16

3–4¼ p.m.

132 (W69°)　　　　　　　**E.B.B. to R.B.**

[*October 17, 1845.*]

Friday.

Do tell me what you mean precisely by your 'Bells and Pomegranates' title. I have always understood it to refer to the Hebraic priestly garment—but Mr. Kenyon held against me the other day that your reference was different, though he had not the remotest idea how. And yesterday I forgot to ask, for not the first time. Tell me too why you should not in the new number satisfy, by a note somewhere, the Davuses of the world who are in the majority ('Davi sumus, non Œdipi')[1] with a solution of this one Sphinx riddle. Is there a reason against it?

Occy continues to make progress—with a pulse at only eightyfour this morning. Are you learned in the pulse that I should talk as if you were? *I*, who have had my lessons? He takes scarcely anything yet but water, & his head is very hot still—but the progress is quite sure, though it may be a lingering case.

Your beautiful flowers!—none the less beautiful for waiting for water yesterday. As fresh as ever, they were; & while I was putting them into the water, I thought that your visit went on all the time. Other thoughts too I had, which made me look down blindly, quite blindly, on the little blue flowers, . . while I thought what I could not have said an hour before without breaking into tears which would have run faster then. To say now that I never can forget,—that I feel myself bound to you as one human being cannot be more bound to another;—& that you are more to me at this moment than all the rest of the world,—is only to say in new words that it would be a wrong against *myself*, to seem to risk your happiness and abuse your generosity. For *me* . . though you threw out words yesterday about the testimony of a " third person," . . it would be monstrous to assume it to be necessary to vindicate my

239

trust of you—*I trust you implicitly*—& am not too proud to owe all things to you. But now let us wait & see what this winter does or un-does—while God does His part for good, as we know—I will never fail to you from any human influence whatever—*that* I have promised—but you must let it be different from the other sort of promise which it would be a wrong to make. May God bless you—you, whose fault it is, to be too generous. You *are* not like other men, as I could see from the beginning—no—

Shall I have the proof tonight, I ask myself.

And if you like to come on Monday rather than Tuesday, I do not see why there should be a 'no' to that. Judge from your own conveni-ence. Only we must be wise in the general practice, & abstain from too frequent meetings, for fear of difficulties. I am Casandra you know, & smell the slaughter in the bathroom.[2] It would make no difference in fact,—but in comfort, much.

Ever your own—

1. "We are Davuses, not Oedipuses." The line is pluralized from Terence, *Andria* l. 194. Davus is the stock name for the none-too-acute slave in Greek and Roman comedy; Oedipus in his wisdom solved the Sphinx's riddle.

2. A reference to the *Agamemnon* of Aeschylus, where Cassandra foretells the King's murder in his bath. Browning's 1877 translation of the play stresses the image here; Cassandra says: "Slaughter blood-dripping does the household smell of!" (l. 1333.)

133 (*W65*)   **R.B. to E.B.B.**

[October 18, 1845.]

Saturday.

I must not go on tearing these poor sheets one after the other,—the proper phrases *will not* come,—so let them stay, while you care for my best interests in their best, only way, and say for me what I would say if I could—dearest,—say it, as I feel it!

I am thankful to hear of the continued improvement of your

brother—So may it continue with him! Pulses I know very little about —I go by your own impressions which are evidently favourable.

I will make a note as you suggest—or, perhaps, keep it for the clos-ing number, (the next) when it will come fitly in with two or three parting words I shall have to say.[1] The Rabbis make Bells & Pome-granates symbolical of Pleasure and Profit, the Gay & the Grave, the Poetry & the Prose, Singing and Sermonizing—such a mixture of effects as in the original hour (that is quarter of an hour) of confidence & crea-tion, I meant the whole should prove at last: well, it *has* succeeded beyond my most adventurous wishes in one respect—"Blessed eyes mine eyes have been, if[2]—" if there was any sweetness in the tongue or flavour in the seeds to *her*. But I shall do quite other & better things, or shame on me! The proof has not yet come . . I should go, I suppose, and enquire this afternoon—and probably I will.

I weigh all the words in your permission to come on Monday . . do not think *I* have not seen *that* contingency from the first! Let it be Tuesday—no sooner!—Meanwhile you are never away—never from your place here.

God bless my dearest.

Ever yours

R. B.

1. The note was reserved for the last number; see Letter 313, note 1. Exodus 28:33–34 is the ultimate source of the title but does not explain the symbolism. Browning may have derived it from the tenth of Francis Quarles's *Eleuen Pious Meditations* (*Works*, ed. A. B. Grosart [3 vols., 1880], II, 29).

2. E.B.B.'s *Catarina to Camoens*, st. ii.

The following note was sent as an enclosure in a package of proof sheets for Dramatic Romances and Lyrics. *It has no envelope.*

134 (W66)   *R.B. to E.B.B.*

[October 20, 1845.]

Monday M^g

This arrived on Saturday night—I just correct it in time for this our first post—will it do, the new matter? I can take it to-morrow—when I am to see you—if you are able to glance thro' it by then.

The "Inscription,"[1] how does that read?

There is strange temptation, by the way, in the space they please to leave for the presumeable 'motto'—"they but remind me of mine own conception"[2] . . but one must give no clue, of a silk's breadth, to the *"Bower,"* yet. One day![3]

—Which God send you, dearest, & your

R. B.

1. The pamphlet was "Inscribed / to / John Kenyon, Esq., / In a hope that a recollection of his own successful / 'Rhymed Plea for Tolerance' / May induce him to admit good-naturedly this humble prose one of / His very sincere friend, / R.B."
2. *Lear* I. iv. 66.
3. The pamphlet had no motto. Browning apparently means that one from E.B.B. is understood. *The Lost Bower* appeared in *Poems* (1844).

The following letter was begun the evening after the visit Browning noted on the envelope of Letter 132:

+Tuesday, Oct. 21
3–4½ p.m.

135 *(W70°)*   *E.B.B. to R.B.*

_____

[*October 21–22, 1845.*]

Even at the risk of teazing you a little I must say a few words, that there may be no misunderstanding between us—& this, before I sleep tonight. Today and before today you surprised me by your manner of receiving my remark about your visits, for I ⟨had⟩ believed I had sufficiently made clear to you long ago how certain questions were ordered in this house & how no exception was to be expected for my sake or even for yours. Surely I told you this quite plainly long ago. I only meant to say in my last letter, in the same track . . (fearing in the case of your wishing to come oftener that you might think it unkind in me not to seem to wish the same) . . that if you came too often & it was *observed,* difficulties & vexations w^d follow as a matter of course, & it would be wise therefore to run no risk. That was the head & front of what I meant to say. The weekly one visit is a thing established & may go on as long as you please—& there is no objection to your coming twice a week *now* & *then* . . if now & then merely . . if there is no habit . . do you understand. I may be prudent in an extreme perhaps—& certainly everybody in the house is not equally prudent!—but I did shrink from running any risk with that calm & comfort of the winter as it seemed to come on. And was it more than I said about the cloak?¹ was there any newness in it?—anything to startle you? Still I do perfectly see that whether new or old, what it INVOLVES may well be unpleasant to you—& that (however old) it may be apt to recur to your mind with a new increasing unpleasantness. We have both been carried too far perhaps, by late events & impulses—but it is never too late to come back to a right place, & I for my part come back to mine, & entreat you my dearest friend, first, *not to answer this,* & next, to weigh & consider thoroughly "that particular contingency" which (I tell you plainly, I who know) the tongue of men & of angels would not modify so as to render less full of vexations to you. Let Pisa prove the excellent hardness of some marbles!—Judge. From motives of selfrespect, you may well walk an opposite way . . *you!* . . When I told you once . . or twice . . that "no human influence should" &c &c, . . I spoke for myself, quite overlooking you—& now that I turn & see you, I am surprised that I did not see you before . . *there.* I ask you therefore to consider 'that contingency' well—not forgetting the other obvious evils, which the late decision about Pisa has aggravated beyond calculation . . for as the smoke rolls off we see the harm done by the fire. And so, and now . . is it not advisable for you to go abroad at once . . as you always intended, you know . . now that your book is through the press? What if you go next week?—I leave it to you. In any case *I entreat you not to answer this*—neither let your thoughts be too hard on me for what you may call perhaps vacillation—only that I stand excused (I do not say justified) before my own moral sense. May God bless you—If you go, I shall wait to see you till your return, & have letters in the meantime—⟨‖ · · · ‖⟩ I write all this as fast as I can to have it over. What I ask of you is, to consider along and decide advisedly . . for both our sakes. If it should be your ⟨‖ · · · ‖⟩ choice not to make an end now, . . why I shall understand *that* by your not going . . or you may say '*no*' in a word . . for I require no '*protesta-*

tions' indeed—and *you* may trust to *me* . . it shall be as you choose. YOU WILL CONSIDER MY HAPPINESS MOST BY CONSIDERING YOUR OWN . . & that is my last word.

Wednesday morning.—I did not say half I thought about the poems yesterday—and their various power & beauty will be striking & surprising to your most accustomed readers. St. Praxed—Pictor Ignotus—the ride—the Duchess!—Of the new poems I like supremely the first & last . . that "Lost Leader" which strikes so broadly & deep . . which nobody can ever forget—& which is worth all the journalizing & pamphleteering in the world!—& then, the last 'Thought'[2] which is quite to be grudged to that place of fragments . . those grand sea-sights in the long lines—Should not these fragments be severed otherwise than by numbers?—The last stanza but one of the 'Lost Mistress' seemed obscure to me.[3] Is it so really? The end you have put to 'England in Italy'[4] gives unity to the whole . . just what the poem wanted. Also you have given some nobler lines to the middle than met me there before. The Duchess appears to me more than ever a new-minted golden coin—the rhythm of it answering to your own description,
'Speech half asleep, or song half awake?'[5]
You have right of trove to these novel effects of rhythm. Now if people do not cry out about these poems, what are we to think of the world?
May God bless you always—send me the next proof *in any case.*
Your E. B. B.

---

1. In Letter 118.

2. *Home-Thoughts from the Sea,* published in 1845 as the third of three pieces under the single title *Home-Thoughts.* The first was its still better known companion piece and the second later became part III of *Nationality in Drinks.* The poems E.B.B. mentions were all published in *Bells and Pomegranates* VII a month later.

3. Though Browning "changed a word" (Letter 147), the stanza still troubled E.B.B. and was altered to substantially its present form in 1849. In 1845 it read:
For tho' no glance of the eyes so black
But I keep with heart's endeavour,—
If only you wish the snowdrops back
That shall stay in my heart forever!—

4. The last seven lines, referring to the Corn Laws. E.B.B.'s critique of the manuscript (Macmillan ed., p. 1344) quotes line 271, but speaks of the poem as still "unfinished."

5. *Garden Fancies* I (*The Flower's Name*), st. iii.

R.B. to E.B.B.

—————————————

[*October 23, 1845.*]

But I *must* answer you, and be forgiven, too, dearest. I was (to begin at the beginning) surely not '*startled*' . . only properly *aware* of the deep blessing I have been enjoying this while, and not disposed to take its continuance as pure matter of course, and so treat with indifference the first shadow of a threatening intimation from without, the first hint of a possible obstruction from the quarter to which so many hopes & fears of mine have gone of late: in this case, knowing you, I was sure that if any imaginable form of displeasure could touch you without reaching me, I should not hear of it too soon—so I spoke—so *you* have spoken—and so now you get—'excused'?—No—wondered at, with all my faculty of wonder for the strange exalting way you will persist to think of me; now, once for all, I *will* not pass for what I make no least pretence to: I quite understand the grace of your imaginary self-denial, and fidelity to a given word, and noble constancy,—but it all happens to be none of mine, none in the least. I love you because I *love* you; I see you "once a week" because I cannot see you all day long; I think of you all day long, because I most certainly could not think of you once an hour less, if I tried, or went to Pisa, or "abroad" (in every sense) in order to 'be happy' . . a kind of adventure which you seem to suppose you have in some way interfered with: do, for this once, think, and never after, on the impossibility of your ever . . (you know I must talk your own language, so I shall say . .) hindering any scheme of mine, stopping any supposeable advancement of mine: do you really think that before I found you, I was going about the world seeking ₊whom₊ I might devour;[1] that is, be devoured by, in the shape of a wife . . do you suppose I ever dreamed of marrying?—what would it mean for me, with my life I am hardened in,—considering the rational chances,—how the land is used to furnish its contingent of Shakespeare's-women: or by 'success,' 'happiness' &c &c you never never can be seeing for a moment with the world's eyes and meaning "getting rich" & all that?—Yet, put that away, and what do you meet at every turn, if you are hunting about in the dusk to catch my good, but *yourself?*——

I know who has got it, caught it, & means to keep it on his heart—

the person most concerned—*I*, dearest, who cannot play the disinterested part of bidding *you* forget your "protestation" .. what should I have to hold by, come what will, thro' years, thro' this life, if God shall so determine, if I were not sure, *sure* that the first moment when you can suffer me with you "in that relation," you will remember and act accordingly—I will, as you know, conform my life to *any* imaginable rule which shall render it possible for your life to move with it and possess it, all the little it is worth—⟨that is no engagement⟩

For your friends .. whatever can be "got over," whatever opposition may be rational, will be easily removed, I suppose: you know when I spoke lately about the "selfishness" I dared believe I was free from, I hardly meant the low faults of .. I shall say, a different organization to mine—which has vices in plenty, but not those: beside half a dozen scratches with a pen make one stand up an apparent angel of light, from the lawyer's parchment—, and Doctors' Commons[2] is one bland smile of applause. The selfishness I deprecate is one which a good many women, & men too, call "real passion"—under the influence of which, I ought to say "be mine, what ever happens to *you*"—but I know better, and you know best—and you know me, for all this letter, which is no doubt in me, I feel, but dear entire goodness and affection, of which God knows whether I am proud or not—and now you will 'let me be,' will not you. Let me have my way, life [live] my life, love my love

Whose I am, praying God to bless her ever,

R. B.

1. An allusion to I Peter 5:8.
2. The civil court dealing with such matters as divorce.

137 (W71°)   **E.B.B. to R.B.**

[*October 23, 1845.*]

"*And be forgiven*" .. yes! and be thanked besides—if I knew how to thank you worthily & as I feel .. only that I do not know it, & cannot say it. And it was not indeed "doubt" of you .. oh no! .. that made me write as I did write; it was rather because I felt you to be ₊surely₊ noblest,

.. & therefore fitly dearest, .. ⟨‖ · · · ‖⟩ ⁺that⁺ it seemed to me detestable & intolerable to leave you on this road where the mud must splash up against you, & never cry 'gare.' Yet I was quite enough unhappy yesterday, & before yesterday .. I will confess to-day, .. to be too gratefully glad to 'let you be' .. to "let you have your way"—you who overcome always!—Always, but where you tell me not to think of you so & so!—as if I could help thinking of you *so*, & as if I should not take the liberty of persisting to think of you just so. 'Let me be'—'Let me have my way'—I am unworthy of you perhaps in everything except one thing—& *that*, you cannot guess. May God bless you—Ever I am yours.

The proof does not come?

138 (W72°) **E.B.B. to R.B.**

[*October 24, 1845.*]

Friday.

I wrote briefly yesterday not to make my letter longer by keeping it; & a few last words which belong to it by right, must follow after it .. must—for I want to say that you need not indeed talk to me about squares being not round, and of YOU being not "selfish"! You know it is foolish to talk such superfluities, & not a compliment, .. I wont say to my knowledge of you & faith in you .. but to my understanding generally. Why should you say to me at all .. much less for this third or fourth time .. "I am not selfish"—to *me* who never .. when I have been deepest asleep & dreaming .. never dreamed of attributing to you any form of such a fault? Promise not to say so again—now promise. Think how it must sound to my ears, when really & truly I have sometimes felt jealous of myself .. of my own infirmities, .. and thought that you cared for me only because your chivalry touched them with a silver sound[1]—& that, without them, you would pass by on the other side:—why twenty times I have thought *that* & been vexed—ungrateful vexation!—In exchange for which too frank confession, I will ask for another silent promise .. a silent promise—no, but first I will say another thing.

First I will say that you are not to fancy any . . the least . . danger of my falling under displeasure through your visits—there is no sort of risk of it *for the present*—& if I ran the risk of making you uncomfortable about *that,* I did foolishly, & what I meant to do was different. I wish you also to understand that EVEN IF YOU CAME HERE EVERY-DAY, my brothers & sisters would simply care to know if I liked it, & then be glad if I was glad:—the caution referred to one person alone. In relation to WHOM, however, there will be no 'getting over'—you might as well think to sweep off a third of the stars of Heaven with the motion of your eye-lashes—this, for matter of fact & certainty—& this, as I said before, the keeping of a general rule and from no disrespect towards individuals—: a great peculiarity *in the individual* of course. But . . though I have been a submissive daughter, & this from no effort, but for love's sake . . be-cause I loved him tenderly, (& love him), . . & hoped that he loved me back again even if the proofs came untenderly sometimes—yet I have reserved for myself ALWAYS that right over my own affections which is the most strictly personal of all things, and which involves principles & consequences of infinite importance & scope—even though I NEVER thought (except perhaps when the door of life was just about to open . . before it opened) never thought it probable or possible that I should have occasion for the exercise,—from without & from within at once— I have too much need to look up. For friends, I can look any way . . round, & *down* even—the merest thread of a sympathy will draw me sometimes—or even the least look of kind eyes over a dyspathy— ↑" Cela se peut facilement "↓ But for another relation—it was all different —& rightly so—& so very different—'Cela ne se peut nullement'—as in Malherbe.

And now we must agree to 'let all this be,' & set ourselves to get as much good & enjoyment from the coming winter (better spent at Pisa!) as we can—and I begin my joy by being glad that you are not going since I am not going, & by being proud of these new green leaves in your bay which came out with the new number—And then will come the tragedies[2]—& then, . . what beside? We shall have a happy winter after all . . *I* shall at least; and if Pisa had been better, London might be worse: & for *me* to grow pretentious & fastidious & critical about various sorts of *purple* . . I, who have been used to the *brun foncé* of Mad^me de Sevigné, *(foncé & enfoncé . .)*—would be too absurd. But why does not the proof come all this time? I have kept this letter to go back with it—

I had a proposition from the New York booksellers about six weeks ago (the booksellers who printed the poems) to let them re-print those prose papers of mine in the Athenæum, with additional matter on American literature, in a volume by itself—to be published at the same time both in America & England by Wiley and Putnam in Waterloo Place—& meaning to offer liberal terms, they said. Now what shall I do?—Those papers are not fit for separate ⟨re⟩publication, & I am not inclined to the responsibility of them,—& in any case, they must give as much trouble as if they were re-written ↑(trouble and not poetry!),↓ before I could consent to such a thing. Well!—and if I do not . . /they⟩these/ ↑people↓ are just as likely to print them without leave . . & so without correction.[3] What do you advise? What shall I do?—All this time they think me sublimely indifferent, they who pressed for an answer by return of packet—& now it is past six . . eight weeks,—and I must say something.

Am I not "femme qui parle"[4] today? And let me talk on ever so, the proof won't come. May God bless you—& me as I am

Yours, E. B. B.

And the silent promise I would have you make is this—that if ever you should leave me, it shall be (though you are not "selfish") for your sake—& not for mine: for your good, & not for mine. I ask it—not because I am disinterested,—but because one class of motives would be valid, and the other void—simply for that reason.

Then the 'femme qui parle' (looking back over the parlance) did not mean to say on the first page of this letter that she was ever for a moment *vexed in her* PRIDE that she should owe anything to her adversities. It was only because adversities are accidents & not essentials. If it had been prosperities, it would have been the same thing—no, not the same thing!—but far worse.

Occy is up to-day & doing well.

1. Cf. *Sonnets from the Portuguese*, I: "The silver answer . . ."
2. *Luria* and *A Soul's Tragedy*, published together in April 1846 as the eighth and last number of *Bells and Pomegranates*.
3. Henry G. Langley was interested in eleven prose papers published in the *Athenæum* during 1842. Four were the series on *The Greek Christian Poets* (February 26, March 5, 12, and 19); five were "a Survey of the English Poets, under the pretence of a review of 'The Book of the Poets,' a bookseller's selection published lately" (*Letters of EBB*, I, 105), followed immediately by a review of Wordsworth's

1842 volume (June 4, 11, 25; August 6, 13, and 27). They were not republished until
after E.B.B.'s death.
    4. The phrase is echoed from Letters 80 and 81.

139 (W68)   **R.B. to E.B.B.**

[*Postmarked October 27, 1845.*]

How does one make "silent promises" . . or, rather, how does the
maker of them communicate that fact to whomsoever it may concern?
I know, there have been many, very many unutterable vows & promises
made,—that is, THOUGHT down upon—the white slip at the top of my
notes,—such as of this note,—and not trusted to the pen,—that always
comes in for the shame,—but given up, and replaced by the poor forms
to which a pen is equal—and a glad minute I should account *that,* in
which you collected and accepted *those* "promises"—because they
would not be all so unworthy of me—much less you: I would receive,
in virtue of *them,* the ascription of whatever worthiness is supposed to
lie in deep, truest love, and gratitude—
      Read my silent answer there too!—[1]
    All your letter is one comfort: we will be happy this winter, and
after, do not fear. I am most happy, to begin, that your brother is so
much better: he must be weak and susceptible of cold, remember.
    It was on my lip, I do think, *last* visit, or the last but one, to beg you
to detach those papers from the "Athenæum's" gâchis: certainly this
opportunity is *most* favourable, for every reason: you cannot hesitate,
surely: at present those papers are lost—*lost* for practical purposes: do
pray reply without fail to the proposers ⟨who would be very apt to⟩;
No, no harm of these really fine fellows, who *could* do harm (by printing
incorrect copies, and perhaps eking out the column by supposititious
matter . . ex-gr. They strengthened & lengthened a book of Dickens', in
Paris, by adding quant. suff. of Thackeray's "Yellowplush Papers" . . as
I discovered by a Parisian somebody praising the latter to me as Dickens'
best work!)—and who *do* really a good straightforward un-American
thing: you will encourage "the day of small things"—tho' this is not
small, nor likely to have small results. I shall be impatient to hear that

you have decided. I like the progress of these Americans in taste, their amazing leaps, like grasshoppers up to the sun—from . . what is the "*from*," what depth, do you remember, say, ten or twelve years back?—*to*—Carlyle, & Tennyson, & you! So children leave off Jack of Cornwall and go on just to Homer.

I can't conceive why my proof does not come—I must go to-morrow and see. In the other, I have corrected all the points you noted,—to their evident improvement. Yesterday I took out 'Luria' & read it thro'—the skeleton—I shall hope to finish it soon now. It is for a purely imaginary Stage,—very simple and straightforward. Would you . . no, Act by Act, as I was about to propose that you should read it,—that process would affect the oneness I most wish to preserve. ⟨‖ · · · ‖⟩

On Tuesday—at last, I am with you—Till when be with me ever, dearest—God bless you ever—

R. B.

1. Browning is not quoting, but centering for effect.

The following note lacks an envelope. It was enclosed in the package of long-awaited proof to which it refers.

140 (W69)   *R.B. to E.B.B.*

[October 28, 1845.]

Tuesday 9 a.m.

I got this on coming home last night—have just run thro' it this morning, and send it that time may not be lost. Faults, faults; but I don't know how I have got tired of this. The Tragedies will be better, at least the second—

R. B.

At 3—this day! Bless you—

The envelope for this letter is unaddressed, and internal evidence in the letter indicates the probable reason—that it was enclosed with the proof that

E.B.B. is returning. Though it does not refer to the visit recorded on the envelope of Letter 138,

+Tues. Oct. 28
3–4½ p.m.

it seems to have been written the next morning or later the same day, since Browning refers to the proofs already marked by E.B.B. in his next letter, written on Wednesday night.

141 *(W73°)*   *E.B.B. to R.B.*

[? *Wednesday, October 29, 1845.*]

I write in haste, not to lose time about the proof. You will see on the papers[1] here my doubtfulnesses such as they are—but silence swallows up the admirations . . & there is no time. 'Theocrite'[2] overtakes that wish of mine which ran on so fast—and the 'Duchess' grows and grows the more I look—and 'Saul' is noble & must have his full royalty some day. Would it not be well, by the way, to print it in the meanwhile as a fragment confessed . . sowing asterisks at the end. Because as a poem of yours it stands there & wants unity, and people can't be expected to understand the difference between incompleteness & defect, unless you make a sign. For the new poems—they are full of beauty. You throw largesses out on all sides without counting the coins—how beautiful that 'Night & Morning' . . and the 'Earth's Immortalities' . . & the 'Song' too. And for your 'Glove,' all women should be grateful,—& Ronsard, honoured, in this fresh shower of music on his old grave . . though the chivalry of the interpretation, as well as much beside, is so plainly yours, . . could only be yours perhaps. And even *you* are forced to let in a third person . . close to the doorway . . before you can do any good. What a noble lion you give us too, with the "flash on his forehead," & "leagues in the desert already" as we look on him!—And then, with what a 'curious felicity' you turn the subject 'glove' to another use & strike De Lorge's blow back on him with it, in the last paragraph of your story!—And the versification! And the lady's speech —(to return!) so calm, & proud—yet a little bitter!
     Am I not to thank you for all /the⟩my/ pleasure & pride in these

poems?—while you stand by and try to talk them down, perhaps.

Tell me how your mother is—tell me how you are . . you who never were to be told twice about walking. Gone the way of all promises, is that promise?

Ever yours, E. B. B.

1. E.B.B.'s critical notes. See Letter 66, note 1.
2. In other words, *The Boy and the Angel.*

142 (W70)   **R.B. to E.B.B.**

_____

[*October 29, 1845.*]

Wednesday Night.

Like your kindness,—too, far too generous kindness,—all this trouble and correcting,—and it is my proper office now, by this time, to sit still and receive, by right *Human* (as opposed to Divine). When you see the pamphlet's self, you will find your own doing,—but where will you find the proofs of the best of all helping and counselling and inciting, unless in new works which shall justify the *unsatisfaction,* if I may not say shame, at these, these written before your time, my best love—

Are you doing well to-day? For I feel well & have walked some eight or nine miles—and my mother is very much better . . is singularly better. You know whether you rejoiced me or no by that information about the exercise *you* had taken yesterday—Think what telling one that you grow stronger would mean—

"Vexatious" with you! Ah, prudence is all very right, and one ought, no doubt, to say, "of course, we shall not expect a life exempt from the usual proportion of &c. &c.—" but truth is still more right, and includes the highest prudence besides, and I do believe that we shall be happy; that is, that *you* will be happy: you see I dare confidently expect *the* end to it all . . so it has always been with me in my life of wonders,—absolute wonders, with God's hand over all . . And this last and best of all would never have begun so, and gone on so, to break off abruptly even here, in this world, for the little time.

So try, try, dearest, every method, take every measure of hastening such a consummation—Why, we shall see Italy together! I could, would,

will shut myself in four walls of a room with you and never leave you
and be most of all *then* "a lord of infinite space"[1]—but, to travel with
you to Italy, or Greece—very vain, I know that, all such day dreaming!
And ungrateful, too; with the real sufficing happiness here of being, and
knowing that you know me to be, and suffer me to tell you I am yours,
ever your own.

God bless you, my dearest—

1. See *Hamlet* II. ii. 257.

143 *(W74°)*   *E.B.B. to R.B.*

_____

[*October 31, 1845.*]

All today, friday, Miss Mitford has been here! She came at two &
went away at seven—& I feel as if I had been making a five-hour speech
on the corn laws in Harriet Martineau's parliament;[1] . . so tired I am.
Not that dear Miss Mitford did not talk both for me & herself, . . for
that, of course she did. But I was forced to answer once every ten minutes at least—& Flush, my usual companion, does not exact so much—&
so I am tired & come to rest myself on this paper—Your name was not
once spoken today; a little from my good fencing: when I saw you at
the end of an alley of associations, I pushed the conversation up the next
—because I was afraid of questions such as every moment I expected,
with a pair of woman's eyes behind them; & those are worse than Mr.
Kenyon's, when he puts on his spectacles. So your name was not once
spoken: not thought of, I do not say—perhaps when I once lost her at
Chevy Chase & found her suddenly with Isidore the queen's hairdresser,
my thoughts might have wandered off to you & your unanswered letter
while she passed gradually from that to this—I am not sure of the contrary. And Isidore, they say, reads Bérenger,[2] & is supposed to be the
most literary person at court—& wasn't at Chevy Chase one must
needs think.

One must needs write nonsense rather—for I have written it there.
The sense, & the truth is, that your letter went to the bottom of my
heart, & that my thoughts have turned round it ever since & through all

the talking today. Yes indeed, dreams! But what *is* not dreaming is this & this—this reading of these words—this proof of this regard—all this that you are to me in fact, & which you cannot guess the full meaning of, dramatic poet as you are . . cannot . . since you do not know what my life meant before you touched it, . . O my angel at the gate of the prison!³ My wonder is greater than your wonders, . . I who sate here alone but yesterday, so weary of my own being that to take interest in my very poems I had to lift them up by an effort & separate them from myself & cast them out from me into the sunshine where I was not—feeling nothing of the light which fell on them even—making indeed a sort of pleasure & interest about that factitious personality associated with them . . but knowing it to be all far on the outside of *me . . myself* . . not seeming to touch it with the end of my finger . . & receiving it as a mockery & a bitterness when people persisted in confounding one with another. Morbid it was if you like it—perhaps very morbid—but all these heaps of letters which go into the fire one after the other, & which, because I am ₊a₊ woman & have written verses, it seems so amusing to the letter-writers of your sex to write & see 'what will come of it,' . . some, from kind good motives I know, . . well, . . how could it all make for me even such a narrow strip of sunshine as Flush finds on the floor sometimes, & lays his nose along, with both ears out in the shadow? It was not for *me . . me . .* in any way!—it was not within my reach—I did not seem to touch it as I said. Flush came nearer, & I was grateful to him . . yes, grateful . . for not being tired! I have felt grateful & flattered . . yes flattered . . when he has chosen rather to stay with me all day than go down stairs. Grateful too, with reason, I have been & am to my own family for not letting me see that I was a burthen. These are facts. And now how am I to feel when you tell me what you have told me—& what you " could would & will " do, & SHALL NOT do? . . but when you tell me . . ?

Only remember that such words make you freer & freer—if you can be freer than free—just as every one makes me happier & richer— too rich by you, to claim any debt. May God bless you always—When I wrote that letter to let you come the first time, do you know, the tears ran down my cheeks . . I could not tell why: partly it might be mere nervousness. And then, I was vexed with you for wishing to come as ⟨‖ · · · ‖⟩ other people did, & vexed with myself for not being able to refuse you as I did them.

When does the book come out? Not on the first, I begin to be glad.
Ever yours,   E. B. B.

I trust that you go on to take exercise—& that your mother is still better. Occy's worst symptom now is too great an appetite . . a monster-appetite indeed—

1. Miss Martineau favored allowing women to vote and hold seats in Parliament. *Harriet Martineau's Autobiography,* with Memorials by Maria Weston Chapman (2d ed.; 3 vols., London, 1877), I 401f.
2. Pierre Jean de Béranger (1780–1857), a French poet who wrote many popular songs by fitting new lyrics to familiar tunes.
3. Acts 5:19.

On the envelope of the preceding letter Browning recorded the visit which intervened between it and Letter 144:
+Monday, Nov. 3
3–4¼ p.m.

144 (W71)   *R.B. to E.B.B.*

_____

[*November 4, 1845.*]

Tuesday.

Only a word to tell you Moxon promises the books for to-morrow, Wednesday—so towards evening yours will reach you—'parve liber, sine me ibis'[1] . . would I were by you, then and ever!—You see, and know, and understand why I can neither talk to you, nor write to you *now,* as we are now;—from the beginning, the personal interest absorbed every other, greater or smaller—but as one cannot well,—or should not,—sit quite silently, the words go on, about Horne, or what chances—while you are in my thought.

But when I have you . . so it seems . . *in* my very heart,—when you are entirely with me—oh, the day—then it will all go better, talk and writing too.

Love me, my own love,—not as I love you—not for—but I cannot write that: nor do I ask anything, with all your gifts here, except for the luxury of asking. Withdraw nothing, then, dearest, from your R. B.

1. "Little book, you will go without me." Martial, *Epigrams* III. v. 1–2.

145 (W75°)   **E.B.B. to R.B.**

———————————

[*November 5, 1845.*]

Wednesday.

I had your note last night, & am waiting for the book to-day,—a true living breathing book, let the writer say of it what he will. Also when it comes it wont certainly come 'sine te.' Which is my comfort.

And now—not to make any more fuss about a matter of simple restitution—may I have my letter back? . . I mean the letter which if you did not destroy . . did not punish for its sins long & long ago . . belongs to me—which if destroyed, I must lose for my sins, . . but, if undestroyed, which I may have back,—may I not? is it not my own? must I not?— that letter I was made to return & now turn to ask for again in further expiation. Now do I ask humbly 'nough? And send it at once, if undestroyed—do not wait till Saturday.

I have considered about Mr. Kenyon & it seems best, in the event of a question or of a remark equivalent to a question, to confess to the visits 'generally once a week' . . because he may hear, one, two, three different ways, . . not to say the other reasons & Chaucer's charge against "doubleness."[1] I fear . . I fear that he (not Chaucer) will wonder a little— & he has looked at me with scanning spectacles already & talked of its being a mystery to him how you made your way here; & *I*, who though I can *bespeak* selfcommand, have no sort of presence of mind (not so much as one would use to play at Jack straws) did not help the case at all. Well—it cannot be helped. Did I ever tell you what he said of you once— '*that you deserved to be a poet*—being one in your heart and life:' he said *that* of you to me, & I thought it a noble encomium & deserving its application.

For the rest . . yes!—you know I do—God knows I do—Whatever I can feel is for you—& perhaps it is not less, for not being simmered away in too much sunshine as with women accounted happier—*I* am happy besides now—happy enough to die now.

    May God bless you, dear—dearest—

                            Ever I am yours—

The book does not come—so I shall not wait. Mr. Kenyon came instead, & comes again on *friday* he says, & Saturday seems to be clear still.

    1. *Beware of Doublenesse* is now excluded from the Chaucerian Canon. Skeat attributes it to Lydgate.

There is no envelope for Letter 146 which was enclosed in a large paper wrapper with the presentation copy of Dramatic Romances and Lyrics *referred to in its opening sentence.*

146 (W72)   **R.B. to E.B.B.**

[*November 6, 1845.*]

Just arrived . . (mind, the *silent writing* overflows the page, and laughs at the black words for Mr. Kenyon to read!)—[1] But your note arrived earlier——more of that, when I write after this dreadful dispatching-business that falls on me—friend A. & B. & C. must get their copy, and word of regard, all by next post!—

    Could you think ↑*that*↓ that untoward letter lived one *moment* after it returned to me? I burned it and cried 'serve it right'! Poor letter,—yet I should have been vexed & offended *then* to be told I *could* love you better than I did already. 'Live and *learn!*' Live and love you . . dearest, as loves you R. B.

You will write to reassure me about Saturday, if not for other reasons. See your corrections . . and understand that in one or two instances in which they would seem not to be adopted, they *are* so, by some modification of the previous, or following line . . as in one of the Sorrento lines . . about a "turret"[2]—see! (Can you give me Horne's address—I would send then)

1. See Letter 134, notes 1 and 3.
2. *England in Italy*, line 219. E.B.B.'s comment was: "The square black tower on the largest. / Did you write '*built* on the largest' because [of] the eternal rhythm? *How tired you are!* | *as you once said to me*." (Macmillan ed., p. 1344.) Browning's revision reads: "On the largest, the strange square black turret."

147 (W76°)   **E.B.B. to R.B.**

_____

[*November 6, 1845.*]

Thursday evening.

I see & know,—read & mark,—& only hope there is no harm done by my meddling,—& lose the sense of it all in the sense of beauty & power everywhere, which nobody could kill, if they took to meddling more even. And now, what will people say to this & this & this—or 'O seclum insipiens et impietum!'[1] or rather, O ungrateful right hand which does not thank you first!—I do thank you. I have been reading everything with new delight,—& at intervals remembering in inglorious complacency (for which you must try to forgive me) that Mr. Forster is no longer anything like an enemy.[2] And yet (just see what contradiction!) the British Quarterly has been abusing me[3] so at large, that I can only take it to be the achievement of a very particular friend indeed,—of someone who positively never reviewed before & tries his new sword on me out of pure friendship. Only I suppose it is not the general rule, & that there are friends "with a difference." Not that you are to fancy me pained—oh no!—merely surprised. I was prepared for anything almost from the quarter in question, but scarcely for being hung 'to the crows' so publicly . . though within the bounds of legitimate criticisms, mind. But oh—the creatures of your sex are not always magnanimous—*that* is true. And to put *you* between me & all . . the thought of *you* . . in a great eclipse of the world . . THAT is happy . . only, . . too happy for such as I am—as my own heart warns me hour by hour.

"Serve *me* right"—I do not dare to complain. I wished for the safety of that letter so much that I finished by persuading myself of the probability of it: but 'serve *me* right' quite clearly. And yet—but no more 'and yets' about it. 'And yets' fray the silk.

I see how the "turret" stands in the new reading, triumphing over the "tower," & unexceptionable in every respect. Also I do hold that nobody with an ordinary understanding has the slightest pretence for attaching a charge of obscurity to this new number—there are lights enough for the critics to scan one another's dull blank of visage by. One verse indeed in that expressive lyric of the 'Lost Mistress,' does still seem questionable to me,[4] though you have changed a word since I saw it; & still I fancy that I rather leap at the meaning than reach it—but it is my own fault probably . . I am not sure. With that one exception I *am quite* sure that people who shall complain of darkness are blind . . I mean, that the construction is clear & unembarrassed everywhere. Subtleties of thought which are not directly apprehensible by minds of a common range, are here as elsewhere in your writings—but if to utter things 'hard to understand' from *that* cause, be an offence, why we may begin with "our beloved brother Paul," you know, & go down through all the geniuses of the world, & bid them put away their inspirations. You must /go d>descend/ to the level of critic A or B, that he may look into your face . . Ah well!—"Let them rave."[5] You will live when all *those* are under the willows. In the meantime there is something better, as you said, even than your poetry . . as the giver is better than the gift, & the maker than the creature, & YOU than YOURS. Yes—*you* than *yours* . . (I did not mean it so when I wrote it first . . but I accept the 'bona verba,' & use the phrase for the end of my letter) . . as *you* are better than *yours;* even when so much yours as your own E. B. B.

⌈May I see the first act first? Let me!—And you walk?
Mr. Horne's address is Hill Side, Fitzroy Park Highgate.
There is no reason against Saturday so far. Mr. Kenyon comes to-morrow, friday, & therefore . .!! and if Saturday sh^d become impracticable, I will write again.⌉[6]

1. "O stupid and boorish age!" Catullus, *Carmen* XLIII. 8.
2. For the enmity, see Letter 107, note. E.B.B. anticipates a sympathetic review in the *Examiner*.
3. The 1844 volumes were reviewed in the issue for November 1845 and praised for right motives and sound sentiments, but "surely never was gold so disguised and overlaid with tinsel . . . never was real merit made to look so like what Carlyle would call a 'sham.'" And, in a tone rather of sorrow than anger, E.B.B. was called "unintelligible."
4. See Letter 135, note 3.
5. From Tennyson's, *A Dirge* (1830).
6. Added at the top of the first page.

The envelope of the foregoing letter logs the next visit:
+Sat^y Nov. 8
3–4.5m. p.m.

148 (W73)   **R.B. to E.B.B.**

──────────────

[*November 9, 1845.*]

Sunday Evening.

When I come back from seeing you, and think over it all, there never is a least word of yours I could not occupy myself with, and wish to return to you with some .. not to say, all .. the thoughts & fancies it is sure to call out of me: there is nothing in you that does not draw out all of me: you possess me, dearest .. and there is no help for the expressing it all, no voice nor hand, but these of mine which shrink and turn away from the attempt: so you must go on, patiently, knowing me, ⸣more and more,⸤ and your entire power on me, and I will console myself, to the full extent, with your knowledge,—penetration, intuition .. *somehow* I must believe you can get to what is here, in me, without the pretence of my telling or writing it—But, because I give up the great achievements, there is no reason I should not secure any occasion of making clear one of the less important points that arise in our intercourse .. if I fancy I can do it with the least success: for instance, it is on my mind to explain what I meant yesterday by trusting that the entire happiness I feel in the letters, and the help in the criticising might not be hurt by the surmise, even, that those labours to which you were born, might be suspended, in any degree, thro' such generosity to me: dearest, I believed in your glorious genius and knew it for a true star from the moment I saw it,—long before I had the blessing of knowing it was MY star, with my fortune and futurity in it—And, when I draw back from myself, and look better and more clearly, then I *do* feel, with you, that the writing a few letters more or less, reading many or few rhymes of any other person, would not interfere in any material degree with that power of yours—that you might easily make one so happy and ⸣yet⸤ go on writing "Geraldines" and "Berthas"—but—how can I, dearest, leave my heart's treasures long, even to look at your genius? .. and when I come back and find all safe, find the comfort of you, the traces of you .. *will* it do—tell me—to trust all that as a light effort, an easy matter?

Yet, if you can lift me with one hand, while the other suffices to crown you—there is queenliness in *that*, too!

Well, I have spoken. And I told you, your turn comes now: how have you determined respecting the American Edition?[1] .. You tell me nothing of yourself!—It is all ME you help, me you do good to .. and I take it all! Now see, if this goes on!—I have not had *every* love-luxury, I now find out .. where is the proper, rationally to-be-expected— "*lovers' quarrel?*" Here, as you will find! "Iræ amantium" .. I am no more "at a loss with my Naso," than Peter Ronsard.[2] Ah, but then they are to be "reintegratio amoris"—and to get back into a thing, one must needs get for a moment first out of it .. trust me, no! And now, the natural inference from all this? The consistent inference .. the "self-denying ordinance"?—Why—do you doubt? even this,—you must just put aside the Romance,[3] and tell the Americans to wait, and make my heart start up when the letter is laid to it, the letter full of your news, telling me you are well and walking, and working for my sake towards *the time*—informing me, moreover, if Thursday or Friday is to be my day—.

May God bless you, my own love—

I will certainly bring you an Act of the Play[4] .. for this serpent's reason, in addition to the others .. that—No, I will *tell* you that—I can tell you now more than even lately!

                                        Ever your own R. B.

1. See Letter 138.
2. See *The Glove* (1845) ll. 11–12. Browning, however, is recalling, not Ovid, but Terence, *Andria* III. ii. 23: "Amantium irae amoris integratio est": "A lover's quarrel is a renewal of love."
3. The "novel-poem"; see Letter 10, and note 7.
4. *Luria;* see Letter 150.

149 (W77°)   *E.B.B. to R.B.*

[*November 10, 1845.*]

Monday.

If it were possible that you could do me harm in the way of work, (but it isn't) it would be possible, not through writing letters & reading manuscripts, but because of a reason to be drawn from your own great line

"What man is strong until he stands alone?"[1]
What man .. what woman? For have I not felt twenty times the desolate advantage of being insulated here & of not minding anybody when I made my poems?—of living a little like a disembodied spirit, & caring less for supposititious criticism than for the black fly buzzing in the pane?—*That* made me what dear Mr. Kenyon calls 'insolent,'—untimid, & unconventional in my degree; and not so much by strength, you see, as by separation—*You* touch your greater ends by mere strength; breaking with your own hands the hampering threads which, in your position w^d have hampered *me*.

Still .. when all is changed for me now, & different, it is not possible, .. for all the changing .. nor for all your line & my speculation, .. that I should not be better & stronger for being within your influences & sympathies, in this way of writing as in other ways. We shall see—you will see. Yet I have been idle lately I confess,—leaning half out of some turret-window of the castle of Indolence & watching the new sunrise— as why not?—Do I mean to be idle always?—no!—and am I not an industrious worker on the average of days? Indeed yes!—Also I have been less idle than you think perhaps, even this last year, though the results seem so like trifling: and I shall set about the prose papers for the New York people, and the something rather better besides we may hope .. may *I* not hope, if *you* wish it? Only there is no 'crown' for me, be sure, except what grows from this letter & such letters .. this sense of being anything to *One!* there is no room for *another* crown. Have I a great head like Goethe's that there should be room? & mine is bent down already by the unused weight—& as to bearing it, .. 'Will it do,— tell me,—to treat *that* as a light effort, an easy matter?'

Now let me remember to tell you that the line of yours I have just quoted, which has been present with me since you wrote it, Mr. Chorley has quoted too in his new novel of "Pomfret."[2] You were right in your identifying of servant & waistcoat—& Wilson waited only till you had gone on Saturday, to give me a parcel & note;—the novel itself in fact, which Mr. Chorley had the kindness to send me 'some days or weeks,' said the note, 'previous to the publication.' Very good-natured of him certainly!—and the book seems to me his best work in point of sustainment & vigour, & I am in process of being interested in it. Not that he is a *maker*, even for this prose. A feeler . . an observer . . a thinker even, in a certain sphere—but a maker . . no, as it seems to me—and if I were he, I would rather herd with the essayists than the novelists where he is too good to take inferior rank & not strong enough to 'go up higher.' Only it would ⸝be⸜ more right in me to be grateful than to talk so—now w^d'nt it?——

And here is Mr. Kenyon's letter back again—a kind good letter . . a letter I have liked to read, (so it was kind and good in you to let me!)—and he was with me to-day & praising the ride to Ghent, and praising the Duchess, & praising you altogether as I liked to hear him. The Ghent-ride was 'very fine'—& the

'Into the midnight they galloped abreast'
drew /you⟩us/ out into the night as witnesses. And then, the 'Duchess' . . the conception of it was noble, & the vehicle, rhythm & all, most characteristic & individual . . though some of the rhymes . . oh, some of the rhymes did not find grace in his ears—but the incantation-scene, 'just trenching on the supernatural,' *that* was taken to be 'wonderful,' . . "showing extraordinary power, . . as indeed other things did . . works of a highly original writer & of such various faculty!"—Am I not tired of writing your praises as he said them? So I shall tell you, instead of any more, that I went down to the drawing-room yesterday (because it was warm enough) by an act of supererogatory virtue for which you may praise *me* in turn. What weather it is! & how the year seems to have forgotten itself into April.

But after all, how have I answered your letter?—& how *are* such letters to be answered? Do we answer the sun when he shines?—May God bless you . . it is my answer—with one word besides . . that I am wholly and ever your E. B. B.

On thursday as far as I know yet—& you shall hear if there sh^d be an obstacle—*Will you walk?*—If you /do⟩will/ not, you know, you must be forgetting me a little—Will you remember me too in the act of the play?—but above all things in taking the right exercise, & in not overworking the head—!—And this for no serpent's reason.

    1. *Colombe's Birthday* (1844), III, 231: "When is man strong until he feels alone?"
    2. Chorley had quoted the line (correctly) as motto for chap. iii, Bk. II, of his novel.

Browning came to call between the two parts of the following letter and recorded his visit on the envelope of Letter 149:
+Thursday Nov 13
3–4½ p.m.

150 (W78°)   **E.B.B. to R.B.**

[*November 12, 1845.*]

         Two letters in one—*Wednesday.*
    I shall see you to-morrow & yet am writing what you will have to read perhaps. When you spoke of 'stars' & 'geniuses' in that letter, I did not seem to hear,—I was listening to those words of the letter which were of a better silver in the sound than even your praise could be: and now that at last I come to hear them in their extravagance (oh such pure extravagance about 'glorious geniuses'—) I cant help telling you they were heard last, & deserved it.
    Shall I tell you besides?—The first moment in which I seemed to admit to myself in a flash of lightning the *possibility* of your affection for me being more than dream-work .. the first moment was *that* when you intimated (as you have done since repeatedly) that you cared for me not for a reason, but because you cared for me.[1] Now such a 'parceque' which reasonable people w^d take to be irrational, /is⟩was/ just the only one fitted to the uses of my understanding on the particular question we were upon .. just 'the woman's reason' suitable to the woman .. : for I could ⟨‖ · · · ‖⟩ understand that it might be as you said, &, if so, that it was altogether unanswerable .. do you see?—If a fact includes its own

cause . . why there it stands for ever—one of 'earth's immortalities'[2]—
as long as it includes it.

And when unreasonableness stands for a reason, it is a promising
state of things, we may both admit, & proves what it would be as well
not too curiously to enquire into. /And⟩But/ then . . to look at it in a
brighter aspect, . . I do remember how, years ago, when talking the
foolishnesses which women will talk when they are by themselves, &
↑not↓ forced to be sensible, . . one of my friends thought it "safest to
begin with a little aversion," & another, wisest to begin with a great deal
of esteem, & how the best attachments were produced so & so, . . I took
it into my head to say that the best was where there was no cause at all
for it, & the more wholly unreasonable, the better still, . . that the motive
sh^d lie in the feeling itself & not in the object of it—& that the affection
which could (if it could) throw itself out on an idiot with a goître would
be more admirable than Abelard's—Whereupon everybody laughed,
& someone thought it affected of me & no true opinion, & others said
plainly that it was immoral, and somebody else hoped, ↑in a sarcasm,↓
that I meant to act out my theory for the advantage of the world. To
which I replied quite gravely that I had not virture enough—& so,
people laughed as it is fair to laugh when other people are esteemed to
talk nonsense. And all this came back to me in the south wind of your
'parceque,' & I tell it as it came . . now.

Which ⟨all⟩ proves, if it proves anything, . . ⟨‖ · · · ‖⟩ while I have
every sort of natural pleasure in your praises & like you to like my
poetry just as I should, & perhaps more than I should; yet *why* it is all
behind . . & in its place—& *why* I have a tendency moreover to sift &
measure any praise of yours & to separate it from the superfluities,
far more than with any other person's praise in the world.

Friday evening [November 14].—Shall I send this letter or not?—I
have been 'tra 'l si e 'l no,'[3] & writing a new beginning on a new sheet
even—but after all you ought to hear the remote echo of your last letter . .
far out among the hills, . . as well as the immediate reverberation, & so I
will send it,—& ⟨it⟩↑what I send↓ is not to be answered, remember!——

I read Luria's first act twice through before I slept last night, & feel
just as a bullet might feel, ↑not because of the lead of it but because↓ shot
into the air and suddenly ↑arrested &↓ suspended. It ↑(' Luria ')↓ is all life,
& we know (that is, the reader knows) that there must be results here &
here. How fine that sight of Luria is upon the lynx hides[4]—how you see

the Moor in him just in the glimpse you have by the eyes of another—&
that laugh when the horse drops the forage, what wonderful truth &
character you have in *that!*—And then, when *he* is in the scene—!
'Golden-hearted Luria' you called him once to me,[5] & his heart shines
already .. wide open to the morning sun. The construction seems to me
very clear everywhere—and the rhythm, even over-smooth in a few
verses, where you invert a little artificially—but *that* shall be set down on
a separate strip of paper: & in the meantime I am snatched ⁺up⁺ into
'Luria' & feel myself driven on to the ends of the poet, just as a reader
should.

But *you* are not driven on to any ends?—so as to be tired, I mean?—
You will not suffer yourself to be overworked because you are 'interested' in this work. I am so certain that the sensations in your head
demand repose,—& it must be so injurious to you to be perpetually calling, calling these new creations, one after another, that you must consent
to be called *to,* & not hurry the next act, no, nor any act—let the people
have time to learn the last number by heart. And how glad I am that
Mr. Fox should say what he did of it[6] .. though it wasn't true, you
know .. not exactly. Still, I do hold that as far as construction goes, you
never put together so much unquestionable, smooth glory before, ..
not a single entanglement for the understanding .. unless 'the snowdrops'
make an exception[7]—while for the undeniableness of genius it never
stood out before your readers more plainly than in that same number!—
Also you have extended your sweep of power—the sea-weed is thrown
farther ⁺(if not higher)⁺,—than it was found before,—& one may calculate surely now how a few more waves will cover the brown stones &
float the sight up away through the fissure of the rocks—The rhythm
(to touch one of the various things) the rhythm of that 'Duchess' does
more & more strike me as a new thing; something like (if like anything)
what the Greeks called *pedestrian-metre,*[8] .. between metre & prose .. the
difficult rhymes combining too quite curiously with the easy looseness
of the general measure. Then the Ride—with that touch of natural feeling at the end, to prove that it was not in brutal carelessness that the poor
horse was driven through all that suffering .. yes, & how that one touch
of softness acts back upon the energy & resolution & exalts both, instead
of weakening anything, as might have been expected by the vulgar of
writers or critics. And then 'Saul'—& in a first place 'St. Praxed'—&
for pure description, 'Fortù'[9] and the /noble⟩deep/ 'Pictor Ignotus'—

& the noble, serene 'Italy in England,' which grows on you the more you know of it—& that delightful 'Glove'—and the short lyrics . . for one comes to '*select*' *everything* at last, & certainly I do like these poems better & better, as your poems are made to be liked. But you will be tired to hear it said over & over so, . . & I am going to 'Luria,' besides.

When you write will you say exactly how you are?—and will you write?—And I want to explain to you that although I don't make a profession of equable spirits, ⟨yet⟩ (as a matter of temperament, my spirits were always given to rock a little, up & down) yet that I did not mean to be so ungrateful & wicked as to complain of low spirits now & to you. It would not be true either: & I said "low" to express a merely bodily state. My opium comes in to keep the pulse from fluttering & fainting . . to give the right composure & point of balance to the nervous system. I dont take it for 'my spirits' in the usual sense,—you must not think such a thing. The medical man who came to see me made me take it the other day when he was in the room, before the right hour & when I was talking quite cheerfully, just for the need he observed in the pulse—'It was a necessity of my position,' he said. Also I do not suffer from it in any way, as people usually do who take opium. I am not even subject to an opium-headache—As to the low spirits I will not say that mine *have not* been low enough & with cause enough; but *even then,* . . why if you were to ask the nearest witnesses . . say, even my own sisters, . . everybody would tell you, I think, that the 'cheerfulness' ₊even *then,*₊ was the remarkable thing in me . . certainly it has been remarked about me again and again. Nobody has known that it was an effort (a habit of effort) to throw the light on the outside—I do abhor so that ignoble groaning aloud of the "groans of Testy and Sensitive"[10]—yet I may say that for three years I never was conscious of one movement of pleasure in anything. Think if I could mean to complain of 'low spirits' now, and to you. ⟨‖ · · · · ‖⟩ Why it would be like complaining of not being able to see at noon—which would simply prove that I was very blind. And you, who are not blind, cannot make out what is written—[11] so you *need not try.* May God bless you long after you have done blessing me!——Your own E. B. B.

Now I am half tempted to tear this letter in two (& it is long enough for three) & to send you only the latter half. But you will understand—you will not think that there is a contradiction between the first

& last . . you *cannot*. One is a truth /in⟩of/ me—and the other a truth /in⟩of/ you—and we two are different, you know.

You are not over-working in 'Luria'? That you *should not*, is a truth, too—

I observed that Mr. Kenyon put in '*Junior*' to your address. Ought that to be done?—or does my fashion of directing find you without hesitation?—

Mr. Kenyon asked me for Mr. Chorley's book, or you should have it—Shall I send it to you presently?—

1. See Letter 136 and cf. *Sonnets from the Portuguese*, XIV: "If thou must love me, let it be for nought / Except for love's sake only." Browning's letter (148) in praise of her "glorious genius" seems to have called forth not only this demurrer but the sonnet as well. The opening sentence also recalls—as does Letter 138—the "silver answer" of the first sonnet.

2. An allusion to the just-published poem.

3. "Between yes and no."

4. *Luria*, I, 103–107 (Jacopo speaking):

> I see him stand and eat, sleep stretched an hour
> On the lynx-skins yonder; hold his bared black arms
> Into the sun from the tent-opening; laugh
> When his horse drops the forage from his teeth
> And neighs to hear him sing old Moorish songs.

E.B.B. praised the passage a second time (Macmillan ed., p. 1347), and Forster quoted it in his *Examiner* review (April 25, 1846).

5. Letter 9.

6. Not identified. W. J. Fox's remark was probably passed in conversation or in a letter that has not come to light, but there is a possibility that one of his Sunday lectures had touched on *Dramatic Romances and Lyrics* as a later one (Letter 244, note 1) did on E.B.B.'s 1844 *Poems*.

7. See Letter 135 and note 3.

8. Perhaps E.B.B. means the *scazon* (Gr. "limping"), a variant of iambic trimeter ending in a spondee. Browning's "difficult rhymes" also weight the line-endings. The comparison of the meter of *The Flight of the Duchess* with any Greek measure is, however, less than inevitable.

9. The small Italian girl addressed by name in *England in Italy*.

10. James Beresford's *The Miseries of Human Life, or the Groans of Timothy Testy and Samuel Sensitive. In Twelve Dialogues* (1806) devotes each dialogue to all the possible complaints on a particular subject, contributed in turn by the two principals and members of their families. Each item is called a "groan" and numbered.

11. In the effaced passage.

151 *(W74)*   *R.B. to E.B.B.*

_____

[*November 16, 1845.*]

Sunday Morning.

At last your letter comes—and the deep joy—(I know and use to analyse my own feelings, and be sober in giving distinctive names to their varieties; this is *deep* joy,)—the true love with which I take this much of you into my heart, . . *that* proves what it is I wanted so long, and find at last, and am happy for ever. I must have more than "intimated"—I must have spoken plainly out the truth, if I do myself the barest justice, and told you long ago that the admiration at your works went *away,* quite another way and afar from this hope of you: if I could fancy some method of what I shall say happening without all the obvious stumbling-blocks of falseness, &c. which no foolish fancy dares associate with you . . if you COULD tell me when I next sit by you —"I will undeceive you,—I am not *the* Miss B.—she is upstairs and you shall see her—I only wrote those letters, and am what you see, that is all now left you" (all the misapprehension having arisen from *me,* in some inexplicable way) . . I should . . not begin by *saying* anything, dear, dearest—but *after that,* I should assure you—soon make you believe that I did not much wonder at the event, for I have been all my life asking what connection there is between the satisfaction at the display of power, and the sympathy with—ever-increasing sympathy with—all imaginable weakness? Look now: Coleridge writes on and on,—at last he writes a note to his "War-Eclogue,"[1] in which he avers himself to have been actuated by a really—on the whole— *benevolent* feeling to Mr. Pitt when he wrote that stanza in which "Fire" means to "cling to him everlastingly"—where is the long line of admiration now that the end snaps?—And now—here I refuse to fancy—you KNOW whether, if you never write another line, speak another intelligible word, recognize me by a look again—whether I shall love you less or *more* . . MORE; having a right to expect more strength with the strange emergency. And it is because I know this, build upon this entirely, that as a reasonable creature, I am bound to look first to what hangs farthest and most loosely from me . . what *might* go from you to your loss, and so to mine, to say the least . . be-

cause I want ALL of you, not just so much as I could not live without
—and because I see the danger of your entirely generous disposition
and cannot quite, yet, bring myself to profit by it in the quiet way you
recommend. Always remember, I never wrote to you, all the years, on
the strength of your poetry . . tho' I constantly heard of you thro' Mr.
K., and was near seeing you once, and might have easily availed myself of his intervention to commend any letter to your notice, so as to
reach you out of the foolish crowd of rushers-in upon genius . . who
come and eat their bread and cheese on the high-altar—and talk of
reverence without one of its surest instincts—never quiet till they cut
their initials on the cheek of the Medicean Venus to prove they worship her. My admiration, as I said, went its natural way in silence—but
when on my return to England in December, late in the month, Mr.
K. sent those Poems to my sister, and I read my name there[2]—and
when, a day or two after, I met him and, beginning to speak my mind
on them, and getting on no better than I should now, said quite naturally—"if I were to *write* this, now?"—and he assured me with his perfect kindness, you would be even "pleased" to hear from me under
those circumstances . . nay,—for I will tell you all, in this, in everything—when he wrote me a note soon after to re-assure me on that
point . . THEN I *did* write, on *account of my purely personal obligation,* tho'
of course taking that occasion to allude to the general and customary
delight in your works: I did write, on the whole, UNWILLINGLY . . with
consciousness of having to *speak* on ₊a₊ subject which I *felt* thoroughly
concerning, and could not be satisfied with an imperfect expression
of: as for expecting THEN what has followed . . I shall only say I was
scheming how to get done with ‖ · · · ‖[3] and go to my heart in Italy.[4]
And now, my love—I am round you . . my whole life is wound up
and down and over you . . I feel you stir everywhere: I am not conscious of thinking or feeling but *about* you, with some reference to you
—so I will live, so may I die! And you have blessed me *beyond* the *bond,*
in more than in giving me yourself to love; inasmuch as you believed
me from the first . . what you call "dream-work" *was* real of its kind,
did you not think? and now you believe me, *I* believe and am happy,
in what I write with my heart full of love for you: why do you tell me
of a doubt, as now, and bid me not clear it up, "not answer you?"—
Have I done wrong in thus answering? Never, never do *me* direct
wrong and hide for a moment from me what a word can explain as

now: you see, you thought, if but for a moment, I loved your intellect,— or what predominates in your poetry and is most distinct
from your heart,—better, or as well as you—did you not? and I have
told you every thing,—explained everything . . have I not? And now
I will dare . . yes, dearest, kiss you back to my heart again; my own.
There—and there!

And since I wrote what is above, I have been reading among other
poems that sonnet—"Past and Future"[5]—which affects me more than
any poem I ever read. How can I put your poetry away from you, even
in these ineffectual attempts to concentrate myself upon, and better
apply myself to what remains?—poor, poor work it is,—for is not
that sonnet to be loved as a true utterance of yours? I cannot attempt
to put down the thoughts that rise;—may God bless me, as you pray,
by letting that beloved hand shake the less . . I will only ask, *the less* . .
for being laid on mine thro' this life! And, indeed, you write down,
for me to calmly read, that I make you happy! Then it is—as with all
power—God thro' the weakest instrumentality . . and I am past expression proud and grateful—My love, I am your R. B.

I must answer your questions: I am better—and will certainly
have your injunction before my eyes and work quite moderately.
Your letters come *straight* to me—my father's go to Town, except on
extraordinary occasions, so that *all* come for my first looking-over. I
saw Mr. K., last night at the Amateur Comedy[6]—and heaps of old
acquaintances—and came home tired and savage—and *yearned* literally, for a letter this morning, and so it came and I was well again. So,
I am not even to have your low spirits leaning on mine? It was just
because I always find you alike, and ever like yourself, that I seemed to
discern a depth, when you spoke of "some days" and what they made
uneven where all / imaginable⟩is agreeable to me / : do not, now,
deprive me of a right—a right, to find you as you *are*;—get no habit
of being cheerful with me—I have universal sympathy and can show
you a SIDE of me, a true face, turn as you may: if you *are* cheerful . . so
will I be . . if sad, my cheerfulness will be all the while *behind*, and
propping up, any sadness that meets yours, if that should be necessary.
As for my question about the opium . . you do not misunderstand *that*
neither: I trust in the eventual consummation of my—shall I not say,
our—hopes; and all that bears upon your health immediately or pro-

spectively, affects me—how it affects me! Will you write again? *Wednesday*, remember! Mr. K. wants me to go to him one of the three next days ꜜafterꜜ. I will bring you some letters . . one from Landor.[7] Why should I trouble you about "Pomfret"?

And Luria . . does it so interest you? Better is to come of it. How you lift me up!—

1. *Fire, Famine, and Slaughter,* which was first published in the *Morning Post* for January 8, 1798, is 81 lines long; the "Apologetic Preface" Coleridge added in *Sibylline Leaves* (1817) runs to 490 prose lines in the Oxford Standard Authors edition of his poems.

2. Introduction, pp. xxxiv–xxxv.

3. The original word here may have been "England," as was conjectured in 1899, but another word written over it has made it indecipherable. The imposed word appears to end in *-and* or *-und* (possibly *-ard* or *-ord*) and to begin with *Staff-* or *Straff-*. If the chronology made any sense, one might conjecture that it was the title of Browning's first play.

4. This is reminiscent of the closing lines of "*De Gustibus——*" (1855). That poem describes scenery Browning had not seen since 1844 (DeVane, pp. 258f.) and had just described in *England in Italy*. It is possible that the 1855 poem was suggested when Browning re-read this letter or even began with this recollection of his love for Italy.

5. This 1844 sonnet was a resigned acceptance of the idea that life had, in effect, ended for E.B.B. There is surely a connection between this reference to it and *Sonnets from the Portuguese,* XLII, which quotes it and reassesses E.B.B.'s life from the new perspective. In the British Museum manuscript the sonnet is seventeenth in the sequence, a position that probably reflects more exactly its place in the chronology of composition than does the order in which E.B.B. arranged the poems for publication.

6. Another performance of *Every Man in His Humour* (see Letter 107 and note) was given on November 15, 1845. *Athenæum,* November 22, 1845.

7. Landor's letter says in part: "My dear kind Friend, before I have half read thro' your *Dramatic Romances* I must acknowledge the delight I am receiving . . . What a profusion of imagery, covering what a depth of thought. You may stand quite alone, if you will: And I think you will." H. C. Minchin, *Walter Savage Landor* (London: Methuen, 1934), pp. 18–20. Landor also enclosed the following lines, the last two of which came to sound like prophecy to the two poets when they were planning their marriage and escape to Italy. As a result, the Siren became a recurrent image in these letters from here on.

> There is delight in singing, though none hear
> Beside the singer; and there is delight
> In praising, though the praiser sit alone
> And see the prais'd far off him, far above.
> Shakespeare is not our poet, but the world's.
> Therefore on him no speech; and short for thee,
> Browning! Since Chaucer was alive and hale,

No man hath walk'd along our roads with step
So active, so inquiring eye, a tongue
So varied in discourse. But warmer climes
Bring brighter plumage, stronger wing; the breeze
Of Alpine heights thou playest with, borne on
Beyond Sorrento and Amalfi, where
The Siren waits thee, singing song for song.

152 (W79°)   *E.B.B. to R.B.*

[November 17, 1845.]

Monday.

How you overcome me as always you do—& where is the answer
to anything except too deep down in the heart for even the pearl-
divers? But understand . . what you do not quite . . that I did not mistake
you as far even as you say here & ⟨not⟩ even "for a moment." I did
not write any of that letter in a 'doubt' of you—not a word . . I was
simply looking back in it on my own states of feeling, . . looking back
from that point of your praise to what was better . . (or I should not
have looked back)—and, so, coming to tell you, by a natural association, how the completely opposite point to that of any praise was the
one which struck me first & most, viz. the no-reason of your reasoning
. . acknowledged to be yours. Of course I acknowledge it to be yours,
. . that high reason of no reason—I acknowledged it to be yours (didn't
I?) in acknowledging that it made an impression on me. And then,
referring to the traditions of my experience such as I told them to you,
I meant, so, farther to acknowledge that I would rather be cared for in
that ₊unreasonable₊ way, than for the best reason in the world. But all
that was history & philosophy simply—was it not?—& not *doubt of you*.

The truth is . . since we really are talking truths in this world . .
that I never have doubted you—ah, you *know!*—I felt from the beginning so sure of the nobility & integrity in you that I would have
trusted you to make a path for my soul—*that,* you *know.* I felt certain
that you believed of yourself every word you spoke or wrote—& you
must not blame me if I thought ₊besides₊ sometimes (it was the extent
of my thought) that you were selfdeceived as to the nature of your own
feelings. If you could turn over every page of my heart like the pages

of a book, you would see nothing there offensive to the least of your feelings . . not even to the outside fringes of your man's vanity . . should you have any vanity like a man,—which I DO doubt. I never wronged you in the least of things—never . . I thank God for it. But 'selfdeceived,' it was so easy for you to be!—see how on every side & day by day, men are—& women too . . in this sort of feelings. 'Self-deceived,' it was so possible for you to be, & while I thought it possible, could I help thinking it *best* for you that it should be so—& was it not right in me to persist in thinking it possible?—It was my reverence for you that made me persist!—What was *I* that I should think otherwise? I had been shut up here too long face to face with my own spirit, not to know myself, &, so, to have lost the common illusions of vanity. All the men I had ever known could not make your stature among them. So it was not distrust, but reverence rather. I sate by while the angel stirred the water, & I called it Messiah. Do not blame me now, . . *my* angel!———[1]

Nor say, that I "do not lean" on you with all the weight of my "past" . . because I do!—You cannot guess what you are to me—you cannot—it is not possible:—& though I have said *that* before, I must say it again . . for it comes again to be said. It is something to me between dream & miracle, [all of it][2]—as if some dream of my earliest brightest dreaming-time had been lying through these dark years to steep in the sunshine, returning to me in a double light. *Can* it be, I say to myself, that *you* feel for me *so?* can it be meant for me? this from YOU?

If it is your "right" that I should be gloomy at will with you, you exercise it, I do think—for although I cannot promise to be very sorrowful when you come, (how could that be?—) yet from different motives it seems to me that I have written to you quite superfluities about my "abomination of desolation,"[3]—yes indeed, & blamed myself afterwards. And now I must say this besides—When grief came upon grief, I never was tempted to ask "How have I deserved this of God," as sufferers sometimes do: I always felt that there must be cause enough . . corruption enough, needing purification . . weakness enough, needing strengthening . . *nothing* of the chastisement could come to me without cause and need. But in this different hour, when joy follows joy, & God makes me happy, as you say, *through* you . . I cannot repress the . . 'How have I deserved THIS of Him?'—I know I have not—I know I do not. ⟨‖ · · · ‖⟩

Could it be that heart & life were devastated to make room for you?—If so, it was well done,—dearest!—They leave the ground fallow before the wheat.

'Were you wrong in answering?'—Surely not . . unless it is wrong to show all this goodness . . & too much, it may be for *me*. When the plants droop for drought & the ⟨too⟩ copious showers fall suddenly, silver upon silver, . . they die sometimes of the reverse of their adversities. But no—*that*, even, shall not be a danger! And if I said 'Do not answer,' I did not mean that I would not have a doubt removed—(having NO doubt!—) but I was simply unwilling to seem to be asking for golden words . . going down the aisles with that large silken purse, as *quêteuse*—Try to understand.

On Wednesday then!—George is invited to meet you on thursday at Mr. Kenyon's.

The *Examiner* speaks well, upon the whole,[4] & with allowances . . oh, that absurdity about metaphysics apart from poetry!—'Can such things be' in one of the best reviews of the day? Mr. Kenyon was here on sunday & talking of the poems with real living tears in his eyes & on his cheeks. But I will tell you. Luria is to climb to the place of a great work, I see. And if I write too long letters, is it not because you spoil me, & because (being spoilt) I cannot help it?—May God bless you always!—Your E. B. B.

1. See John 5:4 for the allusion. Cf. *Sonnets from the Portuguese,* XLII, and see note 5 to the preceding letter.

2. A late erasure in the manuscript, probably by the first transcriber, has made these three words illegible; the reading here is from the 1899 printing.

3. Matthew 24:15.

4. The issue of November 15 gave Forster's review of *Dramatic Romances and Lyrics* first place and most of three columns:

"There is little to encourage . . . poets in these railway days; but the true poet cannot help singing; and it is his best chance for a little honest sympathy, to be dramatic in his song. There is a busy life, a stir of human interest, in all these romances and lyrics, and it is not a sleepy tune.

"We are disposed to admire this little book . . . very much. Our readers know how high we have ranked [Browning's] muse; and how we have grieved when she lost her way in transcendental or other fogs, and, like poor Origen's fallen star, 'rayed out' only darkness. Here she has found the path again.

"Mr. Browning's metaphysics have been too abundant for his poetry. That is the substance of the objection to be urged against him. And it is not a slight one . . . The analytic and imaginative powers never yet worked well together. But it is a fault (not an inglorious one) of youth: the fault of which Shelley himself became conscious before he died, and from which Mr. Browning is freeing himself. Nothing but this has retarded his advance.

"His writing has always had the stamp and freshness of originality. It is in no respect imitative or commonplace. Whatever the verse may be, the man is in it: the music of it echoing to his mood. When he succeeds there have been few so successful in the melodious transitions of his rhythms . . .

"These *Romances and Lyrics* form the seventh part of the collection . . . which Mr. Browning has been publishing for some years. . . . On the whole, they are a remarkable collection, and proof of a very different as well as original genius . . . They look as though already packed up [the format was fine print in double column] and on their way to posterity; nor are we without a confident expectation that some of them will arrive at that journey's end."

On the envelope of the preceding letter Browning noted a visit:
+ Wed. Nov. 19
3–4½ p.m.
Though Browning addressed Letter 153, it bears no postmark. This suggests that, on second thought, he enclosed it in the parcel of books referred to in the postscript.

153 (W75)   **R.B. to E.B.B.**

[*November 20, 1845.*]

Thursday M^{g}

Here is the copy of Landor's verses.

You know thoroughly, do you not, why I brought all those good-natured letters, desperate praise and all? Not, *not* out of the least vanity in the world—nor to help myself in your sight with such testimony: would it seem very extravagant, on the contrary, if I said that perhaps I laid them before your eyes in a real fit of compunction at not being, in my heart, thankful enough for the evident motive of the writers,— and so was determined to give them the "last honours," if not the first, and not make them miss *you* because, through my fault, they had missed *me?* Does this sound too fantastical? Because it is strictly true: the most laudatory of all, I *skimmed* once over with my flesh CREEPING—it seemed such a death-struggle, that of good nature over—well, it is fresh ingratitude of me, so here it shall end—

I am not ungrateful to *you*—but you must wait to know that:—I can speak less than nothing with my living lips.

I mean to ask your brother how you are to-night .. so quietly!

God bless you, my dearest, and reward you.

Your R. B.

Mrs. Shelley—with the "Ricordi."[1]

Of course, Landor's praise is altogether a different gift,—a gold vase from King Hiram;[2] beside he has plenty of conscious rejoicing in his own riches, and is not left painfully poor by what he sends away: *that* is the unpleasant point with some others—they spread you a board and want to gird up their loins and wait on you there: Landor says 'come up higher and let us sit and eat together.'[3]—Is it not that?

Now—you are not to turn on me because the first is my proper feeling to *you*, .. for poetry is not the thing given or taken between us —it is heart and life and *myself,* not *mine,* I give—give? That you glorify and change and, in returning then, give *me!*

1. Browning was returning Mrs. Shelley's book (Letter 100, note 6) and enclosing *Ricordi dei fratelli Bandiera e dei loro compagni di martirico in Cosenza,* ed. Mazzini (Paris, 1844), a memorial to Attilio and Emilio Bandiera, officers in the Austrian navy and members of the Young Italy Society who in June 1844 had led an abortive revolt against the Austrians. When captured and shot by the Naples government in July, they became popular martyr heroes and stirred British sympathies. Browning must have been in Naples within a few weeks of the execution, and Sir Frederic Kenyon suggests that event as the inspiration of *The Italian in England.* (*The Works of Robert Browning*, Centenary Edition, ed. F. G. Kenyon [10 vols.; London: Smith, Elder, 1912], III, xxxiv.) Mazzini presented the book to Browning (*Browning Collections,* p. 115, Lot #913) and the famous undated letter (*ibid.*, p. 55, Lot #255) in which he speaks of reading the poem to his fellow exiles must have accompanied it. Mazzini's intimacy with the Carlyles would explain so early an acquaintance with the poem.

2. The King of Tyre who sent cedar trees and carpenters to build David a house (II Samuel 5: 11) and from whom Solomon bought timber for the Temple (I Kings 5).

3. Luke 14: 10.

[*November 20, 1845.*]

Thursday.

Thank you!—and will you, if your sister made the copy of
Landor's verses for *me* as well as for you, thank *her* from me for another
kindness, . . not the second nor the third? For my own part, be sure that
if I did not fall on the right subtle interpretation about the letters, at
least I did not "think it vain" of you!—vain!—when, supposing you
really to have been overgratified by such letters, it could have proved
only an excess of *humility!*—But . . besides the subtlety . . you meant to
be kind to *me,* you know,—& I had a pleasure & an interest in reading
them—only that . . mind!—Sir John Hanmer's,[1] I was half angry
with!—Now *is* he not cold?—and is it not easy to see / how⟩*why* / he
is forced to write his own scenes five times over & over? He might have
mentioned the 'Duchess' I think,—& he a poet!—Mr. Chorley speaks
some things very well—but what does he mean about 'execution,' *en
revanche?* but I liked his letter & his candour in the last page of it. Will
Mr. Warburton review you?[2]—does he mean *that?*—Now do let me
see any other letters you receive—*May I?* Of course Landor's "dwells
apart" from all: & besides the reason you give for being gratified by it,
it is well that one prophet should open his mouth & prophesy & give
his witness to the inspiration of another. See what he says in the letter
. . "*You may stand quite alone if you will—and I think you will.*" That is a
noble testimony to a *truth.* And he discriminates—he understands &
discerns—they are not words thrown out into the air. The "profusion
of imagery covering the depth of thought" is a true description. And,
in the verses, he lays his finger just on your characteristics—just ↑on↓
those which, when you were only a poet to me, (only a poet!—does it
sound irreverent? almost, I think!) which, when you were only a poet
to me, I used to study, characteristic by characteristic, & turn myself
round & round in despair of being ever able to approach, taking them
to be so essentially & intensely masculine that like effects were unattainable, even in a lower degree, by any female hand. Did I not tell
you so once before? or oftener than once? And must not these verses of
Landor's be printed somewhere—in the Examiner? & again in the

Athenæum if in the Examiner, certainly again in the Athenæum . . it would be a matter of course. Oh those verses!—how they have pleased me! It was an act worthy of him—& of you.

George has been properly "indoctrinated," and, we must hope, will do credit to my instructions. Just now . . just as I was writing . . he came in to say good-morning & good-night (he goes to chambers earlier than I receive visitors generally), & to ask with a smile, if I had 'a message for my friend' . . *that* was *you* . . & so he was indoctrinated. He is good & true, honest & kind, but a little over-grave & reasonable, as I and my sisters complain continually. The great Law lime kiln dries human souls all to one colour—& he is an industrious reader among law books & knows a good deal about them, I have heard from persons who can judge; but with a sacrifice of impulsiveness & liberty of spirit, which *I* should regret for him if he sate on the woolsack even. Oh— that law!—how I do detest it! I hate it & think ill of it—I tell George so sometimes—and he is good-natured & only thinks to himself (a little audibly now & then) that I am ↑a↓ woman & talking nonsense. But the morals of it, & the philosophy of it!—And the manners ↑of it!↓ in which the whole host of barristers looks down on the attorneys & the rest of the world!—how long are these things to last!—

Theodosia Garrow, I have seen face to face once or twice. She is very clever—very accomplished—with talents & tastes of various kinds—a musician & linguist, in most modern languages I believe—& a writer of fluent graceful melodious verses, . . you cannot say any more. At least *I* cannot—& though I have not seen this last poem in the "Book of Beauty," I have no more trust ready for it than for its predecessors, of which Mr. Landor said as much. It is the personal feeling which speaks in him, I fancy—simply the personal feeling—&, *that* being the case, it does not spoil the discriminating appreciation on the other page of his letter. I might have the modesty to admit besides that I may be wrong & he, right, all through. But . . 'more intense than Sappho?!'—more intense than intensity itself!—to think of *that!*[3]— Also the word 'poetry' has a clear meaning to me, & all the fluency & facility and quick ear-catching of a tune which one can find in the world, do not ⟨‖ · · · ‖⟩ ↑answer to↓ it—no.

How is the head? will you tell me?—I have written all this without a word of it, & yet ever since yesterday I have been uneasy, . . I cannot help it. You see you are not better but worse. "Since you were in Italy"—Then is it England that disagrees with you? & is it change away from England that you want? . . *require,* I mean. If so—why what follows & ought to follow? You must not be ill indeed—*that* is the first necessity. Tell me how you are, exactly how you are,—& remember to walk, & not to work too much—for my sake—if you care for me— if it is not too bold of me to say so—I had fancied you were looking better rather than otherwise: but those sensations in the head are frightful & ought to be stopped by whatever means,—even by the worst, as they would seem to *me*. Well—it was bad news to hear of the increase of pain,—for the amendment was a "passing show" I fear, & not caused even by thoughts of mine or it would have appeared before,—: while on the other side (the sunny side of the way) I heard on that same yesterday, what made me glad as good news, a whole gospel of good news, & from *you* too who profess to say 'less than nothing;' and THAT was that "*the times seemed longer to you*"—do you remember saying it? And it made me glad . . happy—perhaps too glad & happy—& surprised: yes, surprised!—for if you had told me (but you would not have told me) if you had let me guess . . just the con- trary, . . "*that the times | were⟩seemed | shorter,*" . . why it would have seemed to *me* as natural as nature—oh, believe me it would, & I could not have thought hardly of you for it in the most secret or silent of my thoughts. How am I to feel towards you, . . do you imagine . . , who have the world round you & yet make me this to you? I never can tell you how,—& you never can know it without having my heart in you with all its experiences: we measure by those weights. ⟨‖ · · · · ‖⟩ May God bless you! & save *me* from being the cause to you of any harm or grief! . . I choose / that⟩it / for *my* blessing instead of another. What should I be if I could fail willingly to you in the least thing? But I *never will,* & you know it. I will not move, nor speak, nor breathe, so as willingly & consciously to touch, with one shade of wrong, that precious deposit of "heart and life" . . which may yet be recalled.

And, so, may God bless you and your E. B. B.

Remember to say how you are.

I sent 'Pomfret'—& Shelley is returned, and the letters, in the same parcel—but my letter goes by the post as you see. Is there contrast enough between the two rival female personages of 'Pomfret.' *I* fancy not. Helena should have been more 'demonstrative' than she appeared in Italy, to secure the 'new modulation' with Walter. But you will not think it a strong book, I am sure, with all the good & pure intention of it. The best character . . most life-like . . as conventional life goes . . seems to *me* "Mr. Rose" . . beyond all comparison—and the best point, the noiseless, unaffected manner in which the acting out of the "private judgement" ⊦in Pomfret himself⊦ is made no heroic virtue but simply an integral part of the love of truth. As to Grace she is too good to be interesting, I am afraid—& people say of her more than she expresses—& as to 'generosity,' she could not do otherwise in the last scenes—

But I will not tell you the story after all.

At the beginning of this letter I meant to write just one page,—but my generosity is like Grace's, & could not help itself. There were the letters to write of, & the verses! and then, you know, 'femme qui parle'[4] never has done. *Let* me hear! and I will be as brief as a monument next time for variety.

1. Hanmer (1809–81) was a prominent M.P. and amateur poet. One of his three volumes, *Fra Cipolla and Other Poems* (1839), furnished the motto for *Colombe's Birthday*.

2. Bartholomew Elliott George Warburton (1810–52), better known as Eliot Warburton, was one of Procter's law students who had just gained fame with *The Crescent and the Cross* (1845), an account of eastern travels. He was an early friend of Browning's. For probable identification of the review, see Letter 165, note 1.

3. E.B.B. refers to the closing paragraph of Landor's letter: "I confess to you I do not greatly like our sub-Shakespearean poets . . . We have better poetry from the living. Even the despised and ridiculed *Annuals* contain it. This very year there is in the *Book of Beauty* a poem by my friend Theodosia Garrow on Italy, far surpassing those of M. Angelo and Filicaia. Sappho is far less intense; Pindar is far less animated." Landor's enthusiasm often bordered on outrage, and E.B.B. herself lived to be compared with Sappho (*Landor's Poetical Works,* ed. S. Wheeler [3 vols., London: Oxford University Press, 1937], II, 459–460).

4. An allusion to Letter 80.

155 (W76)   *R.B. to E.B.B.*

[*November 21, 1845.*]

Friday Night.
How good and kind to send me these books! (The letter I say noth-

ing of, according to convention: if I wrote down " best & kindest " . . oh, what poorest words!) I shall tell you all about " Pomfret," be sure. Chorley talked of it, as we walked homewards together last night,— modestly and well, and spoke of having given away two copies only . . to his mother one, and the other to—Miss Barrett, and "she seemed interested in the life of it, entered into his purpose in it," and I listened to it all, loving Chorley for his loveability which is considerable at other times, and saying to myself what might run better in the child's couplet —" Not more than others I deserve, Tho' God has given me more"![1]— Given me the letter which expresses surprise that I shall feel these blanks between the days when I see you longer and longer! So am *I* surprised— that I should have mentioned so obvious a matter at all; or leave un- mentioned a hundred others its correlatives which I cannot conceive you to be ignorant of, you! When I spread out my riches before me, and think *what* the hour and more means that you endow one with, I *do* . . not to say *could,*—I *do* form resolutions, and say to myself—" If next time I am bidden stay away a FORTNIGHT, I will not reply by a word beyond the grateful assent." I *do,* God knows, lay up in my heart these priceless treasures,—shall I tell you? I never in my life kept a journal, a register of sights, or fancies, or feelings; in my last travel I put down on a slip of paper a few dates . . that I might remember in England, on such a day I was on Vesuvius, in Pompeii, at Shelley's grave; all that should be kept in memory is, with *me*, best left to the brain's own process: but I have, from the first, recorded the date and the duration of every visit to you,—the numbers of minutes you have given me . . and I put them together till they make . . nearly two days now,—four-and-twenty- hour-long-days, that I have been *by you*—and I enter the room deter- mining to get up and go sooner . . and I go away into the light street repenting that I went so soon by I don't know how many minutes—for, love, what is it all, this love for you, but an earnest desiring to include you in myself, if that might be,—to feel you in my very heart and hold you there for ever, thro' all chance and earthly changes?

There, I had better leave off; the words!

I was very glad to find myself with your brother yesterday; I like him very much and mean to get a friend in him—(to supply the loss of my friend . . Miss Barrett—which is gone, the friendship, so gone!) But

I did not ask after you because I heard Moxon do it. Now of Landor's verses: I got a note from Forster yesterday telling me that he, too, had received a copy . . so that there is no injunction to be secret. So I got a copy for dear Mr. Kenyon, and, lo! what comes! I send the note to make you smile! I shall reply that I felt in duty bound to apprise you; as I did. You will observe that I go to that too facile gate of his on Tuesday, *my day* . . from your house directly. The worst is that I have got entangled with invitations already, and must go out again, *hating* it, to more than one place.

I am *very* well—quite well: yes, dearest! The pain is quite gone; and the inconvenience, hard on its trace. You will write to me again, will you not? And be as brief as your heart lets you, to me who hoard up your words and get remote and imperfect ideas of what . . shall it be written? . . anger at you could mean, when I see a line blotted out; a *second-thoughted* finger-tip rapidly put forth upon one of my gold pieces!

I rather think if Warburton reviews me it will be in the "Quarterly" which I know he writes for. Hanmer is a very sculpturesque passionless highminded and amiable man . . this coldness, as you see it, is part of him. I like his poems, I think, better than you—"the Sonnets," do you know them? Not "Fra Cipolla"? See what is here, since you will not let me have only you to look at—this is Landor's first opinion[2]—expressed to Forster—see the date! and last of all, see me and know me, beloved! May God bless you!

1. "Praise for Mercies Spiritual and Temporal" from Isaac Watts's *Divine Songs for Children*.
2. On August 10, 1836, Landor, then in Heidelberg, wrote to Forster seconding his praise of *Paracelsus*. Forster excised a fragment for Browning, who is sending it to E.B.B. "When you told us that the author of Paracelsus would be a great poet, you came rather too late in the exercise of prophecy—he was already, and will be among the greatest. I hope he does not relax in the sirocco of faint praise which brother poets are fond of giving. Such as yours will brace him against it." H. C. Minchin, *Walter Savage Landor* (London: Methuen, 1934), p. 16.

156 (W81°)   *E.B.B. to R.B.*

_____

[*November 22, 1845.*]

Saturday.

Mr. Kenyon came yesterday—& do you know when he took out those verses[1] & spoke his preface & I understood what was to follow, I had a temptation from my familiar Devil not to say I had read them before—I had the temptation strong & clear. For he ʌ(Mr. K.)↓ told me that your sister let him see them—.

But no—My 'vade retro'[2] prevailed, and I spoke the truth and shamed the devil[3] & surprised Mr. Kenyon besides, as I could observe. Not an observation did he make till he was just going away half an hour afterwards, & then he said rather dryly . . "And now may I ask how long ago it was when you first read these verses?—was it a fortnight ago?—" It was better, I think, that I should not have made a mystery of such a simple thing, . . & yet I felt half vexed with myself & with him besides. But the verses,—how he praised them! more than I thought of doing . . as verses—though there is beauty & music & all that ought to be. Do you see clearly now that the latter lines refer to the combination in you,—the qualities over & above those held in common with Chaucer?—And I have heard this morning from two or three of the early readers of the Chronicle (I never care to see it till the evening) that the verses are there—so that my wishes have fulfilled themselves *there* at least—strangely, for wishes of mine . . which generally 'go by contraries' as the soothsayers declare of dreams. How kind of you to send me the fragment to Mr. Forster!—& how I like to read it. Was the Hebrew[4] yours *then . . written then,* I mean . . or written *now?*

Mr. Kenyon told me that you were to dine with him on tuesday, & I took for granted, at first hearing, that you would come on wednesday perhaps to me—& afterwards I saw the possibility of the two ends being joined without much difficulty—Still, I was not sure, before your letter came, how it might be.

That you really are better is the best news of all—thank you for telling me. It will be wise not to go out *too* much—'aequam servare mentem' as Landor quotes,[5] . . in this as in the rest—Perhaps that worst pain was a sort of crisis . . the sharp turn of the road about to end . . oh, I do trust it may be so.

Mr. K. wrote to Landor to the effect . . that it was not because he (Mr. K.) held you in affection . . nor because the verses expressed critically the opinion entertained of you by all who could judge . . nor because they praised a book with which his own name was associated . . but for the abstract beauty of those verses . . for *that* reason he could not help naming them to Mr. Landor. All of which was repeated to me yesterday.

Also I heard of you from George, who admired you—admired you . . as if you were a chancellor in *posse,* a great lawyer in *esse*—& then he thought you . . what he never could think a lawyer . . . '*unassuming.*' And *you* . . you are so kind!—Only *that* makes me think bitterly what I have thought before, but cannot write to-day.

It was goodnatured of Mr. Chorley to send me a copy of his book, & he sending so few—very! George who admires *you*, does not /like⟩tolerate/ Mr. Chorley . . (did I tell ever?—) declares that the affectation is 'bad,' & that there is a dash of vulgarity . . which I positively refuse to believe, & *should*, I fancy, though face to face with the most vainglorious of waistcoats. How can there be vulgarity even of manners, with so much mental refinement? I never c^d believe in those combinations of contradictions.

'An obvious matter,' you think! as obvious, as your "green hill" . . which I cannot see. For the rest . . my thought upon your 'great *fact*' of the "two days," is quite different from yours . . for I think directly, "'So little'! so dreadfully little!—What shallow earth for a deep root! What can be known of me in that time?" 'So *there,* is the only good, you see, that comes from making calculations on a slip of paper!' "It is not and it cannot come to good."[6] I would rather look at my seventyfive[7] letters—there is room to breathe in them. And this is my idea (ecce!) of monumental brevity—and *hic jacet* at last your E. B. B.

1. Landor's; see Letter 151, note 7.
2. "Get thee behind [me]." Matthew 16:23, slightly misquoted from the Vulgate.
3. *I Henry IV* III. i. 59.
4. On the back of the fragment of Landor's 1836 letter, Browning wrote in Hebrew the last half of Proverbs 15:30: ". . . a good report maketh the bones fat." The editor is indebted to Baylor University and the late Dr. A. J. Armstrong for photostats of the fragment.
5. Landor had quoted the opening of Horace's *Ode to Delius* (II. iii) in his 1845 letter:

November, 1845

"*Aequam memento rebus in arduis*
        Servare mentem [To preserve a calm mind in stress]
is a difficult rule to keep in poetry, where it is as much wanted as anywhere."
H. C. Minchin, *Walter Savage Landor* (London: Methuen, 1934), p. 19.
    6. *Hamlet* I. ii. 158.
    7. She has seventy-five of the seventy-six he has written. For the fate of the
sixteenth, see the note before Letter 30.

157 (*W77*)   *R.B. to E.B.B.*

                [*November 23, 1845.*]

                                                Sunday Night.
    But a word to-night, my love—for my head aches a little,—I had
to write a long letter to my friend at New Zealand,[1] and now I want to
sit and think of you and get well—but I must not quite lose the word I
counted on.
    So, *that* way you will take my two days and turn them against me?
Oh, you! Did I say the "root" had been striking then, or not rather, that
the seeds, whence the roots take leisure and grow, *they* had been planted
then—and might not a good heart & hand drop acorns enough to grow
up into a complete Dodona-grove,[2]—when the very rook, say farmers,
hides and forgets whole navies of shipwood one day to be, in his summer
storing-journeys? But this shall do—I am not going to prove what *may*
be, when here it *is,* to my everlasting happiness.
    —And "I am kind"—there again! Do I not know what you mean
by that? Well it is some comfort that you make all even in some degree,
and take from my faculties here what you give them, spite of my protesting, in other directions. So I could not when I first saw you admire
you very much, and wish for your friendship, and be willing to give
you mine, and desirous of any opportunity of serving you, benefitting
you,—I could not think the finding myself in a position to feel this, just
this and no more, a sufficiently fortunate event . . but I must needs get
up, or imitate, or . . what is it you fancy I do? . . an utterly distinct, unnecessary, inconsequential regard for you, which should,—when it got
too hard for shamming at the week's end,—should simply spoil, in its
explosion and departure, all the real and sufficing elements of an honest

life-long attachment and affections! that I should do this, and think it a piece of kindness does . .

Now, I'll tell you what it *does* deserve, and what it shall get. Give me, dearest beyond expression, what I have always dared to think I would ask you for . . one day! Give me . . wait—for your own sake, not mine who never, never dream of being worth such a gift . . but for your own sense of justice, and to *say*, so as my heart shall hear, that you were wrong and are no longer so, give me so much of you—all precious that you are—as may be given in a lock of your hair—I will live and die with it, and with the memory of you—this *at* the *worst!* If you give me what I beg,—shall I say next Tuesday . . when I leave you, I will not speak a word: if you do not, I will not think you unjust, for all my light words, but I will pray you to wait and remember me one day—when the power to deserve more may be greater . . never the will. God supplies all things: may he bless you, beloved! So I can but pray, kissing your hand.

R. B.

Now pardon me, dearest, for what is written . . what I cannot cancel, for the love's sake that it grew from.

The "Chronicle" was thro' Moxon, I believe[3]—Landor had sent the verses to Forster at the same time as to me, yet they do not appear. I never in my life less cared about people's praise or blame for myself, and never more for its influence on *other people* than now—I would stand as high as I could in the eyes of all about you—yet not, after all, at poor Chorley's expense whom your brother, I am sure, unintentionally, is rather hasty in condemning; I have told you of my own much rasher opinion and how I was ashamed and sorry when I corrected it after. C. is of a different species to your brother, differently trained, looking different ways—and for some of the peculiarities that strike at first sight, C. himself gives a good reason to the enquirer on better acquaintance. For 'Vulgarity'—NO! But your kind brother will alter his view, I know, on further acquaintance . . and,—woe's me!—will find that "assumption's" pertest self would be troubled to exercise its quality at such a house as Mr. K.'s, where every symptom of a proper claim is met half way and helped onward far too readily.

Good night, now. Am I not yours—are you not mine? And *can* that make *you* happy too?

Bless you once more and for ever.

That scrap of Landor's being for no other eye than mine—I made the foolish comment, that there was no blotting out—made it some four or five years ago, when I could read what I only guess at now,—thro' my idle opening the hand and letting the caught bird go—but there used to be a real satisfaction to me in writing those grand Hebrew characters—the noble languages!

1. Domett; for the letter, see *Robert Browning and Alfred Domett*, pp. 115ff.

2. The oracle at Dodona in Epirus interpreted the rustling of oak branches or the clanging of brazen vessels suspended in the trees.

3. Browning sent Moxon a copy of Landor's verses on Wednesday night, November 19, and they were published in the *Morning Chronicle* on Saturday. (D & K, p. 37). Landor had sent a copy to Forster, presumably with the idea that they would be published in the *Examiner,* but they never appeared.

158 (W82°)   **E.B.B. to R.B.**

———————————

[*November 24, 1845.*]

Monday.

But what unlawful things have I said about 'kindness'? I did not mean any harm—no, indeed!—And as to thinking . . as to having ever thought, that you could 'imitate' (can this word be 'imitate'?) an unfelt feeling or a feeling unsupposed to be felt . . I may solemnly assure you that I never, never did so. 'Get up'—'imitate'!!—But it was the contrary . . *all* the contrary! From the beginning, now *did* I not believe you too much?—Did I not believe you even in your contradiction of yourself . . in your *yes* & *no* on the same subject, . . & take the world to be turning round backwards & myself to have been shut up here till I grew mad, . . rather than disbelieve you either way? Well!—You know it as well as I can tell you, & I will not, any more. If I have been 'wrong,' it was not *so* . . nor indeed *then* . . it is not so, though it is *now*, perhaps.

Therefore . . but wait!—I never gave away what you ask me to give *you*, to a human being, except my nearest relatives & once or twice or thrice to female friends,[1] . . never, though reproached for it,—and it is just three weeks since I said last to an asker that I was "too great ↑a↓ prude for such a thing"! it was best to anticipate the accusation!—And, prude or not, I could not—I never could—*something* would not let me. And now . . what am I to do . . "for my own sake and not yours"? Should you have it, or not? Why I suppose . . YES. I suppose that "for my own /sake⟩sense/ of justice & in order to show that I was wrong" (which is wrong—you wrote a wrong word there . . 'right,' you meant!) "to show that I was *right* and am no longer so," . . I suppose you must have it, 'Oh, YOU,' . . who have your way in everything! Which does not mean . . Oh, vous, qui avez toujours raison . .!—far from it.

Also . . which does not mean that I shall give you what you ask for, *to-morrow*,—because I shall not—& one of my conditions is (with others to follow) that *not a word be said to-morrow*—you understand. Some day I will send it perhaps . . as you *knew* I should . . ah, as you knew I should . . notwithstanding that 'getting up' . . that "imitation" . . of humility: as you knew TOO well I should!

Only I will not teaze you as I might perhaps; & now that your headache has begun again—the headache again!—the worse than head-ache! See what good my wishes do!—And try to understand that if I speak of my being 'wrong' now in relation to you . . of my being right before, & wrong now, . . I mean wrong for your sake, & not for mine . . wrong in letting you come out into the desert here to me, you whose place is by the waters of Damascus. But I need not tell you over again— you *know*—May God bless you till to-morrow & past it for ever. Mr. Kenyon brought me your note yesterday to read about the 'order in the button-hole'[2]—ah!—or 'oh, *you*,' may I not re-echo? It enrages me to think of Mr. Forster; publishing too as he does, at a moment, the very sweepings of Landors desk!—Is the motive ↑of the reticence↓ to be looked for somewhere among the cinders?[3]—Too bad it is.—So, till to-morrow! & you shall not be 'kind' any more.

Your E. B. B.

But how, '*a foolish* comment'? Good & true rather! And I admired the *writing*[4] . . worthy of the reeds of Jordan!——

1. Cf. *Sonnets from the Portuguese*, XVIII.
2. E.B.B. is quoting Browning's own metaphor for Landor's verses from an unpublished letter, now in the Wellesley College Library, that Browning wrote to Kenyon the preceding Friday.

3. Of recent ill feeling; see Letter 107 and its note 1.
4. The endorsement in Hebrew (Letter 156, note 4).

*Browning visited E.B.B. the day after the preceding letter and marked
its envelope:*

+Nov. 25, 1845

$3\frac{1}{4}$–$4\frac{1}{2}$ p.m.

*That visit occurred on Tuesday, while the following letter was in progress, and
E.B.B. added to it that evening and the next day. It is postmarked November 27
(Thursday). Before the spring of 1846 her sister Henrietta usually mailed each
morning the letters E.B.B. had completed the day before.*

159 (W83°)   **E.B.B. to R.B.**

[*November 24, 1845.*]

monday evening.

Now you must not blame me—you must not. To make a promise
is one thing, & to keep it, quite another: & the conclusion you see 'as
from a tower.' Suppose I had an oath in heaven somewhere . . near to
'coma Berenices,'[1] . . never to give you what you ask for! . . would not
such an oath be stronger than a mere half promise such as I sent you a
few hours ago?—Admit that it would—& that I am not to blame for
saying now . . (listen!) that I *never can* nor *will give you this thing;*—only
that I will, if you please, exchange it for another thing—you understand. *I* too will avoid being 'assuming'; I will not pretend to be generous, ↑no, nor "kind."↓ It shall be pure merchandise[2] or nothing at all—
Therefore determine!—remembering always how our 'ars poetica,'
after Horace, recommends "dare et petere vicissim"[3]—which is making
a clatter of pedantry to take advantage of the noise . . because perhaps I
ought to be ashamed to say this to you, & perhaps I *am!* . . yet say it
none the less.

And . . less lightly . . if you have right & reason on your side, may I
not have a little on mine too?—And shall I not care, do you think? . .
Think!

291

Then there is another reason for me, entirely mine. You have come to me as a dream comes, as the best dreams come .. dearest—& so there is need to me of 'a sign' to know the difference between dream & vision —and *that* is my completest reason, my own reason—you have none like it,—none. A ticket to know the horn-gate from the ivory,[4] .. ought I not to have it? Therefore send it to me before I send you anything, & if possible by that Lewisham post which was the most frequent bringer of your letters until these last few came, & which reaches me at eight in the evening when all the world is at dinner & my solitude most certain. Everything is so still then, that I have heard the footsteps of a letter of yours ten doors off .. or more, perhaps. Now beware of imagining from this which I say, that there is a strict police for my correspondence .. (it is not so—) nor that I do not like hearing from you at any & every hour: it *is* so. Only I would make the smoothest & sweetest of roads for .. and you *understand*, & do not *imagine* beyond.

Tuesday evening [November 25].—What is written is written, .. all the above: and it is forbidden to me to write a word of what I could write down here .. forbidden for good reasons. So I am silent on *conditions* .. those being .. first .. that you never do such things again .. no, you must not & shall not .. I *will not let it be:* & secondly, that you try to hear the unspoken words, & understand how your gift[5] will remain with me while *I* remain .. they need not be said—just as *it* need not have been so beautiful, for that. The beauty drops 'full fathom five'[6] into the deep thought which covers it. So I study my Machiavelli to contrive the possibility of wearing it, without being put to the question violently by all the curiosity of all my brothers;—the questions 'how' .. 'what' .. 'why' .. put round & edgeways—They are famous, some of them, for asking questions. I say to them—'well!— how many more questions?' And now .. for *me*—have I said a word?—*have* I not been obedient? And by rights & in justice, there should have been a reproach .. if there could!—Because, friendship or more than friendship, Pisa or no Pisa, it was unnecessary altogether from you to me .. but I have done, & you shall not be teazed.

Wednesday [November 26].—Only .. I persist in the view of the *other* question. This will not do for the 'sign,' .. this, which, so far from being qualified for disproving a dream, is the beautiful image of a dream in itself . . *so* beautiful: & with the very shut eyelids, and the "little folding of the hands to sleep."[7] You see at a glance it will not do. And so—

Just as one might be interrupted while telling a fairytale, . . in the midst of the "and so's" . . just *so,* I have been interrupted by the coming in of Miss Bayley, & here she has been sitting for nearly two hours, from twelve to two nearly, & I like her, do you know. Not only she talks well, which was only a thing to expect, but she seems to *feel* . . to have great sensibility—& her kindness to me . . kindness of manner & words & expression, all together . . quite touched me.—I did not think of her being so loveable a person. Yet it was kind & generous, her proposition about Italy; (did I tell you how she made it to me through Mr. Kenyon long ago—when I was a mere stranger to her?—) the proposition to go there with me herself—It was quite a grave, earnest proposal of hers—which was one of the reasons why I could not even *wish* not to see her to-day. Because you see, it was a tremendous degree of experimental generosity, to think of going to Italy by sea with an invalid stranger, "seule à seule." And she was wholly in earnest,—wholly. Is there not good in the world after all?

Tell me how you are, for I am not at ease about you—You were not well even yesterday, I thought. If this goes on . . but it must'nt go on—oh, it must not. May God bless us more!—

Do not fancy, in the meantime, that you stay here 'too long' for any observation that can be made. In the first place there is nobody to 'observe'—everybody is out till seven, except the one or two who will not observe if I tell them not. My sisters are glad when you come, because it is a gladness of mine, . . they observe. I have a great deal of liberty, to have so many chains,—we all have, in this house: & though the liberty has melancholy motives, it saves some daily torment, & *I* do not complain of it for one.

May God bless you!—Do not forget me. Say how you are. What good ⟨may⟩ can I do you with all my thoughts, when you keep unwell? See!—Facts are against fancies. As when I would not have the lamp lighted yesterday because it seemed to make it later, & you proved directly that it would not make it *earlier,* by getting up & going away!

Wholly & ever your E. B. B.

1. When Berenice, sister-wife to Ptolemy Euergetes (247–222 B.C.), hung her hair in the Temple of Arsinoë in accordance with a vow to sacrifice it in return for

Egyptian success in Asia, it disappeared, and Conon of Samos told the King it had become a constellation. The seven stars near the tail of Leo are called *Coma Berenices*.

　　2. Cf. *Sonnets from the Portuguese*, XIX, l. 1.

　　3. "Giving and taking by turns." Cf. *Ars Poetica*, l. 11.

　　4. False dreams come by the ivory gate, genuinely prophetic ones by the horn. See *Aeneid* VI. 893–901.

　　5. Not identified. E.B.B.'s opening words on Wednesday suggest a carved ivory pin or cameo.

　　6. *Tempest* I. ii. 394.

　　7. Proverbs 6:10.

160 (W78)　　　　　　　*R.B. to E.B.B.*

───────────────

[*November 27, 1845.*]

Thursday M^g

　　How are you and Miss Bayley's visit yesterday, and Mr. K.'s to-day —(He told me he should see you this morning—and *I* shall pass close by, having to be in Town and near you,—but only the thought will reach you and be with you—) tell me all this, dearest.

　　How kind Mr. Kenyon was last night and the day before! He neither wonders nor is much vexed, I dare believe—and I write now these few words to say so—My heart is set on next Thursday, remember . . and the prize of Saturday! Oh, dearest, believe for truth's sake, that I *would* most frankly own to any fault, any imperfection in the beginning of my love of you,—in the pride and security of this present stage it has reached—I *would* gladly learn, by the full lights now, what an insufficient glimmer it grew from, . . but there *never has been change,* only developement and increased knowledge and strengthened feeling—I was made and meant to look for you and wait for you and become yours for ever. God bless you, and make me thankful!

　　And you *will* give me *that?* What shall "save me from wreck"— but truly? How must I feel to you!

Yours R. B.

E.B.B. wrote the word "hair" on the envelope of the following letter.

[*November 28, 1845.*]

Take it, dearest,—what I am forced to think you mean—and take *no more* with it—for I gave all to give long ago—I am all yours—and now, *mine,*—give me *mine* to be happy with!

You will have received my note of yesterday.—I am glad you are satisfied with Miss Bayley, whom I, too, thank . . that is, sympathize with, . . (not wonder at, though)—for her intention . . Well, may it all be for best—here or at Pisa, you are my blessing and life.

. . How all considerate you are, *you* that are the kind, kind one! The post arrangement I will remember—to-day, for instance, will this reach you at 8? I shall be with you then, in thought. "Forget you!"— *What* does that mean, dearest?

And I might have stayed longer and you let me go. What does *that* mean, also tell me? Why, I make up my mind to go, always, like a man, and praise myself as I get thro' it—as when one plunges into the cold water—ONLY . . ah, *that* too is no more a merit than any other thing I do . . there is the reward, the last and best! Or is it the "lure"?

⟨However⟩ I would not be ashamed of my soul if it might be shown you,—it is wholly grateful, conscious of you.

But another time, do not let me wrong myself *so!* Say, "one minute more—"

On Monday?—I am MUCH better—and, having got free from an engagement for Saturday, shall stay quietly here and think the post never intending to come—for you will not let me wait longer?

Shall I dare ⟨speak⟩ write down a grievance of my heart, and not offend you?—Yes, trusting in the right of my love—you tell me, sweet, here in the letter, "I do not look so well"—and sometimes, I "look better" . . *how do you know?* When I first saw you—*I saw your eyes*— since then, *you*, it should appear, see mine—but I only *know* yours are there, and have to use that memory as if one carried dried flowers about when fairly inside the garden-enclosure: and while I resolve, and hesitate, and resolve again to complain of this—(kissing your foot . . not boldly complaining, nor rudely)—while I have this on my mind, on my heart, ever since that May morning . . can it be?

—No, nothing *can be* wrong now—you will never call me 'kind' again, in that sense, you promise! Nor think 'bitterly' of my kindness, that word!

Shall I *see* you on Monday?

God bless you my dearest—I see her now—and *here* and *now* the eyes open, wide *enough*, and I will kiss them—*how* gratefully!

Your own R. B.

162 (W84°[a])[1]

E.B.B. to R.B.

[*November 28, 1845.*]

Friday.

It comes at eight oclock—the post says eight . . *I* say nearer half past eight . . : it *comes*—and I thank you, thank you, as I can. Do you remember the purple lock of a king on which hung the fate of a city?[2] *I* do! And I need not in conscience—because this one here did not come to me by treason—'ego et rex meus'[3] on the contrary, do fairly give & take.

I meant at first only to send you what is in the ring[4] . . which, by the way, will not fit you I know—(not certainly in the finger which it was meant for . .) as it would not Napoleon before you—but can easily be altered to the right size . . I meant at first to send you only what was in the ring: but your fashion is best so you shall have it both ways. Now dont say a word on Monday . . nor at all. As for the ring, recollect that I am forced to feel blindfold into the other world, and take what is nearest . . by chance, not choice . . or it might have been better—a little better—perhaps. The *best* of it is that it's the colour of your blue flowers. Now you will not say a word—I trust to you.

It is enough that you should have said these others, I think. Now *is* it just of you? isn't it hard upon me? ↑And if the charge is true,↓ whose fault is it, pray?—I have been ashamed & vexed with myself fifty times for being so like a little girl, . . for seeming to have "affectations"; & all in vain: 'it was stronger than I,' as the French say. And for *you* to complain!—As if Haroun Alraschid after cutting off a head, should complain of the want of an obeisance!—Well!—I smile notwithstanding. Nobody / can〉could / help smiling—both for my foolishness which is great I confess, though somewhat exaggerated in your statement—(because if it was quite as bad as you say, you know, I never should have *seen you* . . & *I have!*) & also for yours . . because you take such a very preposterously wrong way for overcoming anybody's shyness. Do you know, I have laughed . . really laughed at your letter—No—it has not been so bad. I have seen you at every visit, as well as I could with both eyes wide open—only that by a supernatural influence they won't stay open with *you* as they are used to do with other people . . so now I tell you. And for the rest I promise nothing at all—as how can I, when it is quite beyond my controul—& you have not improved my capabilities . . do you think you have?—Why what nonsense we have come to—we, who ought to be 'talking Greek!' said Mr. Kenyon . . !!

Yes—he came and talked of you, & told me how you had been speaking of . . me; & I have been thinking how I should have been proud of it a year ago, & how I could half scold you for it now. Ah yes—& Mr. Kenyon told me that you had spoken exaggerations—such exaggerations!—Now should there not be some scolding . . some?

But how did you expect Mr. Kenyon to 'wonder' at *you,* or be 'vexed' with *you?* That would have been strange surely. You are & always have been a chief favorite in that quarter . . appreciated, praised, loved, I think.

While I write . . a letter from America is put into my hands, & having read it through with shame & confusion of face . . not able to help a smile though notwithstanding, . . I send it to you to show how you have made me behave!—to say nothing of my other offences to the kind people at Boston—& to a stray gentleman in Philadelphia who is to perform a pilgrimage next year, he says, . . to visit the Holy Land & your E.B.B. I was naughty enough to take *that* letter to be a circular . . for the address of various "Europaians." In any case . . just see how I have behaved!—and if it has not been worse than . . not opening one's eyes!—Judge. Really & gravely I am ashamed—I mean as to Mr. Mathews,[5] who has been an earnest, kind friend to me—& I do mean to behave better. I say *that* to prevent your scolding, you know. And think of Mr. Poe, with that great Roman justice of his, (if not rather American!), dedicating a book to one & abusing one in the preface of the same. He wrote a review of me in just that spirit—the

two extremes of laudation & reprehension, folded in on one another—
You would have thought that it had been written by a friend & foe,
each stark mad with love & hate, & writing the alternate paragraphs—
a most curious production indeed.[6]

And here I shall end. I have been waiting . . waiting for what does
not come . . the ring . . sent to have the hair put in; but it won't come
(now) until too late for the post, and you must hear from me before
monday . . you ought to have heard to-day. It has not been my fault—
I have waited. Oh these people—who wont remember that it is possible
to be out of patience! So I send you my letter now . . & what is in the
paper now . . and the rest, you shall have after monday. And you *will
not say a word* . . not then . . not at all!—I trust you. And may God
bless you.

If ever you care less for me—I do not say it in distrust of you . . I
trust you wholly—but you are a man, & free to care less, . . & if ever
you *do* . . why in that case you will destroy, burn, . . do all but send
back . . enough is said for you to understand.

May God bless you. You are *best* to me . . best . . as I see . . in the
world—& so, dearest aright to

Your E. B. B.

Finished on saturday evening. Oh—this thread of silk—And to
post!! After all you must wait till tuesday. I have no silk within reach
& shall miss the post. Do forgive me.

---

1. Perhaps because E.B.B. called the following letter a "postscript" and he received them the same day, Browning assigned only one number to it and to this.

2. A purple lock grew in the white hair of Nisus, King of Megara, on which
depended both his life and the safety of his kingdom. His daughter Scylla, mad with
love for Minos, who was leading his Cretans against Megara, cut off the lock and
offered it to him. He rejected it in horror, and Scylla was changed into a bird (Virgil,
Ciris; Ovid, *Metamorphoses* VIII ll. 1–151). The epithet "purply black" in *Sonnets
from the Portuguese,* XIX, probably indicates a tie to this letter.

3. Cardinal Wolsey referred thus to himself and Henry VIII. *Henry VIII* III.
ii. 315.

4. Not traced. A lock of E.B.B.'s hair in a silver reliquary was sold at Sotheby's
in 1913 (*Browning Collections,* Lot #1370, p. 151).

5. Cornelius Mathews (1817–89) was in 1845 editor of *Graham's Illustrated
Magazine.* E.B.B. took the motto for her *Rhapsody of Life's Progress* (1844) from one
of his poems, and through him gained entry to some American periodicals. She wrote
him in April 1845, "My great debt [for my reception] in America, I always consider,

is to you" (manuscript letter, Yale library). He also saw her 1844 volumes through the press in America.

6. Poe dedicated *The Raven and Other Poems* (1845) "To the Noblest of her Sex — / To the Author of / "The Drama of Exile"— / To Miss Elizabeth Barrett / of England, / . . . / With the most enthusiastic admiration / And with the most sincere esteem." The abusive preface never appeared. Poe twice reviewed the 1844 collection —for the New York *Evening Mirror* (October 8, 1844) and for his own *Broadway Journal* (January 4 and 11, 1845). In the latter adverse judgments are lustily rendered but mixed with the highest praise: "Miss Barrett has done more, in poetry, than any other woman, living or dead . . . [and] that she has surpassed all her poetical contemporaries of either sex [except Tennyson] is our deliberate opinion."

163 (W84°[b])   E.B.B. to R.B.
_____

[*November 29, 1845.*]

Saturday evening.

This is the mere postscript to the letter I have just sent away. By a few minutes too late, comes what I have all day been waiting for, . . & besides (now it is just too late!) now I may have a skein of silk if I please, to make that knot with, . . for want of which, two locks meant for you, have been devoted to the infernal gods already . . fallen into a tangle & thrown into the fire . . & all the hair of my head might have followed, for I was losing my patience & temper fast, . . & the post to boot. So wisely I shut my letter, (after unwisely having driven everything to the last moment!)—& now I have silk to tie fast with . . to tie a 'nodus' . . 'dignus'[1] of the celestial interposition—& a new packet shall be ready to go to you directly.

At last I remember to tell you that the first letter you had from me this week, was forgotten, (not by *me*) forgotten, & detained, so, from the post—a piece of carelessness which Wilson came to confess to me too frankly for me to grumble as I should have done otherwise.

For the staying longer, I did not mean to say you were wrong not to stay. In the first place you were keeping your father 'in a maze,' as you said yourself—& then, even without that, I never know what oclock it is . . never. Mr. Kenyon tells me that I must live in a dream— which I do—time goes . . seeming to go round rather than go forward. The watch I have, broke its spring two years ago, & there I leave it in the drawer . . & the clocks all round strike out of hearing, or at best, when the wind brings the sound, one upon another in a confusion. So you know more of time than I do or can.

Till Monday then!—I send the 'Ricordi'[2] to take care of the rest . . of mine. It is a touching story—& there is an impracticable nobleness from end to end in the spirit of it. How *slow* (to the ear & mind) that Italian rhetoric is! a language for dreamers & declaimers. Yet Dante made it for action, & Machiavelli's prose can walk & strike as well as float & faint.

The ring is smaller than I feared at first, & may perhaps—

Now you will not say a word. My excuse is that you had nothing to remember me by, while I had this & this & this & this . . how much too much! If I could be too much

Your E. B. B.

1. "Knot . . . worthy," an allusion to Horace, *Ars Poetica*, ll. 191–192.
2. See Letter 153, note 1.

On the envelope of Letter 163 Browning noted his visit on
Monday Dec. 1, 1845
$3-4\frac{1}{4}$ p.m.
The enigmatic small cross was probably present originally, but the envelope corner, brittle with age, has flaked away.

164 (W80)   *R.B. to E.B.B.*

_____

[*December 2, 1845.*]

Tuesday.

I was happy, so happy before! But I am happier and richer now— My love—no words could serve here, but there is life before us, and to the end of it the vibration now struck will extend—I will live and die with your beautiful ring, your beloved hair—comforting me, blessing me—

Let me write to-morrow—when I think on all you have been and are to me, on the wonder of it and the deliciousness, it makes the paper words that come seem vainer than ever—To-morrow I will write.

May God bless you, my own, my precious—

I am all your own R. B.

I have thought again, and believe it will be best to select the finger *you* intended . . as the alteration will be simpler, I find,—and ⟨there are occasions⟩ ↑one is less liable to↓ observation and comment.

Was not that Mr. Kenyon last evening? And did he ask, or hear, or say anything?

165 (W81)   **R.B. to E.B.B.**

[*Postmarked December 3, 1845.*]

See, dearest, what the post brings me this minute! Now, is it not a good omen, a pleasant inconscious prophecy of what is to be? Be it well done, or badly—there are you, leading me up and onward, in his review as everywhere, at every future time![1] And our names will go together—be read together. In itself this is nothing to *you*, dear poet— but the unexpectedness, unintended significance of it has pleased me very much—*does* it not please you?—I thought I was to figure in that cold "Quarterly" all by myself, (for he writes for it)—but here you are close by me,—it cannot but be for good. He has no knowledge whatever that I am even a friend of yours. Say you are pleased!

There was no writing yesterday for me—nor will there be much to-day: in some moods, you know, I turn and take a thousand new views of what you say . . and find fault with you to your surprise—at others, I rest on you, and feel *all* well, all *best* . . now, for one instance, even that phrase of the *possibility* "and what is to follow,"—even *that* I cannot except against—I am happy, contented; too well, too prodi- gally blessed to be even able to murmur just sufficiently loud to get, in addition to it all, a sweetest stopping of the mouth! I will say quietly and becomingly 'Yes—I do promise you'—yet it is some solace to— NO—I will *not* even couple the promise with an adjuration that you, at the same time, see that they care for me properly at Hanwell Asylum[2] . . the best by all accounts:—yet I feel so sure of *you*, so safe and confident in you! If any of it had been *my* work, my own . . distrust and foreboding had pursued me from the beginning,—but all is *yours*—you crust me round with gold and jewelry like the wood of a sceptre; and why should you transfer your own work? Wood enough to choose from in the first instance, but the choice once made! . . . So I rest on you, for life, for death, beloved—beside you do stand, in my solemn belief, the direct miraculous gift of God to me—that is my solemn belief; may I be thankful!

I am anxious to hear from you . . when am I not?—but *not* before the American letter[3] is written and sent—Is that done? And who was the visitor on Monday—and if &c *what* did he remark?—And what is right or wrong with Saturday—is it to be mine?

Bless you dearest—now and for ever—words cannot say how much I am your own.

1. Browning apparently is forwarding a note from Eliot Warburton indicating that the promised article (see Letter 154 and its note 2) will include comments on E.B.B. It appeared in the *English Review, or Quarterly Journal of Ecclesiastical and General Literature* for December 1845. For an account of it, see the note which precedes Letter 193.

2. The lunatic asylum for London County.

3. Probably a reference to Browning's eagerness to have E.B.B. publish her critical essays from the *Athenæum* in America. See Letter 138 and note 3 and Browning's reaction in Letter 139. Though a letter from Cornelius Mathews is mentioned in Letter 162, there is nothing to suggest the kind of urgency in answering it that Browning seems to recommend here.

166 (W85°) **E.B.B. to R.B.**

[*December 2, 1845.*]

Tuesday evening.

No Mr. Kenyon after all—not yesterday, not today; & the knock at the door belonged perhaps to the post, which brought me a kind letter from Mrs. Jameson to ask how I was, & if she might come—but she wont come on saturday . . I shall 'provide'—she may as well (& better) come on a free day. On the other side, are you sure that Mr. Procter may not stretch out his hand & seize on saturday (he was to dine with you, you said), or that some new engagement may not start up suddenly in the midst of it? . . I trust to you, in such a case, to alter *our* arrangement, without a second thought. Monday stands close by, remember . . & there's a saturday to follow monday . . and I should understand at a word, or apart from a word.

Just as YOU understand how to 'take me with guile,' when you tell me that anything in me can have any part in making you happy . . you, who can say such words & call them 'vain' words!—Ah, well! If I only knew certainly, . . more certainly than the thing may be known by either me or you;—that nothing in me / can⟩could / have any part in making you *un*happy . ., would it not be enough . . *that* knowledge . . to content me, to overjoy me?—but *that* lies too high & out of reach, you see, and one can't hope to get at it except by the ladder Jacob saw,[1] and which an archangel helped to hide away behind the gate of Heaven afterwards.

Wednesday [December 3].—In the meantime I had a letter / of yours⟩from you / yesterday & am promised another to-day. How . . I was going to say 'kind' and pull down the thunders . . how *unkind* . . will *that* do? . . how good you are to me!—how dear you must be!— Dear—dearest—if I feel that you love me, can I help it if, without any other sort of certain knowledge, the world grows lighter round me? —being but a mortal woman, can I help it?—no—certainly.

I comfort myself by thinking sometimes that I can at least understand you, . . comprehend you in what you are and in what you possess & combine,—& that, if doing this better than others who are better otherwise than I, I am, so far, worthier of the ⟨‖ · · · ‖⟩ . . I mean that to understand you is something, & that I account it something in my own favour . . mine.

Yet when you tell me that I ought to know some things, tho' untold, you are wrong, & speak what is impossible. My imagination sits by the roadside ἀπέδιλος like the startled sea nymph in Æschylus,[2] but never dares to put one unsandalled foot, unbidden, on a certain tract of ground—never takes a step there unled!—& never (I write the simple truth) even as the alternative of the probability of your ceasing to care for me, have I touched ↑(untold)↓ on the possibility of your caring *more* for me . . never! That you should *continue* to care, was the /extremest⟩utmost/ of what I saw in that direction. So, when you spoke of a "strengthened feeling," judge how I listened with my heart— judge!

Luria is very great. You will avenge him with the sympathies of the world,—that, I foresee . . And for the rest, it is ↑a↓ magnanimity which grows & grows, & which will, of a wordly necessity, fall by its own weight at last; nothing less being possible. The scene with Tiburzio & the end of the act with its great effects, are more pathetic than professed pathos—When I come to criticize, it will be chiefly on what I take to be a little occasional flatness in the versification, which you may remove if you please, by knotting up a few lines here & there. But I shall write more of Luria,—& well remember in the meanwhile, that you wanted smoothness, you said—

May God bless you. I shall have the letter to-night, I think gladly. Yes,—I thought of the greater safety from 'comment'—it is best in every way.

I lean on you and trust to you, and am always, as to one who is all to me, Your own—

1. Genesis 28:11–13.
2. See E.B.B.'s translation of *Prometheus,* ll. 153–154. The Greek means "unsandaled."

167 (W86°)   **E.B.B. to R.B.**

[*Postmarked December 4, 1845.*]

Why of course I am pleased—I should have been pleased last year, for the vanity's sake of being reviewed in your company. Now, as far as that vice of vanity goes . . shall I tell you . . , I would infinitely prefer to see you set before the public in your own right solitude, & supremacy, apart from me or any one else, . . this, as far as my vice of vanity goes, . . & because, vainer I am of my poet than of my poems . . *pour cause.* But since, according to the Quarterly regime you were to be not apart but with somebody of my degree, I am glad, pleased, that it should be with myself:—and since I was to be there at all, I am pleased, very much pleased that it should be with *you,*—oh, of course I am pleased!—I am pleased that the "names should be read together" as you say, . . & am happily safe from the apprehension of that ingenious idea of yours about 'my leading you &c' . . quite happily safe from the apprehension of that idea's occurring to any mind in the world, except just your own—. Now if I "find fault" with you for writing down such an extravagance, such an ungainly absurdity, (oh, I shall abuse it just as I shall choose!) *can* it be "to your surprise"?—*can* it? Ought you to say such things, when in the first place they are unfit in themselves & inapplicable, & in the second place, abominable in my eyes—?—The qualification for Hanwell Asylum is different perad-venture from what you take it to be—we had better not examine it too nearly. You never will say such words again?—It is your promise to me? Not those words—& not any in their likeness.

Also . . nothing is *my* work . . if you please!—What an omen you take in calling anything my work! If it is my work, woe on it—for everything turns to evil which I touch. Let it be God's work & yours, & I may take breath & wait in hope—& indeed I exclaim to myself about the miracle of it far more even than you can do. It seems to me (as I say over & over . . I say it to my own thoughts oftenest) it seems to me still a dream how you came here at all, . . the very machinery of it seems miraculous. Why did I receive you & only you? Can I tell?—no, not a word.

Last year I had such an escape of seeing Mr. Horne; and in this way it was. He was going to Germany, he said, for an indefinite time, and took the trouble of begging me to receive him for ten minutes before he went. I answered with my usual 'no,' like a wild Indian—where-upon he wrote me a letter so expressive of mortification & vexation . . "mortification" was one of the words used, I remember, . . that I grew ashamed of myself & told him to come any day (of the last five or six days he had to spare) between two & five. Well!—he never came. Either he was overcome with work & engagements of various sorts & had not a moment, (which was his way of explaining the matter & quite true I dare say) or he was vexed & resolved on punishing me for my caprices. If the latter was the motive, I cannot call the punishment effective, . . for I clapped my hands for joy when I felt my danger to be passed—& now of course, I have no scruples . . I may be as capricious as I please, . . may I not?—Not that I ask you. It is a settled matter. And it is useful to keep out Mr. Chorley with Mr. Horne, & Mr. Horne with Mr. Chorley, & the rest of the world with those two. Only the miracle is that *you* should be behind the enclosure—within it . . & so!—

That is *my* side of the wonder! of the machinery of the wonder, . . as *I* see it!—But there are greater things than these—

Speaking of the portrait of you in the 'Spirit of the Age'[1] . .
which is not like . . no!—which has not your character, in a line of it . .
something in just the forehead & eyes & hair, . . but even *that,* thrown
utterly out of your order, by another bearing so unlike you . ! speaking
of that portrait . . shall I tell you?—Mr. Horne had the goodness to
send me all those portraits, & I selected the heads which, in right hero-
worship, were anything to me, & had them framed after a rough
fashion & hung up before my eyes,—Harriet Martineau's . . because
she was a woman & / amiable⟩admirable / , & had written me some
kind letters—& for the rest, Wordsworth's, Carlyle's, Tennyson's &
yours. The day you paid your first visit here, I, in a fit of shyness not
quite unnatural, . . though I have been cordially laughed at for it by
everybody in the house . . pulled down your portrait, . . (there is the
nail, under Wordsworth!—) & then pulled down Tennyson's in a fit
of justice,—because I would not have his hung up & yours away. It was
the delight of my brothers to open all the drawers & the boxes, &
whatever they could get access to, & find & take those two heads &
hang them on the old nails & analyze my 'absurdity' to me, day after
day,—but at last I tired them out, ⟨with⟩being obstinate; & finally
settled the question one morning by fastening the print of you inside
your Paracelsus. Oh no, it is not like—& I knew it was not, before I
saw you, though Mr. Kenyon said, "Rather like!"

By the way Mr. Kenyon does not come. It is strange that he
should not come: when he told me that he could not see me 'for a
week or a fortnight,' he meant it, I suppose.

So it is to be on saturday?—And I will write directly to America—
the letter will be sent by the time you get this. May God bless you ever.

It is not so much a look of "ferocity," . . as you say, . . in that head,
as of *expression by intention.* Several people have said of it what nobody
would say of you . . "How affected-looking"! Which is too strong—
but it is not like you, in any way, & there's the truth.

So until Saturday. I read Luria & feel the life in him. But *walk* &
do not *work!* do you? Wholly your E. B. B.

1. This was the rather boyish-looking profile engraved by Armytage from an
1835 pen sketch by Beard. See Grace E. Wilson, "Robert Browning's Portraits . . .,"
Baylor University Browning Interests, Series XIV (December 1943), pp. 28–30.

Yours very truly,
Robert Browning.

The picture that hung in E.B.B.'s room
From " The New Spirit of the Age"

National Portrait Gallery

John Kenyon
From a bust by Thomas Crawford

Though there is no notation on the envelope of Letter 167, Browning pretty surely made a visit on Saturday, December 6. It is anticipated in Letters 166 and 167 and recalled in 169. In addition, Browning's own numbering, beginning with his note on the envelope of Letter 185, includes one visit for which there is no (surviving) record.

168 (W82)   R.B. to E.B.B.

[*December 7, 1845.*]

Sunday Night.

Well, I did see your brother last night . . and very wisely neither spoke nor kept silence in the proper degree, but said that "I hoped you were well"—from the sudden feeling that I must say *something* of you . . not pretend indifference about you *now* . . and from the impossibility of saying the *full* of what I might; because other people were by—and after, in the evening, when I should have remedied the first imperfect expression, I had not altogether the heart. So, you, dearest, will clear me with him if he wonders, will you not?—But it all hangs together; speaking of you—, to you—, writing to you—all is helpless and sorrowful work by the side of what is in my soul to say and to write—or is it not the natural consequence? If these vehicles of feelings sufficed—*there* would be the end!—And that my feeling for you should end! . . For the rest, the headache which kept away while I sate with you, made itself amends afterward, and as it is unkind to that warm Talfourd to look blank at his hospitable endeavours, all my power of face went *à qui de droit*—

Did your brother tell you . . yes, I think . . of the portentous book, lettered II, and thick as a law-book, of congratulatory letters on the appearance of 'Ion'?[1]—But how under the B's in the Index came "Miss Barrett" and, woe's me, "R. B."! I don't know when I have had so ghastly a visitation: there was the utterly *forgotten* letter, in the as thoroughly disused hand-writing, in the . . I fear . . still as completely obsolete feeling . . no, not so bad as that—but at first there was all the novelty, and social admiration at the friend—it is truly not right to pluck all the rich soil from the roots and hold them up clean and dry as if they came *so* from all you now see, which is nothing at all . . like the Chinese Air-plant! Do you understand this? And surely 'Ion' is a *very, very* beautiful and noble conception, and finely executed,—a beautiful work—what has come after, has lowered it down by grade after grade . . it don't stand apart on the hill, like a wonder, now it is *built up* to by other attempts; but the great difference is in myself . . Another maker of another Ion, finding me out and behaving as Talfourd did, would not find *that me*,—so to be behaved to, so to be honored—tho' he should have all the good will! Ten years ago!

And ten years hence!

Always understand that you do *not* take me as I was at the beginning . . with a crowd of loves to give to *something* and so get rid of their pain & burthen: I have KNOWN what that ends in—a handful of anything may be as sufficient a sample, serve your purposes and teach you its nature, as well as whole heaps—and I know what most of the pleasures of this world are—so that I *can* be surer of myself, and make you surer, on calm demonstrated grounds, than if I had a host of objects of admiration or ambition *yet* to become acquainted with: you say, "I am a man & may change"—I answer, yes—but, while I hold my senses,—only change for the *presumeable* better . . not for the *experienced worst*—

Here is my Uncle's foot on the stair[2] . . his knock hurried the last sentence—here is by me!—Understand what this would have led to, how you would have been *proved logically* my own, best, extreme want, my life's end—YES; dearest! Bless you ever—

R. B.

1. *Ion,* a tragedy Talfourd had printed privately in 1835, was produced by Macready in 1836 and was an extraordinary success.
2. Probably Reuben, but see Letter 126, note 3.

169 (W87°)   *E.B.B. to R.B.*
                  ———————————

[*December 7, 1845.*]

Sunday.

Let me hear how you are, & that you are better instead of worse for the exertions of last night. After you left me yesterday I considered how we might have managed it more conveniently for you, & had the

lamp in, & arranged matters so as to interpose less time between the
going & the dining, even if you and George did not go together, which
might have been best, but which I did not like quite to propose. Now,
supposing that on thursday you dine in town, remember not to be un-
necessarily 'perplext in the extreme'[1] where to spend the time before ..
five, .. shall I say, at any rate? We will have the lamp, & I can easily
explain if an observation should be made .. only it will not be, because
our goers out here never come home until six, & the head of the house,
not until seven .. as I told you. George thought it worth while going to
Mr. Talfourd's yesterday, just to see the author of 'Paracelsus' dance
the Polka .. should I not tell you?

I am vexed by another thing which he tells *me*—vexed, if amused a
little by the absurdity of it. I mean that absurd affair of the "Autography"
—now *isn't* it absurd?—⟨‖···‖⟩ And for neither you nor George to
have the chivalry of tearing out that letter of mine, which was absurd
too in its way, & which, knowing less of the world than I know now, I
wrote as if writing for my private conscience, & privately repented
writing in a day, & have gone on repenting ever since when I happened
to think enough of it for repentance. !—Because if Mr. Serjeant Talfourd
sent then his "Ion" to *me,* he did it in mere goodnature, hearing by
chance of me through the publisher of my 'Prometheus' at the moment,
& of course caring no more for my 'opinion' than for the rest of me—
and it was excessively bad taste in me to say more than the briefest word
of thanks in return, even if I had been competent to say it. Ah well!—
you see how it is, & that I am vexed *you* should have read it, .. as George
says you did .. he laughing to see me so vexed. So I turn round & avenge
myself by crying aloud against the editor of the 'Autography'! Surely
such a thing was never done before .. even by an author in the last stage
of a mortal disease of selflove. To edit the common parlance of conventional flatteries, .. lettered in so many volumes, bound in green morocco,
& laid on the drawingroom table for one's own particular private
public,—is it not a miracle of vanity .. neither more nor less?

I took the opportunity of the letter to Mr. Mathews (talking of
vanity .. *mine!*) to send Landor's verses to America .. yours—so they
will be in the American papers .. I know Mr. Mathews. I was speaking
to him of your last number of Bells and Pomegranates, & the verses
came in naturally,—just as my speaking did, for it is not the first time
nor the second nor the third even that I have written to him of you,

though I admire how in all those previous times I did it in pure disinterestedness, . . purely because your name belonged to my country & to her literature, . . & how I have a sort of reward at this present, in being able to write what I please without anyone's saying "it is a new fancy." As for the Americans, they have 'a zeal without knowledge' for poetry. There is more love for *verse* among them than among the English. But they suffer themselves to be led in their choice of poets by English critics of average discernment,—this is said of them by their own men of letters. Tennyson is idolized deep down in the bush woods (to their honour be it said), but to understand *you* sufficiently, they wait for the explanations of the critics. So I wanted them to see what Landor says of you. The comfort in these questions is, that there can be *no* question, except between the sooner & the later—a little sooner, & a little later: but when there is real love & zeal it becomes worth while to try to ripen the knowledge. They love Tennyson so much that the colour of his waistcoats is a sort of minor Oregon question[2] . . & I like that—do not *you?*—

Monday [December 8].—Now I have your letter: & you will observe, without a finger post from me, how busily we have both been preoccupied in disavowing our own letters of old on 'Ion'—Mr. Talfourd's collection goes to prove too much, I think—& you, a little too much, when you draw inferences of no-changes, from changes like these. Oh yes—I perfectly understand that every sort of inconstancy of purpose regards a "presumably better" thing—but I do not so well understand how any presumeable doubt is to be set to rest by that fact, . . I do not indeed. Have you seen all the birds & beasts in the world? have you seen the 'unicorns'[3]—?—Which is only a pebble thrown down into your smooth logic; & we need not stand by to watch the bubbles ⊹born⊹ of it. And as to the Ion-letters, I am delighted that you have anything to repent, as I have everything. Certainly it is a noble play—there is the moral sublime in it: but it is not the work of a poet, . . & if he had never written another to show what was *not* in him, this might have been 'predicated' of it as surely, I hold. Still, it is a noble work—& even if you over-praised it, (I did not read your letter, though you read mine, alas!) you, under the circumstances, would have been less noble yourself not to have done so—only, *how* I agree with you in what you say against the hanging up of these dry roots . . the soil shaken off!—Such abominable taste—now isn't it? . . though you do not use that word.

I thought Mr. Kenyon would have come yesterday & that I might have something to tell you, of him at least.

And George never told me of the thing you found to say to him of me, & which makes me smile, & would have made him wonder if he had not been suffering probably from some legal distraction at the moment, inasmuch as *he knew perfectly that you had just left me.* My sisters told him downstairs & he came into this room just before he set off on Saturday, with a, .. "*So* I am to meet Mr. Browning" But he made no observation afterwards—none: & if he heard what you said at all, (which I doubt) he referred it ⁺probably⁺ to some enforced civility on 'Yorick's' part[4] when the 'last chapter' was too much with him.

I have written about 'Luria' in another place—you shall have the papers when I have read through the play. How different this living poetry is from the polished rhetoric of *Ion*. The man & the statue are not more different. After all poetry is a distinct thing: it is here or it is not here .. it is not a matter of '*taste,*' but of sight & feeling.

As to the 'Venice'[5] it gives proof (does it not?) rather of poetical sensibility than of poetical faculty?—or did you expect me to say more? —/oh⟩of/ ⟨I⟩ the perception of the poet, rather than of his conception. Do you think more than this? There are fine, eloquent expressions, and the tone of sentiment is good & high everywhere.

Do not write 'Luria' if your head is uneasy—& you cannot say that it is not .. can you?—Or will you if you can? In any case you will do what you can .. take care of yourself & not suffer yourself to be tired either by writing or by too much going out, & take the necessary exercise .. this, you will do—I entreat you to do it.

May God bless & make you happy, as .. you will lose nothing if I say .. as I am yours—

   1. *Othello* V. ii. 345.
   2. The controversy—finally settled in June 1846—about the boundary between Canada and the U.S. Feeling on the matter ran very high in both England and America.
   3. See Letter 104, note 1.
   4. A reference, but apparently only a very general one, to Laurence Sterne.
   5. Alfred Domett's poem of that name (1832), which Browning must have taken on his Saturday visit.

[*December 9, 1845.*]

Tuesday M^g

Well, then, I am no longer sorry that I did *not* read *either* of your letters . . for there were two in the collection: I did not read one word of them—and hear why: when your brother & I took the book between us in wonderment at the notion—we turned to the index, in large text-hand, and stopped at "Miss B."—and *he* indeed read them, or some of them, but holding the volume at a distance which defied my short-sighted eye[1]—all *I* saw was the *faint* small charactery—and, do you know . . I neither trusted myself to ask a nearer look . . nor a second look . . as if I were studying unduly what I had just said was most unfairly exposed to view!—so I was silent, and lost you (in that)—then, and for-ever, I promise you, now that you speak of vexation it would give you. *All* I know of the notes, that *one* is addressed to Talfourd in the third person—and when I had run thro' my own . . not far off . . (BA–BR)—I was sick of the book altogether—You are generous to me—but, to say the truth, I might have remembered the most justifying circumstance in my case . . which was, that my own "Paracelsus," printed a few months before, had been as dead a failure as "Ion" a brilliant success—for, until just before . . Ah, really I forget!—but I know that until Forster's notice in the "Examiner"[2] appeared, *every* journal that thought worth while to allude to the poem at all, treated it with entire contempt . . beginning, I think, with the "Athenæum" which *then* made haste to say, a few days after its publication, "that it was not with-out talent but spoiled by obscurity and only an imitation of—Shelley!" —something to this effect, in a criticism of about three lines among their "Library Table" notices:[3] and that first taste was a most flattering sample of what the "craft" had in store for me—since my publisher[4] and I had fairly to laugh at *his* 'Book'—(quite of another kind than the Serjeant's—) in which he was used to paste extracts from newspapers & the like—seeing that, out of a long string of notices, one vied with its predecessor in disgust at my "rubbish," as their word went: but Forster's notice altered a good deal—which I have to recollect for his good. Still, the contrast between myself and Talfourd was so *utter*—you remember

the world's-wonder ⟨/he⟩it/⟩ ↑"Ion"↓ made,—that I was determined
not to pass for the envious piece of neglected merit I really *was not*—
and so!—

But, dearest, why should you leave your own especial sphere of
doing me good for another than yours?

Does the sun rake and hoe about the garden as well as shine steadily
over it? *Why* must you, who give me heart and power, as nothing else
did or could, to do well—concern yourself with what might be done by
any good, kind ministrant *only* fit for such offices? Not that I *feel*, even
more bound to you for them—they have their weight, I *know* . . but
what weight beside the divine gift of yourself?—Do not, dear, dearest,
care for making me known: *you* know me!—and *they* know so little,
after all your endeavour, who are ignorant of what *you* are to me—if
you . . well, but that *will* follow, . . if I do greater things one day—what
shall they serve for, what range themselves under of right?—

Mr. Mathews sent me two copies of his poems—and, I believe, a
newspaper, "when time was," about the "Blot in the 'Scutcheon"[5]—
and also, thro' Moxon—(I *believe* it was Mr. M.)—a proposition for
reprinting—to which I assented of course—and there was an end to
the matter.

And might I have stayed *till five?*—dearest, I will never ask for
more than you give—but I feel every single sand of the gold showers . .
spite of what I say above! I *have* an invitation for Thursday which I
/have⟩had/ no intention of remembering (it admitted of such liberty)—
but *now* . .

⟨‖ · · · · ‖⟩ (Something I will *say!*) "Polka," forsooth!—one lady
whose *head* could not, and another whose feet could not, dance!—But
I talked a little to your brother whom I like⟨d⟩ more and more: it
comforts me that he is yours.

So, *Thursday,*—thank you from the heart! I am well, and about to
go out. This week I have done nothing to "Luria"—is it that my *ring* is
gone? There surely *is* something to forgive in me—for that shameful
business—or I should not feel as I do in the matter: but you *did* forgive
me.

       God bless my own, only love—ever—
                         Yours wholly
                                R. B.

N.B. An antiquarian friend of mine in old days picked up a non-descript wonder of a coin . . I just remember he described it as Rhomboid in shape—cut, I fancy, out of church-plate in troubled times. What did my friend do but get ready a box, lined with velvet, and properly *compartmented,* to have always about him, so that the *next such coin he picked up,* say in Cheapside, he might at once transfer to a /prop⟩place/ of safety . . his waistcoat pocket being no happy receptacle for the same. I saw the box—and encouraged the man to keep a vigilant eye.

Parallel. R. B. having found an unicorn.[6] . . . . .

Do you forgive these strips of paper?[7] I could not wait to send for more—having exhausted my stock.

1. "Browning's eyes were . . . unequal in their power of vision; one was unusually long-sighted; the other, with which he could read the most microscopic print, unusually short-sighted," Dowden, p. 72 n. Cf. Letter 459.

2. Forster reviewed *Paracelsus* in the *Examiner* for September 5, 1835. His was surely the warmest of the poem's reviews, but Browning perversely credited it with more influence than it actually had and recalled all other reviews with more bitterness than was justified. See the following note.

3. The *Athenæum* notice actually appeared two weeks before Forster's, on ˈ August 22. It is quoted in full by G & M (p. 73). "Our Library Table" was the column of brief notices which, on this occasion, dealt with fourteen other books.

4. *Paracelsus* (1835) was published by Effingham Wilson, a strong liberal whose services were secured by W. J. Fox (G & M, p. 72).

5. The quotation is *Tempest* II. ii. 137. Mathews' short-lived newspaper, the *Pathfinder,* printed a notice of *A Blot in the 'Scutcheon* in early 1843 (*Letters of EBB,* I, 133), and in the same year he published *Poems on Man.* On November 14, 1844, E.B.B. wrote to him that Browning was out of the country, "so that whatever you send for *him* must await his return" (*ibid.,* p. 214).

6. See Letter 104, note 1.

7. Browning's letter is on the two halves of one of his regular sheets torn lengthwise.

171 *(W88°)*   *E.B.B. to R.B.*

_____

[*December 9, 1845.*]

Tuesday evening.

It was right of you to write . . (now see what jangling comes of not using the fit words . . I said 'right,' not to say 'kind') . . right of you

to write to me to-day—and I had begun to be disappointed already because the post *seemed* to be past, when suddenly the knock brought the
letter which deserves all this praising. If not 'kind' . . then *kindest* . . will
that do better? Perhaps.

    Mr. Kenyon was here to-day & asked when you were coming
again—& I, I answered at random . . 'at the end of the week—thursday
or friday'—which did not prevent another question about 'what we
were consulting about.' He said that he "must have you," & had written
to beg you to go to his door on days when you came here—, only mur-
muring something besides of neither thursday nor friday being disengaged days with him. Oh, my disingenuousness!— Then he talked
again of 'Saul'— A true impression the poem has made on him!—He
reads it every night, he says, when he comes home & just before he goes
to sleep, to put his dreams into order, & observed very aptly, I thought,
that it reminded him of Homer's shield of Achilles,[1] thrown into lyrical
whirl & life. Quite ill he took it of me the ⟨‖ · · · ‖⟩ 'not expecting him
to like it so much' & retorted on me with most undeserved severity (as I
felt it), that ⟨nobody⟩ I 'never understood anybody to have any sensibility except myself'—Wasn't it severe, to come from dear Mr. Kenyon?
But he has caught some sort of evil spirit from your Saul perhaps;
though admiring the poem enough to have a good spirit instead. And
do *you* remember of the said poem, that it is there only as a first part,[2] &
that the next parts must certainly follow & complete what will be a
great lyrical work—now remember—And forget 'Luria' . . if you are
better forgetting. And forget *me* . . *when* you are happier forgetting. I
say *that* too.

    So your idea of an unicorn is . . one horn broken off. And you a
poet!—one horn broken off—or hid in the blackthorn hedge!—

    Such a mistake, as our enlightened public, on their part, made,
when they magnified the divinity of the brazen chariot, just under the
thunder-cloud! I don't remember the Athenæum, but can well believe
that it said what you say. The Athenæum admires only what gods, men
& columns reject. It /acclaims⟩applauds/ nothing but mediocrity—
mark it, as a general rule!—The good, they see—the great escapes them.
Dare to breathe a breath above the close, flat conventions of literature,
& you are "put down" & instructed how to be like other people—
By the way, see by the very last number, that you never think to write
'peoples,' on pain of writing what is obsolete[3]—& these the teachers of

the public! If the public does not learn, where is the marvel of it? An imitation of Shelley!—when if 'Paracelsus' was anything it was the expression of a new mind, as all might see—as *I* saw, let me be proud to remember, & ⟨‖ · · · ‖⟩ I was not overdazzled by *Ion*.

Ah, indeed if I could 'rake & hoe' . . or even pick up weeds along the walk, . . which is the work of the most helpless children . . if I could do any of this, there would be some good of me: but as for 'shining' . . shining! . . when there is not so much light in me as to do 'carpet work'[4] by, why let anyone in the world, ↑except you,↓ tell me to shine, & it will just be a mockery! But you have studied astronomy with your favourite snails, who are apt to take a dark-lanthorn for the sun, & so.—

And so, you come on thursday, and I only hope that Mrs. Jameson will not come too, (the carpet work makes me think of her,—&, not having come yet, she may come on thursday by a fatal cross-stitch!) for I do not hear from her, and my precautions are "watched out." May God bless you always Your own

[But no—I did not forgive. Where was the fault to be forgiven, except in *me*, for not being right in my meaning?—][5]

1. *Iliad* XVIII, ll. 462–608.
2. The first nine sections; the entire poem was not published until 1855.
3. "No writer of eminence now uses the plural in question." "Miscellanea," *Athenæum*, December 6, 1845.
4. Mrs. Jameson's phrase, reported in Letter 56.
5. Inserted at the top of the first page.

On the envelope of the preceding letter Browning recorded a call on E.B.B.:
+Thursday Dec. 11
3–4¾ p.m.

172 *(W84)*   *R.B. to E.B.B.*

[*December 12, 1845.*]

Friday.

And now, my heart's love, I am waiting to hear from you,—my heart is *full* of you. When I try to remember what I said yesterday, *that* thought, of what fills my heart—only *that* makes me bear with the memory . . I know that even such imperfect, poorest of words *must* have come *from* thence if not bearing up to you all that is there—and I know you are ever above me to receive, and help, and forgive, and *wait* for the one day which I will never say to myself cannot come, when I shall speak what I feel—more of it—or *some* of it—for now nothing is spoken.

My all-beloved—

Ah, you opposed very rightly, I dare say, the writing that paper I spoke of!¹ The process should be so much simpler! I most earnestly EXPECT of you, my love, that in the event of any such necessity as was then alluded to, you accept at once in my name *any* conditions possible for a human will to submit to—there is no imaginable condition to which you allow me to accede that I will not joyfully bend all my faculties to comply with—And you know this—but so, also do you know *more* . . and yet 'I may tire of you'—'may forget you'!

I will write again, having the long, long week to wait! And one of the things I must say, will be, that with my love, I cannot lose my pride in you—that nothing *but* that love could balance that pride—and that, blessing the love so divinely, you must minister to the pride as well; yes, my own—I shall follow your fame,—and, better than fame, the good you do—in the world—and, if you please, it shall all be mine—as your hand, as your eyes—

I will write and pray it from you into a promise . . and your promises I live upon.

May God bless you! your R. B.

1. These remarks and E.B.B.'s in the following letter indicate that Browning had proposed some document to be given Mr. Barrett in the event that he discovered and violently objected to the frequency of Browning's visits.

173 (W89°)   *E.B.B. to R.B.*

[*December 12, 1845.*]

Friday.

Do not blame me in your thoughts for what I said yesterday or wrote a day before, or think perhaps on the dark side of some other days when I cannot help it . . always when I cannot help it—you could not blame me if you saw the full motives as I feel them. If it is distrust, it is not of *you,* dearest of all!—but of myself rather:—it is not doubt *of* you, but *for* you. From the beginning I have been subject to the too reasonable fear which rises as my spirits fall, that your happiness might suffer in the end through your having known me:—it is for *you* I fear, whenever I fear:—and if you were less to me, . . *should* I fear do you think?—if you were to me only what I am to myself for instance, . . if your happiness were only as precious as my own in my own eyes, . . should I fear, do you think, *then?* Think, & do not blame me.

To tell you to "forget me when forgetting seemed happiest for you," . . (was it not *that,* I said?) proved more affection than might go in smoother words . . I could prove the truth of *that* out of my heart.

And for the rest, you need not fear any fear of mine—my fear will not cross a wish of yours, be sure! Neither does it prevent your being all to me . . all!—more than I used to take for all when I looked round the world, . . almost more than I took for all in my earliest dreams.[1] You stand in between me & not merely the living who stood closest, but between me & the closer graves, . . & I reproach myself for this sometimes, &, so, ask you not to blame me for a different thing.

As to unfavourable influences, . . I can speak of them quietly, having foreseen them from the first, . . & it is true, I have been thinking since yesterday, that I might be prevented from receiving you here, & *should,* if all were known: but with that act, the adverse power would end. It is not my fault if I have to choose between two affections,—only my pain: & I have not to choose between two duties, I feel, . . since I am yours, while I am of any worth to you at all. For the plan of the sealed letter, it would correct no evil,—ah, you do not see, you do not understand. The danger does not come from the side to which a reason may go. Only one person holds the thunder—& I shall be thundered at;

I shall not be reasoned with—it is impossible. I could tell you some dreary chronicles made for laughing & crying over; and you know that if I once thought I might be loved enough to be spared above others, I cannot think so now. In the meanwhile we need not ⊹for the present⊹ be afraid—Let there be ever so many suspectors, there will be no informers . . I suspect the suspectors, but the informers are out of the world, I am very sure:—and then, the one person, by a curious anomaly, *never* draws an inference of this order, until the bare blade of it is thrust /full⟩palpably/ into his hand, point outwards. So it has been in other cases than our's—& so it is, at this moment in the house, with others than ourselves.

I have your letter to stop me—If I had my whole life in my hands with your letter, could I thank you for it, I wonder, at all worthily?—I cannot believe that I could. Yet in life and in death I shall be grateful to you.—

But for the paper—no. Now, observe, that it would seem like a prepared apology for something wrong—And besides, . . the apology would be nothing but the offence in another form . . unless you said it was all a mistake . . (*will* you, again?) . . that it was all a mistake and you were only calling for your boots![2] Well, if you said *that,* it would be worth writing,—but anything less would be something worse than nothing—, & would not save me . . which you were thinking of, I know,—would not save me the least of the stripes—For 'conditions'— now I will tell you what I said once in a jest . .

"If a prince of Eldorado should come, with a pedigree of lineal descent from some signory in the moon in one hand, & a ticket of good-behaviour from the nearest Independent chapel, in the other"—?— —

"Why even *then,*" said my sister Arabel, "it would not *do.*" And she was right, & we all agreed that she was right. It is an obliquity of the will—& one laughs at it till the turn comes for crying. Poor Henrietta has suffered silently, with that softest of possible natures, which hers is indeed,—beginning with implicit obedience, & ending with something as unlike it as possible: but, you see, where money is wanted, & where the dependance is total . . see! And when once, in the case of the one dearest to me,[3] . . when just at the last he was involved in the same grief, & I attempted to make over my advantages to him; (it could be no sacrifice, you know—*I* did not want the money, and could buy nothing with it so good as his happiness,—) why then, my hands were seized &

tied—& then & there, in the midst of the trouble . . came the end of all!
I tell you all this, just to make you understand a little. Did I not tell you
before?—But there is no danger at present—& why ruffle this present
with disquieting thoughts? Why not leave that future to itself? For me,
I sit in the track of the avalanche quite calmly . . so calmly as to surprise
myself at intervals—& yet I know the reason of the calmness well.

For Mr. Kenyon . . dear Mr. Kenyon . . he will speak the softest of
words, if any—only he will think privately that you are foolish & that I
am ungenerous—but I will not say so any more now, so as to teaze you.

There is another thing, of more consequence than HIS thoughts,
which is often in my mind to ask you of—but there will be time for such
questions—let us leave the winter to its own peace. If I should be ill
again you will be reasonable & we both must submit to God's necessity.
Not, you know, that I have the least intention of being ill, if I can help it
—& in the case of a tolerably mild winter, & with all this strength to use,
there are /possibilities⟩probabilities/ for me—& then I have sunshine
from *you*, which is better than Pisa's.

And what more would you say? Do I not hear & understand! It
seems to me that I do both—or why all this wonder & gratitude? If the
devotion of the remainder of my life could prove that I hear, . . would
it be proof enough?—Proof enough perhaps—but not gift enough.

May God bless you always——

I have put *some* of the hair into a little locket which was given to
me when I was a child by my favorite uncle,[4] Papa's only brother, who
used to tell me that he loved me better than my own father did, & was
jealous when I was not glad. It is through him in part, that I am richer
than my sisters—through him & his mother—& a great grief it was &
trial, when he died a few years ago in Jamaica, proving by his last act
that I was unforgotten. And now I remember how he once said to me . .
'Do you beware of ever loving!—If you do, you will ⊦not⊦ do it half:
it will be for life & death.'

So I put the hair into his locket, ⊦which I wear habitually,⊦ & which
never had hair before—the natural use of it being for perfume:—& this
is the best perfume for all hours, besides the completing of a prophecy.

Your E. B. B.

1. Cf. *Sonnets from the Portuguese*, XXVI.
2. A reference to the destroyed letter and Browning's apology for it. See the
note before Letter 30 and the close of Letter 31.

3. Edward ("Bro"), whose death is recounted by E.B.B. in Letter 87.

4. Samuel Barrett Moulton-Barrett (1787–1837). Browning was wearing the locket when he died. Dorothy Hewlett, *Elizabeth Barrett Browning* (London: Cassell's, 1953), p. 158.

174 (W85)   **R.B. to E.B.B.**

[*December 15, 1845.*]

Monday Morning.

Every word you write goes to my heart and lives there: let us live so, and die so, if God will. I trust many years hence to begin telling you what I feel now;—that the beam of the light will have *reached* you!—meantime it *is* here. Let me kiss your forehead, my sweetest, dearest.

Wednesday I am waiting for—how waiting for!

After all, it seems probable that there was no intentional mischief in that jeweller's management of the ring[1]—the divided gold must have been exposed to fire,—heated thoroughly, perhaps,—and what became of the contents then! Well, all is safe now, and I go to work again of course—My next act is just done; that is, *being* done—but, what I did not foresee, I cannot bring it, copied, by Wednesday, as my sister went this morning on a visit for the week—

On the matters, the others, I will not think, as you bid me,—if I can help, at least. But your kind, gentle, good sisters!—and the provoking sorrow of the *right* meaning at bottom of the wrong doing—wrong to itself and its plain purpose—and meanwhile, the real tragedy and sacrifice of a life!

If you should see Mr. Kenyon, and can find if he will be disengaged on Wednesday evening, I shall be glad to go in that case—

But I have been writing, as I say, and will leave off this, for the better communing with you: don't imagine I am unwell,—I feel quite well—but a little tired, and the thought of you waits in such readiness! So, may God bless you, beloved! I am all your own

R. B.

1. See Letter 162.

[*December 15, 1845.*]

Monday.

Mr. Kenyon has not come—he does not come so often, I think. Did he *know* from *you* that you were to see me last thursday? If he did it might be as well . . do you not think? . . to go to him next week—Will it not seem frequent, otherwise? But if you did *not* tell him of thursday distinctly (*I* did not—remember!), he might take the wednesday's ↑visit↓ to be the substitute ↑for↓ rather than the successor of thursday's:—and in that case, why not write a word to him yourself to propose dining with him as he suggested? He really wishes to see you—of that, I am sure. But you will know what is best to do—& he may come here to-morrow perhaps, & ask a whole set of questions about you; so my right hand may forget its cunning[1] for any good it does. Only don't send messages by *me*, please! . .

How happy I am with your letter to-night.

When I ↑had↓ sent away my last letter I began to remember . . & could not help smiling to do so . . that I had totally forgotten the great subject of my "fame," & the oath you administered about it . . totally!! —Now how do you read that omen?—If I forget myself, who is to remember me, do you think? . . except *you* . . ? which brings me where I would stay. Yes—"yours" it must be—but *you*, it had better be! / And⟩But /, to leave the vain superstitions, let me go on to assure you that I did mean to answer that part of your former letter, & do mean to behave well & be obedient. Your wish would be enough, even if there could be likelihood without it of my doing nothing ever again. Oh, certainly I have been idle—it comes of lotos-eating . . &, besides, of sitting too long in the sun. Yet 'idle' may not be the word—: silent I have been, through too many thoughts to speak . . just *that!* . . As to writing letters & reading manuscripts' filling all my time, why I must lack 'vital energy' indeed . . you do not mean seriously to fancy such a thing of me!—For the rest. . . Tell me—Is it your opinion that when the apostle Paul saw the unspeakable things, being snatched up into the third Heavens "whether in the body or out of the body he could not tell,"[2] . . is it your opinion that, all the week after, he worked particularly hard at the tent-making?—For my part, I doubt it.

I would not speak profanely or extravagantly—it is not the best way to thank God. But to say only that I was in the desert & that I am among the palm-trees,[3] is to say nothing. . . because it is easy to *under-stand how,* after walking straight on . . on . . furlong after furlong . . dreary day after dreary day, . . one may come to the end of the sand & within sight of the fountain:—there is nothing miraculous in *that,* you know!——

Yet even in that case . . to doubt whether it may not all be *mirage,* would be the natural first thought . . the recurring dream-fear! now would it not? And you can reproach me for *my* thoughts . . as if *they* were unnatural!——!!

Never mind about the third act—the advantage is that you will not tire yourself perhaps the next week—What gladness it is that you should really seem better—& how much better *that* is than even 'Luria'!—

Mrs. Jameson came to-day—but I will tell you—

May God bless you now & always—

Your E. B. B.

1. Psalms 137:5.

2. II Corinthians 12:2–4.

3. This may be related to the somewhat different palm-tree reference in *Sonnets from the Portuguese,* XXIX, which was surely written before April 28, 1846. See Letter 335.

176 (W91°)   *E.B.B. to R.B.*

[*December 16, 1845.*]

Tuesday evening.

Henrietta had a note from Mr. Kenyon to the effect that he was 'coming to see *Ba*' to-day if in any way he found ⊹it⊹ possible. Now he has not come—and the inference is that he will come to-morrow—in which case you will be convicted of not wishing to be with him perhaps. So . . would it not be advisable for you to call at his door for a moment

—& *before* you come here? Think of it. You know it would not do to vex him—would it?

Your E. B. B.

Browning noted a visit to E.B.B. on the envelope of the preceding letter:

+Wednesday Decr 17
$3\frac{1}{4}$–$4\frac{1}{2}$ p.m.

177 (*W92°*) *E.B.B. to R.B.*

[*December 18, 1845.*]

Thursday evening.

Dearest you know how to say what makes me happiest, you who never think, you say, of making me happy! For my part I do not think of it either—I simply understand that you *are* my happiness, & that therefore you could not make another happiness for me, such as would be worth having—not even *you!* Why, how could you?—*That* was in my mind to speak yesterday, but I could not speak it—to write it, is easier.

Talking of happiness, . . shall I tell you?—Promise not to be angry & I will tell you. I have thought sometimes that, if I considered myself wholly, I should choose to die this winter . . now . . before I had disappointed you in anything. But because you are better & dearer & more to be considered than I, I do *not* choose it. I CANNOT choose to give you any pain, even on the chance of its being a less pain, a less evil, than what may follow perhaps (who can say?) if I should prove the burden of your life.

For if you make me happy with some words, you frighten me with others . . as with the extravagance yesterday—& seriously—; *too* seriously, when the moment for smiling at them is past, . . I am frightened . . I tremble! When you come to know me as well as I know myself, what can save me, do you think, from disappointing & displeasing you? I ask the question, & find no answer—

It is a poor answer, to say that I can do one thing well . . that I have one capacity largely. On points of the general affections, I have ↑in thought↓ applied to myself the words of M^dme de Stael . . not fretfully, I hope . . not complainingly, I am sure . . (I can thank God for most affectionate friends!) not complainingly, /but⟩yet/ mournfully & in profound conviction . . those words . . '*jamais je n' ai ↑pas↓ été aimée comme j'aime.*' The capacity of loving is the largest of my powers I think—I thought so before knowing you & one form of feeling. And although any woman might love you . . *every* woman, . . with understanding enough to discern you by—(oh, do not fancy that I am unduly 'magnifying mine office')[1] yet I persist in persuading myself that . . . .! Because I have the capacity, as I said!—& besides I owe more to you than others could, it seems to me!—let me boast of it. To many, you might be better than all things while one of all things:—to me you are instead of all!—to many, a crowning happiness—to me, the happiness itself. From out of the deep dark pits men see the stars more gloriously—and de profundis amavi[2]— — — — —

It is a very poor answer—! Almost as poor an answer as yours could be if I were to ask you to teach me to please you always:—or rather, how not to displease you, disappoint you vex you—what if all those things were in my fate?—

And . . (to begin!)—*I* am disappointed to-night—I expected a letter which does not come—& I had felt so sure of having a letter to-night . . unreasonably sure perhaps, which means doubly sure.

Friday [December 19].—Remember you have had two notes of mine, & that it is certainly not my turn to write, though I am writing.

Scarcely you had gone on wednesday when Mr. Kenyon came. It seemed best to me, you know, that you should go . . I had the presentiment of his footsteps—&, so near they were, that if you had looked up the street in leaving the door, you must have seen him!—Of course I told him of your having been here & also at his house; whereupon he enquired eagerly if you meant to dine with him, seeming disappointed by my negative. "Now I had told him," he said . . & murmured on to himself loud enough for me to hear, that "it would have been a peculiar pleasure &c"—The reason I have not seen him lately is the eternal 'business,' just as you thought, & he means to come "oftener now"—so nothing is wrong as I half thought.

As your letter does not come it is a good opportunity for asking what sort of ill humour, or (to be more correct) bad temper, you most particularly admire?—sulkiness? . . the divine gift of sitting aloof in a

cloud like any god for three weeks together perhaps—? pettishness . .
which will get you up a storm about a crooked pin or a straight one
either? obstinacy . . which is an agreeable form of temper I can assure
you, & describes itself?—or the good open passion which lies on the
floor & kicks, like one of my cousins?[3]—Certainly I prefer the last, &
should, I think, prefer it, (as an evil) even if it were not the born weakness of my own nature—though I humbly confess (to *you*, who seem
to think differently of these things) that ⟨‖ · · · ‖⟩ ⭭never⭭ since I was a
child have I upset all the chairs & tables & thrown the books about the
room in a fury—I am afraid I do not even 'kick' . . like my cousin, now.
Those demonstrations were all done by the "light of other days"—not
a very full light, I used to be accustomed to think:—but *you*, . . *you*
think otherwise . . *you* take a fury to be the opposite of 'indifference' . .
as if there could be no such thing as self-controul! . . Now for my part, I
do believe that the worst-tempered persons in the world are less so
through sensibility than selfishness—they spare nobody's heart, on the
ground of being themselves pricked by a straw. Now see if it isn't so.
What, after all, is a good temper but generosity in trifles—& what,
without it, is the happiness of life?—We have only to look round us. I
saw a woman, once, burst into tears, because her husband cut the bread
& butter too thick. I saw *that* with my own eyes. ⟨‖ · · · ‖⟩ ⭭Was⭭ it
sensibility, I wonder!—They were at least real tears & ran down her
cheeks. "You ALWAYS do it"! she said.

　　Why how you must sympathize with the heroes & heroines of the
French romances . . (*do* you sympathize with them very much? . . .)
when at the slightest provocation they break up the tables & chairs, (a
degree beyond the deeds of my childhood!—*I* only used to upset them)
⟨‖ · · · ‖⟩ break up the tables & chairs & chiffoniers, & dash the china to
atoms. The men *do* the furniture, & the women the porcelain:—& pray
observe that they always set about this as a matter of course! When they
have broken everything in the room, they sink down quite (& very
naturally) *abattus!*—I remember a particular case of a hero of Frederic
Soulié's,[4] who, in the course of an "emotion," takes up a chair ⟨‖ · · · ‖⟩
unconsciously, & breaks it into very small pieces, & then proceeds with
his soliloquy. Well!—the clearest idea this excites in *me*, is of the low condition ⭭in Paris⭭ of moral government and of ⟨Parisian⟩ upholstery.
Because . . just consider for yourself . . how *you* would succeed in breaking to pieces even a three-legged stool if it were properly put together

↑as stools are in England↓ . . just yourself, without a hammer & a screw!
—You might work at it "comme quatre," & find it hard to finish, I
imagine—And then . . as a demonstration . . . a child of six years old
might demonstrate just so (in his sphere) & be whipped accordingly.

How I go on writing!—& you, who do not write at all!—two
extremes, one set against the other.

But I must say, though in ever such an ill temper (which you know
is just the time to select for writing a panegyric upon good temper) that
I am glad you do not despise my own right name too much, because I
never was called Elizabeth by any one who loved me at all, & I accept
the omen—So little it seems my name that if a voice said suddenly
'Elizabeth,' I should as soon turn round as my sisters would . . no sooner.
Only, my own right name has been complained of for want of euphony
. . *Ba* . . now & then it has—& Mr. Boyd makes a compromise & calls
me *Elibet* . . because nothing could induce him to desecrate his organs
accustomed to Attic harmonies, with a *Ba*. So I am glad, & accept the
omen.

But I give you no credit for not thinking that I may forget you . .I!
—As if you did not see the difference!—Why, *I* could not even forget
to *write* to *you*, observe!—

Whenever you write, say how you are. Were you wet on wednesday?

Your own . .

1. An echo of Romans 11:13.
2. "Out of the depths have I loved." Altered from the Vulgate text of Psalm
130: "De profundis clamavi . . ."
3. Elizabeth Georgina ("Lizzie") Barrett (1833–1918) was a permanent
member of the Wimpole Street household. "Lizzie is . . . the daughter of a cousin
of Papa's—and as her father is in the West Indies and her mother insane . . . she is
next to an orphan, . . and we are not likely to lose her" (*EBB to MRM*, p. 246). She
married E.B.B.'s brother Alfred in 1855.
4. Soulié (1800–47) specialized in melodramatic horror novels.

[*December 19, 1845.*]

Friday Morning.

I ought to have written yesterday—so to-day when I need a letter and get none, there is my own fault besides, and the less consolation— A letter from you would light up this sad day: shall I fancy how, if a letter lay *there* where I look,—rain might fall and winds blow while I listened to you, long after the *words* had been laid to heart? But here you are in your place—with me who am your own—your own—and so the rhyme joins on,

> She shall speak to me in places lone
> With a low and holy tone—
>
> Ay: when I have lit my lamp at night
> She shall be present to my sprite:
> And I will say, whate'er it be,
> Every word she telleth me!¹

Now, is that taken from your book? No—but from *my* book, which holds my verses as I write them; and as I open it, I read that—

And speaking of verse—somebody gave me a few days ago that Mr. Lowell's book² you once mentioned to me: anyone who "admires" *you* shall have my sympathy at once—even though he *do* change the laughing wine-*mark* into a "stain" in that perfectly beautiful triplet³— nor am I to be indifferent to his good word for myself⁴ (tho' not very happily connected with the criticism on the epithet in that "Yorkshire Tragedy" (which has better things, by the way)—seeing that "white boy," in old language, meant just "good boy," a general epithet—as Johnson notices in the life of Dryden⁵—whom the schoolmaster Busby was used to class with his "white boys" . . this is hypercriticism, how- ever)—But these American books should not be reprinted here—one asks, what and where is the class to which they address themselves? for, no doubt, we have our congregations of ignoramuses that enjoy the profoundest ignorance imaginable on the subjects treated of—but *these* are evidently not the audience Mr. Lowell reckons on;—rather, if one may trust the manner of his setting to work,—he would propound his doctrine to the class always to be found, of spirits instructed up to a certain height and there resting—vines that run up a prop and there tangle and grow to a knot—which want supplying with fresh poles; so the provident man brings his bundle into the grounds, and sticks them in laterally or a-top of the others, as the case requires, and all the old stocks go on growing again—but here, with us, whoever *wanted* Chaucer, or Chapman, or Ford, got him long ago—what else have Lamb, & Coleridge, & Hazlitt & Hunt and so on to the end of their generations .. what else been doing this many a year? What one passage of all these, cited with the very air of a Columbus, but has been known to all who know anything of poetry this many, many a year? The others, who don't know anything, are the stocks that have got to *shoot*, not climb higher—*compost*, they want in the first place!—Ford's & Crashaw's rival Nightingales[6]—why they have been dissertated on by Wordsworth & Coleridge—then by Lamb & Hazlitt—then worked to death by Hunt, who printed them entire and quoted them to pieces again, in every periodical he was ever engaged upon—and yet after all, here " Philip "— " must read " (out of a roll of dropping papers with yellow ink tracings, so old!) something at which "John" claps his hands and says "Really— that these ancients should own so much wit &c"! The *passage* no longer looks its fresh self after this veritable passage from hand to hand: as when, in old dances, the belle began the figure with her own partner, and by him was transferred to the next, and so to the next—*they* ever *beginning* with all the old alacrity and spirit—, but she bearing a still-accumulating weight of tokens of galantry, and none the better for every fresh pushing and shoving and pulling and hauling—till, at the bottom of the room .. —

To which Mr. Lowell might say, that—No, I will say the true thing against myself—and it is, that—when I turn from what is in my mind, and determine to write about anybody's book to avoid writing that I love & love & love again my own, dearest love—because of the cuckoo-song[7] of it,—*then*, I shall be in no better humour with that book than with Mr. Lowell's!

(But I *have* a new thing to say or sing—you never before heard me love and bless and send my heart after .. "Ba"[8]—did you?) Ba .. and that is you! I TRIED .. (more than *wanted*) to call you *that*, on Wednesday! I have a flower here—rather, a star, a mimosa, which must be turned and turned, the side to the light changing in a little time to the *leafy* side, where all the fans lean and spread . . so I turn your name to me, that side I have not last seen : you cannot tell how I feel glad that you will not part with the name—Barrett—seeing you have two of the same—and must always, moreover, remain my EBB!

Dearest "E. B. C."——no, no! and so it will never be!

Have you seen Mr. Kenyon? I did not write . . knowing that such a procedure would draw the kind cure letter in return, with the invitation &c, as if I had asked for it! I had perhaps better call on him some morning very early—

Bless you, my own sweetest. You will write to me, I know in my heart! Ever may God bless you!

R. B.

1. E.B.B.'s *The Past* (1826), published with the *Essay on Mind.*

2. James Russell Lowell (1819–91) sent a presentation copy of his *Conversations on Some of the Old Poets* (1844), to E.B.B. in February 1845 (*Browning Collections*, p. 113).

3. "Elizabeth Barrett, a woman whose genius I admire, says very beautifully of Chaucer,

> 'Old Chaucer, with his infantine
> Familiar clasp of things divine
> That stain upon his lips is wine.'

I had rather think it pure grape-juice." Lowell, *Conversations*, p. 37. The quotation is ll. 388–390 of *A Vision of Poets.*

4. "*Philip.* 'What you say reminds me of a passage in the "Yorkshire Tragedy" . . . attributed to Shakespeare. . . . The touch of nature in it is worthy of him [though] nothing in the rest of the drama [sustains] the hypothesis. A spendthrift father, in a fit of madness, murders his children. As he seizes one of them, the little fellow . . . calls himself by the name his father had doubtless given him in happier days. "O, what will you do, father? I am your white boy."'

"*John.* 'That is very touching. How is it that this simpleness, the very essence of tragic pathos, has become unattainable of late? I know only one modern dramatist capable of it . . . Robert Browning.'" Lowell, *Conversations*, pp. 67–68.

5. This appears to be a mistaken attribution.

6. Lowell (*Conversations*, pp. 261–264) compares the passage (I. i. 98ff.) from John Ford's *The Lover's Melancholy* in which a musician vies with a nightingale with Richard Crashaw's *Music's Duel,* another paraphrase of the same story from Strada's *Profusions.*

7. Cf. *Sonnets from the Portuguese*, XXI.

8. Cf. *Sonnets from the Portuguese*, XXXIII.

179 (W87)   *R.B. to E.B.B.*

[*December 20, 1845.*]

Saturday.

I do not, nor will not think, dearest, of ever "making you happy" —I can imagine no way of working to that end, which does not go straight to my own truest, only true happiness: yet in every such effort there is implied some distinction, some supererogatory grace, or why speak of it at all? *You* it is, are my happiness, and all that ever can be: YOU—dearest!

But never, if you would not . . what you will not do I know, never revert to *that* frightful wish.—"Disappoint me?"—"I speak what I know and testify what I have seen"[1]—you shall "mystery" again & again—I do not dispute that, but do not *you* dispute, neither, that mysteries are: but it is simply because I do most justice to the mystical part of what I feel for you . . because I consent to lay most stress on that fact of facts that I love you, beyond admiration, and respect, and esteem and affection even—and do not adduce any reason which stops short of accounting for *that*, whatever else it would account for . . because I do this, in pure logical justice—*you* are able to turn and wonder . . (if you *do . . now*) what causes it all! My love, only wait, only believe in me, and it cannot be but I shall, little by little, become known to you—after long years, perhaps, but still one day—I *would* say *this* now—but I will write more to-morrow. God bless my sweetest—ever, love, I am your R.B.

But my letter came last night, did it not?

⟨Another thing⟩—no, *to-morrow*—for time presses, and, in all cases, *Tuesday*—remember!

⟨My letter shall reach you on that⟩

1. Cf. John 3 : 11.

[December 20, 1845.]

Saturday.

I have your letter now, & now I am sorry I sent mine. If I wrote that you had "forgotten to write," I did not mean it,—not a word!—If I had meant it I should not have written it. But it would have been better for every reason to have waited just a little longer before writing at all. A besetting sin of mine is an impatience which makes people laugh when it does not entangle their silks, pull their knots tighter, & tear their books in cutting them open.

How right you are about Mr. Lowell!—He has a refined fancy & is graceful for an American critic, but the truth is, otherwise, that he knows nothing of English poetry or the next thing to nothing, & has merely had a dream of the early dramatists. The amount of his reading in that direction is an article in the Retrospective Review[1] which contains extracts,—& he re-extracts the extracts, re-quotes the quotations, &, 'a pede Herculem,' from the foot infers the man, or rather from the sandal-string of the foot, infers & judges the soul of the man—it is comparative anatomy under the most speculative conditions. How a /man\writer/ of his talents & pretentions could make up his mind to make up a book on such slight substratum, is a curious proof of the state of literature in America. Do you not think so?—Why a lecturer on the English Dramatists for a "Young Ladies' academy" here in England, might take it to be necessary to have better information than he could gather from an odd volume of an old review! And then, Mr. Lowell's naïveté in showing his authority . . as if the Elizabethan poets lay mouldering in inaccessible manuscript somewhere below the lowest deep of Shakespeare's grave . . is curious beyond the rest!—Altogether, the fact is an epigram on the surface-literature of America. As you say, their books do not suit us:—Mrs. Markham might as well send her compendium of the History of France to M. Thiers.[2] If they *knew* more they could not give parsley crowns to their own native poets when there is /more\greater/ merit among the rabbits. Mrs. Sigourney[3] has just sent me . . just this morning . . her "Scenes in my native land" and, peeping between the uncut leaves, I read of the poet Hillhouse[4] of "sublime spirit & Miltonic energy," standing in "the temple of Fame" as if it were built on purpose for him!—I suppose he is like most of the American poets .. who are shadows of the true, as flat as a shadow, as colourless as a shadow, as lifeless & as ⟨‖ · · ‖⟩ transitory. Mr. Lowell himself is, in his verse-books, poetical, if not a poet—& certainly this little book we are talking of is grateful enough in some ways—you would call it a *pretty book*—would you not?—Two or three letters I have had from him .. all very kind!—& *that* reminds me, alas! of some ineffable ingratitude on my own part! When one's conscience grows too heavy, there is nothing for it but to throw it away!—

Do you remember how I tried to tell you what he said of you, & how you would not let me?

Mr. Mathews said of *him* .. having met him once in society .. that he was the concentration of conceit in appearance & manner. But since then they seem to be on better terms.

Where is the meaning, pray, of E. B. C.?—*your* meaning, I mean ..?

My true initials are *E.B.M.B.*—my long name, as opposed to my short one, being: .. Elizabeth Barrett Moulton Barrett!—there's a full length to take away one's breath!—Christian name .. Elizabeth Barrett: —surname, Moulton Barrett. So long it is, that to make it portable, I fell into the habit of doubling it up & packing it closely, .. & of forgetting that I was a *Moulton*, altogether. One might as well write the alphabet as all four initials. Yet our family-name is *Moulton Barrett,* & my brothers reproach me sometimes for sacrificing the governorship of an old town in Norfolk with a little honorable verdigris from the Heralds' Office— As if I cared for the *Retrospective Review!* Nevertheless it is true that I would give ten towns in Norfolk (if I had them) to own some purer lineage than that of the blood of the slave!—Cursed we are from generation to generation!—I seem to hear the 'Commination Service.'[5]

May God bless you always, always!—beyond the always of this world!—   Your E. B. B.

Mr. Dickens's 'Cricket' sings repetitions, &, with considerable beauty, is extravagant—It does not appear to me by any means one of his most successful productions, though quite free from what was reproached as bitterness & one-sidedness, last year.[6]

You do not say how you are—not a word!—And you are wrong in saying that you "ought to have written"—as if "ought" could be in place *so!*—You *never' ought' to write to me you know!*—or rather . . if you ever /feel⟩think/ you ought, you ought not!—Which is a speaking of mysteries on my part!—

1. An English magazine (published 1820–28) which printed critiques of very old books—e.g., Feltham's *Resolves*—and, in its latter years, a section on heraldry and genealogy..

2. "Mrs. Markham" (Elizabeth Cartwright Penrose, 1780–1837) wrote *A History of France . . . for the Use of Young Persons* (2 vols., London, 1828); Thiers's exhaustive *History of the Consulate and Empire* was published in England in 1845.

3. Lydia Howard Sigourney (1791–1865), a prolific American writer and friend of Cornelius Mathews, had written E.B.B. in April (*Letters of EBB*, I, 251). The book mentioned here had just been published in Boston.

4. James Abraham Hillhouse (1789–1841).

5. "A recital of the Divine threatenings against sinners; part of an office to be read in the Church of England on Ash-Wednesday and at other times" (*Oxford Universal Dictionary*).

6. *The Cricket on the Hearth* succeeded *A Christmas Carol* (1843) and *The Chimes* (1844) as the third of Dickens' Christmas stories. The latter painted so bitter a picture of the treatment of the poor that it roused controversy. The *Athenæum*, on the day this letter was written, expressed relief that Dickens had this time decided not to "risk a new controversy on matters of opinion or practice."

181 (W88) **R.B. to E.B.B.**

[*December 21, 1845.*]

Sunday Night.

Now, *"ought"* you to be "sorry you sent that letter," which made, & makes me so happy—so happy—can you bring yourself to turn round and tell one you have so blessed with your bounty that there was a mistake, and you meant only half that largess? If you are not sensible that you *do* make me most happy by such letters, and do not warm in the reflection of your own rays, then I *do* give up indeed the last chance of procuring *you* happiness. ⟨‖ · · · ‖⟩ My own "ought," which you object to, shall be withdrawn—being only a pure bit of selfishness; I felt, in missing the letter of yours, next day, that I *might* have drawn it down by one of mine,—if I had begged never so gently, the gold would have fallen—*there* was my omitted duty to myself which you properly blame

—I should stand silently and wait and be sure of the ever-remembering goodness.

Let me count my gold now—and rub off any speck that stays the full shining. First—*that thought* . . I told you; I pray you, pray you, sweet—never that again—or what leads never so remotely or indirectly to it! On *your own fancied ground*—the fulfilment would be of necessity fraught with every woe that can fall in this life. I am yours for ever—if you are not *here,* with me—what then? Say, you take all of yourself away but—just enough to live on,—then, *that* defeats every kind purpose . . as if you cut away all the ground from my feet but so much as serves for bare standing room . . why still, I *stand* there—and is it the better that I have no broader space, when off *that* you cannot force me? —I have your memory, the knowledge of you, the idea of you printed into my heart and brain,—on that, I can live my life—but it is for you, the dear, utterly generous creature I know you, to give me more and more beyond mere life—to extend life and deepen it—as you do, and will do. Oh, *how* I love you when I think of the entire truthfulness of your generosity to me—how, meaning, and willing to *give*, you gave *nobly!* Do you think I have not seen in this world how women who *do* love will manage to confer that gift on occasion? And shall I allow myself to fancy how much alloy such pure gold as *your* love would have rendered endurable?—Yet it came, virgin ore, to complete my fortune! And what but this makes me confident and happy? *Can* I take a lesson by your fancies, and begin frightening myself with saying . . "But if she saw all the world—the worthier, better men there . . those who would" &c &c No, I think of the great, dear *gift* that it was,—how I "*won*" NOTHING (the hateful word, and *French* thought)—did nothing by my own arts or cleverness in the matter . . so what pretence have the *more* artful or more clever for—but I cannot write out this folly—I am yours for ever, with the utmost sense of gratitude—to say I would give you my life joyfully is little . . I would, I hope, do that for two or three other people—but I am not conscious of any imaginable point in which I would not implicitly devote my whole self to you—be disposed of by you as for the best. There! It is not to be spoken of—let me *live* it into proof, beloved!

And for 'disappointment and a burthen' . . now—let us get quite away from ourselves, and not see one of the filaments, but only the *cords* of love with the world's horny eye—Have we such jarring tastes, then?

Does your inordinate attachment to gay life interfere with my deep passion for society? "Have they common sympathy in each other's pursuits?"—always asks Mrs. Tomkins![1] Well, here was I when you knew me, fixed in my way of life, meaning with God's help to write what may be written and so die at peace with myself so far. Can you help me or no? Do you *not* help me so much that, if you saw the more likely peril for poor human nature, you would say, "He will be jealous of all the help coming from me,—none from him to me!"—And *that would* be a consequence of the help, all-too-great for hope of return, with any one less possessed than I with the exquisiteness of being *transcended* and the *blest* one.

But—"here comes the Selah and the voice is hushed"[2]—I will speak of other things: when we are together one day—the days I believe in—I mean to set about that reconsidering "Sordello"[3]—it has always been rather on my mind—but yesterday I was reading the "Purgatorio" and the first speech of the group of which Sordello makes one struck me with a new significance, as well describing the man and his purpose and fate in my own poem—see; one of the burthened, contorted souls tells Virgil & Dante—

> Noi fummo già tutti per forza morti,
> E *peccatori infin' all' ultim' ora:*
> Quivi—*lume del ciel ne fece accorti;*
> *Si chè, pentendo e perdonando, fora*
> *Di vita uscimmo a Dio pacificati*
> *Che del disio di se veder n'accora.*[4]

Which is just my Sordello's story . . could I "*do*" it off hand, I wonder—

> And sinners ↑were we↓ to the extreme hour⟨were we⟩;
> *Then*, light from heaven fell, making us aware,
> So that, repenting us and pardoned, out
> Of life we passed to God, at peace with Him
> Who fills the heart with yearning Him to see.

There were many singular incidents attending my work on that subject—thus, quite at the end, I found out there *was* ⟨publis⟩↑*printed* and↓ not published, a little historical tract by a Count V—— something, called "Sordello"—with the motto "Post fata resurgam"!⟨⟩[5] "I hope he prophesied." The main of this—biographical notices—is extracted by Muratori,[6] I think. Last year when I set foot in Naples I found after a few minutes that at some theatre, that night, the opera was to be "one act of Sordello"[7] and I never looked twice, nor expended a ⟨muzz⟩ couple of carlines on the *libretto!*

I wanted to tell you, in last letter, that when I spoke of people's tempers *you* have no concern with "people"—I do not glance obliquely at *your* temper—either to discover it, or praise it, or adapt myself to it— I speak of the relation one sees in other cases—how one opposes passionate foolish people, but hates cold clever people who take quite care enough of themselves: I myself am born supremely passionate—so I was born with light yellow hair—all changes; that is the passion changes its direction and, taking a channel large enough, looks calmer, perhaps, than it should—and all my sympathies go with quiet strength, of course —but I know what the other kind is. As for the breakages of chairs, and the appreciation of Parisian *meubles;* manibus, pedibusque descendo in tuam sententiam, Ba, mî ocelle![8] ('What was E. B. *C?*' why, the first letter after, and *not,* E. B. *B,* my own *B!* There was no latent meaning in the C—but I had no inclination to go on to D, or E, for instance!)

And so, love, Tuesday is to be our day—one day more—and then! And meanwhile *"care"* for me! a good word for you—but *my* care, what is that! One day I aspire to *care,* though! I shall not go away at any dear Mr. K.'s coming! They call me down-stairs to supper—and my fire is out, and you keep me from feeling cold and yet ask if I am well? Yes, well—yes, happy—and your own ever—I must bid God bless you —dearest!

R. B.

1. Not identified, but referred to several times in this correspondence as if a proverbial vehicle for commonplaces.

2. Cf. *An Essay on Mind* (1826), line 1229 and E.B.B.'s own note on it.

3. See Letter 99 and its note 4.

4. *Purgatorio* V. 52–57.

5. Actually Giovanni Battista Gherardo, Count d'Arco, *Sordello* (Cremona: per Lorenzo Manini Regio Stampatore, 1783). The motto means, "After my allotted span of days, I shall arise again."

6. Ludovico Antonio Muratori (1672–1750), editor of *Rerum italicarum scriptores* (25 vols., 1723–38). Browning used this compendium of source materials in writing *Sordello* (DeVane, p. 82).

7. Not identified.

8. "I acquiesce completely in your opinion, Ba, my little eye!" The epithet is a not readily translatable expression of approval.

The visit noted by Browning on the envelope of Letter 180 occurred before E.B.B. wrote the Wednesday portion of the following letter:
+Tuesday
Dec 23
3–4¾ p.m.

182 (W94°)   *E.B.B. to R.B.*

[*December 21, 1845.*]

Sunday Night.

But did I dispute? Surely not. Surely I believe in you and in 'mysteries.' Surely I prefer the no–reason to ever so much rationalism . . (rationalism & infidelity go together they say!). All which I may do, & be afraid sometimes notwithstanding— —& when you overpraise me *(not* over*love)* I must be frightened as I told you.

It is with me as with the theologians. I believe in you & can be happy and safe *so:* but when my 'personal merits' come into question in any way, even the least, . . why then the position grows untenable:— it is no more 'of grace.'

Do I teaze you? as I teaze myself sometimes? But do not wrong me in turn!—Do not keep repeating that 'after long years' I shall know you—know you!—as if I did not without the years. If you are forced to refer me to those long ears, I must deserve the thistle besides. The thistles are the corollary.

For it is obvious . . manifest . . that I cannot doubt of you—that I may doubt of myself, of happiness, of the whole world, . . but of YOU— NOT: it is obvious that if I could doubt of you & *act so* I should be a very idiot, or worse indeed. And *you* . . you think I doubt of you whenever I make an interjection!—now do you not? . . And is it reasonable?— Of *you*, I mean?

Monday [December 22].—For my part, you must admit it to be too possible that you may be, as I say, 'disappointed' in me—it *is* too possible. And if it does me good to say so, even now perhaps . . if it is mere weakness to say so & simply torments you, why do *you* be magnanimous & forgive *that* . . let it pass as a weakness & forgive it *so*. Often I think painful things which I do not tell you & . . . . . .

338

While I write, your letter comes. Kindest of you it was, to write me such a letter, when I expected scarcely the shadow of one!—this makes up for the other letter which I expected unreasonably & which you '*ought not*' to have written, as was proved afterwards. And now why should I go on with that sentence?—What had I to say of "painful things," I wonder? all the painful things seem gone .. vanished .. I forget what I had to say. Only do you still think of this, dearest beloved—, that I sit here in the dark but for *you*, & that the light you bring me (from *my* fault!—from the nature of *my* darkness!) is not a settled light as when you open the shutters in the morning, but a light made by candles which burn some of them longer & some shorter, & some brighter & briefer, at once—being "double-wicks," & that there is an intermission for a moment now & then between the dropping of the old light into the socket & the lighting of the new—Every letter of yours is a new light which burns so many hours .. & *then!*—I am morbid, you see—or call it by what name you like .. too wise or too foolish. 'If the light of the body is darkness, how great is that darkness.'[1] Yet even when I grow too wise, I admit always that while you love me it is an answer to all. And I am never so much too foolish as to wish to be worthier for my own sake—only for yours!—not for my own sake, since I am content to owe all things to you—

And it could be so much to you to lose me!—& you say so,—& THEN think it needful to tell me not to think the other thought.!! As if /I had ever⟩*that* were/ possible!—Do you remember what you said once of the flowers—that you 'felt a respect for them when they had passed out of your hands'?—And must it not be so with my life, which if you choose to have it, must be respected too?—Much more with my life!—Also, see that I, who had my warmest affections on the other side of the grave, feel that it is otherwise with me now—quite otherwise. I did not like it at first to be so much otherwise. And I could not have had any such thought through a weariness of life or any of my old motives, but simply to escape the 'risk' I told you of. Should I have said to you instead of it .. '*Love me for ever*'?[2]—Well then, .. I *do*—

As to my 'helping' you, my help is in your fancy,—& if you go on with the fancy, I perfectly understand that it will be as good as deeds. We *have* sympathy too—we walk one way—oh, I do not forget the advantages. Only Mrs. Tomkins's ideas of happiness are below my ambition for you— —

So often as I have said, (it reminds me) that in this situation I should be more exacting than any other woman—so often I have said it—& so different everything is from what I thought it would be!—Because if I am exacting it is for *you* & not for *me*—it is altogether for *you*—you understand *that,* dearest of all . . it is for YOU *wholly.* It never crosses my thought, in a lightning even, the question whether I may be happy so & so—*I.* It is the other question which comes always—too often for peace.

People used to say to me, "You expect too much—you are too romantic—" And my answer always was that "I could not expect too much when I expected nothing at all" . . which was the truth—for I never thought (& how often I have SAID *that!*) I never thought that anyone whom *I* could love, would stoop to love ME . . the two things seemed clearly incompatible to my understanding.

And now when it comes in a miracle, you wonder at me for looking twice, thrice, four times, to see if it comes through ivory or *horn*[3]— You wonder⟨ed⟩ that it should seem to me at first all illusion—illusion for you . . illusion for me as a consequence. But how natural—

It is true of me . . very true . . that I have not a high appreciation of what passes in the world (& not merely the Tomkins-world!) under the name of love; & that a distrust of the thing had grown to be a habit of mind with me when I knew you first. It has appeared to me, through all the seclusion of my life & the narrow experience it admitted of, that in nothing, men . . & women too! . . were so apt to mistake their own feelings, as in this one thing. Putting *falseness* quite on one side . . quite out of sight & consideration, an honest mistaking of feeling appears wonderfully common—& no mistake has such frightful results—none can. Selflove & generosity, a mistake may come from either—from pity, from admiration, from any blind impulse—oh, when I look at the histories of my own female friends . . to go no step further!—And if it is true of the *women,* what must the other side be?—To see the marriages which are made every day!—worse than solitudes & more desolate! In the case of the two happiest I ever knew, one of the husbands said in confidence ↑to a brother of mine↓—not much in confidence or I should not have heard it, but in a sort of smoking frankness . . that he had "ruined his prospects by marrying"; & the other said to himself at the very moment of professing an extraordinary happiness, . . "But I should have done as well if I had not married *her.*"

Then for the falseness——the first time I ever, in my own experience, heard that word which rhymes to glove & comes as easily off and on ↑(on some hands!)↓—it was from a man of whose attentions to another woman I was at that *time her confidante*. I was bound so to silence for her sake, that I could not even speak the scorn that was in me—and in fact my uppermost feeling was a sort of horror . . a terror—for I was very young then, & the world did, at the moment, look ghastly!

The falseness and the calculations!—why how can you, who are *just, blame women* . . when you must know what the "system" of man is towards them,—& of men not ungenerous otherwise? Why are women to be blamed if they act as if they had to do with swindlers?—is it not the mere instinct of preservation which makes them do it? These make women what they are. And your 'honorable men,' the most loyal of them, (for instance) . . is it not a rule with them (unless when taken unaware through a want of selfgovernment) to force a woman (trying all means) to force a woman to stand committed in her affections . . (they with their feet lifted all the time to /tread upon〉trample on/ her for want of delicacy—) before *they* risk the pin-prick to their own personal pitiful vanities? Oh—to see how these things are set about by *men!* to see how a man carefully holding up on each side the skirts of an embroidered vanity to keep it quite safe from the wet, will contrive to tell you in so many words that he . . might love you if the sun shone! And women are to be blamed!—Why there are, to be sure, cold & heartless, light & changeable, ungenerous & calculating women in the world!—that is sure. But for the most part, they are only what they are made . . & far better than the nature of the making . . of that I am confident. The loyal make the loyal, the disloyal the disloyal. And I give no more discredit to those women you speak of, than I myself can take any credit in this thing—I—Because who could be disloyal with YOU . . with whatever corrupt inclination? *you,* who are the noblest of all? If you judge me so, . . it is my privilege rather than my merit . . as I feel of myself.

Wednesday [December 24].—All but the last few lines of all this was written before I saw you yesterday, ever dearest—& since, I have been reading your third act which is perfectly noble & worthy of you both in the conception & expression, & carries the reader on triumphantly . . to speak for one reader. It seems to me too that the language is freer—there is less inversion & more breadth of rhythm. It just strikes me so for the first impression: at any rate the interest grows & grows. You have a secret about Domizia, I guess—which will not be told till the last perhaps. And that poor, noble Luria, who will be equal to the leap . . as it is easy to see. It is full, altogether, of magnanimities:—noble, & nobly put. I will go on with my notes, & those, you shall have at once . . I mean together . . presently. And don't hurry & chafe yourself for the fourth act—now that you are better! To be ill again—think what that would be!—Luria will be great now whatever you do—◦or whatever you do *not*. Will he not?↓

And never, never for a moment (I quite forgot to tell you) did I fancy that you were talking at *me* in the temper-observations—never. It was the most unprovoked egotism, all that I told you of my temper—, for certainly I never suspected you of asking questions so—I was simply amused a little by what you said, & thought to myself (if you *will* know my thoughts on that serious subject) that you had probably lived among very goodtempered persons, to hold such an opinion about the innocuousness of illtemper. It was all I thought, indeed. Now to fancy that I was capable of suspecting you of such a maneuvre!—Why you would have *asked* me ◦directly;—◦ if you had wished 'curiously to enquire.'

An excellent solemn chiming, the passage from Dante makes with your Sordello and the Sordello *deserves* the labour which it needs, to make it appear the great work it is. I think that the principle of association is too subtly in movement throughout it—so that *while* you are going straight forward you go at the same time round & round, until the progress involved in the motion is lost sight of by the lookers on. Or did I tell you that before?

You have heard, I suppose, how Dickens's 'Cricket' sells by nineteen thousand copies at a time, though he takes Michael Angelo to be 'a humbug'[4]—or for "though" read "because." Tell me of Mr. Kenyon's dinner—And Moxon?

Is not this an infinite letter?—I shall hear from you, I hope . . I *ask* you to let me hear soon. I write all sorts of things to you, rightly & wrongly perhaps; when wrongly, forgive it. I think of you always. May God bless you. "Love me for ever," as

Your

Ba

1. Matthew 6:23.
2. She is quoting Browning's *Earth's Immortalities* (1845).
3. See Letter 159, note 4.
4. Cf. *Pictures from Italy* (1846), pp. 208–209, where Dickens says he cannot

imagine how a truly sensitive man "can discern in Michael Angelo's Last Judgment . . . any general idea or one pervading thought, in harmony with the stupendous subject."

183 (W89)　　　　　　　*R.B. to E.B.B.*

———————

25th Dec. [1845.]

My dear Christmas gift of a letter! I will write back a few lines, (all I can, having to go out now)—just that I may forever,—certainly during our mortal "forever"—mix my love for you, and, as you suffer me to say, your love for me . . dearest! . . these shall be mixed with the other loves of the day and live therein—as I write, and trust, and know— forever! While I live I will remember what was my feeling in reading, and in writing, and in stopping from either . . as I have just done . . to kiss you and bless you with my whole heart— Yes, yes, bless you, my own!

———————

All is right, all of your letter . . admirably right and just in the de- fence of the women I *seemed* to speak against; and only seemed—because that is a way of mine which you must have observed; that foolish con- centrating of thought and feeling, for a moment, on some one little spot of a character or anything else indeed, and—in the attempt to do justice and develop whatever may seem ordinarily to be overlooked in it,— that over vehement *insisting* on, and giving an undue prominence to, the same—which has the effect of taking away from the importance of the rest of the related objects which, in truth, are not considered at all . . or they would also rise proportionally when subjected to the same (. . that is, correspondingly magnified and dilated . .) light and concen- trated feeling: so, you remember, the old divine, preaching on "/little⟩ small/ sins," in his zeal to expose the tendencies & consequences usually made little account of, was led to maintain the said small sins to be "greater than great ones." *But then* . . if you look on the world *altogether,* and accept the small natures, in their usual proportion with the greater . . things do not look *quite* so bad; because the conduct which *is* atrocious in those higher cases, of proposal and acceptance, *may* be no more than the claims of the occasion justify—(wait and hear)—in certain other cases where the thing sought for and granted is avowedly less by a million degrees: it shall all be traffic, exchange—(counting spiritual gifts as only coin, for our purpose)—but surely the formalities and policies and decencies all vary with the nature of the thing trafficked for—if a man makes up his mind during half his life to acquire a Pitt-diamond or a Pilgrim-pearl[1]—[he] gets witnesses and testimony and soforth—but, surely, when I pass a shop where oranges are ticketed up seven for six-pence I offend no law by sparing all words and putting down the piece with a certain authoritative ring on the counter: if instead of diamonds you want—(being a king or queen)—provinces with live men on them .. there is so much more diplomacy required; new interests are appealed to .. high motives *supposed,* at all events—whereas, when, in Naples, a man asks leave to black your shoe in the dusty street "purely for the honor of serving your Excellency" you laugh and would be sorry to find yourself without a "grano" or two—(six of which, about, make a farthing)—Now do you not see! Where so little is to be got, why offer much more? If a man knows that .. but I am teaching you! All I mean is, that, in Benedick's phrase, "the world must go on."[2]—He who honestly wants his wife to sit at the head of his table and carve .. that is be his *help-meat* (not "help mete for him")—he shall assuredly find a girl of his degree who wants the table to sit at—, and some dear friend to mortify, who *would* be glad of such a piece of fortune—and if that man offers that woman a bunch of orange-flowers and a sonnet, instead of a buck-horn-handled sabre-shaped knife, sheathed in a 'Every Lady Her Own *Market-Woman,* Being a Table of' &c &c *then,* I say he is—

　　Bless you, dearest—the clock strikes—and time is none—but—bless you! Your own R. B.

　　1. The Regent or Pitt diamond, one of the French Crown Jewels, weighed 410 carats when found. The Pilgrim pearl—"La Pellegrina"—was perhaps the largest perfectly globular pearl ever found: 28 carats.
　　2. "The world must be peopled." *Much Ado* II. iii. 244.

184 (W90)   R.B. to E.B.B.

───────────────

[December 27, 1845.]

Saturday, 4. p. m.

I was forced to leave off abruptly on Christmas Morning—and now I have but a few minutes before our inexorable post leaves: I hoped to return from Town earlier. But I can say something—and Monday will make amends.

"Forever" and for ever I *do* love you, dearest—love you with my whole heart—in life, in death—

Yes; I did go to Mr. Kenyon's—who had a little to forgive in my slack justice to his good dinner, but was for the rest his own kind self—and I went, also, to Moxon's—who said something about my number's going off "rather heavily"—so let it!

Too good, too, too indulgent you are, my own Ba, to "acts" first or last; but all the same, I am glad and encouraged. *Let* me get done with these, and better things will follow—

Now, bless you, ever, my sweetest—I have you ever in my thoughts —And on Monday, remember, I am to see you—

Your own R. B.

See what I cut out of a Cambridge Advertiser of the 24th—to make you laugh![1]

1. The cutting is the heading and four epigraphs from the December 24 issue of a Christmas poem: "The Original [black-letter head] / A FEW RHYMES FOR THE PRESENT CHRISTMAS. / BY J. PURCHAS, ESQ., B.A. / (Written for 'The Cambridge Advertiser.')

'This age shows, to my thinking, still more infidels
to Adam,
Than directly, by profession, simple infidels to God.'
ELIZABETH B. BARRETT [*Lady Geraldine*, st. lxxiii]
'φωνᾶντα συνετοῖσι,' κ.τ.λ. ["A message to those who
comprehend," &c.]
PINDAR, OLYMP[IAN ODES] II.'

Browning underscored the second Greek word ("those who comprehend") and set an exclamation mark in the margin. The other epigraphs—from Lear and Mrs. Norton—have no real pertinence and the seven stanzas of the poem were not included in the cutting.

E.B.B. to R.B.

———————————

[December 27, 1845.]

Saturday.

Yes, indeed, I have "observed that way" in you, & not once, & not twice, & not twenty times, but oftener than any,—& almost every time . . do you know, . . with an uncomfortable feeling from the reflection that *that* is the way for making all sorts of mistakes dependent on ↑& issuing in↓ exaggeration. It is the very way!—the highway.

For what you say in the letter here otherwise, I do not deny the truth . . as partial truth:—I was speaking generally quite. Admit that I am not apt to be extravagant in my 'esprit de sexe': the Martineau doctrines of intellectual equality &c, I gave them up, you remember, like a woman—most disgracefully, as Mrs. Jameson would tell me. But we are not on that ground now—we are on ground worth holding a brief for!—& when women fail *here* . . it is not so much our fault. Which was all I meant to say from the beginning.

It reminds me of the exquisite analysis in your Luria, this third act, of the worth of a woman's sympathy,—indeed of the exquisite double-analysis of unlearned & learned sympathies. Nothing could be better, I think, than this:—

> To the motive, the endeavour, the heart's self
> Your quick sense looks; you crown and call aright
> The soul of the purpose ere 'tis shaped as act,
> Takes flesh i' the world, and clothes itself a king—[1]

except the characterizing of the 'learned praise,' which comes afterwards in its fine subtle truth. What would these critics do to you, to what degree undo you, who would deprive you of the exercise of the ⟨‖ · · · ‖⟩ discriminative faculty of the metaphysicians? As if a poet could be great without it! They might as well recommend a watchmaker to deal only in faces, in dials, & not to meddle with the wheels inside!— You shall tell Mr. Forster so—[2]

And speaking of 'Luria,' which grows on me the more I read, . . how fine he is when the doubt breaks on him—I mean, where he begins . . 'Why then, all is very well'—It is most affecting, I think, all that process of doubt . . & that reference to the friends at home (which at once

346

proves him a stranger, & intimates, by just a stroke, that he /does⟩will/ not look home for comfort out of the new foreign treason) is managed by you with singular ⟨‖ · · · ‖⟩ dramatic dexterity . . . .

> . . . 'so slight, so slight,
> And yet it tells you they are dead & gone'—

And then, the direct approach . .

> You now, so kind here, all you Florentines,
> What is it in your eyes?—[3]

Do you not feel it to be success, . . '*you* now'?—*I* do, from my low ground as reader. The whole breaking round him of the cloud, & the manner in which he *stands*, facing it, . . I admire it all thoroughly. Braccio's /personifica⟩vindication/ of Florence strikes me as almost too *poetically* subtle for the man—but nobody could have the heart to wish a line of it away—*that* would be too much for critical virtue!—

I had your letter yesterday morning early. The postoffice people were so resolved on keeping ⟨their⟩ Christmas that they would not let me keep mine. No post all day, after that general post before noon, which never brings me anything worth the breaking of a seal!

Am I see you on monday?—If there should be the least, least crossing of that day, . . anything to do, anything to see, anything to listen to,—remember how tuesday stands close by, & that another monday comes on the following week. Now I need not say *that* every time, & you will please to remember it—Eccellenza!—

> May God bless you—

> Your E. B. B.

From the *New Monthly Magazine*. "The admirers of Robert Browning's poetry, & they are now very numerous, will be glad to hear of the issue by Mr. Moxon of a *seventh* series of the renowned Bells & delicious Pomegranates, under the title of "Dramatic Romances & Lyrics."[4]

1. Lines 68–71; the ensuing reference is to ll. 79–89.
2. See Forster's review, Letter 152, note 4.
3. The quotations are ll. 110–111 and 114–115 of *Luria*, III.
4. Quoted from "Miscellaneous" on the last page of the December 1845 issue.

With the notation on the envelope of Letter 185, Browning began numbering his visits:

+Mon. Dec. 29, 1845
3–4¾ p.m. (37.)

186 (W96°)   **E.B.B. to R.B.**

[*December 30, 1845.*]

Tuesday.

When you are gone I find your flowers; & you never spoke of nor showed them to me—so instead of yesterday I thank you to-day—thank you. Count among the miracles that your flowers live with me—I accept *that* for an omen, dear—dearest! Flowers in general, all other flowers, die of despair when they come into the same atmosphere[1] . . used to do it so constantly & observably that it made me melancholy & I left off for the most part having them here. Now, you see how they put up with the close room, & condescend to me & the dust—it is true and no fancy! To be sure they know that I care for them & that I stand up by the table myself to change their water & cut their stalks freshly at intervals—*that* may make a difference perhaps. Only the great reason must be that they are yours, & that you teach them to bear with me patiently.

Do not pretend even to misunderstand what I meant to say yesterday of dear Mr. Kenyon. His blame would fall as my blame of myself has fallen: he would say . . will say . . "it is ungenerous of her to let such a risk be run! I thought she would have been more generous." There, is Mr. Kenyon's opinion as I forsee it! Not that it would be spoken, you know! he is too kind. And then, he said to me last summer, somewhere *à propos* to the flies or butterflies, that he had "long ceased to wonder at any extreme of foolishness produced by—*love*."—He will of course think you very very foolish, but not ungenerously foolish like other people—

Never mind. I do not mind indeed. I mean, that, having said to myself worse than the worst perhaps of what can be said against me by any who regard me at all, & feeling it put to silence by the fact that you *do* feel so & so for me;—feeling that fact to be an answer to all . . I cannot mind much, in comparison, the railing at second remove.—There will be a nine days railing of it and no more!—and if on the ninth day you should not exactly wish never to have known me, the better reason will be demonstrated to stand with us. On this one point the wise man cannot judge for the fool his neighbour. If you *do* love me, the inference is that you would be happier with than without me—& whether you do, you know better than another: so I think of *you* and not of *them*—always of YOU! When I talked of being afraid of dear Mr. Kenyon, I just meant that he makes me nervous with his all-scrutinizing spectacles, put on for great occasions, & his questions which seem to belong to the spectacles, they go together so:—and then I have no presence of mind, as you may see without the spectacles. My only way of hiding (when people set themselves to look for me) would be the old child's way of getting behind the windowcurtains or under the sofa:—& even *that* might not be effectual if I had recourse to it now. Do you think it would? Two or three times I fancied that Mr. Kenyon suspected something—but if he ever *did*, his only reproof was a reduplicated praise of *you*—he praises you always and in relation to every sort of subject.

What a *misomonsism*[2] you fell into yesterday, you who have so much great work to do which no one else can do except just yourself!—& you, too, who have courage & knowledge, & must know that every work, with the principle of life in it, *will* live, let it be trampled ever so under the heel of a faithless & unbelieving generation—yes, that it will live like one of your toads, for a thousand years in the heart of a rock. All men can teach at second or third hand, as you said . . by prompting the foremost rows . . by tradition & translation:—all, *except* poets, who must preach their own doctrine & sing their own song, to be the means of any wisdom or any music, & therefore have stricter duties thrust upon them, & may not lounge in the στοά[3] like the conversation-teachers. So much I have to say to you, till we are in the Siren's island . . . & *I,* jealous of the Siren!—

"The Siren waits thee singing song for song," says Mr. Landor.[4] A prophecy which refuses to class you with the 'mute fishes,' precisely as I do.

And are you not my 'good'—all my good now—my only good ever? The Italians would say it better without saying more.

I had a letter from Miss Martineau this morning who accounts for her long silence by the supposition . . put lately to an end by ↑scarcely credible↓ information from Mr. Moxon, she says . . that I was out of England,—gone to the South from the 20th of September. She calls herself the strongest of women, & talks of " walking fifteen miles one day & writing fifteen pages another day without fatigue "—also of mesmerizing & of being infinitely happy except in the continued alienation of two of her family who cannot forgive her for getting well by such unlawful means. And she is to write again to tell me of Wordsworth, & promises to send me her new work in the meanwhile—all very kind.

So here is my letter to you which you asked for so " against the principles of universal justice "—Yes, very unjust—very unfair it was— only, you make me do just as you like in everything. Now confess to your own conscience that even if I had not a lawful claim of a debt against you, I might come to ask charity with another sort of claim, oh " son of humanity." Think how much more need of a letter *I* have than you can have; & that if you have a giant's power, ' 'tis tyrannous to use it like a giant.'[5]—Who would take tribute from the desert?— How I grumble. *Do* let me have a letter directly! remember that no other light comes to my windows, & that I wait " as those who watch for the morning "[6]—" lux mea ! "

May God bless you—and mind to say how you are *exactly,* and dont neglect the walking, *pray* do not! your own—

And after all, those women!—A great deal of doctrine commends and discommends itself by the delivery: & an honest thing may be said so foolishly as to disprove its very honesty. Now after all, what did she mean by that very silly expression about books, but that she did not feel as she considered herself capable of feeling—& what else but *that* was the meaning of the other woman? Perhaps it should have been spoken earlier—nay, clearly it should—but surely it was better spoken even in the last hour than not at all . . surely it is always & under all circumstances, better spoken at whatever cost—I have thought so steadily since I could think or feel at all. An entire openness to the last moment of possible liberty, at whatever cost & consequence, is the most honorable & most merciful way, both for men & women! perhaps for men in an especial manner. But I shall send this letter away, being in haste to get change for it—

1. Cf. the closing sonnet of *Sonnets from the Portuguese*. ". . . all flowers forswear

me—and die either suddenly or gradually as soon as they become aware of the want of fresh air and light in my room." E.B.B. to Mrs. Martin, January 30, 1843. *Letters of EBB*, I, 121.

    2. Apparently a neologism of unclear derivation. Browning's remarks in the following letter help to define it as an indifference to, or distate for, society.

    3. The portico or promenade from which the Stoics took their name.

    4. The last line of Landor's verse tribute to Browning. See Letter 151 and its note 7.

    5. *Measure for Measure* II. ii. 108–109.

    6. Psalms 130:6.

187 (W91)   **R.B. to E.B.B.**

Wednesday, December 31, 1845.

I have been properly punished for so much treachery as went to that re-urging the prayer that *you* would begin writing, when all the time—after the first of those words had been spoken which bade *me* write—I was full of purpose to send my own note last evening; one which should do its best to thank you: but see, the punishment! At home I found a note from Mr. Horne—on the point of setting out for Ireland, too unwell to manage to come over to me; anxious, so he said, to see me before leaving London, and with only ⟨Wednesday⟩ ↑Tuesday↓ or to-day to allow the opportunity of it, if I should choose to go and find him out: so I considered all things and determined to go—but not till so late, did I determine, on Tuesday, that there was barely time to get to Highgate ⟨‖···‖⟩ . . wherefore no letter reached you to beg pardon . . and now this undeserved—beyond the usual undeservedness —this last-day-of-the-year's gift—do you think or not think my grati- tude weighs on me? When I lay this with the others, and remember what you have done for me—I do bless you—so as I cannot but believe must reach the all-beloved head all my hopes and fancies and cares fly straight to. Dearest, whatever change the new year brings with it, we are together—I can give you no more of myself—indeed, you give me now—(back again if you choose, but changed and renewed by your possession—) the powers that seemed most properly mine: I could only mean that, by the expressions to which you refer—only could mean that you were my crown and palm branch, now and for ever, and so, that it was a very indifferent matter to me if the world took notice of that fact or no—Yes, dearest, that *is* the meaning of the prophecy—which I was stupidly blind not to have read and taken comfort from long ago—You ARE the veritable Siren—and you "wait me," and will sing "song for song"[1]—And this is my first song, my true song—this love I bear you—I look into my heart and then let it go forth under that name—love—I am more than mistrustful of many other feelings in me: they are not earnest enough; so far, not true enough—but this is all the flower of my life which you call forth and which lies at your feet.

Now let me say it . . what you are to remember. That if I had the slightest doubt, or fear, I would utter it to you on the instant—secure in the incontested stability of the main *fact,* even though the heights at the verge in the distance should tremble and prove vapour—and there would be a deep consolation in your forgiveness—indeed, yes,—but I tell you, on solemn consideration, it does seem to me that,—once take away the broad & general words that admit in their nature of any freight they can be charged with,—put aside love, and devotion, and trust—and *then* I seem to have said *nothing* of my feeling to you —nothing whatever.

⟨Indeed I so far conform myself to your pleasure, as I understand it, as never to *try,* even to express⟩ I will not write more now on this subject—believe you are my blessing and infinite reward beyond possible desert in intention,—my life has been crowned by you, as I said.

May God bless you ever—thro' you I shall be blessed. May I kiss your cheek and pray this, my own, all-beloved?

I must add a word or two of other things: I am very well now, quite well—am walking and about to walk. Horne—or rather his friends—reside in the very lane Keats loved so much—Millfield Lane: Hunt lent me once the little copy of the first Poems dedicated to him— and on the title-page was recorded in Hunt's delicate charactery that "Keats met him with this, the presentation-copy, or whatever was the odious name,—in M. Lane—called Poets' Lane by the gods—Keats came running, holding it up in his hand"—Coleridge had an affection for the place, and Shelley *"knew"* it—and I can testify it is green and silent, with pleasant openings on the grounds and ponds, thro' the old trees that line it—But the hills here are far more open and wild and hill-like—, not with the eternal clump of evergreens and thatched summer house—to say nothing of the "invisible railing" miserably visible everywhere.

You very well know *what* a vision it is you give me—when you speak of *standing up by the table* to care for my flowers . . (which I will never be ashamed of again, by the way—I will say for the future; "here are my best"—in this as in other things) . . Now, do you remember, that once I bade you not surprize me out of my good behaviour by standing to meet me unawares, as visions do, some day—but now— omne *ignotum?*[2] No, dearest!

Ought I to say there will be two days more? till Saturday—and if one word comes, *one* line—think!

I am wholly yours—yours, beloved!

R. B.

1. See Landor's verse tribute to Browning, Letter 151, note 7.
2. "Omne ignotum pro magnifico est." ("Everything unknown is supposed magnificent.") Tacitus, *Agricola*, 30. Also alluded to in Letter 77, note 6.

188 (W97°)   *E.B.B. to R.B.*

January 1, 1845 [1846].

How good you are—how best!—it is a favorite play of my memory to take up the thought of what you were to me (to my mind gazing!) years ago, as the poet in an abstraction . . then the thoughts of you, a little clearer, in concrete personality, as Mr. Kenyon's friend, who had dined with him on such a day, or met him at dinner on such another, and said some great memorable thing 'on wednesday last,' & enquired kindly about *me* perhaps on thursday . . till I was proud! & so, the thoughts of you . . nearer & nearer (yet still afar!) as the Mr. Browning who meant to do me the honor of writing to me, & who did write; & who asked me once in a letter (does he remember?) "not to lean out of the window while his foot was on the stair"![1] . . to take up all those thoughts, & more than those, one after another, & tie them together with all *these*, which cannot be named so easily—which cannot be classed in botany & Greek—It is a nosegay of mystical flowers, looking strangely & brightly . . & keeping their May-dew through the Christ-mases—better even than *your* flowers!—And I am not 'ashamed' of mine, . . be very sure! no!

For the siren, I never suggested to you any such thing—why you do not pretend to have read such a suggestion in my letter certainly. *That* would have been most exemplarily modest of me!—would it not, O Ulysses?

And you meant to write, . . you *meant!* & went to walk in 'Poet's lane' instead, ⸆(in the "Aonias of Highgate")⸅ which I remember to have read of—does not Hunt speak of it in his memoirs?[2]—& so now there is another track of light in the traditions of the place, & people may talk of the pomegranate-smell between the hedges. So you really have *hills* at New Cross, & not hills by courtesy?—I was at Hampstead once—& there was something attractive to me in that fragment of heath with its wild smell, thrown down . . like a Sicilian rose from Proserpine's lap when the car drove away, . . into all that arid civilization, "laurel-clumps & invisible ⸆visible⸅ fences," as you say!—& the grand, eternal smoke rising up in the distance, with its witness against nature!—People grew severely in jest about cockney landscape—but is it not true that the trees & grass in the close neighbourhood of great cities must of necessity excite deeper emotion than the woods & valleys will, a hundred miles off . . where human creatures ruminate ⸆stupidly⸅ as the cows do . . the 'county families' es-*chewing* all men who are not 'landed proprietors' . . & the farmers never looking higher than to the fly on the uppermost turnip-leaf! Do you know at all what English country-life is, which the English praise so, & 'moralize upon into a thousand similes,'[3] as that one greatest, purest, noblest thing in the world . . the purely English and excellent thing?—It is to my mind simply & purely abominable, & I would rather live in a street than be forced to live it out . . that English country-life; for I don't mean life in the country. The social exigencies . . why, nothing *can* be so bad—nothing!—That is the way by which Englishmen grow up to top the world in their peculiar line of respectable absurdities.

Think of my talking so as as if I could be vexed with any one of them!—*I!*—On the contrary I wish them all a happy new year to abuse one another, or visit each of them his nearest neighbour whom he hates, three times a week, because 'the distance is so convenient' . . & give great dinners in noble rivalship: (venison from the Lord Lieutenant against turbot from London!) & talk popularity and gamelaws by turns to the tenantry, & beat down tithes to the rector. This glorious England of ours,—with its peculiar glory of the rural districts!!—And *my* glory of patriotic virtue, who am so happy in spite of it all . . & make a pretence of talking .. talking .. while I think the whole time of your letter. I think of your letter—I am no more a patriot than *that!*—

May God bless you, best & dearest! You say things to me which I am not worthy to listen to for a moment .. even if I was deaf dust the next moment .. I confess it humbly and earnestly as before God—

Yet He knows .. if the entireness of a gift means anything .. that I have not given with a reserve—that I am yours in my life & soul, for this year & for other years.—Let me be used *for* you rather than *against* you!—& that unspeakable, immeasurable grief of feeling myself a stone in your path, a cloud in your sky .. may I be saved from it!—pray it for *me* .. for *my* sake rather than *yours*. For the rest, I thank you, I thank you—You will be always to me, what to-day you are—& that is all!—! I am your own—

1. See the close of Letter 11.
2. Leigh Hunt's *Lord Byron and Some of His Contemporaries, with Recollections of the Author's Life* (2 vols., London, 1828). The lane is mentioned several times and the story in the preceding letter told in a chapter on Keats (I, 413–414).
3. Cf. *As You Like It* II. ii. 137.

The next visit is noted on the envelope of Letter 188:
+Saturday, Jan. 3. 1846
3–5 p.m. 38.

189 (W92)   **R.B. to E.B.B.**

                    ─────────────────

[*January 4, 1846.*]

Sunday Night.

Yesterday, nearly the last thing, I bade you "think of me"—I wonder if you could misunderstand me in that?—As if my words or actions or any of my ineffectual outside-self *should* be thought of, unless to be forgiven! But I do—dearest—feel confident that while I am in your mind,—cared for, rather than thought about,—no great harm can happen to me—and as, for great harm to reach me, it must pass thro' you,— you will care for yourself; *myself*, best self!

Come, let us talk: I found Horne's book[1] at home, and have had time to see that fresh beautiful things are there—I suppose "Delora"[2] will stand alone still—but I got pleasantly smothered with that odd shower of wood-spoils at the end, the dwarf-story; cup-masses and fern and spotty yellow leaves,—all that, I love heartily—and there is good sailor-speech in the "Ben Capstan"—though he does knock a man down with a "crow-bar"—instead of a marlingspike or, even, a belaying-pin! The first tale, tho' good, seems least new and individual .. but I must know more. At one thing I wonder—his not reprinting a quaint clever *real* ballad, published before 'Delora,' on the "Merry Devil of Edmonton"[3]—the first of his works I ever read—the very first piece was a single stanza, if I remember, in which was this line ⟨‖ · · · ‖⟩ 'When bason-crested Quixote, lean and bold,' .. good, is it not?[4] Oh, while it strikes me, good, too, *is* ⟨‖ · · · ‖⟩ that Swineshead-Monk-ballad! Only I miss the old chronicler's touch on the method of concocting the poison: "Then stole this Monk into the Garden and ⊦under a certain herb,↓ found out a Toad, which, squeezing into a cup," &c. something to that effect. I suspect, *par parenthèse*, you have found out by this time my odd liking for "vermin"—you once wrote "*your* snails" —and certainly snails are old clients of mine—but efts!—Horne traced a line to me—in the rhymes of a ''prentice-hand' I used to look over and correct occasionally[5]—taxed me (last week) with having altered the wise line "Cold as a *lizard* in a *sunny* stream" to "Cold as a newt hid in a shady brook"—for 'what do *you* know about newts?'—he asked of the author—who thereupon confessed. But never try and catch a speckled gray lizard when we are in Italy, love —and you see his tail hang out of the chink of a wall, his winter-house—because the strange tail will snap off, drop from him and stay in your fingers—and tho' you afterwards learn that there is more desperation in it and glorious determination to be free, than positive pain—(so people say who have no tails to be twisted off)—and tho', moreover, the tail grows again after a sort—*yet* .. don't do it, for it will give you a thrill! What a fine fellow our English water-eft is; "Triton paludis Linnaei"—*e come guizza*[6] (*that* you can't say in another language; cannot preserve the little in-and-out motion along with the straightforwardness!)—I always loved all those wild creatures God "*sets up for themselves*" so independently of us, so successfully, with their strange happy minute inch of a candle, as it were, to light them; while we run about and against each other with our great cressets and fire-pots. I once saw a solitary bee nipping a leaf round till it exactly fitted the front of a hole; his nest, no doubt; or tomb, perhaps— "Safe as Œdipus's grave-place, 'mid Colone's olives swart"[7]—(Kiss me, my Siren!)—Well, it seemed awful to watch that bee—he seemed so *instantly* from the teaching of God! Ælian[8] says that . . a *frog,* does he say?—some animal, having to swim across the Nile, never fails to provide himself with a bit of reed, which he bites off and holds in his mouth transversely and so puts from shore gallantly . . because when the water-serpent comes swimming to meet him, there is the reed, wider than his ✝serpent's✝ jaws, and no hopes of a swallow that time—now fancy the two meeting heads, the frog's wide eyes and the vexation of the snake!

Now, see! do I deceive you? Never say I began by letting down my dignity "that with no middle flight intends to soar above the Aonian Mount"![9]—

My best, dear, dear one,—may you be better, less *depressed,* . . I can hardly imagine frost reaching you if I could be by you. Think what happiness you mean to give me,—what a life,—what a death! "I may change"—too true,—yet, you see, as an eft was to me at the beginning so it continues—I *may* take up stones and pelt the next I see—but—do you much fear that?—Now, *walk,* move, *guizza, anima mia dolce.*[10] Shall I not know one day how far your mouth will be from mine as we walk? May I let that stay . . dearest, (the *line* stay, not the mouth).

I am not very well to-day—or, rather, have not been so—*now,* I am well and *with you.* I just say that, very needlessly, but for strict frankness' sake. Now, you are to write to me soon, and tell me all about yourself, and to love me ever, as I love you ever, and bless you, and leave you in the hands of God—My own love!—

Tell me if I do wrong to send *this* by a morning post—so as to reach you earlier than the evening—when you will . . write to me?

[Don't let me forget to say that I shall receive the Review to-morrow, and will send it directly.][11]

1. Richard Henry Horne's *Ballad Romances,* which had just been published.
2. *The Ballad of Delora; or, the Passion of Andrea Como,* collected in *Ballad Romances,* had first appeared in the *Monthly Repository* for December 1836.
3. " *The Rime of the Merry Devil of Edmonton, by Pyckle Smyth, sometime Clerk of that Parish*" appeared in the same number (January 1836) of the *Monthly Repository* with *Johannes Agricola* and *Porphyria.*
4. Horne's *Stanzas to a Ruined Windmill* immediately followed Browning's

sonnet *Eyes Calm Beside Thee* in the October 1834 *Monthly Repository*. Browning quotes from the first of five stanzas.

5. Very likely Thomas Powell; Browning's autograph corrections of two poems Powell published in 1842 are in the Yale library, and Horne was, or had been, an intimate of Powell's.

6. "And how it darts." The verb is a special one to suggest the rapid movement of a fish in water.

7. E.B.B.'s *Lost Bower*, st. lvi, slightly misquoted.

8. Claudius Aelianus, a Roman rhetorician of the second and third centuries, whose *Historiae Variae* is full of odd anecdotes of men and animals. The canny frog is in I. iii. Aelian is mentioned often in these letters and in *Aurora Leigh*.

9. *Paradise Lost* I. 14–15.

10. "Dart, my sweet soul."

11. Written on an outside edge after the letter was folded. For "the Review," see Letter 165, note 1, and the note preceding Letter 193.

190 *(W98°)*   **E.B.B. to R.B.**

[*January 4, 1846.*]

Sunday—

When you get Mr. Horne's book you will understand how, after reading just the first & the last poems, I could not help speaking coldly a little of it—& in fact, estimating his power as much as you can do, I did think & do, that the last was unworthy of him, & that the first might have been written by a writer of one tenth of his faculty. But last night I read the 'Monk of Swineshead Abbey' & the 'Three Knights of Camelott' & 'Bedd Gelert' & found them all of different stuff, better, stronger, more consistent, & read them with pleasure & admiration. Do you remember this application, among the countless ones of shadow to the transiency of life? I give the first two lines for clearness—

> "Like to the cloud upon the hill
> We are a moment seen
> Or the *shadow of the windmill*
> *Across yon sunny slope of green*"——

New or not, & I don't remember it elsewhere, it is just & beautiful I think. Think how the shadow of the windmill-sail just touches the ground on a bright windy day! the shadow of a bird flying is not faster!

—Then the 'Three Knights' has beautiful things, with more definite & distinct images than he is apt to show—for his character is a vague grand massiveness, . . like Stonehenge—or at least, if 'towers & battlements he sees' they are 'bosomed high' in dusky clouds . . it is a "passion-created imagery" which has no clear outline. In this ballad of the 'Knights,' & in the Monk's too, we may *look at* things, as on the satyr who swears by his horns & mates not with his kind afterwards, '/And⟩While/, *holding beards,* they dance in pairs' . . & that is all excellent & reminds one of those fine sylvan festivals, in Orion. But now tell me if you like altogether 'Ben Capstan' & if ↦you consider↤ the sailor-idiom to be lawful in poetry . . because I do not indeed. On the same principle we may have Yorkshire & Somersetshire 'sweet Doric' & do recollect what it ended in of old, in the Blowsibella heroines[1]—Then for the Elf story . . why should such things be written by men /of⟩like/ Mr. Horne? I am vexed at it. Shakespeare & Fletcher did not write so about fairies:—Drayton did not. Look at the exquisite Nymphidia, with its subtle sylvan consistency, & then at the lumbering coarse . . 'machina intersit'[2] . . Grandmama Grey! . . to say nothing of the 'small dog' that isn't the 'small boy'—Mr. Horne succeeds better on a larger canvass, & with weightier material . . with blank verse rather than lyrics—He cannot make a fine stroke. He wants subtlety & elasticity in the thought & expression— Remember, I admire him honestly & earnestly. No one has admired more than I the 'Death of Marlowe,' scenes in Cosmo, & Orion in much of it. But now tell me if you can accept with the same stretched out hand all these lyrical poems?—I am going to write to him as much homage as can come truly. Who combines different faculties as you do, striking the whole octave?—No one, at present in the world—

Dearest, after you went away yesterday & I began to consider, I found that there was nothing to be so over-glad about in the matter of the letters, for that, Sunday coming next to Saturday, the best now is only as good as the worst before, & I cant hear from you, until Monday . . Monday!—Did you think of *that* . . you who took the credit of acceding so meekly!—I shall not praise you in return at any rate. I shall have to wait . . till what oclock on Monday . . tempted in the meanwhile to fall into controversy against the "new moons & sabbath days" & the pausing of the post in consequence.

You never guessed perhaps . . what I look back to at this moment in the physiology of our intercourse . . . the curious double feeling I had about you . . you personally, & you as the writer of these letters, . . & the crisis of the feeling, when I was positively vexed & jealous of myself for not succeeding better in making a unity of the two. I could not!— And moreover I could not help but that the writer of the letters seemed nearer to me, long . . long . . & in spite of the postmark . . than did the personal visitor who confounded me, & left me constantly under such an impression of its being all dream-work on his side, that I have stamped my feet on this floor with impatience to think of having to wait so many hours before the 'candid' closing letter c^d come with its confession of an illusion. 'People say,' I used to think, 'that women *always* know . . & certainly I do not know . . & therefore . . therefore' —The logic /came⟩crushed/ on like Juggernaut's car. But in the letters it was different—the dear letters took me on the side of my own ideal life where I was able to stand a little upright & look round —I could read such letters for ever & answer them after a fashion . . that, I felt from the beginning. But *you*—!

Monday [January 5].—Never too early can the light come. Thank you for my letter!—Yet you look askance at me over "newt & toad," & praise so the Elf-story that I am ashamed to send you my ill humour on the same head. And you really like *that?* admire it? Grandmama Grey & the night cap & all? & "shoetye & blue sky?" & is it really wrong of me to like certainly some touches & images, but not the whole . . not the poem as a whole? I can take delight in the fantastical, & ⟨even⟩ in the grotesque—but here there is a want of life & consistency, as it seems to me!—the elf is no elf & speaks no elf-tongue!—it is not the right key to touch, . . this, . . for supernatural music. So I fancy at least— but I will try the poem again presently. You must be right—unless it should be your over-goodness opposed to my over-badness—I will not be sure. Or you wrote perhaps in an accidental mood of most excellent critical smoothness such as Mr. Forster did his last Examiner in, when he gave the all-hail to Mr. Harness as one of the best dramatists of the age!!³ Ah no!—not such as Mr. Forster's. Your soul does not enter into his secret—There can be nothing in common between you. For him to say such a word—he who knows—or ought to know!—And now let us agree & admire the bowing of the old minstrel over Bedd Gelert's unfilled grave—

> 'The *long* beard *fell* like *snow* into the grave
>   With solemn grace'

A poet, a friend, a generous man Mr. Horne is, even if no laureate for the fairies.

I have this moment a parcel of books via Mr. Moxon—Miss Martineau's two volumes[4]—& Mr. Bailey sends his 'Festus'[5] very kindly, . . and 'Woman in the Nineteenth Century' from America from a Mrs. or a Miss Fuller[6]—how I hate those 'Women of England,' 'Women & their Mission' & the rest. As if any possible good were to be done by such expositions of rights & wrongs.

Your letter would be worth them all, if *you* were less *you*! I mean, just this letter, . . all alive as it is with crawling buzzing wriggling cold-blooded warmblooded creatures . . as all alive as your own pedant's book in the tree.[7] And do you know, I think I like frogs too—particularly the very little leaping frogs, which +are+ so highhearted as to emulate the birds. I remember being scolded by my nurses for taking them up in my hands & letting them leap from one hand to the other— But for the toad!—why, at the end of the row of narrow beds which we called our gardens when we were children, grew an old thorn, & in the hollow of the root of the thorn, lived a toad, a great ancient toad, whom I, for one, never dared approach too nearly. That he 'wore a jewel in his head'[8] I doubted nothing at all. You must see it glitter if you stooped & looked steadily into the hole. And on days when he came out & sate swelling his black sides, I never looked steadily,—I would run a hundred yards round through the shrubs, deeper than knee-deep in the long wet grass & nettles, rather than go past him where he sate; being steadily of opinion, in the profundity of my natural history-learning, that if he took it into his toad's head to spit at me I should drop down dead in a moment, poisoned as by one of the Medici.

Oh—and I had a field-mouse for a pet once, & should have joined my sisters in a rat's nest if I had not been ill at the time: (as it was, the little rats were tenderly smothered by over-love!) & blue-bottle flies I used to feed, & hated your spiders for them,—yet no, not much. My aversion proper . . call it horror rather . . was for the silent, cold, clinging, gliding *bat,*—& even now, I think, I could not sleep in the room with that strange bird-mouse-creature, as it glides round the ceiling silently, silently as its shadow does on the floor—If you listen or look, there is not a wave of the wing—the wing never waves!—A bird without a feather! a beast that flies!—and so cold!—as cold as a fish!—It is the most supernatural-seeming of natural things. And then to see how

when the windows are open at night /they⟩those/ ⁺bats⁺ come sailing . .
without a sound—& go . . you cannot guess where!—fade with the
night-blackness!

 You have not been well—which is my first thought if not my first
word. Do walk, & do not work,—& think . . what I could be thinking
of, if I did not think of *you* . . dear—dearest!—'As the doves fly to the
windows,'[9] so I think of you!—As the prisoners think of liberty, as the
dying think of Heaven, so I think of you. When I look up straight to
God . . nothing, no one, used to intercept me—now there is *you*—only
you under Him! Do not use such words as those therefore any more,
nor say that you are not to be thought of so & so. You are to be thought
of every way. You must know what you are to me if you know at all
what *I* am,—and what I should be but for you.

 So . . love me a little, with the spiders & the toads & the lizards!
love me as you love the efts—and I will believe in *you* as you believe . .
in Ælian—Will *that* do?

Your own—

Say how you are when you write—& *write.*

---

 1. A confusion of John Gay's satiric *Blowzalinda* in the *Shepherd's Week* and the
Elizabethan term "dowsabell" for a country girl, as in Michael Drayton's *Ballad of
Dowsabell.*

 2. An allusion to Horace, *Ars Poetica,* ll. 191–192: "Nec deus intersit nisi dignus
vindici nodus / Inciderit" (Nor let a god interfere, unless a knot worthy such a
champion occurs).

 3. "Daborne, in Shakespeare's time, was a most successful playwright; so was
Jasper Maine; so was William Cartwright, the 'florid and seraphical preacher'; so
are Mr. Milman, Mr. Harness, and others of more modern days." (Forster's review
of the Rev. James White's *Earl of Gowrie,* January 3, 1846.) The Rev. William James
Harness (1790–1869) was an admirer and friend of Browning's, but there was
apparently some coolness at this time. D & K, pp. 37–38.

 4. The first two volumes of Harriet Martineau's *Forest and Game Law Tales,*
published by Moxon in December and January.

 5. Philip James Bailey (1806–1902) gained a considerable contemporary reputation with this poem, an English version of the Faust legend. It had originally been
published in 1839, but a new, enlarged edition occasioned the gift.

 6. Margaret Fuller (1810–50), the feminist and Transcendentalist author and
critic, who, as the Marchioness Ossoli, became a good friend of the Brownings.

 7. *Sibrandus Schafnaburgensis.*

 8. *As You Like It* II. 1. 13–14.

 9. Isaiah 60:8.

The envelope for Letter 191 bears no postmark or stamp; its text implies the sending of a package whose contents can be fairly certainly identified as the December 1845 issue of the English Review. *The state of the envelope is most logically accounted for by the hypothesis that the letter was an enclosure in the package. The* English Review *had printed an article dealing with both Browning and E.B.B., and with Coventry Patmore as well. A thread of evidence running through these letters seems to indicate that Browning had known of the article's forthcoming publication for over a month and that it was written by his friend Eliot Warburton. See E.B.B's question about Warburton in Letter 154, Browning's response in Letter 155, referring to " the ' Quarterly,'" and his pleasure in Letter 165 at having learned that E.B.B. would be with him in " that cold ' Quarterly,'" where he had thought to appear alone. For an account of this review, see the editorial link between Letters 192 and 193.*

191 (W93)　　　　　　　R.B. to E.B.B.

[*January 6, 1846.*]

Tuesday Morning.

I this minute receive the Review—a poor business, truly! Is there a reason for a man's wits dwindling the moment he gets into a critical High-place to hold forth?—I have only glanced over the article however. Well, oneday *I* am to write of you, dearest, and it must come to something rather better than *that!*

I am forced to send now what is to be sent at all. Bless you, dearest. I am trusting to hear from you—Your R. B.

[And I find by a note from a fairer friend and favourer of mine that in the "New Quarterly" "Mr. Browning" figures pleasantly as "one without any sympathy for a human being!"[1]—Then, for newts and efts, at all events!][2]

1. "[His] total absence of all sympathy with the efforts, wishes, and struggles of his fellow-man is a great defect in the poetry of Robert Browning." "Poetical Contrasts," *New Quarterly Review; or, Home, Foreign, and Colonial Journal* (January 1846).
2. Written across the outside of the already folded note.

192 (*W94*)   R.B. *to* E.B.B.
                        _____

[*January 6, 1846.*]

Tuesday Night.

But, my sweet, there is safer going in letters than in visits, do you
not see? In the letter, one may go to the utmost limit of one's supposed
tether without danger—there is the distance so palpably between the
most audacious step *there,* and the next . . which is no where, seeing it is
not in the letter: quite otherwise in personal intercourse, where any
indication of turning to a certain path, even, might possibly be checked
not for its own fault but lest, the path once reached and proceeded in,
some ↑other↓ forbidden turning might come into sight, we will say: in
the letter, all ended *there,* just there . . and you may think of that, and
forgive; at all events, may avoid speaking irrevocable words—and
when, as to me, those words are intensely *true, doom-words*—think,
dearest! Because, as I told you once, what most characterizes my feeling
for you is the perfect *respect* in it, the full *belief* . . (I shall get presently to
poor Robert's very avowal of "owing you all esteem"!)[1]—It is on that
I build, and am secure—for how should I know, of myself, how to serve
you and be properly yours if it all was to be learnt by my own interpreting, and what you professed to dislike you were to be considered as
wishing for, and what liking, as it seemed, you were loathing at your
heart, and if so many "noes" made a "yes," and "one refusal no rebuff"
and all that horrible bestiality which stout gentlemen turn up the whites
of their eyes to, when they rise after dinner and, pressing the right hand
to the left side say, "The toast be dear woman!" Now, love, with this
feeling in me from the beginning,—I do believe,—*now,* when I am
utterly blest in this gift of your love, and least able to imagine what I
should do without it,—I cannot but believe, I say, that had you given
me /one⟩once/ ↑a↓ "refusal"—clearly derived from your own feelings,
and quite apart from any fancied consideration for my interests,—had
this come upon me, whether slowly but inevitably in the course of
events, or suddenly as precipitated by any step of mine,—I should,
believing you, have never again renewed directly or indirectly such solici-
tation,—I should have begun to count how many other ways were yet
open to serve you and devote myself to you . . but *from the outside,* now,

and not in your livery! Now, if I should have acted thus under *any* circumstances, how could I but redouble my endeavours at precaution after my own foolish[2] . . you know, and forgave long since, and I, too, am forgiven in my own eyes, for the cause, tho' not the manner—but could I do other than keep ⟨‖ · · · ‖⟩ "farther from you" than in the letters, dearest? For your own part in that matter, seeing it with all the light you have since given me (and *then,* not inadequately by my own light) I could, I do kiss your feet, kiss every letter in your name, bless you with my whole heart and soul if I could pour them out, from me, before you, to stay and be yours,—when I think on your motives and pure perfect generosity—It was the plainness of *that* which determined me to wait and be patient and grateful and your own for ever in any shape or capacity you might please to accept. Do you think that because I am so rich now, I could not have been most rich, too, *then*—in what would seem little only to *me,* only with this great happiness? I should have been proud beyond measure & happy past all desert, to call and be allowed to see you simply, speak with you and be spoken to—what am I more than others? Don't think this mock humility—*it is not*—you take me in your mantle, and we shine together, but I know my part in it! All this is written breathlessly on a sudden fancy that you *might* . . if not now, at some future time—, give other than this, the true reason, for that discrepancy you see, that nearness in the letters, that early farness in the visits! And, love, all love is but a passionate *drawing closer*—I would be one with you, dearest,—let my soul press close to you, as my lips, dear life of my life—

 Wednesday [January 7, 1846.]/You are entirely right about those poems of Horne's—I spoke only of the effect of the first glance, and it is a principle with me to begin by welcoming any strangeness, intention of originality in men—the other way of safe copying precedents being *so* safe! So I began by praising all that was at all questionable in the form . . reserving the ground-work for after consideration. The Elf-story turns out a pure mistake, I think—and a common mistake, too. Fairy stories, the good ones, were written for men & women, and, being true, pleased also children—now, people set about writing for children and miss them and the others too,—with that detestable irreverence and plain mocking all the time at the very wonder they profess to want to excite—All obvious bending down to the lower capacity,—determining not to be the great complete man one is, by half,— ⸌any⸍ patronizing

minute to be spent in the nursery over the books and work and healthful
play, of a visitor who will presently bid goodbye and betake himself to
the Beefsteak Club—keep us from all that! The Sailor-Language is good
in its way; but as wrongly used in Art as real clay & mud would be, if
one plastered them in the foreground of a landscape in order to attain
to so much truth . . at all events—the true thing to endeavour is the
making a golden colour which shall do every good in the power of the
dirty brown—Well, then, what a veering weathercock am I, to write
so and now, *so!*—Not altogether,—for first it was but the stranger's
welcome I gave, the right of every new comer who must stand or fall
by his behavior once admitted within the door—And then—when I
know what Horne thinks of—you, dearest,—how he knew you first,
and from the soul admired you,—and how little he thinks of my good
fortune . . I *could* NOT begin by giving you a bad impression of anything
he sends—he has such very few rewards for a great deal of hard excellent
enduring work, and *none,* no reward, I do think, would he less willingly
forego than your praise and sympathy—But your opinion once expressed—truth remains the truth—so, at least, I excuse myself . . and
quite as much for what I say *now* as for what was said *then!* King John
is very fine and full of purpose . . The Noble Heart, sadly faint and un-
characteristic. The chief incident, too, turns on that poor conventional
fallacy about what constitutes a proper wrong to resist—a piece of
morality, after a different standard, is introduced to complete another
fashioned morality—a segment of a circle of larger dimensions is fitted
into a smaller one—now, you may have your own standard of morality
in this matter of resistance to wrong, how and when +if at all—+ and you
may quite understand and sympathize with quite different standards
innumerable of other people; but go from one to the other abruptly,
you cannot, I think—" Bear patiently all injuries—revenge in no case"
—that is plain. " Take what you conceive to be God's part, do his evident
work, stand up for good & destroy evil, and coöperate with this whole
scheme here"—*that* is plain, too,—but, call Otto's conduct *no* wrong,
or being one, not such as should be avenged—and then, call the remark
of a stranger that one is a "recreant"—, just what needs the slight
punishment of instant death to the remarker—and . . where is the way?
What *is* clear?

 —Not my letter! which goes on and on—" dear letters"—sweetest? because they cost all the precious labour of making out? Well, I

shall see you to-morrow, I trust—bless you, my own—I have not half said what was to say even in the letter I thought to write, and which proves only what you see! But at a thought I fly off with you, "at a cock-crow from the Grange."[3]—Ever your own.

Last night, I received a copy of the New Quarterly—now here is popular praise, a sprig of it! Instead of the attack I supposed it to be, from my foolish friend's account, the notice is outrageously eulogistical,[4] a stupidly extravagant laudation from first to last—and in *three other* articles,[5] as my sister finds by diligent fishing, they introduce my name with the same felicitous praise (except one instance, though, in a good article by Chorley I am certain)—and *with* me I don't know how many poetical *crétins* are praised as noticeably—and, in the turning of a page, somebody is abused in the richest style of scavengering—only Carlyle![6] And I love him enough not to envy him nor wish to change places, and giving him mine, mount into his—

All which, let me forget in the thoughts of to-morrow! Bless you, my Ba.

1. Browning is quoting E.B.B.'s *Bertha in the Lane* (1844), st. xix.
2. "Letter" understood; see the note before Letter 30.
3. *Lady Geraldine's Courtship,* st. xlvi.
4. Two paragraphs of the article cited in note 1 to Letter 191 will indicate how Browning was treated: "It is always refreshing to meet with the poetry of Robert Browning: we may be quite sure that we shall meet with no soundings, commonplaces, or simple drivellings; all is firm, vigorous, original, and daring. Alas! that we do not meet with the 'sensuous.' The poetry of the 'Bells and Pomegranates' wants 'flesh and blood;' wants that coming home to men's bosoms which makes the poet for the million. No! Browning is the poet of the mind. . . . He is possibly the most intellectual poet of the day; and certainly the most singular (may we say *original?*) in the treatment of his subject. . .

"One remarkable peculiarity . . . is the finish of his style. In the mechanical he was perfect from the first: his 'Paracelsus' is an astonishing performance for a poet of eighteen [*sic*]; and a little work called 'Pauline,' written and published still earlier, is full of the most wonderful writing."

This must be the first open attribution of *Pauline* to Browning and the ground of his conviction that Powell had a hand in the article (see Letter 198). This review first made E.B.B. aware of the poem's existence.

5. One is the article Browning attributes to Chorley—a review of four volumes of Irish poetry. It lists Browning, with Burns, Byron, Shelley, Coleridge, and Tennyson, as a modern Minnesinger. A review of the Rev. James White's *Earl of Gowrie* remarks that the *Edinburgh* and *Quarterly* have proclaimed "Mr. Taylor [the greatest dramatic poet of the day] to the utter confusion, no doubt, of such *scribblers*

as . . . Browning." Finally, a review of the anonymous "*My Life*. Part the First" praises it extravagantly for "pregnant thoughts," "bursts of lyrical power," and "more, in fine, of the purely grand and beautiful than any poetical work . . . for years, if we except the magnificent productions of Browning, and perhaps the lays of Tennyson."

6. A review of *Oliver Cromwell's Letters and Speeches* begins: "Mr. Carlyle visits us now but rarely, and we had hoped that the long interval . . . would have been followed by some grand mental effort, in which, although we might distrust the conclusions, and put down much to that fine phrenzy in which he utters his fragmental notices, yet we trusted that longer time would have chastened his excesses, purified his style, subdued extravagant hypotheses, and, at least, have brought him out of the almost bedlamite ravings in which he indulged in the 'Hero Worship.'"

E.B.B.'s following letter is an extended commentary on Warburton's article in the English Review, *with which Browning had sent Letter 191, and can best be understood in the light of a brief summary of it augmented by later notes on particular details. The article was a review of* "Poems London *1833–44 By Miss* BARRETT," "Paracelsus, and other Poems. London, *1835–45. By* ROBERT BROWNING," *and* "Poems London, *1845. By* COVENTRY PATMORE."

The article opens with a discussion of the "un-poetical" nature of the age. The writer feels that the poets—by virtue of their lack of "universality" and clarity—are responsible for the state of affairs, rather than the public. "Milnes, DeVere, and Robert Browning, for example, have too frequently preferred to glimmer as nebulae, rather than to shine as stars." Then follows about nine and a half pages of comment on E.B.B.'s 1838 and 1844 collections. "As Christian, poet, woman, scholar, this lady has done justice to each attribute; her versification is varied and harmonious; her imagination powerful, if not always well controlled; her arrangement is generally artistic; and over and through all her works there is a classic spirit not a little uncommon in authors of her sex: her scholarship, solid and genuine, can defy the charge of female pedantry." The reviewer praises the imaginative conception of such poems as The Seraphim *(1838) but turns "with some sensation of relief to the more human poems," his favorite being* Isobel's Child *(1838). The* Poet's Vow *(also 1838) and a* Vision of Poets *(1844) have "many Tennysonian faults and graces," and the* Drama of Exile *(1844) something of both Shelley's power and his obscurity.*

There is an interesting transition to Browning: " And now we must leave Miss Barrett for Robert Browning. We do so with somewhat of the sensation experienced in issuing from a cathedral into the open air: the one consecrated all over, its atmosphere incense—its sounds, chants—its solemn glooms only lighted through the painted effigies of saint or angel:—the other nature's own wide temple,—fresh, genial, invigorating, and free.

" Mr. Browning unites within himself more of the elements of a true poet than perhaps any other of those whom we call 'modern' amongst us ; yet there are few writers so little read, so partially understood. He came into the literary forum in such a mysterious guise, (that Paracelsus of his,) and carried his great gifts about him with such a careless air, that men took but little notice of the unostentatious stranger." Paracelsus, the writer thinks, is almost as obscure as its subject, yet its diction is remarkably simple, the style has " nobleness, energy, and polish," and the " delicate delineation of character" is even more remarkable. Sordello is dismissed as a puzzle. The best of Browning's work is declared to be in the various number of Bells and Pomegranates (whose riddling title the reviewer regrets): " They abound in almost every variety of composition, from the most stately tragic to the airiest lyric . . . [the] two lyrical numbers (three and seven) would and will alone vindicate his fame . . . . If he copies at all, he does so from the early fathers of our poetry, which lends a dignity, and yet a freshness to his style, that is too rare amongst us now."

193 (W99°)   *E.B.B. to R.B.*

[January 7, 1846.]

Wednesday.

But some things are indeed said very truly, & as I like to read them —of *you,* I mean of course,—though I quite understand that it is doing no manner of good to go back so to Paracelsus, heading the article 'Paracelsus & other poems,' as if the other poems could not front the reader broadly by a divine right of their own. Paracelsus is a great work & will *live,* but the way to do you good with the stiffnecked public (such good as critics can do in their degree) w^d have been to hold fast & conspicuously the gilded horn of the last living crowned creature led by you to the altar, saying 'Look HERE.' What had he to do else, as a critic? Was he writing for the Retrospective Review?[1] And then, no attempt at analytical criticism—or ↑a↓ failure, at the least attempt!—all slack & in sentences! Still there are right things true things, worthy things, said of you as a poet, though your poems do not find justice: & I like, for my own part, the issuing from my cathedral into your great world . . the outermost temple of divinest consecration—I like that figure & association, & none the worse for its being a sufficient refutation of what he dared to impute, of your poetical sectarianism,[2] in another place— *yours!!*

For me, it is all quite kind enough—only I object, on my own part also, to being reviewed in the *Seraphim,* when my better books are nearer: & also it always makes me a little savage when people talk of Tennysonianisms!—I have faults enough as the Muses know . . but let them be *my* faults!—When I wrote the 'Romaunt of Margret,' I had not read a line of Tennyson. I came from the country with my eyes only half open, & he had not penetrated where I had been living & sleeping: & in fact when I afterwards tried to reach him here in London, nothing c^d be found except one slim volume, so that, till the collected works appeared . . favente Moxon,[3] . . I was ignorant of his best *early* productions ⟨even⟩; and not even for the rhythmetical form of my Vision of the Poets, was I indebted to the Two Voices,—three pages of my Vision having been written several years ago . . at the beginning of my illness . . & thrown aside, & taken up again in the spring of 1844. Ah, well!— there's no use talking!—In a solitary review which noticed my Essay on Mind,[4] somebody wrote . . 'this young lady imitates Darwin'—& I never could *read* Darwin, . . was stopped always on the second page of the 'Loves of the Plants' when I tried to read him /as⟩to/ ⟨‖ · · · ‖⟩ 'justify myself in having an opinion'—the repulsion was too strong. Yet the " young lady imitated Darwin" of course, as the infallible critic said so—

And who are Mr. Helps & Miss Emma Fisher[5] & the 'many others,' whose company brings one down to the right plebeianism?—The 'three poets in three distant ages born'[6] may well stare amazed!

After all you shall not by any means say that I upset the inkstand on your review in a passion—because pray mark that the ink has over-run some of your praises, & that if I had been angry to the overthrow of an inkstand, it would not have been *precisely there*. It is the second book spoilt by me within these two days—& my fingers were so dabbled in blackness yesterday that to wring my hands w^d only have made matters worse. Holding them up to Mr. Kenyon they looked dirty enough to befit a poetess—as black 'as bard beseemed'[7]—& he took the review away with him to read and save it from more harm.

How could it be that you did not get my letter which would have reached you, I thought, on monday evening, or on tuesday at the very very earliest?—and how is it that I did not hear from you last night again when I was unreasonable enough to expect it? is it true that you *hate* writing to me?

At that word, comes the review back from dear Mr. Kenyon, & the letter which I enclose[8] to show you how it accounts reasonably for the ink—I did it 'in a pet,' he thinks!—And I ought to buy you a new book . . certainly I ought—only it is not worth doing justice for . . & I shall therefore send it back to you spoilt as it is,—and you must forgive me as magnanimously as you can.

'Omne ignotum pro magnifico'[9] . . do you think *so?* I hope not indeed! *vo guizzando*[10] . . & everything else that I ought to do—except of course, *that* thinking of you which is so difficult.

May God bless you. Till to-morrow!——

Your own always——

Mr. Kenyon refers to Festus—of which I had said that the fine things were worth looking for, the design manqué.

1. See Letter 180, note 1.

2. The only evident imputation of the kind is placing Browning among "those whom we call modern."

3. "With Moxon's help." E.B.B.'s word is the one Romans used for the gods.

4. The *Eclectic Review* thought her style too much like Pope's and Erasmus Darwin's (Gardner B. Taplin, *The Life of Elizabeth Barrett Browning* [New Haven: Yale University Press, 1957], p. 14). Charles Darwin's grandfather and his precursor in evolutionary theory (1731–1802) wrote very respectable natural history in very bad heroic couplets. There was at least one other review; the *Literary Gazette* of July 15, 1826, compared her favorably with Akenside. In addition, *La Belle Asemblée* for August of the same year (p. 85) devoted two disapproving sentences to the poem.

5. "Notwithstanding its unpoetical reputation, perhaps no country or period can produce such a number of living poets as our own," said the *English Review* article, and gave an extensive list including these two: Helps, later Sir Arthur (1813–75), had by 1845 written two mediocre plays, some liberal essays on labor, and an aphoristic poem, *Thoughts in the Crowd and Cloister*. Miss Fisher seems swallowed up in total anonymity.

6. Dryden, *Lines Under the Portrait of Milton*.

7. Thomson, *Castle of Indolence*, Bk. I, st. lxviii.

8. No longer with the letters.

9. Tacitus, *Agricola*, 30: "Everything unknown is supposed magnificent."

10. "I am darting about." The verb is Browning's, Letter 189.

On the envelope of Letter 193 Browning logged the visit which intervened at this point :

+Thursday Jan. 8 '46
3–5 p.m. (39)

194 (W100°)   E.B.B. to R.B.

[*January 9, 1846.*]

Friday morning.
You never think, ever dearest, that I ' repent'—why what a word to use!—You never could *think* such a word for a moment! If you were to leave me even, . . to decide that it is best for you to do it, & do it, . . I should accede at once of course, but never should I nor could I ' repent' . . regret anything . . be sorry for having known you and loved you . . no! Which I say simply to prove that, in *no* extreme case, could I repent for my own sake—For yours, it might be different—

Not out of ' generosity' certainly, but from the veriest selfishness, I choose here, before God, any possible present evil, rather ＋than＋ the future consciousness of feeling myself less to you, on the whole, than another woman might have been.

Oh, these vain & most heathenish repetitions!—do I not vex you by them, *you* whom I would always please, & never vex?—Yet they force their way because you are the best noblest & dearest in the world, & because your happiness is so precious a thing.

Cloth of frieze, be not too bold,
Though thou'rt matched with cloth of gold!—[1]
. . that, beloved, was written for *me*. And you, if you would make me happy, . . *always* will look at yourself from my ground & by my light, as I see you, & consent to be selfish in all things. Observe, that if I were *vacillating,* I sh^{d} not be so weak as to teaze you with the process of the vacillation: I should wait till my pendulum ceased swinging. It is precisely because I am your own, past any retraction or wish of retraction, . . because I belong to you by gift & ownership, & am ready & willing to prove it before the world at a word of yours, . . it is precisely for this, that I remind you too often of the necessity of using this right of yours,

not to your injury . . of being wise & strong for both of us, & of guarding your happiness which is mine—I have said these things ninety & nine times over, & over & over have you replied to them, . . as yesterday! . . & now, do not speak any more. It is only my preachment for general use, & not for particular application,—only to be *ready* for application. I love you from the deepest of my nature—the whole world is nothing to me beside you—& what is so precious, is not far from being terrible. "How *dreadful* is this place."[2]

To hear you talk yesterday, is a gladness in the thought for to-day, . . it was with such a full assent that I listened to every word. It is true, I think, that we see things (things apart from ourselves) under the same aspect & colour—and it is certainly true that I have a sort of instinct by which I seem to know your views of such subjects as we have never looked at together. I know *you* so well (yes, I boast to myself of that intimate knowledge) that I seem to know also the *idola*[3] of all things as they are in your eyes—so that never, scarcely, I am curious, . . never anxious, to learn what your opinions may be—Now, HAVE I been curious or anxious? It was enough for me to know *you*.

More than enough! You have "left undone" . . do you say?—On the contrary, you have done too much,—you *are* too much—My cup, . . which used to hold ˄at the bottom of it˅ just the drop of Heaven dew mingling with the absinthus, . . has overflowed all this wine—& *that* makes me look out for the vases, which would have held it better, had you stretched out your hand for them.

Say how you are . . & do take care & exercise—& write to me, dearest!

Ever your own—
Ba

How right you are about Ben Capstan,—and the illustration by the *yellow clay*. That is precisely what I meant . . said with more precision than I could say it. Art without an ideal is neither nature nor art. The ⟨whole⟩ question involves the whole difference between Madame Tussaud and Phidias.

I have just received Mr. Edgar Poe's book—& I see that the deteriorating preface which was to have saved me from the vanity-fever produceable by the dedication, is cut down & away—perhaps in this particular copy only!—

Tuesday is so near, as men count, that I caught myself just now being afraid lest the week should have no chance of appearing long to you!—Try to let it be long to you—will you? My consistency is wonderful.

1. Not identified; but cf. *Aurora Leigh*, IV, 538–539.
2. Genesis 28:17: Jacob awaking from his dream.
3. "Images."

The envelope of the following letter is not stamped or postmarked, since it was enclosed in a parcel containing the New Quarterly Review *for January 1846, referred to in the letter's second sentence and already alluded to and quoted in Letters 191 and 192 and in their notes. Browning's reluctance to let E.B.B. see the* Review *is probably attributable primarily to the fact that it disclosed the existence of* Pauline, *about which he suffered from extreme diffidence, and perhaps secondarily to his distaste for Powell, one of the magazine's proprietors.*

195 (W95)   R.B. to E.B.B.

[*January 9, 1846.*]

Friday Mᵍ
/Can⟩As if/ I could deny you anything!—Here is the Review—indeed it was foolish to mind your seeing it at all—But now, may I stipulate?—You shall not send it back—but on your table I shall find and take it next Tuesday—*c'est convenu!* The other precious volume[1] has not come to hand (nor to foot—) all thro' your being so sure that to carry it home would have been the death of me last evening!

I cannot write my feelings in this large writing, begun on such a scale for the Reviews' sake—and just now . . there is no denying it . . and spite of all I have been incredulous about . . it does seem that the feat *is* achieved and that I DO love you, plainly, surely, more than ever, more than any day in my life before—It is your secret, the why, the how,—the experience is mine: what are you doing to me?—in the heart's heart—

Rest—dearest—bless you—

1. The *English Review;* see Letter 193 and the note preceding it.

196 (*W101°*) *E.B.B. to R.B.*

[*January 10, 1846.*]

Saturday.

Kindest & dearest you are!—that is "my secret" and for the others, I leave them to you!—only it is no secret that I should & must be glad to have the words you sent with the book,—which I should have seen at all events, be sure, whether you had sent it or not—Should I not, do you think?—And considering what the present generation of critics really is, the remarks on you may stand, although it is the dreariest impotency to complain of the want of flesh & blood & of human sympathy in general. Yet suffer them to say on—it is the stamp on the critical knife. There must be something eminently stupid, or farewell criticdom! And if anything more utterly untrue could be said than another, it is precisely that saying, which Mr. Mackay stands up to catch the reversion of!—Do you indeed suppose that Heraud could have done this?[1] I scarcely can believe it, though some things are said rightly as about the 'intellectuality,' & how you stand first by the brain,—which is as true as truth can be. Then, I *shall have 'Pauline' in a day or two*—yes, I shall & must . . & *will* . .

The 'Ballad Poems & Fancies,' the article calling itself by that name, seems indeed to be Mr. Chorley's, & is one of his very best papers, I think. There is to me a want of colour & thinness about his writings in general, with a grace & savoir faire nevertheless, & ↑always↓ a rightness & purity of intention—Observe what he says of 'many-sidedness' seeming to trench on opinion & principle. That, he means for himself I know, for he has said to me that through having such largeness of sympathy he has been charged with want of principle—yet 'many-sidedness' is certainly no word for him. The effect of ⟨wide⟩ ↑general↓ sympathies may be evolved both from an elastic fancy & from breadth of mind, & it seems to me that he rather *bends* to a phase of ⟨‖ · · · ‖⟩ ↑humanity & literature↓ than contains it . . than comprehends it. Every part of a truth implies the whole; & to accept truth all round, does not mean the recognition of contradictory things: universal sympathies cannot make a man inconsistent, but, on the contrary, sublimely consistent—A church tower may stand between the mountains and the sea, looking to either, & stand fast: but the willowtree at the gable-end, blown now toward the north & now toward the south while its natural leaning is due east or west, is different altogether . . *as* different as a willowtree from a church tower.

Ah, what nonsense!—There is only one truth for me all this time, while I talk about truth & truth. And do you know, when you have told me to think of you, I have been feeling ashamed of thinking of you so much, of thinking of only you——which *is* too much, perhaps. Shall I tell you?—it seems to me, to myself, that no man was ever before to any woman what you are to me—the fulness must be in proportion, you know, to the vacancy . . & only *I* know what was behind . . the long wilderness *without* the footstep, . . without the blossoming rose . . and the capacity for happiness, like a black gaping hole, before this silver flooding. Is it wonderful that I should stand as in a dream, & disbelieve . . not *you*—but my own fate? Was ever any one taken suddenly from a lampless dungeon & placed upon the pinnacle of a mountain, without the head turning round & the heart turning faint, as mine do?—And you love me *more*, you say?— Shall I thank you or God?—Both, . . indeed—& there is no possible return from me to either of you!—I thank you as the unworthy may . . & as we all thank God. How shall I ever prove what my heart is to you? how will you ever see it as I feel it? I ask myself in vain.

Have so much faith in me, my only beloved, as to use me simply for your own advantage & happiness, & to your own ends without a thought of any others—*that* is all I could ask you with any disquiet as to the granting of it—May God bless you!—

Your Ba

But you have the review *now*—surely?

The Morning Chronicle attributes the authorship of 'Modern Poets' (*our* article) to Lord John Manners[2]—so I hear this morning. I have not yet looked at the paper myself. The Athenæum, still abominably dumb!—

1. Charles Mackay (1814–89) was a Scots journalist, editor of the Glasgow *Arms,* and the volume being reviewed was his first. The article cited in note 1 to Letter 191 contrasts Browning and Mackay on the point of sympathy noted there and also because "[Mackay's] verses are light, elegant, graceful, and intelligible; you have no

rough, Herculean thoughts [such as] jostle you in every page of 'Bells and Pomegranates,' no burning madnesses . . . which you . . . read over and over again, sometimes to reduce to an intelligible shape [or] to feel its full galvanic shock . . . here all is elegant repose."

James Abraham Heraud (1799–1887) was a not very successful poet and dramatist and editor of various periodicals in the course of his career. In 1846 he was literary critic for the *Athenæum*.

2. "The first article [in the *English Review*] 'On Modern English Poets,' is such a one as Lord John Manners might write; for it abounds with those frank admissions and commonsense notions which his lordship associates with his chivalric and sentimental affection for the past." *Morning Chronicle*, January 10, 1846. John James, Lord Manners, seventh Duke of Rutland (1818–1906), was a political disciple of Disraeli's and a minor poet. Browning seems to have had direct knowledge that the review was by Eliot Warburton (Letter 165 and its note 1).

197 *(W96)*   *R.B. to E.B.B.*

[*January 10, 1846.*]

Saturday.

This is *no* letter—love,—I make haste to tell you—tomorrow I will write: for here has a friend been calling and consuming my very destined time, and every minute seemed the last that was to be,—and an old, old friend he is, beside—so—you must understand my defection, when only this scrap reaches you to-night!—Ah, love,—you are my unutterable blessing,—I discover you, more of you, day by day,—hour by hour, I do think!——I am entirely yours,—one gratitude, all my soul becomes when I see you over me as now—God bless my dear, dearest.

My "Act Fourth"[1] is done—but too roughly this time! I will tell you—

One kiss more, dearest!

Thanks for the Review.

1. Of *Luria*.

198 *(W97)*   *R.B. to E.B.B.*

———————————

[*January 11, 1846.*]

Sunday.

I have no words for you, my dearest,—I shall never have—

You are mine, I am yours. Now, here is one sign of what I said:
that I must love you more than at first . . a little sign, and to be looked
narrowly for or it escapes me, but then the increase it shows *can* only be
little, so very little now—and as the fine French Chemical Analysts
bring themselves to appreciate matter in its refined stages by *millionths,*
so—! At first I only thought of being *happy* in you,—in your happiness:
now I most think of you in the dark hours that must come—I shall grow
old with you, and die with you—as far as I can look into the night I see
the light with me: and surely with that provision of comfort one should
turn with fresh joy and renewed sense of security to the sunny middle
of the day,—I am in the full sunshine now,—and *after*, all seems cared
for—is it too homely an illustration if I say the day's visit is not crossed
by uncertainties as to the return thro' the wild country at nightfall?—
Now Keats speaks of 'Beauty, that *must* die—and Joy whose hand is
ever at his lips, bidding farewell.'[1] And *who* spoke of—looking up into
the eyes and asking "And *how long* will you love us"?[2]—There is a
Beauty that will not die, a Joy that bids no farewell, dear dearest eyes
that will love for ever!

And *I*—am to love no longer than I can—Well, dear—and when I
can no longer—you will not blame me?—You will do only as ever,
kindly and justly; hardly more: I do not pretend to say I have chosen
to put my fancy to such an experiment, and consider how *that* is to
happen, and what measures ought to be taken in the emergency—because in the "universality of my sympathies" I certainly number a very
lively one with my own heart and soul, and cannot amuse myself by
such a spectacle as their ↑supposed↓ extinction or paralysis—there is no
doubt I should be an object for the deepest commiseration of you or any
more fortunate human being:—and I hope that because such a calamity
does not obtrude itself on me as a thing to be prayed against, it is
↑no less↓ duly implied with all the other visitations from which no
humanity can be altogether exempt—just as God bids us ask for the

continuance of the "daily bread"—"battle, murder and sudden death"
lie behind doubtless—I repeat, and perhaps in so doing, only give one
more example of the instantaneous conversion of that indignation we
bestow in another's case, into wonderful lenity when it becomes our
own, . . that I only contemplate the *possibility* you make me recognize,
with pity, and fear . . no anger at all,—and imprecations of vengeance,
for what?—Observe, I only speak of cases *possible;* of sudden impotency
of mind; that *is* possible——there *are* other ways of "*changing,*" "ceasing to love" &c. which it is safest not to think of nor believe in. A man
may never leave his writing desk without seeing safe in one corner of it
the folded slip which directs the disposal of his papers in the event of
his reason suddenly leaving him—or he may never go out into the street
without a card in his pocket to signify his address to those who may
have to pick him up in an apoplectic fit—but if he once begins to fear
he is growing a glass bottle, and, *so*, liable to be smashed,—do you see?
And now, love, dear heart of my heart, my own, only Ba—see no more
—see what I *am*, what God in his constant mercy ordinarily grants to
those who have, as I, received already so much,—much, past expression!
It is but . . if you will so please . . at worst, forestalling the one or two
years, for my sake; but you *will* be as sure of me *one* day as I can be now
of myself—and why not *now* be sure? See, love—a year is gone by—
we were in one relation when you wrote at the end of a letter "Do not
say I do not tire you" (by writing)—"*I am sure I do.*"[3] A year has gone
by—*Did you tire me then? Now,* you tell me what is told; for my sake,
sweet, let the few years go by,—we are married, and my arms are round
you, and my face touches yours, and I am asking you, "*Were you not
to me*, in that dim beginning of 1846, a joy behind all joys, a life added
to and transforming mine, the good I choose from all the possible gifts
of God on this earth, for which I seemed to have lived; which accepting,
I thankfully step aside and let the rest get what they can; what, it is very
likely, they esteem more—for why should my eye be evil because God's
is good,—why should I grudge that, giving them, I do believe, infinitely
less, he gives them a content in the inferior good and belief in its worth—
I should have wished *that* further concession, that illusion as I believe it,
for their sakes—but I cannot undervalue my own treasure and so scant
the only tribute of mere gratitude which is in my power to pay."—Hear
this said *now before* the few years, and believe in it *now, for then,* dearest!

Must you see "Pauline"? A least then let me wait a few days,—
to correct the misprints which affect the sense, and to write you the
history of it;[4] what is necessary you should know before you see it.
That article I suppose to be by Heraud . . about two thirds . . and the
rest, ⟨‖ · · · ‖⟩ a little less—by that Mr. Powell—whose unimaginable,
impudent vulgar stupidity you get some inkling of in the "Story from
Boccaccio"[5]—of which the *words* quoted were *his,* I am sure—as sure
as that he knows not whether Boccaccio lived before or after Shakspeare,
whether Florence or Rome be the more northern city,—one word of
Italian in general, or letter of Boccaccio's in particular.—When I took
pity on him once on a time and helped his verses into a sort of grammar
and sense, I did not think he was a *buyer* of other men's verses, to be
printed as his own,—thus he *bought* two modernizations of Chaucer—
"Ugolino" & another story from Leigh Hunt . . and one, "Sir Thopas"
from Horne . . and printed them as his own,[6] as I learned only last week:
he paid me extravagant court and, seeing no harm in the mere folly of
the man, I was on good terms with him—till ten months ago he grossly
insulted a friend of mine who had written an article for the Review[7]—
(which is as good as *his,* he being a large proprietor of the delectable
property, and influencing the voices of his co-mates in council)—well,
he insulted my friend, who had written that article at my special solici-
tation, and did all he could to avoid paying the price of it—Why?—
Because the poor creature had actually taken the article to the Editor *as
one by his friend Serjt Talfourd contributed for pure love of him, Powell the
aforesaid,*—cutting, in consequence, no inglorious figure in the eyes of
Printer & Publisher! Now I was away all this time in Italy or he would
never have ventured on such a piece of childish impertinence: and my
friend being a true gentleman, and quite unused to this sort of "practice," in the American sense, held his peace and went without his
"honorarium"—But on my return, I enquired—and made him make
a proper application—which Mr. Powell treated with all the insolence
in the world . . because, as the event showed, the having to write a
cheque for "the Author of *the* Article"—that author's name *not* being
Talfourd's . . *there* was certain disgrace! Since then (ten months ago) I
have never seen him—and he accuses *himself,* observe, of "sucking my
plots while I drink his tea"[8]—one as much as the other! And now why
do I tell you this, all of it? Ah,—now you shall hear! Because, it has
often been in my mind to ask you what YOU know of this Mr. Powell,

or ever knew : for he, (being profoundly versed in every sort of untruth, as every fresh experience shows me, and the rest of his acquaintance—) he told me long ago, "he used to correspond with you, and that he quarrelled with you"—which I supposed to mean—that he began by sending you his books (as with one and everybody)—and that, in return to your note of acknowledgement, he had chosen to write again, and perhaps, again—is it so? Do not write one word in answer to me—the name of such a miserable nullity, and husk of a man, ought not to have a place in your letters . . and *that way* he would get near to me again—, near indeed this time!—So *tell* me, in a word—or do not tell me.

How I never say what I sit down to say! How saying the little makes me want to say the more! How the least of little things, once taken up as a thing to be imparted to you, seems to need explanations and commentaries,—all is of importance to me—every breath you breathe, every little fact (like this) you are to know!

I was out last night—to see the rest of Frank Talfourd's theatricals[9]—, and met Dickens and his set—so my evenings go away! If I do not bring the *Act* you must forgive me—yet I shall . . I think; the roughness matters little in this stage—Chorley says very truly that a tragedy implies as much power *kept back* as brought out—very true that is—I do not, on the whole, feel dissatisfied . . as was to be but expected . . with the effect of this last[10]—the *shelve* of the hill, whence the end is seen, you continuing to go down to it . . so that at the very last you may pass off into a plain and so away—not come to a stop like your horse against a church wall. It is all in long speeches—the *action, proper*, is in them— they are no descriptions, or amplifications—but here . . in a drama of this kind, all the *events*, (and interest), take place in the *minds* of the actors . . somewhat like Paracelsus in that respect: you know, or don't know, that the general charge against me, of late, from the few quarters I thought it worth while to listen to, has been that of abrupt, spasmodic writing—they will find some fault with this, of course.

How you know Chorley! That is precisely the man, that willow blowing now here now there—precisely! I wish he minded the Athenæum, its silence or eloquence, no more nor less than I—but he goes on painfully plying me with invitation after invitation, only to show me, I feel confident, that *he* has no part nor lot in the matter : I have *two* kind little notes asking me to go on Thursday & Saturday . . See the absurd position of us both; he asks more of my presence than he can want, just to show his own kind feeling, of which I do not doubt, —and I must try and accept more hospitality than suits me, only to prove my belief in that same! For myself—if I have vanity which such Journals can raise; would the praise of them raise it, they who praised Mr. Mackay's own, own Dead Pan,[11] quite his own, the other day? (—By the way, Miss Cushman informed me the other evening that the gentleman had written a certain 'Song of the Bell' . . "singularly like Schiller's; *considering that Mr. M. had never* seen it!" I am told he writes for the Athenæum, but don't know)—would that sort of praise be flattering, or his holding the tongue—which Forster, deep in the mysteries of the craft, corroborated my own notion about—as pure willingness to hurt, and confessed impotence and little clever spite, and enforced sense of what may be safe at the last— You shall see they will not notice . . unless a fresh publication alters the circumstances—⟨‖ · · · ‖⟩ ↑until↓ some seven or eight months—as before; and then they *will* notice, and *praise*, and tell anybody who cares to enquire, "*So* we noticed the work." So do not you go expecting justice or injustice till I tell you: it amuses me to be found writing so, so anxious to prove I understand the laws of the game, when that game is only "Thimble-rig" and for prizes of gingerbread-nuts—Prize or no prize, Mr. Dilke *does* shift the pea, and so did from the beginning—as Charles Lamb's pleasant *soubriquet*—(Mr. *Bilk*, he would have it)—testifies.[12] Still he behaved kindly to that poor Frances Brown[13]—let us forget him.

And now, my Audience, my crown-bearer, my path-preparer—I am with you again and out of them all—there, *here*, in my arms, is my *proved palpable success!*—My life, my poetry,—gained nothing, oh no! —but this found them, and blessed them. On Tuesday I shall see you, dearest—I am much better; well to-day—are you well—or "scarcely to be called an invalid"? Oh, when I *have* you, am by you—

Bless you, dearest—And be very sure you have your wish about the length of the week—still Tuesday must come! And with it your own, happy, grateful R. B.

1. *Ode on Melancholy*, ll. 21–23.
2. Not identified; perhaps a reference to a remark at one of the meetings.
3. Letter 4.
4. See Letter 207 and its note 5.
5. Among the eight works reviewed in the *New Quarterly* article (Letter 191, note 1) was an anonymous *Stories from Boccaccio*. For the "*words* quoted," see note 8, below.

6. *Poems of Geoffrey Chaucer, Modernized* (London, 1841) was published under Horne's editorship with contributions from E.B.B., Wordsworth, Hunt, and Powell. *Sir Thopas* carried the initials "Z.A.Z" there but was republished in Powell's 1842 *Poems*. His other contributions are signed.

7. This was probably Joseph Arnould, for whom Browning arranged publication of an article in the *New Quarterly* in January 1845. W. H. Griffin, "Early Friends of Robert Browning," *Contemporary Review*, LXXXVII (March 1905), 429.

8. The *New Quarterly* quoted some lines from the first canto of "The Abbot of Florence" in *Stories from Boccaccio*:

> At four years I began to poetise,
>> And spoke Pindaric odes on 'odds or evens:'
> When I was seven I wrote two comedies,
>> So full of fun all thought them writ by Stephens;
> Jones likened them to Powell's tragedies,
>> Which are made up of Horne's and Browning's leavings;
> For he, I'm told, asks dramatists to tea,
>> And sucks their plots as they suck his Bohea!

9. Serjeant Talfourd's son Francis (1828–62) was later known as the writer of numerous burlesques and travesties.

10. The fourth act of *Luria*.

11. "That Mr. Mackay's volume will avail to dissipate [public indifference to poetry], we cannot hope; but that he has genius capable of better things than the majority of pieces it contains, we need no other proof than his poem 'The Death of Pan,' which has the true heroic ring in its blank verse, and indicates power both to perceive and in a degree to realize the presence of the sublime." *Athenæum*, August 2, 1845. Mackay's poem was based on the same legend as E.B.B..s *The Dead Pan* (1844) but had appeared in *Hood's Magazine* four months before her poem was published, so that Browning's implication is mistaken.

12. Charles Wentworth Dilke (1789–1864), antiquary and critic and friend of Keats and Leigh Hunt, joined the *Athenæum* staff in 1829 and assumed control of the paper the next year. Though Lamb is on record with several uncomplimentary remarks about Dilke, this one must have been relayed verbally by one of Browning's several friends who had been close to Lamb.

13. A self-taught blind poetess from Stranorlar, County Donegal, who had sent Dilke some poems, requesting the *Athenæum* in return. Thereafter she became a quite successful minor poet, regularly printed in the journals, and in 1844 Lady Peel granted her a pension of £20 a year.

A visit at this point is recorded on the envelope of Letter 196:
+Tuesday Jany 13—'46
$3\frac{1}{2}$–$5\frac{1}{2}$ p.m. (40)

199 *(W102°)*   *E.B.B. to R.B.*

[*January 13, 1846.*]

Tuesday Night.

Ah Mr. Kenyon!—how he vexed me to-day. To keep away all the
ten days before, & to come just at the wrong time after all!—It was
better for you . . I suppose . . I believe . . to go with him down stairs—
yes, it certainly was better: it was disagreeable enough to be very wise!
Yet I, being addicted to every sort of superstition turning to melancholy, did hate so breaking off in the middle of that black thread . .
(do you remember what we were talking of when they opened the
door?) that I was on the point of saying "Stay one moment," which
I should have repented afterwards for the best of good reasons. Oh, I
should have liked to have 'fastened off' that black thread, and taken
one stitch with a blue or a green one!—

You do not remember what we were talking of? what *you*, rather,
were talking of?—And what *I* remember, at least, because it is exactly
the most unkind & hard thing you ever said to me . . ever dearest, so I
remember it by that sign!—That you should say such a thing to me—!
think what it was, for indeed I will not write it down here—it would be
worse than Mr. Powell! Only the foolishness of it (I mean, the foolishness of it alone) saves it, smooths it to a degree!—the foolishness being
the same as if you asked a man where he would walk when he lost his
head. Why, if you had asked St. Denis *beforehand,* he would have thought
it a foolish question.[1]

And you!—you, who talk so finely of never, never doubting,—
of being such an example in the way of believing & trusting—it appears,
after all, that you have an imagination apprehensive (or comprehensive)
of "glass bottles" like other sublunary creatures, & worse than some of
them. For mark, that I never went any farther than to the stone-wall-
hypothesis of your forgetting me!—*I* always stopped there—& never
climbed to the top of it over the broken-bottle fortification, to see which
way you meant to walk afterwards. And you, to ask me so coolly—
think what you asked me. That you should have the heart to ask such a
question!—

And the reason—! and it could seem a reasonable matter of doubt to you whether I would go to the south for my health's sake!—And I answered quite a common 'no' I believe—for you bewildered me for the moment—& I have had tears in my eyes two or three times since, just through thinking back /of⟩on/ it all . . of your asking me such questions. Now did I not tell you when I first knew you, that I was leaning out of the window?² True, *that* was—I was tired of living . . unaffectedly tired. All I cared to live for was to do better some of the work which, after all, was out of myself, and which I had to reach across to do. But I told you. Then, last year . . for duty's sake I would have *consented* ⟨perhaps⟩ to go to Italy!—but if you really fancy that I /should⟩would/ have struggled in the face of all that ↑difficulty↓—or struggled, indeed, anywise, to compass such an object as *that* . . except for the motive of your caring for it & me . . why you know nothing of me after all—nothing!—And now, take away the motive . . & I am where I was—leaning out of the window again. To put it in plainer words . . (as you really require information), I should let them do ↑what↓ they liked to me till I was dead—only I *wouldn't go to Italy* . . if anybody proposed Italy out of contradiction. In the meantime I do entreat you never to talk of such a thing to me any more.

You know, if you were to leave me by your choice & for your happiness, it would be another thing. It would be very lawful to talk of *that*.

& observe!—I perfectly understand that you did not think of *doubting me*—so to speak!—But you thought, all the same, that if such a thing happened, I should be capable of doing so & so.

Well—I am not quarrelling—I am uneasy about your head rather. That pain in it . . what can it mean? I do beseech you to think of me just so much as will lead you to take regular exercise every day, never missing a day,—since to walk till you are tired on tuesday & then not to walk ↑at all↓ until friday is *not* taking exercise, nor the thing required. Ah, if you knew how dreadfully natural every sort of evil seems to my mind, you would not laugh at me for being afraid. I do beseech you . . dearest!—And then, Sir John Hanmer invited you, besides Mr. Warburton . . & suppose you went to *him* for a very little time . . just for the change of air?—or if you went to the coast somewhere. Will you consider, & do what is right, *for me?* I do not propose that you should go to Italy, observe, nor any great thing at which you might reasonably hesitate. And . . did you ever try smoking as a remedy?—If the nerves of the head ⟨are⟩ chiefly ↑are↓ affected it might do you good, I have been thinking—Or without the smoking, to breathe where tobacco is burnt, —*that* calms the nervous system in a wonderful manner, as I experienced once myself when, recovering from an illness, I could not sleep, & tried in vain all sorts of narcotics & forms of hop-pillow & inhalation, yet was tranquillized in one half hour by a *pinch* of *tobacco* being burnt in a shovel near me. Should you mind it very much? the trying I mean?

Wednesday [January 14].—For '*Pauline*' . . when I had named it to you I was on the point of sending for the book to the booksellers—then suddenly I thought to myself that I should wait & hear whether you very, very much would dislike my reading it—See now! Many readers have done virtuously, but ⟨until⟩ I, (in this virtue I tell you of) surpassed them all!—And now, because I may, I "*must* read it"—: & as there are misprints to be corrected, will you do what is necessary, or what you think is necessary, & bring me the book on Monday? Do not send—bring it,—!—In the meanwhile I send back the review[3] which I forgot to give you yesterday in the confusion—Perhaps you have not read it in your house, & in any case there is no use in my keeping it . .

Shall I hear from you, I wonder! Oh my vain thoughts, that will not keep you well!—And, ever since you have known me, you have been worse—*that*, you confess!—& what if it should be the crossing of my bad star? *You* of the 'Crown' and the 'Lyre,'[4] to seek the influences from the 'chair of Cassiopeia'!!—I hope she will forgive me for using her name so!—I might as well have compared her to a professorship of poetry in the university of Oxford, according to the latest election.[5] You know, the qualification there, is, . . . *not to be a poet.*

How vexatious, yesterday: the stars (talking of *them*) were out of spherical tune, . . through the damp weather, perhaps—and that scarlet sun was a sign!—First, Mr. Chorley!—& last, dear Mr. Kenyon; who *will* say tiresome things without any provocation. Did you walk with him his way, or did he walk with you yours? or did you only walk down stairs together?

Write to me!—Remember that it is a month to Monday. Think of your very own, who bids God bless you when she prays for herself!—

E. B. B.

Say particularly how you are—now do not omit it. And will you have Miss Martineau's books[6] when I can lend them to you? Just at this moment I *dare* not, because they are reading them here.

Let Mr. Mackay have his full proprietary in his 'Dead Pan'—which is quite a different conception of the subject, & executed in blank verse too. I have no claims against him, I am sure!—

But for the *man!*—To call him a poet!—A prince & potentate of Commonplaces, such as he is!—I have seen his name in the Athenæum attached to a lyric or two . . poems, correctly called fugitive,—more than usually fugitive!—but I never heard before that his hand was in the prose department.

1. Tradition says that after being beheaded at Paris in 272, France's patron saint carried his severed head some six miles and laid it on the spot where a cathedral bearing his name now stands in the suburb of St. Denis.

2. Letter 10, close.

3. The *New Quarterly Review*.

4. See Letter 62, note 7.

5. James Garbett, M.A., had been elected for a second term, to begin January 27, 1846. (*Oxford Calendar*, 1847).

6. For identification see Letter 190, note 4.

200 (W98)   **R.B. to E.B.B.**

[January 14, 1846.]

Wednesday.

Was I in the wrong, dearest, to go away with Mr. Kenyon? I *well knew and felt* the price I was about to pay . . but the thought *did* occur that he might have been informed my probable time of departure was that of his own arrival—and that he would not know how very soon, alas, I should be *obliged* to go—so . . to save you any least embarrassment in the world, I got—just that shake of the hand, just that look—and no more! And was it all for nothing, all needless after all? So I said to my-self all the way home—

When I am away from you—a crowd of things press on me for utterance . . 'I will say them, not write them,' I think:—when I see you —all to be said seems insignificant, irrelevant,—"they can be written, at all events"—I think *that* too. So, feeling so much, I say so little!—

I have just returned from Town and write for the Post—but *you* mean to write, I trust—

That was not obtained, that promise, to be happy with, as last time!
How are you?—tell me, dearest; a long week is to be waited now!
Bless you, my own, sweetest Ba.

I am wholly your R.

201 (*W99*) *R.B. to E.B.B.*

[*January 15, 1846.*]

Thursday.

Dearest, dearer to my heart minute by minute, I had no wish to
give you pain, God knows. No one can more readily consent to let a
few years more or less of life go out of account,—be lost—but as I sate
by you, you so full of the truest life, for this world as for the next,—and
was struck by the possibility, all that might happen were I away, in the
case of your continuing to acquiesce—dearest, it *is* horrible,—I could
not but speak—if in drawing you, all of you, closer to my heart, I hurt
you whom I would—*outlive* . . yes,—I cannot speak here—forgive
me, Ba.

My Ba, you are to consider now for me: your health, your strength
—it is all wonderful; that is not my dream, you know—but what all
see: now, steadily care for us both—take time, take counsel if you
choose; but at the end tell me what you will do for your part—thinking
of me as utterly devoted, soul and body, to you, living wholly in your
life, seeing good and ill, only as you see,—being yours as your hand is,—
or as your Flush, rather. Then I will, on my side, prepare. When I say
"take counsel"—I reserve my last right, the man's right of first speech.
I stipulate, too, ↑and require to say my own speech in my own words or
by letter—↓ remember! But this living without you is too tormenting
now. So begin thinking—, as for Spring, as for a New Year, as for a
new life.

I went no farther than the door with Mr. Kenyon—he must see
the truth; and—you heard the playful words which had a meaning all
the same.

No more of this; only, think of it for me, love!

One of these days I shall write a long letter—on the omitted matters, unanswered questions, in your past letters: the present joy still makes me ungrateful to the previous one; but I remember. We are to live together one day . . love!

Will you let Mr. Poe's book lie on the table on Monday, if you please, that I may read what he *does* say, with my own eyes? *That* I meant to ask, too!

How too, too kind you are—how you care for so little that affects me! I am very much better—I went out yesterday, as you found: to-day I shall walk, beside seeing Chorley. And certainly, certainly I would go away for a week, if so I might escape being ill (and away from you) a fortnight—but I am *not* ill—and will care, as you bid me, beloved! So, you will send, and take all trouble,—and all about that crazy Review! Now, you should not!—I will consider about your goodness. I hardly know if I care to read that kind of book just now.

Will you, and must you have "Pauline"? If I could pray you to revoke that decision! For it is altogether foolish and *not* boylike—and I shall, I confess, hate the notion of running over it—yet commented it must be; more than mere correction! I was unluckily *precocious*—but I had rather you *saw* real infantine efforts . . (verses at six years old, and drawings still earlier)[1] than this ambiguous, feverish— Why not wait? When you speak of the "Bookseller"—I smile, in glorious security—having a whole bale of sheets at the house-top: he never knew my name even!—and I withdrew these after a very little time.

And now—here is a vexation: may I be with you (for this once) next Monday, at *two* instead of *three* o'clock? Forster's business with the new Paper[2] obliges him, he says, to restrict his choice of days to *Monday* next—and give up *my* part of Monday I will never for fifty Forsters . . now, sweet, mind that! Monday is no common day, but leads to a *Saturday* . . and if, as I ask, I get leave to call at 2—and to stay till 3½— though I then lose nearly half an hour—yet all will be comparatively well. If there is any difficulty—one word and I re-appoint our party, his and mine,—for the day the paper breaks down—not so long to wait, it strikes me!

Now, bless you, my precious Ba—I am your own

—Your own R.

1. Browning drew at the age of two (G & M, p. 11) and wrote an imitation of Ossian at five (Letter 520, below).

2. Forster and Dickens collaborated on the *Daily News,* which commenced publication on January 21, 1846. Forster succeeded Dickens as editor on February 9, without relinquishing his tie with the *Examiner.*

202 (W103°[a])[1]   **E.B.B. to R.B.**

[January 15, 1846.]

Thursday Morning.
    Our letters have crossed; &, mine being the longest, I have a right to expect another directly, I think. I have been calculating—& it seems to me . . now what I am going to say may take its place among the paradoxes . . that I gain most by the short letters. Last week the only long one came last, & I was quite contented that the 'old friend' should come to see you on saturday and make you send me two instead of the single one I looked for: it was a clear gain, the little short note, and the letter arrived all the same. I remember, when I was a child, liking to have two shillings & sixpence better than half a crown—and now it is the same with this fairy money . . which will never turn all into pebbles, or beans . . whatever the chronicles may say of precedents.
    Arabel did tell Mr. Kenyon (she told me) that "Mr. Browning would soon go away" . . in reply to an observation of his, that 'he would not stay as I had company'; & altogether it was better:—the lamp made it look late. But you do not appear in the least remorseful for being tempted of my black devil, my familiar, to ask such questions & leave me under such an impression—'mens conscia recti'[2] too!!—
    And Mr. Kenyon will not come until next Monday perhaps. How am I? But I am too well to be asked about. Is it not a warm summer? The weather is as 'miraculous' as the rest, I think—It is you who are unwell and make people uneasy . . dearest. Say how you are, & promise me to do what is right & try to be better. The walking, the changing of the air, the leaving off Luria . . do what is right, I earnestly beseech you. The other day, I heard of Tennyson being ill again,[3] . . too ill to write a simple note to his friend Mr. Venables,[4] who told George. A little more than a year ago, it would have been no worse a thing to me to hear of your being ill than to hear of his being ill!—How the world has changed since then! To *me,* I mean.

Did I say *that* ever . . that "I knew you must be tired"? And it was not even so true as that the coming event threw its shadow before?——

Thursday night
[January 15].—

I have begun on another sheet—I could not write here what was in my heart—yet I send you this paper besides to show how I was writing to you this morning. In the midst of it came a female friend of mine & broke the thread—the visible thread, that is.

And now, even now, at this safe eight oclock, I could not be safe from somebody, who, in her goodnature & my illfortune, must come and sit by me—& when my letter was come . . "why wouldn't I read it? What wonderful politeness on my part. She would not & could not consent to keep me from reading my letter—She would stand up by the fire rather."

No, no, three times no. Brummel got into the carriage before the Regent, . . (didn't he?) but I persisted in /my>not/ ⟨politeness⟩ reading my letter in the presence of my friend. A notice on my punctiliousness may be put down to-night in her 'private diary.' I kept the letter in my hand & only read it with those sapient ends of the fingers which the mesmerists make so much ado about, & which really did seem to touch a little of what was inside. Not *all*, however, happily for me!—Or my friend would have seen in my eyes what *they* did not see.

May God bless you!—Did I ever say that I had an objection to read the verses at six years old . . or see the drawings either? I am reasonable, you observe!—Only, 'Pauline' I must have *some day*—why not without the emendations?—But if you insist on them, I will agree to wait a little . . if you promise *at last* to let me see the book which I will not show . . Some day, then!—you shall not be vexed nor hurried for the day—some day—Am I not generous? And *I* was 'precocious' too, & used to make rhymes over my bread & milk when I was nearly a baby . . only really it was mere echo-verse, that of mine, & had nothing of mark or of indication, such as I do not doubt that yours had. I used to write of virtue with a large 'V,' & 'Oh Muse' with a harp—, & things of that sort. At nine years old I wrote what I called 'an epic'—& at ten, various tragedies, French & English, which we used to act in the nursery—There was a French 'hexameter,' tragedy on the subject of Regulus[5]—but I cannot even smile ↑to think↓ /at>of/ it now, there are so many grave memories . . which time has made grave . . hung around it. How I remember sitting in "my house under the sideboard," in the dining-room, concocting one of the soliloquies beginning

> "Que suis je? autrefois un general Romain:
> Maintenant esclave de Carthage je souffre en vain."

Poor Regulus!—Cant you conceive how fine it must have been alto-gether?—And these were my 'maturer works,' you are to understand, . . and "the moon was bright at ten oclock at night" years before— As to the gods & goddesses, I believed in them all quite seriously, & reconciled them to Christianity, which I believed in too after a fashion, as some greater philosophers have done—& went out one day with my pinafore full of little sticks (& a match from the housemaids' cupboard) to sacrifice to the blue eyed Minerva who was my favorite goddess on the whole because she cared for Athens. As soon as I began to doubt about my goddesses, I fell into a vague sort of general scepticism, . . & though I went on saying "the Lord's prayer" at nights & mornings, & the "Bless all my kind friends" afterwards, by the childish custom . . yet I ended this liturgy with a supplication which I found in 'King's Memoirs' & which took my fancy & met my general views exactly . . "O God, if there be a God, save my soul if I have a soul."[6] Perhaps the theology of many thoughtful children is scarcely more orthodox than /mine⟩this/ : but indeed it is wonderful to myself sometimes how I came to escape, on the whole, as well as I have done, considering the com-monplaces of education in which I was set, with strength & opportunity for breaking the bonds all round into liberty & license. Papa used to say . . 'Dont read Gibbon's history—it's not a proper book. Dont read "Tom Jones"—& none of the books on *this* side, mind'! So I was very obedient and never touched the books on *that* side, & only read instead Tom Paine's Age of Reason, & Voltaire's Philosophical Dictionary, & Hume's Essays, & Werther, & Rousseau, & Mary Wollstonecraft . . books, which I was never suspected of looking towards, & which were not "on *that* side" certainly, but which did as well.

How I am writing!—And what are the questions you did not answer? I shall remember them by the answers I suppose—but your letters always have a fulness to me & I never seem to wish for what is not in them.

But this is the end *indeed*——

1. This letter and 203 were evidently sent as one; Browning assigned them a single number.

2. "A mind aware of the right." This three-word adaptation of the *Aeneid* I. 608, was a popular heraldic motto.

3. Apparently a relapse of his serious 1844 illness. "Tennyson, they say, professed to be quite well on his arrival in London, cured by hydropathy, but has since relapsed, & been very unwell indeed." *Letters to Geo. Barrett*, p. 126.

4. George Stovin Venables (1810–88) was a successful lawyer, anonymous journalist, and amateur poet, a particularly close friend of Tennyson's after Hallam's death (*Tennyson: A Memoir*, I, 122–123).

5. Three scenes, both French and English versions, are reprinted in *Elizabeth Barrett Browning: Hitherto Unpublished Poems and Stories* (2 vols., Bibliophile Society, Boston, 1914), I, 110–122.

6. "Sir William Wyndham [said] that the shortest prayer he had ever heard was the prayer of a common soldier just before the battle of Blenheim, 'O God, if there be a God, save my soul, if I have a soul!'" Dr. William King, *Political and Literary Anecdotes of His Own Times* (Boston, 1819), pp. 17–18. Cf. *Aurora Leigh*, I, 796–797. The whole account of Aurora's early reading in the last 450 lines of Book I has interesting parallels to this letter.

203 (W103°[b])   **E.B.B. to R.B.**

[January 15, 1846.]

Thursday Night.

Ever dearest—how you can write touching things to me,—& how my whole being vibrates, as a string, to these!—How have I deserved from God & you all that I thank you for? Too unworthy I am of all!— Only, it was not, dearest beloved, what you feared, that was "horrible," . . it was what you *supposed*, rather!—It was a mistake of yours. And now we will not talk of it any more.

Friday morning
[January 16].—

For the rest, I will think as you desire: but I have thought a great deal, & there are certainties which I know; & I hope we *both* are aware that nothing can be more hopeless than our position in some relations & aspects, though you do not guess perhaps that the very approach to the subject is shut up by dangers, & that from the moment of a suspicion entering *one mind,* we should be able to meet never again in this room, nor to have intercourse by letter through the ordinary channel. I mean, that letters of yours, addressed to me here, would infallibly be stopped & destroyed—if not opened. Therefore it is advisable to hurry on nothing—on these grounds it is advisable. What should I do if I did not see you nor hear from you, without being able to feel that it was for your happiness? What should I do for a month even?—And then, I might be thrown out of the window or its equivalent—I look back shuddering to the dreadful scenes in which poor Henrietta was involved who never offended as I have offended .. years ago which seem as present as to-day. She had forbidden the subject to be referred to until that consent was obtained—& at a word she gave up all—at a word. In fact she had no true attachment, as I observed to Arabel at the time: a child never submitted more meekly to a revoked holiday. Yet how she was made to suffer— Oh, the dreadful scenes!—and only because she had seemed to feel a little. I told you, I think, that there was an obliquity .. an eccentricity—or something beyond .. on one class of subjects. I hear how her knees were made to ring upon the floor, now!—she was carried out of the room in strong hysterics, & I, who rose up to follow her, though I was quite well at that time & suffered only by sympathy, fell flat down upon my face in a fainting-fit. Arabel thought I was dead.

I have tried to forget it all—but now I must remember—& throughout our intercourse *I have remembered*. It is necessary to remember so much as to avoid such evils as are evitable, & for this reason I would conceal nothing from you. Do *you* remember, besides, that there can be no faltering on my /"side">"part"/ & that, if I should remain well, which is not proved yet, I will do for you what you please & as you please to have it done. But there is time for ⟨‖ · · · ‖⟩ considering! ⟨‖ · · · ‖⟩

Only .. as you speak of 'counsel,' I will take courage to tell you that my SISTERS KNOW.—Arabel is in most of my confidences, & being often in the room with me, taxed me with /that>the/ ₊truth₊ long ago— she saw that I was affected from some cause—& I told her. We are as safe with both of them as possible—& they thoroughly understand that *if there /were>should/ ₊be₊ any change it would not be* YOUR *fault* .. I made them understand that thoroughly. From themselves I have received nothing but the most smiling words of kindness & satisfaction—(I thought I might tell you so much—) they have too much tenderness for me to fail in it now. My brothers, it is quite necessary not to draw into a dangerous responsibility: I have felt that from the beginning, & shall continue to feel it—though I hear & can observe that they are full of suspicions & conjectures, which are never unkindly expressed. I told you once that we held hands the faster in this house for the weight over our heads. But the absolute *knowledge* would be dangerous for ⟨themselves⟩ ↑my brothers↓: with my sisters it is different, & I could not continue to conceal from *them* what they had under their eyes—and then, Henrietta is in a like position—It was not wrong of me to let them know it?—no?—

Yet of what consequence is all this to the other side of the question? What, if *you* should give pain & disappointment where you owe such pure gratitude—But we need not talk of these things now. Only you have more to consider than *I*, I imagine, while the future comes on.

Dearest, let me have my way in one thing: let me see you on *tuesday* instead of on Monday—on tuesday at the old hour. Be reasonable & consider—Tuesday is almost as near as the day before it; & on Monday, I shall be hurried at first, lest Papa should be still in the house, (no harm, but an excuse for nervousness: & I cant quote a noble Roman as you can, to the praise of my conscience!) & *you* will be hurried at last, lest you should not be in time for Mr. Forster. On the other hand, I will not let you be rude to the Daily News, . . no, nor to the *Examiner*. Come on tuesday, then, instead of monday, & let us have the usual hours in a peaceable way, . . & if there is no obstacle, . . that is, if Mr. Kenyon or some equivalent authority should not take note of your being here on tuesday, why you can come again on the saturday afterwards . . I do not see the difficulty. Are we agreed? On tuesday, at three oclock. Consider, besides, that the Monday arrangement would hurry you in every manner, & leave you fagged for the evening—no, I will not hear of it. Not on my account, not on yours!—

Think of me on Monday instead, & write before. Are not these two lawful letters? And do not they deserve an answer?

My life was ended when I knew you, & if I survive myself it is for your sake:—*that* resumes all my feelings & intentions in respect to you. No "counsel" could make the difference of a grain of dust in the balance. It *is so,* & not otherwise. If you changed towards me, it would be better for you I believe—& I should be only where I was before. /If⟩While/ you do *not* change, I look to you for my first affections & my first duty—& nothing but your bidding me, could make me look away.

In the midst of this, Mr. Kenyon /comes⟩came/ & I felt as if I could not talk to him. No—he does not "see how it is." He may have passing thoughts sometimes, but they do not stay long enough to produce . . even an opinion. He asked if you had been here long.

It may be wrong & ungrateful, but I do wish sometimes that the world were away . . even the good Kenyon-aspect of the world—

And so, once more—may God bless you!——

I am wholly yours—

Tuesday, remember!—And say that you agree.

204 (W100)   **R.B. to E.B.B.**

———————————————

[*January 17, 1846.*]

Saturday.

Did my own Ba, in the prosecution of her studies, get to a book on the forb . . no, *un*forbidden shelf—wherein Voltaire pleases to say that "si Dieu n'existait pas, il faudrait l'inventer"?[1] I feel, after reading these letters . . as ordinarily after seeing you, sweetest, or hearing from you, . . that if *marriage* did not exist, I should infallibly *invent* it. I should say, no words, no *feelings* even, do justice to the whole conviction and *religion* of my soul—and tho' they may be suffered to represent some one minute's phase of it, yet, in their very fulness and passion they do injustice to the *unrepresented, other minute's,* depth and breadth of love . . which let my whole life (I would say) be devoted to telling and proving and exemplifying, if not in one, then in another way—let me have the plain palpable power of this; the assured time for this . . something of the satisfaction . . (but for the fantasticalness of the illustration) . . something like the earnest joy of some suitor in Chancery if he could once get Lord Lyndhurst[2] into a room with him, and lock the door on them both, and know that his whole story *must* be listened to now, and the "rights of it,"—dearest, the love unspoken now you are to hear "in all time of our tribulation, in all time of our wealth . . at the hour of death, and"—[3]

If I did not *know* this was so,—nothing would have been said, or sought for—(your friendship, the perfect pride in it, the wish for, and eager co-operation in, your welfare, all that is different, and, seen now, nothing.)

⟨‖···‖⟩ I will care for it no more, dearest—I am wedded to you now. I believe no human being could love you more—that thought consoles me for my own imperfection—for when *that* does strike me, as so often it will—I turn round on my pursuing self, and ask "What if ↑it↓ were a claim then,—what is in Her, demanded rationally, equitably, in return for what were in you—do you like *that* way!"—And I do *not,* Ba—you, even, might not—when people everyday buy improveable ground, and eligible sites for building, and don't want every inch filled up, covered over, done to their hands! So take me, and make me what you can and will—and tho' never to be *more* yours, yet more *like* you, I may and must be—Yes, indeed . . best, only love!

And am I not grateful to your sisters—entirely grateful for that crowning comfort; it is "miraculous," too, if you please—for *you* shall know me by finger-tip intelligence or any art magic of old or new times—but they do not see me, know me—and must moreover be jealous of you, chary of you, as the daughters of Hesperus, of wonderers and wistful lookers up at the gold apple—yet instead of "rapidly levelling eager eyes"[4]—they are indulgent? Then—shall I wish capriciously they were *not* your sisters, not so near you, that there might be a kind of grace in loving them for it?—but what grace can there be when . . yes, I will tell you—*no*, I will not—it is foolish!—and it is *not* foolish in me to love the table and chairs and vases in your room—

Let me finish writing to-morrow; it would not become me to utter a word against the arrangement . . and Saturday promised, too—but though all concludes against the early hour on Monday, yet—but this is wrong—on Tuesday it shall be, then,—thank you, dearest! you let me keep up the old proper form, do you not?—I shall continue to thank, and be gratified &c. as if I had some untouched fund of thanks at my disposal to cut a generous figure with on occasion! And so, now, for your kind considerateness *thank you* . . *that I* say, which, God knows, *could* not say, if I died ten deaths in one to do you good, "you are repaid"—

To-morrow I will write, and answer more. I am pretty well, and will go out to-day—to-night. My Act is done, and copied—I will bring it. Do you see the Athenæum?[5] By Chorley surely—and kind and satisfactory. I did not expect any notice for a long time—all that about the "mist," "unchanged manner" and the like is politic concession to the Powers that Be . . because he might tell me that and much more with

his own lips or unprofessional pen, and be thanked into the bargain—
yet he does not—But I fancy he saves me from a rougher hand—the
long extracts answer every purpose—

There is all to say yet—to-morrow!—

And ever, ever your own,—God bless you!

R.

Admire the clean paper . . I did not notice that I have been writing
on a desk where a candle fell! See the bottoms of the other pages!

1. *Epître* (*A l'auteur des livres des trois imposteurs*), *Oeuvres complètes de Voltaire,*
ed. L. Moland (52 vols., Paris, 1877–85), x, 403.

2. John Singleton Copley, first Baron Lyndhurst (1772–1863), was Lord
Chancellor.

3. Slightly misquoted from the Litany in the *Book of Common Prayer.*

4. Tennyson's *Hesperides* (1833), l. 60.

5. Which reviewed *Dramatic Romances and Lyrics* in the January 17 issue (pp.
58–59). There were extensive extracts of *How They Brought the Good News . . .,
England in Italy, Home Thoughts from Abroad, The Laboratory, The Confessional,* and
The Flight of the Duchess. The bulk of critical comment was "Though his manner
changes less than might be wished—since the mist, if it rises and reveals a clear prospect for half a page, as certainly falls again,—there are few of his contemporaries who
embrace so wide a field of subjects; be they of thought, or description, or passion, or
character."

205 (W101)   **R.B. to E.B.B.**

[*January 18, 1846.*]

Sunday Evening.

You may have seen, I put off all the weighty business-part of the
letter—but I shall do very little with it now: to be sure, a few words will
serve, because you understand me, and believe in *enough* of me—
First, then, I am wholly satisfied, thoroughly made happy in your assurance. I would build up an infinity of lives, if I could plan them, one on
the other, and all resting on you, on your word—I fully believe in it,—
of my feeling, the gratitude, let there be no attempt to speak. And for
"waiting"; "not hurrying", . . I leave all with you henceforth—all you
say is most wise, most convincing.

On the saddest part of all,—silence. You understand, and I can understand thro' you. Do you know, that I never *used* to dream unless indisposed, and rarely then—(of late I dream of you, but quite of late)—and *those* nightmare dreams have invariably been of *one* sort—I stand by (powerless to interpose by a word even) and see the infliction of tyranny on the unresisting—man or beast (generally the last)—and I wake just in time not to die : let no one try this kind of experiment on me or mine! Tho' I have observed that by a felicitous arrangement, the man with the whip puts it into use with an old horse commonly : I once knew a fine specimen of the boilingly passionate, desperately respectable on the Eastern principle that reverences a madman—and this fellow, whom it was to be death to oppose, (some bloodvessel was to break)—he, once at a dinner party at which I was present, insulted his wife (a young pretty simple believer in his awful immunities from the ordinary terms that keep men in order)—brought the tears into her eyes and sent her from the room . . purely to "show off" in the eyes of his guests . . (all males, law-friends &c., he being a lawyer.) This feat accomplished, he, too, left us with an affectation of compensating relentment, to "just say a word and return"—and no sooner was his back to the door than the biggest, stupidest of the company began to remark "what a fortunate thing it was that Mr. So-&-so had such a submissive wife—not one of the women who would resist—that is, attempt to resist—and so exasperate our gentleman into . . Heaven only knew what!"—I said it *was*, in one sense, a fortunate thing,—because one of those women, without necessarily being the lion-tressed Bellona, would richly give him his desert, I thought—"Oh, indeed?" No—*this* man was not to be opposed—wait, you might, till the fit was over, and then try what kind argument would do—and so forth to unspeakable nausea. Presently we went upstairs—there sate the wife with dried eyes, and a smile at the tea table—and by her, in all the pride of conquest, with her hand in his, our friend—disposed to be very good-natured of course. I listened *arrectis auribus,*[1] and in a minute he said he did not know somebody I mentioned—I told him, *that* I easily conceived—such a person would never condescend to know *him, &c,* and treated him to every consequence ingenuity could draw from that text—and at the end marched out of the room,—and the valorous man, who had sate like a post, got up, took a candle, followed me to the door, and only said in unfeigned wonder, "What *can* have possessed you, my *dear* B?"[2]—All which I as much expected beforehand, as that the above mentioned man of the whip keeps quiet in the presence of an ordinary-couraged dog—All this is quite irrelevant to *the* case . . indeed, I write to get rid of the thought altogether: but do hold it the most stringent of all who can, to stop a condition, a relation of one human being to another which God never allowed to exist between Him and ourselves—*Trees* live and die, if you please, and accept will for a law—but with us, all commands surely refer to a previously-implanted conviction in ourselves of their rationality and justice—Or why declare that "the Lord *is* holy, just and good" unless there is recognised and independent conception of holiness and goodness, to which the subsequent assertion is referable? "You know what *holiness* is, what it is to be good? Then, He *is* that"—not, "*that* is so—because *he* is that"; tho' of course, when once the converse is demonstrated, this, too, follows, and may be urged for practical purposes—All God's urgency, so to speak, is on the *justice* of his judgments, *rightness* of his rule: yet why? one might ask—if one does believe that the rule *is* his; why ask further?—Because, his is a "reasonable service," once for all.

Understand why I turn my thoughts in this direction—if it is indeed as you fear,—and no endeavour, concession, on my part will avail, under any circumstances—(and by endeavour, I mean all heart & soul could bring the flesh to perform)—in that case, you will not come to me with a shadow past hope of chasing——

The likelihood is, I over frighten myself for you, by the involuntary contrast with those here—you allude to them—if I went with this letter downstairs and said simply "I want this taken to the direction to-night—and am unwell & unable to go, will you take it now?" My father would not say a word,—or rather would say a dozen cheerful absurdities about his "wanting a walk," "just having been wishing to go out" &c—At night he sits studying my works—illustrating them (I will bring you drawings to make you laugh)—and *yesterday* I picked up a crumpled bit of paper . . "his notion of what a criticism on this last number ought to be—, none, that have appeared, satisfying him!"— So judge of what he will say!—(And my mother loves me just as much more as must of necessity be—)

Once more, understand all this . . for the clock scares me of a sudden—I meant to say more—far more—

But may God bless you ever—my own dearest, my Ba—

I am wholly your R.

(Tuesday)

1. "With ears pricked."
2. See the close of Letter 207, which indicates that the friend had been an intimate one and that he may have been someone known at least by name to E.B.B.

206 (W104°)   **E.B.B. to R.B.**

[January 18, 1846.]

Sunday.

Your letter came just after the hope of one had past—the latest Saturday post had gone, they said: & I was beginning to be as vexed as possible, looking into the long letterless Sunday. Then, suddenly came the knock—the postman redivivus . . just when it seemed so beyond hoping for—it was half past eight, observe . . & there had been a post at nearly eight—suddenly came the knock, & your letter with it. Was I not glad, do you think?

And you call the Athenæum "kind and satisfactory"? Well—I was angry instead. To make us wait so long for an 'article' like *that*, was not over-kind certainly, nor was it "satisfactory" to class your peculiar qualities with other contemporary ones,[1] as if they were not peculiar— It seemed to me cold & cautious . . from the causes perhaps which you mention . . but the extracts will work their own way with everybody who knows what poetry is, & for ⟨the⟩ others, let the critic do his worst with them. For what is said of "mist" I have no patience,—because I who know when you are obscure & never think of denying it in some of your former works, do hold that this last number is as clear & self-sufficing to a common understanding, as far as the expression & medium goes, as any book in the world, & that Mr. Chorley was bound in verity to say so. If I except that one stanza,[2] you know, it is to make the general observation stronger. And then "mist" is an infamous word for your kind of obscurity—You never *are* misty, not even in Sordello—never vague. Your graver cuts deep sharp lines always—& there is an extra-distinctness in your images & thoughts, from the midst of which, cross-

401

ing each other infinitely, the general significance seems to escape. So that to talk of a 'mist,' when you are obscurest, is an impotent thing to do—Indeed it makes me angry.

But the suggested virtue of "selfrenunciation"[3] only made me smile, because it is simply nonsense . . nonsense which proves itself to be nonsense at a glance. So genius is to renounce itself . . *that* is the new critical doctrine, is it? Now is it not foolish? To recognize the poetical faculty of a man, & then to instruct him in "selfrenunciation" in that very relation—or rather, to hint the virtue of it, and hesitate the dislike of his doing otherwise?[4] What atheists these critics are after all—& how the old heathens understood the divinity of gifts, better, beyond any comparison—We may take shame to ourselves, looking back—

Now, shall I tell you what I did yesterday. It was so warm, so warm, the thermometer at 68 in this room, that I took it into my head to call it April instead of January, & put on a cloak & walked down stairs into the drawing room—walked, mind!—Before, I was carried by one of my brothers . . even to the last autumn-day when I went out . . I never walked a step for fear of the cold in the passages. But yesterday it was so wonderfully warm, & I so strong besides—it was a feat worthy of the day—& I surprised them all as much as if I had walked out of the window instead. That kind dear Stormie who with all his shyness & awkwardness has the most loving of hearts in him, said that he was '*so* glad to see me'!—

Well!—setting aside the glory of it, it would have been as wise perhaps if I had abstained . . . our damp detestable climate reaches us otherwise than by cold, & I am not quite as well as usual this morning after an uncomfortable feverish night—⟨but⟩ not very unwell, mind, nor unwell at all in the least degree of consequence: & I tell you, only to show how susceptible I really am still, though "scarcely an invalid," say the complimenters.

What a way I am from your letter . . that letter . . or seem to be rather—for one may think of ⟨‖ · · · ‖⟩ ↑one↓ thing & yet go on writing distractedly of other things. So you are 'grateful' to my sisters . . *you!*—Now I beseech you not to talk such extravagances; I mean such extravagances as words like these *imply*—& there are far worse words than these, in the letter . . such as I need not put my finger on; words which are sense on my lips, but no sense at all on yours, & which make me disquietly sure that you are under an illusion. Observe!—*certainly* I should not choose to have a "*claim*," see! Only, what I object to, in 'illusions,' 'miracles,' & things of that sort, is the want of continuity common to such. When Joshua caused the sun to stand still, it was not for year even!⁵—Ungrateful, I am!

And 'pretty well. means 'not well' I am afraid—or I should be gladder still of the new act—You will tell me on tuesday what "pretty well" means, & if your mother is better—or I may have a letter to-morrow . . dearest! May God bless you!—

To-morrow too, at half past three oclock, how joyful I shall be that my "kind considerateness" decided not to receive you until tuesday. My very kind considerateness, which made me eat my dinner to-day!—

Your own Ba—

A hundred letters I have, by this last, . . to set against Napoleon's Hundred Days—did you know *that?*

So much better I am to-night: it was nothing but a little chill from the damp—the fog, you see!—

1. E.B.B. apparently objects to the phrase "few of his contemporaries."
2. The penultimate one of *The Lost Mistress.*
3. "His art is sometimes consummate—'Wherefore not always?' is a question, the reply to which might lead to threadbare discussions on taste, self-renunciation, and the like. Instead of these, we shall be more just to our author if we give him room to exhibit himself in his strength, and in his variety." *Athenæum,* January 17, 1846, p. 58.
4. An allusion to Pope's *Epistle to Dr. Arbuthnot,* l. 204.
5. Joshua 10:12–14.

207 (W102)   R.B. to E.B.B.

[*January 19, 1846.*]

Monday Mᵍ

Love, if you knew but how vexed I was, so very few minutes after my note left last night; how angry with the unnecessary harshness into which some of the phrases might be construed—you would forgive me, indeed. But, when all is confessed and forgiven, the fact remains—that it would be the one trial I *know* I should not be able to bear,—the repeti-

tion of those "scenes"—intolerable—not to be written of, even—my
mind *refuses* to form a clear conception of them—

   My own loved letter is come—and the news; of which the reassur-
ing postscript lets the interrupted joy flow on again—Well, and I am
not to be grateful for that,—nor that you *do* "eat your dinner"?—Indeed you will be ingenious to prevent me! I fancy myself meeting you
on "the stairs"—stairs and passages generally, and galleries (ah, those
indeed!—) all, with their picturesque *accidents*, of landing-places, and
spiral heights & depths, and sudden turns and visions of half open doors
into what Quarles calls "mollitious chambers"[1]—and above all, *landing-
places*—they are my heart's delight—I would come upon you unaware
on a landing-place in my next dream! One day we may walk on the
galleries round and over the innercourt of the Doges' Palace at Venice,—
and read, on tablets against the wall, how such an one was banished for
an "enormous dig (intacco) into the public treasure"—another for . .
what you are not to know because his friends have got chisels and chip-
ped away the record of it—underneath the "giants" on their stands,
and in the midst of the *cortile*[2] the bronze fountains whence the girls
draw water—

   So *you* too wrote French verses?—Mine were of less lofty argument—one couplet makes me laugh now for the reason of its false
quantity—I translated the Ode of Alcæus;[3] and the last couplet ran thus . .
   Harmodius, et toi, cher Aristogĭton!

   .   .   .   .

   .   .   .   .

            Comme l'astre du jour, brillera votre nom!
The fact was, I could not bear to hurt my French Master's feelings—
who inveterately maltreated "αι's and οι's"[4] and in this instance, an
"ει." But "Pauline" is altogether of a different sort of precocity—you
shall see it when I can muster resolution to transcribe the explanation
which I know is on the fly-leaf of a copy here.[5] Of that work, the
Athenæum said ⟨‖ · · · ‖⟩—[6] now, what outrageous folly,—I care, and
you care, precisely nothing about its saying and doings—yet here I talk!

   Now to you—Ba! When I go thro' sweetness to sweetness, at "Ba"
I stop last of all, and lie and rest. That is the quintessence of them all,—
they all take colour and flavour from that. So, dear, dear Ba, be glad as
you can to see me to-morrow—God knows how I embalm every such
day,—I do not believe that one of the *forty* is confounded with another

in my memory. So, *that* is gained and sure for ever. And of letters, this ↑makes↓ my 104th and, like Donne's Bride, "I take my jewels from their boxes; call / My Diamonds, Pearls, and Emeralds, and make / Myself a constellation of them all!"[7] Bless you my own Beloved!

—I am much better to-day—having been not so well yesterday— whence the note to you, perhaps! I put that to your charity for construction. By the way, let the foolish and needless story about my whilome friend be of this use, that it records one of the traits in that same generous lover of me, I once mentioned, I remember—one of the points in his character which, I told you, *would* account, if you heard them, for my parting company with a good deal of warmth of attachment to myself—

What a day! But you do not so much care for rain, I think. My Mother is no worse, but still suffering sadly—

Ever your own, dearest—ever—R.

1. Quarles uses the adjective several times but not for "chambers." Much closer than anything in Quarles is Browning's own "mollitious alcoves" (*Sordello*, III, 129).

2. "Courtyard."

3. Not identified; the subject matter postdates Alcaeus.

4. An allusion to E.B.B.'s *Wine of Cyprus*, st. ix. Browning's French tutor was a M. Loradoux, (G & M, p. 47), whose failure to understand Greek quantitative verse is indicated in the spelling "Aristogĭton" for what is normally transliterated "Aristogeiton."

5. There is no way of knowing what copy of this very rare book Browning is thinking of, but we can be pretty sure of the "explanation," which exists in several forms. The basic text of it seems to be that found in the copy, annotated by John Stuart Mill (see above, p. xxvii), which had been in Forster's possession about four years earlier (DeVane, p. 46, n. 17) and which is now in the Forster and Dyce Collection at the Victoria and Albert Museum:

"The following poem was written in pursuance of a foolish plan which occupied me mightily for a time, and which had for its object the enabling me to assume and realize I know not how many different characters;—meanwhile the world was never to guess that 'Brown, Smith, Jones and Robinson' (as the spelling books have it) the respective authors of this poem, the other novel, such a speech, etc., etc., were no other than one and the same individual. The present abortion was the first work of the *Poet* of the batch, who would have been more legitimately *myself* than most of the others; but I surrounded him with all manner of (to my then notion) poetical accessories, and had planned quite a delightful life for him.

"Only this crab remains of the shapely Tree of Life in this Fool's Paradise of mine.—R. B."

Browning condensed this text a bit for the copy of the poem now in the Turnbull Library, Wellington, N.Z. (F. J. Furnivall, "Chronological List of Browning's

Works," *Browning Society Papers* [1881], p. 38) and expanded it slightly in a letter to Ripert-Monclar dated August 9, 1837 (manuscript in the possession of Professor Richard L. Purdy of Yale).

6. The *Athenæum* for April 6, 1833, devoted just over a column to Allan Cunningham's unsigned review, which, though it regretted "a touch of the mysterious," "now and then a want of true melody," and "more abruptness than . . . necessary," dismissed such shortcomings as "a grain of sand in a cup of pure water." Cunningham declared that "fine things abound" and quoted two passages of thirty and forty-nine lines in demonstration. He recognized the anonymous work as that of a new poet and hoped his next work would be "as original" but "more cheerful." He closed with the remark that "to one who sings so naturally, poetry must be as easy as music is to a bird, and no doubt it has a solace all its own."

7. Donne's *Epithalamion* "St. Valentine's Day," st. iii.

Browning recorded the next day's visit on the envelope of Letter 206:
+Tuesday Jan. 20
3–5 p.m. (41.)
On that occasion he took along four acts of Luria.

208 (*W105°*)   **E.B.B. to R.B.**

———————————

[*January 21, 1846.*]

Wednesday.

Ever since I ceased to be with you . . ever dearest . . I have been with your Luria, if *that* is ceasing to be with you . . which it *is*, I feel at last. Yet the new act is powerful & subtle, & very affecting, it seems to me, after a grave, suggested pathos; the reasoning is done on every hand with admirable directness & adroitness, & poor Luria's iron baptism under such a bright crossing of swords, most miserably complete. Still . . is he to die *so?* can you mean it? Oh—indeed I foresaw *that*—not a guess of mine ever touched such an end—and I can scarcely resign myself to it as a necessity, even now . . I mean, to the act, as Luria's act, whether it is final or not—the act of suicide being so unheroical. But you are a dramatic poet & right perhaps, where, as a didactic poet, you would have been wrong, . . & after the first shock, I begin to see that your Luria is the man Luria & that his "sun" lights him so far & not farther than so,

& to understand the natural reaction of all that generous trust & hopefulness, what naturally it would be. Also, it is satisfactory that Domizia, having put her woman's part off to the last, should be too late with it— it will be a righteous retribution. I had fancied that her object was to isolate him, . . to make ⟨‖ · · · ‖⟩ /the⟩his/ military glory & national recompense ring hollowly to his ears, & so, commend herself, drawing back the veil—

Puccio's scornful working out of the low work, is very finely given, I think, . . & you have 'a cunning right hand,' to lift up Luria higher in the mind of your readers, by the very means used to pull down his fortunes—you show what a man he is by the very talk of his rivals . . by his "natural god"ship over Puccio. Then Husain is nobly characteristic—I like those streaks of Moorish fire in his speeches. "Why 'twas all fighting" &c. . . *that* passage perhaps is over-subtle for a Husain— but too nobly right ⸂in the abstract⸃ to be altered, if it is so or not. Domizia talks philosophically ⟨too⟩ besides, & how eloquently;—& very noble she is where she proclaims

> "The angel in thee & rejects the sprites
> That ineffectual crowd about his strength,
> And mingle with his work & claim a share,—"

But why not "spirits" rather than "sprites," which has a different association by custom?[1] 'Spirits' is quite short enough, it seems to me, for a last word—it sounds like a monosyllable that trembles . . or thrills, rather. And, do you know, I agree with yourself a little when you say . . (did you *not* say? . .) that some of the speeches . . Domizia's for instance . . are too lengthy. I think I should like them to coil up their strength, here & there, in a few passages. Luria . . poor Luria . . is great & pathetic when he stands alone at last, & "all his waves have gone over him"—Poor Luria!—And now, I wonder where Mr. Chorley will look, in this work, . . along all the edges of the hills, . . to find, or prove, his favorite 'mist!' On the glass of his own opera-/glass⟩lognon,/ perhaps:—shall we ask him to try *that?*

But first, I want to ask *you* something—I have had it in my head a long time, but it might as well have been in a box—& indeed if it had been in the box with your letters, I should have remembered to speak of it long ago. So now, at last, tell me—how do you write, O my poet? —with steel pens, or Bramah pens,[2] goosequills or crowquills?—Because I have a penholder which was given to me when I was a child, &

which I have used both then & since in the production of various great
epics & immortal 'works,' until in these latter years it has seemed to me
too heavy & I have taken into service, instead of it, another two-inch-
long instrument which makes Mr. Kenyon laugh to look at—& so, my
fancy has run upon your having the heavier holder, which is not very
heavy after all, & which will make you think of me whether you choose
it or not, besides being made of a splinter from the ivory gate of old, &
therefore not unworthy of a true prophet . . Will you have it . . dearest?
Yes—because you can't help it. When you come . . on saturday!—

And for 'Pauline,' . . I am satisfied with the promise to see it some
day . . when we are in the isle of the sirens, or ready for wandering in
the Doges' galleries . . . I seem to understand that you would really rather
wish me not to see it now . . & as long as I *do* see it.! So *that shall* be!—
Am I not good now, & not a teazer? If there is any poetical justice in
'the seven worlds,'³ I shall have a letter tonight.

By the way, you owe me two letters by your confession. A hundred
& four of mine you have, and I, only a hundred & two of yours . . which
is a 'deficit' scarcely creditable to me, (now is it? . .) when, according
to the law & ordinance, a woman's hundred & four letters would take
two hundred & eight at least, from the other side, to justify them—
Well—I feel inclined to wring out the legal per centage to the uttermost
farthing,—but fall into a fit of gratitude, notwithstanding, thinking of
monday, & how the second letter came beyond hope. Always better,
you are, than I guess you to be,—& it was being *best*, to write, as you
did, for me to hear twice on one day!—best & dearest!—

But the first letter was not what you feared—I know you too well
not to know how that letter was written & with what intention. Do
you, on the other hand, endeavour to comprehend how there may be
an eccentricity & obliquity in certain relations and on certain subjects,
while the general character stands up worthily of esteem & regard . .
—even of yours. Mr. Kenyon says broadly that it is monomania . .
neither more nor less. Then the principle of passive filial obedience is
held . . drawn (& quartered) from Scripture. He *sees* the law & the gospel
on his side. Only the other day, there was a setting forth of the whole
doctrine, I hear, down stairs—"passive obedience, & particularly in
respect to marriage." One after the other, my brothers all walked out
of the room, & there was left for sole auditor, Captain Surtees Cook,⁴
who had especial reasons for sitting it out against his will,—so he sate

and asked "if children were to be considered slaves" as meekly as if he were asking for information. I could not help smiling when I heard of it. ⟨‖ · · · ‖⟩ He is just *succeeding* in obtaining what is called an "adjutancy," which, with the half pay, will put an end to many anxieties—

Dearest—when, in the next dream, you meet me in the "landing-place," tell me why I am to stand up to be reviewed again. What a fancy, *that* is of yours, for 'full-lengths'—& what bad policy, if ⟨‖ · · · ‖⟩ a fancy, to talk of it so!—because you would have had the glory & advantage, & privilege, of seeing me on my feet twenty times before now, if you had not impressed on me, in some ineffable manner, that to stand on /one's⟩my/ head ⟨is⟩ ↟wᵈ↡ scarcely ↟be↡ stranger. Nevertheless you shall have it your own way, as you have everything—which makes you so very, very, exemplarily submissive, you know!—

Mr. Kenyon does not come—puts it off to *Saturday* perhaps.

The Daily News I have had a glance at.[5] A weak leading article, I thought . . & nothing stronger from Ireland:—but enough advertisements to promise a long future. What do you think? or have you not seen the paper? No broad principles laid down. A mere newspaper-support of the 'League.'[6]

May God bless you—Say how you are—& *do* walk & 'care' for yourself

&, so, for your own *Ba*

Have I expressed to you at all how Luria impresses *me* more & more? You shall see the 'remarks' with the other papers[7]—the details of what strikes me.

1. *Luria*, IV, 196–198. The change from "sprites" to "spirits" was not made.
2. Invented by Joseph Bramah (1749–1814).
3. The seven planets of the old astrologers.
4. See the account of Henrietta Barrett in the Introduction.
5. The first issue appeared the day this letter was written.
6. The Anti-Corn Law League.
7. See Letter 66, note 1.

[*January 22, 1846.*]

Thursday M^g

But you did *not* get the letter last evening—no, for all my good intentions—because somebody came over in the morning and forced me to go out . . and . . perhaps . . I *knew* what was coming, and had all my thoughts *there* ⊦that is,—*here* now, with my own letter from you.↓: I think so—for this punishment, I will tell you, came for some sin or other last night. I woke—late, or early—and, in one of those lucid moments when all things are thoroughly *perceived,*—whether suggested by some forgotten passage in the past sleep itself, I don't know—but I seem to *apprehend,* comprehend entirely, for the first time, what would happen if I lost you—the whole sense of that *closed door* of Catarina's came on me at once, and it was *I* who said—not as quoting or adapting another's words, but spontaneously, unavoidably, ' *In that door, you will not enter, I have* '[1] . . . And, dearest, the

Unwritten it must remain. ⟨‖ · · · ‖⟩

What is on the other leaf[2] is no ill-omen, after all,—because I strengthened myself against a merely imaginary evil—as I do always: and *thus*—I know I never can lose you,—you surely are more mine . . there is less for the future to give or take away than in the ordinary cases, where so much less is known, explained, possessed, as with us. Understand for me, my dearest.

And do you think, sweet, that there *is* ⟨‖ · · · ‖⟩ ⊦any free↓ movement of my soul which your pen-holder is to secure?—Well, try,—it will be yours by every right of discovery—and I, for my part, will religiously report to you the first time I think of you "which, but for your present I should not have done"—or is it not a happy, most happy way of ensuring a better fifth act to Luria than the foregoing? See the absurdity I write—when it will be more probably the ruin of the whole —for was it not observed in the case of a friend of mine once—who wrote his own part in a piece for private theatricals, and had ends of his own to serve in it,—that he set to work somewhat after this fashion:

410

'Scene 1st. A breakfast chamber—Lord & Lady A. at table—Lady A. / No more coffee, my dear?—Lord A. / One more cup! *(Embracing her)*. Lady A. / I was thinking of trying the ponies in the Park—are you engaged? Lord A. / Why, there's that bore of a Committee at the House till 2. *(Kissing her hand)*.' And so forth, to the astonishment of the auditory, who did not exactly see the "sequitur" in either instance—Well, dearest—whatever comes of it, the "aside," the bye-play, the digression, will be the best, and only true business of the piece. And tho' I must smile at your notion of securing *that* by any fresh appliance, mechanical or spiritual, yet I do thank you, dearest, thank you from my heart indeed—(and I write with Bramahs *always*—not being able to make a pen!)

If you have gone so far with 'Luria,' I fancy myself nearly or altogether safe: I must not tell you, but I wished just these feelings to be in your mind about Domizia, and the death of Luria: the last act throws light back on all, I hope. Observe only, that Luria *would* stand, if I have plied him effectually with adverse influences, in such a position as to render any other end impossible without the hurt to Florence which his religion is, to avoid inflicting—passively awaiting, for instance, the sentence and punishment to come at night, would as surely inflict it as taking part with her foes: his aim is to prevent the harm she will do herself by striking him—so he moves aside from the blow—But I know there is very much to ⟨‖ · · · ‖⟩ ↑improve and heighten↓ in this fourth act, as in the others—but the right aspect of things seems obtained and the rest of the work is plain and easy—

I am obliged to leave off—the rest to-morrow—and then dear, Saturday! I love you utterly, my own best, dearest—

R.

1. The opening words of E.B.B.'s *Catarina to Camoens* (1844), and an allusion to the unquoted remainder of the first stanza:

> On the door you will not enter
> I have gazed too long; adieu!
> Hope withdraws her peradventure;
> Death is near me,—and not *you*.

This mood of despair is so directly reversed in these same terms by *Sonnets from the Portuguese*, I, where the "silver answer" is "Not Death, but Love," that this letter may have inspired it. Browning's feeling that E.B.B.'s "condition in certain respects . . . resembled those of the Portuguese Catarina" led him to suggest the title for the sonnet sequence. Rowland Grey, Browning's Answer," *Cornhill*, n.s. LXVIII (April 1930), 430.

2. This sentence opens the second page of the letter.

210 (W106°) **E.B.B. to R.B.**

[January 22, 1846.]

Thursday Night.

Yes, I understand your Luria—& there is to be more light; & I open the window to the east & wait for it . . a little less gladly than for *you* on saturday,—dearest.—In the meanwhile you have "lucid moments," & "strengthen" yourself into the wisdom of learning to lose me . . &, upon consideration, it does not seem to be so hard after all . . there is 'less for the future to take away' than you had supposed—so *that* is the way? Ah, "these lucid moments, in which all things are thoroughly *perceived*";—what harm they do me!—And I am to 'understand for you,' you say!—Am I?—

On the other side, & to make the good omen complete, I remembered, after I had sealed my last letter, having made a confusion between the ivory & horn gates, the gates of false & true visions,[1] as I am apt to do—& my penholder belongs to the ivory gate, . . as you will perceive in your lucid moments—poor /pen⟩holder/! But, as you forget me on wednesdays, the post testifying, . . the sinecure may not be quite so certain as the thursday's letter says. And *I* too, in the meanwhile, grow wiser, . . having learnt something which you cannot do,—you of the Bells & Pomegranates— —*You cannot make a pen*—Yesterday I looked round the world in vain for it.

Mr. Kenyon does not come . . *will* not perhaps until Saturday—!— Which reminds me . . . Mr. Kenyon told me about a year ago that he had been painfully employed ↑that morning↓ in *parting* two—dearer than friends—& he had done it he said, by proving to either, that he or she was likél[y] to mar the prospects of the other. "If I had spoken to each, ⟨of their⟩ of himself or herself," he said, "I *never could have done it*."

Was not *that* an ingenious cruelty? The rememberance rose up in me like a ghost, and made me ask you once to promise what you promised[2] . . (you recollect?) because I could not bear to be stabbed with my own dagger by the hand of a third person . . *so!* When people have lucid moments themselves, you know, it is different.

January, 1846

And *shall* I indeed have a letter to-morrow? Or, not having the pen holder yet, will you . . .

Goodnight. May God bless you—

ever & wholly your

Ba—

1. See *Aeneid* VI, ll. 893–901.
2. Not to reveal their relationship to Kenyon. Letter 186 (paragraphs 2 and 3) suggests that such a promise was exacted on December 29.

211 *(W104)* **R.B. to E.B.B.**

[*January 23, 1846.*]

Now, of all perverse interpretations that ever were and never ought to have been, commend me to this of Ba's—after I bade her generosity "understand me," too!—which meant, "let her pick out of my disjointed sentences a general meaning,—if she can,—which I very well know their imperfect utterance would not give to one unsupplied with the key of my whole heart's-mystery"—and Ba, with the key in her hand, to pretend and poke feathers and pen-holders into the key-hole, and complain that the wards are wrong! So—when the poor scholar, one has read of, ╪uses not very dissimilar language and argument╪—who being threatened with the deprivation of his Virgil learnt the Æneid by heart and then said "Take what you can now"!—*that* Ba calls "feeling the loss would not be so hard after all"!—*I* do not, at least: and if at any future moment I should again be visited . . as I earnestly desire may never be the case . . with a sudden consciousness of the entire inutility of all earthly love: (since of *my* love) to hold its object back from the decree of God, if such should call it away,—one of those known facts which, for practical good, we treat as supremely common-place—but which, . . like those of the uncertainty of life,—the very existence of God, I may say,—if they were *not* commonplace, and could they be thoroughly apprehended (except in the chance minutes which make one grow old, not the mere years)—the business of the world would cease; (but when you find Chaucer's graver at his work of "graving smale seles"[1] by the sun's light, you know that the sun's self could not have been *created* on

413

that day—do you "understand" that, Ba? And when I am with you, or here or writing or walking—and perfectly happy in the sunshine of you, I very well know I am no wiser than is good for me and that there seems no harm in feeling it impossible this should change, or fail to go on increasing till this world ends and we are safe, I with you, for ever—)— But when . . if only *once,*—as I told you, recording it for its very strangeness, I *do* feel—in a flash—that words are words, and could not alter *that* decree . . will you tell me how, after all, that conviction and the true woe of it are better met than by the as thorough conviction that, for one blessing, the extreme woe is *impossible* now—that you *are,* and have been, *mine,* and *me*—one with me, never to be parted—so that the complete separation not being to be thought of,—such an incomplete one as is yet in Fate's power may be the less likely to attract her notice? And, dearest, in all emergencies, see, I go to you for help; for your gift of better comfort than is found in myself. Or ought I, if I could, to add one more proof to the Greek proverb "that the half is greater than the whole"[2]—and only love you for myself . . (it is absurd; but if I *could* disentwine you from my soul in that sense) . . only see my own will, and good (not in *your* will and good, as I now see them and shall ever see) . . should you say I *did* love you then? Perhaps.—And it would have been better for me, I know—I should not have *written* this or the like— there being no post in the Siren's isle, as you will see—

And the end of the whole matter is—what? Not by any means what my Ba expects or ought to expect; that I say with a flounce "Catch me blotting down on paper, again, the first vague impressions in the weakest words and being sure I have only to bid her 'understand'!— when I can get 'Blair on Rhetoric,'[3] and the additional chapter on the proper conduct of a letter"! On the contrary I tell you, Ba, my own heart's dearest, I will provoke you tenfold worse; will tell you all that comes uppermost, and what frightens me or reassures me, in moments lucid or opaque—and when all the pen-stumps and holders refuse to open the lock,—out will come the key perforce; and once put that knowledge—of the entire love and worship of my heart and soul—to its proper use,—and all will be clear—tell me to-morrow that it will be clear when I call you to account and exact strict payment for every word and phrase and full-stop and partial stop, and no stop at all, in this wicked little note which got so treacherously the kisses and the thankfulness— written with no penholder that is to belong to me, I hope—but with the

feather, possibly, which Sycorax wiped the dew from, as Caliban remembered when he was angry![4]—All but . . (that is, all was wrong
but)—to be just . . the old, dear, so dear ending which makes my heart
beat now as at first . . and so, pays for all! Wherefore, all is right again,
is it not? and you are my own priceless Ba, my very own—and I will
have you—if you like that style, and want you, and must have you
every day and all day long—much less see you to-morrow *stand*—

. . Now, there breaks down my new spirit—and, shame or no, I
must pray you, in the old way, *not to receive me standing*—I should not
remain master of myself I do believe!

You have put out of my head all I intended to write—and now I
slowly begin to remember the matters they seem strangely unimportant
—that poor impotency of a Newspaper![5] No—nothing of that for the
present. To-morrow, my dearest! (Ba's first comment—" *To-morrow?
To-day* is too soon, it seems—yet it is wise, perhaps, to avoid the satiety
&c. &c. &c. &c. &c.")

Does she feel how I kissed that comment back on her dear self as
fit punishment?

1. *Troilus and Criseyede* III. 1461–63.
2. Hesiod, *Works and Days*, 40.
3. Hugh Blair's *Lectures on Rhetoric* (1783) was a standard handbook, often
reprinted.
4. *Tempest* I. ii. 321–323.
5. *The Daily News.*

The following letter was begun the evening after Browning's next visit:
× Saturday Jan 24
3.5–5¼ p.m. (42)
*he noted on the envelope of Letter 210, altering for some reason his usual initial
symbol.*

212 (W107°)   **E.B.B. to R.B.**

[*January 24–25, 1846.*]

I must begin by invoking my own stupidity! To forget after all the pen-holder! I had put it close beside me too on the table, & never once thought of it afterwards from first to last—just as I should do if I had a common-place book, the memoranda all turning to obliviscenda as by particular contract. So I shall send the holder with Miss Martineau's books[1] which you can read or not as you like,—they have beauty in passages . . but, trained up against the wall of a set design, want room for branching & blossoming, great as her skill is. I like her "Playfellow" stories twice as well.[2] Do you know *them?*—Written for children, and in such a fine heroic child-spirit as to be too young & too old for nobody. Oh, & I send you besides a most frightful extract from an American magazine sent to me yesterday . . no, the day before . . on the subject of mesmerism—& you are to understand, if you please, that the Mr. Edgar Poe who stands committed in it, is my dedicator[3] . . whose dedication I forgot, by the way, with the rest—so, while I am sending, you shall have his poems with his mesmeric experience & decide whether the outrageous compliment to /me>EBB/ or the experiment on M. Vande-leur [Valdemar][4] goes furthest to prove him mad. There is poetry in the man, though, now & then, seen between the great gaps of bathos . . 'Politian' will make you laugh[5]—as the 'Raven' made *me* laugh, though with something in it which accounts for the hold it took upon people such as Mr. N. P. Willis[6] & his peers—it was sent to me from *four* differ-ent quarters besides the author himself, before its publication in this form, & when it had only a newspaper life.[7] Some of the other lyrics have power of a less questionable sort. For the author, I do not know him at all—never heard from him nor wrote to him—and in my opinion, there is more faculty shown in the account of that horrible mesmeric experience (mad or not mad) than in his poems. Now do read it from the beginning to the end. That *"going out"* of the hectic, struck me very much . . & the writing *away* of the upper lip. Most horrible!— Then I believe so much of mesmerism, as to give room for the full acting of the story on me . . without absolutely giving full credence to it, understand.

Ever dearest, you could not think me in earnest in that letter? It was because I understood you so perfectly that I felt at liberty for the jesting a little—for had I not thought of *that* before, myself, & was I not reproved for speaking of it, when I said that I was content, for my part, even so? Surely you remember—and I should not have said it if I had not felt with you, felt & known, that "there is, with us, less for the future to give or take away than in the ordinary cases." So much less!—

All the happiness I have known has come to me through you, & it is enough to live for or die in—therefore living or dying I would thank God, & use that word *"enough"* . . being yours in life & death. And always understanding that if either of us should go, you must let it be this one here who was nearly gone when she knew you, since I could not bear—

Now see if it is possible to write on this subject, unless one laughs to stop the tears. I was more wise on friday.

Let me tell you instead of my sister's affairs, which are so publicly talked of in this house that there is no confidence to be broken in respect to them—yet my brothers only see & hear, & are told nothing, to keep them as clear as possible from responsibility. I may say of Henrietta that her only fault is . . her virtues being written in water—I know not of one other fault: She has too much softness to be able to say 'no' in the right place—& thus, without the slightest levity . . perfectly blameless in that respect, . . she says half a yes or a quarter of a yes, or a yes in some sort of form, too often—but I will tell you. Two years ago, three men were loving her, as they called it. After a few months, & the proper quantity of interpretations, one of them consoled himself by giving /epithets⟩nic-names/ to his rivals. Perseverance[8] & Despair he called them . . & so, went up to the boxes to see out the rest of the play. Despair ran to a crisis, was rejected in so many words, but appealed against the judgment & had his claim admitted—it was all silence & mildness on each side . . a tacit gaining of ground,—Despair 'was ⟨quite⟩ ↑at least↓ a gentleman,' said my brothers. On which Perseverance came on with violent re-iterations . . insisted that she loved him without knowing it, or *should* . . elbowed poor Despair into the open streets . . who being a gentleman wouldn't elbow again—swore that "if she married another he would wait till she became a widow, trusting to Providence" . . *did* wait every morning till the head of the house was out, & sate day by day, in spite of the disinclination of my sisters & the rudeness of all my brothers, four hours in the drawing-room . . let himself be refused once a week & sate all the longer . . allowed everybody in the house (& a few visitors) to see & hear him in fits of hysterical sobbing, & sate on ⟨‖· · ·‖⟩ unabashed, the end being that he sits now sole regnant, my poor sister saying softly, with a few tears of remorse for her own instability, that she is 'taken by storm & cannot help it.' I give you only the resumé of this military movement—& though I seem to smile, /as⟩which/

it was impossible to avoid at some points of the evidence as I heard it from first one person & then another, yet I am woman enough rather to be glad that the decision is made *so*—He is sincerely attached to her, I believe; & the want of refinement & sensibility (for he understood her affections to be engaged to another at one time) is covered in a measure by the earnestness, . . & justified too by the event . . everybody being quite happy & contented, even to Despair, who has ⟨boug⟩ a new horse & takes lessons in music.

That's love—is it not? And that's my answer (if you look for it) to the question you asked me yesterday.

Yet do not think that I am turning it all to game. I could not do so with any real earnest sentiment . . I never could . . & now least, & with my own sister whom I love so. One may smile to oneself & yet wish another well—and so I smile to *you*—& it is all safe with you I know— He is a second or third cousin of ours and has golden opinions from all his friends & fellow-officers—& for the rest, most of these men are like one another . . I never could see the difference between fuller's earth and common clay, among them all.

What do you think he has said since—to *her* too?—"I always persevere about everything. Once I began to write a farce . . which they told me was as bad as could be. Well!—I persevered!—*I finished it.*" Perfectly unconscious, both he & she were of there being anything mal à propos in *that*—& no kind of harm was meant,—only it expresses the man.

Dearest—it had better be thursday I think—*our* day! I was showing to-day your father's drawings[9] . . & my brothers, & Arabel besides, admired them very much on the right grounds. Say how you are. You did not seem to me to answer frankly this time, & I was more than half uneasy when you went away. Take exercise, dear, dearest . . think of me enough for it,—& do not hurry Luria. May God bless you!—Your own *Ba*——

1. *Forest and Game Law Tales*. See Letter 190, note 4.
2. Published 1841.
3. Edgar Allan Poe's "Facts in the Case of M. Valdemar," *American Whig Review*, December 1845.
4. So identified in the 1899 edition.
5. "Scenes from *Politian*," an "unpublished drama," in Poe's 1845 collection.
6. Nathaniel Parker Willis (1806–67), American journalist, editor, and dramatist,

was a close friend of Poe's and, as editor of the *Evening Mirror,* his employer for a time.

7. In an effort to gain publicity, *The Raven* was printed "in advance of publication" in the New York *Evening Mirror* for January 29, 1845, and widely reprinted. Hervey Allen, *Israfel: The Life and Times of Edgar Allan Poe* (2 vols., New York: George H. Doran, 1927), II, 631–634.

8. Captain Surtees Cook.

9. See Letter 205.

213 (W105)   **R.B. to E.B.B.**

[*January 25, 1846.*]

Sunday E^g

I will not try and write much to-night, dearest, for my head gives a little warning—and I have so much to think of!—(spite of my penholder being kept back from me after all! Now, ought I to have asked for it? Or did I not seem grateful enough at the promise? This last would be a characteristic reason, seeing that I reproached myself with feeling *too* grateful for the "special symbol"—the "essential meaning" of which was already in my soul: well then, I will—I do pray for it—next time;—and I will keep it for that one yesterday and all its memories—and it shall bear witness against me, if, on the Siren's isle, I grow forgetful of Wimpole Street.[)] And when is "next time" to be—Wednesday or Thursday? When I look back on the strangely steady widening of my horizon—how no least interruption has occurred to visits or letters—oh, care *you*, sweet—care for us both!

That remark of your sister's delights me—you remember?—that the anger would not be so formidable. I have exactly the fear of encountering *that,* which the sense of having to deal with a ghost would induce: there's no striking at it with one's partizan—Well, God is above all! It is not my fault if it so happens that by returning my love you make me exquisitely blessed; I believe—more than hope, I am *sure* I should do all I ever *now* can do, if you were never to know it—that is, my love for you was in the first instance its own reward—if one must use such phrases—and if it were possible for that . . not *anger,* which is of no good, but that *opposition*—that adverse will—to show that your good would be attained by the—

But it would need to be *shown* to me.

You have said thus to me—in the very last letter, indeed. But with me, or any *man,* the instincts of happiness develop themselves too unmistakeably where there is anything like a freedom of will: the man whose heart is set on being rich or influential after the wordly fashion, may be found far enough from the attainment of either riches or influence—but he will be in the presumed way to them . . pumping at the pump, if he is really anxious for water, even tho' the pump be dry . . but not sitting still by the dusty roadside—

I believe—first of all, *you*—but when that is done, and I am allowed to call your heart *mine,* I cannot think you would be happy if parted from me—and that belief, coming to add to my own feeling in *that* case— So, this will *be*—I trust in God.

In life, in death, I am your own, *my* own! My head has got well already! It is so slight a thing, that I make such an ado about! Do not reply to these bodings—they are gone—they seem absurd! All steps secured but the last, and that last the easiest! Yes—far easiest! For first you had to be created, only that; and then, in my time; and then, not in Timbuctoo but Wimpole Street, and then . . the strange hedge round the Sleeping Palace keeping the world off—and then . . all was to begin, all the difficulty only *begin:*—and now . . see where is reached! And I kiss you, and bless you, my dearest, in earnest of the end!

214 (W108°)   **E.B.B. to R.B.**

_____

[*January 26, 1846.*]

Monday.
You have had my letter & heard about the penholder. Your fancy of "not seeming grateful enough," is not wise enough for YOU, dearest; when you know that *I* know your common fault to be the undue magnifying of everything that comes from me, & I am always complaining of it outwardly & inwardly. That suddenly I should set about desiring you to be more grateful . . even for so great a boon as an old penholder . . would be a more astounding change than any to be sought or seen in a prime minister.

Another mistake you made concerning Henrietta & her opinion—

& there's no use nor comfort in leaving you in it. Henrietta says that the "anger would not be so formidable after all!—" Poor dearest Henrietta, who trembles at the least bending of the brows . . who has less courage than I, & the same views of the future!! What she referred to, was simply the infrequency of the visits.—"Why was I afraid," she said—"where was the danger? who would be the *informer*"?—Well! I will not say any more. It is just natural that you, in your circumstances & associations, should be unable to see what I have seen from the beginning—only you will not hereafter reproach me, in the most secret of your thoughts, for not having told you plainly. If I could have told you with greater plainness I should blame myself (& I do not:) because it is not an opinion I have, but a perception. I see, I know. The result . . the end of all . . perhaps now and then I see *that* too . . in the "lucid moments" which are not the happiest for anybody. Remember, in all cases, that I shall not repent of any part of our past intercourse,—& that, therefore, when the time for decision comes, you will be free to look at the question as if you saw it then for the first /time⟩moment/, without being hampered by considerations about "all those yesterdays."

For *him* . . he would rather see me dead at his foot than yield the point: & he will say so, & mean it, & persist in the meaning.

Do you ever wonder at me . . that I should write such things, & have written others so different? *I have thought* THAT *in myself very often.* Insincerity & injustice may seem the two ends, while I occupy the straight betwixt two—& I should not like you to doubt how this may be!—Sometimes I have begun to show you the truth, & torn the paper,— I *could* not— Yet now again I am borne on to tell you, . . to save you from some thoughts which you cannot help perhaps—

There has been no insincerity . . nor is there injustice. I believe, I am certain, I have loved him better than the rest of his children . . I have heard the fountain within the rock, & my heart has struggled in towards him through the stones of the rock . . thrust off . . dropping off . . turning in again & clinging! Knowing what is excellent in him well, loving him as my only parent left, & for himself dearly, notwithstanding that hardness & the miserable 'system' which made him appear harder still— I have loved him & been proud of him for his high qualities, for his courage & fortitude when he bore up so bravely years ago under the wordly reverses which he yet felt ⟨so⟩ acutely . . more than you & I could feel them—but the fortitude was admirable. Then came the trials

of love—then, I was repulsed too often, . . made to suffer in the suffering
of those by my side . . depressed by petty daily sadnesses & terrors, from
which it is possible however for an elastic affection to rise again as past . .
Yet my friends used to say "You look broken-spirited"—& it was true.
In the midst, came my illness,—and when I was ill he grew gentler &
let me draw nearer than ever I had done—& after that great stroke[1] . .
you *know* . . though *that* fell in the middle of a storm of emotion &
sympathy on my part, which drove clearly against him . . God seemed
to strike our hearts together by the shock,—& I was grateful to him for
not saying aloud what I said to myself in my agony, '*If it had not been
for* YOU' . . ! And comparing my selfreproach to what I imagined his
selfreproach must certainly be (for if *I* had loved selfishly, *he* had not
been kind) I felt as if I could love & forgive him for two . . (I knowing
that serene generous departed spirit, & seeming left to represent it) . . &
I did love him better than all those left to ME to love in the world here.
I proved a little my affection for him, by coming to London at the risk
of my life rather than diminish the comfort of his home by keeping a
part of my family away from him[2]—And afterwards for long & long
he spoke to me kindly & gently, & of me affectionately & with too much
praise,—& God knows that I had as much joy as I imagined myself
capable of again, in the sound of his footstep on the stairs, & of his voice
when he prayed in this room,—my best hope, as I have told him since,
/was⟩being/, to die beneath his eyes. Love is so much to me naturally—
it is, to all women! & it was so much to *me* to feel sure at last that *he*
loved me—to forget all blame . . to pull the weeds up from that last
illusion of life . . & this, till the Pisa-business, which threw me off, far
as ever, again—farther than ever—when George said "he could not
flatter me" & I dared not flatter myself—But do *you* believe that I never
wrote what I did not feel: I never did. And I ask one kindness more . .
do not notice what I have written here. Let it pass—We can alter nothing by ever so many words. After all, he is the victim. He isolates himself—& now and then he feels it . . the cold dead silence all round, which
is the effect of an incredible system. If he were not stronger than most
men, he could not bear it as he does. With such high qualities too!—so
upright & honorable—you would esteem him, you would like him, I
think. And so . . dearest . . let *that* be the last word.

    I dare say you have asked yourself sometimes, why it was that I
never managed to draw you into the house here, so that you might

make your own way—Now *that* is one of the things impossible to me.
I have not influence enough for *that*. George can never invite a friend of
his even—Do you see? The people who do come here, come by particular license & association . . Capt. Surtees Cook being one of them.
Once . . when I was in high favour too . . I asked for Mr. Kenyon to be
⟨‖ · · · ‖⟩ invited to dinner—he an old college friend, & living close by
& so affectionate to me always—I felt that he must be hurt by the
neglect, & asked. *It was in vain.* Now, you see—

    May God bless you always!—I wrote all my spirits away in this
letter yesterday, and kept it to finish to-day . . being yours/Wednesday⟩
everyday/, glad or sad, ever beloved!—

Your Ba

1. The death of her brother Edward.
2. See *Letters of EBB,* I, 88.

215 (W106)   **R.B. to E.B.B.**

[*January 27, 1846.*]

Tuesday.

    Why will you give me such unnecessary proofs of your goodness?
Why not leave the books for me to take away, at all events? No—you
must fold up, and tie round, and seal over, and be at all the pains in the
world with those hands I see now—But you only threaten,—say you
"shall send"—as yet, and nothing having come, I do pray you, if not
too late, to save me the shame—add to the gratitude you never can now,
I think . . only *think,* for you are a siren, and I don't know certainly to
what your magic may not extend. Thus, in not so important a matter,—
I should have said, the day before yesterday, that no letter from you
could make my heart rise within me, more than of old . . unless it should
happen to be of twice the ordinary thickness . . and *then* there's a fear at
first lest the over-running of my dealt-out measure should be just a note
of Mr. Kenyon's, for instance!—But yesterday the very seal began with
"Ba"[1]—Now, always seal with that seal my letters, dearest! Do you
recollect Donne's pretty lines about seals—

> Quondam fessus Amor loquens Amato,
> Tot et tanta loquens amica, scripsit:
> Tandem et fessa manus dedit Sigillum.[2]

And in his own English,

> When love, being weary, made an end
> Of kind expressions to his friend,
> He writ; when hand could write no more,
> He gave the seal—and so left o'er.

(By the way, what a mercy that he never noticed the jingle *in posse* of ending "expressions" and beginning "impressions.")

How your account of the actors in the "Love's Labour Lost" amused me! I rather like, tho', the notion of that steady, business-like pursuit of love under difficulties,—and the *sobbing* proves something surely! Serjt. Talfourd says . . is it not he who says it? . . "All tears are not for sorrow."[3] I should incline to say, from my own feeling, that no tears were . . they only express joy in me, or sympathy with joy—and so is it with you too, I should think—

Understand that I do *not* disbelieve in Mesmerism—I only object to insufficient evidence being put forward as quite irrefragable—I keep an open sense on the subject—ready to be instructed,—and should have refused such testimony as Miss Martineau's if it had been adduced in support of something I firmly believed—"non *tali* auxilio"[4]—indeed, so has truth been harmed, and only so, from the beginning. So, I shall read what you bid me, and learn all I can.

I am not quite so well this week—yesterday some friends came early and kept me at home—for which I seem to suffer a little,—less, already, than in the morning—so I will go out and walk away the whirring . . which is all the mighty ailment. As for Luria I have not looked at it since I saw you—which means, saw you in the body, because last night I saw you; as I wonder if you know!

Thursday, and again I am with you—and you will forget nothing . . how the farewell is to be returned? Ah, my dearest, sweetest Ba; how entirely I love you!

May God bless you ever—

R.

2. p.m. Your parcel arrives . . the penholder,—now what shall I say? How am I to use so fine a thing even in writing to you? I will give

it you again in our Isle, and meantime keep it where my other treasures
are—my letters and my dear ringlet.

Thank you—all I can think—

1. E.B.B. for the first time, had used a seal imprinted with her pet name on
Letter 214.
2. Really George Herbert's reply to Donne's *To Mr. George Herbert, With One
of My Seals, of the Anchor and Christ* but attributed to Donne until reassigned by
Grosart in his edition of Donne (2 vols., private circulation, 1872–73, II, 346).
3. The remark is apparently not in any of Talfourd's published works.
4. "Not with *such* assistance." *Aeneid* II. 521.

216 (W107)　　　　　　　**R.B. to E.B.B.**

[*January 28, 1846.*]

Wednesday.

Ever dearest—I will say, as you desire, nothing on that subject—
but this strictly for myself: you engaged me to consult "my own good"
in the keeping or breaking our engagement; not *your* good as it might
even seem to me; much less seem to another: my only good in this
world,—that against which all the world goes for nothing—is to spend
my life with you, and be yours. You know that when I *claim* anything,
it is really yourself in me—you *give* me a right and bid me use it, and I,
in fact, am most obeying you when I appear most exacting on my own
account—so, in that feeling, I dare claim, once for all, and in all possible
cases (except that dreadful one of your becoming worse again . . in
which case I wait till life ends with both of us . .)—I claim your promise's
fulfilment—say, at the summer's end: it cannot be for your good that
this state of things should continue. We can go to Italy for a year or two
and be happy as day & night are long. For me, I adore you. This is all
unnecessary, I feel as I write: but you will think of the main fact as
ordained, granted by God, will you not, dearest?—so, not to be put in
doubt *ever again*—Then, we can go quietly thinking of after matters.
Till to-morrow, and ever after, God bless my heart's own, own Ba. All
my soul follows you, love!—encircles you—and I live in being yours.

R.

Browning's call the next day is logged on the envelope of Letter 214, but without the usual initial symbol:
Thursday Jan. 29.
3–5 p.m. (43.)

217 (W109°) *E.B.B. to R.B.*

[*January 30, 1846.*]

Friday Morning.

Let it be this way, ever dearest—If in the time of fine weather, I am not ill, .. THEN .. *not now* .. you shall decide, & your decision shall be duty & desire to me, both—I will make no difficulties. Remember, in the meanwhile, that I *have* decided to let it be as you shall choose .. *shall* choose. That I love you enough to give you up "for your good," is proof (to myself at least) that I love you enough for any other end:— but you thought *too much of* ME *in the last letter*—Do not mistake me— I believe & trust in all your words—only you are generous unawares, as other men are selfish.

More, ⟨‖ · · · ‖⟩ I meant to say of this,—but you moved me as usual yesterday into the sunshine, & then I am dazzled & cannot see clearly. Still I see that you love me & that I am bound to you!—& "what more need I see," you may ask,—while I cannot help looking out to the future, to the blue ridges of the hills, to the *chances* of your being happy with me. Well!—I am yours as *you* see .. & not yours to teaze you. You shall decide everything when the time comes for doing anything—and from this to then, I do not, dearest, expect you to use "the liberty of leaping out of the window," unless you are sure of the house being on fire—! Nobody shall push you out of the window—least of all, *I.*

For Italy .. you are right—We should be nearer the sun, as you say, & further from the world, as I think—out of hearing of the great storm of gossiping, when "scirocco is loose."[1] Even if you liked to live altogether abroad, coming to England at intervals, it would be no sacrifice for me—and whether in Italy or England, we should have sufficient or more than sufficient means of living, without modifying by a line that "good free life" of yours which you reasonably praise—which, if it

426

had been necessary to modify, *we must have parted,* . . because I could not /bear⟩have/ borne to see you do it,—though, that you once offered it for my sake, I never shall forget.

Mr. Kenyon stayed half an hour, & asked after you went, if you had been here long. I reproached him with what they had been doing at his club (the Athenæum) in blackballing Douglas Jerold,[2] for want of something better to say—& he had not heard of it—There were more black than white balls, & Dickens was so enraged at the repulse of his friend that he gave in his own resignation like a privy councillor.

But the really bad news is of poor Tennyson—I forgot to tell you— I forget everything—He is seriously ill with an internal complaint & confined to his bed, as George heard from a common friend.[3] Which does not prevent his writing a new poem—he has finished the second book of it—and it is in blank verse & a fairy tale, & called the 'University,'[4] the university-members being all females. If George has not diluted the scheme of it with some law from the Inner Temple, I dont know what to think—it makes me open my eyes. Now isn't the world too old & fond of steam, for blank verse poems, in ever so many books, to be written on the fairies? I hope they may cure him, for the best deed they can do. He is not precisely in danger, understand—but the complaint may *run* into danger—so the account went.

And you? how are you? Mind to tell me. May God bless you. Is monday or tuesday to be *our* day? If it were not for Mr. Kenyon I should take courage & say monday—but tuesday & saturday would do as well—would they not? Your own Ba

Shall I have a letter?—

1. *England in Italy,* l. 116.
2. If this story was true, the trouble must have blown over. Dickens remained a member of the Athenæum; Jerrold apparently never belonged; and the incident seems not to be mentioned elsewhere.
3. Venables.
4. *The Princess* (1847).

218 *(W108)*   *R.B. to E.B.B.*

[*January 31, 1846.*]

Saturday.

It is a relief to me this time to obey your wish, and reserve further remark on *that* subject till by and bye.—And, whereas some people, I suppose, have to lash themselves up to the due point of passion, and choose the happy minutes to be as loving in as they possibly can . . (that is, in *expression;* the just correspondency of word to fact & feeling; for *it,*—the love,—may be very truly *there,* at the bottom, when it is got at, and spoken out)—quite otherwise, I do really have to guard my tongue and set a watch on my pen . . that so I may say as little as can well be likely to be excepted to by your generosity: dearest, *love* means *love,* certainly, and adoration carries its sense with it—and *so,* you may have received my feeling in that shape—but when I begin to hint at the merest putting into practice one or the other profession, you "fly out" —instead of keeping your throne—So let this letter lie awhile, till my heart is more used to it, and after some days or weeks I will find as cold and quiet a moment as I can, and by standing as far off you as I shall be able—see more—"si *minus propè* stes, te capiet magis"[1]—Meanwhile, silent or speaking, I am yours to dispose of as that *glove*—not that hand—

I must think that Mr. Kenyon sees, and knows, and . . in his goodness . . hardly disapproves—he knows I could not avoid,—escape you— for he knows, in a manner, what you are . . like your American,[2] and early in our intercourse, he asked me (—did I tell you?)—"what I thought of his young relative"—and I /thought⟩considered/ half a second to this effect—"if he asked me what I thought of the Queendiamond[3] they showed me in the crown of the Czar"—, and I answered truly—he would not return,—'then of course you mean to try and get it to keep.'" So I *did* tell the truth in a very few words—Well, it is no matter.

I am sorry to hear of poor Tennyson's condition—the projected book,—title, scheme, all of it,—*that* is astounding;—and fairies? If "Thorpès and barnes, sheep-pens and dairies—*this* maketh that there

428

ben no fairies"[4]—locomotives and the broad or narrow guage must keep the very ghosts of them away—But how the fashion of this world passes; the forms its beauty & truth take; if *we* have the making of such! I went last night, out of pure shame at a broken promise,—to hear Miss Cushman and her sister in "Romeo and Juliet."[5] The whole play goes . . horribly,—"speak" bids the Poet, and so M. Walladmir [Valdemar][6] moves with his tongue and dispenses with his jaws: whatever is slightly touched in, indicated, to give relief to something actually insisted upon and drawn boldly . . *here,* you have it gone over with an unremitting burnt-stick,—/then⟩till/ it stares black forever! Romeo goes whining about Verona by broad daylight: yet when a schoolfellow of mine, I remember, began translating in class Virgil after this mode, 'Sic fatur— so said Æneas,—lachrymans—*a-crying*' . . our pedagogue[7] turned on him furiously—"D'ye think Æneas made such a noise—as *you* shall, presently?"—How easy to conceive a boyish half-melancholy, smiling at itself—

    Then *Tuesday,* and not Monday . . and Saturday will be the nearer afterward. I am singularly well to-day—head quite quiet—and yesterday your penholder began its influence and I wrote about half my last act. Writing is nothing, nor praise, nor blame, nor living, nor dying, but you are all my true life; May God bless you ever—

R.

    1. "The *less near* you stand, the more it will strike you." An adaptation of Horace, *Ars Poetica,* ll. 361–362.

    2. A reference to Poe's dedication.

    3. Probably the Orloff diamond, given to Catherine the Great by Prince Orloff. It was a yellowish stone of over 194 carats.

    4. Chaucer, *Wife of Bath's Tale,* ll. 15–16.

    5. Charlotte Cushman was currently appearing as Romeo, with her sister Susan as Juliet.

    6. So identified in the 1899 edition.

    7. Probably the Rev. Thomas Ready (G & M, pp. 29–33).

219 (W110°[a])[1]   *E.B.B. to R.B.*

[*January 30, 1846.*]

Friday evening.

Something, you said yesterday, made me happy—"that your liking for me did not come & go"—do you remember? Because there was
a letter, written at a crisis long since, in which you showed yourself
awfully, as a burning mountain,[2] & talked of "making the most of your
fire-eyes," & of having at intervals "deep black pits of cold water"!—
and the lava of that letter has kept running down into my thoughts of
you too much, until quite of late—while even yesterday I was not too
well instructed to be "happy," you see!—Do not reproach me! I would
not have 'heard your enemy say so'!—it was your own word!—And
the other long word *idiosyncrasy* seemed long enough to cover it; and it
might have been a matter of temperament, I fancied, that a man of
genius, in the mystery of his nature, ⟨‖ · · · ‖⟩ /had⟩should/ find his feelings sometimes like dumb notes in a piano . . should care for people at
half past eleven on tuesday, and on wednesday at noon prefer a black
beetle—How you frightened me with your "fire-eyes"! "making the
most of them" too!—and the 'black pits,' which gaped . . *where* did
they gape?—who could tell?—Oh—but lately I have not been crossed
so, of course, with those fabulous terrors—lately that horror of the
burning mountain has grown more like a superstition than a rational
fear!—and if I was glad . . happy . . yesterday, it was but as a tolerably
sensible nervous man might be glad of a clearer moonlight, showing
him that what he had half shuddered at /as⟩for/ a sheeted ghoule, was
only a white horse on the moor. Such a great white horse!—call it the
"mammoth horse"—the "*real* mammoth," this time!—

Dearest, did I write you a cold letter the last time? Almost it seems
so to me!—the reason being that my feelings were near to overflow, &
that I had to hold the cup straight to prevent the possible dropping on
your purple underneath. *Your* letter, the letter I answered, was in my
heart . . *is* in my heart——& all the yeses in the world would not be too
many for such a letter, as I felt & feel. Also, perhaps, I gave you, at last,
a merely formal distinction—& it comes to the same thing practically
without any doubt!—but I shrank, with a sort of instinct, from appear-

ing (to myself, mind) to take a security from your words now (said too on an obvious impulse) for what should, would, +*must*,+ depend on your deliberate wishes hereafter—You understand—you will not accuse me of over-cautiousness and the like. On the contrary, you are all things to me, . . instead of all & better than all!—You have fallen like a great luminous blot on the whole leaf of the world . . of life & time . . & I can see nothing beyond you, nor wish to see it. As to all that was evil & sadness to me, I do not feel it any longer—it may be raining still, but I am in the shelter & can scarcely tell. If you *could* be *too dear* to me you would be now—but you could not—I do not believe in those supposed excesses of pure affections—God cannot be too great.

Therefore it is a conditional engagement still—all the conditions being in your hands, except the necessary one, of my health. And shall I tell you what is "not to be put in doubt *ever*"?—your goodness, *that* is . . & every tie that binds me to you. "Ordained, granted by God" it is, that I should owe the only happiness in my life to you, & be contented & grateful (if it were necessary) to stop with it at this present point. Still I *do not*—there seems no necessity yet—

May God bless you, ever dearest!—

Your own Ba

1. Sent with Letter 220; Browning assigned one number to the two.
2. See the opening of Letter 31.

220 (*W110°[b]*)   *E.B.B. to R.B.*

———————————————

[*January 31, 1846.*]

Saturday.

Well—I have your letter—& I send you the postscript to my last one, written yesterday you observe . . & being simply a postscript in some parts of it, *so* far it is not for an answer. Only I deny the 'flying out' —perhaps you may do it a little more . . in your moments of starry centrifugal motion.

So you think that dear Mr. Kenyon's opinion of his "young relative" . . (neither young nor his relative . . not very much of either!)

is to the effect that you couldn't possibly "escape" her—? It looks like the sign of the Red Dragon, put *so* . . & your burning mountain is not too awful for the scenery.

Seriously . . gravely . . if it makes me three times happy that you should love me, yet I grow uneasy & even saddened when you say infatuated things such as this & this . . unless after all you mean a philosophical sarcasm on the worth of Czar diamonds——! No—do not say such things!—If you do, I shall end by being jealous of some ideal ↑Czarina↓ /which〉who/ must stand between you & me . . I shall think that it is not *I* whom you look at . . & *pour cause*. "Flying out," *that* would be!

And for Mr. Kenyon, I only know that I have grown the most ungrateful of human beings lately, & find myself almost glad when he does not come, certainly uncomfortable when he does—yes, REALLY I would rather not see him at all, & when you are not here. The sense of which & the sorrow for which, turn me to a hypocrite, & make me ask why he does not come &c. . . questions which never came to my lips before . . till I am more & more ashamed & sorry. Will it end, I wonder, by my ceasing to care for any one in the world, except . . except . . ? or is it not rather that I feel trodden down by either his too great penetration or too great unconsciousness, both being overwhelming things from him to me—from a similar cause I hate writing letters to any of my old friends—I feel as if it were the merest swindling to attempt to give the least account of myself to anybody, & when their letters come & I know that nothing very fatal has happened to them, scarcely I can read to an end afterwards through the besetting care of having to answer it all. Then I am ignoble enough to revenge myself on people for their stupidities . . which never in my life I did before nor felt the temptation to do . . & when they have a distaste for your poetry through want of understanding, I have a distaste for *them*[1] . . cannot help it—& you need not say it is wrong, because I know the whole iniquity of it, persisting nevertheless. As for dear Mr. Kenyon—with whom we began, & who thinks of you as appreciatingly & admiringly as one man can think of another, . . do not imagine that, if he *should* see anything, he can 'approve' of either your wisdom or my generosity, . . *he,* with his large organs of caution, & his habit of looking right & left, & round the corner a little way. Because, you know, . . if I should be ill *before* . . why there, is a conclusion!—but if AFTERWARD . . what? You, who talk wildly

of my generosity, whereas I only & most impotently TRIED to be generous, must see how both suppositions have their possibility—Nevertheless you are the master to run the latter risk—You have overcome . . to
your loss perhaps—unless the judgment is revised. As to taking the half
of my prison . . I could not even smile at THAT if it seemed probable . . I
should recoil from your affection even, under a shape so fatal to you . .
dearest!—No! There is a better probability before us I hope & believe—
in spite of the *possibility* which it is impossible to deny. And now we
leave this subject for the present.——

Sunday [February 1].—You are "singularly well." You are very
seldom quite well, I am afraid—yet Luria seems to have done no harm
this time, as you are singularly well the day *after* so much writing. Yet
do not hurry that last act . . I wont have it for a long while yet—

Here I have been reading Carlyle upon Cromwell & he is very fine,
very much himself, it seems to me, everywhere. Did Mr. Kenyon make
you understand that ↑I had said↓ there was nothing in him but *manner* . .
I thought he said so—& I am confident that he never heard such an
opinion from me, for good or for evil, ever at all. I may have observed
upon those vulgar attacks ⟨on him⟩ on account of the so-called *mannerism,* the obvious fact . . that an individuality, carried into the medium,
the expression, ⟨was⟩ /a⟩is/ a feature in all men of genius . . as Buffon
teaches . . "Le style, c'est *l'homme.*" But if the *whole man* /was⟩were/
style . . if all Carlyleism were manner . . why there would be no man,
no Carlyle worth talking of—I wonder that Mr. Kenyon should mis-
represent me so. Euphuisms there may be to the end of the world . .
affected parlances . . just as a fop at heart may go without shoestrings to
mimic the distractions of some great wandering soul—although *that* is
a bad comparison, seeing that what is called Carlyle's mannerism, is not
his dress, but his physiognomy—or more than *that* even.

But I do not forgive him for talking ↑here↓ against the "ideals of
poets" . . opposing their ideal ⟨against⟩ ↑by↓ a mis-called *reality,* which
is another sort, a baser sort, of ideal after all. He sees things in broad
blazing lights . . but he does not analyze them like a philosopher . . do
you think so? Then his praise for dumb heroic action as opposed to
speech & singing,[2] what is *that*—when all earnest thought, passion, belief, & their utterances, are as much actions surely as the cutting off of
fifty heads by one right hand. As if Shakespeare's actions were not
greater than Cromwell's!—

But I shall write no more. Once more . . may God bless you.

Wholly & only your Ba

1. E.B.B. is most likely thinking of Mary Russell Mitford; see the account of her in the Biographical Appendix and in Letter 223.

2. "The Intelligence that can, with full satisfaction to itself, come out in eloquent speaking, in musical singing, is, after all, a small Intelligence. He that works and *does* some Poem, not merely he that *says* one, is worthy of the name of Poet." *Oliver Cromwell's Letters and Speeches, with Elucidations,* Centenary edition of Carlyle's *Works* (30 vols., London, 1896), VI, 78.

There is some confusion about the visit which intervenes here, because Browning appears to have made (in quick succession) two errors which bear upon the matter. On the envelope of Letter 219 he noted

+ Tuesday Feb. 2

3–5 p.m. (44.)

Tuesday was actually February 3, and the close of Letter 218 makes it pretty clear that the error must be as to date rather than day. At the head of Letter 221 he must be in error about the day, since the letter is postmarked February 4 (Wednesday) and Browning's other morning letters are all postmarked the day written. His letter must therefore follow the visit.

221 (W109)   R.B. to E.B.B.

[*Postmarked February 4, 1846.*]

Tuesday [Wednesday?] Morning.

You ought hardly,—ought you, my Ba?—to refer to *that* letter or any expression in it,—I had—and *have,* I trust . . your forgiveness for what I wrote, meaning to be generous or at least just, God knows: that, and the other like exaggerations were there to serve the purpose of what you properly call a *crisis.* I *did* believe, . . taking an expression, in the note that occasioned mine, in connection with an excuse which came in the postscript for not seeing me on the day previously appointed, I did fully believe that you were about to deny me admittance again unless I blotted out,—not merely softened down,—the past avowal. All was wrong, foolish, but from a good motive, I dare to say. And then, that particular exaggeration you bring most painfully to my mind—*that* does not, after all, disagree with what I said and you repeat—does it, if you will think? I said my other "*likings*" (as you rightly set it down) *used* to "come & go," and that my love for you *did not,* and that is true, the first clause as the last of the sentence, for my sympathies are very wide and general,—always have been—and the natural problem has been the giving unity to their object, concentrating them instead of dispersing. I seem to have foretold, *foreknown* you in other likings of mine —now here . . when the liking "*came*" . . and now elsewhere . . when as surely the liking "*went*" : and if they had stayed before the time would that have been a comfort to refer to? On the contrary, I am as little likely to be led by delusions as can be,—for Romeo *thinks* he loves Rosaline, and is excused on all hands—whereas I saw the plain truth without one mistake, and "looked to like, if looking liking moved—and no more deep *did* I endart mine eye"[1]—about which, first I was very sorry, and after rather proud—all which I seem to have told you before—And now, when my whole heart and soul find you, and fall on you, and fix forever,—I am to be dreadfully afraid the joy cannot last, seeing that . . it is so baseless a fear that no illustration will serve! Is it gone now, dearest, ever-dearest?—

And as you amuse me sometimes, as now, by seeming surprised at some chance expression of a truth which is grown a veriest commonplace to ME—like Charles Lamb's "letter to an elderly man whose education had been neglected"[2]—when he finds himself involuntarily communicating truths above the capacity and acquirements of his friend, and stops himself after this fashion—"If you look round the world, my dear Sir . . (for it *is* round—)["] so I will make you laugh at me, if you will, for *my* inordinate delight at hearing the success of your experiment with the opium,—I never dared, nor shall dare inquire into your use of that—for, knowing you utterly as I do, I know you only bend to the most absolute necessity in taking more or less of it—so that increase of the quantity must mean simply increased weakness, illness —and diminution, diminished illness—And now there *is* diminution! Dear, dear Ba—you speak of my silly head and its ailments . . well, and what brings on the irritation? A wet day or two spent at home,—and what ends it all directly?—just an hour's walk! So with *me:* now,— fancy me shut in a room for seven years . . it is—no, *don't* see, even in

fancy, what is left of me then! But *you,* at the end; this is *all* the harm!
I wonder . . I confirm my soul in its belief in perpetual miraculousness . .
I bless God with my whole heart that it is thus with you! And so, I will
not even venture to say,—so superfluous it were, tho' with my most
earnest, most loving breath,—(I who *do* love you more at every breath
I draw,—indeed, yes dearest,)—I *will not* bid you,—that is, pray you—
to persevere!—You have all my life bound to yours—save me from
my "seven years"—and God reward you!

Your own R.

1. *Romeo and Juliet* I. iii. 97–98.
2. *London Magazine,* N.S., I (January 1825), 95. It seems never to have been
collected.

222 (W111°)   *E.B.B. to R.B.*

[Wednesday, February 4, 1846.]

But I did not . . dear dearest . . no indeed, I did not mean any harm
about the letter. I wanted to show you how you had given me pleasure
—& so . . did I give you pain? was *that* my ingenuity? Forgive my un-
happiness in it, & let it be as if it had not been—Only I will just say that
what made me take [talk] about 'the thorn in the flesh' from that letter
so long, was a sort of conviction of your having put into it as much of
the truth, *your* truth, as admitted of the ultimate purpose of it . . & not
the least, slightest doubt of the key you gave me to the purpose ⟨& spirit⟩
in question. And so forgive me. Why did you set about explaining, as
if I were doubting you?—When you said once that it "did not come &
go," . . was it not enough?—enough to make me feel happy as I told
you?—Did I require you to write a letter like this?—Now think for a
moment, & know once for all, how from the beginning to these latter
days & through all possible degrees of crisis, you have been to my apprehension & gratitude, the best, most consistent, most noble . . . the words
falter that would speak of it all. In nothing & at no moment have you . .
I will not say . . failed to *me* . . but spoken or acted unworthily of yourself at the highest—What have you ever been to me except too generous?
—Ah—if I had been only half as generous, it is true that I never could

have seen you again after that first meeting—it was the straight path perhaps. But I had not courage—I shrank from the thought of it—& then . . besides . . I could not believe that your mistake was likely to last,—I concluded that I might keep my friend.

Why should any rememberance be painful to *you*? I do not understand. Unless indeed *I* should grow painful to you . . I myself!—seeing that every remembered separate thing has brought me nearer to you, & made me yours with a deeper trust & love.

And for that letter . . do you fancy that in *my* memory the sting is not gone from it?—& that I do not carry the thought of it, as the Roman maidens, you speak of, their cool harmless snakes, at my heart always?[1] —So let the poor letter be forgiven, for the sake of the dear letter that was burnt,[2] forgiven by *you*—until you grow angry with me instead . . just till then.

And what you should care so much about the opium—! Then *I* must care, & get to do with less . . at least. On the other side of your goodness & indulgence (a very little way on the other side) . . it might strike you as strange that I who have had no pain . . no acute suffering to keep down from its angles . . should need opium in any shape. But I have had restlessness till it made me almost mad—at one time I lost the power of sleeping quite . . and even in the day, the continual aching sense of weakness ↑has been intolerable . .↓ besides palpitation . . as if one's life, instead of giving movement to the body, were imprisoned ↑undiminished↓ within it, & beating & fluttering impotently to get out, at all the doors & windows. So the medical people gave me opium . . a preparation of it, called morphine, & ether—& ever since I have been calling it my amreeta draught,[3] my elixir . . because the tranquillizing power has been ⟨so⟩ wonderful. Such a nervous system I have . . so irritable naturally, & so shattered by various causes . . that the need has continued ↑in a degree↓ until now—& it would be dangerous to leave off the calming remedy, Mr. Jago[4] says, except very slowly & gradually. But slowly & gradually something may be done—& you are to understand that I never *increased* upon the prescribed quantity . . prescribed in the first instance—no!—Now think of my writing all this to you!—

And after all the lotus-eaters are blessed beyond the opium-eaters, & the best of lotuses are such thoughts as I know—

Dear Miss Mitford comes to-morrow, & I am not glad enough. Shall I have a letter to make me glad? She will talk, talk, talk . . & I shall be hoping all day that not a word may be talked of . . *you:*—a forlorn hope indeed!—There's a hope for a day like thursday which is just in the middle between a tuesday & a saturday!——

Your head . . . is it . . *how* is it? tell me. And consider again if it could be possible that I could ever desire to reproach *you* . . in what I said about the letter.

May God bless you, best & dearest. If you are the *compensation*, blessed is the evil that fell upon me: and *that*, I ⟨could⟩ ↑can↓ say before God.

Your Ba——

1. A letter from Browning to Miss Haworth, April 1839, apparently refers to the same pet snakes: "*I* . . . can tie and untie English as a Roman girl a tame serpent's tail." (D & K, p. 15.)
2. See the note preceding Letter 30.
3. In Hindu mythology, the drink that conferred immortality.
4. Charles Trelawny Jago was also E.B.B.'s physician in Florence in 1847 (*EBB: Letters to Her Sister*, pp. 52, 54). He was a grandson of the Trelawny who knew Byron and Shelley.

223 (W110)   R.B. *to* E.B.B.
———————————

[*February 6, 1846.*]

Friday.

If I said you 'gave me pain' in anything, it was in the only way ever possible for you, my dearest—by giving *yourself*, in me, pain—being unjust to your own right and power as I feel them at my heart: and in that way, I see you will go on to the end . . I getting called—in this very letter—"generous" &c. Well, let me fancy you see very, very deep into future chances and how I should behave on occasion: I shall hardly imitate you,—I whose sense of the present and its claims of gratitude, already is beyond expression.

All the kind explaining about the opium makes me happier. "Slowly and gradually" what may *not* be done? Then see the bright weather while I write—lilacs, hawthorn, plum-trees all in bud,—elders in leaf, rose-bushes with great red shoots; thrushes, whitethroats, hedge sparrows in full song—there can, let us hope, be nothing worse in store than a sharp wind, a week of it perhaps—and then comes what shall come—

And Miss Mitford yesterday—and has she fresh fears for you of my evil influence and Origenic power of "raying out darkness" like a swart star?[1] Why, the common sense of the world teaches that there is nothing people at fault in any faculty of expression are so intolerant of as the like infirmity in others—whether they are unconscious of, or indulgent to their own obscurity and fettered organ, the hindrance from the fettering of their neighbour's is redoubled: a man may think he is not deaf, or, at least, that you need not be so much annoyed by his deafness as you profess—but he will be quite aware, to say the least of it, when another man can't hear him,—he will certainly not encourage him to stop his ears: and so with the converse; a writer who fails to make himself understood, as presumably in my case, may either believe in his heart that it is *not* so . . that only as much attention and previous instructedness as the case calls for, would quite avail to understand him,—or he may open his eyes to the fact and be trying hard to overcome it: but on which supposition is he led to confirm another in his unintelligibility? By the proverbial tenderness of the eye with the mote for the eye with the beam? If that beam were just such another mote—*then* one might sympathize and feel no such inconvenience—but, because I have written a "Sordello"—do I turn to just its *double,* Sordello the second, in your books, and so perforce see nothing wrong? "No"—it is supposed—"but something *as* obscure in its way." Then down goes the bond of union at once, and I stand no nearer to view your work than the veriest proprietor of one thought and the two words that express it without obscurity at all—"bricks and mortar." Of course an artist's whole problem must be, as Carlyle wrote to me, "the expressing with articulate clearness the thought in him"[2]—I am almost inclined to say that *clear expression* should be his only work and care—for he is born, ordained, such as he is—and not born learned in putting what was born in him into words—what ever *can* be clearly spoken, ought to be: but "bricks and mortar" is very easily said—and some of the thoughts in "Sordello" not so readily even if Miss Mitford were to try her hand on them—

I look forward to a real life's work for us both: *I* shall do all,—under your eyes and with your hand in mine,—all I was intended to do: may but *you* as surely go perfecting—by continuing—the work begun so wonderfully—"a rose-tree that beareth seven-times seven"—

I am forced to dine in town to-day with an old friend—"to-morrow" always begins half the day before, like a Jewish sabbath: did your sister tell you that I met her on the stairs last time? She did *not* tell you that I had almost passed by her—the eyes being still elsewhere and occupied. Now let me write out that—no—I will send the old ballad I told you of,[3] for the strange coincidence—and it is very charming beside, is it not? Now goodbye, my sweetest, dearest—and tell me good news of yourself to-morrow, and be but half a quarter as glad to see me as I shall be blessed in seeing you. God bless you ever.

Your own R.

1. A letter from E.B.B. to Miss Mitford perhaps reflects Miss Mitford's constant worry: "As to my friend Mr. Browning, you make me smile a little at your anxiety about the influence of this cloud-compelling Jupiter among my clouds. You seem to think that, between us, reasonable people have no chance of ever seeing the sun!" ([June 4, 1845.] *EBB to MRM*, p. 245.) Browning's phraseology is taken from Forster's review, quoted in note 4 to Letter 152. Origen (ca. 185–ca. 254) was one of the Greek fathers of the Church whose doctrines were anathematized in 553. Thereafter, of course, his prolific writings were considered to propagate error ("darkness") rather than truth. Browning's special kind of darkness is the obscurity he was regularly accused of after *Sordello* (1840).

2. "Unless I very greatly mistake, judging from these two works [*Sordello* and *Pippa Passes*], you seem to possess a rare spiritual gift, poetical, historical, intellectual . . . to unfold which into articulate clearness is naturally the problem of all problems for you." (Letter of June 21, 1841, *Browning Collections*, p. 45, Lot #202.)

3. The ballad is no longer with the letters; in Letter 240, however, E.B.B. identifies the "strange coincidence" as a similarity to *The Flight of the Duchess,* so that it was probably a version of the Scottish ballad *The Gypsie Laddie.* See DeVane, pp. 172–173.

224 (W111) R.B. to E.B.B.

[*February 7, 1846.*]

Saturday M[g]

Dearest, to my sorrow I must, I fear, give up the delight of seeing you this morning. I went out unwell yesterday, and a long noisy dinner with speech-making, /with⟩and/ a long tiresome walk at the end of it— these have given me such a bewildering headache that I really see some reason in what they say here about keeping the house. Will you forgive me—and let me forget it all on Monday? On *Monday*—unless I am told otherwise by the early post—And God bless you ever

Your own—

R.

225 (W112)   *R.B. to E.B.B.*

[*February 7, 1846.*]

The clock strikes—*three,*—and I am here, not with you—and my "fractious" headache at the very worst got suddenly better just now, and is leaving me every minute—as if to make me aware, with an undivided attention, that at this present you are waiting for me, and soon will be wondering—and it would be so easy now to dress myself and walk or run or ride—do anything that led to you . . but by no haste in the world could I reach you, I am forced to see, before a quarter to five— by which time I think my letter must arrive. Dear, dearest Ba, did you but know how vexed I am—with myself, with—this is absurd, of course. The cause of it all was my going out last night—yet that, neither, was to be helped, the party having been twice put off before—once solely on my account. And the sun shines, and you would shine—

Monday is to make all the amends in its power, is it not? Still, still I have lost my day.

Bless you, my ever-dearest.

Your R.

226 (W112°)   *E.B.B. to R.B.*

[*February 7, 1846.*]

Saturday.

I felt it must be so . . that something must be the matter, . . & I had been so really unhappy for half an hour, that your letter which comes now at four, seems a little better, with all its bad news, than my fancies took upon themselves to be, without instruction. Now *was* it right to go out yesterday when you were unwell, & to a great dinner?—but I shall not reproach you, dearest, dearest—I have no heart for it at this moment. As to monday, of course it is as you like . . if you are well enough on monday . . if it should be thought wise of you to come to London through the noise . . if . . you understand all the *ifs* . . & among them the greatest if of all, . . for if you do love me . . *care* for me even, you will not do yourself harm or run any risk of harm by going out *anywhere too soon*. On monday, in case you are *considered well enough* . . and otherwise tuesday, wednesday—I leave it to you.—Still I *will* ask one thing, whether you come on monday or not. *Let* me have a single line by the nearest post to say how you are. Perhaps for to-night it is not possible—oh no, it is nearly five now!—but a word written on Sunday would be with me early on Monday morning, & I know you will let me have it, to save some of the anxious thoughts . . to break them in their course with some sort of certainty!—May God bless you dearest of all!—I thought of you on thursday, but did not speak of you, not even when Miss Mitford called Hood the greatest poet of the age . . she had been depreciating Carlyle, so I let you lie & wait on the same level, . . that shelf of the rock which is above tide mark!—I was glad even, that she did not speak of you, &, under cover of her speech of others, I had my thoughts of you deeply & safely—When she had gone at half past six, moreover, I grew over-hopeful, & made up my fancy to have a letter at eight!—The branch she had pulled down, sprang upward sky-ward[1] . . to that high possibility of a letter!—Which did not come that day . . no!—& I revenged myself by writing a letter to *you,* which was burnt afterwards because I would not torment you for letters. Last night, came a real one—dearest!—So we could not keep our sabbath to-day!—It is a fast day instead, . . on my part. How should I feel (I have been thinking to myself), if I did not see you on saturday, and could not hope to see you on monday, nor on tuesday, nor on wednesday, nor thursday nor friday, nor saturday again—if all the sabbaths were gone out of the world for me!—May God bless you!—it has grown to be enough prayer—as *you* are enough (& all, besides) for your own Ba—

1. Cf. *Aurora Leigh,* V, 1173–78.

227 (W113)   *R.B. to E.B.B.*

[*February 8, 1846.*]

Sunday M^g

My dearest—there are no words,—nor will be to-morrow, nor even in the Island—I know that! But I do love you

My arms have been round you for many minutes since the last word—

I am quite well now—my other note will have told you when the change began—I think I took too violent a shower bath, with a notion of getting better in as little time as possible,—and the stimulus turned mere feverishness to headache: however, it was no sooner gone, in a degree, than a worse plague came—I sate thinking of you—but I knew my note would arrive at about four o'clock or a little later—and I thought the visit for the quarter of an hour would as effectually prevent to-morrow's meeting as if the whole two hours blessing had been laid to heart—to-morrow I shall see you, Ba—my sweetest. But there are cold winds blowing to-day—how do you bear them, my Ba? "*Care*" you, pray, pray, care for all *I* care about—and be well, if God shall please, and bless me as no man ever was blessed! Now I kiss you, and will begin a new thinking of you—and end, and begin, going round and round in my circle of discovery,—*My* lotos-blossom! because they *loved* the lotos, were lotos-lovers,— λωτοῦ τ'ἔρωτες as Euripides writes in the Τρωάδες —[1]

Your own R.

P.S. See those lines in the Athenæum on Pulci with Hunt's translation[2]—all wrong—"*che non si sente,*" being—"that one does not *hear* him" i.e. the ordinarily noisy fellow—and the rest, male, pessime![3] Sic verte, meo periculo, mî ocelle![4]

Where's Luigi Pulci, that one don't the man see?
He just now ↑yonder↓ in the copse has '*gone it*' (*n*'andò)
Because across his mind there came a fancy;
He'll wish to fancify, perhaps, a sonnet!

Now Ba thinks nothing can be worse than that? Then read *this* which I really told Hunt and got his praise for. Poor dear wonderful persecuted

Pietro d'Abano[5] wrote this quatrain on the people's plaguing him about his mathematical studies and wanting to burn him—he helped to build Padua Cathedral, wrote a Treatise on Magic still extant, and passes for a conjuror in his country to this day—when there is a storm the mothers tell the children that he is in the air; his pact with the evil one obliged him to drink no *milk*; no natural human food! You know Tieck's novel about him?[6] Well, this quatrain is said, I believe truly, to have been discovered in a well ↑near Padua↓ some fifty years ago.[7]

> Studiando le mie cifre, col compasso
> Rilevo, che presto sarò sotterra—
> Perchè del mio saper si fa gran chiasso,
> E gl'ignoranti m'hanno mosso guerra.

Affecting, is it not, in its simple, child like plaining? Now so, if I remember, I turned it—word for word—

> Studying my ciphers, with the compass
> I reckon—who soon shall be below ground,
> Because of my lore they make great "rumpus,"
> And against me war makes each dull rogue round.

Say that you forgive me to-morrow!

> [With my compass I take up my ciphers, poor scholar, . .
> Who myself shall be taken down ↑soon↓ under the ground . .
> Since the world at my learning roars out in its choler,
> And the blockheads have fought me all round.][8]

---

1. *Trojan Women* (Troades).
2. The February 7 *Athenæum* printed the second part of a review of Leigh Hunt's *Stories from the Italian Poets: with Lives of the Writers*. It quotes the following lines of Lorenzo de Medici's *La caccia col falcone* and Hunt's translation of them.

> Luigi Pulci ov'è, che non si sente?
> Egli se n'ando dianzi in qual boschetto,
> Che qualche fantasia ha per la mente;
> Vorr a fantasticar forse un sonnetto.

> And where's Luigi Pulci? I saw *him.*
> Oh, in the wood there. Gone, depend upon it,
> To vent some fancy in his brain—some whim,
> That will not let him rest till it's a sonnet.

3. "Bad, very bad."
4. "Translate thus, on my responsibility, my little eye!" The epithet is simply approving.

5. Pietro d'Abano (ca. 1250–ca. 1316), philosopher and physician, a founder of Padua's medical school, was twice summoned before the Inquisition and died before his second trial.

6. Johann Ludwig Tieck (1773–1853), German romantic writer—novelist, poet, and critic. A translation of his *Pietro von Abano oder Petrus Apone* (1825) was published in the August 1839 *Blackwood's*.

7. Browning introduced this quatrain, with a translation very like the one he gives here, into his *Pietro of Abano* (1880). See DeVane, pp. 452–453.

8. Added in E.B.B.'s hand.

Browning noted a visit on the envelope of Letter 225:
+Monday. Feb. 9.
3–5¼ p.m. (45.)

228 (W113°)   *E.B.B. to R.B.*

──────────────

[*February 10, 1846.*]

Tuesday.

Ever dearest, I have been possessed by your Luria just as you would have me, & I should like you to understand, not simply how fine a conception the whole work seems to me, so developed, but how it has moved & affected me, without the ordinary means & dialect of pathos, by that calm attitude of moral grandeur which it has—it is very fine. For the execution, *that* too is worthily done . . although I agree with you, that a little quickening & drawing in closer here & there, especially toward the close where there is no time to lose, the reader feels, would make the effect stronger—but you will look to it yourself—and such a conception *must* come in thunder & lightning, as a chief god would—*must* make its own way . . & will not let its poet go until he speaks it out to the ultimate syllable. Domizia disappoints me rather. You might throw a flash more of light on her face—might you not? But what am I talking? I think it a magnificent work—a noble exposition of ↑the↓ ingratitude of men against their "heroes," & (what is peculiar) an *humane* exposition . . not misanthropical, after the usual fashion of such things: for the return, the remorse, saves it—& the 'Too late" of the repentance & compensation covers with its solemn toll the fate of per-

445

secutors & victim—We feel that Husain himself could only say after-ward . . *" That is done."* And now . . surely you think well of the work as a whole? You cannot doubt, I fancy, of the grandeur of it—& of the *subtilty* too, for it is subtle—too subtle perhaps for stage purposes, though as clear, . . as to expression . . as to medium . . as "bricks and mortar"[1] . . shall I say?

> "A people is but the attempt of many
> To rise to the completer life of one."[2]

There is one of the fine thoughts. And how fine *he* is, your Luria, when he looks back to his East, ⟨with⟩ /that⟩through/ the halfpardon and halfdisdain of Domizia—Ah—Domizia! would it hurt her to make her more a woman . . a little? . . I wonder!—

So I shall begin from the beginning, from the first act, and read *through* . . since I have read the fifth twice over. And remember, please, that I am to read, besides, the 'Soul's Tragedy,' & that I shall dun you for it presently. Because you told me it was finished . . otherwise I would not speak a word, . . feeling that you want rest, & that I, who am anxious about you, would be crossing my own purposes by driving you into work. It is the overwork the overwear of mind & heart, (for the feelings come as much into use as the thoughts in these productions) that makes you so pale, . . dearest!—that distracts your head . . & does all the harm on saturdays & so many other days beside.

To-day . . how are you? It *was* right & just for me to write this time, after the two dear notes . . the one on saturday night which made me praise you to myself & think you kinder than kindest, & the other on Monday morning which took me unaware . . such a note, *that* was! Oh it WAS right & just that I should not teaze you to send me another after those two others,—yet I was very near doing it—yet I should like in-finitely to hear to-day how you are—unreasonable!—Well!—you will write now—you will answer what I am writing, & mention yourself particularly & sincerely—Remember!—Above all, you will care for your head—I have been thinking since yesterday that, ⟨you⟩ coming out of the cold, you might not have refused as usual to take something . . hot wine & water, or coffee? Will you have coffee with me on saturday? "Shunning the salt," will you have the sugar?—And do tell me—for I have been thinking,—are you careful as to diet . . & will such sublunary things as coffee & tea & cocoa affect your head . . *for* or *against?* Then you do not touch wine—and perhaps you ought. Surely something may be found or done to do you good—If it had not been for me, you would be travelling in Italy by this time & quite well perhaps.

This morning I had a letter from Miss Martineau[3] & really read it to the end without thinking it too long, which is extraordinary for me just now, & scarcely ordinary in the letter . . & indeed it is a delightful letter, as letters go, which are not yours! You shall take it with you on Saturday to read, & you shall see that it is worth reading, & interesting for Wordsworth's sake & her own—Mr. Kenyon has it now, because he presses on to have her letters, & I should not like to tell him that you had it first from me. Also saturday will be time enough.

Oh—poor Mr. Horne! shall I tell you some of his offences?—That he desires to be called at four in the morning, & does not get up till eight. That he pours libations on his bare head out of the water-glasses at great dinners. That being in the midst of sportsmen . . rural aristo-crats . . lords of soil,—& all talking learnedly of pointers' noses & spaniels' ears,—he has exclaimed aloud in a mocking paraphrase . . "If I were to hold up a horse by the tail." (The wit is certainly doubtful!)— That being asked to dinner on tuesday, he will go on wednesday in-stead.—That he throws himself at full length with a gesture approaching to a "summerset" on satin sofas. That he giggles. That he only *thinks* he can talk. That his ignorance on all subjects is astounding. That he never read the old ballads, nor saw Percy's collection. That he asked *who* wrote "Drink to me only with thine eyes." That after making himself ridicu-lous in attempting to speak at a public meeting, he said to a compassion-ate friend "I got very well out of THAT" . . That, in writing his work on Napoleon,[4] he employed a man to study the subject for him . . That he cares for nobody's poetry or fame except his own, & considers Tennyson chiefly illustrious as being his contemporary. That, as to politics, he doesn't care *"which* side"—That he is always talking of "my shares," "my income," as if he were a Kilmansegg.[5] Lastly (& understand, this is *my* 'lastly' & not Miss Mitford's, who is far from being out of breath so soon) that he has a mania for heiresses—that he has gone out at half past five & 'proposed' to Miss M or N with fifty thousand pounds, & being rejected (as the lady thought fit to report herself) came back to tea & ˄the same evening˅ 'fell in love' with Miss O or P . . with forty thousand—went away for a few months, & upon his next visit, did as much to a Miss Q or W, on the promise of four blood horses—has a prospect now of a Miss R or S . . . with hounds, perhaps.

Too, too bad—isn't it? I would repeat none of it except to you—& as to the worst part, the last, why some may be coincidence, & some, exaggeration, for I have not the least doubt that every now & then a fine poetical compliment was turned into a serious thing by the listener, . . & then the poor poet had critics as well as listeners all round him. Also, he rather 'wears his heart on his sleeve,' there is no denying—& in other respects he is not much better, perhaps, than other men. But for the base traffic of the affair . . I do not believe a word. He is too generous—has too much real sensibility. I fought his battle, poor Orion. "And so," she said, 'you believe it possible for a disinterested man to become really attached to two women . . heiresses . . on the same day?' I doubted the *fact*. And then she showed me a note, an autograph note ↑from the poet↓ confessing the M or N part of the business—while Miss O or P confessed herself, said Miss Mitford. But I persisted in doubting, notwithstanding the lady's confessions & convictions, as they /might⟩may/ be. And just think of Mr. Horne, not having tact enough to keep out of these multitudinous scrapes, for those few days which on three separate occasions he paid Miss Mitford in a neighbourhood where all were strangers to him!—& never outstaying his week! He must have been *foolish,* . . read it all how we may.

And so am *I*, to write this 'personal talk' to you when you will not care for it—yet you asked me, & it may make you smile, though Wordsworth's teakettle outsings it all.

When your Monday letter came, I was reading the criticism on Hunt and his Italian poets, in the Examiner. How I liked to be pulled by the sleeve to your translations!—How I liked everything!—Pulci, Pietro . . & you, best!

Yet here's a naïveté which I found in your letter! I will write it out that you may read it—

"However" (the headache) "was no sooner gone in a degree, than a worse plague came—*I sate thinking of you.*"

Very satisfactory *that* is, & very clear.

May God bless you dearest dearest! Be careful of yourself. The cold makes me *languid* . . as heat is apt to make everybody; but I am not unwell, & keep up the fire & the thoughts of you.

Your worst . . worst plague

Your own
Ba—

I shall hear? yes! And admire my obedience /to have⟩in having/ written "a long letter" *to* the letter!

1. Quoted from Letter 223.
2. *Luria*, V, 299–300.
3. Printed before Letter 233.
4. *A History of Napoleon* (London, 1841) with 500 illustrations, edited by Horne with the assistance of Mary Gillies. Eric J. Shumaker, *Concise Bibliography* . . . (Granville, Ohio, 1943), p. 3.
5. See Thomas Hood's satire on riches, *Miss Kilmansegg and Her Precious Leg* (1840).

229 (W114)　　　　　　　*R.B. to E.B.B.*

──────────────

[*February 11, 1846*.]

Wednesday Morning.

My sweetest 'plague,' *did* I really write that sentence so, without gloss or comment in close vicinity? I can hardly think it—but you know well, well, where the real plague lay,—that I thought of you as thinking, in your infinite goodness, of untoward chances which had kept me from you—and If I did not dwell more particularly on that thinking of *yours*, which became as I say, in the knowledge of it, a plague when brought before me *with* the thought of you,—if I passed this slightly over it was for pure unaffected shame that I should take up the care and stop the "reverie serene" of . . ah, the rhyme *lets* me say—"sweetest eyes were ever seen"[1]—were *ever* seen! And yourself confess, in the Saturday's note, to having been "unhappy for half an hour till" &c &c.—and do not I feel *that* here, and am not I plagued by it?

Well, having begun at the end of your letter, dearest, I will go back gently (that is, backwards) and tell you I 'sate thinking' too, and with no greater comfort, on the cold yesterday. The pond before the window was frozen ("so as to bear sparrows" somebody said) and I knew you would feel it—"but you are not unwell"—really? thank God—and the month wears on: beside I have got a reassurance—you asked me once if I were superstitious, I remember . . (as what do I forget that you say?)— However that may be, yesterday morning as I turned to look for a book, an old fancy siezed me to try the "sortes" and dip into the first page of the first I chanced upon, for my fortune; I said "what will be the event of my love for Her"—in so many words—and my book turned out to be—"Cerutti's Italian Grammar"[2]—a propitious source of information . . the best to be hoped, what could it prove but some assurance that you were in the Dative Case, or I, not in the ablative absolute? I do protest that, with the knowledge of so many horrible pitfalls, or rather spring guns with wires on every bush . . such dreadful possibilities of stumbling on "conditional moods" . . "imperfect tenses" . . "singular numbers,"—I should have been too glad to put up with the safe spot for the sole of my foot tho' no larger than afforded by such a word as "Conjunction," "possessive pronoun—," secure, so far, from poor Tippet's catastrophe: well, I ventured—and what did I find? *This*—which I copy from the book now—"*If we love in the other world as we do in this, I shall love thee to eternity*"—from "Promiscuous Exercises," to be translated into Italian, at the end.

And now I reach Horne and his characteristics—of which I can tell you with confidence that they are grossly misrepresented where not altogether false—whether it proceed from inability to see what one may see, or disinclination, I cannot say. I know very little of Horne, but my one visit to him a few weeks ago would show the uncandidness of those charges—for instance, he talked a good deal about horses, meaning to ride in Ireland,—and described very cleverly an old hunter he had hired once,—how it galloped and could not walk—also he propounded a theory of the true method of behaving in the saddle when a horse rears, which I besought him only to practise in fancy on the sofa, where he lay telling it—so much for professing his ignorance in that matter! On a sofa he does throw himself—but when thrown there, he *can* talk, with Miss Mitford's leave, admirably,—I never heard better stories than Horne's—some Spanish-American incidents of travel want printing—or have been printed, for aught I know. That he cares for nobody's poetry is *false*—he praises more unregardingly of his own retreat, more unprovidingly for his own fortune,—(do I speak clearly?)—less like a man who himself has written somewhat in the "line" of the other man he is praising—which "somewhat" has to be guarded in its interests, &c, less like the poor professional praise of the 'craft' than *any* other I ever met—instance after instance starting into my mind as I write: to his income I never heard him allude—unless one should so interpret a remark to me this last time we met, that he had been on some occasion

put to inconvenience by somebody's withholding ten or twelve pounds
due to him for an article, and promised in the confidence of getting
them to a tradesman, which does not look like "boasting of his income"! As for the "heiresses"—I don't believe one word of it, of the
succession and transition and trafficking. Altogether, what miserable
"set-offs" to the achievement of an "Orion," a "Marlowe," a
"Delora"! Miss Martineau understands him better.

Now I come to myself and my health. I am quite well now—at all
events, much better, just a little turning in the head—since you appeal
to my sincerity. For the coffee—thank you,—indeed thank you, but
nothing after the "œnomel"[3] and before half past six! *I* know all
about that song and its Greek original[4] if Horne does not—and can
tell you—, how truly. . !

> The thirst that from the soul doth rise
> Doth ask a drink divine—
> But might I of Jove's nectar sup
> I would not change for thine! *No, no, no!*

(And by the bye, I have misled you as my wont is, on the subject of
wine, "that I do not touch it"—not habitually, nor so as to feel the
loss of it, that on a principle: but every now and then of course.)

And now, Luria, so long as the parts cohere and the whole is discernible, all will be well yet. I shall not look at it, nor think of it, for a
week or two, and then see what I have forgotten. Domizia is all wrong
—I told you I knew that her special colour had faded,—it was but a
bright line, and the more distinctly deep that it was so narrow—One
of my half dozen words on my scrap of paper "pro memoriâ" was,
under the "Act V," "*she loves*"—to which I could not bring it, you
see! Yet the play requires it still,—something may yet be effected,
though: I meant that she should propose to go to Pisa with him, and
begin a new life. But there is no hurry—I suppose it is no use publishing much before Easter—I will try and remember what my whole
character *did* mean—it was, in two words, understood at the time by
"panther's-beauty"—on which hint I ought to have spoken! But
the work grew cold, and you came between, and the sun put out the
fire on the hearth "nec vult panthera domari!"[5]

For the Soul's Tragedy—*that* will surprise you, I think—There is
no trace of you there,[6]—you have not put out the black face of *it*—it
is all sneering and *disillusion*—and shall not be printed but burned if

you say the word—now wait and see and then say! I will bring the first of the two parts next Saturday.

And now, dearest, I am with you—and the other matters are forgotten already. God bless you, I am ever your own R. (You will write to me I trust? And tell me how to bear the cold.)

1. A current refrain from E.B.B.'s *Catarina to Camoens* (1844).
2. Angelo Cerutti, a native Italian, was Browning's own tutor (G & M p. 20). The text of the *sortes* may have suggested the close of *Sonnets from the Portuguese*, XLIII; see E.B.B.'s reaction in the following letter.
3. A mixture of wine and honey; Browning alludes to E.B.B.'s *Wine of Cyprus*, final stanza.
4. Jonson's lyric paraphrases a prose passage in Philostratus, *Epistles* XXIV.
5. "Nor does the panther wish to be tamed!"
6. The play was written "two or three years" earlier. See Letter 231 and DeVane, pp. 190ff.

230 (W114°)   *E.B.B. to R.B.*

[*Postmarked February 12, 1846.*]

Ah, the 'sortes'!—Is it a double oracle . . . 'swan & shadow,'[1] . . do you think? . . or do my eyes see double, dazzled by the light of it? —"I shall love thee to eternity"—I *shall*.

And as for the wine, I did not indeed misunderstand you "as my wont is," because I understood simply that "habitually" you abstained from wine . . & I meant exactly that perhaps it would be better for your health to take it habitually—It *might*, you know—not that I pretend to advise. Only when you look so much too pale sometimes, it comes into one's thoughts that you ought not to live on cress & cold water. Strong coffee, which is the nearest to a stimulant that I dare to take, as far as ordinary diet goes, will almost always deliver *me* from the worst of headaches . . but there is no likeness, no comparison. And your 'quite well' means that dreadful 'turning' still . . still!—Now do not think any more of the Domizias, nor 'try to remember,' which is the most wearing way of thinking. The more I read & read your Luria, the grander it looks—and it will make its own road with all understanding men, you need not doubt . . & still less need you try to make me uneasy about the harm I have done in "coming between," & all the rest of it—I wish never to do you greater harm than just *that*,—& then with a white conscience 'I shall love thee to eternity!' . . dearest! You have made a golden work out of your 'goldenhearted Luria' . . as once you called him to me,—& I hold it in the highest admiration—*should*, if you were precisely nothing to me. And still, the fifth act *rises!*—That is certain. Nevertheless I seem to agree with you that your hand has vacillated in your Domizia—We do not know her with as full a light on her face, as the other persons—we do not see the *panther*, . . no, certainly we do not—but you will do a very little for her which will be everything, after a time . . & I assure you that if you were to ask for the manuscript ↑before↓ you should not have a page of it—⟨nor a⟩ *now*, you are only to rest. What a work to rest upon! Do consider what a triumph it is!—The more I read, the more I think of it, the greater it grows—and as to "faded lines," you never cut a pomegranate that was redder in the deep of it—Also, no one can say 'This is not clearly written.' The people who are at "words of one syllable" may be puzzled by you & Wordsworth together this time . . as far as the expression goes. Subtle thoughts you always must have, in & out of Sordello—& the objectors would find even Plato (though his medium is as lucid as the water that ran beside the beautiful plane-tree!) a little difficult perhaps.

To-day Mr. Kenyon came . . & do you know, he has made a beatific confusion between last Saturday & next Saturday, & said to me he had told Miss Thomson to mind to come on friday if she wished to see me . . "remembering" (he added) 'that Mr. Browning took *Saturday!!*' —So I let him mistake the one week for the other— 'Mr. Browning took Saturday,' it was true, both ways. Well—and then he went on to tell me that he had heard from Mrs. Jameson who was at Brighton & unwell, & had written to say this & that to him, & to enquire besides . . now what do you think, she enquired besides? "how you and . . Browning were" said Mr. Kenyon—I write his words. He is coming . . perhaps to-morrow, or perhaps Sunday—Saturday is to have a twofold safety—That is, if you are not ill again. Dearest, you will not think of coming if you are ill . . unwell even. I shall not be frightened next time, as I told you—I shall have the precedent. Before, I had to think!! 'It has never happened *so*—there must be a cause—and if it is a very, very, bad cause, why no one will tell *me* . . ↑it will not seem *my* concern'—↓ *that* was my thought on Saturday. But another time . .

only, if it is possible to keep well, do keep well, beloved, & think of me instead of Domizia, & let there be no other time for your suffering . . my waiting is nothing. I shall remember for the future that you may have the headache—& do you remember it too!—

For Mr. Horne I take your testimony gladly & believingly. SHE *blots* with her *eyes* sometimes. She hates . . and loves, in extreme degrees. We have, once or twice or thrice, been on the border of mutual displeasure, on this very subject, . . for I grew really vexed to observe the trust on one side & the *dyspathy* on the other . . using the mildest of words. You see, he found himself, down in Berkshire, in quite a strange element of society,—he, an artist in his good & his evil,—& the people there, "county families," smoothly plumed in their conventions, & classing the ringlets & the aboriginal way of using waterglasses among offences against the Moral Law. Then . . meaning to be agreeable . . or fascinating perhaps, made it twenty times worse. Writing in albums about the Graces discoursing meditated impromptus at picnics, playing on the guitar in fancy dresses, . . all these things which seemed to poor Orion as natural as his own stars I dare say, & just the things suited to the *genus* poet, and to himself ⟨in⟩ specifically . . were understood by the natives & their 'rural deities' to signify, that he intended to marry one half ⟨of⟩ the county, to run away with the other. But Miss Mitford should have known better—*she* should—And she *would* have known better, if she had liked him—for the liking could have been unmade by no such offences. She is too fervent a friend—she can be. Generous too, she can be without an effort—& I have had much affection for her—& accuse myself for seeming to have less— but . .

May God bless you!—I end in haste after this long lingering.

—Your Ba

Not unwell—*I* am not! I forgot it, which proves how I am not.

---

1. Wordsworth's *Yarrow Unvisited*, ll. 3–4. "[Let] The swan on still St. Mary's Lake / Float double, swan and shadow."

231 (W115)   R.B. to E.B.B.
_____

[*February 13, 1846.*]

Friday M^g

Two nights ago I read the 'Soul's Tragedy' once more—and
though there were not a few points which still struck me as successful
in design & execution, yet on the whole I came to a decided opinion—
that it will be better to postpone the publication of it for the present: it
is not a good ending,—an auspicious wind-up of this series,—subject-
matter & style are alike unpopular even for the literary *grex*[1] that stands
aloof from the purer *plebs*,[2] and uses that privilege to display & parade
an ignorance which the other is altogether unconscious of—so that, if
Luria is *clearish*, the Tragedy would be an unnecessary troubling the
waters: whereas, if I printed it first in order, my readers, according to
custom, would make the (comparatively) little they did not see into, a
full excuse for shutting their eyes at the rest—and we may as well part
friends, so as not to meet enemies: but, at bottom, I believe the proper
objection is to the immediate, *first* effect of the whole—its moral effect,—
which is dependent ⟨of⟩ on the contrary supposition of its being really
understood, in the main drift of it—yet I don't know; for I wrote it with
the intention of producing the best of all effects—perhaps the truth is, that
I am tired, rather, and desirous of getting done, and Luria will answer
my purpose so far: will not the best way be to reserve this unlucky
play and, in the event of a second edition,—as Moxon seems to think
such an apparition possible,—might not this be quietly inserted?—in
its place, too, for it was written two or three years ago. I have lost, of
late, interest in dramatic writing, as you know—and, perhaps, occasion.
And, dearest, I mean to take your advice and be quiet awhile and let
my mind get used to its new medium of sight—, seeing all things, as
it does, thro' you: and then, let all I have done be the prelude and the
real work begin—I felt it would be so before, and told you ⟨the⟩
₊at₊ the very beginning—do you remember? And you spoke of Io
"in the proem"[3]—How much more should follow now!

And if nothing follows, I have *you*.

I shall see you to-morrow and be happy. To-day—is it the
weather or what?—something depresses me a little—to-morrow

brings the remedy for it all. I don't know why I mention such a matter; except that I tell you everything without a notion of after-consequences—, and because your dearest, dearest presence seems under any circumstances as if created just to help me *there*,—if my spirits rise they fly to you; if they fall, they hold by you and cease falling—as now. Bless you, Ba—my own best blessing that you are! But a few hours and I am with you, beloved!

Your own
R.

1. "Herd."
2. "Common people."
3. See Letter 6.

E.B.B.'s following letter was begun a few hours after the visit recorded on the envelope of Letter 230:

+Sat^y Feb 14
3–5.5 p.m. (46.)

232 (W115°)   *E.B.B. to R.B.*

[*February 14, 1846.*]

Saturday evening.

Ever dearest, though you wanted to make me say one thing dis-pleasing to you today, I had not the courage to say two instead .. which I might have done indeed & indeed!—For I am capable of thinking both thoughts of "next year," as you suggested them :—because while you are with me I see only *you*, & you being you, I cannot doubt a power of yours nor measure the deep loving nature which I feel to be so deep—so that there may be ever so many 'mores,' & no 'more' wonder of mine! —but afterwards, when the door is shut & there is no 'more' light nor speaking until thursday, why *then*, that I do not see *you* but *me*, .. *then* come the reaction, .. the natural lengthening of the shadows at sunset .. & *then*, the "less, less, less" grows to seem /so>as/ natural to my fate, as the "more" seemed to your nature—I being I!—

Sunday [February 15].—Well!—you are to try to forgive it all! And the truth, over & under all, is, that I scarcely ever do think of the future . . scarcely ever further than to your next visit . . & almost never ⊦beyond⊣ except for your sake & in reference to that view of the question which I have vexed you with so often, in fearing for your happiness. Once it was a habit of mind with me to live altogether in what I called the future—but the tops of the trees that looked towards Troy, were broken off in the great winds, & falling down into the river beneath, where now after all this time they grow green again, I let them float along the current gently & pleasantly.—Can it be better I wonder! —And if it becomes worse, can I help it? Also the future never seemed to belong to me so little—never!—It might appear wonderful to most persons, it is startling even to myself sometimes, to observe how free from anxiety I am . . from the sort of anxiety which might be well connected with my own position *here* . . & which is personal to myself. *That* is all thrown behind . . into the bushes—long ago it was, . . & I think I told you of it before. Agitation comes from indecision—and *I* was decided from the first hour when I admitted the possibility of your loving me really.—Now, . . as the Euphuists used to say, . . I am "more thine than my own" . . it is a literal truth—& my future belongs to you: if it was mine, it was mine to give, and if it was mine to give, it was given, . . and if it was given . . beloved . . . .

So you see!

Then I will confess to you that all my life long I have had ⟨two⟩ ⊦a⊣ rather strange sympathy & dyspathy—the sympathy having concerned the genus *jilt* (as vulgarly called) male and female—and the dyspathy the whole class of heroically virtuous persons who make sacrifices of what they call 'love' to what they call 'duty.' There are exceptional cases of course—but, for the most part, I listen incredulously or else with a little contempt to those latter proofs of strength . . or weakness . . as it may be :—people are not usually praised for giving up their religion . . for unsaying their oaths . . for desecrating their 'holy things' ⊦while believing them still to be religious and sacramental!⊣ On the other side I have always & shall always ⟨‖ · · · ‖⟩ understand how it is possible for the most earnest & faithful of men & even of women perhaps, to err in the convictions of the heart as well as of the mind, to profess an affection which is an illusion, and to recant & retreat loyally at the eleventh hour, on becoming aware of the truth which is in them. Such men are the truest of men, . . & the most courageous for the truth's sake, . . & instead of blaming them I hold them in honour, for me, & always did & shall.

And while I write, you are 'very ill'—very ill!—how it looks, written down *so!*—When you were gone yesterday & my thoughts had tossed about restlessly for ever so long, I was wise enough to ask Wilson how *she* thought you were looking, . . & she "did not know" . . she "had not observed" . . "only certainly Mr. Browning ran upstairs instead of walking as he did the time before"—

Now promise me dearest, dearest—not to trifle with your health . . not to neglect yourself . . not to tire yourself . . & besides to take the advice of your medical friend as to diet & general treatment—because there must be a wrong & a right in everything, & the right is very important under your circumstances . . if you have a tendency to illness— It may be right for you to have wine for instance. Did you ever try the putting your feet into hot water at night, to prevent the recurrence of the morning headache . . for the affection of the head comes on early in the morning . . does it not? . . just as if the sleeping did you harm. Now I have heard of such a remedy doing good—and could it *increase* the evil?—mustard mixed with the water, remember. Everything approaching to *congestion* is full of fear—I tremble to think of it . . & I bring no remedy by this teazing neither!—But you will not be "wicked" nor "unkind," nor provoke the evil consciously—you will keep quiet & forswear the going out at nights, the excitement & noise of parties, & the worse excitement of composition—you promise. If you knew how I keep thinking of you, & at intervals grow so frightened!—Think *you*, that you are three times as much to me as I can be to you at best & greatest, . . because you are more than three times the larger planet . . & because too, you have known other sources of light & happiness . . . but I need not say this—& I shall hear on monday, & may trust to you every day . . may I not? Yet I would trust my soul to you sooner than your own health.

May God bless you, dear, dearest. If the first part of the 'Soul's Tragedy' should be written out, I can read *that* perhaps, without drawing you in to think of the second. Still it may be safer to keep off altogether for the present—& let it be as you incline. I do not speak of Luria.

Your own Ba

If it were not for Mr. Kenyon, I should say . . almost . . wednesday, instead of thursday . . I want to see you so much, & to see for myself about the looks & spirits—only it would not do if he found you here on wednesday. Let him come to-morrow or on tuesday, & wednesday will be safe— shall we consider? what do you think?

> *Browning sent his next letter in a paper wrapper and enclosed the one from Harriet Martineau to E.B.B. mentioned in Letter 228 which had been given to him on the previous Saturday. The manuscript original is now in the Yale Library. Since Browning's letter is a running commentary on Miss Martineau's the text of her letter is here given in full, save for the brief portion already cited in a note to Letter 54.*

Ambleside
Feby 8th

Dear Miss Barrett,
Here I come at last, with my news of our Happy Valley. And it is such a day that I shall be wishing for you to see the valley when I go out, on finishing this, & walk around one of our own commonest circuits. As I look out now, there are the highest peaks glittering in a rose tinted snow,—the lower ranges red & brown, with dark hollows, & the lake blue & breezy, & the wild ducks scudding over it. The rocky promontories with their tall & graceful fir clumps are a perpetual delight to my eye, in all seasons; & now espec^y, when in the evg^s the slender moon hangs over the finest of them, & the brightest of planets casts its tail of light on the waters. But, beautiful as the view is here, & grateful as one might be to pass one's life in a house w^h has such windows, I much prefer the view from my own cottage. The lake is there seen only from afar, & thro' trees, a streak of blue in winter: but Wansfell rises so nobly,—its woods running along its hollows, & Ambleside nestles so charmingly under it, & the stretch of meadows to the South, & the paradisy valley to the west, with its streamlets leap^g down Loughrigg, & the Rotha rushing & winding at once, & the rocky knotts & noble clumps of trees make up such a picture that I daily wonder at my own bliss in being permitted to live with such a heaven before my Eyes. And now very soon I shall be living there. Next month, my maids & I hope to be inhabiting the upper rooms. Yes^y I sent in a couple of chairs, & to-morrow I shall put in a dust pan & brush,—signs of habitation! The reason of them is that there are to be fires kept every day now; & my good Jane (from

*Tynemouth) is to have the charge thereof, & [I am] going to help her to make
the blinds & kitchen linen &c, & to keep the dust down for varnishing (for I
choose to have no paint, except in the offices.) The drive & terrace have been
finished this last week, & some of my larches are in. The rest of the planting
will be done this week, we hope. I can't afford to spend anything on garden^g.—
the little that I can spare being all wanted for planting. But Jane & I can make
something pretty with our own hands, I am persuaded, & this very year, of the
tempting slopes & platforms & quarry. The little quarry has yielded the stones
for the terrace wall; & now it offers a pretty shelter for the delicate plants & has
a western aspect. We mean to hang it all with ivies, & honeysuckles & roses,
& tuft it with ferns, & then we will see what it shall guard. I have a beautiful
southern exposure from fruit trees . . . .*

*Evg/ Here entered a neighbour of mine—that rare sort of person, a happy
governess—to challenge me for a walk. And O! how I have walked today!
She & I went to my cottage; & afterw^{ds} I went alone for a glorious scramble up
Windermere. My walks have an additional interest now. I peep & pry every
where to find what I can help myself with for my rocks & nooks & slopes. In a
few days, my field will be empty of carts &c, & given over to me; & then Archy
Davy & his mother & I go, with our trowels & baskets, up into the woods, &
along the brooks, to get ivies, wood anemones & primroses, & such ferns as I
never saw before, & pansies, & such foxgloves as Wordsworth cherishes, pin-
ning them up against the wall—for they break down with their own beauty.
—But I won't write any more of my place,—except just to say that we hope to
be in before April. I assure you that gay as is my delight in it, the plan is a very
serious & even solemn one to me. It is my desire to keep up that union of practical domestic life with literary labour w^h has been such a blessing to me ever
since I held the pen: but I feel pretty confident that such work (authorship) of a
kind very serious & important to myself will be done on that spot where I so
lately sat on the grass, & resolved there to pitch my tent. I have a horror of a
mere booklife; or a life of books & society. I like a need to have some express &
daily share in somebody's comfort: & trust to find much peace & satisfaction as
a housekeeper, in making my maids happy, & perhaps a little wiser,—in
receiv^g overworked or delicate friends & relations to rest in my paradise, & in
the sort of strenuous handwork w^h I like better than authorship. I am fond of
making & mending,—never let anyone mend my stockings, gloves, &c,—like
making preserves, gingerbread & custards, cleaning pictures, gardening &c &c.
And across all these things, I see a pleasant prospect of congenial work. To-
morrow, I begin a new series of " The Playfellow": & this is all I w^d promise*

for the year. Next year a novel. In the summer, some of my family & friends are coming to see me, & we must be under the open sky all day. In the autumn, I must tear myself away from my paradise, for a few weeks, to see some of my brothers & sisters, & visit friends in & near town. About Nov^{br} I may be in town, choosing that dead time on purpose. I ought to wish that you may not be there; & indeed I do wish it. Of course, I cannot understand anything of the painful circums^s of disappointment you refer to; but I hope their influence may not extend into another season, but that you may be able to leave town,—able in health & in oppor^y. How much better you seem to show me you are! Surely almost everything may be hoped for you now,—perhaps even that you may one day sit on my terrace, with old Wordsworth stretched by your side, play^g with a flower, & discoursing of things great or trivial, as may happen. I have written freely to you of our wealth of delights,—partly because I know by experience that such images will yield refreshm^t to the prisoner, & yet more with a strong hope that the day is not far distant when you will enjoy many of these pleasures yourself.—I have never for a moment wondered, as you suppose, that you have not tried Mesmerism. Yours was a case in w^h I did not think it right to urge it; & tho' I imagine that in your present condition it might be exactly the best means of restoring you completely, I w^d never urge it, & certainly can never wonder at your reluctance. I think you overrate much the possibility of curious mental phenomena occurring. In the vast majority of cases nothing occurs but a felt infusion of strength & ease, with, pretty often, sleep; but the cases of an ulterior experience are comparatively very few. If I were by your side, I believe you w^d let me mesmerize you; & I believe you w^d thereupon quietly, & from day to day, grow strong: & that w^d be all: & that objectors w^d say that there was nothing in it, & you would have improved just the same without it.—I won't write more now about Mes^m, Except just to say that we all—except the physician's family—are seeing & learning more & more continually, & believ^g that the researches of Reichenbach, Gregory, Pacini & other scientific men are penetrat^g to the secret of the nature of the influence [for the passage omitted here, see note 2 to Letter 54].

*   The Wordsworths are an affliction just now. His only brother [Christopher] died a few days ago; & a nephew here is dying & they have had accounts from their sick daughter-in-law in Italy. But, as you can well conceive, he can lose himself completely in any interesting subject of thought, so as to forget his griefs. His mind is always completely full of the thing that may be in it; & there he was on Wed^y, his face all gloom & tears at two o'clock from the tidings of his brother's death rec^d an hour before, & lo! at three he was all animation, dis-*

*cussing the rationale of my extraor^y discourses (in the mesmeric state)—his
mind so wholly occupied that he was quite happy for the time. He is very
interest^g—merely as an old poet, without Wordsworthianism,—to those who
have seen him oftener than once or twice. His mind must always have been
essentially liberal; but now it is more obviously & charmingly so than I understand it used to appear. The mildness of age has succeeded to what used to be
thought a rather harsh particularity of opinion & manners. His conversⁿ can
never be anticipated. Sometimes he flows on in the utmost grandeur that even
you can conceive—leaving a strong impression of inspiration. At other times,
we blush & are annoyed at the extremity of bad taste with w^h he pertinaciously
dwells on the most vexatious & vulgar trifles. The first mood is all informed &
actuated by knowledge of Man; the other a strange & ludicrous proof of his
want of knowledge of men. I, deaf, can hardly conceive how he, with eyes &
ears, & a heart w^h leads him to converse with the poor in his incessant walks,
can be so unaware of their moral state. I dare say you need not be told how
sensual vice abounds in rural districts. Here it is flagrant bey^d any thing I ever
C^d have looked for; & here, while every Justice of the peace is filled with disgust, & every clergyⁿ with (almost) despair at the drunkenness, quarrelling &
extreme licentiousness with women,—here is dear good old Wordsworth for
ever talking of rural innocence, & deprecating any intercourse with towns, lest
the purity of his neighbours sh^d be corrupted! He little knows what elevation,
selfdenial & refinement accrue in towns from the superior culture of the people.
The virtues of the people here are also of a sort different, we think, from what
he supposes. The people are very industrious, thrifty, prudent, & so well off
as to be liberal in their dealings. They pride themselves on doing their work
capitally; & in this point of honour, they are exemplary.*

*You know W's affairs are most comfortable in his old age. His wife is
perfectly charming & the very angel he sh^d have to tend him. His life is a most
serene & happy one, on the whole, & while all goes* methodically, *he is
happy & cheery & courteous & benevolent,—so that one C^d almost worship
him. But to secure this, every body must be punctual, & the fire must burn
bright, & all go orderly,—his angel takes care that everything shall, as far as
depends on her. He goes every day to Miss Fenwick, (he always needs some
such daily object,—& she is the worthiest possible)—gives her a smacking
kiss, & sits down before the fire to open his mind. Think what she could tell,
if she survives him! He does me the honour (to my amazement & to his great
honour) to be fond of me; but I see less of them than I shall do when I get to
the Knoll;—I don't ask him to come so far as my lodg^{gs}, & so only meet him in*

comp^y or when I call at the Mount ; & then only hear *him when he talks expressly to me. So I miss a good deal. I feel a growing love & tenderness for him, but cannot yet thoroughly connect—incorporate—him with his works ;—cannot yet feel him to be so great as they. But I shall ere long, if we live, & he takes to coming to my cottage.—I have not yet 1/2 done ; but I must stop for this time. God bless you, dear friend. Write when you can & like. Yours ever, H.M.*

[Postscript, added above the heading on the first page] Mr. Chorley & I are so kind you w^d be amused. I really doubt whether I shall ever have any quarrells if I can get people to join in my plan & practice of plain speaking,—in good humour, of course.

> *Miss Martineau prides herself on not quarreling with Chorley even though as a staff member of the* Athenæum *he was a party to its energetic attacks on her for her faith in mesmerism.*

233 (W116)   **R.B. to E.B.B.**

[*February 15, 1846.*]

Sunday Afternoon.

Here is the letter again, dearest: I suppose it gives me the same pleasure, in reading, as you—and Mr. K. as me, and anybody else as him ; if all the correspondence which was claimed again and burnt on some principle or other some years ago[1] be at all of the nature of this sample, the measure seems questionable: burn anybody's *real* letters, well & good—they move & live—the thoughts, feelings, & expressions even,— in a self-imposed circle limiting the experience of two persons only— *there* is the standard, and to *that* the appeal—how should a third person know ? His presence breaks the line, so to speak, and lets in a whole tract of country on the originally inclosed spot—so that its trees, which were from side to side there, seem left alone and wondering at their sudden unimportance in the broad land,— while its "ferns such as I never saw before" and ⁺which⁺ have been petted proportionably, /seem⟩look/ extravagant enough amid the new spread of good honest grey grass that is now the earth's general wear: so that the significance is lost at once, and whole value of such letters—the cypher changed, the

vowel-points removed: but how can that affect clever writing like this?
What do you, to whom it is addressed, see in it more than the world that
wants to see it and shan't have it? One understands shutting an un-
privileged eye to the ineffable mysteries of those "upper-rooms," now
that the broom & dust pan, stocking-mending and gingerbread-making
are invested with such unforeseen reverence . . but the carriage-sweep
and quarry, together with Jane and our baskets, and a pleasant shadow
of Wordsworth's Sunday hat preceding his own rapid strides in the
direction of Miss Fenwick's[2] house—surely, "men's eyes were made to
see, so let them gaze" at all *this*! And so I, gazing with a clear conscience,
am very glad to hear so much good of a very good person and so well
told: she plainly sees the proper use and advantage of a country-life; and
that knowledge gets to seem a high point of attainment doubtless by the
side of the Wordsworth she speaks of—for *mine* he shall not be as long as
I am able! Was ever such a *"great"* poet before? Put one trait with the
other—the theory of rural innocence—alternation of "vulgar trifles"
with dissertating with style of "the utmost grandeur that *even you* can
conceive" (speak for yourself, Miss M. . . !)—and that amiable transition
from two o'clock's grief at the death of one's brother to three o'clock's
happiness in the "extraordinary mesmeric discourse" of one's friend.
All this, and the rest of the serene & happy inspired daily life which a
piece of "unpunctuality" can ruin, and to which the guardian "angel"
brings as crowning qualification the knack of poking the fire adroitly—
of this—what can one say but that—no—best hold one's tongue and
read the Lyrical Ballads with finger in ear: did not Shelley say long ago
"He had no more *imagination* than a pint-pot"[3] tho' in those days he
used to walk about France and Flanders like a man—*Now*, he is "most
comfortable in his worldly affairs" and just this comes of it! He lives the
best twenty years of his life after the way of his own heart—and when
one presses in to see the result of the rare experiment . . what the *one*
alchemist whom fortune has allowed to get all his coveted materials and
set to work at last in earnest with fire and melting-pot what *he* produces
after all the talk of him and the like of him/well⟩why/—you get
pulvis et cinis[4]—a man at the mercy of the tongs and shovel!

Well! Let us despair at nothing, but, wishing success to the newer
aspirant, expect better things from Miss M. when the "knoll," and
"paradise," and their facilities, operate properly; and that she will make
a truer estimate of the importance & responsibilities of "authorship"

than she does at present, if I understand rightly the sense in which she describes her own life as ⟨‖ · · · ‖⟩ ⊦it means↓ to be—for in one sense it is all good and well—and quite natural that she should like "that sort of strenuous handwork" better than book-making; like the play better than the labour, as we are apt to do: if she realises a very ordinary scheme of literary life, planned under the eye of God not "the public," and prosecuted under the constant sense of the Night's coming which ends it good or bad—then, she will be sure to "like" the rest and sport—teaching her maids and sewing her gloves and making delicate visitors comfortable—so much more rational a resource is the worst of them than gin-and-water, for instance. But if, as I rather suspect, these latter are to figure as a virtual *half* duty of the whole Man—as of equal importance ⊦(on the ground of the innocence and utility of such occupations)↓ with the book-making aforesaid . . always supposing *that* to be of the right kind . . *then* I respect Miss M. just as I should an Archbishop of Canterbury whose business was the teaching A.B.C. at an infant-school —he who ⊦might↓ set on the Tens to instruct the Hundreds how to convince the Thousands of the propriety of doing that and many other things: of course one will respect him only the more if when *that* matter is off his mind he relaxes at such a school instead of over a chess-board; as it will increase our love for Miss M. to find that making "my good Jane (from Tyne-mouth)"—"happier and—I hope—wiser" is an amusement, or more, after the day's progress towards the "novel for next year" which is to inspire thousands, beyond computation, with the ardour of making innumerable other Janes and delicate relatives happier & wiser—who knows but as many as Burns did, and does, so make happier and wiser? Only, *his quarry* and after-solace was that "marble bowl often replenished with whiskey" on which Dr. Currie discourses mournfully.[5] "Oh, be wiser Thou!"—and remember it was only *after* Lord Bacon had written to an end *his* Book— given us for ever the Art of Inventing—whether steam-engine or improved dust-pan,—that he took on himself to do a little exemplary "hand work"; got out on that cold St. Alban's road to stuff a fowl with snow and so keep it fresh, and got into his bed and died of the cold in his hands ("strenuous *hand* work"—) before the snow had time to melt: he did not begin in his youth by saying—"I have a horror of merely writing Novum Organums and shall give half my energies to the stuffing fowls"!

All this it is *my* amusement, of an indifferent kind, to put down solely on the pleasant assurance contained in that postscript, of the one way of never quarrelling with Miss M.—"by joining in her plan and practice of plain speaking"—could she but "get people to do it!" Well, she gets me for a beginner: the funny thing would be to know what Chorley's desperate utterance amounted to! Did you ever hear of the plain speaking of some of the continental lottery-projectors? An estate on the Rhine, for instance, is to be disposed of, and the holder of the lucky ticket will find himself suddenly owner of a mediæval castle with an unlimited number of dependencies, vineyards, woods, pastures, and so forth[6]—all only waiting the new master's arrival—while inside, all is swept and garnished (not to say, varnished)—the tables are spread, the wines on the board, all is ready for the reception *but* . . here "plain speaking" becomes necessary—it prevents quarrels, and, could the projector get people to practise it as he does all would be well—, so he, at least, will speak plainly—you hear what *is* provided but, he cannot, dares not withhold what is *not*—there is then, to speak plainly,—no night cap! You *will* have to bring your own night cap. The projector furnishes somewhat, as you hear, but not *all*—and now—the worst is heard,—will you quarrel with him? Will my own dear, dearest Ba please and help me here, and fancy Chorley's concessions, and tributes, and recognitions, and then, at the very end, the "plain words," to counterbalance all, that have been to overlook and pardon?

Oh, my own Ba, hear *my* plain speech—and how this is *not* an attempt to frighten you out of your dear wish to "*hear* from me"—no, indeed—but a whim, a caprice,—and now it is out! over, done with! And *now* I am with you again—it is to *you* I shall write next. Bless you, ever—my beloved. I am much better, indeed—and mean to be well. And you! But I will write—this goes for nothing—or only *this*, that I am your very own—

R.

1. About 1841 Miss Martineau began to fear that her voluminous correspondence would fall into the hands of possible biographers. "She wrote all her correspondents to tell them that in the interest of the general sacredness of private correspondence she begged that they would be so good as to burn every letter they might receive in the future. She added that if they did not comply with the request they could never hope to hear from her again." Theodora Bosanquet, *Harriet Martineau: An Essay in Comprehension* (London: Etchels & H. Macdonald, 1927), pp. 141–142.

2. Isabella Fenwick (c. 1780–1856) was an intimate of the Wordsworth

household in the 1830's and 1840's and to her the poet dictated in 1843 the extended first-person notes and comments on his poems often reprinted with them. George McLean Harper, *William Wordsworth: His Life, Works, and Influence* (2 vols., New York: Chas. Scribner's Sons, 1916), II, 404–411.

3. *Peter Bell the Third*, IV, viii.

4. "Dust and ashes."

5. Dr. James Currie (1756–1805) edited the first collected edition (1800) of Burns's works and correspondence. In the prefixed life he tells of two Englishmen who visited Burns at Ellisland in 1791, of a punchbowl made of Inverary marble, and of how Burns and his guests emptied the bowl several times before midnight. But the "mournful" note seems to be Browning's addition. *The Works of Robert Burns*, ed. J. Currie (2nd ed.; 4 vols., London, 1801), I, 196–197.

6. Cf. *Aurora Leigh*, II, 1069ff.:

> Perhaps she . . .
>
> . . . .
>
> . . . touched a lottery with her finger-end,
> Which tumbled on a sudden into her lap
> Some old Rhine town or principality?

234 (W117)   **R.B. to E.B.B.**

[*February 16, 1846.*]

Monday.

My long letter is with you, dearest, to show how serious my illness was 'while you wrote': unless you find that letter too foolish, as I do on twice thinking—or at all events a most superfluous bestowment of "handwork" while the heart was elsewhere, and with you—never more so! Dear, dear Ba, your adorable goodness sinks into me till it nearly pains,—so exquisite and strange is the pleasure: *so* you care for me, and think of me, and write to me!—I shall never die for you,—and if it could be so, what would death prove? But I can live on, your own as now,—utterly your own.

Dear Ba, do you suppose we differ on so plain a point as that of the superior wisdom, and generosity, too, of announcing such a change &c at the eleventh hour? There can be no doubt of it: and now, what of it to me?

But I am not going to write to-day—only this—that I am better, having not been quite so well last night—so I shut up books . . (that is, of my own)—and mean to think about nothing but you, and you, and still you, for a whole week—so all will come right, I hope!— MAY I take Wednesday? And do you say that,—hint at the possibility of that, because you have been reached by my own remorse at feeling that if I had kept my appointment *last* Saturday (but one)—Thursday would have been my day this past week, and this very Monday had been gained?—Shall I not lose a day for ever unless I get Wednesday and Saturday?—Yet . . care . . dearest—let nothing horrible happen—

If I do not hear to the contrary to-morrow—or on Wednesday early—

But write and bless me, dearest, most dear Ba. God bless you ever—

R.

235 *(W116°[a])*[1]   *E.B.B. to R.B.*

[*February 15, 1846.*]

Monday Morning.

Méchant comme quatre! you are, & not deserving to be let see the famous letter— — —is there any grammar in *that* concatenation, can you tell me, now that you are in an arch-critical humour?—And re-member (turning back to the subject) that personally she & I are stran-gers & that therefore what she writes for me is naturally scenepainting to be looked at from a distance, done with a masterly hand & most amiable intention, but quite a different thing of course from the intimate revelations of heart & mind which make a living thing of a letter—If she had sent such to me, I should not have sent it to Mr. Kenyon . . but then, she would not have sent it to me in any case. What she *has* sent me might be a chapter in a book & has the life proper to itself . . & I shall not let you try it by another standard, even if you wished, but you don't— for I am not so *bête* as not to understand how the jest crosses the serious all the way ⟨in what⟩ you write. Well—& Mr. Kenyon wants the letter the second time, not for himself, but for Mr. Crabb Robinson who promises to let me have a new sonnet of Wordsworth's in exchange for the loan,[2] & whom I cannot refuse because he is an intimate friend of Miss Martineau's and once allowed me to read a whole packet of letters from her to him. She does not object (as I have read under her hand) to

her letters being shown about in MS., notwithstanding the anathema
against all printers of the same (which completes the extravagance of
the unreason, I think) & people are more anxious to see them from their
presumed nearness to annihilation. I, for my part, value letters . . (to talk
literature) . . as the most vital part of biography . . & for any rational
human being to put his foot on the traditions of his kind in this particular
class, does seem to me as wonderful as possible . . Who would put away
one of those multitudinous volumes, even, which stereotype Voltaire's
⟨witty⟩ wrinkles of wit . . even Voltaire?—I can read book after book
of such reading—or could . . ! And if her principle were carried out,
there would be an end!—Death would be deader from henceforth.
Also it is a wrong selfish principle & unworthy of her whole life &
profession, because we should all be ready to say that if the secrets of
our daily lives & inner souls may instruct other surviving souls, let
them be open to men hereafter, even as they are to God now. Dust to
dust, & soul-secrets to humanity—there are natural heirs to all these
things. Not that I do not intimately understand the shrinking back
from the idea of publicity on any terms—not that I would not myself
destroy papers of mine which were sacred to *me* /from⟩for/ personal
reasons—but then I never would call this natural ⟨failing⟩ ↑weakness,↓
virtue—nor would I, as a teacher of the public, announce it & attempt
to justify it as an example to other minds & acts, I hope.

How hard you are on the mending of stockings & the rest of it!—
Why not agree with me & like that sort of homeliness & simplicity in
combination with such large faculty as we must admit *there?* Lord Bacon
did a great deal of trifling besides the stuffing of the fowl you mention
. . which I did not remember: & in fact, all the great work done in the
world, is done just by the people who know how to trifle . . do you not
think so? When a man makes a principle of 'never losing a moment,'
he is a lost man. Great men are eager to find an hour, & not to avoid
losing a moment—"What are you doing" said somebody once (as I
heard the tradition) to the beautiful Lady Oxford as she sate in her open
carriage on the race-ground—"Only a little algebra," said she. People
who do a little algebra on the raceground are not likely to do much of
anything with ever so many hours for meditation. Why, you must
agree with me in all this, so I shall not be sententious any longer. Mending stockings is not exactly the sort of pastime *I* should choose . .
/but⟩who/ ⟨I⟩ do things quite as trifling without the utility . . & even

your Seigneurie peradventure . . . . I stop there for fear of growing impertinent. The 'argumentum ad hominem' is apt to bring down the 'argumentum ad baculum,'[3] it is as well to remember in time.

For Wordsworth . . you are right in a measure & by a standard— but I have heard such really desecrating things of him, of his selfishness, his love of money, his worldly *cunning* (rather than prudence) that I felt a relief & gladness in the new chronicle;—& you can understand how *that* was. Miss Mitford's doctrine is that everything put into the poetry, is taken out of the man +& lost utterly by him+ . . her general doctrine about poets, quite amounts to that . . I do not say it too strongly. And knowing that such opinions are held by minds not /obtuse⟩feeble/, it is very painful (as it would be indeed in any case) to see them apparently justified by royal poets like Wordsworth.— Ah, but I know an answer—I see one in my mind!—

So again for the letters. Now ought I not to know about letters, I who have had so many . . from chief minds too, as society goes in England & America?[4] And *your* letters began by being first to my intellect, before they were first to my heart. All the letters in the world are not like yours . . & I would trust them +for that verdict+ with any jury in Europe, if they were not so far too dear!—Mr. Kenyon wanted to make me show him your letters—I did show him the first, & resisted gallantly afterwards, which made him say what vexed me at the moment, . . 'oh—you let me see only *women's* letters!'—till I observed that it was a breach of confidence, except in some cases, . . & that *I* should complain very much ⟨myself⟩ if anyone, man or woman, acted to by myself. But nobody in the world writes like you . . not so *vitally*—and I have a right, if you please, to praise my letters, besides the reason of it which is as good.

Ah—you made me laugh about Mr. Chorley's free speaking— &, without the personal knowledge, I can comprehend how it could be nothing very ferocious . . some 'pardonnez moi, vous êtes un ange'——. The amusing part is that by the same post which brought me the Ambleside document, I heard from Miss Mitford "that it was an admirable thing of Chorley to have persisted in not allowing Harriet Martineau to quarrel with him" . . so that there are laurels on both sides, it appears.

And I am delighted to hear from you today just *so*, though I reproach you in turn just *so* . . because you were not 'depressed' in writing all this and this & this which has made me laugh—you were not, . . dearest—& you call yourself better, 'much better,' which means a very little perhaps, but is a golden word, let me take it as I may. May God bless you. Wednesday seems too near (now that this is Monday & you are better) to be *our* day . . perhaps it does,—& thursday *is* close beside it at the worst.

Dearest I am your own
Ba

1. This and the following letter arrived together and were assigned a single number.

2. Henry Crabb Robinson (1775–1867) was an intimate of the Lake Poets, Blake, and other eminent contemporaries. The identity of the newest Wordsworth sonnet at the time is disclosed in Mary Moorman, *William Wordsworth: Later Years* (Oxford: Clarendon Press, 1965) pp. 569–570: "[Wordsworth's] son John brought back from Italy in February [1846] a picture of Endymion and Diana, by Lucca Giordano. Wordsworth . . . gave it a sonnet"; this was *Evening Voluntaries* XIV, to be published in 1850.

3. Argument to the man (attacking the opponent, not his argument) and argument to the stick (threatening physical violence).

4. A joking reference to Horne's account of her in *A New Spirit of the Age;* see Letter 6, note 1.

236 (W116°[b])　　　　　　　**E.B.B. to R.B.**

――――――――――

[*February 15, 1846.*]

Monday evening.

　　Now forgive me, dearest of all, but I must teaze you just a little, & entreat you, if only for the love of me, to have medical advice & follow it *without further delay*. I like to have recourse to these medical people quite as little as you can . . but I am persuaded that it is necessary—that it is at least *wise*, for you to do so now . . &, you see, you were "not quite so well" again last night! So will you, for me? Would *I* not, if you wished it?—And on wednesday, yes, on wednesday, come—that is, if coming on wednesday should really be not bad for you . . for you *must* do what is right & kind . . and I doubt whether the omnibus-driving & the noises of every sort betwixt us, should not keep you away for a little while . . I trust you to do what is best for both of us.

And it is not best . . it is not good even, to talk about "dying for me" . . oh, I do beseech you never to use such words—You make me feel as if I were choking—Also it is nonsense—because nobody puts out a candle for the light's sake—

Write *one line* to me to-morrow literally so little . . just to say how you are. I know by the writing here, what *is*. Let me have the one line by the eight oclock post to-morrow, tuesday.

For the rest it may be my "goodness" or my badness, but the world seems to have sunk away beneath my feet and to have left only you to look & hold by—Am I not to *feel*, then, any trembling of the hand?—the least trembling?

May God bless both of us—which is a double blessing for me notwithstanding my badness—

I trust you about wednesday—& if it should be wise & kind not to come quite so soon, we will take it out of other days & lose not one of them. And as for anything "horrible" being likely to happen, do not think of that either:—there can be nothing horrible while you are not ill. So be well—try to be well . . use the means . . &, well or ill, let me have the one line to-morrow . . tuesday. I send you the foolish letter I wrote to-day ⸗in answer⸗ to your too long one—too long, was it not, as you felt? And I, the writer of the foolish one, am twice-foolish, and push poor 'Luria' out of sight, & refuse to finish my notes on him[1] till the harm he has done shall have passed away—In my badness I bring false accusation, perhaps, against poor Luria.

So till wednesday—or as you shall fix otherwise—

Your Ba

1. See Letter 66, note 1.

237 (W118)   R.B. to E.B.B.

[*February 17, 1846.*]

6½ Tuesday E[g]

My dearest, your note reaches me only now—with an excuse from the postman: the answer you expect, you shall have the only way

possible. I must make up a parcel so as to be able to knock & give it.
I shall be with you to-morrow, God willing—being quite well.

Bless you ever—

R.

The preceding letter lacks stamp or postmark, having been delivered personally at the door by Browning, as his text indicates. His record of the next day's visit is on the envelope of Letter 235:

+Wednesday, Feb. 17 [18]

3–5¼ p.m. (47.)

238 (W119)   R.B. to E.B.B.

[*February 19, 1846.*]

Thursday M^g

My sweetest, best, dearest Ba I *do* love you less, much less already,
and adore you more, more by so much more as I see of you, think of
you: I am yours just as much as those flowers; and you may pluck
those flowers to pieces or put them in your breast; it is not because
you so bless me now that you may not if you please one day——you
will stop me here; but it is the truth and I live in it.

I am quite well; indeed, this morning, *noticeably* well, they tell
me, and well I mean to keep if I can—

When I got home last evening I found this note—and I have
accepted, that I might say I could also keep an engagement, if so minded,
at Harley St.—thereby insinuating that other reasons *may* bring me into
the neighbourhood than *the* reason—but I shall either not go there, or
only for an hour at most. (I also found a note headed "Strictly private
and confidential"—so here it goes from my mouth to my heart—
pleasantly proposing that I should "start in a few days" for St.
Petersburg, as secretary to somebody going there on a "mission of
humanity"—*grazie tante!*)[1]

Did you hear of my meeting someone at the door whom I take
to have been one of your brothers?

One thing vexed me in your letter—I will tell you, the praise of *my* letters: now, one merit they have—in language mystical—that of having *no* merit. If I caught myself trying to write finely, graphically &c &c, nay, if I found myself conscious of having in my own opinion, so written—all would be over! yes, over! I should be respecting you inordinately, paying a proper tribute to your genius, summoning the necessary collectedness,—plenty of all that!—But the feeling with which I write to you, not knowing that it is writing,—with *you*, face and mouth and hair and eyes opposite me, touching me, knowing that all *is* as I say, and helping out the imperfect phrases from your own intuition—*that* would be gone—and *what* in its place? "Let us eat and drink for to-morrow we write to Ambleside."[2] No, no, love, nor can it ever be so, nor *should* it ever be so if—even if, preserving all that intimate relation, with the carelessness, *still*, somehow, was obtained with no effort in the world, graphic writing and philosophic and what you please—for I *will* be—*would* be, better than my works and words with an infinite stock beyond what I put into convenient circulation whether in fine speeches fit to remember, or fine passages to quote. For the rest, I had meant to tell you before now, that you often put me "in a maze" when you particularize letters of mine—"such an one was kind" &c. I know, sometimes I seem to give the matter up in despair—I take out paper and fall thinking on you, and bless you with my whole heart and then begin—'What a fine day this is"! I distinctly remember having done that repeatedly—but the converse is not true by any means, that (when the expression may happen to fall more consentaneously to the mind's motion) that less is felt; oh no! But the particular thought at the time has not been of the *insufficiency* of expression, as in the other instance—

Now I will leave off—to begin elsewhere—for I am always with you, beloved, best beloved! Now you will write? And walk much, and sleep more? Bless you, dearest—ever—

Your own,

R.

1. "Thanks so much."
2. To Harriet Martineau, see the note preceding Letter 233.

E.B.B.'s bad luck with the mail, which led Browning to deliver his own note on Tuesday evening and so provided the opening subject of the Letter 239, did not end there. The envelope of 239 bears postmarks for February 19 and 20 and the longhand notation " Missent to Mitcham."

239 (W117°)   **E.B.B. to R.B.**

──────────────

[*February 19, 1846.*]

Best and kindest of all that ever were to be loved in dreams, & wondered at & loved out of them, you are indeed!—I cannot make you feel how I felt that night when I knew that to save me an anxious thought you had come so far so late—it was almost too much to feel, & *is* too much to speak. So let it pass. You will never act so again, ever dearest—you shall not. If the post sins, why leave the sin to the post; & I will remember for the future, will be ready to remember, how post-men are ⟨in⟩fallible & how you live at the end of a lane—& not be uneasy about a silence if there should be one unaccounted for. For the tuesday coming, I shall remember that too—who could forget it? . . I put it in the niche of the wall, one golden lamp more of your giving, to throw light purely down to the end of my life—I do thank you. And the truth is, I *should* have been in a panic, had there been no letter that evening—I was frightened the day before, then reasoned the fears back & waited: & if there had been no letter after all— . . But you are supernaturally good & kind. How can I ever "return" as people say . . (as they might say in their ledgers) . . any of it all? How indeed can I . . who have not even a heart left of my own, to love you with?—

I quite trust to your promise in respect to the medical advice, if walking & rest from work do not prevent at once the recurrence of those sensations—it was a promise, remember. And you will tell me the very truth of how you are—& you will try the music, & not be nervous, dearest. Would not *riding* be good for you . . consider. And why should you be 'alone' when your sister is in the house? How I keep thinking of you all day—you cannot really be alone with so many thoughts . . such swarms of thoughts, if you could but see them, drones and bees together!

George came in from Westminster Hall after we parted yesterday & said that he had talked with the junior counsel of the wretched plaintiffs in the Ferrers case,[1] & that the belief was in the mother being implicated, although not from the beginning. It was believed too that the miserable girl had herself taken step after step into the mire, involved herself gradually, the first guilt being an extravagance in personal expenses, which she lied & lied to account for in the face of her family. "Such a respectable family," said George, "the grandfather in court looking venerable, and everyone indignant upon being so disgraced by her"! But for the respectability in the best sense, I do not quite see. That all those people should acquiesce in the indecency (according to every standard of English manners in any class of society) of thrusting the personal expenses of a member of their family on Lord Ferrers, she still bearing their name . . & in those peculiar circumstances of her supposed position too . . where is the respectability?—And they are furious with her . . which is not to be wondered at after all. Her counsel had an interview with her previous to the trial, to satisfy themselves of her good faith, . . & she was quite resolute & earnest, persisting in every statement. On the coming out of the anonymous letters, Fitzroy Kelly said to the juniors . . that if anyone could suggest a means of explanation, he would be eager to carry forward the case, . . but for him he saw no way of escaping from the fact of ↑the↓ guilt of their client. Not a voice could speak for her—So George was told. There is no ground for a prosecution for a conspiracy, he says, but she is open to the charge for *forgery*, of course, & to the dreadful consequences, though it is not considered at all likely that Lord Ferrers could wish to disturb her /into\>beyond/ the ruin she has brought on her own life—

Think of Miss Mitford's growing quite cold about Mr. Chorley who has spent two days with her lately, & of her saying in a letter to me this morning that he is very much changed and grown to be "a presumptuous coxcomb."[2] He has displeased her in some way—that is clear. What changes there are in the world.

Should I ever change to *you*, do you think, . . even if you came to "love me less"—not that I meant to reproach you with that possibility. May God bless you, dear dearest. It is another miracle (beside the many) that I /grow\>get/ nearer to the mountains yet still they seem more blue. Is not *that* strange?

Ever and wholly Your Ba

1. Mary Elizabeth Smith vs. Washington Sewallis Shirley, Earl Ferrers, for

breach of promise, had gone to trial on February 14, but Fitzroy-Kelly, the Solicitor General, suddenly withdrew it on February 18. Miss Smith had told her family that Ferrers had proposed and asked her to assemble appropriate clothes, which cost her stepfather £100. When Ferrers married some one else, the family brought suit. The case against the Earl was supported by highly circumstantial letters identified by his own former chaplain, who supported Miss Smith's claim in other respects. Nevertheless, the case collapsed when she broke down and admitted forging the incriminating letters. She had been trapped by her family's faith in her story. See *The Times*, February 16–19, 1846.

2. Chorley was one of Miss Mitford's closest friends and the editor of two volumes of her letters after her death. No details of this coolness have come to light, but Miss Mitford was prone to such spells of disaffection.

240 *(W118°)*   **E.B.B. to R.B.**

[*February 19, 1846.*]

Thursday Evening.

And I offended you by praising your letters . . or rather *mine*, if you please . . as if I had not the right!—Still, you shall not, shall not fancy that I meant to praise them in the way you seem to think . . by calling them "graphic," "philosophic" . . why, did I ever use such words? I agree with you that if I could play critic upon your letters, it would be an end!—but no, no . . I did not, for a moment. In what I said I went back to my first impressions—& they were *vital* letters, I said—which was the resumé of my thoughts upon the early ones you sent me . . because I felt your letters to be *you* from the very first, & I began, from the beginning, to read every one several times over— Nobody, I felt, nobody of all these writers, did write as you did— Well!—& had I not a right to say *that* now at last . . & was it not natural to say just *that*, when I was talking of other people's letters & how it had grown almost impossible for me to read them; and do I deserve to be scolded . . . No indeed—

And if I had the misfortune to think now, when you say it is a fine day, that *that* is said in more music than it could be said in by another . . where is the sin against *you*, I should like to ask. It is yourself who is the critic, I think, after all. But over all the brine, I hold my letters . . just as Camoens did his poem.[1] They are *best to* ME—and they are *best*. I knew what *they* were, before I knew what *you* were . . all of you. And I like to think that I never fancied anyone on a level with you, even in a letter.

What makes you take them to be so bad, I suppose, is just feeling in them how near we are—YOU *say that!*—not I.

Bad or good, you *are* better—yes, "better than the works & words"!—though it was very shameful of you to insinuate that I talked of fine speeches & passages & graphical & philosophical sentences, as if I had proposed a publication of 'Elegant Extracts' from your letters . . . See what blasphemy one falls into through a beginning of light speech! —It is wiser to talk of St. Petersburgh; ⟨though⟩ ₊for all Voltaire's₊ . . *"ne disons pas de mal de Nicolas."*

Wiser—because you will not go. If you were going . . . well!—but there is no danger:—it would not do you good to go, I am so happy this time as to be able to think—& your 'mission of humanity' lies nearer— 'strictly private & confidential'? but not in Harly Street—so if you go *there*, dearest, keep to the 'one hour' & do not suffer yourself to be tired and stunned in those hot rooms & made unwell again—it is plain that you cannot bear that sort of excitement. For Mr. Kenyon's note, . . it was a great temptation to make a day of friday—but I resist both for monday's sake & for yours, because it seems to me safer not to hurry you from one house to another till you are tired completely. I shall think of you so much the nearer for Mr. Kenyon's note—which is something gained. In the meanwhile you are better, which is everything . . or seems so. Ever dearest, do you remember what it is to me that you should be better, & keep from being worse again—I mean, of course, *try* to keep from being worse—be wise . . & do not stay long in those hot Harley St. rooms.—Ah—now you will think that I am afraid of the unicorns!—[2]

Through your being ill the other day I forgot . . , & afterwards went on forgetting . . to speak of and to return the ballad . . which is delightful . . I have an unspeakable delight in those suggestive ballads, which seem to make you touch with the end of your finger the full warm life of other times . . so near they bring you, yet so suddenly all passes in them. Certainly there is a likeness to your Duchess—it is a curious crossing.[3] And does it not strike you that a verse or two must be wanting in the ballad—there is a gap, I fancy.

Tell Mr. Kenyon (if he enquires) that you come here on monday instead of saturday—& if you can help it, do not mention wednesday —it will be as well, not. You met Alfred at the door—he came up to me afterwards & observed that "at last he had seen you"! 'Virgilium tantum vidi!'[4]

As to the thing which you try to say in the first page of this letter, & which you "stop" yourself in saying . . *I* need not stop you in it. . . .

And now there is no time, if I am to sleep to-night. May God bless you, dearest, dearest.

I must be your own while He blesses *me*.

1. In October 1559 Camoëns—then an exile—sailed for India, but "the ship in which he had embarked was wrecked at the mouth of the river Mecon, and he with difficulty reached shore on a plank, having lost everything but the manuscript of [the *Lusiads*]." John Adamson, *Memoirs of the Life and Writings of Luis de Camoens* (2 vols., London, 1820), II, 155. There are references to this misfortune in the *Lusiads* (VII. 80; X. 128).

2. See Letter 104, note 1.

3. See Letter 223, note 3.

4. "Virgil I only saw." Ovid, *Tristia* IV. ix. 51.

241 (W120)   R.B. to E.B.B.
_____

[*February 20, 1846.*]

Friday Afternoon.

Here is my Ba's dearest *first* letter come four hours after the second, with *"Mis-sent to Mitcham"* written on its face as a reason: one more proof of the negligence of somebody! But I *do* have it at last: what should I say? what do you expect me to say? And the first note seemed quite as much too kind as usual!

Let me write to-morrow, sweet? I am quite well, and sure to mind all you bid me. I shall do no more than look in at that place ↑(they are the cousins of a really good friend of mine, Dr. White[1]—I go for *him*)↓ if even that—(for to-morrow night I must go out again, I fear—to pay the ordinary compliment for an invitation to the R. S.'s *soirée* at Lord Northampton's!—)[2] ⟨but it will surely ‖ · · · ‖⟩ And then comes Monday—and to-night any unicorn I may see I will not find myself at liberty to catch— (N.B.—should you meditate really an addition to the Elegant Extracts—, mind this last joke is none of mine but my father's; when walking with me when a child, I remember, he bade a little urchin we found fishing with a stick and a string for sticklebacks in a ditch—"to mind that he brought any sturgeon he might catch to the King"—he having a claim on such a prize, by courtesy if not right).

As for Chorley, he is neither the one nor the other of those ugly things—One remembers Regan's "Oh Heaven—so you will rail at *me*, when you are in the mood"[3]—But what a want of self-respect such judgments argue, or rather, want of knowledge what true self-respect is—"So I believed yesterday, and *so* now—and yet am neither hasty, nor inapprehensive, nor malevolent"—*what then?*——

—But I will say more of my mind—(not of that)—to-morrow, for time presses a little—so bless you my ever ever dearest—I love you wholly.

R. B.

1. Letter 374 locates him in Doctors' Commons. *The Post Office London Directory* for 1846 indicates, by elimination, that he must have been "White Wm Fredk., D.C.L., Advocate, 15 Regent & 1 College, Doctors' Commons." Perhaps he was a brother of the Rev. Edward White whom Browning knew as a child (G & M, p. 50 and note 2).

2. Spencer Joshua Alwyne Compton, 2nd Marquess of Northampton (1790–1851), was president of the Royal Society. Browning apparently attended on April 4 (Letter 300, postscript).

3. *Lear* II. iv. 168–169.

242 (W119°)   **E.B.B. to R.B.**

[*February 20, 1846.*]

Friday Morning.

As my sisters did not dine at home yesterday & I see nobody else in the evening, I never heard till just now & *from Papa himself*, that "George was invited to meet Mr. Browning & Mr. Procter." How surprised you will be. It must have been a sudden thought of Mr. Kenyon's.

And I have been thinking, thinking since last night that I wrote you then a letter all but . . . insolent . . which, do you know, I feel half ashamed to /think>look/ back upon this morning—particularly what I wrote about "missions of humanity"—now was it not insolent of me to write so? If I could take my letter again I would dip it into Lethe between the lilies, instead of the post office:—but I can't . . so if you wondered, you must forget as far as possible, & understand how it was, & that I was in brimming spirits when I wrote, from two causes . . first, because I had your letter which was a pure goodness of yours, & secondly because you were "noticeably" better you said, or "noticeably well" rather, to mind my quotations. So I wrote what I wrote, & gave it to Arabel when she came in at midnight, to give it to Henrietta who goes out before eight in the morning & often takes charge of my letters, . . & it was too late, at the earliest this morning, to feel a little ashamed.

Miss Thomson told me that she had determined to change the type of the few pages of her letterpress which had been touched, & that therefore Mr. Burges's revisions of my translations should be revised back again. She appears to be a very acute person, full of quick perceptions . . naturally quick, & carefully trained—a little over anxious perhaps about mental lights, & opening her eyes still more than she sees—which is a common fault of clever people, if one must call it a fault. I like her—& she is kind and cordial. Will she ask you to help her book with a translation or two, I wonder. Perhaps—if the courage should come. Dearest, how I shall think of you this evening—& how near you will seem, not to be here. I had a letter from Mr. Mathews the other day, & smiled to read in it just what I had expected . . , that he immediately sent Landor's verses on you to a *few editors*, friends of his, in order to their communication to the public. He received my apology for myself with the utmost graciousness,—A kind good man he is.

After all, do you know, I am a little vexed that I should have even *seemed* to do wrong in my speech about the letters. I must have been wrong, if it seemed so to you, I fancy now—Only I really did no more mean to try your letters . . mine . . such as they are to me now . . by the common critical measure, . . than the shepherds praised the pure tenor of the angels who sang "Peace upon earth" to them. It was enough that they knew it for angels' singing. So do *you* forgive me, beloved, & put away from /me\>you/ the thought that I have let in between us any miserable stuff 'de metier,' which I hate as you hate. And I will not say any more about it, not to run into more imprudences of mischief—

On the other hand I warn you against saying again what you began to say yesterday & stopped—do not try it again. What may be quite good sense from me, is from *you* very much the reverse—& pray observe that difference. Or did you think that I was making my own road clear in the thing I said about . . 'jilts'?—No, you did not.—Yet I am ready to repeat of myself as of others, that if I ceased to love you, I certainly ⟨‖ · · · ‖⟩ would act out the whole consequence—but *that* is an impossible "if" to my nature, supposing the conditions of it otherwise to be /possible⟩probable/. I never loved anyone much and ceased to love that person—Ask ⟨any⟩ every friend of mine, if I am given to change even in friendship! *And to* you . . ! Ah—but you never think of such a thing seriously . . & you are conscious that you did not say it very /wisely⟩sagely/. You & I are in different positions. Now let me tell you an apologue in exchange for your Wednesday's stories which I liked so—& mine perhaps may make you "a little wiser"—who knows?

It befell that there stood in hall a bold baron, & out he spake to one of his serfs . . "Come thou; & take this baton of my baronie, & give me instead thereof that sprig of hawthorn thou holdest in thine hand." Now the hawthorn-bough was no larger a thing than might be carried by a wood-pigeon to the next, when she flieth low—and the baronial baton was covered with fine gold . . and the serf, turning it in his hands, marvelled greatly.

And he answered & said, "Let not my lord be in haste, . . nor jest with his servant. Is it verily his will that I should keep his golden baton?—Let him speak again—lest it repent him of his gift."

And the baron spake again that it was his will. "And I" . . he said once again—"shall it be lawful for me to keep this sprig of hawthorn—and will it not repent thee of thy gift?"——

Then all the servants who stood in hall, laughed, & the serf's hands trembled till they dropped the baton into the rushes, knowing that his lord did but jest. . .

Which mine did not. Only, "de te fabula narratur"[1] up to a point . .

And I have your letter—"What did I expect?" Why I expected just *that* . . a letter in turn. Also I am graciously pleased (yes, & very much pleased!) to "*let* you write to-morrow." How you spoil me with goodness . . which makes one 'insolent' as I was saying, . . now & then.

The worst is, that I write "too kind" "letters" . . I! . . . & what does that criticism mean, pray?—It reminds me, at least, of . . now I will tell you what it reminds me of.

A few days ago Henrietta said to me that she was quite uncomfortable. She had written to somebody a not ⟨‖ · · · ‖⟩ kind ⸝enough⸝ letter, she thought . . & it might be taken ill. "Are *you* ever uncomfortable, Ba, after you have sent letters to the post?" she asked me.

"Yes," I said, "sometimes, but from a reason just the very reverse of your reason—*my* letters, when they get into the post, seem too kind . . rather." And my sisters laughed . . laughed . .

But if *you* think so beside, I must seriously set to work, you see, to correct that flagrant fault . . & shall do better in time 'deis faventibus,'[2] though it will be difficult.

Mr. Kenyon's dinner is a riddle which I cannot read. *You* are invited to meet Miss Thomson & Mr. Bayley[3] & "*no one else.*" George is invited to meet Mr. Browning & Mr. Procter and "*no one else*"— just those words. The "*absolu*" ⸝(do you remember Balzac's beautiful story?)⸝[4] is just *you* & no one else," the other elements being mere uncertainties . . shifting while one looks for them.

Am I not writing nonsense to-night?—I am not 'too *wise*' in any case . . which is some comfort. It puts one in spirits to hear of your being "well," ever & ever dearest. Keep so for *me*. May God bless you hour by hour. In every one of mine I am your own

Ba

For Miss Mitford . .
       "Best people are not angels quite . ."[5]
and she sees the whole world in stripes of black & white . . it is her way. I feel very affectionately towards her . . love her sincerely. She is affectionate to *me* beyond measure. Still, always I feel that if I were to vex her, the lower deep below the lowest deep would not be low enough for me . . I always feel *that*. She would advertise me directly for a wretch proper.

Then, for all I said about never changing, I have ice enough over me just now to hold the sparrows[6]—in respect to a great crowd of people . . & she is among them—for reasons—for reasons.—

1. "The story is about you." Horace, *Satires* I. i. 69. The fable seems to be original.
2. "The gods assisting."
3. Not identified; perhaps a brother of Miss Bayley's.
4. *La Recherche de l'absolu* (1833–34).
5. *Pippa Passes,* IV, 281.
6. An allusion to the second paragraph of Letter 229.

243 (W121)   R.B. to E.B.B.
                        ─────────────

[*February 21, 1846.*]

Saturday M^g

So all was altered, my love—and, instead of Miss T. and the other
friend, I had your Brother & Procter—to my great pleasure—After, I
went to that place, and soon got away, and am very well this morning in
the sunshine; which I feel with you, do I not? Yesterday after dinner we
spoke of Mrs. Jameson, and, as my wont is—(Here your letter reaches
me—let me finish this sentence now I have finished kissing you, dearest
beyond all dearness—My own heart's Ba!)—oh, as I am used, I left the
talking to go on by itself, with the thought busied elsewhere, till at last
my own voice startled me for I heard my tongue utter "Miss Barrett..
that is, Mrs. Jameson says".. or "does".. or "does not." I forget which!
And if anybody noticed the *gaucherie* it must have been just your brother!

Now to these letters! I do solemnly, unaffectedly wonder how you
can put so much pure felicity into an envelope so as that I shall get it as
from the fount head. This to-day, those yesterday—there is, I see, and
know, thus much goodness in line after line, goodness to be scientifically
appreciated, *proved there*—but over and above, is it in the writing, the
dots and traces, the seal, the paper,—here does the subtle charm lie
beyond all rational accounting for? The other day I stumbled on a
quotation from J. Baptista Porta—wherein he avers that any musical
instrument made out of wood possessed of medicinal properties
retains, being put to use, such virtues undiminished,—and that, for
instance, a sick man to whom you should pipe on a pipe of elder-tree
would so receive all the advantage derivable from a decoction of its
berries.[1] From whence, by a parity of reasoning, I may discover, I
think, that the very ink and paper were.. ah, what were they? ⟨The
finding of⟩ curious thinking won't do for me and the wise head which
is mine, so I will lie and rest in my ignorance of content and understand
that without any magic at all you simply wish to make one person—,
which of your free goodness proves to be your R.B,—to make me
supremely happy, and that you have your wish—you *do* bless me! More
and more—for the old treasure is piled undiminished and still the new
comes glittering in—dear, dear heart of my heart, life of my life, *will*

this last, let *me* begin to ask? Can it be meant I shall love thee to the end? Then, dearest, care also for the life beyond, and put in my mind how to testify *here* that I have felt, if I could not deserve that a gift beyond all gifts! I hope to work hard, to prove I do feel, as I say—it would be terrible to accomplish nothing now.

With which conviction—, renewed conviction time by time, of your extravagance of kindness to me unworthy,—will it seem characteristically consistent when I pray you not to begin frightening me, all the same, with threats of writing *less* kindly? That must not be, love, for *your* sake now—if you had not thrown open those windows of heaven I should have no more imagined than that Syrian lord on whom the King leaned "how such things might be"[2]—but, once their influence showered, I should know, too soon & easily, if they shut up again! You have committed your dear, dearest self to that course of blessing, & blessing on, on, for ever—so let all be as it is, pray, *pray!*

No—not *all*—No more, ever, of that strange suspicion—"insolent"—oh, what a word!—nor suppose I shall particularly wonder at its being fancied applicable to *that,* of all other passages of your letter! It is quite as reasonable to suspect the existence of such a quality *there* as elsewhere: how *can* such a thing, *could* such a thing come, —from you to me?—But, dear Ba, *do* you know me better! *Do* feel that I know you, I am bold to believe, and that if you were to run at me with a pointed spear I should be sure it was a golden sanative Machaon's touch,[3] for my entire good, that I was opening my heart to receive! As for words, written or spoken—I, who sin forty times a day by light words, and untrue to the thought, I am certainly not used to be easily offended by other people's words, people in the world. But *your* words! And about the "mission";[4] if it had not been a thing to jest at, I should not have begun, as I did—as you felt I did. I know now, what I ↑only↓ suspected then, and will tell you all the matter on Monday if you care to hear—the 'humanity' however, would have been unquestionable if I had chosen to exercise it towards the poor weak incapable creature that wants *somebody,* and urgently I can well believe—

As for your apologue, it is naught—as you felt, and so broke off— for the baron knew well enough it was a spray of the magical tree which once planted in his domain would shoot up, and out, and all round, and be glorious with leaves and musical with birds' nests, and a fairy safeguard and blessing thenceforward and for ever, when the foolish baton had been broken into ounces of gold, even if gold it *were,* and spent and vanished . . for, he said, such gold lies in the highway, men pick it up, more ✝of it✝ or less—, but this one slip of the flowering tree is all of it on this side Paradise. Whereon he laid it to his heart and was happy (in spite of his disastrous chase the night before, when so far from catching an unicorn,[5] he saw not even a respectable prize-heifer, worth the oil-cake and rape-seed it had doubtless cost to rear her—"insolence!")

I found no opportunity of speaking to Mr. K. about Monday—but nothing was said of last Wednesday, and he must know I did not go yesterday—So, Monday is laughing in sunshine surely! Bless·you, my sweetest. I love you with my whole heart; ever shall love you.

R.

1. Giovanni Battista della Porta (c. 1538–1615), Italian natural philosopher, traveler, and author of many scientific and pseudo-scientific works under the Latin version of his name used here. The strange theory Browning refers to is in his *Magiae Naturalis* XX. vii. Cf. *Sonnets from the Portuguese,* XVII: "antidotes / Of medicated music. . . ."

2. For the quoted words, see John 3:9, but the "Syrian lord" seems to be Naaman. See II Kings 5:18.

3. Machaon was the son of Aesculapius and a physician with the Greeks at Troy. *Iliad* II. 729–733.

4. See Letter 238, and note 2 to Letter 244.

5. See Letter 104 and its note 1.

The visit E.B.B. alludes to in the first sentence of the following letter is logged on the envelope of Letter 242:

+Mon. Feb. 23

3–5½ p.m. (48.)

244 (W120°)   **E.B.B. to R.B.**

[*Monday, February 23, 1846.*]

Ever dearest, it is only when you go away, when you are quite gone, out of the house & the street, that I get up and think properly, & with the right gratitude of your flowers. Such beautiful flowers you

brought me this time too!—looking like summer itself, and smelling!—
Doing the 'honour due' to the flowers, makes your presence a little
longer with me—the sun shines back over the hill just by that time . . ,
& then drops, till the next—letter's oriency—

If I had had the letter on Saturday as ought to have been . . no!—
I could *not* have answered it so that you should have my answer on
sunday—no, I should still have had to write first . .

Now you understand that I do not object to the writing first, but
only to the hearing second. I would rather write than not . . I! But to be
written to is the chief gladness of course; & with all you say of liking to
have my letters (which I like to hear quite enough indeed) you cannot
pretend to think that *yours* are not more to *me,* most to *me!* Ask my
guardian-angel & hear what he says!—Yours will look another way for
shame of measuring joys with him!—Because as I have said before, &
as he says now, you are all to me . . all the light . . all the life—I am
living for you now. And before I knew you, what was I & where? What
was the world to me do you think? and the meaning of life? And now . .
when you come and go, & write & do not write . . all the hours are
chequered accordingly in so many squares of white & black, as if for
playing at fox & goose . . only there is no fox, & I will not agree to be
goose for one . . *that* is *you* perhaps, for being 'too easily' satisfied.

So my claim is that you are more to me than I can be to you at any
rate. Mr. Fox said on sunday that I was a "religious hermit" who wrote
"poems which ought to be read in a Gothic alcove"[1]—and religious
hermits, when they care to see visions, do it better, they all say, through
fasting & flagellation & seclusion in dark places. St. Theresa, for instance,
saw a clearer glory by such means, than your Sir Moses Montefiore[2]
through his hundred-guinea telescope[3] Think then, his [how] every
shadow of my life has helped to throw out into brighter, fuller significance, the light which comes to me from you . . think how it is the one
light, seen without distractions—

I was thinking the other day that certainly & after all (or rather
before all) I had loved you all my life unawares . . that is, the idea of you.
Women begin for the most part, (if ever so very little given to reverie)
by meaning, in an aside to themselves, to love such & such an ideal, seen
sometimes in a dream & sometimes in a book . . & forswearing their
ancient faith as the years creep on. I say a book . . because I remember
a friend of mine who looked everywhere for the original of Mr. Ward's

Tremaine,[4] because nothing would do for *her,* she insisted, except just *that* excess of ↑so-called↓ refinement . . with the book-knowledge & the conventional ⟨knowledge⟩ manners—('loue qui peut,' Tremaine), & ended by marrying a lieutenant in the Navy who could not spell. Such things happen every day, & cannot be otherwise, say the wise:—and *this* ↑being otherwise↓ with *me,* is miraculous compensation for the trials of many years, . . though such abundant, overabundant compensation, that I cannot help fearing it is too much ⟨for me⟩ . . as I know that you are too good & too high for me, & that by the degree in which I am raised up you are let down, for us two to find a level to meet on. One's ideal must be above one, as a matter of course, you know. It is as far as one can reach with one's eyes (soul-eyes) not reach to touch. And here is mine . . shall I tell you? . . even to the visible outward sign of the black hair & the complexion—(why you might ask my sisters!—) yet I would not tell you, if I could not tell you afterwards that, if it had been red hair quite, it had been the same thing—only I prove the coincidence out fully & make you smile half—

Yet indeed I did not fancy that *I* was to love *you* when you came to see me—no indeed . . any more than I did your caring on your side. My ambition when we began our correspondence, was simply that you should forget I was a woman (being weary & blasée of the empty written gallantries, of which I have had my share & all the more perhaps from my peculiar position which made them so without consequence) that you should forget *that* & let us be friends, & consent to teach me what you knew better than I, in art & human nature, & give me your sympathy in the meanwhile. I am a great hero-worshipper & had admired your poetry for years, & to feel that you liked to write to me & be written to was a pleasure & a pride, as I used to tell you I am sure, & then your letters were not like other letters . . as I must not tell you again. Also you *influenced* me, in a way in which no one else did. For instance, by two or three halfwords you made me see you, & other people had delivered orations on the same subject quite without effect. I surprised everybody in this house by consenting to see you—Then, when you came . . you never went away—I mean I had a sense of your presence constantly. Yes . . & to prove how free that feeling was from the remotest presentiment of what has occurred . . I said to Papa in my unconsciousness the next morning . . 'it is most extraordinary how the idea of Mr. Browning does beset me—I suppose it is not being used to

see strangers, in some degree—but it haunts me . . it is a persecution.'
On which he smiled & said that "it was not grateful to my friend to use
such a word." When the letter came . . .

Do you know that all that time I was frightened of you?—frightened in this way. I felt as if you had a power over me & meant to use it,
& that I could not breathe or speak very differently from what you
chose to make me: As to my thoughts, I had it in my head somehow
that you read *them* as you read the newspaper—examined them, &
fastened them down writhing under your long entomological pins—
ah, do you remember the entomology of it all?

But the power was used upon *me*—& I never doubted that you had
mistaken your own mind, the strongest of us having some exceptional
weakness. Turning the wonder round in all lights, I came to what you
admitted yesterday . . yes, I saw *that* very early . . that you had come
here with the intention of trying to love whomever you should find, . .
& also that what I had said about exaggerating the amount of what I
could be to you, had just operated in making you more determined to
justify your own presentiment in the face of mine. Well—& if that last
clause was true a little, too . . why should I be sorry now . . and why
should you have fancied for a moment, that the first could make me
sorry. At first & when I did not believe that you really loved me . . when
I thought you deceived yourself . . *then,* it was different. But now . .
now . . when I see & believe your attachment for me . . do you think
that any cause in the world (except what diminished it) could render it
less a source of joy to me?—I mean as far as I myself am considered—
Now if you ever fancy that I am *vain* of your love for me . . you will be
unjust, remember. If it were less dear, & less above me, I might be vain
perhaps. But I may say *before* God & you, that of all the events of my
life . . inclusive of its afflictions . . nothing has humbled me so much as
your love. Right or wrong it may be, but true it *is* . . & I tell you. Your
love has been to me like God's own love, which makes the receivers of
it kneelers.

Why all this should be written, I do not know—but you set me
thinking yesterday in the backward line, which I lean back to very
often . . & for once, as you made me write directly, why I wrote, as my
thoughts went, that way.

Say how you are, beloved—& do not brood over that 'Soul's
Tragedy'—which I wish I had here with Luria, because, so, you should

not see it for a month at least. And take exercise & keep well—&
remember how many letters I must have before saturday. May God
bless you. Do you want to hear me say

I cannot love you less . . ?

That is a doubtful phrase. And

I cannot love you more

is doubtful too, for reasons I could give. More or less, I really love you . .
but it does not sound right, even *so* . . does it? . . I know what it ought
to be, & will put it into the 'seal' & the 'paper' with the ineffable other
things.

  Dearest, do not go to St. Petersburgh. Do not think of going, for
fear it should come true & you should go: & while you were helping
the Jews & teaching Nicholas, what (in that case) would become

of Your Ba?

---

 1. "Her volumes should be taken into solitude; they should be read in some
Gothic recess, when twilight begins to gloom over the scene." "On Living Poets;
and Their Services to the Cause of Political Freedom and Human Progress—No. 10,"
People's Journal, I (March 7, 1846), 132. W. J. Fox was delivering on Sunday evenings
at the National Hall of the Working Men's Association in Holborn a series of talks,
some of which were published in the *People's Journal* and collected as *Lectures
Addressed Chiefly to the Working Classes* (4 vols., London, 1845–1849). The one quoted
above, on E.B.B. and Sarah Flower Adams, was delivered on February 22, 1846.

 2. Sir Moses Haim Montefiore (1784–1885) retired from the London Exchange
with a considerable fortune in 1824, and spent the rest of his life helping distressed
European and Middle Eastern Jews. He served as Sheriff of London in 1837 and was
knighted in the same year.

 It is clear in the context of these letters that Browning was offered a post as
secretary to Sir Moses in 1846, when the latter undertook the "mission of humanity"
to St. Petersburgh referred to in Letter 238. On March 1 (see the postscript to Letter
252) he set out to urge Czar Nicholas to rescind a ukase ordering the withdrawal of
all Jews from an area of some thirty miles from the German and Austrian borders.
His success earned him a baronetcy. The offer to Browning is probably accounted
for by two facts: Sir Moses had both family and financial connection with the House
of Rothschild, where Browning's two uncles held important posts, and Browning
had been to St. Petersburg in 1834. The apparent tone of both E.B.B.'s and
Browning's remarks on the mission and Sir Moses is a mystery. He was almost
universally esteemed.

 3. Not identified, but Sir Moses was a member of the Royal Society and
one-hundred guineas was about the price of a seven-foot "Newtonian telescope"
of the kind owned by some early Victorian amateurs in astronomy.

 4. *Tremaine; or the Man of Refinement,* by Robert Plumer Ward (1825).

245 (*W122*)   R.B. to E.B.B.

[*February 24, 1846.*]

Tuesday.

Ah, sweetest, in spite of our agreement, here is the note that sought not to go, but must—because, if there is no speaking of Mrs. Jamesons and such like without bringing in your dear name—(not *dearest* name, my Ba!)—what is the good of not writing it down, now, when I, tho' possessed with the love of it no more than usual, yet *may* speak, and to a hearer? And I have to thank you with all my heart for the good news of the increasing strength and less need for the opium—how I do thank you, my dearest—and desire to thank God thro' whose goodness it all is! This I could not but say now, tomorrow I will write at length,—having been working a little this morning, with whatever effect. So now I will go out and see your elm-trees and gate, and think the thoughts over again—and coming home I shall perhaps find a letter.

Dearest, dearest—my perfect blessing you are!

May God continue his care for us. R.

246 (*W123*)   R.B. to E.B.B.

[*February 25, 1846.*]

Wednesday M^g

Once you were pleased to say, my own Ba, that "I made you do as I would"—I am quite sure, you make me *speak* as you would, and not at all as I mean—and for one instance, I never surely spoke anything half so untrue as that "I came with the intention of loving whomever I should find"—No!—wreathed shells, and hollows in ruins, and roofs of caves may transform a voice wonderfully, make more of it or less, or so change it as to almost alter . . but turn a "no" into a "yes" can no echo (except the Irish one)—and I said "no" to such a charge, and still say "no."—I *did* have a presentiment—and tho' it is hardly possible for me to look back on it now without lending it the true colours given to it by the event, yet I *can* put them aside, if I please, and remember that I not merely hoped it would not be so—(*not* that the effect I expected to be produced would be *less* than in anticipation . . certainly I did not hope *that*—but that it would range itself with the old feelings of simple reverence and sympathy and friendship—that I should love you as much as I supposed I *could* love, and no more)—but in the confidence that nothing could occur to divert me from my intended way of life, I made . . went on making arrangements to return to Italy. You know—did I not tell you I wished to see you before I returned?—And I had heard of you just so much as seemed to make it impossible such a relation could ever exist: I know very well, if you choose to refer to my letters you may easily bring them to bear a sense in parts, more agreeable to your own theory than to mine, the true one—but that was instinct, Providence—anything rather than foresight: now I will convince you! yourself have noticed the difference between the *letters* and the *writer*—the greater "distance of the latter from you"—why was that? Why if not because the conduct *begun* with *him*, with one who had now seen you,—was no continuation of the conduct, as influenced by the feeling, of the letters —else, they, if *near*, should have enabled him;—if but in the natural course of time and with increase of familiarity, to become *nearer*—but it was not so! The letters began by loving you after their way—but what a world-wide difference *that* love and the true, the love from seeing and hearing and feeling . . since you make me resolve, what now lies blended so harmoniously, into its component parts—Oh, I know what is old from what is new, and how chrystals may surround and glorify other vessels meant for ordinary service than Lord N's![1] But I *don't* know that handling may not snap them off, some of the more delicate ones—and if you let me, love, I will not again, ever again, consider how it came and whence, and when, so curiously, so pryingly,—but believe that it was always so; and that it all came at once, all the same; the more unlikelinesses the better, for they set off the better the truth of truths that here, ("how begot? how nourished?")[2]—here is the whole wondrous Ba filling my whole heart and soul; and over-filling it, because she is in all the world, too, where I look, where I fancy. At the same time, because all is so wondrous and so sweet, do you think that it would be *so* difficult for me to analyse it, and give causes to the effects in sufficiently numerous instances, even to "justify my presentiment"? Ah, dear, dearest Ba, I could, could indeed . . could account for all, or enough! But you are unconscious, I do believe, of your power—and the knowledge of it would be no added grace,—perhaps! So let us go on—taking a lesson out of the world's book in a difference sense—you shall think I love you for—(tell me, you must, what for)—while in my secret heart I know what my "mission of humanity" means, and what telescopic & microscopic views it procures me—Enough!—Wait, one word about the "too kind letters"—could not the same Montefiore understand that tho' he deserved not one of his thousand guineas, yet that he is in disgrace if they bate him of his next gift by merely *ten*? It *is* all too kind—but I shall feel the diminishing of the kindness, be very sure! Of that there is, however, not too alarming a sign in this dearest, because last, of all—dearest letter of all—till the next! I looked yesterday over the "Tragedy"—and think it will do after all. I will bring one part at least next time,—and "Luria" take away, if you let me, so all will be off my mind—and April and May be the welcomer! Don't think I am going to take any extraordinary pains—there are some things in the "Tragedy" I should like to preserve and print now, leaving the future to spring as it likes, in any direction,—and these half-dead, half-alive works fetter it, if left behind—

Yet one thing will fetter +it+ worse, only one thing—if *you*, in any respect, stay behind! You that in all else help me and will help me, beyond words—beyond dreams,—if, because I find you, your own works *stop*—"then comes the Selah and the voice is hushed"[3]—Oh, no, no, dearest, *so* would the help cease to be help,—the joy to be joy, Ba herself to be *quite* Ba, and my own Siren singing song for song.[4] Dear love, will that be kind, and right, and like the rest? Write and promise that all shall be resumed, the romance-poem[5] chiefly, and I will try and feel more yours than ever now. Am I not with you in the world, proud of you—and *vain*, too, very likely, which is all the sweeter if it is a sin as you teach me. Indeed dearest, I have set my heart on your fulfilling your mission—my heart is on it! Bless you, my Ba—

Your R. B.

I am so well as to have resumed the shower-bath (this M^g)—and I walk, especially near the elms and stile—and mean to walk, and be very well—and you, dearest?

1. Apparently Lord Northampton.
2. *Merchant of Venice* III. ii. 65.
3. See Letter 181, note 2.
4. See Letter 151, note 7.
5. *Aurora Leigh*. See Letter 10.

247 *(W121°)*   *E.B.B. to R.B.*

[*Postmarked February 26, 1846.*]

I confess that while I was writing those words I had a thought that they were not quite yours as you said them. Still it comes to something in their likeness, . . but we will not talk of it and break off the chrystals . . they *are* so brittle, then? do you know *that* by an "instinct"? But I agree that it is best not to talk—I "gave it up" as a riddle long ago. Let there be 'analysis' even, & it will not be solution. I have my own thoughts of course . . & you have yours, & the worst is that a third person looking down on us from some snow-capped height, & free from personal influences, would have *his* thoughts too, . . & *he* would think that if you had been reasonable as usual you would have gone to Italy—I have by heart (or by head at least) what the third person would think. The third person thundered to me in an abstraction for ever so long, & at intervals I hear him still . . only you shall not to-day, because he talks 'damnable iterations'[1] & teazes you. Nay . . the first person is teazing you now perhaps, without going any further . . and yet I must go a little further, just to say (after accepting all possible unlikelinesses & miracles, because everything was miraculous & impossible) that it was agreed between us long since that you did not love me for anything—your having no reason for it is the only way of your not seeming unreasonable. Also *for my own sake*. I like it to be so—I cannot have peace with the least change from it. Dearest take the baron's hawthorn bough[2] which, in spite of his fine dream of it is dead since the other day & so much the worse than when I despised it last—. . take that dead stick & push it ⸆upright⸆ into the sand as the tide rises . . & the whole blue sea draws up its glittering breadth & length towards & around it. But what then? What does *that prove?* . . as the philosopher said of the poem. So we ought not to talk of such things; & we get warned off even in the accidental illustrations ⟨we⟩ taken up to light us. Still, the stick certainly did not draw the sea.

Dearest & best you were yesterday, to write me the little note! You are better than the imaginations of my heart . . & *they,* as far as they relate to you (not further) are *not* desperately wicked, I think. I always expect the kindest things from you, & you always are doing some kindness beyond what is expected—& this is a miracle too, like the rest—now

is'nt it? When the knock came last night, I knew it was your letter, &
not another's. Just another little leaf of my Koran! How I thank you . .
thank you!—If I write too kind letters, as you say . . why they may be
too kind for me to send, but not for you to receive—& I suppose I think
more of you than of me, which accounts for my writing them . .
accounts & justifies. And *that* is my reflection not now for the first time.
For we break rules very often—as that exegetical third person might
expound to you clearly out of the ninety-sixth volume of the Code of
Conventions . . only you are not like another, nor have you been to
me like another—you began with most improvident & (will you let
me say?) UN*masculine* generosity . . and Queen Victoria does not sit
upon a mat after the fashion of Queen Pomare,[3] nor should.

But . . but . . you know very fully that you are breaking faith in the
matter of the 'tragedy' & Luria—you promised to rest—& *you rest for
three days.* Is it *so* that people get well? or keep well? Indeed I do not
think I shall let you have Luria. Ah—be careful, I do beseech you—be
careful. There is time for a pause, & the works will profit by it themselves. And *you!* And I . . . if you are ill!—

For the rest I will let you walk in my field, & see my elms as much
as you please . . though I hear about the shower bath with a little
suspicion. Why, if it did you harm before, should it not again? and why
should you use it, if it threatens harm? Now tell me if it has'nt made you
rather unwell since the new trial!—tell me, dear dearest.

As for myself, I believe that you set about exhorting me to be busy,
just that I might not reproach *you* for the over-business—confess that
that was the only meaning of the exhortation. But now . . you are quite
serious, you say. You even threaten me in a sort of underground
murmur, which sounds like a nascent earthquake; & if I do not write
so much a day directly, your stipendiary magistrateship will take
away my license to be loved . . I am not to be Ba to you any longer . .
you say!—And is *this* right?—now I ask you. Ever so many chrystals
fell off by that stroke of the baton, I do assure you. Only you did not
mean quite what you /said>say/ so too articulately, & you will unsay
it, if you please, & unthink it near the elms.

As for the writing, I will write . . I have written . . I am writing.
You do not fancy that I have given up writing?—No. Only I have
certainly been more loitering & distracted than usual in what I have
done . . which is not my fault—nor yours directly—and I feel an

indisposition to setting about the romance—the hand of the soul shakes. I am too happy & not calm enough, I suppose, to have the right inclination. Well—it will come. But all in blots & fragments there are verses enough, to fill a volume done in the last year.[4]

And if there were not . . if there were none . . I hold that I should be Ba, and also *your* Ba . . which is "insolence" . . . will you say?

1. *I Henry IV* I. ii. 92.
2. See E.B.B.'s fable, Letter 242, and Browning's ending for it, Letter 243.
3. Pomare IV of Tahiti was forced in 1843 to accept a French protectorate and then to abdicate, despite her pleas to the British for help. Popular feeling on the matter ran high in England, and it was much in the press. Pomare is mentioned in *Aurora Leigh* (V, 823).
4. This is a response to Browning's remark at the close of Letter 246 and pretty surely means a volume of verses for *Aurora Leigh,* not a quantity of shorter pieces. It would be an apt description of the Wellesley manuscript of the poem.

248 (W124)   **R.B. to E.B.B.**

───────────

[*February 26, 1846.*]

Thursday.

As for the "third person," my sweet Ba, he was a wise speaker from the beginning; and in our case he will say, turning to me—'the late Robert Hall, when a friend admired that one with so high an estimate of the value of intellectuality in woman should yet marry some kind of cook-maid-animal, as did the said Robert; wisely answered, "you can't kiss Mind"!'[1] May *you* not discover eventually,' (this is to me) . . 'that mere intellectual endowments,—tho' incontestably of the loftiest character,—mere Mind, tho' that Mind be Miss B's—cannot be *kissed*— nor, repent too late the absence of those humbler qualities, those softer affections which, like flowerets at the mountain's foot, if not so proudly soaring as, as, as" . . and so on, till one of us died, with laughing or being laughed at! So judges the third person! and if, to help him, we let him into your room at Wimpole St., suffered him to see with Flush's eyes, he would say with just as wise an air—" True, mere personal affections may be warm enough . . but does it augur well for the durability of an attachment that it should be *wholly, exclusively* based on such perishable attractions as the sweetness of a mouth, the beauty of an eye? I could wish, rather, to know that there was something of less transitory nature co-existent with this—some congeniality of Mental pursuit, some—" Would he not say that? But I can't do his platitudes justice because here is our post going out and I have been ↑all the morning↓ walking in the perfect joy of my heart—with your letter—and under its blessing— dearest, dearest Ba—let me say more to-morrow—only this now, that you—ah, what are you not to me! My dearest love, bless you—till to-morrow when I will strengthen the prayer; (no, *lengthen* it!)

Ever your own R.B.

'Hawthorn'—[2]to show how Spring gets on!

1. An English Baptist divine (1764–1831) noted for his erudition and pulpit oratory. He married the servant of a fellow divine in 1808 after a very brief acquaintance.
2. "Sprig of Hawthorn enclosed with letter." Footnote, 1899 edition.

249 (W122°)   *E.B.B. to R.B.*

[*February 26, 1846.*]

Thursday evening.

If all third persons were as foolish as this third person of yours, ever dearest, first & second persons might follow their own devices without losing much in the way of good counsel. But you are unlucky in your third person as far as the wits go—he talks a great deal of nonsense . . & Flush, who is sensible, will have nothing to do with him, he says, any more than you will with Sir Moses:[1]—he is quite a third person *singular* for the nonsense he talks!

So, instead of him, you shall hear what I have been doing to-day. The sun, which drew out you & the hawthorns, persuaded me that it was warm enough to go down stairs—& I put on my cloak as if I were going into the snow, & went into the drawing-room & took Henrietta by surprise as she sate at the piano singing. Well,—I meant to stay half an hour and come back again . . for I am upon 'Tinkler's ground'[2] in the drawing room and liable to whole droves of morning visitors—&

Henrietta kept me, kept me, because she wanted me, besought me, to stay & see the great sight of Capt. Surtees Cook . . *plus* his regimentals . . fresh from the royal presence at St. James's . . & I never saw him in my life, though he is a sort of cousin. So, though I hated it as you may think, . . not liking to be unkind to my sister, I stayed & stayed one ten minutes after another, till it seemed plain that he wasn't coming at all (as I told her) and that Victoria had kept him to dinner, enchanted with the regimentals. And half laughing & half quarreling, still she /kept⟩held/ me by force, until a knock came most significantly . . & "*There* is Surtees" said she . . "now you must & shall stay! So foolish . ." (I had my hand on the door-handle to go out) "he, your own cousin too! who always calls you Ba . . except before Papa"—Which might have encouraged me perhaps, but I cant be sure of it, as the very next moment apprized us both that no less a person than Mrs. Jameson was standing out in the passage. The whole 36th. regiment could scarcely have been more astounding to me. As to saying to see her in that room, with the prospect of the military descent in combination, . . I couldn't have done it for the world! . . so I made Henrietta, who had drawn me into the scrape, take her up stairs, & followed myself in a minute or two—& the corollary of this interesting history is, that being able to talk at all after all that 'fuss,' & after walking "upstairs and downstairs" like the ancestor of your spider,[3] proves my gigantic strength—now doesn't it?

For the rest, 'here be proofs'[4] that the first person can be as foolish as any third person in the world—What do you think?

And Mrs. Jameson was kind beyond speaking of, & talked of taking me to Italy—What do you say? It is somewhere about the fifth or sixth proposition of the sort which has come to me—I shall be embarrassed, it seems to me, by the multitude of escorts ↑to Italy↓. But the kindness, one cannot laugh at so much kindness.

I wanted to hear her speak of you, & was afraid. I *could not* name you. Yet I *did* want to hear the last 'Bell' praised—

She goes to Ireland for two months soon, but prints a book first . . a collection of essays.[5] I have not seen Mr. Kenyon, with whom she dined yesterday . . The Macreadys were to be there—& he told me a week ago that he very nearly committed himself in a "social mistake" by inviting you to meet them.[6]

Ah my hawthorn spray!—Do you know, I caught myself pitying it for being gathered, with that green promise of leaves on it!—There is room too on it for the feet of a bird!—Still I shall keep it longer than it would have stayed in the hedge . . *that* is certain!

The first you ever gave me was a yellow rose sent in a letter[7]—and shall I tell you what *that* means—the yellow rose? "*Infedility*," says the dictionary of flowers. You see what an omen, . . to begin with!—

Also you see that I am not tired with the great avatar[8] to-day—the 'fell swoop' rather—mine, into the drawing-room, & Mrs. Jameson's on *me*.

And shall I hear to-morrow again, . . really? I "*let*" you. And you are best, kindest, dearest, every day. Did I ever tell you that you /make⟩made/ me do what you choose? I fancied that I ⟨had⟩ only *thought* so. May God bless you. I am your own.

Shall I have the "Soul's Tragedy" on saturday?—any of it? But *do not work*—I beseech you to take care.

1. Montefiore.
2. Perhaps a use of *tinkler* as slang for a bell *(OED)*. Though 50, Wimpole Street seems not to have had a bell, the sense is clearly "too close to the front door to retreat if visitors come."
3. *The Oxford Dictionary of Nursery Rhymes* (revised ed., 1952) gives a version of "Goosey, Goosey Gander" which has "Old father long legs" instead of the old man. In Britain the term is used for the crane-fly, but if E.B.B. were thinking of the long-legged arachnid to which Americans give the name, it would explain this confusing passage. For Browning's spider, see Letter 10 and its note 8.
4. See Letter 31, note 9.
5. *Memoirs and Essays, Illustrative of Art, Literature and Social Morals* (1846).
6. William Charles Macready (1793–1873), one of the leading actors of his day, became a friend of Browning's after *Paracelsus* (1835). At his request the poet wrote *Strafford,* which Macready produced in 1837. However, they quarreled so bitterly over *A Blot in the ' Scutcheon* that it would have been hazardous to entertain them together. (For an example see Letter 394, note 4.)
7. Letter 42.
8. Apparently used to mean only "descent."

250 (W125)   **R.B. to E.B.B.**

[*Friday, February 27, 1846.*]

To be sure my "first person" was nonsensical, and, in that respect made speak properly, I hope—only he was cut short in the middle of his performance by the exigencies of the post. So, never mind what such persons say, my sweetest, because they know nothing at all—*quod erat demonstrandum*. But you, love, you speak roses, and hawthorn-blossoms when you tell me of the cloak put on, and the descent, and the entry, and staying and delaying—I will have had a hand in all that . . I know what I wished all the morning, and now this much came true! But you should have seen the regimentals, if I could have so contrived it, for I confess to a Chinese love for bright red—the very names "vermilion" "scarlet" warm me,—yet in this cold climate nobody wears red to comfort one's eye save soldiers and fox hunters, and old women fresh from a Parish Christmas Distribution of cloaks. To dress in floating loose crimson silk, I almost understand being a Cardinal! Do you know anything of Nat Lee's Tragedies? In one of them a man angry with a Cardinal, cries—

> Stand back, and let me mow this poppy down,
> This rank red weed that spoils the Churches' corn![1]

Is not that good? and presently, when the same worthy is poisoned (that is, the Cardinal)—they bid him—'now, Cardinal, lie down and roar!

> "Think of thy scarlet sins!"[2]

Of the justice of all which, you will judge with no Mrs. Jameson for guide when we see the Sistina together, I trust! By the way, yesterday I went to Dulwich to see some pictures, by old Teniers, Murillo, Gainsborough, Raffaelle!—then twenty names about, and last but one, as if just thought of—"Correggio"—The whole collection, including "a *divine* picture by Murillo," and Titian's Daughter (hitherto supposed to be in the Louvre) ⟨But⟩ the whole I would, I think, have cheerfully given a pound or two for the privilege of not possessing—so execrable as sign-paintings even! Are there worse poets in their way than painters? Yet the melancholy business is here—that the bad poet goes out of his way, writes his verses in the language he learned in order to do a hundred other things with it, all of which we can go on and do afterwards—but the painter has spent the best of his life in learning even how to produce such monstrosities as these, and to what other good do his acquisitions go? This short minute of life our one chance, an eternity on either side! and a man does not walk whistling and ruddy by the side of hawthorn hedges in spring, but shuts himself up and comes out after a dozen years with "Titian's Daughter" and, there, gone is his life, let somebody else try!

I have tried—my trial is made, too—

To-morrow you shall tell me, dearest, that Mrs. Jameson wondered to see you so well,—did she not wonder? Ah, to-morrow! There is a lesson from all this writing and mistaking and correcting and being corrected: and what, but that a word goes safely only from lip to lip, dearest? See how the cup slipped from the lip and snapped the chrystals, you say! But the writing is but for a time—" a time and times and half a time!"[3]—would I knew when the prophetic weeks end! Still, one day, as I say, no more writing, (and great scandalization of the third person, peeping thro' the fringes of Flush's ears!)—meanwhile, I wonder whether if I meet Mrs. Jameson I may practise diplomacy and say carelessly "I should ⟨‖ · · · ‖⟩ ↑be glad to↓ know what Miss B. is like—" No, that I must not do, something tells me, "for reasons, for reasons"—

I do not know—you may perhaps have to wait a little longer for my "divine Murillo" of a Tragedy. My sister is copying it as I give the pages, but—in fact my wise head does ache a little—it is inconceivable! As if it took a great storm to topple over some stone, and once the stone pushed from its right place, any bird's foot, which would hardly bend the hawthorn spray, may set it trembling! The aching begins with reading the presentation-list at the Drawing-room quite naturally, and with no shame at all! But it is gentle, well-behaved aching now, so I *do* care, as you bid me, Ba, my Ba, whom I call Ba to my heart but could not, I really believe, ⟨‖ · · · ‖⟩ ↑call so be↓fore another, even your sister, if—if—

But Ba, I call you boldly here, and I dare kiss your dear, dear eyes, till to-morrow—Bless you, my own!—

R.

1. *Caesar Borgia,* Act I (slightly misquoted). Cf. *The Ring and the Book,* Bk. II, ll. 939–940:
> "Such are the red-clothed milk-swollen poppy-heads
> That stand and stiffen 'mid the wheat o' the Church!"
2. *Caesar Borgia,* Act V.
3. Daniel 12:7 and Revelations 12:14.

The record of the next day's visit is on the envelope of Letter 249:
+Feb. 28. Sat^y
3–5¼ p.m. (49.)

251 (W123°)   E.B.B. to R.B.

[March 1, 1846.]

Sunday.

You never could think that I meant any insinuation against you by a word of what was said yesterday, or that I sought or am likely to seek a 'security'! . . . do you know it was not right of you to use such an expression—indeed no. You were angry with me for just one minute, or you would not have used it—and why? Now what did I say that was wrong or unkind even by construction? If I did say anything, it was three times wrong, & unjust as well as unkind, & wronged my own heart & consciousness of all that you are to me,—more than it could *you*. But you began speaking of yourself just as a woman might speak under the same circumstances . . you remember what you said . . & then *I*, remembering that all the men in the world would laugh such an idea to scorn, said something to that effect . . you *know*. I once was in company with a man, however, who valued himself very much on his constancy to a woman who was so deeply affected by it that she became his wife at last . . & the whole neighbourhood came out to stare at him on that ground as a sort of monster. And can you guess what the constancy meant? Seven years before, he loved that woman, he said, & she repulsed him . . "And in the meantime—*how many?*" I had the impertinence to ask a female friend who told me the tale. "Why," she answered with the utmost simplicity, "I understand that Miss A & Miss B & Mrs. C would not listen to him, but he took Miss D's rejection most to heart." That was the head & front of his "constancy" to Miss E, who had been loved she boasted, for seven years . . that is, once at the beginning & once at the end. It was just a coincidence of the 'premier pas' & the 'pis aller.'

Beloved, I could not mean this for you—you are not made of such stuff—, as we both know.

And for myself, it was my compromise with my own scruples, that you should not be "chained" to me . . not in the merest metaphor . . that you should not seem to be bound, in honour or otherwise, . . so that if you stayed with me it should be your free choice to stay, not the *consequence* of a choice so many months before. That was my compromise with my scruples . . & not my doubt of your affection—& least of all, was it /my⟩an/ intention of trifling with you sooner or later that made me wish to suspend ⟨your ‖ · · · ‖⟩ ⸋all⸌ *decisions* as long as possible. I have decided (for me) to let it be as you shall please—now I told you that before—Either we will live on as we are . . until an obstacle arises, . . for indeed I do not look for a "security" where you suppose . . & the very appearance of it THERE is what most rebuts me; or I will be yours in the obvious way, & go out of England the next half-hour if possible. As to the steps to be taken (or not taken) before the last step, we must think of those—The worst is that the only question is about a *form.* Virtually the evil is the same all round, whatever we do. Dearest, it was plain to see yesterday evening when he came into this room for a moment at seven oclock, before going to his own to dress for dinner . . plain to see, that he was not altogether pleased at finding you here in the morning.[1] There was no pretext for objecting gravely—but it was plain that he was not pleased. Do not let this make you uncomfortable . . he will forget all about it, & I was not *scolded,* do you understand—It was more manner:—by my sisters thought as I did of the significance:—& it was enough to prove to me (if I had not known) what a desperate game we should be playing if we depended on a yielding nerve *there.*

And to-day I went down stairs (to prove how my promises stand) though I could find at least ten good excuses for remaining in my own room . . for our cousin, Sam Barrett,[2] who brought the interruption yesterday & put me out of humour (it wasn't the fault of the dear little cousin Lizzie . . my "Portrait"[3] . . who was *"so sorry,"* she said, dear child, . . to have missed Papa somewhere on the stairs!) the cousin who should have been in Brittainy yesterday instead of here, sate in the drawingroom all this morning, & had visitors there, . . & so I had excellent excuses for never moving from my chair. Yet, the field being clear at *half-past two*—, I went for half an hour . . just . . just for *you.* Did you think of me, I wonder? It was to meet your thoughts that I went, dear dearest.

How clever these sketches are.[4] The expression produced by such apparently inadequate means is quite striking!—& I have been making my brothers admire them, and they "wonder you don't think of employing them in an illustrated edition of your works." Which might be, really!—Ah . . you did not ask for 'Luria'! Not that I should have let you have it!—I think I should not indeed. Dearest, you take care of the head . . & dont make that tragedy of the soul one for mine, by letting it make you ill. Beware too of the shower bath—it plainly does not answer for you at this season. And walk, & think of me for *your* good, . . if such a combination should be possible.

And *I* think of *you* . . if I do not of Italy. ⟨‖ · · · ‖⟩ Yet I forget to speak to you of the Dulwich Gallery. I never saw those pictures, but am astonished that the whole world should be wrong in praising them. "Divine" is ↑a↓ bad word for Murillo in any case—because he is intensely human in his most supernatural subjects. His beautiful Trinity in the National Gallery, which I saw the last time I went out to look at pictures, has no deity in it—& I seem to see it now. And do you remember the visitation of the angels to Abraham (the Duke of Sutherland's picture—is it not?) where the mystic visitors look like shepherds who had not even dreamt of God? But I always understood that that Dulwich Gallery was famous for great works: you surprise me! And for painters . . their badness is more ostentatious than that of poets—they stare idiocy out of the walls, & set the eyes of sensitive men on edge. For the rest, however, I very much doubt whether they wear their lives more to rags, than writers who mistake their vocation in poetry do. There is a mechanism in poetry as in the other ↑art↓—&, to men not native to the way of it, it runs hard & heavily. The "cudgelling of the brain" is as good labour as the grinding of the colours, . . do you not think?

If ever I am in the Sistine Chapel, it will not be with Mrs. Jameson—no. If ever I should be there, what teaching I shall want, *I* who have seen so few pictures, & love them only as children do, with an unlearned love, just for the sake of the thoughts they bring. Wonderfully ignorant I am, to have had eyes & ears so long! There is music, now, which lifts the hair on my head, I feel it so much, . . yet all I know of it as art all I have of the works of the masters in it, has been the mere sign & suggestion, such as the private piano may give. I never heard an oratorio, for instance, in my life—judge by *that!* It is a guess, I make, at all the greatness and divinity . . feeling in it, though, distinctly & certainly, that a composer like Beethoven *must* stand above the divinest painter in soul-godhead, & nearest to the true poet, of all artists. And this I felt in my guess, long before I knew you—But observe how, if I had died in this illness, I should have left a sealed world behind me! *you,* unknown too . . unguessed at, *you* ↑in many respects,↓ . . wonderfully unguessed at! Lately I have learnt to despise my own instincts. And apart from those—

& *you*, . . it was right for me to be melancholy, in the consciousness of passing blindfold under all the world-stars, & of going out into another side of the creation, with a blank for the experience of this . . the last revelation, unread! How the thought of it used to depress me sometimes!—

Talking of music, I had a proposition the other day from certain of Mr. Russell's[5] (the singer's) friends, about his setting to music my "Cry of the Children." His programme exhibits all the horrors of the world, I see! Lifeboats . . madhouses . . gamblers wives . . all done to the right sort of moaning. His audiences must go home delightfully miserable, I should fancy. He has set the 'Song of the Shirt' . . and my 'Cry of the Children' will be acceptable, it is supposed, as a climax of agony. Do you know this Mr. Russell, & what sort of music he suits to his melancholy? But to turn my 'Cry' to a 'Song,' a burden, it is said, is required—he can't sing it without a burden!—& behold what has been sent "for my approval" . . I shall copy it *verbatim* for you . .

> And the threads twirl, twirl, twirl,
>   Before each boy & girl;
> And the wheels, big & little, still whirl, whirl, whirl.

. . accompaniment *agitato,* imitating the roar of the machinery——

This is not endurable . . ought not to be . . should it now? Do tell me.

May God bless you, ever dearest! . . Let me hear how you are—and think how I am your own . .

1. Mr. Barrett had apparently returned from the City before Browning left on February 28. E.B.B. is using *morning* in the archaic sense of before dinner.

2. Miss Marks (p. 544) identifies this cousin as Samuel Goodin Barrett, from Jamaica.

3. "Lizzie" was the subject of *A Portrait* (1844).

4. By Browning's father. See Letters 205 and 212.

5. Henry Russell (1812–1900), who studied with Rossini, gained fame with a successful series of dramatic "vocal entertainments," including "Woodman, Spare That Tree." Miss Mitford called him a "great tragic actor" (*Letters of Mary Russell Mitford,* ed. R. Brimley Johnson [London: John Lane, 1925], p. 203). He never set E.B.B.'s poem.

252 (W127)   *R.B. to E.B.B.*

[March 1, 1846.]

Sunday E^g

One or two words, if no more, I must write to dearest Ba, the night would go down in double blackness if I had neither written nor been written to! So here is another piece of 'kindness' on my part, such as I have received praise for of late! My own sweetest, there is just this good in such praise—that by it one comes to something pleasantly definite amid the hazy uncertainties of mere wishes and possibilities—while my whole heart does, *does* so yearn, love, to do something to prove its devotion for you; and, now and then, amuses itself with foolish imaginings of real substantial services to which it should be found equal if fortune so granted,—suddenly you interpose with thanks, in such terms as would all too much reward the highest of even those services which are never to be; and for what?—for a note, a going to Town, a——! Well, there are definite beginnings certainly, if you will recognize them —I mean, that since you *do* accept, far from "despising—this day of small things,"—then I may take heart, and be sure that even tho' none of the great achievements should fall to my happy chance, still the barrenest, flattest life will,—*must* of needs produce in its season better fruits than those poor ones—I keep it, value it, now, that it may produce such.

Also I determine never again to 'analyse,' nor let you analyse if the sweet mouth can be anyway stopped—the love shall be one and indivisible—and the Loves we used to know from

One another huddled lie . . . .

Close beside Her tenderly[1]—(which is surely the next line!) Now am I not anxious to know what your Brothers said?—And if anybody else said or wondered . . how should I know? Of all fighting,—the warfare with shadows,—what a work is *there!* But tell me,—and,—with you for me—

Bless me dearest ever, as the face above mine blesses me—

Your own R. B.

Sir Moses[2] set off this morning, I hear—somebody yesterday

506

called the telescope an "optical delusion," anticipating many more of the kind! So much for this "wandering Jew."

1. E.B.B.'s *The Dead Pan* (1844), ll. 114, 116.
2. Montefiore.

253 (*W126*)   **R.B. to E.B.B.**

_____

[*Monday, March 2, 1846.*]

Dearest, I have been kept in Town and just return in time to say why you have *no* note . . to-morrow I will write . . so much there is to say on the subject of this letter I find.

Bless you, all beloved—

R. B.

Oh, do not sleep another night on that horrible error I have led you into! . . The 'Dulwich Gallery"?—! ! !—Oh, no. Only some pictures to be sold at the Greyhound Inn, Dulwich—"the genuine property of a gentleman deceased."

254 (*W124°*)   **E.B.B. to R.B.**

_____

[*March 2, 1846.*]

Monday evening.

Upon the whole, I think, I am glad when you are kept in town & prevented from writing what you call 'much' to me. Because in the first place, the little from *you,* is always much to *me*—& then, besides, *the letter* comes . . & with it the promise of another! Two letters have I had from you today, ever dearest!—How I thank you!—yes, *indeed!* It was like yourself to write yesterday . . to remember what a great gap there would have been otherwise, as it looked on this side—here. The worst of Saturday is (when you come on it) that Sunday follows—Saturday night bringing no letter. Well—it was very good of you . . best of you . . !

For the 'analyzing' I give it up willingly—only that I must say what altogether I forgot to say in my last letter . . that it was not *I, if* you please, who spoke of the chrystals breaking away! And you, to quote me with that certainty!—"The chrystals are broken off, ⟨as⟩ *you say.*" ⟨as⟩ *I* say! ! When it was in your letter, and not at all in mine! !

The truth is that I was stupid, rather, about the Dulwich collection —it was my fault. I caught up the idea of the gallery out of a heap of other thoughts, & really might have known better if I had given myself a chance, by considering.

Mr. Kenyon came to-day, & has taken out a license, it seems to me, for praising you, for he praised & praised. Somebody has told him (who had spent several days with you in a house with a large library) that he came away "quite astounded by the versatility of your learning"—& that, to complete the circle, you discoursed as scientifically on the training of greyhounds & breeding of ducks as if you had never done anything else all your life. Then dear Mr. Kenyon talked of the poems; & hoped, very earnestly I am sure, that you would finish 'Saul' . . . which you ought to do, . . must do—*only not now.* By the way Mrs. Coleridge had written to him to enquire whether you had authority for the 'blue lilies' . . rather than white.[1] Then he asked about 'Luria' & 'whether it was obscure'; & I said, not unless the people, who considered it, began by blindfolding themselves.

And where do you think Mr. Kenyon talks of going next February . . a long way off to be sure? To Italy of course. Everybody I ever heard of seems to be going to Italy ⟨for⟩ next winter. He visits his brother at Vienna, & 'may cross the Alps & get to Pisa:—it is the shadow of a scheme—nothing certain, so far.

I did not go down stairs today because the wind blew and the thermometer fell. Tomorrow perhaps I may. And *you,* dearest dearest, might have put into the letters how you were when you wrote them. You might—but you did not feel well and would not say so. Confess that that was the reason. Reason or no reason, mention yourself tomorrow, & for the rest, do not write a long letter so as to increase the evil—There was nothing which I can remember as requiring an answer in what I wrote to you & though I *will* have my letter of course, it shall be as brief as possible, if briefness is good for you;—*now always remember that.* Why if I, who talk against Luria, should work the mischief myself . . what should I deserve? I should be my own jury directly & not recommended to mercy . . . not to mine. Do take care—care for *me* just so much.

And, except that taking care of your health, what would you do for me that you have not done? ⟨With my hair⟩ You have given me the best of the possible gifts of one human soul to another . . you have made my life new . . & am I to count these things as small & insufficient? Ah, you *know,* you KNOW that I cannot, ought not, will not.

May God bless you. He blesses me in letting me be grateful to you

as your Ba

1. The inquiry is about line 12 of *Saul* (as presently numbered).

255 *(W128)*   *R.B. to E.B.B.*

[*March 3, 1846.*]

Tuesday.

First and most important of all,—dearest, "angry"—with you, and for THAT! It is just as if I had spoken contemptuously of that Gallery I so love and so am grateful to—having been used to go there when a child, far under the age allowed by the regulations—those two Guidos, the wonderful Rembrandt of Jacob's vision, such a Watteau, the triumphant three Mutrillo [Murillo] pictures, a Giorgione music-lesson group, all the Poussins with the "Armida" and "Jupiter's nursing"—and—no end to "ands"—I have sate before one, some *one* of those pictures I had predetermined to see—, a good hour and then gone away . . it used to be a green half-hour's walk over the fields. So much for one error, now for the second like unto it; what I meant by charging you with *seeing,* (not *not* "*looking* for")—*seeing* undue "security" in *that,* in the form,—I meant to say "you talk about me being "free" now, free till *then* . . and I am rather jealous of the potency attributed to the *form,* with all its solemnity, because it *is* a form, and no more—yet you frankly agree with me that *that* form complied with, there is no redemption; yours I am *then* sure enough, to repent at leisure &c. &c. So I meant to ask, "then, all *now* said, all short of that particular form of saying it, all goes for comparatively nothing"? Here it is written down—you "wish to *suspend* all decisions as long as possible"—*that* form effects the decision, then,—till then, "where am I?"—Which is just what Lord Chesterfield cautions people against asking when they tell stories.[1] Love, Ba, my own heart's dearest, if all is *not* decided *now*—why—hear /par⟩story/ à propos of storytelling, and deduce what is deducible—a very old Unitarian minister met a still older Evangelical brother .. John Clayton[2] (from whose son's mouth I heard what you shall hear)—the two fell to argument about the true faith to be held—after words enough, 'Well,' said the Unitarian, as winding up the controversy with an amicable smile—"at least let us hope we are both engaged in the *pursuit* of Truth!" —"*Pursuit* do you say?" cried the other, "here am I with my years eighty and odd—if I haven't *found* Truth by this time where is my chance, pray?"—My own Ba, if I have not already decided alas for me and the solemn words that are to help! (Tho' in another point of view there would be some luxurious feeling, beyond the ordinary, in knowing one was kept safe to one's heart's good by yet another wall than the hitherto recognized ones,—is there any parallel in the notion I once *heard* a man deliver himself of in the street—a labourer talking with his friends about "*wishes*"—and this one wished, if he might get his wish, "to have a nine gallon cask of strong ale set running that minute and his own mouth to be *tied* under it"—the exquisiteness of the delight was to be in the security upon security,—the being "tied.") Now, Ba says I shall not be "chained" if she can help!

But now—here all the jesting goes—You tell me what was observed in the "moment's" visit; by you, and (after, I suppose) by your sisters. First, I *will* always see with your eyes *there*—next, what I see I will *never* speak, if it pain you: but just this much truth I ought to say, I think. I always give myself to you for the worst I am,—full of faults as you will find, if you have not found them: but I *will* not affect to be so bad, so wicked, as I count wickedness, as to call that conduct other than intolerable—*there*, in my conviction of *that*, is your real "security" and mine for the future as the present. That a father choosing to give out of his whole day some /fif⟩five/ minutes to a daughter, supposed to be prevented from participating in what he, probably, in common with the whole world of sensible men, as distinguished from poets and dreamers, consider *every* pleasure of life,— by a complete foregoing of society—that he, after the Pisa business and the enforced continuance, and as he must believe, permanence of this state in which any other human being would go mad,—I do dare say, for the justification of God, who gave the mind to be *used* in this world,—where it saves us, we are taught, or destroys us,—and not to be sunk quietly, overlooked, and forgotten,—that, under these circumstances, finding . . what, you say, unless he thinks he *does* find, he would close the door of his house instantly,—a mere sympathizing man, of the same literary tastes, who comes goodnaturedly, on a proper and unexceptionable introduction, to chat with and amuse a little that invalid daughter, once a month, so far as is known, for an hour perhaps,—that such a father should show himself "*not pleased* plainly," at such circumstances . . . my Ba, it is SHOCKING! See, I go *wholly* on the supposition that the real relation is not imagined to exist between us. I so completely could understand a repugnance to trust you to me were the truth known, that, I will confess, I have several times been afraid the very reverse of this occurrence would befall,—that your father would have at some time or other thought himself obliged, by the usual feeling of people in such cases, to see me for a few minutes and express some commonplace thanks after the customary mode . . (just as Capt. Domett sent a heap of unnecessary thanks to me not long ago for sending now a letter now a book to his son in New Zealand—keeping up the spirits of poor dear Alfred now he is cut off from the world at large)—and if *this* had been done, I shall not deny that my heart would have accused me . . unreasonably I *know* but still, suppression, and reserve, and apprehension . . the whole of *that is* horrible always! But this way of looking on the endeavour of anybody, however humble, to just preserve your life, remedy in some degree the first . . if it *was* the first . . unjustifiable measure,—this being "displeased"—is exactly what I did *not* calculate upon. Observe, that in this *only* instance I am able to do as I shall be done by,—to take up the arms furnished by the world, the usages of society—this is monstrous on the *world's* showing! I say this now that I may never need recur to it—that you may understand why I keep *such* entire silence henceforth.

Get but well, keep but *as* well, and all is easy now. This wonderful winter—the spring—the summer—you will take exercise, go up and down stairs, get strong. *I pray you, at your feet, to do this, dearest!* Then comes Autumn, with the natural expectations, as after *rouge* one expects *noir:* the LIKELIHOOD of a *severe* winter after this mild one, which to prevent, you reiterate your demand to go and save your life in Italy . . ought you not to do that? And the matters brought to issue, (with even, if possible, less shadow of ground for a refusal than before, if you are *well,* plainly well enough to bear the voyage)—*there* I *will* bid you "be mine in the obvious way"—if you shall preserve your belief in me— and you *may* in much, in all important to you. Mr. Kenyon's praise is undeserved enough, but yesterday Milnes said I was the only literary man he ever knew, tenax propositi,[3] able to make out a life for himself and abide in it—"for," he went on, "you really do live without any of this 'titillation' ↑and fussy dependence upon adventitious excitement of all kinds,↓ they all say they can do without"—that is *more* true—and I *intend* by God's help to live wholly for you,—to spend my whole energies in reducing to practise the feeling which occupies me, and in the practical operation of which, the other work I had proposed to do will be found included, facilitated—I shall be able . . but of this there is plenty [of] time to speak hereafter . . I shall, I believe, be able to do this without even allowing the world to *very much* misinterpret— against pure lying there is no defence, but all up to that I hope to hinder or render unimportant—as you shall know in time & place.

I have written myself grave—but write to *me,* dear, dearest, and I will answer in a lighter mood—even now I can say how it was yesterday's hurry happened. I called on Milnes—who told me Hanmer had broken a bone in his leg and was laid up, so I called on him too—on Moxon, by the way, (his brother telling me strangely cheering news, from the grim- mest of faces, about my books selling and likely to sell . . your wishes, Ba!)—then in Bond Street about some business with somebody, then on Mrs. Montagu[4] who was out—walking all the time, and home too. I found a letter from Mr. Kenyon, perfectly kind, asking me to go on Monday to meet friends, and with yours today comes another confirm- ing ↑the↓ choice of the day. How entirely kind he is!

I am very well, much better, indeed—taking that bath with sensibly good effect, to-night I go to Montagu's again; for shame, having kept away too long.

And the rest shall answer *yours*—dear! Nor "much to answer?" And Beethoven, and Painting and—what *is* the rest and shall be answered! Bless you, now, my darling—I love you, ever shall love you, ever be your own. R.

1. Not found.
2. The Rev. John Clayton (1754–1843), whose son was minister of the Congregational Church at Walworth attended by Browning's parents.

3. "Persisting in the intention."
4. The third wife of Basil Montagu.

256 (W125°)   *E.B.B. to R.B.*

_____

[*March 3, 1846.*]

Tuesday Evening.
Yes, but, dearest, you mistake me, or you mistake yourself. I am
sure I do not over-care for forms—it is not my way to do it—and in this
case . . no. Still you must see that there is a fact as well as a form, & in-
volving a frightful quantity of social inconvenience (to use the mildest
word) if too hastily entered on. I deny altogether looking for, or 'seeing'
any 'security' in it for myself—it is a mere form for the heart & the
happiness: illusions may pass after as before. Still the truth is that if they
were to pass with you now, you stand free to act according to the wide-
awakeness of your eyes, & to reform your choice . . see!—whereas afterward you could not carry out such a reformation while I was alive, even
if I helped you. All I could do for you would be to walk away—And
you pretend not to see this broad distinction?—ah . . For me I have seen
just this & no more, & have felt averse to forstall, to seem to forstall even
by an hour, or a word, that stringency of the legal obligation from
which there *is* in a certain sense no redemption. Tie up your drinker
under the pour of his nine gallons, & in two minutes he will moan &
writhe (as you perfectly know) like a Brinvilliers under the water-
torture.[1] That he *asked* to be tied up, was unwise on his own principle of
loving ale. And *you* sha'n't be "chained" up, if you were to ask twenty
times; if you have found truth or not in the water-well.
You do not see aright what I meant to tell you on another subject.
If he was /not pleased⟩displeased/, (and it was expressed by a shadow,
a mere negation of pleasure . .) it was not with you as a visitor & my
friend. You must not fancy such a thing. It was a sort of instinctive
indisposition towards seeing you here—unexplained to himself, I have
no doubt—of course unexplained, or he would have desired me to
receive you never again . . *that* would have been done at once & un-
scrupulously. But without defining his own feeling, he rather disliked

seeing you here—it just touched one of his vibratory wires . . brushed by & touched it—oh, we understand in this house. He is not a nice observer, but, at intervals very wide, he is subject to lightnings . . call them fancies, sometimes right, sometimes wrong. Certainly it was not in the character of a 'sympathising friend' that you made him a very little cross on monday[2]—And yet you never were nor will be in danger of being *thanked* . . he would not think of it. For the reserve, the apprehension . . dreadful those things are, & desecrating to one's own nature —but we did not make this position . . we only endure it—The root of the evil is the miserable misconception of the limits & character of parental rights—it is a mistake of the intellect rather than of the heart. Then, after using one's children as one's chattels for a time, the children drop lower & lower toward the level of the chattels, & the duties of human sympathy ↑to them↓ become difficult in proportion. And (it seems strange to say it, yet it is true) *love,* he does not conceive of at all. He has feeling . . he can be moved deeply . . he is capable of affection in a peculiar way—but *that,* he does not understand, any more than he understands Chaldee, respecting it less of course.

And you fancy that I could propose Italy again?—after saying too that I never would? Oh no no—yet there is time to /talk⟩think/ of this, a superfluity of time, . . 'time, times & half a time'[3] and to make one's head swim with leaning over a precipice is not wise. The roar of the world comes up too, as you hear & as I heard from the beginning. There will be no lack of 'lying,' be sure . . 'pure lying' too—& nothing you can do, dearest dearest, shall hinder my being torn to pieces by most of the particularly affectionate friends I have in the world. Which I do not think of much . . any more than of Italy. You will be mad, & I shall be bad . . . & *that* will be the effect of being poets!—"Till when, where are you?"—why in the very deepest of my soul . . wherever in it is the fountain head of loving!—beloved, *there* you are!—

Some day I shall ask you 'in form,' . . as I care so much for forms, it seems, . . what your "faults" are . . these immense multitudinous faults of yours . . which I hear such talk of, & never, never, can get to see. Will you give me a catalogue raisonnée of your faults?—I should like it, I think. In the meantime they seem to be faults of obscurity . . that is, invisible faults . . like those in the poetry . . which do not keep it from selling as I am *so, so* glad to understand. I am glad too that Mr. Milnes knows you a little——

Now I must end—there is no more time to-night. God bless you, very dearest!—Keep better . . try to be well—as *I* do for you since you ask me. Did I ever think that *you* would think it worth while to ask me *that?* What a dream! reaching out into the morning! Today however I did not go down stairs, because it was colder & the wind blew its way into the passages:—if I can to-morrow without risk, I will, . . be sure . . be sure. Till Thursday then!—till eternity!

'Till when, where am I,' but with you? & what, but yours

Your Ba

I have been writing 'autographs' (save my *mark*) for the North & the South to-day . . the Fens, & Golden Square. Somebody asked for a verse . . from either 'Caterina' or 'Flush'[4] . . "those poems" &c. &c.! Such a concatenation of criticisms. So I preferred Flush of course . . i.e. gave him the preferment.

1. Marie Marguerite d'Aubray, marquise de Brinvilliers (1630–76), plotted to poison her husband and family. When her lover's sudden death disclosed the plot, the Marquise fled to Belgium, but was lured into a police trap, returned to Paris, and beheaded. She had undergone the "water question," in which her hands and feet were secured to the wall, a three-foot bench wedged under her, and three gallons of water forced down her throat. Albert Richard Smith had given a circumstantial account of the torture in his *Marchioness of Brinvilliers,* serialized in 1845. The marquise's torture is mentioned in *Aurora Leigh,* I, 465–470.
2. A slip of the pen—or memory—for Saturday: see Letter 251.
3. Daniel 12:7 and Revelations 12:14; quoted by Browning in Letter 250.
4. *Catarina to Camoens* and *To Flush, My Dog,* both from the 1844 collection.

257 (W129)   R.B. to E.B.B.

[*March 4, 1846.*]

Wednesday M^g

Ah, sweetest, don't mind people and their lies any more than I shall—if the toad *does* "take it into his toad's head to spit at you"—you will not "drop dead,"[1] I warrant,—all the same, if one may make a circuit thro' a flower-bed and see the less of his toad-habits and general ugliness, so much the better—no words can express my entire indifference (far below *contempt*) for what can be said or done—But one thing, only one, I choose to hinder being said, if I can: the others I would not if I could—why prevent the toad's puffing himself out thrice his black bigness if it amuses him among those wet stones? We shall be in the sun.

I dare say I am unjust—, hasty certainly, in the other matter—but all faults are such inasmuch as they are "mistakes of the intellect"—toads may spit or leave it alone,—but if I ever see it right, exercising my intellect, to treat any human beings like my "chattels"—I shall pay for that mistake one day or another, I am convinced—and I very much fear that you would soon discover what one fault of mine is, if you were to hear anyone assert such a right in my presence—

Well, I shall see you to-morrow . . had I better come a little later, I wonder? . . half-past three, for instance,—staying, as last time, till . . ah, it is ill policy to count my treasure aloud! Or shall I come at the usual time to-morrow? If I do *not* hear,—at the usual time!—because, I think you would—am sure you would have considered and suggested it, were it necessary.

Bless you, dearest—ever your own.

R.

I said nothing about that Mr. Russell and his proposition—by all means, yes—let him do more good with that noble, pathetic "lay"—and do not mind the "burthen," if he is peremptory—so that he duly specify—*"by the singer"*—with *that* precaution nothing but good can come of his using it.

1. An allusion to Letter 190.

The visit immediately preceding the following letter is noted on the envelope of Letter 256:

+Thursday, March 5
$3\frac{1}{4}$–$5\frac{3}{4}$ p.m. (50.)

258 (W126°)   *E.B.B. to R.B.*

———————————

[*March 5, 1846.*]

Thursday.

Ever dearest I lose no time in writing, you see, so as to be written to
at the soonest—and there is another reason which makes me hasten to
write . . it is not all mercantile calculation. I want you to understand me.

Now listen! I seem to understand myself: it seems to me that every
word I ever said to you on one subject, is plainly referable to a class of
feelings of which you could not complain . . could not. But this is *my*
impression; and yours is different:—you do not understand . . you do
not see by my light—& perhaps it is natural that /we⟩you/ should not,
as we stand on different steps of the argument. Still I, who said what I
did, *for you,* & from an absorbing consideration of what was best *for you,*
cannot consent, even out of anxiety for your futurity, to torment you
now . . to vex you by a form of speech which you persist ⟨too⟩ ↑in↓
translating into a want of trust in you . . (*I,* want trust in you!!) into a
need of more evidence about you from others . . (*could* you say no?) &
even into an indisposition on my part to fulfil my engagement—no,
dearest dearest, it is not right of you. And therefore, as you have these
thoughts reasonably or unreasonably, I shall punish you for them at
once, & "chain" you . . (as you wish to be chained), chain you, rivet
you—do you feel how the little fine chain twists round & round you?
do you hear the stroke of the riveting?—& you may *feel that* too. Now,
it is done—now, you are chained—βία[1] has finished the work . . *I, Ba!*
(observe the anagram!) and not a word do you say, O Prometheus,
though you have the conscience of it all, I dare say. Well!—you must
be pleased; . . as it was "the weight of too much liberty"[2] which
offended you: & now you believe, perhaps, that I trust you, love you,
& look to you over the heads of the whole living world, without any
one head needing to stoop,—you MUST, if you please, because you belong to me now & shall believe as I choose. There's a ukase[3] for you!
Cry out . . repent . . and I will loose the links, & let you go again—*shall
it be "My dear Miss Barrett"?—*

Seriously, you shall not think of me such things as you halfsaid,
if not whole-said, today. If all men were to speak evil of you, my heart

would speak ⟨to me⟩ of you the more good—*that* would be the
/only⟩one/ result with *me*. Do I not know you, soul to soul?—should
I believe that any of them could know you as I know you? Then for the
rest . . I am not afraid of 'toads' now, not being a child any longer . . I
am not inclined to mind, if *you* do not mind, what may be said about us
by the benevolent world—nor will other reasons of a graver kind affect
me otherwise than by the necessary pain. Therefore the whole rests with
you—unless illness should intervene—and you will be kind & good
(will you not?) & not think hard thoughts of me ever again—no—
It wasn't the sense of being less than you had a right to pretend to, which
made me speak what you disliked—for it is *I* who am 'unworthy,' &
not another—not certainly that other!!—

I meant to write more tonight of subjects farther off us, but
/they⟩my/ sisters have come up stairs & I must close my letter quickly.
Beloved, take care of your head!—Ah, do not write poems, nor read,
nor neglect the walking, nor take that shower bath. *Will* you, instead,
try the warm bathing?—Surely the experiment is worth making for a
little while. Dearest beloved, do it for your

own Ba

1. The silent character—E.B.B. translated his name as "Force"—who at the
opening of *Prometheus Bound* helps chain Prometheus to the rock.
2. Wordsworth, "Nuns Fret Not at Their Convent's Narrow Room."
3. The Russian word had a current topical significance for Browning and
E.B.B. because of the "mission of humanity" to St. Petersburg. See Letter 244,
note 2.

259 *(W130)* R.B. *to* E.B.B.

[*March 6, 1846.*]

Friday M^g

I am altogether your own, dearest—the words were only words
⊦and the playful feelings were play—while⊦ the *fact* has always been so
irresistibly obvious as to make them *break* on and off it, fantastically like
water turning to spray and spurts of foam on a great solid rock—*Now*
you *call* the rock, a rock, but you must have known what chance you

had of pushing it down when you sent all those light fancies and free-leaves, and refusals-to-hold-responsible . . to do what they could. It *is* a rock; and may be quite barren of good to you,—not large enough to build houses on, not small enough to make a mantelpiece of, much less a pedestal for a statue,—but it is real rock, that is all.

It is always *I* who "torment" *you*—instead of taking the present and blessing you, and leaving the future to its own cares—I certainly am not apt to look curiously into what next week is to bring, much less next month or six months—but you, the having you, my own, dearest beloved—*that* is as different in kind as in degree from any other happiness or semblance of it that even seemed possible of realization. Then, now, the health is all to stay, or retard us—oh, be well, my Ba!

(Let me speak of that letter[1]—I am ashamed at having mentioned those circumstances, and should not have done so, but for their insignificance—for I knew that if you ever *did* hear of them, all any body *would* say would not amount to enough to be repeated to me and so get explained at once. Now that the purpose is gained, it seems little worth gaining: you bade me not send the letter—I will not.) — — —

As for 'what people say'—ah—Here lies a book, Bartoli's 'Simboli'[2]—and this morning I dipped into his Chapter XIX. His "Symbol" is "Socrate fatto ritrar su' Boccali" and the theme of his disertating, 'L'indegnità del mettere in disprezzo i più degni filosofi dell' antichità.' He sets out by enlarging on the horror of it—then describes the character of Socrates, then tells the story of the representation of the "Clouds," and thus gets to his "symbol"—"le pazzie fatte spacciare a Socrate in quella commedia . . . il misero in tanto scherno e derisione del pubblico, che perfino i vasai dipingevano il suo ritratto sopra gli orci, i fiaschi, i boccali, e ogni vasellamento da più vile servigio. Così quel sommo filosofo . . fu condotto a far di se par le case d'Atene una continua commedia, con solamente vederlo comparir così scontraffato e 'ridicolo, come i vasai sel formavano d' invenzione'"—

There you have what a very clever man can say in choice Tuscan on a passage in Ælian[3] which he takes care not to quote nor allude to, but which is the sole authority for the fact. Ælian, speaking of Socrates' magnanimity, says that on the first representation, a good many foreigners being present who were at a loss to know "who ⟨might⟩ ₊could₊ be this Socrates"—the sage himself stood up that he might be pointed out to them by the auditory at large . . "which" says Ælian—

"was no difficulty for them, to whom his features were most familiar,—
the very potters being in the habit of decorating their vessels with his likeness"
—no doubt out of a pleasant and affectionate admiration. Yet see how
"people" can turn this out of its sense,—"say" their say on the
simplest, plainest word or deed, and change it to its opposite! "God's
great gift of speech abused" indeed!

But what shall we hear of it *there*, my Siren?

On Monday—is it not?—(*Who* was it looked into the room just
at our leave-taking?)

Bless you, my ever dearest,—remember to walk, to go down
stairs—and be sure that I will endeavour to get well for my part—
To-day I am very well—with this letter!

Your own R.

1. The real discussion of this mysterious letter took place at Thursday's visit, so
that we can only conjecture about it. In a like discussion in December E.B.B. had
opposed a "sealed letter" of some kind (Letter 172). The continuing discussion of
Mr. Barrett's irritation the previous Saturday (Letter 251) might suggest, but for the
fact that E.B.B. had clearly indicated the folly of such a step on the earlier occasion,
that Browning planned a direct approach to Mr. Barrett. Browning's words, "those
circumstances," could refer to a possible misconstruction of his relation to some
other woman, but when such a situation arises in May, his reaction seems clearly
to indicate that the topic is being discussed for the first time (Letter 371).

2. Daniello Bartoli (1608–85) was the Jesuit author of the *Simboli*, which
Browning's Italian teacher used as a text. The material quoted from him may be
translated thus (the ellipsis points represent Browning's interpolations in English):
"Socrates pictured on pots . . . The indignity of demeaning the worthiest
philosophers of antiquity . . . the crazy things Socrates is made to say and do in that
comedy . . . the poor man, held in such public scorn and derision that even the
potters were picturing his features on the pitchers, flasks, jugs, and every vessel of the
vilest use. Thus that greatest philosopher . . . was led to wear a constant comic mask
among the households of Athens, only seeing him so disguised was 'ridiculous, as
the potters moulded him in their imaginations.'"

3. Aelian's *Historiæ Variae* (II. xiii) tells how Socrates stood to be identified at
a performance of *The Clouds*, but does not mention the potters. It merely says that
the mask used in the play was a good likeness.

[*March 6, 1846.*]

Friday evening.

Always *you*, is it, who torments me?—always *you?* Well!—I agree to bear /those⟩the/ torments as Socrates his persecution by the potters:—& by the way he liked those potters, as Plato shows, & was fain to go to them for his illustrations . . as I to you for all my light. Also, while we are on the subject, I will tell you another fault of your Bartoli . . his 'choice Tuscan' filled one of my pages, ⟨‖ · · · ‖⟩ in the place of my English better than Tuscan.

For the letter you mentioned, I meant to have said in mine yesterday, that I was grateful to you for telling me of it—*that* was one of the prodigalities of your goodness to me . . not thrown away, in one sense, however superfluous. Do you ever think how I must feel when you overcome me with all this generous tenderness, only beloved!—I cannot say it.

Because it is colder to-day I have not been down-stairs, but let to-morrow be warm enough & 'facilis descensus.'[1] There's something infernal to me really, in the going down,—& now too that our cousin is here![2] Think of his beginning to attack Henrietta the other day . . '*So* Mr. C. has retired & left the field to Surtees Cook. Oh . . you needn't deny . . it's the news of all the world except your father. And as to *him*, I don't blame you—he never will consent to the marriage of son or daughter.—Only you should consider, you know, because he won't leave you a shilling, &c &c . . .' You hear the sort of man. And then in a minute after . . "And what is this about Ba?" 'About Ba' said my sisters, 'why who has been persuading you of such nonsense?' "Oh, my authority is very good,—perfectly unnecessary for you to tell any stories, Arabel,—a literary friendship, is it?" . . . and so on . . after that fashion! This comes from my brothers of course, but we need not be afraid of its passing *beyond*, I think, though I was a good deal vexed when I heard first of it last night & have been in cousinly anxiety ever since to get our Orestes safe away from those Furies his creditors, into Brittainy again. He is an intimate friend of my brothers besides the relationship, & they talk to him as to each other, only they oughtn't to have talked *that* . . . & without knowledge too.

I forgot to tell you that Mr. Kenyon was in an immoderate joy the ⟨other⟩ day ↑I saw him last,↓ about Mr. Poe's 'Raven' as seen in the Athenæum extracts,[3] & came to ask what I knew of the poet & his poetry, & took away the book. It's the rhythm which has taken him with 'glamour' I fancy—Now you will stay on monday till the last moment, & go to him for dinner at six.

Who "looked in at the door"? Nobody. But Arabel a little way opened it, & hearing your voice, went back. There was no harm—*is* no fear of harm. Nobody in the house would find his or her pleasure in running the risk of giving me pain . . I mean my brothers & sisters would not.

Are you trying the music to charm the brain to stillness? Tell me. And keep from that 'Soul's Tragedy' which did so much harm—oh, that I had bound you by some Stygian oath not to touch it.

So my rock . . may the birds drop into your crevices the seeds of all the flowers of the world——only it is not for *those*, that I cling to you as the single rock in the salt sea.

Ever I am
Your own.

1. An allusion to *Aeneid* VI. 126: "facilis decensus Averno"—"The descent [to Hell] is easy."
2. See Letter 251, note 2.
3. A review in the February 28 issue (pp. 215–216) quoted most of the poem.

261 (W131)   **R.B. to E.B.B.**

[*March 7, 1846.*]

Saturday M^g

You call me "kind"; and by this time I have no heart to call you such names: I told you, did I not once? that "Ba" had got to convey infinitely more of you to my sense than "dearest," "sweetest," all or any epithets that break down with their load of honey like bees—to say you are "kind," you that so entirely and unintermittingly bless me,—it will never do now, "Ba"—(All the same, one way there is to make even "Ba" dearer,—"*my* Ba," I say to myself!)

About my *fears*—whether of opening doors or entering people—one thing is observable and prevents the possibility of any misconception—I desire, have been in the habit of desiring, to *increase* them, far from diminishing—they relate, of course, entirely to *you*—and only thro' *you* affect me the least in the world: put your well-being out of the question, so far as I can understand it to be involved,—and the pleasure & pride I should immediately choose would be that the whole world knew our position . . what pleasure, what pride! But I endeavour to remember on all occasions,—and perhaps succeed in too few,—that it is very easy for me to go away and leave you who cannot go. I only allude to this because some people are "naturally nervous" and all that—and I am quite of another kind.

Last evening I went out . . having been kept at home in the afternoon to see somebody . . went walking for hours. I am quite well to-day and, now your letter comes, my Ba, most happy. And, as the sun shines, you are perhaps making the perilous descent now, while I write—oh, to meet you on the stairs! And I shall really see you on Monday, dearest? So soon, it *ought* to feel, considering the dreary weeks that now get to go between our days! For music, I made myself melancholy ↑just now↓ with some "Concertos for the Harpsichord by Mr. Handel"—brought home by my father the day before yesterday;—what were light, modern things once! Now I read not very long ago a french memoir of 'Claude Le Jeune'[1] called in his time the Prince of Musicians,—no, '*Phœnix*'—the unapproachable wonder to all time . . that is, twenty years after his death about—and to this pamphlet was prefixed as motto this startling axiom—"In Music, the Beau Idéal changes every thirty years"[2]—well,—is not that *true?* The *Idea*, mind, changes,—the general standard . . so that it is no answer that a single air, such as many one knows, may strike as freshly as ever—they were *not* according to the Ideal of their own time,—just now, they drop into the ready ear,—next hundred years, who will be the Rossini? who is no longer the Rossini even I remember—his early overtures are as purely Rococo as Cimarosa's or more—The sounds remain, keep their character perhaps—the scale's proportioned notes affect the same, that is,—the major third, or minor seventh—but the arrangement of these, the sequences—the law—for *them*,—if it *should* change every thirty years! To Corelli nothing seemed so

conclusive in Heaven or earth as this

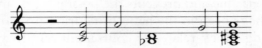

I don't believe there is one of his sonatas wherein that formula does not do duty. In these things of Handel that seems replaced by

—that was the only true consummation! Then,—to go over the hundred years,—came Rossini's unanswerable *coda:*

which serves as base to the infinity of songs, gone, gone—*so* gone by!—From all of which Ba draws *this* "conclusion" that these may be worse things than Bartoli's Tuscan to cover a page with!—yet, yet the pity of it! Le Jeune, the Phœnix . . and Rossini who directed his letters to his mother as "mother of the famous composer"—and Henry Lawes,[3] and Dowland's Lute,[4] ah me!

Well, my conclusion is the best, the everlasting, here and I trust elsewhere—I am your own, my Ba, ever your

R.

1. Claude (or Claudin) Le Jeune (ca. 1523–ca. 1600), a Huguenot musician whose settings for some of the Psalms were used in the Geneva Psalter. The memoir was probably *Esquisse biographique sur Claude Lejeune, surnommé le Phénix des musiciens, compositeur de la musique des rois Henri III et Henri IV* (Valenciennes, 1845). William C. DeVane, *Browning's Parleyings* (New Haven: Yale University Press, 1927), p. 257.

2. Dean DeVane has shown the importance of this idea in Browning's poems about musicians (*ibid.*, pp. 257–259).

3. Lawes (1596–1662) composed the music for Milton's *Comus* and is the subject of one of his sonnets.

4. John Dowland (1563–1626) was "not only the greatest composer of the English Lutenist school, but . . . stands, perhaps, among the first half-dozen of the world's song-writers." *Grove's Dictionary of Music and Musicians,* ed. Eric Blom (5th ed.; London: Macmillan, 1954), II, 758.

E.B.B.'s "Now you will stay on monday till the last moment, & go to him for dinner at six" is reflected in Browning's notation on the envelope of that letter (260):

+Monday, March 9.
$3\frac{1}{2}$–$6\frac{1}{4}$ p.m. (51.)

262 (W128°)   *E.B.B. to R.B.*

[*March 10, 1846.*]

Tuesday Morning.

Now I shall know what to believe when you talk of very bad & very indifferent doings of yours. Dearest, I read your 'Soul's Tragedy' last night & was quite possessed with it, & fell finally into a mute wonder how you could for a moment doubt about publishing it. It is very vivid, I think, & vital, & impressed me more than the first act of 'Luria' did . . though I do not mean to compare such dissimilar things, . . & for pure nobleness 'Luria' is unapproachable . . will prove so, it seems to me . . But this "Tragedy" shows more heat from the first . . & then, the words beat down more closely . . well! I am struck by it all as you see. If you keep it up to this passion, if you justify this high key-note . . it is a great work, & worthy of a place next Luria. Also do observe how excellently balanced the two will be, & how the tongue of this next silver Bell will swing from side to side. And *you* to frighten me about it—!—Yes!— and the worst is (because it was stupid in me) the worst is that I half believed you & took the manuscript to be something inferior . . for YOU . . & the adviseableness of its publication, a doubtful case. And yet, after all, the really worst is, that you should prove yourself such an adept

at deceiving!—For can it be possible that the same
                    'Robert Browning'
who (I heard the other day) said once that he could ⟨afford to⟩ "wait
three hundred years," . . should not feel the life of centuries in this work
too—can it be? Why all the pulses of the life of it are beating in even *my*
ears!—

Tell me, beloved, how you are—I shall hear it to-night—shall I not?
To think of your being unwell, & forced to go here & go there to visit
people to whom your being unwell falls in at best among the secondary
⟨things⟩ ↑evils↓! . . makes me discontented . . which is one shade more to
the uneasiness I feel. Will you take care, & not give away your life to
these people? Because I have a better claim than they . . and shall put it
in, if provoked . . *shall*. Then you will not use the showerbath again—
you promise? I dare say Mr. Kenyon observed yesterday how unwell
you were looking—tell me if he didn't! Now do not work . . dearest!
Do not think of Chiappino, leave him behind . . he has a good strong
life of his own, & can wait for you. Oh—but let me remember to say of
him, that he & the other personnages appear to me to articulate with
perfect distinctness & clearness . . you need not be afraid of having been
obscure in this first part. It is all as lucid as noon.

Shall I go down stairs to-day? 'No' say the privy councillors . .
'because it is cold,'—but I *shall* go peradventure, because the sun
brightens & brightens, & the wind has gone round to the west.

George had come home yesterday before you left me, but the stars
were favorable to us & kept him out of this room . . Now he is at
Worcester—went this morning . . on those never ending "rounds,"
poor fellow, which weary him I am sure.

And why should music & the philosophy of it make you "melancholy," ever dearest, more than the other arts, which each has the seal of
the age, modifying itself after a fashion & *to* one? Because it changes
more, perhaps. Yet all the Arts are mediators between the soul &
the Infinite, . . shifting always like a mist, between the Breath on this
side, & the Light on that side . . /shifted⟩shifting/ and coloured:—
mediators, messengers, projected from the Soul, to go & feel, for Her,
out there!

You dont call me "kind" I confess—but then you call me "too
kind" which is nearly as bad, you must allow on your part. Only you
were not in earnest when you said *that*, as it appeared afterward. *Were*

you, yesterday . . in pretending to think that I owed you nothing . . *I?*

May God bless you. He knows that to give myself to you, is not to pay you. Such debts are not so paid. Yet I am your

Ba

"People's Journal" for March 7th.[1]

1. See Letter 244, note 1.

---

263 (W132)   **R.B. to E.B.B.**

————————

[March 10, 1846.]

Tuesday Morning.

Dear, dear Ba, if you were here I should not much *speak* to you,—not at first,—nor, indeed, at last,—but as it is . . sitting alone, only words can be spoken, or (worse) written—and, oh how different to look into the eyes and imagine what *might* be said, what ought to be said, tho' it never can be—and to sit and say and write, and only imagine who looks above me, looks down, understanding and pardoning all! My love, my Ba, the fault you found once with some expressions of mine about the amount of imperishable pleasures already hoarded in my mind, the indestructible memories of you; that fault, which I refused to acquiesce under the imputation of, at first, you remember—well, *what* a fault it was, by this better light! If all stopped here and now; horrible! complete oblivion were the thing to be prayed for, rather! As it is, *now,* I must go on, must live the life out, and die yours. And you are doing your utmost to advance the event of events,—the exercise, and consequently—(is it not?)—necessarily improved sleep, and the projects for the fine days, the walking . . a pure bliss to think of! Well, now—I think I shall show seamanship of a sort, and "try another tack"—do not be over bold, my sweetest,—the cold *is* considerable,—taken into account the previous mildness . . one ill-advised (I, the *adviser,* I should remember!) too early, or too late descent to the drawing-room, and all might be ruined,—thrown back so far . . seeing that our flight is to be prayed for "not in the winter"[1]—and one would be called on to wait, wait—in this world where nothing waits, rests, as can be counted on. Now think of this, too, dearest, and never mind the slowness,—for the

sureness' sake! How perfectly happy I am as you stand by me, as yesterday you stood, as you seem to stand now!

I will write to-morrow more: I came home last night with a head
rather worse; which ⟨‖ · · · ‖⟩ ↑in the event was↓ the better, for I took a
little medicine and all is very much improved to-day,—I shall go out
presently, and return very early and take as much care as is proper—for
I thought of Ba, and the sublimities of Duty, and that gave myself airs
of importance, in short, as I looked at my mother's inevitable arrow-
root this morning. So now I am well,—so now, is dearest Ba well? I
shall hear to-night . . which will have its due effect, that circumstance,
in quickening my retreat from Forster's Rooms. All was very pleasant
last evening—and your letter &c. went *à qui de droit,* and Mr. W.
Junior[2] had to smile good naturedly when Mr. Burges began laying
down this general law, that the sons of all men of genius were poor
creatures—and Chorley & I exchanged glances after the fashion of two
Augurs meeting at some street-corner in Cicero's time, as he says. And
Mr. Kenyon was kind, kinder, kindest, as ever, "and thus ends a
wooing"![3]—no, a dinner—my wooing ends never, never,—and so
prepare to be asked to give, and give, and give till all is given in
Heaven! And all I give *you* is just my heart's blessing; God bless you,
my dearest, dearest Ba!

1. Cf. Matthew 24:20 and Mark 13:18.
2. William Wordsworth, Jr.
3. An allusion to E.B.B.'s *Lay of the Brown Rosary* (1844), III, ii.

264 (W129°)　　　　　　　**E.B.B. to R.B.**

[*March 10, 1846.*]

Tuesday evening.
You find my letter I trust—for it was written this morning in
time: & if these two lines should not be flattery . . oh, rank flattery! . .
why happy letter is it, to help to bring you home ten minutes earlier,
when you never ought to have left home—no, indeed! I knew how it
would be yesterday, & how you would be worse & not better. You are

not fit to go out, dear dearest, to sit in the glare of lights & talk & listen, & have the knives & forks to rattle all the while & remind you of the chains of necessity. Oh—should *I bear* it, do you think? I was thinking, when you went away—*after* you had quite gone. You would laugh to see me at my dinner .. Flush & me—Flush placing in me such an heroic confidence, that, .. after he has cast one discriminating glance on the plate, &, in the case of 'chicken,' wagged his tail with an emphasis, .. he goes off to the sofa, shuts his eyes & allows a full quarter of an hour to pass before he returns to take his share. Did you ever hear of a dog before who did not persecute one with beseeching eyes at mealtimes? And remember, this is not the effect of *discipline*. Also if another than myself happens to take coffee or break bread in the room here, he teazes straightway with eyes & paws, .. teazes like a common dog & is put out of the door before he can be quieted by scolding. But with *me* he is sublime! Moreover he has been a very useful dog in his time,—(in the point of capacity)—causing to disappear supererogatory dinners & impossible breakfasts which .. to do him justice, is a feat accomplished without an objection on his side, always.

So, when you write me such a letter, I write back to you about Flush. Dearest beloved, but I have read the letter & felt it in my heart, through & through! & it is as wise to talk of Flush foolishly, as to fancy that I *could say* HOW it is felt .. this letter! Only .. when you spoke last of breaking off with such & such recollections, it was the melancholy of the breaking off which I protested against .. was it not? & *not* the insufficiency of the recollections. There might have been something besides in jest .. Ah .. but *you* remember, if you please, that *I* was the first to wish (wishing for my own part, .. if I could wish exclusively) to break off in the middle the silken thread, .. & you told me, not .. you forbade me .. do you remember? For, as happiness goes, the recollections were enough, .. *are* enough for *me!*—I mean that I should acknowledge them to be full compensation for the bitter gift of life, *such as it was*, to me! if/they〉that/ ↑subject-matter↓ were broken off here!—'Bona verba'[1] let me speak nevertheless. You mean, you say, to run all risks with me, & I don't mean to draw back from my particular risk of .. what am I to do to you hereafter to make you vexed with me?—What is there in marriage to make all these people on every side of us .. (who all began, I suppose, by talking of love ..) look askance at one another from under the silken mask .. & virtually hate one another through the tyranny of the stronger & the hypocrisy of the weaker party. It never could be so with *us—I know that*. But you grow awful to me sometimes with the very excess of your goodness & tenderness . . & still, I think to myself, if you do not keep lifting me up quite off the ground by the strong faculty of love in you, I shall not help falling short of the hope you have placed in me—it must be "supernatural" of you, to the end! . . or I fall short & disappoint you. Consider this, beloved. Now if I could put my soul out of my body, just to stand up before you & make it clear!—

I did go to the drawing-room to-day . . would . . should . . did. The sun came out, the wind changed . . where was the obstacle? I spent a quarter of an hour in a fearful solitude, listening for knocks at the door, as a ghost-fearer might at midnight, & 'came home' none the worse in any way. Be sure that I shall 'take care' better than you do . . & there, is the worst of it all—for *you* let people make you ill, & do it yourself upon occasion.

You know from my letter how I found you out in the matter of the 'Soul's Tragedy.' Oh! so bad . . so weak, so unworthy of your name!—If some other people were half a quarter as much the contrary . . !

And so, good-night, dear dearest. In spite of my fine speeches about 'recollections,' I should be unhappy enough to please you, with *only those* . . without you beside—! I could not take myself back from being Your own——

1. "Words of good omen."

265 (W133) **R.B. to E.B.B.**

[*Wednesday, March 11, 1846.*]

Dear, dear Ba, but indeed I *did* return home earlier by two or three good hours than the night before—and to find *no* letter,—none of yours! *That* was reserved for this morning early, and then a rest came, a silence, over the thoughts of you,—and now again, comes this last note! Oh, my love—why . . what is it you think to do, or become "afterward," that you may fail in and so disappoint me? It is not very unfit that you should thus punish yourself, ↑and that,↓ sinning by your own ambition of growing something beyond my Ba even, you should "fear" as you say! For, sweet, why wish, why think to alter ever by a line, change by a shade, turn better if that were possible, and so only rise the higher above me, get further from instead of nearer to my heart? What I expect, what I build my future on, am quite, quite prepared to "risk" everything for,—is that one belief that you *will not alter,* will just remain as you are—meaning by '*you,*' the love in you, the qualities I have *known* . . (for you will stop me, if I do not stop myself)—what I have evidence of in every letter, in every word, every look. Keeping these, if it be God's will that the body passes,—what is that?—Write no new letters, speak no new words, look no new looks,—only tell me, years hence, that the present is alive, that what was once, still is—and I am, must needs be, blessed as ever! You speak of my feeling as if it were a pure speculation—as if because I *see somewhat* in you I make a calculation that there must be more to see somewhere or other—where bdellium is found, the onyx-stone mày be looked for in the mystic land of the four rivers![1] And perhaps . . ah, poor human nature!—perhaps I *do* think at times on what *may* be to find! But what is that to you? I *offer* for the *bdellium*—the other may be found or not found . . what I see glitter on the ground, *that* will suffice to make me rich as,—rich as—

So bless you my own Ba! I would not wait for paper, and you must forgive half-sheets instead of a whole celestial quire to my love and praise. Are you so well? So adventurous? Thank you from my heart of hearts. And I am quite well to-day (and have received a note from Procter *just* this *minute* putting off his dinner on account of the death of his wife's sister's husband abroad—) Observe *this* sheet I take as I find[2]— I mean, that the tear tells of no improper speech repented of—what English, what sense, what a soul's tragedy! but then, what real, realest love and more than love for my ever dearest Ba possesses her own—

1. Genesis 2:10–14.
2. Browning is continuing his letter on a sheet torn in half.

[*Postmarked March 12, 1846.*]

When my Orpheus writes Περὶ λίθων[1] he makes a great mistake
about onyxes—there is more true onyx in this letter of his . . that I have
just read . . than he will ever find in the desert land he goes to.—And for
what "glitters on the ground," it reminds me of the yellow metal sparks
found in the Malvern Hills, & how we used to laugh years ago at
⟨some⟩ one of our ⸗geological⸗ acquaintances, who looked mole-hills
up that mountain-range in the scorn of his eyes, saying . . . 'Nothing
but mica!!' Is anybody to be rich through 'mica', I wonder? through
'Nothing but mica?' "As rich as . . as rich as" . . . . . . *Walter the Penny-
less?*[2]

Dearest, best you are nevertheless, and it is a sorry jest which I can
break upon your poverty, with that golden heart of yours so apprehended of mine! Why if I ⸗am⸗ 'ambitious' . . is it not because you love
me as if I were worthier of your love, . . & that, *so,* I get frightened of
the opening of your eyelids to the *un*worthiness? "A little sleep, a little
slumber, a little folding of the hands ⟨in sleep⟩ to sleep'[3]—*there,* is my
'ambition for ⟨the⟩ /future⟩afterward/.' Oh—you do not understand
how with an unspeakable wonder, an astonishment which keeps me
from drawing breath, I look to this Dream, & 'see your face as the face
of an angel,'[4] and fear for the vanishing, . . because dreams & angels *do*
pass away in this world. But *you* . . *I* understand *you* . . & all your goodness past expression . . past belief of mine . . if I had not known you . .
just YOU. If it will satisfy you that I should know you, love you, love
you . . why then indeed . . . because I never bowed down to any of the
false gods—I know the gold from the mica, . . I! My own beloved!—
you should have my soul to stand on if it could make you stand higher.
Yet you shall not call me 'ambitious.'

Today I went down stairs again, & wished to know whether you
were walking in your proportion—& your letter does call you 'better,'
whether you walked enough or not . . & it bears the Deptford postmark. On Saturday I shall see how you are looking. So pale you were
last time!—I know Mr. Kenyon must have observed it,—(dear Mr.
Kenyon . . for being 'kinder & kindest') & that one of the 'augurs'

marvelled at the other!—By the way I forgot yesterday to tell you how Mr. Burges's 'apt remark' did amuse me. And Mr. Kenyon who said much the same words to me last week in relation to this very Wordsworth junior, writhed, I am sure, & wished the ingenious observer with the lost plays of Æschylus—oh, I seem to see Mr. Kenyon's face!—He was to have come to tell me how you all behaved at dinner that day . . but he keeps away . . you have given him too much to think of perhaps.

I heard from Miss Mitford today that Mr. Chorley's hope is at an end in respect to the theatre, & (. . I must tell you . .) she praises him warmly for his philosophy & fortitude under the disappointment. How much philosophy does it take, . . please to instruct me, . . in order to the decent bearing of such disasters? Can I fancy one, shorter than you by a whole head of the soul, condescending to '*bear*' such things? No, indeed.

Be good & kind, & do not work at the 'Tragedy' . . do not.

So you and I have written out all the paper in London! At least, I send & send in vain to have more envelopes 'after my kind,' & the last answer is, that a 'fresh supply will arrive in eight days from Paris, & that in the meanwhile they are quite *out* in the article." An awful sign of the times, is this famine of envelopes . . not to speak of the scarcity of little sheets:—& the augurs look to it all of course.

For MY part I think more of Chiappino—Chiappino holds fast.

But I must let *you* go—it is too late. This dearest letter, which you sent me! I thank you for it with ever so much dumbness. May God bless you & keep you, & make you happy for me——Your Ba—

1. "Concerning stones."
2. A leader of the Peasants' Crusade (1096).
3. Proverbs 6:10.
4. Cf. Acts 6:15.

267 (W134)   *R.B. to E.B.B.*

———————————

[*Postmarked March 12, 1846.*]

How I get to understand this much of Law—that prior possession is nine points of it! Just because your infinite adroitness got first hold of the point of view whence our connection looks like "a dream" . . I find myself shut out of my very own, unable to say what is oftenest in my thought,—whereas the dear, miraculous dream *you* were, and are, my Ba! Only, *vanish—that* you will never! My own, and for ever!

Yesterday I read the poor, inconceivably inadequate notice in the "People's Journal,"—How curiously wrong, too, in the personal guesses! Sad work truly. For my old friend Mrs. Adams—⟨in the first place⟩ no, I must be silent: the lyrics seem doggerel in its utter purity.[1]— And so the people are to be instructed in the new age of gold! I *heard* two days ago precisely what I told you—that there was a quarrel, &c which this service was to smooth over, no doubt? Chorley told me, in a hasty word only, that all was over, Mr. Webster would not have anything to do with his play:[2] the said W. is one of the poorest of poor creatures, and as Chorley was certainly forewarned, forearmed I will hope him to have been likewise—still it is very disappointing—he was apparently nearer than most aspirants to the prize,—having the best will of the actresses on whose shoulder the burthen was to lie. I hope they have been quite honest with him—knowing as I do the easy process of transferring all sorts of burthens, in that theatrical world, from responsible to irresponsible members of it, actors to manager, manager to actors, as the case requires. And it is a "hope deferred" with Chorley,—not for the second or third time—I am very glad that he cares no more than you tell me.

Still you go down stairs, and still return safely, and every step leads us nearer to *my* 'hope.' How unremittingly you bless me—a visit promises a letter, a letter brings such news, crowns me with such words, and speaks of another visit—and so the golden links extend! Dearest words, dearest letters—as I add each to my heap, I say,—I *do* say—"I was *poor,* it now seems, a minute ago, when I had not *this*" Bless you, dear, dear Ba. On Saturday I shall be with you, I trust—may God bless you! Ever your own R.

1. See Letter 244, note 1. Sarah Flower Adams was a ward of Fox's and had been Browning's friend since his boyhood. (G & M, pp. 45–47.) Two of her lines quoted by Fox will substantiate Browning's charge of doggerel: "Who are the happy, and who are the free? / You tell me, and I will tell thee!"
2. Probably *Old Love and New Fortune,* finally produced with some success in 1850. (*Henry Fothergill Chorley: Autobiography, Memoir and Letters,* ed. H. G. Hewlett

[2 vols., London, 1873], II, 14–20.) Benjamin Nottingham Webster (1797–1882) was manager of the Haymarket Theatre. For Browning's probable reason for calling him a "poor creature," see D & K, p. 23, note 14.

The visit occurred as scheduled and is noted on the envelope of Letter 266:
+ Sat^y March 14.
3–5¾ p.m. (52.)

268 (W131°)   *E.B.B. to R.B.*

[*March 15, 1846.*]

Sunday.

Ever dearest I am going to say one word first of all lest I should forget it afterward, of the two or three words which you said yesterday & so passingly that you probably forget to-day having said them at all. We were speaking of Mr. Chorley & his house . . & you said that you did not care for such and such things for yourself, but that for others . . . now you remember the rest. And I just want to say what it would have been simpler to have said at the time . . only not so easy . . (I *couldn't* say it at the time) . . that you are not if you please to fancy that because I am a woman I have not the pretension to do with as little in any way as you yourself . . no, it is not *that* I mean to say . . I mean that you are not, if you please, to fancy that, because I am a woman, I look to be cared for in those outside things, or should have the slightest pleasure in any of them.—So never wish nor regret in your thoughts to be able or not to be able to care this & this for *me*,—for while you are thinking so, our thoughts go different ways,—which is wrong. Mr. Fox did me a great deal too much honour in calling me 'a religious hermit'[1] he was 'curiously' in fault, as you saw. It is not my vocation to sit on a stone in a cave—I was always too fond of lolling upon sofas or in chairs nearly as large,—& this, which I sit in, was given to me when I was a child by my uncle, the uncle I spoke of to you once,[2] & has been lolled in nearly ever since . . when I was well enough. Well—*that* is a sort of luxury, of course—but it is more idle than expensive, as a habit, & I do believe that it is the 'head and foot of my offending' in ⟨respect to⟩ that matter. Yes—'confiteor tibi'[3] besides, that I do hate white dimity curtains, which is highly improper for a religious hermit of course, but excusable in ME who would accept brown serge as a substitute with ever so much indifference. It is the white light which comes in the dimity which is so hateful to me—To " go mad in white dimity' "[4] seems perfectly natural, & consequential even. Set aside these foibles, & one thing is as good as another with me, & the more simplicity in the way of living, the better. If I saw Mr. Chorley's satin sofas & gilded ceilings I should call them very pretty I dare say, but never covet the possession of the like—it would never enter my mind to do so. Then Papa has not kept a carriage since I have been grown up—(they grumble about it here in the house, but when people have once had great reverses they get nervous about spending money)—so I shall not miss the Clarence & greys . . & I do entreat you *not* to put those two ideas together again of *me* & the finery which has nothing to do with me. I have talked a great deal too much of all this, you will think, but I want you, once for all, to apply it broadly to the whole of the future both in the general view & the details, so that we need not return to the subject. Judge for me as for yourself—*what is good for you is good for me*. Otherwise I shall be humiliated, you know; just as far as I know your thoughts.

Mr. Kenyon has been here to-day—& I have been down stairs—two great events!—He was in brilliant spirits & sate talking ever so long, & named you as he always does. Something he asked, & then said suddenly . . " But I dont /know⟩see/ why I should ask *you*, when I ought to know him better than you can." On which I was wise enough to change colour, as I felt, to the roots of my hair. There is the effect of a bad conscience! & it has happened to me before, ↑with↓ Mr. Kenyon, three times—once particularly, when I could have cried with vexation (to complete the effects!) he looked at me with such infinite surprise in a dead pause of any speaking. *That* was in the summer,—& all to be said for it now, is, that it couldn't be helped!—couldn't!

Mr. Kenyon asked of 'Saul.' (By the way, you never answered about the blue lilies.)[5] He asked of 'Saul' & whether it would be finished in the new number. He hangs on the music of your David. Did you read in the Athenæum how Jules Janin . . no, how the critic on Jules Janin . . (was it the critic? was it Jules Janin? the glorious confusion is gaining on me I think) has magnificently confounded places & persons in Robert

Southey's urn by the Adriatic & devoted friendship for Lord Byron?[6]
And immediately the English observer of the phenomenon, after moral-
izing a little on the crass ignorance of Frenchmen in respect to our literature, goes on to write like an ignoramus himself, on M^dme Charles
Reybaud, encouraging that pure budding novelist, who is in fact a hack
writer of romances third & fourth rate, of ⟨a⟩ questionable purity
enough, too. It does certainly appear wonderful that we /do⟩should/
not sufficiently stand abreast here in Europe, to justify ⸲& necessitate⸲
the establishment of an European review . . journal rather . . (the
'Foreign Review,' so called, touching only the summits of the hills . .)
a journal which be on a level with the intelligent readers of all the
countries of Europe, & take all the rising reputations of each, with the
national light on them as they rise, into observation & judgment. If nobody can do this, it is a pity I think to do so much less . . both in France
and England . . to snatch up a French book from over the channel as
ever and anon they do in the Athenæum, & say something prodigiously
absurd of it, till people cry out "oh oh" as in the House of Commons.

Oh—oh—& how wise I am today, as if I were a critic myself!—
Yesterday I was foolish instead—for I couldn't get out of my head all
the evening how you said that you would come 'to see a candle held up
at the window.' Well!—but I do not mean to love you any more just
now—so I tell you plainly. Certainly I will not. I love you already too
much perhaps . . I feel like the turning Dervishes turning in the sun when
you say such words to me—& I *never shall* love you any "less," . . because it is too much to be made less of.

And you write to-morrow? and will tell me how you are? honestly
will tell me? May God bless you, most dear!—I am yours—'Tota tua
est'—Ba

1. See Letter 244, note 1.
2. See Letter 173 and its note 4.
3. "I confess to you."
4. Cf. Sheridan's *The Critic*, III, i: "Enter Tilburina stark mad in white satin,
and her confidant stark mad in white linen."
5. See Letter 254.
6. The "Foreign Correspondence" column of the March 14 *Athenæum* quoted
from the February 2 *Journal des Débats* part of an article by Jules Janin (1804–74), its
famous drama critic: "Cet ami de Lord Byron, Robert Southey, un des beaux
esprits de l'Angleterre moderne, dont le bûcher s'est élevé sur les bords de l'Adriatique
. . . a écrit une poème dans lequel ce Comte Julien joue le grand rôle."

269 (W135)   R.B. to E.B.B.

[March 15, 1846.]

Sunday.

How will the love my heart is full of for you, let me be silent? Insufficient speech is better than no speech, in one regard—the speaker had *tried* words, and if they fail, hereafter he needs not reflect that he did not even try—so with me now, that loving you, Ba, with all my heart and soul,—all my senses being lost in one wide wondering gratitude and veneration, I press close to you to say so, in this imperfect way, my dear dearest beloved! Why do you not help me, rather than take my words, my proper word, from me and call them yours, when yours they are not?—You said lately love of you "made you humble"—just as if to hinder *me* from saying that earnest truth!—entirely true it is, as I feel ever more convincingly. You do not choose to understand it should be so, nor do I much care, for the one thing you must believe, must resolve to believe in its length and breadth, is that I do love you and live only in the love of you—

I will rest on the confidence that you do so believe! You *know* by this that it is no shadowy image of you and *not* you, which having attached myself to in the first instance, I afterward compelled my fancy to see reproduced, so to speak, with tolerable exactness to the original idea, in you, the dearest real *you* I am blessed with—you *know* what the eyes are to me, and the lips and the hair—And I, for my part, know *now,* while fresh from seeing you, certainly *know,* whatever I may have said a short time since, that *you* will go on to the end, that the arm round me will not let me go,—over such a blind abyss—I refuse to think, to fancy, *towards* what it would be to lose you now! So I give my life, my soul into your hand—the giving is a mere form too, it is yours, ever yours from the first—but ever as I see you, sit with you, and come away to think over it all, I find more that seems mine to give,—you give me more life and it goes back to you.

I shall hear from you to-morrow—then, I will go out early and get done with some calls, in the joy and consciousness of what waits me,— and when I return I will write a few words—Are these letters, these merest attempts at getting to talk with you thro' the distance . . yet always with the consolation of feeling that you will know all, interpret all & forgive it and put it right,—can such things be cared for, expected, as you say? Then, Ba, my life *must* be better . . with the closeness to help, and the "finding out the way" for which love was always noted—If you begin making ⟨in fancy⟩ a lover to your mind, I am lost at once—but the one quality of *affection* for you, which would sooner or later have to be placed on his list of component graces; *that* I will dare start supply—the entire love you could dream of *is* here—You think you see some of the other adornments, and only too many,—and you will see plainer one day, but with that I do not concern myself—you shall admire the true heroes—but me you shall love for the love's sake. Let me kiss you, you, my dearest, dearest—God bless you ever—

270 (W136)   *R.B. to E.B.B.*

[Postmarked March 16, 1846.]

Indeed I would, dearest Ba, go with entire gladness and pride to see a light that came from your room—why should that surprise you?— Well, you will *know* one day.

We understand each other too about the sofas and gilding—oh, I know you, my own sweetest! For me, if I had set those matters to heart, I /would⟩should/ have turned into the obvious way of getting them— not *out* of it, as I did resolutely from the beginning. All I meant was, to express a very natural feeling—if one could give you diamonds for flowers, and if you liked diamonds,—then, indeed!—As it is, wherever we are found shall be, if you please, "For the love's sake found therein— sweetest *house* was ever seen"![1]

Mr. Kenyon must be merciful—(lilies are of all colours in Palestine —one sort is particularized as *white* with a dark blue spot and streak— the water lily, lotos, which I think I meant, is *blue* altogether)

I have walked this morning to town & back—I feel much better, "honestly!" The head better—the spirits rising,—as how should they not, when *you* think all will go well in the end,—when you write to me that you go down stairs and are stronger—and when the rest is written? ⟨I am ‖ · · · ‖⟩

539

Not more now, dearest, for time is pressing—but you will answer this,—the love that is not here,—not the idle words—and I will reply to-morrow. Thursday is so far away yet!

Bless you, my very own, only dearest!

R.

1. An echo of E.B.B.'s *Catarina to Camoens* (1844), st. iv. Browning has substituted "*house*" for "eyes."

271 *(W132°)*   *E.B.B. to R.B.*

[*March 16, 1846.*]

Monday evening.

Dearest, you are dearest always! Talk of Sirens, . . there must be some masculine ones 'rari nantes,'[1] I fancy, (though we may not find them in unquestionable authorities like your Ælian!) to justify this voice I hear. Ah—how you speak,—with that pretension, too, to dumbness! What should people be made of, in order to bear such words, do you think?—Will all the wax from all the altar-candles in the Sistine Chapel, keep the piercing danger from their ears? Being tied up a good deal tighter than Ulysses did not save *me*. Dearest dearest!—I laugh, you see, as usual, not to cry!—But deep down, deeper than the Sirens go, deep underneath the tides, *there,* I bless & love you with the voice that makes no sound—

Other human creatures (how often I do think /that⟩it/ to myself!) have their good things scattered over their lives, sown here & sown there, down the slopes, & by the waysides. But with me . . I have mine all poured down on one spot in the midst of the sands!—if you knew what I feel at moments, & at half-hours, when I give myself up to the feeling freely & take no thought of red eyes. A woman once was killed with gifts, crushed with the weight of golden bracelets thrown at her: &, knowing myself, I have wondered more than a little, how it was that I could *bear* this strange & ⟨light &⟩ unused gladness, without sinking as the emotion rose. Only I was incredulous as first, & the day broke slowly . . & the gifts fell like the rain . . softly;—& God gives strength, by His providence, for sustaining blessings as well as stripes. Dearest!——

For the rest I understand you perfectly—perfectly. It was simply to your *thoughts*, that I replied . . & that you need not say to yourself any more, as you did once to me when you brought me flowers, . . that you wished they were diamonds. It was simply to prevent the accident of such a *thought,* that I spoke out mine. You would not wish accidentally that you had a doublebarrelled gun to give me, or a cardinal's hat, or a snuff box—& I meant to say that you *might as well* . . as ⟨for⟩ diamonds & satin sofas à la Chorley. Thoughts are something—& *your* thoughts are something more. To be sure they are!—

You are better you say, which makes me happy of course. And you will not make the 'better' worse again by doing wrong things . . *that* is my petition. It was the excess of goodness to write those two letters for me in one day—& I thank you, thank you. Beloved, when you write, *let* it be, if you choose, ever so few lines. Do not suffer me (for my own sake) to tire you—because two lines or three bring YOU to me . . remember . . just as a longer letter would.

But where, pray, did I say . . & when, . . that "everything would end well"? Was *that* in the dream, when we two met on the stairs?[2] I did not really say so I think. And "well" is how you understand it. If you jump out of the window you ⟨will⟩ succeed in getting to the ground, somehow, dead or alive . . but whether *that* means "ending well," depends on your way of considering matters. I am seriously of opinion nevertheless, that if "the arm," you talk of, *drops*, it will not be for weariness nor even for weakness . . but because it is cut off at the shoulder. *I* will not fail to you,—may God so deal with me, so bless me, so leave me, as I live only for you & *shall*. Do you doubt *that,* my only beloved?—Ah, you know well—*too well,* people would say . . but I do not think it "too well" myself, . . knowing *you*.

Your Ba

Here is a gossip which Mr. Kenyon brought me on Sunday . . disbelieving it himself, he asseverated, though Lady Chantrey said it 'with authority,'—that Mr. Harness had offered his hand heart & ecclesiastical dignities to Miss Burdett Coutts.[3] It is Lady Chantrey's & Mr. Kenyon's *secret,* remember.

And . . will you tell me? . . How can a man spend four or five successive months on the sea, most cheaply . . at the least pecuniary expense, I mean? Because Miss Mitford's friend Mr. Buckingham[4] is ordered by his medical adviser to complete his cure by these means; & he is not rich. Could he go with sufficient comfort by a merchant's vessel to the Mediterranean . . & might he drift about among the Greek islands?

1. "Swimming here and there," *Aeneid* I. 118. For the Sirens, see Letter 151, note 7.

2. See the second paragraph of Letter 207.

3. Angela Georgina Burdett-Coutts, later Baroness Burdett-Coutts, (1814–1906) was a desirable heiress, having inherited a great fortune from her maternal grandfather.

4. Not identified, but he eventually took his trip and fell into disfavor with Miss Mitford. See *EBB to MRM,* pp. 267, 275.

272 (W137)   R.B. to E.B.B.

[*March 17, 1846.*]

Tuesday.

"Out of window" would be well, as I see the leap, if it ended *(so far as I am concerned)* in the worst way imaginable—I would "run the risk" (Ba's other word) rationally,—deliberately,—knowing what the ordinary law of chances in this world justifies in such a case; and if the result after all *was* unfortunate, it would be far easier to undergo the extremest penalty with so little to reproach myself for,—than to put aside the adventure,—waive the wondrous probability of such best fortune, in a fear of the barest possibility of an adverse event, and so go to my grave, Walter the Penniless, with an eternal recollection that Miss Burdett Coutts once offered to wager sundry millions with me that she could throw double-sixes a dozen times running—which wager I wisely refused to accept because it was not written in the stars that such a sequence might never be—I had rather, rather a thousand-fold lose my paltry stake, and be the one recorded victim to such an unexampled unluckiness that half a dozen mad comets, suns gone wrong, and lunatic moons must have come laboriously into conjunction for my special sake to bring it to pass, which were no slight honor, properly considered!

—And this is *my* way of laughing, dearest Ba, when the excess of belief in you, and happiness with you, runs over and froths if it don't sparkle—underneath is a deep, a sea not to be moved—But chance, chance! there is *no* chance here! I *have* gained enough for my life, I can only put in peril the gaining more than enough—You shall change altogether my dear, dearest love, and I will be happy to the last minute on what I can remember of this past year—I *could* do that. *Now,* jump with me out, Ba!—If you feared for yourself—all would be different, sadly different—But saying what you do say, promising "the strength of arm"—do not wonder that I call it an assurance of all being 'well'! All is *best,* as you promise—dear, darling Ba!—and I say, in my degree, with all the energy of my nature, *as you say,* promise as you promise—only meaning a worship of you that is solely fit for me,—fit by position—are not you my "mistress"? Come, some good out of those old conventions, in which you lost faith after the Bower's disappearance[1]—(it was carried by the singing angels, like the House at Loretto,[2] to the Siren's Isle where we shall find it preserved in a beauty "very rare and absolute")—is it not right you should be my Lady, my Queen?—and you are, and ever must be, dear Ba—because I am suffered to kiss the lips, shall I ever refuse to embrace the feet?—I kiss lips, and embrace feet, love you *wholly,* my Ba! May God bless you—Ever your own,——R.

It would be easy for Mr. Buckingham to find a Merchant-ship bound for some Mediterranean port, and after a week or two in harbour, to another and perhaps a third—Naples, Palermo, Syra, Constantinople, & so on. The expense would be very trifling—but the want of comfort *enormous* for an Invalid—the one advantage is the solitariness of the *one* passenger among all those rough new creatures—*I* like it much, and soon get deep into their friendship, but another has other ways of viewing matters—No one article provided by the ship in the way of provisions can *anybody* touch. Mr. B. must lay in his own stock,—and the horrors of dirt and men's ministry are portentous,—yet by a little arrangement beforehand much might be done. Still, I only know my own powers of endurance, and counsel nobody to gain my experience—on the other hand, were all to do again, I had rather have seen Venice *so* —with the five or six weeks' absolute rest of the minds eyes, than any other imaginable way,—except Balloon-travelling.

Do you think they meant Landor's *Count Julian*[3]—the "subject of

his tragedy" sure enough,—and that *he* was the friend of Southey?
So it struck me—

1. An allusion to E.B.B.'s *The Lost Bower* (1844).
2. A house in the Adriatic town of Loreto was shown as the Virgin Mary's
home, said to have been transported from Nazareth in the thirteenth century by
angels. In mid-1844 when Count Rocchi, custodian of its funds, absconded, the
scandal revived British awareness of the legend.
3. Browning's "they" refers to the extract from the *Journal des Débats* in the
March 14 *Athenæum* (Letter 268). E.B.B. has a more plausible explanation of the
confusion in Letter 273.

273 *(W133°)*   **E.B.B. to R.B.**
                          _____

[*March 17, 1846.*]

                                                Tuesday Evening.
        Ah well—we shall see. Only remember that it is not my fault if I
throw the double sixes, & if you, on ⟨some sunshiny day, (a day too late
to help yourself) stand face to face with a milkwhite unicorn.⟩[1] Ah—do
not be angry. It is ungrateful of me to write so—I put a line through it to
prove I have a conscience after all. I know that you love me .. & I know
it so well that I was reproaching myself severely not long ago, for seeming to love your love more than you. Let me tell you how I proved *that,*
or seemed. For ever so long, you remember, I have been talking finely
about giving you up for your good & so on. Which was sincere as far as
the words went—but oh, the hypocrisy of our souls!—of mine, for
instance! 'I would give you up for your good'—*but* when I pressed
upon myself the question whether (if I had the power) I would consent
to make you willing to be given up, by throwing away your love into
the river, in a ring like Charlemagne's,[2] . . . . why I found directly
that I would throw myself there sooner. I could not do it in fact—I
shrank from the test. A very pitiful virtue of generosity, is your Ba's!
Still, it is not possible, I think, that she should "*love your love more than
you,*" There must be a mistake in the calculation somewhere—a
figure, dropt. It would be too bad for her!—
        Your account of your merchantmen, though with Venice in the
distance, will scarcely be attractive to a confirmed invalid, I fear—& yet

                                  544

the steamers will be found expensive beyond his means. The sugar-vessels, which I hear most about, give out an insufferable smell & steam —let us talk of it a little on thursday. On monday I forgot.

For Landor's 'Julian' . . oh no . . I cannot fancy it to be probable that those Parisians should know anything of Landor, even by a mistake. Do you not suppose that the play is founded (confounded) on Shelley's poem,[3] as the French use materials . . by distraction, into confusion? The 'urn by the Adriatic' (which all the French know how to turn upside down) fixes the reference to Shelley—does it not?

Not a word of the head!—what does THAT mean, I wonder. I have not been down stairs to-day—the wind is too cold . . but you have walked? . . there was no excuse for you. God bless you, ever dearest. It is my last word till thursday's first. A fine queen you have, by the way!—a queen Log,[4] whom you had better leave in the bushes! Witness our hand . .

Ba-Regina

1. See Letter 104, note 1.
2. The Eastern princess Frastrada, Charlemagne's fourth wife, held his affection by means of a magic ring which she hid in her mouth as she lay dying. Held by the spell, the Emperor would not let her be buried. Archbishop Turpin found the ring and, embarrassed by the Emperor's consequent affections, threw it into a pool. Charlemagne then built his capital nearby, at Aix-la-Chapelle. The story is told in Southey's poem, *King Charlemain*, drawn from Pasquier's *Recherches de la France*, whose author claims a letter of Petrarch's as his source. See *The Poetical Works of Robert Southey,* Collected by Himself (10 vols., London [1837]), VI, 85–86.
3. *Julian and Maddalo.*
4. In the fable the frogs petition Zeus for a king and are given first a log, then—when they protest—a stork. E.B.B. may be thinking not so much of Aesop as of the end of Book I of the *Dunciad*.

274 (W138)   *R.B. to E.B.B.*

_____

[*Postmarked March 18, 1846*.]

Indeed, dearest, you shall not have *last word* as you think,—all the "risk" shall not be mine, neither,—how can I, in the event, throw ambs-ace[1] (is not that the old word?) and not peril *your* stakes too, when once we have common stock and are partners? When I see the unicorn[2] and grieve proportionately, do you mean to say you are not going to grieve too, for my sake? And if so—why, *you* clearly run exactly the same risk,—*must,*—unless you mean to rejoice in my sorrow! So your chance is my chance; my success your success, you say, and my failure, your failure, will you not say? You see, you see, Ba, my own!—own! What do you think frightened me in your letter for a second or two? You write "Let us talk on Thursday . . Monday I forgot"—which I read,—"no, not on Thursday—I had forgotten! It is to be *Monday* when we meet next"!—whereat

> . . as a goose
> In death contracts his talons close,

as Hudibras sings[3]—I clutched the letter convulsively—till relief came.

So till to-morrow—my all-beloved! Bless you—I am rather hazy in the head as Archer Gurney will find in due season—(he comes, I told you)—but all the morning I have been going for once and for ever thro' the Tragedy, and it is *done*—(done *for*). Perhaps I may bring it to-morrow—if my sister can copy all—I cut out a huge kind of sermon from the middle and reserve it for a better time[4]—still it is very long; so long! So, if I ask, may I have "Luria" back to morrow? So shall printing begin, and headache end—and "/now⟩no/ more for the present from your loving"

R. B.

1. The lowest throw, therefore, figuratively, bad luck.
2. See Letter 104, note 1.
3. I. iii. 527–528. The original has "loose," not "close."
4. See Letter 294 and its note 2.

At this point there was a visit, noted on the envelope of Letter 273:

+Thursday March 19

$3\frac{1}{4}$–$5\frac{1}{4}$ p.m. (53.)

275 (W134°)   *E.B.B. to R.B.*

[March 20, 1846.]

Friday.

I shall be late with my letter this morning because my sisters have been here talking, talking . . & I did not like to say exactly 'Go away that I may write.' Mr. Kenyon shortened our time yesterday too by a whole half hour or three quarters—the stars are against us. He is coming on Sunday, however, he says, and if so, Monday will be safe & clear . . & not a word was said after you went, about you—he was in a good joyous humour—as you saw, . . & the letter he brought was, oh! so complimentary to me . . I will tell you. The writer doesn't see anything "in Browning & Turner,"[1] she confesses . . "*may* perhaps with time and study," but for the present sees nothing, . . only has wide-open eyes of admiration for E. B. B. . . . . now isn't it satisfactory to *me?* Do you understand the full satisfaction of just that sort of thing . . to be praised by somebody who sees nothing in Shakespeare?—to be found on the level of somebody so flat? Better the bad-word of the Britannia,[2] ten times over.! And best, to take no thought of bad or good words . .! except such as I shall have to-night, perhaps!—Shall I?

　　Will you be pleased to understand in the meanwhile a little about the 'risks' I am supposed to run, & not hold to such a godlike simplicity ('gods & bulls,' dearest!) as you made show of yesterday? If we two went to the gaming-table, & you gave me a purse of gold to play with, should I have a right to talk proudly of 'my stakes'? & would any reasonable person say of both of us playing together as partners, that we ran "equal risks"? I trow not—& so do *you* . . when you have not predetermined to be stupid, & mix up the rouge and noir into "one red"[3] of glorious confusion. What had I to lose on the point of happiness when you knew me first?—& if now I lose (as I certainly may according to your calculation) the happiness you have given me, why still I am your debtor for *the* /past⟩*gift*/ . . now see! Yet to bring you down into my ashes . . *that* has been so intolerable a possibility to me from the first . . . Well—perhaps I run *more* risk than you, under that one aspect,— Certainly I never should forgive myself again if you were unhappy. "What had *I* to do," I should think, "with touching your life?" And if ever I am to think so, I /should⟩would/ rather that I never had known you, seen your face, heard your voice—which is the uttermost sacrifice & abnegation. I could not say or sacrifice any more . . not even for YOU! —*You,* for *you* . . is all I can!

　　Since you left me I have been ⟨thinking⟩ making up my mind to your having the headache worse than ever, through the agreement with Moxon. I do, do beseech you to spare yourself, & let "Luria" go as he is,

& above all things not to care for my infinite foolishnesses as you see them in those notes.[4] Remember that if you are ill, it is not so easy to say, "Now I will be well again." Ever dearest, care for me in yourself—say how you are . . . I am not unwell today, but feel flagged & weak rather with the cold . . & look at your flowers for courage & an assurance that the summer is within hearing. May God bless you . . blessing *us*, beloved!

Your own
Ba

Mr. Poe has sent me his poems & tales[5]—so now I must write to thank him for his dedication.—Just now I have the book. As to Mr. Buckingham he will go, Constantinople & back, before we talk of him—

1. Probably the painter, J. M. W. Turner (1775–1851), whose impressionistic later style alienated a large part of the general public and the critics.
2. Probably *Britannia,* "a weekly Journal of News, Politics and Literature," published in London, 1839–1856.
3. An allusion to *Macbeth* II. ii. 64.
4. See Letter 66, note 1.
5. *The Raven and Other Poems* was issued twice in 1845, once separately and a second time in combination with the *Tales.*

276 (W139)   **R.B. to E.B.B.**

[*March 21, 1846.*]

Saturday M^g

Dearest,—it just strikes me that I *might* by some chance be kept in town this morning—(having to go to Milnes' breakfast there)—so as not to find the note I venture to expect, in time for an answer by our last post to-night. But I will try—this only is a precaution against the possibility. Dear, dear Ba! I cannot thank you, know not how to thank you for the notes![1] I adopt every one, of course, not as Ba's notes but as Miss Barrett's, not as Miss Barrett's but as anybody's, everybody's—such incontestable improvements they suggest. When shall I tell you more . . on Monday or Tuesday? *That* I *must* know—because you appointed

Monday, "if nothing happened—" and Mr. K. happened—can you let me hear by our early post to-morrow—as on Monday I am to be with Moxon early, you know—and no letters arrive before $11\frac{1}{2}$ or 12. I was not very well yesterday, but to-day am much better—and you,—I say how *I* am precisely to have a double right to know *all* about you, dearest, in this snow and cold! How do you bear it? And Mr. K. spoke of "*that* being your worst day"—Oh, dear, dearest Ba, remember how I live in you—on the hopes, with the memory of you. Bless you ever!——R.

1. See Letter 66, note 1.

277 (W135°)   *E.B.B. to R.B.*

[*Postmarked March 21, 1846.*]

I do not understand how my letters limp so instead of flying as they ought with the feathers I give them, & how you did not receive last night, nor even early this morning, what left me at two oclock yesterday. But I understand *now* the not hearing from you—you were not well. Not well, not well . . *that* is always "happening" at least. And Mr. Moxon, who is to have his first sheet, whether you are well or ill! . . It is wrong . . yes, very wrong—and if one point of wrongness is touched, we shall not easily get right again—as I think mournfully, feeling confident (call me Casandra, but I cannot jest about it) feeling certain that it will end (the means being so persisted in) by some serious illness—serious sorrow, . . on yours & my part.

As to Monday, Mr. Kenyon said he would come again on Sunday —in which case, Monday will be clear. If he should not come on Sunday, he will or may on Monday,—yet,—oh . . in every case, perhaps you can come on Monday—there will be no time to let you know of Mr. Kenyon—& *probably* we shall be safe . . & your being in town seems to fix the day. For myself I am well enough, & the wind has changed, which will make me better—this cold weather oppresses & weakens me—but it is close to April & cant last and wont last—it is warmer already. Beware of the notes!—They are not Ba's . . except for the insolence,—nor EBB's . . because of the carelessness. If I had known, moreover, that you were going to Moxon's on Monday, they should have gone to the fire rather than provoked you into superfluous work for the short interval. Just so much are they despised of both EBB & Ba.

I am glad I did not hear from you yesterday because you were not well, & you *must* NEVER write when you are not well. But if you had been quite well, should I have heard?—*I doubt it.* You meant me to hear from you only once, from thursday to monday. Is it not the truth now that you hate writing to me?—

The Athenæum takes up the 'Tales from Boccaccio'[1] as if they were worth it, & imputes in an underground way the authorship to the members of the "coterie" so called—do you observe *that?* There is an implication that persons named in the poem wrote the poem themselves. And upon *whom* does the critic mean to fix the song of "Constancy" . . the song which is "not to puzzle anybody" who knows the tunes of the songwriters? The perfection of commonplace it seems to me. It might have been written by the "poet Bunn."[2] Don't you think so?—

While I write this you are in town, but you will not read it till sunday unless I am more fortunate than usual—On monday then!— And no word before? No— I shall be sure not to hear tonight. Now do try not to suffer through Luria. Let Mr. Moxon wait a week rather. There is time enough—Ever your Ba

1. The March 21 issue reviewed the anonymous *Tales from Boccaccio, with Modern Illustrations, and Other Poems,* which (as *Stories*) has been reviewed with Browning's *Dramatic Romances and Lyrics* in the *New Quarterly Review.* (Letter 198 and its notes 5 and 8.)

2. Alfred Bunn (1796–1860) was the almost universally disliked manager of Drury Lane, with whom Macready actually came to blows. His attempts at verse led *Punch* to dub him "the poet Bunn."

278 (*W140*) R.B. *to* E.B.B.

[*March 22, 1846.*]

Sunday.

Oh, my Ba—how you shall hear of this to-morrow—that is all: *I* hate writing? See when presently I *only* write to you daily, hourly if you let me? Just this *now*—I will be with you ⸱to-morrow⸱ in any case—I can go away *at once*, if need be—or stay—if you like you can stop me by sending a note for me *to Moxon's before* 10 o'clock—if anything calls for such a measure.

Now briefly,—I am unwell and entirely irritated with this sad Luria—I thought it a failure at first, I find it infinitely worse than I thought—it is a pure exercise of *cleverness*, even where most successful, —clever ⸱attempted⸱ reproduction of what was conceived by another faculty, and foolishly let pass away. If I go on, even hurry the more to get on, with the printing,—it is to throw out and away from me the irritating obstruction once & forever. I have corrected it, cut it down, and it may stand and pledge me to doing better hereafter. I say, too, in excuse to myself,—*unlike* the woman at her spinning-wheel, "He thought of his *flax* on the whole far more than of his singing"—more of his life's sustainment, of dear, dear Ba he hates writing to, than of these wooden figures—no wonder all is as it is!

Here is a pure piece of the old Chorley leaven for you, just as it reappears ever and anon and throws one back on the mistrust all but abandoned![1] Chorley *knows* I have not seen that Powell for nearly fifteen months—that I never heard of the book till it reached me in a blank cover—that I never contributed a line or word to it directly or indirectly—and I should think ⸱he⸱ *also knows* that all the sham learning, notes &c, all that saves the book from the deepest deep of contempt, was contributed by Heraud *(a regular critic in the Athenæum),*—who received his pay for the same: he knows I never spoke in my life to "Jones or Stephens"—that there is no "côterie" of which I can, by any extension of the word, form a part—that I am in this case at the mercy of a wretched creature who to get into my favor again (to speak the plain truth) put in the gross, disgusting flattery in the notes —yet Chorley, knowing this, none so well,—and what the writer's end is—(to have it supposed I, and the others named—Talfourd, for instance—ARE his friends and helpers)—he condescends to *further* it by such a notice, written with that observable & characteristic duplicity, that to poor gross stupid Powell it shall look like an admiring "Oh, fie—*so* clever but *so* wicked!"—a kind of *D'Orsay's* praise[2]—while to the rest of his readers, a few depreciatory epithets & slight sneers convey his real sentiments, he trusts! And this he does, just because Powell buys an article of him once a quarter and would *expect* notice

—I think I hear Chorley—"You know, I *cannot* praise such a book—
it *is* too bad"—as if, as if—oh, it makes one sicker than having written
Luria, there's one comfort! I shall call on Chorley and ask for *his*
account of the matter. Meantime nobody /will⟩can/ read his foolish
notice without believing as he and Powell desire! Bless you, my own
Ba—tomorrow makes amends to R. B.

1. Browning thought that Chorley, a member of the *Athenæum* staff, wrote the
review of *Tales from Boccaccio*, which hinted that Browning was a member of the
"côterie" by printing the verse quoted in Letter 198, note 8.
2. Alfred Guillaume Gabriel, Count d'Orsay (1801–52), the famous dandy,
was the son of a French general and the daughter by morganatic marriage of the
King of Württemberg. In 1822 his good looks and ready wit led the Earl and
Countess of Blessington, then touring Europe, to attach him to their household,
where he remained even after the collapse of his brief marriage (1827) to the Earl's
fifteen-year-old daughter. After Blessington's death in 1829 d'Orsay and his widow
lived together until her death in 1849. Despite the scandal, d'Orsay managed to
charm even Carlyle, but Browning's references are always critical, like that in
Bishop Blougram's Apology, l. 54.

Browning recorded a visit on the envelope of Letter 277:
+Monday, March 23,
3–5¾ p.m. (54.)

279 (W136°)   **E.B.B. to R.B.**

[*March 24, 1846.*]

Tuesday.
How ungrateful I was to your flowers yesterday, never looking at
them nor praising them till they were put away, & yourself gone away
—& *that* was *your* fault, be it remembered, because you began to tell me
of the good news from Moxon's, &, in the joy of it, I missed the flowers
. . for the nonce, you know. Afterward they had their due, & all the
more that you were not there. My first business when you are out of the
room & the house, & the street perhaps, is to arrange the flowers & to
gather out of them all the thoughts you leave between the leaves & at

the end of the stalks. And shall I tell you what happened, not yesterday, but the thursday before?—no, it was the friday morning, when I found, or rather Wilson found & held up from my chair, a bunch of dead blue violets. Quite dead they seemed!—You had dropped them & I had sate on them, & where we murdered them they had lain, poor things, all the night through. And Wilson thought it the vainest of labours when she saw me set about reviving them, cutting the stalks afresh, & dipping them head & ears into water—but then she did not know how you, & I and ours /are>live/ under a miraculous dispensation, & could only simply be astonished when they took to blowing again as if they never had wanted the dew of the garden, . . yes, & ↑when↓ at last they outlived all the prosperity of the contemporary white violets which flourished in water from the beginning & were free from the disadvantage of having been sate upon. Now you shall thank me for this letter . . it is at once so amusing & instructive. After all, too, it teaches you what the great events of my life are—not that the resuscitation of your violets would not really be a great event to me, even if I led the life of a pirate, between fire & sea, otherwise. But take *you* away . . out of my life!—& what remains? The only greenness I used to have (before you brought your flowers) was as the grass growing in deserted streets, . . which brings a proof, in every increase, of the extending desolation.

Dearest, I persist in thinking that you ought not to be too disdainful to explain your meaning in the Pomegranates. Surely you might say in a word or two that, your title having been doubted about (to your surprise, you *might* say!), you refer the doubters to the Jewish priest's robe, & the Rabbinical gloss . . for I suppose it is a gloss on the robe . . do you not think so? Consider that Mr. Kenyon & I may fairly represent the average intelligence of your readers,—& that *he* was altogether in the clouds as to your meaning . . had not the most distant notion of it,—while I, taking hold of the priest's garment, missed the Rabbins & the distinctive significance, as completely as he did. Then for Vasari, it is not the handbook of the whole world, however it may be Mrs. Jameson's. Now why should you be too proud to teach such persons as only desire to be taught?[1] I persist—I shall teaze you.

This morning my brothers have been saying . . "Ah you had Mr. Browning with you yesterday, I see by the flowers," . . just as if they said "I see queen Mab has been with you."[2] Then Stormie took the opportunity of swearing to me by all his gods that your name was mentioned ↑lately↓ in the House of Commons—*is* that true? or untrue? He forgot to tell me at the time, he says,—& you were named with others & in relation to copyright matters. *Is* it true?

Mr. Hornblower Gill is the author of a Hymn to Passion week,[3] & wrote to me as the "glorifier of pain" to remind me that the best glory of a soul is /seen⟩shown/ in the joy of it, & that all chief poets except Dante have seen, felt, & written it so. Thus & therefore was matured his purpose of writing an "ode to joy," as I told you. The man seems to have very good thoughts, . . but he writes like a colder Cowley still . . no impulse, no heat for fusing . . no inspiration, in fact. Though I have scarcely done more than glance at his 'Passion week,' & have little right to give an opinion.

If you have killed Luria as you helped to kill my violets, what shall I say, do you fancy? Well—we shall see!—Do not kill yourself, beloved, in any case! The ἰοστέφανοι Μοῦσαι[4] had better die themselves first!— Ah—what am I writing? What nonsense! I mean, in deep earnest, the deepest, that you should take care & exercise: & not be vexed for Luria's sake—Luria will have his triumph presently! May God bless you— prays your own

Ba

1. For Browning's response to this request, see Letter 313, note 1.
2. *Romeo and Juliet* I. iv. 52–53.
3. The Rev. Thomas Hornblower Gill (1819–?) had also written *The Fortunes of Faith; or, Church and State* (1841), and subsequently was to produce several hymns. The May 18, 1844,.*Athenæum* reviewed his *Hymn to Passion Week* in one curt sentence.
4. "Violet-crowned muses." E. B. B. omitted the tau before the epsilon.

280 (W141)   **R.B. to E.B.B.**

[*March 24, 1846.*]

Tuesday Afternoon.

My own dearest, if you *do*—(for I confess to nothing of the kind)— but if you *should* detect an unwillingness to write at certain times, what would that prove,—I mean, ↑what↓ that one ⟨should⟩ ↑need↓ shrink from avowing?—If I never had you before me except when writing

letters to you—then! .. Why, we do not even *talk* much now! witness
Mr. Buckingham & his voyage that ought to have been discussed!—
Oh, how coldly I should write,—how the bleak-looking paper would
seem unpropitious to carry my feeling—if all had to begin and try to
find words *this* way!

Now, this morning I have been out—to town & back—and for all
the walking my head aches—and I have the conviction that presently
when I resign myself to think of you wholly, with only the pretext,—
the make-believe of occupation, in the shape of some book to turn over
the leaves of,—I shall see you and soon be well,—so soon! You must
know, there is a chair (one of the kind called gondóla-chairs by uphol-
sterers—with an emphasized o)—which occupies the precise place,
stands just in the same relation to *this* chair I sit on now, that yours
⁺stands in and⁺ occupies—to the left of the fire: and, how often, how
always I turn in the dusk and *see* the dearest real Ba with me—

How entirely kind to take that trouble, give those sittings for me!
Do you think the kindness has missed its due effect? *No,* NO—! I am
glad,—*(knowing what I* now *know,*—what you meant *should be,* and did
all in your power to procure) that I have *not* received the picture,[1] if
anything short of an adequate likeness. 'Nil nisi,—te!'[2] But I have set
my heart on *seeing* it—will you remember next time, next Saturday?

I will leave off now. To-morrow, dearest, only dearest Ba, I will
write a longer letter—the clock stops it this afternoon—it is later than I
thought, and our poor crazy post! This morning, hoping against hope,
I ran to meet our postman coming meditatively up the lane—with *a*
letter, indeed!—but Ba's will come to-night—and I will be happy—,
already *am* happy, expecting it. Bless you, my own love—

Ever your R.

1. Not certainly identified, but see Letters 286 and 287, which indicate that it
was given to Browning on Saturday, March 28. Very probably it was the sketch by
Alfred Barrett that Browning had asked for in September (Letter 100). A sketch of
E.B.B. by Alfred is reproduced as the frontispiece of Dorothy Hewlett's *Elizabeth
Barrett Browning* (London: Cassell, 1953).
2. "Nothing if not—you!"

[*March 24, 1846.*]

Tuesday evening.

Ah; if I '*do*' . . if I '*should*' . . if I *shall* . . if I *will* . . if I *must* . . . . what can all the 'ifs' prove, but a most hypothetical state of the conscience? And in brief, I beg you to stand convinced of one thing, . . that whenever the 'certain time' comes for you to "hate writing to me" confessedly, "avowedly," (oh what words!) *I shall not like it at all*—not for all the explanations . . & the sights in gondola chairs, which the person seen is none the better for!—The εἴδωλον[1] sits by the fire—the real Ba is cold at heart through wanting her letter. And that's the doctrine to be preached now, . . is it? I "shrink," shrink from it.—That's your word!—& mine! Dearest, I began by half a jest & end by half-gravity, . . which is the fault of your doctrine & not of me I think. Yet it is ungrateful to be grave, when practically you are good & just about the letters, & generous too sometimes,—& I could not bear the idea of obliging you to write to me, even once . . when . . . Now do not fancy that I do not understand. I understand perfectly, on the contrary. Only do *you* try not to dislike writing when you write,—or not to write when you dislike it . . *that,* I ask of you—, dear dearest—& forgive me for all this over-writing & teazing & vexing which is foolish & womanish in the bad sense. It is a way of meeting, . . the meeting in letters, . . & next to receiving a letter from you, I like to write one to you . . &, so, revolt from thinking it lawful for you to dislike . . Well! the Goddess of Dulness herself couldn't have written *this* better, anyway, nor more characteristically.

I will tell you how it is: You have spoilt me just as I have spoilt Flush. Flush looks at me sometimes with reproachful eyes 'à fendre le cœur,' because I refuse to give him my fur cuffs to tear to pieces. And as for myself, I confess to being more than half jealous of the εἴδωλον in the gondola chair, who isn't the real Ba after all, & yet is set up there to do away with the necessity "at certain times" of writing to her. Which is worse than Flush. For Flush, though he began by shivering with rage & barking & howling & gnashing his teeth at the brown dog in the glass, has learnt by experience what that image means, . . and now contemplates it, serene in natural philosophy. Most excellent sense, all this is!— & dauntlessly 'delivered"!—

Your head aches, dearest. Mr. Moxon will have done his worst, however, presently, and then you will be a little better I do hope & trust —& the proofs, in the meanwhile, will do somewhat less harm than the manuscript. You will take heart again about Luria . . which I agree with you, is more diffuse . . that is, less close, than any of your works . . not diffuse in any bad sense, . . but round, copious, & another proof of that wonderful variety of faculty which is so striking in you, & which signalizes itself both in the thought & in the medium of the thought. You will appreciate 'Luria' in time—or others will do it for you. It is a noble work under every aspect. Dear Luria! Do you remember how you told me of Luria last year, in one of your early letters?[2] Little I thought that ever, ever, I should feel so, while Luria went to be printed!—A long trail of thoughts, like the rack in the sky, follows his going—Can it be the same Luria, I think, that "golden-hearted Luria," whom you talked of to me, when you complained of keeping "wild company," in the old dear letter?[3] And I have learnt since, that *"golden-hearted"* is not a word for him only, or for him most. May God bless you, best & dearest! I am your own to live & to die—

　　　　　　　　　　　　　　　　　　　　　　　　　　Ba

Say how you are. I shall be down stairs to-morrow if it keeps warm.
Miss Thomson wants me to translate the Hector & Andromache scene from the Iliad for her book; & I am going to try it.—

1. "Image."　　　　　　　2. Letter 7.　　　　　　　3. Letter 9.

282 (W142)　　　　　　　*R.B. to E.B.B.*

[*March 25, 1846.*]

　　　　　　　　　　　　　　　　　　　　　　　　Wednesday.
　　You were right to bid me never again wish my poor flowers were "diamonds"—you could not, I think, speak so to my heart of any diamonds. God knows my life is for you to take just as you take flowers: —these last please you, serve you best when plucked—and "my life's rose" . . if I dared profane *that* expression I would say,—you have but to "stoop" for it. Foolish, as all words are.

You *dwell* on that notion of your being peculiarly isolated,—of any kindness to you, in your present state, seeming doubled and quadrupled —what do I, what could anyone infer from *that* but, most obviously, that it was a very fortunate thing for such kindness, and that the presumeable bestower of it got all his distinction from the fact that no better . . however, I hate this and cannot go on. Dearest, believe that under ordinary circumstances, with ordinary people, all operates differently—the *imaginary* kindness-bestower with his ideal methods of showing and proving his love,—*there* would be the rival to fear!

Do not let us talk of this—you always beat me, beside, turn my own illustrations into obscurations—as in the notable case of the *cards* and stakes and risks[1]—I suppose, (to save my vanity!) that if I knew anything about cards, I might go on, a step at least, with my argument. I once heard a dispute in the street between the proprietor of an oyster-stall and one of his customers—*who* was in the wrong . . that is, *who* used the clenching argument you shall hear presently, I don't remember,— but *one* brought the other to this pass—" *Are* there three shells to an oyster?"—Just that! If there *were not*—he would clearly be found in the wrong, that as all!—" *Why,*" . . began the other; and I regret I did not catch the rest—there was such a clear possibility contained in that " *Why* . . an oyster *might* have three shells!"

(Note the adroitness,—(calm heroic silence of the *act* rather than a merely attempted *word,*)—the mastery with which, taking up Ba's implied challenge, I *do* furnish her with both "amusement and instruction")—moreover I will at Ba's bidding amuse and instruct the world at large, and make them know all to be known—for my purposes— about Bells & Pomegranates—yes, it will be better.

I said rather hastily that my head "ached" yesterday: that meant, only that it was more observable because, after walking, it is usually well—and I had been walking: to-day it is much better; I sit reading "Cromwell"[2]—and the newspaper, and presently I shall go out—all will be better now, I hope—it shall not be my fault, at least, depend on that. All my work (work!)—well, such as it is, it is done—and I scarcely care *how*—I shall be prouder to begin one day—(may it be soon!—) with your hand in mine from the beginning—*that* is a very different thing in its effect from the same hand touching mine *after* I had begun, with no suspicion such a chance could befall! I repeat, both these things, Luria & the other, are *manqué*, failures—the life-incidents ought to have been acted over again, experienced afresh,—and I had no inclination nor ability. But one day, my siren!—

Let me make haste and correct a stupid error. I spoke to my father last night about that tragedy of the STUDS—I was wholly *out* in the story —the sufferer was his *uncle*—⟨not first ‖ · · ‖⟩ ↑and the scene↓ should have been laid on the Guinea coast.³ Apropos of errors—the copyright matter⁴ is most likely a case of copy*wrong* by reporters—I never heard of it before—to be sure, I signed a petition of Miss Martineau's super-intending once on a time—but long ago. "I, I, I"—how, dear, all important "I" takes care of himself, and issues bulletins, and corrects his wise mistakes, and all this to . . just "one of his readers of the average intelligence."⁵ Are you that, so much as that, Ba?—I will tell you—if you do not write to me all about *your* dear, dearest self, I shall sink with shame at the recollection of what this letter and its like prove to be: *must* prove to be! Dear love, tell me—that you walk and are in good spirits—and I will try and write better. May God bless my own beloved! —Ever her own R.

I think, am all but sure, there is a MRS. *Hornblower something!*⁶

Just a minute to say your second note has come, and that I *do* hate *hate* having to write, not kiss my answer /and⟩on/ your dearest mouth— —kindest, dearest—to-morrow I will try—and meantime—tho' Ba by the fire will not be cold at heart, cold *of* heart, at least, and I will talk to *her* & more than talk—My dearest, dearest one!

1. The discussion which opens Letter 272 and is continued in the three succeed-ing letters.
2. Carlyle's *Oliver Cromwell's Letters and Speeches* . . .
3. A letter signed "J.S.K." in the *Spectator* for January 30, 1869, connects these studs with a demonstration of clairvoyance by an Italian nobleman, who associated the "cuff studs" Browning gave him with murder. Browning identified them as "taken from the dead body of a great uncle of mine who was violently killed on his estate at St. Kitts, nearly eighty years ago." (Mrs. Orr, pp. 213–214). The "Guinea coast" may be more trustworthy than Browning's memory twenty-three years later, since the same uncle was "said to have penetrated further into the interior of Africa than any other European of his time" (*ibid.*, p. 9).
4. See Letter 279.
5. *Ibid.*
6. Browning is probably recalling a Mrs. F. Hornblower, whose *Poems* had been reviewed in the *Athenæum* for April 6, 1844.

[*March 25, 1846.*]

Wednesday evening.

But if people half say things, . . intimate things . . as when your disputant in the street (you are felicitous, I think, in your street-*experiences*) suggested the possible case of the "three oyster shells to an oyster," . . why you must submit to be answered a little, & even confuted at need. Now just see—

. . "Got all his distinction from the fact that no better" . . . .

That is precisely *the fact . . so . .* as you have stated it, & implied . . . "The fact that no better" . . *is to be found in the world—no better . . none.* There, is the peculiar combination. The isolation on one side, & ⟨‖ · · ‖⟩ the best in the whole world, coming in for company!—And I "dwell" upon it, never being tired . . & if *you* are tired already, you must be tired of *me*, because the 'dwelling' has grown to be a part of me & I cannot put it away. It is my special miracle *à moi*. "No better?" —No, indeed! not in the seven worlds![1]—and just *there*, lies the miraculous point.

But you mean it perhaps otherwise. You mean that it is a sort of "pis aller" on my part . . . A "pis aller" along the Via lactea . . is *that* what you mean?

Shall I let you off the rest, dearest, dearest? though you deserve ever so much more, for implying such monstrous things, & treading down all my violets, so & so—What did I say to set you writing so? I cannot remember at all? If I 'dwell' on anything, beloved, it is that I feel it strongly, be sure—& if I feel gratitude to you with the /rest⟩other/ feelings, you should not grudge what is a happy feeling in itself, & not dishonoring (I answer for *that*) to the object of it.

Now I shall tell you. I had a visitor to-day . . Mrs. Jameson; & when she went away she left me ashamed of myself . . I felt like a hypocrite . . *I,* who was not born for one, I think. She began to talk of you . . talked like a wise woman, which she is . . led me on to say just what I might have said if I had not known you, . . (she, thoroughly impressed with the notion that we two are strangers! . .) & made me quite leap in my chair with a sudden consciousness, by exclaiming at last . . "I am really glad to hear you speak so—Such appreciation" &c. &c. . . . imagine what she went on to say. Dearest—I believe she rather gives me a sort of credit for *appreciating you* without the jealousy '*de métier.*' Good Heavens . . how humiliating some conditions of praise are!—She *approved* me with her eye—indeed she did. And this, while we were agreeing that you were the best . . "none better" . . ⸓none so good⸣ . . of your country & age. Do you know, while we were talking, I felt inclined both to laugh & to cry . . & if I had "given away" the least, she would have been considerably astounded. As it was, my hands were so marble-cold when she took leave of me, that she observed it & began making /excuses⟩apologies/ for exhausting me. Now here is a strip of the '*world,*' . . see what colour it will turn to presently! We had better, I think, go farther than to your siren's island—into the desert . . shall we say? . . Such stories there will be! For certain . ., I shall have seen you just once out of the window!— Shall you not be afraid? Well—& she talked of Italy too—it was before she talked of *you* . . & she hoped I had not given up the thoughts of going there. To which I said /not⟩that/ "I had not . . but that it seemed like scheming to travel in the moon." She talked of a difference, & set down the moon-travelling as simple lunacy. "And ⸓simply⸣ lunatical," . . I said, . . "my thoughts, ⸓if chronicled,⸣ would be taken to be, perhaps"— "No, no, no, ! . ." she insisted . . "as long as I kept to the earth, everything was to be permitted to me"—

How people talk at cross-purposes in this world . . & act so too!— It's the very spirit of worldly communion. Souls are gregarious in a sense, but no soul touches another, as a general rule. I like Mrs. Jameson nevertheless—I like her *more*. She appreciates you—& it is *my* turn to praise for that, now. I am to see her again tomorrow morning, when she has the goodness to promise to bring some etchings of her own, her illustrations of the new essays,[2] for me to look at.

Ah—your '*failures*' in Luria and the Tragedy!—Proud, we should all be, to fail exactly so.

Dearest, are you better indeed? Walk . . talk to the Ba in the chair . . go on to be better, ever dearest. May God bless you! Ah . . the 'I's.' You do not see that the "I's"—as you make them, . . all turn to "yours" by the time they get to me. The "I's" indeed! How dare you talk against my eyes?—For me, I was going down stairs to-day, but it was wet & windy & I was warned not to go. If I am in bad or good spirits, judge from this foolish letter—foolish & wise, both!—but not melancholy, *anywise*. When one drops into a pun, one might as well come to an end altogether—it cant be worse with one.

Nor can it be better than being

Your own——

"NO BETTER" ! ! .

1. The planets, so called by the old astrologers.
2. *Memoirs and Essays Illustrative of Art, Literature, and Social Morals* (1846).

284 (W143)   R.B. to E.B.B.

[*March 26, 1846.*]

Thursday Morning.

Sometimes I have a disposition to dispute with dearest Ba, to wrench her simile-weapons out of the dexterous hand (that is, try and do so)—and have the truth of things my way and its own way, not hers, if she *be* Ba—(observe, I say nothing about ever meeting with remarkable success in such undertakings,—only, that they *are* entered on sometimes) : but at other times I seem as if I must lie down, like Flush, with all manner of coral necklaces about my neck, and two sweet mysterious hands on my head, and so be forced to hear verses on me, Ba's verses, in which I, that am but Flush of the lower nature, am called loving friend and praised for not preferring to go "coursing hares"—with "other dogs."[1] So I will lie now, as you *will* have it, and say in Flush-like tones (the looks that are dog's tones)—I don't *don't* know how it is, or why, or what it all will end in, but I am very happy and what I hear must mean right, by the music,—tho' the meaning is above me,—and here *are* the hands—which I may, and will, look up to, and kiss—determining not to insist any more this time that at Miss Mitford's were sundry dogs, brighter than "brown" . . . See *where*, just *where*, Flush stops discreetly! "Eter . .—nity" he would have added, "but stern death" &c. &c.

I treat these things lightheartedly, as you see—instead of seriously, which would at first thought seem the wiser course—"for after all, she will find out one day &c." *No*, dearest,—I do NOT fear that! ⟨‖ · · · · ‖⟩ ↑Why make uneasy words of saying simply that I shall continue to

562

give you my best flowers,↓ all I can find—if I bring violets, or grass, when you expected to get roses,—you will know there were none in my garden—that is all.

And for you,—as I may have told you once,—as I tell myself always—you are *entirely* what I love—not just a rose plucked off with an inch of stalk, but presented as a rose should be, with a green world of boughs round,—all about you is "to my heart"—*(to my mind*, as they phrase it)—and were it not that, of course, I know *when* to have done with fancyings and merely flitting permissible "inly-sayings with heart-playing,"[2]—and when ↑it is time↓ to look at the plain "best" thro' the lock of "good" and "better" in circumstances and accidents,—I *do* say,—were the best blessing of all, the blessing I trust and believe God intends, of your perfect restoration to health,—were THAT not so palpably best,—I should catch myself desirous that your present state of *unconfirmed* health might never pass away! Ba *understands*, I know!— After all, it will always stay, that luxury,—if but thro' the memory of what has been, and *may* recur,—that deepest luxury that makes my very heart-strings tremble in the thought of,—that I shall have a right, a duty,—where in another case, they would be uncalled for, superfluous, impertinent: tapers ordinarily burn best *let alone*,—with all your light depending on the little flame, the darkest night but for *it*—why, stand off—what good can you do, so long as there is no extraordinary evil to avert, breaking down of the candlestick to prevent? But *here*—there will be reason as well as a delight beyond delights in always learning to close over, all but holding the flame in the hollow of one's hand! I shall have a right to think it is not mere pleasure, merely for myself, that I care and am close by—and as that which thus is called "not for myself" *is*, after all, in its essence, *most* for myself,—why, it is a luxury, a last delight!—

—In the procurement of which there will be this obstacle, or grave matter to be first taken into consideration,—that the world will "change colour" about it, will have its own thoughts on the subject. I have my own thoughts, on *its* subjects, the affairs of the world and pieces of perfect good fortune it approves of, and stamps for enviable —and on the whole the world has quite a right to treat me unceremoniously,—I having begun it. As for the "seeing out of the window once"—those who knew nothing about us but our names had better think *that* was the way, than most others; and the half-dozen who know a little more, may hear the true account if they please, when they hear anything—those who know *all*, all necessary to know, will understand my 137 letters here and my 54 visits . . see, I write as if this were to be pleaded to-night!—would it were! As if you had to write the *meeting* between Hector and Andromache, not the parting![3] By the way, dearest, what enchanted poetry all your translations for Miss Thomson are:—as Carlyle says! "Nobody can touch them, get at them!" How am I the better for Nonnus, and Apuleius? Now, do you serve me well *there?*

I shall hear to-morrow of Mrs. Jameson's etchings and discourses? and more good news of you, darling? I am *quite* well to-day—going out with my sister to dine next /house⟩door/—then, over to-morrow, and the letter, will come Saturday, my day.

Bless you, my own best, dearest—I am your own.

R.

1. An allusion to *To Flush, My Dog* (1844), st. ix: "Other dogs in thymy dew/ Tracked the hare and followed through . . ."
2. An echo of E.B.B.'s *Catarina to Camoens* (1844), st. ii: "Only saying / In heart-playing . . ."
3. See the postscript to Letter 281.

285 *(W 139°)*   *E.B.B. to R.B.*

_____

[*March 26, 1846.*]

Thursday.

Not the "dextrous hand"—say rather the good cause. For the rest, when you turn into a dog & lie down, are you not afraid that a sorcerer should go by & dash the water & speak the formula of the old tales— "If thou wert born a dog, remain a dog, but if not" . . . . If not . . *what* is to happen? Aminè whipped her enchanted hounds ever so often in the day[1] . . . . ah, what nonsense happens!

Dear, dearest, how you 'take me with guile,' or with stronger than guile . . with that divine right you have, of talking absurdities!—You make it clear at last that I am so much the better for being bad . . . and I . . . shall I laugh?—*can* I? is it possible?—The words go too deep . . .

as deep as death which cannot laugh!—And I am forbidden to 'dwell' on the meaning of them—I!—There are *'I's'* to match yours!—

I shall have the right of doing one thing, . . (passing to *my* rights)—I shall hold to the right of remembering to my last hour, that YOU, ↑who↓ might well have passed by on the other side if we two had met on the road when I was riding at ease, . . *did not* when I was in the dust—I choose to remember *that* to the end of feeling. As for *men*, you are not to take me to be quite ignorant of what they are worth in the gross. The most blindfolded women may see a little under the folds . . & I have seen quite enough to be glad to shut my eyes. Did I not tell you that I never thought that any man whom *I* could love, would stoop to love *me*, even if I attained so far as the sight of such. Which I NEVER *attained* . . until . . until!—Then, that *you* should care for me . .!! Oh—I hold to my rights, though you overcome me in most other things. And it is my right to love you better than I could do if I were more worthy to be loved by you.

Mrs. Jameson came late to-day, . . at five—& was hurried & could not stay ten minutes, . . but showed me her etchings & very kindly left a 'Dead St. Cecilia' which I admired most, for its beautiful lifelessness. She is not to be in town again, she said, till a month has gone—a month, at least. Oh—and "quite uneasy" she was, about my "cold hands"—↑yesterday—↓ she thought she had put me to death with over-talking!—which made me smile a little . . 'sub-ridens.'[2] But she is very kind & affectionate; & you were right to teach me to like her—and now, do you know, I look in vain for the 'steely eyes' I fancied I saw once, & see nothing but two good & true ones.

Well—here is an end till Saturday. It is too late . . or I could go on writing . . which I do not hate indeed. Talking of hating, . . . "what you love entirely" means *that you love entirely* . . & no more & no less. If it did not mean so, I should be unhappy about the *mistake* . . but to 'love entirely' is not a mistake & cannot pass for one either on earth or in Heaven. May God bless you, ever dearest. Such haste I write in—as if the angels were running up Jacob's ladder![3]—or DOWN it, rather, at this close!

Your own Ba

1. In the *Arabian Nights*, Zobeide tells how her two sisters, jealous of her attentions from a prince, threw her into the sea. She managed to survive, however, and a

good fairy delivered the sisters to her, metamorphosed into dogs. On pain of herself becoming a dog, she must give each a hundred lashes a night (Nights 63–66). E.B.B. has confused Zobeide with one of her sisters, Amene.

2. "Smiling." E.B.B. is playing on the literal meaning: "nearly laughing" or "laughing somewhat."

3. Genesis 28. The story is alluded to in Letter 166 and there is a quotation from it in Letter 194.

286 (W144)　　　　　　　　　　**R.B. to E.B.B.**

[*March 27, 1846.*]

Friday.

"Qui laborat, orat";[1] so they used to say, and in that case I have been devotional to a high degree this morning. Seven holes did I dig (to keep up inversions of style)—seven rose-trees did I plant—("Brennus" —and "Madame Laffarge"!)[2] are two names I remember,—very characteristic of old Gaul and young France—) and, for my pains, the first fruits, first blossoms some two or three months hence, will come, & will go to dearest Ba who first taught me what a rose really *was,* how sweet it might become with superadded memories of the room and the chair and the vase, and the cutting stalks and pouring fresh water . . ah, my own Ba!—And did you think to warn me out of the Flush-simile by the hint of Aminè's privilege which it would warrant? If the "ever so much whipping" should please you! . . . And beside it was, if I recollect, for the creature's good, those poor imprisoned sisters, all the time. Moreover, I *was* "born" all this and more, that you *will* know, at least— and only walked glorious & erect on two legs till dear Siren; an old friend of, and deep in the secrets of Circe,—sprinkled the waters . . perhaps on those roses—No, before that!—

Well, to-morrow comes fast now—and I shall trust to be with you my beloved—and, first, you are to show me the portrait, remember—[3]

I am glad you like Mrs. Jameson—do not *I* like her all the better, *much* the better! But it is fortunate I shall not see her by any chance just now—she would be sure to begin and tell me about *you*—and if my hands did not turn cold, my ear-tips would assuredly turn red. I daresay that St. Cecilia is the beautiful statue above her tomb at Rome,— covered with a veil—affectingly beautiful; I well remember how she lies.

Now good-bye; and to-morrow! Bless you, ever dear, dearest Ba—

Your own

R.

1. "He who labors, prays."

2. Browning's roses were named for a Gallic chief who occupied Rome in 390 B.C. and who is mentioned in *Sordello* (III, 588ff.), and the defendant in a sensational and highly complicated murder trial of six years earlier. Madame Laffarge, a young and pretty Frenchwoman, was finally convicted of poisoning her elderly husband but "with extenuating circumstances" and sentenced to hard labor for life. The case and its outcome were a sensation in England (see, e.g., *The Times* letter column, September 26, 1840), and Henry Colburn published a translation of the widow's memoirs which E.B.B. read in early 1846 (*EBB to MRM*, pp. 263–264).

3. See Letter 280, note 1.

The envelope of the following letter, because it was an enclosure with the package of proof mentioned in the text, bears no stamp or postmark. It was written the day after the visit noted on the envelope of Letter 285:

+March 28, Saturday

3¼–5¾ p.m. (55.)

287 (*W145*)   *R.B. to E.B.B.*

[March 29, 1846.]

Sunday Afternoon.

Now, I think, if I had been 'pricked at the heart' by dear, dearest Ba's charge yesterday,—if I did not *certainly* know why it might sometimes seem better to be silent than to speak,—should I not be found taking three or four sheets of paper, and beginning to write, and write! My own, dearest and best,—it is *not* so,—not wrong, my heart's self tells me,—and tells you! But for the rest there shall never pass a day till my death wherein I will not write to you, so long as you let me, excepting those days I may spend with you, partly or . . altogether—Love, shall I have very, very long to be hating to write, yet writing?

You see sometimes how I *talk* to you,—even in mere talking what a strange work I make of it. I go on thinking quite another way; so, generally, I often have thought, the little I *have* written, has been an inconscious scrawling with the mind fixed somewhere else: the subject of the scrawl may have previously been the real object of the mind on some similar occasion,—the very thing which *then* to miss, (finding in its place *such another* result of a still prior fancy-fit)—which then to see escape, or find escaped, was the vexation of the time! One cannot, (or *I* cannot) *finish up* the work in one's mind, put away the old projects and take up new—Well, this which I feel on so many occasions, do you wonder if—if!

I should write on *this* for ever! It is all so strange, such a dream as you say!

Indeed, love, the picture[1] is not like, nor "flattered" by any means, yet I don't know how it is, I cannot be cross with it—there is a touch of truth in the eyes,—would one have believed *that?* I know my own way with portraits; how I let them master eventually my most decided sense of their *unlikeness*—and *this* finds me very prepared—still—it seems already more faithful than last night . . how do I determine where the miraculousness ends? (My Mother was greatly impressed by it—and my sister, coming ⹁(from my room)⹁ into the room where I was with a visitor, before whom she could not speak . . English, said '*È molto bella*'!)[2]

Here is my 'proof'—I found it as I expected: I fear I must put you to that trouble of sending the other two acts—I hate to think of so troubling you! But do not, Ba, hurry yourself—nor take extraordinary pains—what is worth your pains in these poor things? I like Luria better now,—it may do, now,—probably because it *must:* but, as I said yesterday, I seriously hope and trust to shew my sense of gratitude for what is promised my future life, by doing some real work in it,—work of yours, as thro' you. I have felt,—not for the first time now,—but from the beginning vexed, foolishly vexed perhaps, that I could not without attracting undesirable notice, "dedicate," in the true sense of the word, this or the last number to you: but if any really worthy performance *should* follow, then . . my mouth will be unsealed. All is forewritten!

I wonder if you have ventured down this sunny afternoon—tell me how you are, and, once again, do not care about those papers,—any time will do——So, bless you, my own—my all-beloved Ba.

Your R. B.

1. See Letter 280, note 1.   2. "She is very beautiful."